1997

THE SOCIAL WELFARE INSTITUTION

An Introduction

THIRD EDITION

THE SOCIAL WELFARE INSTITUTION

An Introduction

Ronald C. Federico
University of Cincinnati

D. C. HEATH AND COMPANY
Lexington, Massachusetts Toronto

This book is dedicated to

BETTY L. BAER

with thanks for the opportunity to grow
and for modeling the meaning of collegial support
and professional commitment.

Photo Credits:

Chapter 1: Elizabeth Hamlin/Stock, Boston
Chapter 2: © Hap Stewart/Jeroboam, Inc.
Chapter 3: Peter Southwick/Stock, Boston
Chapter 4: Leonard Freed/Magnum Photos, Inc.
Chapter 5: Editorial Photocolor Archives, Inc.
Chapter 6: © Karen Preuss/Jeroboam, Inc.
Chapter 7: © Karen Preuss/Jeroboam, Inc.
Chapter 8: Chris Maynard/Magnum Photos, Inc.
Chapter 9: Charles Harbutt/Magnum Photos, Inc.

Published simultaneously in Canada.

Printed in the United States of America.

International Standard Book Number: 0-669-01916-X

Library of Congress Catalog Card Number: 79-87817

PREFACE

The third edition of *The Social Welfare Institution* is intended for the first course in a baccalaureate social work program. Its overall objective is to help the student attain a conceptual understanding of the scope and major components of the social welfare institution and the profession of social work. More specific objectives are:

1. *To help the student conceptually understand social welfare within a system framework.* Using this framework, an effort is made to look at the causes of need, as well as provisions for their solution or amelioration.
2. *To help the student examine his or her own value orientations, beliefs, value-influenced behaviors, and potential for changing his or her values and behavior.* This is done within the context of professional social work values, diverse group values, and larger societal values.
3. *To help the student develop a logical, rational, information-based analytical approach to understanding situations.* This approach will be used in looking at the full range of the social welfare institution's structure and functioning. This includes specific interactions with people as well as the planning, practice, and policy-related activities that take place in organizations.
4. *To help the student recall information obtained in other courses and through life experience and develop the skills necessary to use this information in practical life situations.* Social science–related information is most directly highlighted, but biological science and basic communications are also reinforced.
5. *To help the student achieve an intellectual and emotional understanding of the meaning of helping, the helping process, and the helping person.*
6. *To help the student understand the demands and rewards of social welfare careers, including a reasonable estimate of future career opportunities.*

Comparing This Book to the Previous Edition

Like the previous editions, the third edition begins with a broad view of social welfare and then focuses on social work's place within the larger social welfare institution. No content area in the previous edition has been omitted from this book. However, some content areas are new, and others have been extensively reorganized.

New content areas. Discussions of two major areas have been added to the book. The first takes up the general concept of professional helping, including the meaning of helping, the helping process, and the helping person. This material has been added in order to engage the student more directly in his or her area of most vital interest—that is, Do I really want to be a professional helping person? The second major new area is a discussion of the process of defining human needs within a systems framework. This discussion reflects a strengthening of two other areas: seeing the social welfare institution as society's response to the needs of its members (or at least those whose needs are identified, recognized, and accepted), and the use of research as an important part of the social worker's practice tools.

Reorganized content areas. Although there has been some reorganization at several points in the book, two areas have been completely rethought and rewritten. One is the whole area of the social science foundations of social work practice. That section now begins with a basic framework useful for integrating relevant social, behavioral, and biological knowledge, and then moves on to a review of specific areas of knowledge that undergird social welfare policy and practice.

The second reorganized area is that on interventive methods. This section conceptualizes social work practice in terms of functions, objectives, and activities appropriate for the entry-level professional practitioner. It identifies competencies and skills needed to practice at the entry level, along with some description of why they are necessary. The section also reviews the historical development of other approaches, and attempts to help the student understand the current reality of many different practice approaches existing simultaneously. However, the view of practice presented is highly integrated and systems related.

I believe that educators who have used the previous editions will continue to find this book easy to use and understand. Indeed, in many ways I think that it is better integrated and more clearly conceptualized. As in the previous editions, I have used a wide variety of illustrative and factual material in the exhibits. The third edition also retains the end-of-chapter features of summary or conclusion, study questions, and a bibliography of relevant contemporary books. In addition to the appendix with case illustrations, two new appendixes have been added. One summarizes major federal income-maintenance programs, while the second presents the National Association of Social Workers personnel standards, material previously incorporated in the Introduction.

Finally, a special effort has been made in this edition to eliminate sexist language. However, the masculine pronoun is used in most of the exhibits, since they are reproduced exactly as originally written.

Two outside forces have helped directly and indirectly to shape this edition. One is the Council on Social Work Education, whose accreditation process has sparked considerable activity in several curriculum areas. The other is the Undergraduate Social Work Curriculum Development Project,* funded by the Department of Health, Education and Welfare. My two years as Associate Director, working with Betty Baer, Project Director, had a profound effect on my thinking about the purposes of social work, the functions of the entry-level professional social worker, and the curriculum structure and content necessary to educate that audience. I hope this edition will lay the foundation for a baccalaureate curriculum that makes operational the view of practice and education described in the Project report.

It has always been my objective to produce a book that students would find appealing, informative, and useful, and this edition tries as hard as the earlier ones. This is a basic textbook whose mission is to stimulate, help, and encourage. I hope that every educator will always feel free to tell me whether or not it accomplishes these goals and to suggest better ways for it to do so. This edition is certainly much richer because of such input in the past.

Acknowledgments

As with the earlier editions of the book, there are more people to thank for its successful completion than there is room to do so. However, several are of particular importance: Robert Berger, Mary Ellen Elwell, Dean Pierce, and Philip Smith, for their careful and insightful reviews of the manuscript; Doug Burnham, Larry Icard, and Marilyn Rifkin, for their patient willingness to discuss ideas and issues; Jane Ann Carter and Jeannie Pritchett, for their expert secretarial support; and Debbie Lewis and Pat Early, for their cooperation and skillful typing. I would also like to thank especially Paul Mills and Ann Jones, for their interest in the book and their willingness to undertake the arduous task of doing an instructor's guide for it. Their fine work provides a valuable resource for instructors and greatly enriches the book's usefulness. I am sincerely grateful to these people, as well as to the countless others who have contributed to this book in its present or earlier editions.

Ronald C. Federico

* The Project report was published as Betty L. Baer and Ronald C. Federico, *Educating the Baccalaureate Social Worker: Report of the Undergraduate Social Work Curriculum Development Project* (Cambridge, Mass.: Ballinger Books, 1978).

CONTENTS

CHAPTER 1

Social Welfare as a Helping Effort

The purpose of this chapter is to define the concept of social welfare and to understand its structural components and characteristics. Growing out of the discussion of the function of social welfare, the concepts of needs and helping are discussed, including strategies for identifying needs. (The nature of the helping process is analyzed in Chapter 6.) After having completed this chapter, readers should have a clear understanding of the place of social welfare in the institutional structure of society as well as a framework to use in assessing social welfare services as they relate to human need. At the value and skill levels, readers should have begun the process of identifying and examining their individual values and the ways in which these values affect behavior.

▶ Social Welfare as a Social Institution

Many attempts have been made to define social welfare. A sampling of the diversity of these definitions, reflecting the breadth of the concept itself, is presented in Exhibit 1-1.* Social welfare is defined in this book as *improving social functioning and minimizing suffering through a system of socially approved financial and social services at all levels in the social structure.* This definition highlights three especially important characteristics of social welfare:

1. The phrase "improving social functioning and minimizing suffering" entails problem solving as well as developmental activities. As people seek to attain their life goals, they frequently confront obstacles that can be conceptualized as problems to be solved. However, the attainment of goals also involves facilitation and resource use rather than problem solving. Therefore, social welfare focuses on helping people to better use their own and societal resources and does not deal only with situations in which problems exist.
2. Saying that social welfare rests on "a system of socially approved . . . " means that there can be no social welfare unless the society approves of such activities. Social groups exist and function because of agreed-upon types of interaction. In that sense, any group, small or large, is constantly renegotiating or reaffirming the collective decisions that created and maintain (or change) it. This process is also true of social welfare activities. They exist because they have been considered desirable, and their form is always dependent on the wishes of the groups of people involved, ranging from societal institutions to the smallest person-to-person interaction. As these wishes change, the mandate of social welfare changes. For example, public education for everyone is considered a basic part of our current social welfare institutional structure, but this was not true in the early history of this society.
3. The phrase "services at all levels in the social structure" suggests that social welfare activities are built into the fabric of society. Where and how they exist in society is very much part of the process of group definition and negotiation. Many social welfare activities are informally provided through such structures as the family and peer groups. Others are highly formalized, existing in formal structures specifically created for that purpose. But whether formal or informal, all are woven into the social structure.

William Robson stated the following about social welfare:[1]

> *The rights of citizens to the benefits of the welfare state must be accompanied by reciprocal duties. The need for complementary rights and obligations is particularly great in the fields of work, law and order, education, and the social services.*

---

* Exhibits are placed throughout the book to supplement the basic text material. They sometimes serve to examine issues in more detail, as in this exhibit. At other times they illustrate concepts discussed in the text, while still others present alternative points of view about a particular issue. Each exhibit is an important companion to the text and should serve to both add information and stimulate thinking about points introduced in the text.

EXHIBIT 1-1 *Defining Social Welfare*

There have been many attempts to formally define social welfare. As stated in the *Encyclopedia of Social Work:*[a]

"Social welfare" generally denotes the full range of organized activities of voluntary and governmental agencies that seek to prevent, alleviate, or contribute to the solution of recognized social problems, or to improve the well-being of individuals, groups, or communities. Such activities use a wide variety of professional personnel such as physicians, nurses, lawyers, educators, engineers, ministers, social workers, and paraprofessional counterparts of each.

Philip Klein refers to social welfare as "the administration of certain services to individuals and families who find it difficult or impossible to maintain themselves and their dependents in material solvency and in health by their own efforts."[b] Crampton and Keiser "define social welfare operationally as a system that embodies a multifaceted approach to social and economic problems, reflecting social values and using the expertise of interrelated disciplines for the collective good."[c] Friedlander defines social welfare as "the organized system of social services and institutions, designed to aid individuals and groups to attain satisfying standards of life and health, and personal and social relationships which permit them to develop their full capacities and to promote their well-being in harmony with the needs of their families and the community."[d] Wilensky and Lebeaux define welfare by distinguishing traits of the contemporary social welfare structure. These are: (1) formal organization; (2) social sponsorship and accountability; (3) absence of a profit motive as a dominant program purpose; (4) an integrated view of human needs; and (5) direct focus on human consumption needs.[e] Finally, Smith and Zeitz say simply that "the social services institutionalize, as public policy, the philanthropic impulse."[f]

The United States Committee Report at the 1974 International Conference on Social Welfare, authored by John Turner, uses the term social welfare to include:

(1) the wide range of services designed to attain ways of life acceptable to individuals and the community, sometimes thought of collectively as the "social aspects of development" and including services designed to strengthen the individual confronted with economic, physical, mental or social disabilities, together with (2) those aimed at influencing the remedy of conditions leading to dependency.

Realistically evaluating its theoretical definition of social welfare, the Report continues:[g]

The scope of social welfare in the U.S. is not as broad as social work professionals concerned with the question would like it to be. While the preferred definition suggests improvements in social conditions for all, [and] *support and enhancement of the social well-being of the total population, in actual practice the scope of social welfare has a narrower, more residual orientation. . . . The principal targets of social welfare are then, in spite of our preferences for a broader view, special groups in the population whose social situation is problematic* [i.e.] *. . . the poor, the handicapped, the dependent, the deprived, the deviant, the disadvantaged, the alienated.*

---

[a] National Association of Social Workers, *Encyclopedia of Social Work* (New York, 1971), Vol. II, p. 1446.

[b] Philip Klein, *From Philanthropy to Social Welfare* (San Francisco: Jossey-Bass, 1968), p. 7.

[c] Helen Crampton and Kenneth Keiser, *Social Welfare: Institution and Process* (New York: Random House, 1970).

[d] Walter A. Friedlander, *Introduction to Social Welfare* (Englewood Cliffs, N.J.: Prentice-Hall, 1961), p. 4.

[e] Harold Wilensky and Charles Lebeaux, *Industrial Society and Social Welfare* (New York: Russell Sage Foundation, 1958), pp. 140–47.

[f] Russell Smith and Dorothy Zeitz, *American Social Welfare Instiututions* (New York: John Wiley, 1970), p. 3.

[g] John Turner, *Development and Participation: Operational Implications for Social Welfare* (New York: United States Committee, International Council on Social Welfare, 1974), p. 19.

His statement expresses well the fact that society exists to meet the needs of its members as they are defined and understood at any particular time (recognizing that they change over time). It also emphasizes that a system of welfare services depends on the willingness of each individual to support it—to believe it is worthwhile, to contribute resources for it, to use its benefits in a responsible way, and to support public policy that makes a social welfare structure possible. Social welfare, therefore, seeks to balance the collective good with individual needs and desires. Finding the point at which this balance is best achieved is an ongoing activity in society. It depends on societal definitions of the good and desirable, which in turn are embedded in societal values, values that evolve over time and sometimes vary between groups in a society.

Keith-Lucas discusses three value bases commonly used in United States society: the capitalist-puritan, the humanist-positivist-utopian, and the Judeo-Christian. His analysis of the tenets of each and their implications for social welfare beliefs and values is presented in Exhibit 1-2. In spite of the diversity of societal values related to helping, Keith-Lucas sees an identifiable core of professional helping values:[2]

1. People should be free to choose [including the choice of failure].
2. The individual matters, and his interests cannot be wholly subjected to those of the community.
3. Man has neither the right nor the ability to judge his fellows in terms of what they deserve.
4. Helping people find their own way is better than controlling them, however subtly.
5. Feelings, and personal relationships, matter.
6. People should be treated as "subjects" and not as "objects."

Thus social welfare has a specific function in society; it is desired and accepted by society, and its activities are structured in orderly ways. These characteristics make it possible to talk about social welfare as a *social institution* (in contrast to what is popularly called an institution, a word used to refer to large organizations, such as mental hospitals or General Motors, as well as to something that is so well established in a group or community that it is taken for granted). As a sociological concept, a social institution (1) develops from efforts to meet one or more identified societal needs; (2) grows out of the normative (value) system that characterizes a society; and (3) is an organized structure of activities.

Everyone is familiar with the five most commonly discussed social institutions: the family, education, religion, and the political and economic institutions. This chapter focuses on a sixth—social welfare. Each social institution is embedded in all of the others. The family has reciprocal relationships with the political and economic institutions through its socialization and resource distribution functions. For example, children learn the political (and other) views of their parents, and their significant life chances and experiences are affected by their family's socioeconomic standing. Similarly, the education institution modifies and extends socialization received in the family, and the religious institution may influence political decisions (as when religious groups lobby for or against social issues like abortion, homosexuality, or drug use).

EXHIBIT 1-2 *Value Systems Underlying Social Welfare's Societal Mandate*

The following discussion of major value systems underlying society's approach to social welfare illustrates the complexity of societal values as well as the difficulty encountered in trying to define a coherent social welfare system based on such opposing values. Yet Keith-Lucas makes it clear that whatever the problems, values form the base upon which our social welfare institution is built.

There are in our culture three . . . more or less logical [value] systems. There are variations on these, and perversions of them, which may be held by some to be distinct belief systems, but for the purposes of this discussion these three may be sufficient.

The first such system, and possibly the most powerful among people as a whole, might be called capitalist-puritan or CP for short. Its basic assumptions might be summarized as follows:

1. Man is responsible for his own success or failure.
2. Human nature is basically evil, but can be overcome by an act of will.
3. Man's primary purpose is the acquisition of material prosperity, which he achieves through hard work.
4. The primary purpose of society is the maintenance of law and order in which this acquisition is possible.
5. The unsuccessful, or deviant, person is not deserving of help, although efforts should be made, up to a point, to rehabilitate him or to spur him to greater efforts on his own behalf.
6. The primary incentives to change are to be found in economic or physical rewards and punishments.

The prevalence of these assumptions needs no emphasis at this time. The 1968 election in the United States is ample evidence of it. It is the creed popularly thought of as "American" or even common sense, and as such is part of the heritage of most of us . . .

So closely have God's favor and worldly success become identified that the successful are thought of as "good" and the unsuccessful as "bad" or inferior. Man takes over what was originally God's prerogatives of judgment and chastisement and those who do not exercise sufficient ambition or will are shamed, exhorted, punished, or left to the workings of the economic system.

Where the CP system of beliefs is associated with certain other religious values it has strong ethical content, in which success and failure to achieve certain ethical goals is thought of in almost exactly the same way as are material achievement and its opposite. The two systems meet in the matter of work, which has both a material and an ethical value, and in statements applying ethical standards to business enterprise, such as the statement, "Honesty is the best policy," or emphasis on the "service" motive in business. . . .

Almost diametrically opposed to this system is the one that can be called humanist-positivist-utopian, or HPU for short. This is the belief of

---

Alan Keith-Lucas, *Giving and Taking Help* (Chapel Hill: University of North Carolina Press, 1972), pp. 138–43. Used by permission.

most social scientists and many liberals, but is also held to some degree by people who profess CP views and by many religious people, despite some inherent contradiction. Summarized, its basic assumptions can be presented as follows:

1. The primary purpose of society is to fulfill man's needs both material and emotional.
2. If man's needs were fulfilled, then he would attain a state that is variously described, according to the vocabulary used by the specific HPU system, as that of goodness, maturity, adjustment, or productivity, in which most of his and society's problems would be solved.
3. What hampers him from attaining this state is external circumstance, not in general under his individual control. This, in various HPU systems, has been ascribed to lack of education, economic circumstance, his childhood relationships, and his social environment.
4. These circumstances are subject to manipulation by those possessed of sufficient technical and scientific knowledge, using, in general, what is known as "the scientific method," and consequently
5. Man, and society, are ultimately perfectible.

HPU-ism is perhaps difficult to see as a unitary theory, since many of its devotees have relied on a single specific for creating the utopia it envisages. Dewey, for instance, a strong HPU-ist, saw education as the answer; Marx, reform of the economic system; and Freud, the early Freud at least, the removal of repressions. . . .

The sources of this system are to be found in the Enlightenment and its first prophets were Rousseau and Comte. Today it is most obvious in the Poverty program, but many of its assumptions are inherent in modern materialism, at which point it joins hands with and lives somewhat uneasily with CP thought.

Behind, and yet parallel with these two systems is a third, for which it is harder to find a name. Perhaps the best that can be devised is the familiar "Judeo-Christian" tradition. . . .

Yet the system is essentially the system of assumptions about man and the universe that are inherent in the Jewish and Christian Scriptures, and is accepted, at least officially, although not always acted upon by the mainstream religious bodies, Catholic, Protestant, and Jewish.

Summarizing its basic assumptions in the same way as we have done for the CP and HPU systems, these might be presented as follows:

1. Man is a created being one of whose major problems is that he acts as if he were not and tries to be autonomous.
2. Man is fallible, but at the same time capable of acts of great courage or unselfishness.
3. The difference between men, in terms of good and bad, is insignificant compared with the standard demanded by their creator, and, as a consequence, man cannot judge his fellow in such terms.
4. Man's greatest good lies in terms of his relationship with his fellows and with his creator.
5. Man is capable of choice, in the "active and willing" sense, but may need help in making his choice.
6. Love is always the ultimate victor over force.

The position of this ethic vis-à-vis the others is a complicated one. In one sense it lies parallel to them and is a viable alternative, or a middle ground, especially in item 2, its recognition of man's simultaneous fallibility and potential. In another, it lies behind them and makes both of them possible. . . .

Probably most people are influenced to some extent by all three of these sets of assumptions. All have some value and it is not so much a matter of saying that one is good and another bad as it is of taking a position nearer or further from one or another extreme. Yet we do need to explore which set of assumptions is more likely to preserve the kind of values we see as important in helping, and which is most compatible with what we can observe in the process of helping as we know it.

Quite obviously the CP position is in general the least likely to lead to help. If man is totally responsible for his own actions, if he can better his condition by an act of will, if he can be induced to change by punishment or reward, then helping becomes a simple matter of us arranging the appropriate rewards and punishments. There is no room for relationships, or concern for another, except in a highly condescending and judgmental way.

This is the view of man that created the workhouse and the pauper's oath, which demands of children in Children's Homes or welfare clients that they work harder and behave better than other people, and which is terrified of any welfare measure that would make the receipt of relief in any way bearable or dignified. It assumes without question that welfare clients will "naturally" lie, cheat, or steal if given the chance, prefer laziness to work, and feign sickness in order to shirk working. And typically it is much more concerned to punish the few who may do such things than help the many who do not.

Yet it is not without some positive features. It does at least recognize that it is the person in trouble who must bear the final responsibility for his own betterment, and as such it has moderated some of the extreme implications of the HPU set of assumptions which, for many helping people, have appeared to supersede it.

In its initial impact on helping theory and practice HPU thought produced a tremendous outpouring of love and understanding. The helped person was freed from the total responsibility he had borne up till then for his own condition. He was no longer a second-class citizen, judged by his fellows. He was valued for his own sake. The particular social science which became the model for helping in the 1930s—analytical psychology—also stressed certain things which, if not strictly HPU—and indeed I shall argue that they are basically Judeo-Christian and not HPU at all—were at least acceptable to those who claimed to be humanists and utopians. These were in general:

1. A sense of man's common vulnerability. There were, and this is one of Freud's greatest contributions to helping, no longer "sick" and "well" people, but people who were in greater or less difficulty with problems that trouble us all.
2. A habit of looking at problems from the point of view of the helped person rather than from the outside, that is, treating him as subject rather than as object.
3. An emphasis on relationship as the principal means of help.
4. At least in the earlier stages a degree of awe in the face of new knowledge of a somewhat mysterious nature. . . .

One of the most important insights of the Judeo-Christian tradition is the nature of man himself. He is neither the evil being of capitalist-puritan belief, nor is he as good as many HPU-ists believe. But it is not so much a matter of steering between an over- and an underestimation of his nature as it is of recognizing two different factors in his makeup. The first is his fallibility and the second his ability, in certain circumstances, to work out for himself something somewhat better than his fallibility would suggest. This is far from saying that he has in him a potential which needs only some triggering, or some favorable circumstance, to tap. It means rather that with help, or where he is put to it, or from the depths of despair, he can sometimes transcend his own fallibility. Moreover this ability is found in the most unlikely places. It is often demonstrated by those whom objectively one would be forced to believe are unequipped or incapable. This is the constant surprise one comes up against in helping. Not infrequently it tends to have the air of the miraculous about it.

The social welfare institution is similarly in reciprocal interaction with all of the other social institutions. Social welfare services may be used to help people when families disintegrate (such as foster home care) or to help prevent the dissolution of families (as with financial assistance payments, family planning counseling, or assistance in budgeting family income). Social welfare services may help children learn in school and may help people obtain basic financial support when elderly. Political decisions affect the social welfare services available, whereas social welfare professionals often influence political decisions through lobbying and other organizing efforts.

In these and many other ways, social institutions reinforce each other's functioning in society. This integration of function can be both problematic and useful. It is useful in that it serves to promote societal stability when all of the social institutions work toward the common goal of defining expected behaviors for people. For example, the family socializes its members to want and expect what they are likely to get in the educational, political, and economic structures of society, given the family's socioeconomic standing. On the other hand, those who are raised in families that are disadvantaged socioeconomically are less likely to have opportunities to improve their lot. Therefore, social institutions tend to be conservative in their effect, generally tending to maintain the status quo.

Social welfare as a social institution can serve to either reinforce the status quo or challenge it. The definition of social welfare used above emphasizes its *manifest* function—helping people to function more effectively. This may be achieved through the existing network of social and societal relationships, or it may necessitate changes in these relationships. Social welfare, like any social institution, may also have *latent* functions, that is, functions that are less visible and less emphasized. For example, to the degree that social welfare maintains a status quo, which in fact impedes the functioning of certain groups of people (the poor, for example) while preserving the advantage of others (such as the rich), social welfare may serve a latent function of social control. Similarly, the manifest function of the family is socialization, but a latent function is the preservation of clearly distinct sex roles.

Perception of the latent functions of a social institution is aided by the use of a *functional* perspective. The manifest functions of a social institution usually emphasize its contributions to the stability of the society, assuming that such stability is useful for everyone in the society. However, what is advantageous (or functional) for some groups may be problematic (or dysfunctional) for others. Criminal justice procedures that more strictly control minority group members are functional for the majority groups in society in that they reduce visible challenges to the status quo but dysfunctional for the minority group members whose civil and human rights are jeopardized. Therefore, a realistic understanding of social welfare as it is embedded in a larger institutional context necessitates a functional analysis of the interplay of forces that produce different effects for different parts of the social structure. A systems approach facilitates this type of analysis, as is illustrated in Exhibit 1-3.

The Social Welfare Institution from a Systems Perspective ◀

A useful contemporary perspective on the social welfare institution as an organized structure of activities is the systems approach. Brill defines a system as "a whole made up of interrelated and interdependent parts. The parts exist in a state of balance, and when change takes place within one, there is compensatory change within the others."[3] There are at least three levels at which social welfare can be understood within a systems framework:

1. *Social welfare as a social institution exists in a larger societal context of institutions.* The internal structure of social welfare impinges on other social institutions and is in turn affected by them. For example, legislative decisions made in the political institution affect the resources available to social welfare agencies, and the effectiveness of social welfare services affect such things as the ability of the family to function when both parents work.

2. *Social welfare organizations exist in community systems made up of many different parts.* A community translates societal values and legislative mandates into local community structures, services, and patterns of interpersonal interaction. Political, economic, educational, religious, and family structures all exist at the community level, and each relates to community social welfare services. For example, schools refer childen who are acting out to social welfare agencies, and social welfare agencies may attempt to organize minority groups in a community so that they can have a better impact on decisions about needed resources.

EXHIBIT 1-3 *Hurting By Helping*

American society has traditionally been protective of women in the sense of defining female roles as primarily homebound and subservient to men. The women's movement has successfully shown the latent functions of these role definitions—preservation of male dominance and male privilege through the limitation of opportunities for females as well as subtle mechanisms to reduce women's self-esteem. In the following excerpts, ways in which the juvenile justice system supports these latent functions are described.

Many people assume that as women increasingly abandon their traditional roles, previously male domains such as burglary, larceny, and auto theft are among those infiltrated by women. Thus they connect women's rights with a rise in the number of female criminals.

In fact, the relationship of sex roles to crime is much more complicated. For example, drug offenses account for the most precipitous rise in arrests of young women, having increased 5,375 percent between 1960 and 1975. A study of police handling of suspected drug users showed that women who cried, blamed their boyfriends, and otherwise acted in stereotypic ways during raids frequently convinced the police not to arrest them. Those young women who displayed "male" traits of hostility and aggression, however, were often arrested and processed.

Thus, the increase in women charged with crimes may reflect increased criminal activity, or it may result from more aggressive behavior on the part of women apprehended—or both.

These ambiguities, however, do not plague the juvenile justice system. There, young women and girls come in contact with police and the

Source: Excerpted from Paz Cohen, "A Double Standard of Justice," *Civil Rights Digest,* Spring 1978, pp. 10–18.

courts for a variety of reasons, and, sooner or later, their sex counts against them.

Three broad categories of youths find themselves involved in the juvenile justice system. Some are judged delinquent; some are deemed to be improperly cared for at home, or have no homes; and some are charged with "status offenses"—acts that, if performed by adults, would not be considered crimes. The word substituted for "conviction" in juvenile cases is "adjudication."

Between 70 and 85 percent of adjudicated girls in detention are status offenders, compared to a detention rate for boys charged with "children's crimes" of less than 20 percent.

Status offenses range from school truancy and running away to refusal to do household chores, use of "vile language," and promiscuity. An informal survey of child advocates throughout the country yielded only one instance of a boy institutionalized for sexual promiscuity, while sexuality appeared to be the underlying cause of most female referrals, even where not directly cited.

Undesirable boyfriends, staying out after curfew, wanting to get married and "incorrigibility" are among the complaints parents take to the courts along with their daughters. Pregnancy, fornication, or an abortion without parental consent falls more obviously under the category of promiscuity, but "truancy and incorrigibility," according to Mary Kaaren Jolly, staff director of the Senate Subcommittee on the Constitution, "are often nothing but buffer charges for promiscuity in girls—or the court's fear of future promiscuity." At home, in school, and throughout the many stages of the juvenile justice system, female sexuality evokes patronizing and/or biased treatment.

The Double Standard Revisited

Carol, 13, is now enrolled in a feminist counseling program. She was institutionalized due to her parent's double standard for male and female sexuality. "Boys do have it better," she says, "comparing my life to my brother's. I got sent up to an institution because I was messing around. He went out and got some girl pregnant. He was only 17 and he never got into any kind of trouble for it. She did, but he didn't."

When she has children of her own, Carol hopes they are boys:

It's just a hassle to raise girls because you've got to worry if they get caught having sex, then of course it's the girl that gets arrested on an unlawful morals charge. What do they do to the guy? Nothing.

It's just like in the family. If a man's daughter comes home and her hair's all messed up and her shirt's unbuttoned, he calls her a little slut. But if a boy comes home and tells his dad he made it with someone tonight, he says, "Oh, that's good. That's my son." That's just how it is.

Treatment of the crime of incest provides another example of the double standard. Most often, it is the girl—the victim—who is sent to a foster home while the father stays behind. And children's-rights advocate Kenneth Wooden estimates that 40 percent of the girls and young women in city and county jails who were picked up as runaways left home after being sexually molested.

Seventeen-year-old Dominica was sexually assaulted by one of her mother's four husbands. She ran away from home. Picked up by the police, she was placed on probation and returned home. Dominica left again, and was charged with violating probation. Thus she became a full-fledged delinquent.

For the young woman who engages in sexual intercourse of her own volition, school hardly offers a more understanding environment than home, should she become pregnant. Many schools suspend pregnant students or encourage them to "voluntarily" withdraw.

For the overwhelmingly male-dominated juvenile justice hierarchy, young women's sexuality is "offensive," as spelled out in the following statement made in 1975 by Hunter Hurst, Director of the Juvenile Justice Division of the National Council of Juvenile Court Judges:

The issue is that status offenses are offenses against our values. Girls are seemingly overrepresented as status offenders because we have a strong heritage of being protective towards females in this country. It offends our sensibility and our values to have a 14-year-old girl engage in sexually promiscuous activity. It's not the way we like to think about females in this country.

As long as it offends our values, be sure that the police, or the church or vigilante groups, or somebody is going to do something about it. For me, I would rather that something occur in the court where the rights of the parties can be protected.

"We play big daddy," confessed another judge.

Carol Zimmerman, Executive Director of the Arizona-based New Directors for Young Women, which compiled the foregoing comments, sees girls caught in a double bind: If they remain in school, they are molded along lines that limit their futures, and if they cut classes or stop going altogether, they can wind up in jail.

A great many young women out of school drop out because school isn't meeting their needs; because they aren't getting any encouragement, because the attitude is "you don't really need to learn a career, you don't really need to go on and work, you're going to be taken care of, you're going to marry."

They find no reason to stay in school, to attend classes. They drop out—and become part of the juvenile justice system. The courts say, "You're a truant, you're a dropout, I remand you to this-and-this facility."

"Sexism," adds Shirley McKuen of the Research Center on Sex Roles in Education, "is clearly a part of the curriculum in all educational agencies and institutions." (Jolly notes that there are 48 Job Corps Centers for young men and only 10 for young women, despite higher unemployment rates for female youth.)

One important factor in the disproportionate detention rate for girls is that many times their parents refuse to take them home. When it comes time for a court hearing, this parental attitude can prejudice the female youth's chances, as Chesney-Lind points out.

"Children charged with crimes have natural allies in their parents at every step in the judicial process," she writes. But, "Parents of young people charged with status offenses are, themselves, the complainants, and they not only impugn the moral character of their children but frequently refuse to take them home in an attempt to force the court official to retain jurisdiction. Since the determination of good moral character is pivotal in the determination of guilt or innocence in the juvenile justice system, this parental orientation is significant."

A parental attitude toward young female offenders and minors in general is reflected in the 1967 U.S. Supreme Court decision awarding children some rights of due process, but not the same ones from which adults benefit. In re Gault, the Court wrote that "The right of the State, as parens patriae, to deny to the child procedural rights available to his elders was elaborated by the assertions that a child, unlike an adult, has a right not to liberty but to custody."

State intervention is warranted, the Justices voted, when "parents default in effectively performing their custodial functions." When the State does inject itself in a child's life, they continued, "it does not deprive the child of any rights, because he has none."

Two years ago, adults receiving a jury trial stood a 48 percent chance of conviction; adults facing only a judge were convicted 65 percent of the time. In juvenile court, the "conviction" rate is a staggering 89 percent, according to Wally Mlyniec, Director of the Juvenile Justice Clinic of the Georgetown University Law Center in Washington, D.C.

Where young women are concerned, this conviction rate, combined with the "protective" or paternal attitude, portends a high probability for confinement.

Author Kenneth Wooden asserts that female juveniles receive longer sentences than male juveniles, although the girls' crimes are usually less serious. The average term of incarceration for a young man is 9 months, Wooden says, on charges ranging from truancy to rape, while the average period of confinement for young women offenders is one year—33 percent longer.

"The alleged justifications (for incarceration in secure facilities) may be diverse and not always apparent," Jolly offers, "but the subcommittee has discovered that the application and results are clearly discriminatory."

"The fact that . . . sexist community norms exist," adds Chesney-Lind, "is no justification for involving agencies of the law in their enforcement, any more than community prejudices would justify judicial racism."

For Judge Lisa Richette of the Court of Common Pleas in Philadelphia, "The offense of most of the young women going before the courts was nonconformity to a social model of what is accepted behavior for young girls. The juvenile courts should no longer act as a legal chastity belt placed around the waists of young women."

3. *Each social welfare organization is itself a system.* It is made up of many categories of people (administrators, clerical staff, professional staff, consumers, and so forth). Each relates to the others in specified ways, and the actions of each affects the ability of the others to function. For example, if a social worker quits and the social agency hires another to fill the position, a series of effects result that are felt both within the agency and by the agency's users. The caseload of the departing worker must be redistributed among other workers so that service is not interrupted. Workers who receive the reallocated cases must then contact the clients involved and start to develop a meaningful relationship with each. The clients in turn must find ways of continuing their activities with minimal disruption or setback. Meanwhile, all members of the agency must help the newly hired person learn agency procedures and establish facilitative relationships within the agency: Agency administrators must try to help the new worker become productive as quickly as possible; other professionals should try to help their new colleague; and clerical personnel must train the new person in the use of forms and other agency procedures.

There have been numerous other attempts to define systems within social welfare. One of the most popular definitions is by Pincus and Minahan, who identify four systems involved in any helping effort:[4]

1. *Change agent system:* The change agent and the people who are part of his agency or employing organization.
2. *Client system:* People who sanction or ask for the change agent's services, who are the expected beneficiaries of services, and who have a working agreement or contract with the change agent.
3. *Target system:* People who need to be changed to accomplish the goals of the change agent.
4. *Action system:* The change agent and the people he works with and through to accomplish his goals and influence the target system.

Regardless of the framework used and the level of specificity chosen, the message of systems is inescapable: Social welfare structures and activities pervade our society, and social welfare cannot be understood without understanding how it relates to the various parts of the larger society.

The interlocking nature of systems, especially social welfare systems, highlights the fact that the social welfare institution affects more than just the people providing and obtaining services; it also, through its various systems, affects many other systems and is in turn affected by them. Professional people are affected by their professional membership, training, and values, as well as by the structure of the specific agency in which work is performed. The consumers of services are affected by their diverse group memberships based on such factors as race, sex, ethnicity, and life-style, as well as by a wide variety of life constraints (such as employment, family, and income). Nonconsumers, who may never enter a social welfare agency and who may never identify themselves as recipients of social welfare services,* are affected by their own life-space realities. Yet, in spite of their differences, the systems to which they belong affect each other. Nonconsumers participate in political decision making, which has important influences on the societal mandate for social welfare. Consumers decide to use or not use services, or to complain or not complain about them, thereby affecting agency operation and even the societal mandate. Professions change service delivery strategies, thus affecting service delivery. Throughout the total social welfare institution, it is necessary to understand the system concept and its application to specific social welfare-related systems. This concept will be studied in more detail in Chapter 4. For the purposes of this chapter, however, it is sufficient to understand the interrelatedness of the social forces that operate on and within the social welfare institution. Exhibit 1-4 attempts to elaborate on this interrelatedness.

* This self-identification is usually incorrect, since practically everyone receives social welfare services in one way or another.

EXHIBIT 1-4 *The Social Welfare System in Action: Skid-Row Alcoholics*

Jacqueline Wiseman, in *Stations of the Lost: The Treatment of Skid-Row Alcoholics*, takes an in-depth look at the organization and operation of the major social welfare agencies that serve skid-row alcoholics. She notes that there are a variety of agencies that serve such alcoholics, ranging from specialized agencies (missions, alcoholism schools) to multipurpose agencies that serve many other types of persons along with alcoholics (hospitals, jails, welfare homes). She also notes that a variety of professions is involved in the provision of services—medical, corrections, social work, religious, and the like. These many agencies and professions are interrelated in a system that contains the alcoholic, and which Wiseman calls the "loop."

Wiseman's general conclusion, supported through extensive interview data, is that the loop is ineffective in meeting the needs of the skid-row alcoholic. The various agencies and professions in the system are so concerned with meeting their own organizational and professional needs that they are frequently insensitive to the needs of the alcoholic. For example, two value approaches determine the services offered: (1) "Punitive-Correctional Strategies," focusing on control and containment when alcoholism is seen as "sheer self-indulgence"; and (2) "Strategies of Therapy," when alcoholism is seen as the result of psychological and physiological problems, or moral and spiritual problems. The use of these approaches bears little relationship to the feelings and preferences of the alcoholic—the agency simply offers service as it sees fit, and the alcoholic must take it or leave it (except when it is actually forced upon him, as when he is arrested).

Another example of the way agency needs dominate in the provision of services is in the selection of services provided. While there are many agencies and services, they are for the most part unrelated to each other. Each agency decides on its services and offers them as it wishes. There may be overlap with other agencies, and some needs may not be met by any agency. The alcoholic has no control over these decisions. He simply has the loop as the professionals decide to structure it. The result is that alcoholics tend to go from agency to agency, getting what they can at each, but nowhere having the multi-faceted totality of their needs met.

As a system, the loop is essentially oriented toward achieving its own equilibrium, in this case each of the agencies involved maintaining its own autonomy in policy-making and service delivery. Alcoholics are part of the system in that they provide the rationale for the existence of many of the agencies and their services, but within the system they have no power they could use to make it more responsive to their needs. In striving to justify their own existence, the agencies are responding to external systems as well, since they depend on public and private sources of funds, and the good-will and mandate of the public (who, among other things, are sources of referrals). In describing the loop, Wiseman clearly illustrates a system, its structure, and its attempt to maintain internal cohesion and external support. She also illustrates some of the dilemmas of professional autonomy referred to in Exhibit 1-1. While the social welfare agencies described by Wiseman are generally successful in maintaining their own autonomy in policy-making and service delivery, they are generally unsuccessful in meeting the needs of those they serve. At the same time, those being served have no power to affect policy or services. What is the solution?

The table below and the figure on p. 16, based on Wiseman's work, illustrate the points above. In the table, the professional contexts in which social welfare services are offered to skid-row alcoholics are shown and briefly described. The figure illustrates the operation of the loop; it is easy to see the hapless and powerless alcoholic making the rounds of the agencies.

Professional Contexts in which Social Welfare Service to Skid-Row Alcoholics is Offered:	*Official Goal is Rehabilitation of the Alcoholic. Means Used in Goal Attainment:*
City jail	Place to sober up and dry out; context in which alcoholic is punished for public drunkenness (norm violation).
Alcoholism school	Education on the evils of alcoholism.
County jail	Same as city jail, except more severe (longer sentences) for repeaters (chronic norm violators).
State mental hospital	Drying out and psychological therapy (emphasis on alcoholism as an illness).
Jail branch clinic	Same as state mental hospital.
Out-patient therapy center	Psychological therapy.
Welfare home for homeless men	Drying out; informal therapy; food and shelter provided.
Clinics and hospitals	Detoxification; treatment for physical problems caused by alcoholism or skid-row life.
Christian missionaries	Spiritual renewal; food and shelter provided; employment.

Routes by Which Skid-Row Alcoholics Enter Treatment Contexts

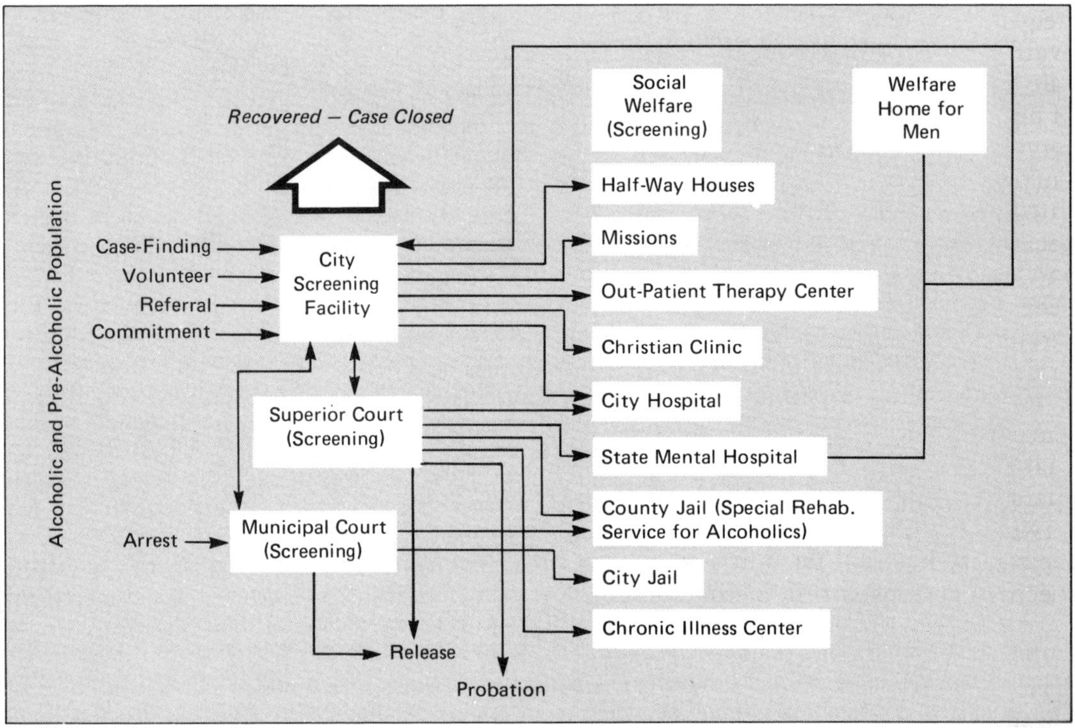

Source: Table on p. 15 and figure above are from Jacqueline P. Wiseman, *Stations of the Lost: The Treatment of Skid-Row Alcoholics*, © 1970, pp. 51 and 55. By permission of Prentice-Hall, Inc., Englewood Cliffs, N.J.

The Structure of Social Welfare Services: An Overview

The structure of social welfare services in United States society is complex and fragmented. Details about specific services are provided at a number of points throughout the book, and such details are not the point of this section. Rather, a full understanding of the nature of the social welfare institution, and ultimately of specific programs, rests on an understanding of the underlying structure of services. This structure can be understood most simply in terms of four continuums: institutional to residual; public or private; income maintenance or social service; and the focus of services. These continuums can be used to "chart" an individual program and illuminate some of the underlying concepts and values of social welfare in this society:

Institutional to Residual

An *institutional* social welfare service is available to all as a normal part of the social environment. Such services are considered *rights* of the members of a society. Institutional services are sometimes called *universal services*, because access is not limited by economic status. Another term frequently used is *public social utility*, meaning that the programs are available at the initiative of the potential consumers.[5] Just as the police, a safe water system, and public education are available to all, so the concept of public social utility suggests that a whole range of other social welfare services can be provided on this basis. On the other hand, institutional/universal/utility services may require that the recipient fall into a certain category—a child, a parent, an elderly person, and so forth. This is simply because the service is structured to meet the needs of a particular group and would not be appropriate for members of other groups. However, all people within the group for which the service is intended may request the service, simply because they are group members. No other criteria are used in deciding whether someone can receive the service.

Residual services are available only to those who can prove the existence of a specific need and who can also prove that they meet the qualifications specified for receipt of that service. Having to prove need and qualifications is called establishing *eligibility*, and in contrast to receiving services as one's right simply by membership in a group (which could be the society itself), it refers to a system in which services are restricted to specified persons within a group.

Public or Private

Services that are funded from public monies, exist by public mandate, or are administered in publicly funded agencies are called *public social welfare services. Private social welfare services*, in contrast, are generally funded from private monies (such as individual contributions, foundation grants, and corporate donations); they exist because an agency's policymaking body mandated them; and they are administered in an agency supported by private funds. The distinction between public and private services is not always clear-cut, however, because private agencies are increasingly providing services for public agencies on a contractual basis. Nevertheless, the basic distinction in conception between public and private services continues to be significant: public agencies are sponsored by and accountable to society as a whole, and private agencies are not.[6]

Kramer notes the following functions generally ascribed to private agencies: (1) introducing innovative programs; (2) guarding values; (3) strengthening and expanding public services; and (4) filling service gaps.[7] Each of these functions deserves a brief elaboration:

Introducing innovative programs. The flexibility that private agencies may have because of their freedom from the legislative process has made it possible for some of them to experiment with programs for which there would not be adequate political support. Behavior modification, birth control counseling, and halfway houses are examples. Some of the innovative programs, having proven their value, are later taken over or supported by public agencies.

Guarding values. Private agencies can be responsive to the needs of special interest groups and are readily accessible to citizen participation. Indeed, many private programs, such as the Red Cross, depend heavily on volunteer participation. In a multicultural society, having the needs of all groups expressed can be very functional.

Strengthening and expanding public services. Private agencies can serve as a stimulus to public agencies to improve their services. They can help people identify and obtain services from public agencies, and they can communicate with the public agency to push for more adequate services when a need has been identified.

Filling service gaps. Because private agencies can be more flexible, they have traditionally tried to provide services that were not provided by public agencies.

Kramer summarizes his review of the traditional functions of private agencies by noting:[8]

> *Both theory and experience suggest that the discretion-potential of the (private agency) is probably its most outstanding feature . . . setting the limits of its responsibility and choosing whom it will serve, to what extent, how, where, and in what ways . . . . Once choices are made, they tend to become institutionalized, resist change, and be subject to a host of constraints and organizational commitments.*

In spite of their potential for innovative, flexible, specialized programs, private agencies have been criticized for several reasons:[9]

1. *Progressive detachment from the poor.* The limited resources of private agencies have combined with their emphasis on professionalism to create a network of services frequently oriented toward the sophisticated consumer rather than the most needy.
2. *Overreliance on individual treatment.* Private agencies have generally been characterized by a belief in individual counseling rather than intervention oriented to the group or community. This is inherently limiting, but all the more so because the effectiveness and efficiency of many of the techniques traditionally used have been seriously questioned.
3. *Neglect of social change.* To the extent that the focus of private agencies has been on the nonpoor, there has been much less emphasis

on social change, since the needs of the nonpoor are not so likely to be a direct result of existing social conditions.

4. *Increasing bureaucratization, unrepresentativeness, and professionalization.* As private agencies have focused on the needs of special groups and on highly professionalized treatment, they have tended to become more rigid and less responsive to the range of needs that may exist in a community. These problems have been accentuated by contracting with public agencies, which then may impose additional service delivery standards and structures.[10]
5. *Dependence on mass, impersonal fund raising.* In an attempt to maximize fund-raising efficiency and minimize antagonism created when many agencies solicit funds from the same people, cooperative community fund-raising efforts, such as the United Fund, have been used. Unfortunately, donors then have little direct contact with the agencies to which they contribute.

In spite of their potential flexibility, private agencies are in trouble, as Exhibit 1-5 will reveal. Public expenditures for social welfare are far in excess of private expenditures. This fact reflects society's commitment to a more adequate social welfare system. Public resources are expanding while private resources are not, and the inability of private agencies to generate resources may well further limit their involvement in change-oriented services for the poor. This tends to make their services even more responsive to the special-interest groups that provide funds and to minimize flexibility and innovation. Nevertheless, Kramer notes that the trend toward more public services may not be altogether desirable because of bureaucratic problems. To summarize this discussion of public and private services, Exhibit 1-5 presents an analysis of some current issues affecting them, while Exhibit 1-6 looks at some of the specific structural differences between them.

Trends in Private Philanthropy **EXHIBIT 1-5**

Private giving to social welfare through organized community drives has been declining in recent years, causing many to fear the demise of private giving and the serious weakening of private social welfare services as a result. In our society in which the federal income tax looms so large, its relationship to charitable contributions is a crucial variable in understanding the future of private philanthropy and hence of private social welfare services. After an overview of public and private giving in the table, this exhibit presents a thoughtful discussion of charitable contributions in their social context.

Source: Wade Greene, "A Farewell to Alms," *New York Times Magazine*, May 23, 1976, pp. 36–46. © 1976 by The New York Times Company. Reprinted by permission.

Public and Private Expenditures for Social Welfare Purposes
(For fiscal years, in millions of current dollars)

Type of expenditure	*1950*	*1955*	*1960*	*1965*	*1970*	*1975*[a]
Total, net[b]	35,337	49,957	78,704	117,871	211,033	388,695
Public	23,508	32,640	52,293	77,175	145,761	286,547
Private	12,160	17,997	27,790	42,766	67,995	107,752
Income maintenance	10,723	17,304	29,827	42,530	72,399	152,794
Public[c]	9,758	15,409	26,292	36,575	60,814	132,094
Private	965	1,895	3,535	5,955	11,585	20,700
Health	12,027	17,330	25,856	38,892	69,201	118,499
Public	3,065	4,421	6,395	9,535	25,237	49,947
Private	8,962	12,909	19,461	29,357	43,964	68,552
Education	10,914	14,206	21,742	34,228	62,368	98,359
Public	9,366	11,863	18,036	28,149	51,922	82,859
Private	1,548	2,343	3,706	6,079	10,446	15,500
Welfare and other services	2,004	1,797	2,658	4,291	9,788	24,647
Public[c]	1,319	947	1,570	2,916	7,788	21,647
Private	685	850	1,088	1,375	2,000	3,000
Public Expenditures as a Percent of All Expenditures						
Total[d]	65.9%	64.5%	65.3%	64.3%	68.2%	72.7%
Income maintenance	91.0	89.0	88.1	86.0	84.0	86.5
Health	25.5	25.5	24.7	24.5	36.5	42.1
Education	85.8	83.5	83.0	82.2	83.3	84.2
Welfare and other services	65.8	52.7	59.1	68.0	79.6	87.8
All Expenditures as Percent of Gross National Product						
Total, net[b]	13.4	13.2	15.9	18.0	22.1	27.3
Income maintenance	4.1	4.6	6.0	6.5	7.6	10.7
Health	4.6	4.6	5.2	5.9	7.2	8.3
Education	4.1	3.7	4.4	5.2	6.5	6.9
Welfare and other services	.8	.5	.5	.7	1.0	1.7

Public Expenditures						
Total	23,508	32,640	52,293	77,175	145,761	286,547
Income maintenance	41.5	47.2	50.3	47.4	41.7	46.1
Health	13.0	13.5	12.2	12.4	17.3	17.4
Education	39.8	36.3	34.5	36.5	35.6	28.9
Welfare	5.6	2.9	3.0	3.8	5.3	7.6
Private Expenditures						
Total	12,160	17,997	27,790	42,766	67,995	107,752
Income maintenance	7.9	10.5	12.7	13.9	17.0	19.2
Health	73.7	71.7	70.0	68.6	64.7	63.6
Education	12.7	13.0	13.3	14.2	15.4	14.4
Welfare	5.6	4.7	3.9	3.2	2.9	2.8
Public and Private Expenditures in Constant (1975) Dollars						
Total, net[b]	73,772	91,833	130,955	185,332	283,266	388,695
Public	49,077	60,000	87,010	121,344	195,652	286,547
Private	25,386	33,082	46,240	67,242	91,268	107,752
Price deflators[e]	47.9	54.4	60.1	63.6	74.5	100.0
	1950–75	*1950–55*	*1955–60*	*1960–65*	*1965–70*	*1970–75*
Average Annual Percent Change in Constant (1975) Dollar Expenditures						
Total, net	6.64	4.38	7.10	6.95	8.48	6.33
Public	7.06	4.02	7.43	6.65	9.55	7.63
Private	5.78	5.30	6.70	7.49	6.11	3.32

Source: U.S. Department of Commerce, *Social Indicators, 1976* (Washington, D.C.: U.S. Government Printing Office), p. 129.

[a] Preliminary data.

[b] Total expenditures adjusted to eliminate duplication resulting from use of cash payments received under public and private social welfare programs to purchase medical care and educational services.

[c] See technical notes for inclusions under these programs.

[d] Before adjustment for elimination of duplication.

[e] See technical notes for explanation.

The moment was exquisitely American. It was a final drawing in New Jersey's bicentennially inspired special lottery, held in the auditorium of Montclair State College. The top prize: $1,776 a week for life. And the winner: holder of finalist ticket No. 10, Eric D. Leek, a 26-year-old hairdresser. "Praise the Lord," Leek shouted as he swept stageward. "I hope to use the money for the betterment of mankind." One project he had in mind was building a youth center "to keep a lot of kids off the streets."

The moment, early this year, was the drawing for the biggest lottery in American history and it seemed to capture the national character not only because it was a celebration of instant wealth—a kind of contemporary Horatio Alger denouement in which blind, mysterious luck rather than planning and perseverance was, contemporarily, the secret of success—but also because instant wealth was accompanied by instant beneficence.

Leek was responding to the widely acclaimed American spirit of philanthropy, a spirit that has moved millions of Americans, from pious Protestant almsgivers who heeded the counsel of Cotton Mather, to John D. Rockefeller, who gave away nickels and dimes, and who, like other founders of great fortunes, bureaucratized philanthropy in a foundation bearing his name, to factory workers who give the United Way through payroll deductions to churchgoers who leave their contributions on felt-bottomed silver plates.

In all, it is estimated that Americans gave close to $27 billion last year and volunteered a roughly equivalent value in services. A wide array of organizations—as many as six million, by one estimate: symphonies, youth centers, Junior Leagues, birth control clinics, etc.—subsist totally, or in part, on such gifts. The dimensions of American generosity and the institutional "third sector" (after government and business) that it has supported are sizable by any reckoning and have been widely recognized as basic to the pluralistic fabric of our society. Some say that they are, indeed, prerequisites of free initiative and responsible citizenship.

Yet, throughout history, Americans have also evidenced considerable uneasiness about philanthropy, as historian Robert Bremner has noted, about its overtones of paternalism and its seeming approval of economic and class distinction. And in this time of rising egalitarian expectations, of widespread disenchantment with our institutions and of expanding government, we are, I believe, attending the disintegration of philanthropy, in its traditional forms, as a major force in American society. . . .

Since the Depression and the growth of the welfare state, nearly all major "philanthropic" or "charitable" functions have become or are becoming the province of government. Higher education, for instance, has been a principal preserve of private institutions, privately supported, through most of American history. As recently as 1950, a majority of American students of higher education attended private colleges and universities. But today, that proportion has shrunk to less than one-quarter, as state universities and colleges have swelled in size and number. At the same time, as their labor-intensive costs have soared far faster than their contributions, private educational institutions have found themselves relying more and more on government funds to balance their own books; they are becoming more and more public in their basic, financial underpinnings. . . .

Private beneficence toward the poor—which historically has been the bedrock function of philanthropy or charity—has become relatively minuscule in relation to the government's immense social insurance and income maintenance programs, thanks largely to the Social Security Act of 1935 and repeated enlargements. Voluntary hospitals, like public and profit-making hospitals, draw increasingly from government programs, principally Medicare and Medicaid.

Aside from religion, the only area of traditional philanthropy that remains mainly private and privately supported is the arts-and-culture field, but financially distressed museums, symphony orchestras, ballet companies and the like are turning to local, state and Federal budget makers to help keep them afloat. National "endowments" and state arts councils are among new governmental bodies that have been set up to channel public funds into these areas.

Underlying these shifts is the fact that Americans, as members of an abundant society, have come to expect a certain standard of living as their birthright and have therefore turned to government for better education, minimum income, health care. They no longer are willing to rely on the beneficence of private organizations and individuals. . . .

As government has increasingly become—or is looked to as—the principal provider of "philanthropy," the question grows as to what, if anything, remains for purely private, nonprofit, "philanthropic" organizations to do. The answer lies in functions that government cannot effectively fill. Religion remains one area that is constitutionally off-limits to government. Keeping a public-interest eye on government itself is another such function. And it is this function, I believe, that provides the major secular frontier for nonprofit activity—in the place of traditional "philanthropy." In recent years, in fact, the voluntary sector has given birth to many thousands of organizations whose major purpose is to conduct research and try to persuade government to act in what they regard as the public interest. . . .

The donor end of philanthropy is also changing, slowly, reluctantly in some cases, but no less profoundly. The most obvious change is in size. Donations are shrinking. . . .

People may be giving less because they feel that government is, or should be, attending to needs they are being asked to support.

A major related change may also be under way in the motivations behind giving. The donor may be becoming more activated by what giving does for him or her than by what it does for the donee. According to conventional wisdom, givers have always given in areas that reinforce their own tastes and values, or that have provided them with direct services. The rich give above all to higher education, voluntary hospitals (which in some cases have had to be legally prodded into accepting poor patients), to art and cultural groups. Lower-income contributors give mostly to religion; they can be regarded as buying celestial insurance or paying dues to what for many are social as well as religious institutions. But self-interest and self-expression may be becoming all the more central to the act of giving as giving itself becomes less essential to the support of traditional philanthropic institutions and causes.

Giving for the giver's sake need not be a cynical notion. In a time when men and women are seen to be alienated from their communities and institutions and to feel impotent in dealing with them, giving can provide the contributor with a means of personal involvement in, and influence over, the world around him or her. The giving of money often tends to be accompanied by the giving of time; those who do one are likely to do the other. The donor's involvement, in other words, often extends well beyond a few moments' thought and the signing of a check. And in its contribution to social cohesion, this involvement may prove to be more valuable than the specific causes it serves. . . .

Since 1917, nearly as long as the progressive income tax has been a fact of American life, we have allowed taxpayers to subtract certain contributions from the income they pay taxes on. The "charitable" deduction plays a central role in influencing both the amount and the direction of giving. According to econometric studies made for the Commission on Private Philanthropy and Public Needs, one-third of all giving is generated by the deduction. . . .

Like all tax deductions under the progressive income tax, the charitable deduction lowers a high-income taxpayer's taxes more, for any deducted amount, than it does the taxes of someone in a lower bracket; the richer the giver the greater encouragement to—or subsidy of—his or her giving. The taxpayer in the maximum, 70 percent bracket, for instance, reduces his taxes by 70 cents for every dollar he or she can deduct, and therefore sacrifices a net of only 30 cents for every dollar given away. While at the other end of the income-tax spectrum, a taxpayer saves only 14 cents in taxes for every dollar deducted: The cost of giving is 86 cents for each dollar. Two-thirds of taxpayers now use the standard deduction—most of them in low-to-middle-income ranks—and they do not reduce their taxes at all by giving; a dollar given costs them a full dollar out of pocket. . . .

If tax changes provide a promising avenue toward redefining and revitalizing giving in America, herein also lies a sizable obstacle. The possibility exists that those institutions that benefit from current tax incentives will, in their understandable efforts to shore up their own, often precarious finances, successfully stifle changes in tax incentives. They may do so until any tax provisions at all for giving are abandoned as the existing ones become increasingly less defensible. If so, an opportunity for establishing a durable underpinning for the independent institutional sector will have become irretrievably lost.

EXHIBIT 1-6 *Differences between Public and Private Agencies*

Arthur Dunham, in *The New Community Organization* (1970), has a very helpful summary of the major differences between public (governmental) and private (voluntary) agencies. The summary reproduced here should help the reader understand the different sanctions, functions, problems, and potential of each.

Governmental (Public)	*Voluntary (Private)*
Sanctions	
1. Established by law: a. Legal authority for its activities. b. Must carry out provisions of the law. c. Cannot go beyond the law.	1. Usually established by interested group of persons. Articles of incorporation, constitution, by-laws, or charter from national agency is usually its instrument of government.
2. Law tends to define powers and duties fairly precisely; relatively inflexible.	2. Objectives and functions may be expressed in fairly general terms; program may be potentially quite flexible.
3. Law is difficult to amend; requires legislative action.	3. Constitution and by-laws usually easy to amend. Articles of incorporation usually stated in general terms. National charter amendable only on national level.
4. Part of the larger structure of local, state, or federal government.	4. Usually more or less autonomous association, sometimes a subsidiary unit of a national agency. The agency's governing board usually determines most of the policies.
5. More tendency toward large size and bureaucratic organization.	5. Size varies, though usually not as large as major governmental agency in same size community.
6. Personnel usually employed under civil service.	6. Employment standards usually determined by agency; may be determined or influenced by national agency or United Fund.
7. Subject to outside administrative controls—chief executive (governor, mayor, etc.), personnel, budgeting, auditing, legislative committees, courts.	7. Outside administrative controls usually limited mainly to United Fund, national agency, laws regarding licensing, etc.
8. Agency is a part of a political "administration." It is related to governmental and political power structure and may be subject to partisan political pressures.	8. Agency is related to the "community power structure"—primarily the economic power structure.

Governmental (Public)	Voluntary (Private)
Support	
9. Income derived primarily from tax funds, appropriated by a legislative body.	9. Income (in the past) usually derived primarily from voluntary contributions, either to the United Fund or the national agency.
10. Funds obtained through governmental budgeting and appropriation process.	10. Funds obtained usually through United Fund budgeting process or through arrangements with national agency. [May also contract with public agencies to provide specified services.]
11. Accounting and auditing procedures subject to law and governmental regulations.	11. Accounting and auditing procedures usually subject to procedures of United Fund or national agency.

Source: From *The New Community Organization,* by Arthur Dunham (Thomas Y. Crowell). Copyright © 1970 by Harper & Row, Publishers, Inc. Reprinted by permission of the publisher.

Income Maintenance or Social Service

Services that improve a recipient's financial situation are called *income maintenance* services. Although they are most often financial in nature, such as a *cash grant* to supplement other income or to provide the only income available to a person or group, they may also be given *in kind,* which is the provision of a needed resource that the person or group would otherwise have had to purchase. Cash grants and in-kind programs usually involve *income transfers,* meaning that money from one segment of the population (collected through taxes or other means) is redistributed to others in the form of grants or in-kind resources. *Tax allowances* is a way of transferring income by allowing certain groups to exclude some of their income from the amount upon which taxes are calculated, thereby forcing the use of tax monies collected from those groups that did not have these exemptions to fund services. A different kind of income maintenance program is a *social insurance,* in which persons who have paid into a fund during one period collect from it during another period. Social security (OASDHI) and unemployment insurance are social insurances. In general, social insurances carry less stigma than either cash grants or in-kind services. In one case, people are receiving their own money back (although in fact any insurance spreads risk, so some receive more than they contributed and others receive less), whereas with cash grants and in-kind services, people are receiving money collected from others. In a society that so highly prizes personal independence and self-responsibility, it is understandable why social insurances carry less stigma. However, the attribution of stigma to those receiving cash grants and in-kind services ignores the very legitimate and unavoidable circumstances that may leave people destitute and helpless. In most cases, the creation of such severe financial need is socially created, as in periods of economic depressions or under circumstances of widespread discrimination against minority groups.

Whereas income maintenance services focus on improving people's financial situation, *social services* are oriented toward helping people with their nonfinancial needs (although some nonfinancial services, such as budget counseling, may effectively improve people's financial situation). Social services, which are sometimes also called *personal social services,* tend to focus on developmental and socialization tasks. Examples include child welfare services (adoption, foster care, protective services, residential facilities), family counseling, homemaker services, protective care for the aged, day care, community centers, congregate meals and meals-on-wheels, self-help and mutual-aid activities, information and referral services, and recreational services.[11] Social services may be provided free, or a fee may be required. Often fees are calculated on a *sliding scale,* being increased or decreased according to an individual's or group's ability to pay.

Income maintenance and social service programs may be either public or private. Social security (OASDHI), an income maintenance program, is public, whereas payments made by Traveler's Aid to help people obtain needed food, lodging, or transportation come from private funds administered through a nonpublic agency. Similarly, AFDC mothers can get personal counseling as well as a check from a state or county Department of Social Services, a public agency, whereas if they went to a family service agency they would receive the same types of services but under private auspices.

The Focus of Services

Services may seek to prevent the occurrence of a need (*preventive*), to meet a current need but to prevent its future occurrence (*rehabilitative*), or simply meet a need after it has occurred (*curative*).

Although any service can be analyzed according to these four continuums, it is often difficult to place any given service at one end or the other of each continuum. Many services fall somewhere in between on one or more of the continuums, reflecting the complex nature of the services that are available. Exhibit 1-7 summarizes several of these concepts and

EXHIBIT 1-7 *The Scope and Focus of Social Welfare*

The magnitude and complexity of the American social welfare system can make it difficult to comprehend. This exhibit illustrates the kinds of social welfare services that would exist in various types of systems using the framework presented in the text. Concrete examples of existing services are provided for illustrative purposes. Further analysis of the distinction between residual and institutional social welfare systems may be found in Harold Wilensky and Charles Lebeaux, *Industrial Society and Social Welfare* (New York: Free Press, 1958).

An Institutionalized Social Welfare System

Social welfare services are built into the normal functioning of the social system. They are available as a matter of course to the participants in the social system. The American social welfare system has some institutionalized segments, such as public education, but most social welfare services are available only upon evidence of need and qualification for the service.

1. *Curative Institutionalized Services.* Institutionalized services to help when a problem arises. Free hospital care would be an example of such a service, since it would provide needed care for all in the event of illness. Few curative institutionalized services actually exist in contemporary North America. The legal system is one of the closest approximations of such an existing service, since it is available to all in times of need. This includes the police as a social service resource available to handle an extremely wide range of personal and social problems.

2. *Preventive Institutionalized Services.* Such institutionalized services prevent the future occurrences of personal and social problems. Free medical care would be an example of such a service, since it would enable everyone to enjoy the benefits of preventive medicine. Preventive institutionalized services are not common in our society, but free public education is one example of such an existing service. It is intended to guarantee an education to a certain level, helping to prepare the individual for a satisfying and productive life in the social system of which that person is a part.

3. *Rehabilitative Institutionalized Services.* Institutionalized social welfare services that help those with an existing problem overcome it and avoid similar problems in the future. An example would be free marital counseling, whereby those experiencing marital problems could be helped to solve these problems and develop the skills to avoid similar problems in the future. One of the very few rehabilitative institutionalized services available in our society is the United States Employment Service. It assists the unemployed to find work, as well as providing job training to try to avoid unemployment in the future.

A Residual Social Welfare System

Residual social welfare services are provided only to those in crisis who also qualify for the service. Therefore, residual social welfare services are only selectively available. The majority of the United States social welfare system is of the residual type.

1. *Curative Residual Services.* These services help those who qualify when a problem arises. Medical care is an excellent example, since medical services are available only to those sick persons who can afford it (either by paying cash, by having health insurance, or by being on public assistance). Disaster victims (floods, tornados, fires, etc.) generally qualify for services to meet their basic needs, another example of a curative residual service.

2. *Preventive Residual Services.* These services help prevent the future occurrence of personal and social problems. Prevention and residual are almost by definition exclusive, but nevertheless, some preventive services do exist for selected groups in American society. Social Security is an example, in that eligible individuals contribute to a fund that will provide income when they are no longer able to work, thereby helping to prevent poverty in old age.

3. *Rehabilitative Residual Services.* These services help selected persons with an existing problem overcome the problem and avoid similar problems in the future. Here again there is a certain inconsistency between rehabilitation and residual, but programs that are both do exist. The WIN (Work Incentive) program for public assistance mothers is an example. The purpose of the program is to help financially needy unemployed mothers obtain job training so that they can hopefully become self-supporting, thereby improving their own self-image as well as their family's standard of living.

The above analytical framework is not completely comprehensive or mutually exclusive. For example, the line between prevention and rehabilitation is not always clearcut, and residual services shade into institutionalized services in some cases. Even so, it is helpful when trying to disentangle some of the complex characteristics of the social welfare system in the United States, since it is such a mixture of all parts of the framework.

continuums; others are illustrated at various points throughout the book. Appendix A provides a selected list of federal programs that seek to improve an individual's or family's income. This is only a partial list, intended to familiarize the reader with some of the major federal programs as well as to illustrate the complexity of our current social welfare system.

▶ Defining Social Welfare Needs

If social welfare is to help people function more effectively in order to achieve their life goals, the specific needs that must be met to accomplish this goal have to be known. Although certain needs seem obvious to most of us—we all know that some people are physically handicapped, that others are poor—defining needs in specific, comprehensive, and verifiable ways is a complex and often elusive process.[12] When attempting to identify needs, at least four characteristics of the needs in question should be considered:

1. *What needs exist.* Needs range from very personal needs to interactional needs to community and society needs. A commonly made distinction is between personal problems versus public issues. If two people are getting a divorce, it is a personal problem, but if close to half the marriages in society are ending in divorce, it is a public issue. In other words, the creation of a comprehensive social welfare institution is dependent on the comprehensive definition of needs existing at all levels in the social structure. Recalling our earlier discussion of systems, if a need is identified in one system but related needs in other systems are ignored, one cannot hope to achieve a really satisfactory solution to the identified need, because it is affected by the other unidentified needs.

2. *Who has needs.* Different groups usually have different needs. This fact results from different groups having had different experiences in the societal structure, resulting in different goals, different resources, and different obstacles. Here, too, however, all of these groups interact in one way or another, so a comprehensive social welfare system depends on the needs of all groups being identified. Although the needs of the coal miners of Appalachia may seem far removed from the needs of urbane San Franciscans, their mutual dependence on adequate energy and social order creates a level of interdependence.

3. *The frequency, severity, and impact of needs.* Some needs result from rare unanticipated events, such as floods. Others are chronic, such as some types of physical incapacity. Some create minor disruptions in behavior, as we experience when our car breaks down and we have no transportation, while other needs prevent us from functioning completely, as is the case with severe mental illness. Here again, the point is that needs come in many different forms, they affect different people differently, and

they have varying impacts on people and situations. Our goal is to try to identify all of them and to build a social welfare structure that offers help in all cases.

4. *Who has defined the needs.* Very often persons who are actually experiencing needs are unable to interpret them to others. This may be because they lack the ability to effectively articulate their needs (children are an example), or because they are denied access to channels through which they can communicate with others. The poor, for example, are generally too powerless and fragmented to gain access to the mass media. As a result, the needs of one group are often interpreted and expressed by others—adults "know" what children need, whereas social researchers frequently define needs based on their research, even though their research procedures may be incompatible with interpersonal and communication patterns generally used in the groups studied.[13] Consequently, *who* defines needs is sometimes an important determinant of *what* needs are expressed and *how* they are expressed.

Although the discussion about needs has so far emphasized the many different kinds of needs, there are certain needs that we all share as human beings. As Charlotte Towle stated many years ago, there are "common human needs."[14] We all need adequate food and shelter. We all need to be nurtured and to be accepted as worthwhile human beings. However, even with these commonalities, there are enormous differences in the ways in which different groups define levels of need and appropriate ways to meet them. The nutritional level considered normal and healthy in the United States is far different from that in many less-developed countries. The foods that are eaten are certainly different. The manner in which nurturance and acceptance is demonstrated in this country—indeed, even in different regions of the country—are also different from patterns accepted as natural elsewhere. Therefore, although we recognize that there are important common human needs, the emphasis in this book is on the different ways in which needs are expressed and the need that this creates for society and the social welfare institution to be sensitive to, accepting of, and helpful with these differences. In a large, culturally diverse society like the United States, difference is the norm.

Given the necessity of defining needs in order to create social welfare services, how might we go about this task in an orderly way? Two major strategies have been used:

Research

One strategy is to use highly codified and systematized methods of scientific research to study behavior and identify need. Two approaches are possible: an objective or a subjective approach.[15] An *objective research approach* uses systematically collected data to identify needs and levels of need. A good example is the concept of a poverty level. One way to try to decide if poverty is a need, and how severe the need is, is to set a base income level below which it is assumed that people will not have adequate financial resources to meet their minimal living needs. Such levels are usually calculated by the fact that it has been determined through systematic data collection that low-income people spend approximately one-third of their income for food. Working from existing food prices as well as a nutritional analysis of food consumption needed to survive, an average amount needed to purchase food in a given area (urban or rural) is determined. Multiplying this by three yields the average minimum income needed to survive—the poverty level (in 1979, this was $6,700 for a United States urban family of four).[16] One can then measure people's incomes and say that those whose income falls below the poverty line are living in poverty—regardless of whether these people actually feel poverty-stricken.

A second approach is more *subjective.* Instead of defining a fixed income level, one can ask people to define for themselves what they feel their needs are and why. Notice, however, that both approaches include the orderly, systematic collection and analysis of information. Even when asking people to evaluate their own situation and its meaning for them, this task is done systematically, and all the responses are analyzed using the same methods. However, the results may be quite different. In general, objective research methods have tended to be more popular. It tends to be easier to collect objective data and to apply set standards to all when attempting to identify needs, especially when dealing with large numbers of people. Nevertheless, we know that this method ignores many of the subtle cultural and life-style differences that exist—and which are often very important. Unfortunately, some things are not easily objectified, and no matter how convenient the objective method may be, the subjective approach remains an important and useful alternative research strategy.

Research may be done at many levels:

1. *Social surveys.* One commonly used research level, especially in previous decades, was social surveys. They were broadly focused community studies that comprehensively examined community life, community resources, and community needs. Charles Booth's pioneering study of London is an example, as is the famous Pittsburgh study in more recent years.[17]

2. *Need studies.* Another technique is to focus only on specific kinds of needs. For example, how many people in a community or a society are poor? How many battered children or battered wives are there? By focusing on only one need, the focus is more narrow, but the scope may be broader, in that the study may be an analysis of an entire society, not just a community.

3. *Client studies.* These studies try to identify the persons and groups who receive the services and get their evaluation of the services. Are most clients elderly? Are they poor? If a community has a large minority popula-

tion, are such persons adequately represented among service recipients? How do recipients of services feel about them? This type of information is helpful in not only identifying unmet needs but also gaps or injustices in the service delivery network.

4. *Service studies.* This technique focuses on studying the services provided in a community, region, or society. Are certain services overrepresented while others don't exist at all? At what levels are services provided? Who provides them? As with client studies, a service approach can identify gaps and obstacles to service.

Research, therefore, can be an extremely useful source of information required to identify needs, either if the needs relate to individual or social-structural functioning or if they result from problems in the service delivery structure of the social welfare systems themselves. If purposefully planned, large and highly technical research studies provide invaluable data for the identification of needs and their ultimate solution, but such studies are not the only way to obtain needed information.

Practice Feedback

Another important source of information about needs is the daily practice of social welfare professionals. In the course of their work, they are exposed to people, structures, and situations. They have the opportunity to experience firsthand the realities of the lives of a wide range of people. They see where needs are not being adequately met or are being ignored entirely or where services are being poorly delivered. Thus it is possible for professional helping people to systematically collect information from their own practice experiences and to organize such information into forms that are helpful to those with decision-making responsibility in social welfare agencies—or, indeed, in other community structures. Being a helping person is not just working with people in need—it is also helping to identify needs and to influence those with decision-making responsibility to be more aware of, and sensitive to, existing needs. Unless this task is accomplished, the daily interactions with people seeking help may be frustrated by inadequate resources.

In spite of increasingly sophisticated methods for obtaining information about needs, we know that many needs continue to be ignored. There are several reasons for this:

1. *Many needs are difficult to locate because they are invisible.* Invisibility may be of many kinds. Geographical isolation characterizes many rural areas, as well as many economically depressed areas in cities. As most people go about their daily affairs, they never have occasion to see the realities of urban slum life and never travel through the most economically depressed rural areas (modern high-speed expressways have increased this type of avoidance). As a result, it is easy to forget that these areas exist,

often with desperate needs within them. A second kind of invisibility lies in needs that are the result of interpersonal behaviors that occur in private. This factor contributes to making child abuse needs so difficult to identify, for example. It usually occurs in the home, where it is invisible to outsiders, and unless there are physical symptoms visible to people who see the child outside the home, it is difficult to detect. In addition, many forms of child abuse are mental rather than physical and may be even more difficult to spot.

A third difficulty making needs difficult to locate is the fact that many personal problems are either not recognized or are denied by the person who has them. Several types of physical and physically related problems are not easily identified, even by health professionals. It is common for people to have such problems and never realize it, and thus they never have occasion to make their needs known. Other problems may be recognized but may be denied because of fear or embarrassment. A woman who is abused by her husband may be afraid to report her need for help because she fears her husband will abuse her even more. A person who is losing the ability to hear may be embarrassed to admit to others that this is happening. In either case, it is difficult for outsiders to spot the problem and identify the need to the appropriate people and agencies. A final difficulty in location results from many people with needs being inarticulate and disenfranchised. Poor people are often inadequately educated and unable to read about the availability of services or to manage to get to available resources. Minority people may be so intimidated that they are reluctant to make their needs known or to participate in service structures. If these needs are not visible to helping people in other ways, these people's inability to identify their needs to others may result in these needs not being identified and therefore ignored.

2. *Some needs are difficult to identify because people find them difficult to accept.* Many needs are unpleasant, and one way to deal with them is to deny their existence. They may be messy or depressing, or they may violate societal values. The resulting response is frequently righteous indignation rather than attempts to carefully identify the need and then try to meet it. The elderly are often seen as depressing, or sometimes as scatterbrained, disheveled, and smelly. Rather than meet their needs for adequate stimulation, physical care, and social acceptance, they may be shunted off to minimal care homes where they can be ignored. An even more dramatic example is provided in Exhibit 1-8. This tragic account of the life and death of a preteen age prostitute exemplifies the way in which a desperate but morally offensive need can be ignored and hidden.

3. *Many needs are not identified because it is impossible to gain agreement on how to define them.* Different groups frequently have different definitions of problematic behavior, which may result from value differences that affect perceptions about what is appropriate or acceptable behavior, as well as perceptions of priorities of needs. Minority groups may

define confrontation as a necessary and legitimate way to deal with oppression and discrimination; nonminority group members may define such behavior as disruptive and illegal. Women may define consciousness raising as their first priority to insure their personal integrity; men may define child rearing as a higher priority for women than the development of self as a woman.

Another source of definitional differences can result from vested interests. Groups tend to define situations in ways that maximize their own self-interests and resist definitions that will result in their own loss of power or resources. Therefore, although corporations may define assembly lines as worthwhile contributors to economic progress for everyone, workers may see them as dehumanizing and demoralizing. As long as groups have the ability to resist each other's definitions of situations, it is unlikely that a consensus will be reached about needs. On the other hand, sometimes precisely this dissensus helps people to realize the diversity of needs that exist.

The Difficulty of Identifying Needs **EXHIBIT 1-8**

In the following account of the life and death of a 12-year-old prostitute, the struggle that people in and out of the social welfare system had in accepting and dealing with the needs being expressed by the young girl involved is evident. Equally evident is the girl's inability to articulate her needs and to find effective social welfare resources to meet them. In the labyrinth streets of Brooklyn and Manhattan—and many other cities—how many similar girls are hidden from view and from help?

The first time Veronica Brunson was arrested she was 11 years old. The charge was prostitution. Before another year passed, the police, unaware of her real age, arrested her 11 more times for prostitution.

At the age of 12 Veronica was dead—killed in a mysterious plunge last July from the 10th floor of a shabby midtown hotel frequented by pimps.

Veronica's death, which is being investigated as a possible murder, is one more grim crime statistic to the police. But Veronica's life, and her encounters with the city's social service and criminal justice systems in the last year, illustrate the problems and dangers confronting thousands of runaway girls and boys who turn to prostitution to survive alone on the streets of New York.

Six public and private agencies were partly aware of Veronica's difficulties and were supposedly providing aid. But none of the agencies knew her entire history and none intervened quickly enough to rescue her.

"The Brunson case is a classic example of how a kid can float through the entire system without getting any help," said Officer Warren McGinniss of the Police Department's Youth Aid Division, a specialist in runaways. "Even a baby-faced obvious child who claims she is 18 can parade through the entire process—arrest, fingerprinting, arraignment—without anyone asking any questions."

The six agencies—the Department of Social Services, the Board of Education, the Probation Department, the Corporation Counsel's Office, the police, and the Brooklyn Center for Psychotherapy—now cite bureaucratic barriers and

---

Source: Excerpted from "Veronica's Short, Sad Life—Prostitution at 11, Death at 12," *The New York Times*, October 3, 1977, p. 1ff. © 1977 by the New York Times Company. Reprinted by permission.

communication breakdowns for their failure to act more effectively.

"You can't tell me appropriate intervention couldn't have saved her life," said the Rev. Bruce Ritter, director of Covenant House, a program assisting runaways. "The juvenile-justice and child-welfare systems in the city are chaotic. Programs just don't exist and everyone knows it."

Prostitution by 13-, 14- and 15-year-olds posing as older persons is no longer rare, but arrest for prostitution at the age of 11 is believed by vice squad detectives to be the youngest recorded here in decades.

In the summer of 1976, Veronica Brunson was 11, living in a fatherless home with her mother, Emma, who is now 34, and her brothers, Carson, 17, Douglas, 18, and Willie, 19.

Mrs. Brunson, unable to find work in her home state of North Carolina, had moved to Brooklyn when Veronica was 2. The family lived in a neatly kept, three-bedroom apartment in the Housing Authority's Marlboro Houses in Bensonhurst. In addition to their rent, the family received $318 monthly from welfare.

No Sign of Delinquency

By 1976 each of the Brunson boys had been arrested several times and had been in the juvenile courts. In contrast, Veronica, her mother, teachers and friends agreed, was well behaved, with no sign of delinquency . . . .

Pinched for money, Mrs. Brunson said she had made most of Veronica's clothing herself. "I tried to give her everything a little girl could want—clothing, food and some pocket money," Mrs. Brunson said in an interview. "She was a good little girl and if I told her to be home by six, she always was."

The Trouble Begins

At school, Veronica was a poor student. She had been left back once in the elementary grades, and in 1975 she was transferred to a special program for slow learners at Public School 253 in the Brighton Beach section. Her first year in the program went reasonably well, according to her teachers, and she was promoted to the sixth grade in June 1976.

Veronica's runaway problem suddenly began in midsummer of 1976, Mrs. Brunson said.

"One evening she came home with an older girl whose name was Diana who she met at Coney Island," Mrs. Brunson recalled. "Diana said she was 18 and wanted Veronica to spend a few days with her over the bridge (in Manhattan). I said no because I didn't think that girl Diana would be a good influence."

Several days later, Mrs. Brunson continued, Veronica disappeared for the first time, staying away from home for three days. On her return, Veronica told her mother she had stayed with her new friend Diana in Manhattan.

That July, Veronica continued to leave home for two- or three-day periods. Mrs. Brunson said that she had failed to report her daughter to the police as a missing person because Veronica would occasionally telephone her.

When the new school year began in September of 1976, Veronica failed to appear at P.S. 253. Checking into Veronica's absence, Bernard Lew, her guidance counselor, said he was told by her mother that she had been missing for more than a month. Mr. Lew said he urged Mrs. Brunson to contact the police.

First Arrested Last Fall

Police records show that Veronica was reported missing for the first time on September 19, 1976, after the school term had begun, and that her family said she had been missing for six weeks.

One day after the missing person report was filed, Veronica was arrested on a prostitution charge. A plainclothes officer said she had solicited him on West 42nd Street. The 11-year-old gave the police her real age and identity, and she was released in Mrs. Brunson's custody, pending action by the Family Court, which hears all criminal matters involving children up to the age of 16.

When Veronica returned to P.S. 253 in the autumn of 1976 her teachers and counselors were unaware of the arrest. Nevertheless, all of them said they noticed significant changes in her.

The year before she had dressed inconspicuously, almost shabbily. Now she used facial makeup and wore expensive looking, color-coordinated clothing, jewelry, high-heeled shoes and nylon stockings . . . .

The teachers, who were ignorant of her arrest, were most concerned about her chronic absenteeism, which eventually reached 121 of 180 school days that year.

Mr. Lew said that numerous telephone inquiries by staff members had been made about Veronica's absences. Her mother or brothers usually replied that the girl was ill, the teachers said.

Case Kept Out of Court

In the aftermath of the first arrest, Veronica and her mother were interviewed on October 8 by a Manhattan Family Court probation department officer. At that time, the officer decided that the matter should be kept out of the court, where Veronica could have been declared a "person in need of supervision," and possibly taken from her mother.

Instead, the probation officer, after consulting with child-welfare officials in the Social Services Department, decided that the case could be "adjusted" by sending Veronica for outpatient counseling at the Brooklyn Center for Psychotherapy, a private institution.

Under a policy of "diversion," the Probation Department tries to help youngsters without exposing them to formal court hearings before a judge.

Last autumn, the department, having made no inquiries at Veronica's school, had no inkling of her increasing truancy, her unorthodox dress or conversations with teachers about being recruited by pimps. Satisfied that the girl was getting adequate attention from the Social Services Department and the private psychotherapy center, the department closed her case in December. . . .

"She Was Still a Child"

Mr. Knepper said that Veronica had made one of her infrequent visits to his classroom on her 12th birthday, December 5, because she knew he was planning a party for her.

"She wanted that kind of attention and affection," the teacher said. "Despite all of her supposed sophistication it was obvious that she was still a child who wanted someone to help her." . . .

With Veronica no longer attending school, Mrs. Brunson and her son, Douglas, said that they were unable to prevent her running from home for brief periods. Mrs. Brunson acknowledged that she "sometimes" failed to report her daughter missing because she was confident of ultimately persuading her to return home and to school.

By May, Veronica was a familiar figure on the "Minnesota strip," a seedy part of Eighth Avenue from 40th to 50th Streets that is favored by street walkers. On the strip, Veronica, now five-feet, two-inches tall and weighing 110 pounds was known to other prostitutes as "Shortie" and by her childhood nickname, "Bay-Bay."

Police and court records show that between May 7 and July 18 Veronica was arrested 11 times in the midtown area. Usually she was charged with loitering for the purpose of prostitution, the most common misdemeanor used by the police to harass and temporarily remove prostitutes from the streets.

Used Fictitious Names

Either through coaching from a pimp or older prostitutes, Veronica carried no identification and gave the police a fictitious name and address and said she was 18 when arrested. Two of her aliases were Vanessa Brown and Paula Brunson.

She always pleaded guilty in Criminal Court and often was released after being held overnight at a police station. But for two convictions she was sentenced to a total of 12 days, which she served among adult prisoners in the Women's House of Detention.

Only once during this series of arrests did Veronica reveal her real identity and age. Police Officer David Olenchalk, who arrested Veronica on May 12 on Eighth Avenue and 46th Street, said she wore a shoulder-length black wig and "easily passed for 18 or 19." While being booked at the Midtown North stationhouse, Veronica abruptly acknowledged her age and asked the police to call her mother.

Released in the custody of her mother, Veronica was referred for a second time to the Family Court. At an interview with a Probation Department Officer on May 20, Veronica disclosed that she had been arrested several times and had been in jail on Rikers Island.

Gerald Hecht, the city's Probation Director, said department files indicated that at the May 20 meeting, Mrs. Brunson "exhibited ambivalence about placement" of Veronica in an institution or a foster home and another interview was scheduled for a month later.

Crucial Postponement

Several hours after the May 20 interview, Veronica, once more using an alias, was arrested on a prostitution charge.

Dr. Judianne Densen-Gerber, a psychiatrist who is president of the Odyssey Institute, a group of private treatment centers for emotionally disturbed children, said that the month-long postponement by the Probation Department may have been crucial for Veronica.

"By admitting she was 12 years old, this child was clearly saying 'Help me, do something for me now.' " Dr. Densen-Gerber asserted, "Time is a critical factor for these children. They can't tolerate delay. It's like telling a person who's just had a heart attack to come back to the hospital in a month or two."

Veronica failed to appear for her scheduled interview at the Probation Department on June 29. Yet none of the three agencies—Probation, the Corporation Counsel or the Social Services Department—would petition the Family Court to have her picked up as a "person in need of supervision". . .

With the Family Court proceedings in legal limbo, Veronica remained on the "Minnesota strip," occasionally getting arrested. Her last known arrest occurred on July 18 when she gave her age as 18. Pleading in Criminal Court to a charge of prostitution, she jumped bail rather than serve a 15-day sentence. . . .

"There are two stories on the street about her death," said Lieut. James Gallagher, the commander of the prostitution squad in Manhattan South area. "One that she was thrown out by a pimp and the other that she was having a fight with her pimp and fell out the window while sitting on the ledge."

"It's not unbelievable that a pimp would throw a girl out a window," he continued. "They brutalize girls if they hold back money, get fresh or try to get away from them."

Even in death, Veronica remained forgotten. It took the police nine days to identify her. Her fingerprints, taken in her "adult" arrests, linked her to fictitious names and addresses. Since no fingerprints are taken of children under the age of 16 there was no way of identifying her through Family Court records.

Neither Veronica's family nor any of the agencies reported her missing even after she failed to appear in Family Court. Detectives traced her after learning from Times Square prostitutes that she came from a Brooklyn Housing project and that her family name might be Brunson. . . .

Major Areas of Identified Need

It is impossible to assemble a list of human needs that would be responsive to the many subtleties of human life. As discussed earlier, different people and groups have different needs growing out of their distinctive characteristics and life situations. Nevertheless, there are some major areas in which needs tend to develop, and they are discussed briefly here. This discussion does not attempt to be comprehensive, and each area discussed can only be understood within a context of human diversity that makes the way in which needs develop in that area different from group to group. The list is useful at the beginning level to begin to sensitize those seeking to understand the social welfare institution to the major parameters of its work, understanding that more advanced study and practical experience is needed to understand the many complexities of human need.

There are many ways to organize and conceptualize major areas of identified need. The approach used here is based on the method used by the Southern Regional Education Board.[18] Three conceptual approaches are used to identify needs:

1. *Domains of living,* which can be thought of as *areas in which needs arise.* In order to function effectively and with a sense of personal satisfaction, the following areas of human life are important: *Health,* both physical and mental, is basic to human activity. Natural physical processes as well as social situations affect our ability to function effectively. Services need to be provided to meet needs arising from natural health processes, as well as from unusual and unexpected health-related situations. *Financial resources* are basic in a complex industrial society that depends on money as a medium of exchange. Inadequate financial resources are a serious obstacle to health, social interaction, and personal happiness, and services are needed that provide for people's financial needs as they arise or can be predicted.

Community integrity refers to the ability of communities to provide basic resources for their members. These resources include employment, housing, education, and leisure opportunities, as well as a sense of group identity and personal well-being. Services are needed to and through communities to ensure the provision of these resources. *Family integrity* is the family's ability to provide for the emotional and relational needs of its members. This need requires possession of basic financial and other life-supporting resources, since family ties are extremely difficult to maintain if resources are chronically missing, inadequate, or uncertain. As used here, the concept of family refers to groups related by blood or legally created relationships, as well as the wide range of voluntarily formed (but not necessarily legally bound) relationships between people to perform the functions of the family. This would include groupings such as unmarried couples, homosexual couples, communes, and similar family-type groups. Finally, *interpersonal integrity* refers to an individual's personal sense of well-being that makes it possible for the person to relate comfortably, effectively, and, where appropriate, intimately, to other people. Services supporting self-identity and the development of feelings of self-worth and of interpersonal skills help to meet this need.

2. *Levels of functioning* may be thought of as *levels at which needs arise.* As noted earlier, needs may be severe or simply discomforting, leading to breakdown or inconvenience. Beginning from a standard of well-being, services are necessary to cope with needs that generate stress,

problems, crises, and disability. During *stress,* a person or group experiences pressures that may be incompatible, anxiety producing, or personally draining. Supportive, coping, informational, and planning services are important when stress is evident. *Problems* require problem-solving services that allow careful analysis based on all the information available and relevant. The problems need to be partialized into component parts so that the person with the problem is not overwhelmed by the seemingly insoluble complex dimensions of one problem or several interwoven problems. *Crises* are situations in which helpful action is needed immediately, whereas *disability* refers to help needed when a person or group is unable to function independently. Needs, then, exist both in substantive areas (financial resources, the family, and so forth) and at different levels of seriousness and immediacy.

3. *"Obstacles to functioning"* are *areas in which solutions to needs may be sought.* Some needs are created by *catastrophes,* which usually strike swiftly and unexpectedly. Organizing social welfare services to deal with such needs usually focuses on meeting specific needs, both physical and emotional, that already exist. For example, a family whose home has burned down needs help to get treatment for possible injuries; housing, food, clothing, and other concrete resources; and the opportunity to work through the fear and anxiety created by such a catastrophe. Other needs are created by *rigid laws or regulations* that prevent people from receiving resources they need. In such situations, services would focus on changing laws and regulations to make them more humane and more compatible with existing needs. *Environmental deficiencies* create needs as a result of lack of developmental opportunities that people need in order to grow and function effectively. An example would be a community's lack of public transportation, which would prevent poor people from reaching needed social welfare services. Another example would be the lack of necessary social welfare services, perhaps including services to help people to organize to get needed public transportation. *Personal deficiencies* include the personal obstacles to functioning that may have been genetically transmitted, as well as deficiencies resulting from adverse social conditions. Social welfare resources would seek to obtain the previously missed resources while growth and change is still possible and to support and guide when personal deficiencies are unchangeable.

This chapter has attempted to show how social welfare systems result from a society's assessment of its resources and priorities in their use and development. Each society establishes a system that reflects its particular history, value system, and needs, resulting in great variation among social welfare systems in different societies. So far this chapter has attempted to describe and analyze the United States social welfare system, but it will now conclude with Exhibit 1-9, which presents a brief overview of the structure of social welfare services in the Federal Republic of Germany.

A Comparative View EXHIBIT 1-9

This exhibit provides a brief view of income maintenance services in the Federal Republic of Germany (commonly called West Germany) so that you can compare the values and resulting social welfare systems in the two societies. What similarities and what differences do you see in the two systems? Why would it be practically impossible to make a similar listing of services for the United States? The exhibit concludes with comparative data for social welfare expenditures for selected countries.

The Federal Republic as a Social State

The Federal Republic is looked upon by the whole world as a social state, a community which has at least mitigated the egregious differences between the rich and the poor and offers to its citizens an exemplary basic social protection scheme. Four aspects of the social program should be mentioned as the most significant here:

a) Social Insurance: Employer and employee contribute, the State fills in the gaps with subsidies (e.g. if the contributions to the Old Age Insurance and Unemployment Insurance are insufficient).

b) State Pensions and Compensation Benefits: Social benefits which compensate the citizen for contributions made to State and Society are financed exclusively by the State from its tax revenues (civil servants and military pensions, assistance for war victims, family benefits out of the "Equalization of War and Post-War Burdens" funds, etc.).

c) Public Welfare: Needy persons who are not insured or are insufficiently covered by other programs receive aid out of tax revenues (when neither parents nor children are in a position to contribute sufficiently to their support).

d) Prevention: A new field of social protection which is being developed increasingly, since politicians and experts agree that timely protection against socio-economic risks (e.g. of illness, of disability, of death of the breadwinner, of unemployment, of large families) minimizes their financial consequences (one who takes advantage of preventive medical examinations, lessens the risk of illness; one who receives children's allowances can open to his children more opportunities; one who acquires property and assets is better armed against the vicissitudes of life). . . .

The History of the Social State

The foundation of the German Social System was laid 100 years ago. In 1881, Kaiser Wilhelm I. issued a proclamation announcing the first social laws. Two factors were responsible for this development: First, it had become clear to the government that the working man was in dire need. Under the pressure of industrialization, close family contacts disintegrated because the individual could no longer sustain himself in his own circle by his own hands but had to move to the place of mass production, usually from the village to the city, where the factories were located. That caused the breakdown of the foundations of the social protection system as it then existed, i.e. in the family and community.

Secondly, the labor movement thrived upon the desperation of the working man. Socialism became a highly important political factor. The 1881 Imperial Proclamation, as prepared by Chancellor Otto von Bismarck, was intended to placate the workers by eroding the basis for their socialist involvement. And the "Socialist Laws" passed in those years did indeed limit considerably the activities of the Social Democratic Party. So that a structure of comprehensive social protection developed, founded on the interest of the

---

Source: Excerpted from Günther Windschild, "Social Policy—A Comprehensive Network," in *Meet Germany,* (17th rev. ed.) (Hamburg: Atlantik-Bruche, 1978), pp. 82–88; and from *Social Indicators 1976,* p. 140.

State in its citizens on the one hand and, simultaneously, in curtailing their civil rights.

Then came the crucial laws in short intervals:

- The Workers' Health Insurance Law (1883);
- The Industrial Accidents Law (1884);
- The Old Age and Disability Insurance Law (1889);
- The Employee Insurance Law (1911).

Later came:

- The Miners' Social Insurance Law (1923);
- The Placement and Unemployment Insurance Law (1927);
- The Craftmen's Social Security Law (1938);
- The Law Reforming Old Age Insurance (1957);
- The Law Reforming Unemployment Insurance (1969);
- The Law on Sick Pay for Workers (1970);
- The Second Reform of the Old Age Insurance Law (1972);
- The Reorganization of the Health Insurance (1977).

The Story of Wells, Into Which No One Should Fall

German Social Policy has experienced many profound changes. The division of Germany after the end of World War II led to the development of two different social protection systems. Each state still bases its social laws on the Bismarck model, but in the Federal Republic a remarkable change has been made. It is based on the idea that it is not sufficient for social policies to be supportive in case of need, but they must, at the same time, be protective. Bismarck, and the politicians following him, wanted in the first place to shield the citizens from the evil consequences of socio-economic risks: sickness, old age, unemployment—with all benefits being also extended to dependents of the person affected (they still are in cases of illness; widows benefits; in determining the amount of unemployment benefits, etc.).

Analogizing to the story of the child who fell into the well and could not get out on his own, the state offered rope and ladder with which he could be helped out. The Federal Republic's social

Who Pays for the Social Benefits?

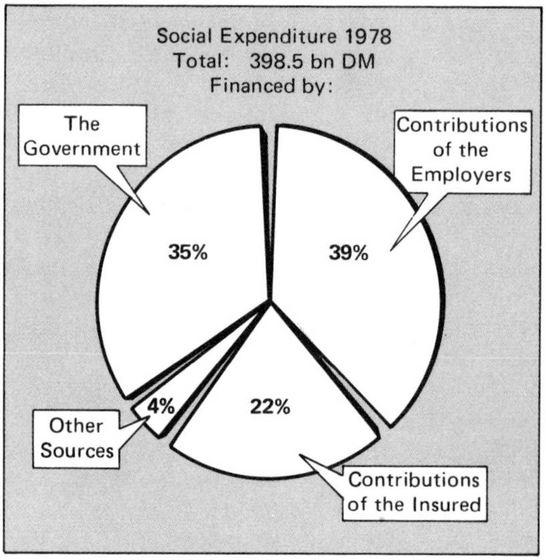

program wants to offer something else: a lid, which covers the well and prevents the child from falling in, in the first place. For example:

Since 1971, early recognition examinations are offered for children up to the age of four and are paid for by the social health insurance. In this way, defects can be discovered and treated promptly and in most cases even healed. Similar early recognition examinations for cancer are offered annually for women after 30 and for men after 45. These examinations are also paid for by the health insurance. Prevention is the motto.

Another example: Rehabilitation has become very important in the social policy within the last four years. What does that entail?—The reintegration of victims of industrial accidents, of the chronically ill, even of the congenitally handicapped, either physically or mentally, into the cultural and working systems with the help of the social institutions. This includes medical cures, vocational training and retraining courses, etc. The aim of the system is to make the affected individual whole again, to the extent possible, to assist him to participate in life and to prevent him from giving up and withdrawing into the existence of a retiree. This is a prophylaxis which relieves not only the community of the insured but also the State. After all, a pension paid over decades costs much more than medical and curative treatment and vocational training. A prophylaxis which at the same time gives the affected party the courage to go on. . . .

The Three Classical Pillars of the Social Policy

1. *Social Insurance*

As had been mentioned before, the social laws of the German Reich in the 1880s are still the basis of the Social Insurance System. Old Age, Health, Accident and Unemployment Insurance have been further developed, but have not significantly deviated from their original pattern. A few details:

OLD AGE INSURANCE. Since 1968, every employed person regardless of income is required to join his appropriate pension plan. Only high-salaried employees are permitted to substitute an exemptive private life insurance for the general social insurance. In 1978, for the compulsory contributions only monthly gross income up to DM* 3,700 is considered; this "contribution ceiling" is adjusted yearly in correspondence with the development of wages and salaries, so that it increases somewhat every year. The rate of contribution is currently 18 per cent. Consequently, this 18 per cent charge is imposed on all incomes up to the ceiling and the employee and his employer each pay one-half. The State participates in the financing of Old Age Insurance with a subsidy which is applied to disability benefits.

The Old Age Insurance pays pensions, participates in the financing of the health insurance for pensioners and pays for vocational and medical rehabilitation. There are different kinds of pensions:

- Old Age Pensions (for those 65 years of age or over);
- the so-called "Flexible Old Age Pension" (available to insured employees at 63, to the disabled at 62, if they have belonged to the Insurance for at least 35 years);
- the advanced pensioners benefits for women 60 years old;
- the advanced pensioners benefit due to unemployment (for insured employees over 60 years old who have been unemployed for at least one year);
- Partial and Permanent Disability Benefits (both of these can be drawn by younger persons, and are therefore somewhat lower than Old Age Pensions);
- Miners' Pensions (for Surface and Underground Miners);
- Survivors Benefits (for widows and orphans).

The amount of the pension varies considerably, but one can roughly count on receiving approximately 60 per cent of the last net income, except for orphans, where other criteria apply.

Every pensioner is automatically included in the health insurance. This is provided by the pension office. Currently it pays approximately 11 per cent of his pension into the sickness fund (Krankenkasse) for him. However, a law requiring pensioners to participate personally, although minimally, in the health insurance beginning in 1980 is presently before the German Parliament. Pensioners enjoy the same complete health protection offered to employed insureds. Pensioners who formerly belonged to the private sickness funds may remain there and receive a subsidy to cover the difference in cost from their pension plans.

The Old Age Insurance is the most important carrier of rehabilitation costs. Insured persons may undergo curative and medical treatments (Heilkuren) at the expense of their respective pension plans. The Old Age Insurance also pays for vocational retraining programs, when such programs increase the chances of a recuperating individual to be re-employed, even if in another profession as that learned.

HEALTH INSURANCE. Membership in the health insurance is compulsory for all blue collar workers and for white collar employees earning up to DM

* DM refers to the monetary unit used in West Germany, the deutsche mark. In February 1979, 1.92 DM were equal to $1.00.

2,775 gross monthly. This figure is not chosen arbitrarily. It it oriented every year to the "contribution ceiling" mentioned in the section on pensions; it increases, in other words, with this figure, which is itself a reflection of the general trends in income. Employees earning more than this amount may join voluntarily. At present, the required contribution is 11 or 12 per cent of income, which is paid by employer and employee jointly. Here, as for pensions, the highest contribution is limited to the respective per cent of the upper limit, even for persons earning more than this amount.

There are approximately 1,600 sickness funds. Most of them (approximately 1,100) are company funds, which cover one or more enterprises. Funds oriented to a specific area are called Regional Sickness Funds ("Allgemeine Ortskrankenkassen"), of which there are approx. 330. Many white collar employees and a smaller number of blue collar workers belong to the Clerical and Laborers' Sickness Funds (Ersatzkassen).

The Sickness Funds offer comprehensive protection. Usually, the individual is not required to pay the doctor himself, rather the patient gives the doctor a form (Krankenschein) which the latter submits to the Sickness Funds for payment. The benefits include:

- Medical and dental care;
- Medical aids, pharmaceuticals, bandages, eye glasses;
- Orthopedic equipment;
- Inpatient hospital care including surgery;
- Curative treatments;
- Sick pay—80 percent of the last net wage or salary (after 6 weeks, since wages or salaries must be paid for this period by the employer);
- Maternity benefits;
- Lump sum payment at death.

In cases of hospitalization, the fund pays for the entire stay. Recently, in an attempt to reduce costs, insureds are required to pay DM 1 for every medicine prescribed; in hardship cases, the Sickness Funds may make exceptions.

ACCIDENT INSURANCE. Companies, not individuals, belong to the Accident Insurance. They pay their contributions directly to the various Industrial Associations (Berufsgenossenschaften) established for the respective branches of industry, commerce, trade and administration. Accident Insurance covers industrial accidents, accidents on the way to or from the workplace, occupational diseases and accident prevention. The Accident Insurance pays for treatment required due to industrial accidents or occupational diseases, including hospital care arising therefrom, and for support and disability payments and benefits (the amounts of which are dependent upon the gravity of the injury). Disability payments are also adjusted yearly according to the general income development.

In 1971, the Accident Insurance was extended to include children in Kindergarten, pupils, and university students within its protection.

UNEMPLOYMENT INSURANCE. All blue and white collar employees, except civil servants, are obligated to join the Unemployment Insurance Fund. The carriers of this insurance are the local Employment Offices (Arbeitsamt), the State Employment Offices, and the Federal Employment Institute in Nuremberg. Three per cent of the earning of every employed member must be paid into the insurance. Of this amount, the employer and employee each pay one-half. Here too, the same "contribution ceiling" as that for the Old Age Insurance applies, and also the same rules.

The Unemployment Insurance pays:

- Unemployment benefits of 68 per cent of the last month's net earning for at most one year;
- Unemployment assistance of 58 per cent of the last month's net earning when the requirements for unemployment benefits are not fulfilled;
- Bankruptcy benefits in varying amounts when jobs are lost due to bankruptcy of the employer;
- Income maintenance payments to compensate for loss of earning when working short weeks;

- Bad weather allowances and winter allowances to compensate for loss of earning in those industries (e.g., construction) which are affected by weather conditions.

Unemployment Insurance is included in the Employment Promotion Act which since 1969 covers all aspects of the labor policy. These include generous grants for continuing education programs, retraining programs, and rehabilitation. The participants in these training programs also receive family support payments when the training seems desirable in terms of labor market trends.

2. *Social Compensation Benefits*

BENEFITS FOR WAR VETERANS. Wars are conducted by countries and not by their citizens. That means that one is compelled to fulfill military service requirements. In Germany, this knowledge had, since the end of the First World War (1914–1918) led to the passage of the Imperial "Social Assistance Law." Needy war victims received aid and assistance from the State. After the Second World War, the Federal Social Assistance Law (Bundesversorgungsgesetz) was passed for the same purpose, to aid the victims of war and their dependents. Even today, injuries to military servicemen are compensated for under this law.

Assistance for war veterans or victims of military service accidents consists primarily of medical as well as rehabilitation care for the individual affected, then welfare (including special emergency aid), and finally pensions for veterans and their dependents. Every injured veteran receives a basic pension regardless of his other income. Additional grants are made to compensate for particular injuries. The amount of the pension is determined by the degree of the disability and by its effect on the capacity to earn. The highest pension in both these categories in 1978 is DM 645 monthly.

CHILDREN'S ALLOWANCES. This allowance is paid to all families with children in the Federal Republic to help carry the additional burden. The amounts paid (regardless of income) are as follows:

- for the first child DM 50;
- for the second child DM 80;
- and for every other child DM 150 monthly.

This allowance may be paid until the child is 27 years old if he or she is still in training, and also when the child is physically or mentally handicapped. Children of foreigners who are employed in the Federal Republic receive the same allowance, if they reside within Germany. Children living in homelands having a lower cost-of-living than that of the Federal Republic receive a smaller allowance.

RENT ALLOWANCE. Every citizen in the Federal Republic should be able to live in premises appropriate for the family condition at a tolerable price. When the family income is less than a certain sum, the family is entitled to a rent subsidy (Wohngeld). Even home or apartment owners are entitled to subsidies when they reside in the premises themselves. In 1976, the average rent subsidy was DM 72 monthly. The procedure for computing the family income for the purpose of qualifying for rent subsidies is such that the larger the family, the better the chances of qualifying.

3. *Welfare*

Along with Insurance and Social Compensation Benefits, Welfare is the classical third pillar of the social policy. This used to be called "Armenpflege" and later "Fürsorge," now the German term is "Sozialhilfe." Every person resident in the Federal Republic who can show evidence of need has a right to welfare (foreigners may in some cases be exempted from certain special benefits). Even recipients of insurance benefits (such as pensioners) or compensation benefits may receive welfare payments if their income is lower than a certain sum set by law. In determining income for this purpose, rental costs are deducted so that in all cases suitable premises are guaranteed.

Social Expenditure in the Federal Republic of Germany 1976 in billion D-Marks

Old age insurance program	114.2	Public welfare assistance	9.7
Health insurance program	68.2	Accident insurance program	7.9
Civil service pensions	28.1	Tax benefits in housing construction	4.5
Continued wage payments in case of illness	19.0	Youth programs	4.0
Unemployment benefits, retraining programs, etc.	16.5	Education allowance (BAFöG)	2.7
Children's Allowance	14.4	Restitution to Nazi victims	2.2
Social benefits in the public service	14.1	Old-age assistance for farmers	2.1
Savings incentives	14.0	Equalization of war burdens	1.9
Assistance to war victims	11.8	Rent allowance	1.7
		Health service	1.4
		Other	18.6
		total:	357 billion DM

= 32 per cent of the Gross National Product. This means that almost one third of all income is spent on social expenditure.

Expenditures for Specified Social Welfare Programs as a Percent of GNP, Selected Countries: 1968 and 1971
(expenditures in international currency units)

Country and currency unit		Old-age, survivors, and disability insurance: Expenditures 1968	Expenditures 1971	Percent of GNP 1968	Percent of GNP 1971	Public aid and other social welfare: Expenditures 1968	Expenditures 1971	Percent of GNP 1968	Percent of GNP 1971	Public health care programs: Expenditures 1968	Expenditures 1971	Percent of GNP 1968	Percent of GNP 1971
Belgium[a]	(francs)	49,467	70,583	4.73	4.97	10,340	14,547	.99	1.03	36,712	56,147	3.51	3.96
Canada[a]	(dollars)	1,625	2,205	2.24	2.36	1,581	1,976	2.18	2.12	4,126	6,194	5.68	6.63
France	(francs)	26,400	38,139	4.19	4.22	(b)	(b)	(b)	(b)	26,082	41,062	4.14	4.54
Germany (Fed. Rep.)[a]	(marks)	43,299	57,599	8.03	7.59	5,652	7,621	1.05	1.00	22,253	35,377	4.13	4.66
Japan[a]	(yen)	171,039	247,490	.33	.31	305,822	505,157	.59	.64	1,753,614	2,719,300	3.39	3.44
Netherlands	(florins)	6,246	8,082	6.91	6.32	841	1,325	.93	1.03	3,338	5,969	3.69	4.66
Sweden	(krona)	7,133	11,045	5.11	6.03	3,091	6,406	2.21	3.50	7,184	11,789	5.15	6.44
United Kingdom	(pounds)	1,648	2,002	3.81	3.55	813	1,097	1.88	1.95	1,518	2,087	3.51	3.68
United States[a]	(dollars)	23,858	35,874	2.76	3.42	14,377	26,415	1.66	2.52	19,665	27,935	2.27	2.66

Source: U.S. Department of Health, Education, and Welfare, Social Security Administration, *Research and Statistics Note,* October 1974.

[a]Some public expenditures for health care are included under public aid.
[b]Public aid expenditures are not separately identified.

Welfare grants assistance towards the costs of living which is paid monthly, and assistance in special situations, which includes assistance during training periods, preventive health care, assistance for the ill and the handicapped, the tubercular, the blind and the aged. Welfare is granted only when neither parents nor children nor other persons are present who can contribute to the individual affected. Personal property is taken into consideration in determining the amount of the payments. Welfare aid may be extended to single individuals whose income is under DM 300 monthly. There are numerous additional rules.

SOCIAL SECURITY—ELEMENT OF THE SOCIAL POLICY. The social benefits in the Federal Republic of Germany are part of a basic social policy which has been proven successful. This is the idea that economic and social achievements are mutually dependent. The model of the social market economy (Soziale Marktwirtschaft) was established on the same foundation: Social benefits should not be handled as "Band-Aids" to cover wounds to individuals caught up in the grinding wheels of the economy. Rather they ought to be formative. This presupposes that social considerations are included in the planning and execution of economic measures.

Chapter Summary ◀

The social welfare institution is an integral part of the United States social structure. In the process of carrying out its societal mandate, it is closely intertwined with the other social institutions of society, and it must be understood within this context. Although the structure of social welfare services is complex and extensive, many human needs remain unmet in whole or in part, and not everyone is equally treated. The human needs that social welfare seeks to meet affect everyone, and everyone is touched by the social welfare institution in one way or another. Yet there is still a great deal of ambivalence in the societal values relating to social welfare, and considerable misunderstanding about its functions in society. In the next chapter, the origins and development of social welfare will be explored, so that the reasons for some of the value and structural inconsistencies that characterize our present system can be better understood.

STUDY QUESTIONS

1. Make a chart that shows as many relationships as you can think of between the social welfare institution and the other major social institutions in our society. Do certain institutions have more of an impact on the social welfare institution than others? Be sure to include the impact the social welfare institution has on other institutions. After you have finished, compare your chart with someone else's chart and discuss the differences between the two with that person.
2. Write down examples of curative, preventive, and rehabilitative institutional and residual social welfare services in your community (six in all). If you do not know one of each, use available resources to find an example of any missing links—interview a social worker, consult a community service directory if available, and so on. Which kinds of services are most common and which are least common? What does this tell you about the social welfare structure of your community?

3. Visit a social welfare agency and record your impressions. Who works there and who goes there to get service? What does the agency look like—is it attractive? Modern? Does it seem well run? How do you think you would feel if you needed to use the services of the agency? Why? Do you think others would be likely to feel as you do? Why or why not?
4. Try writing down your personal value system. How much freedom and responsibility do you think each individual should have? What rights and responsibilities do you think society has? What do you think is an appropriate way to deal with people who are unable to care for themselves adequately? How about people who break the law? Try to project the kind of social welfare system that would result if it were created on the basis of your values.

REFERENCES

1. William A. Robson, *Welfare State and Welfare Society* (London: George Allen and Unwin, 1976), p. 174.
2. Alan Keith-Lucas, *Giving and Taking Help* (Chapel Hill: University of North Carolina Press, 1972), p. 136.
3. Naomi Brill, *Working with People: The Helping Process* (Philadelphia: J. B. Lippincott, 1973), p. 63.
4. Allen Pincus and Anne Minahan, *Social Work Practice: Model and Method* (Itasca, Ill.: F. E. Peacock Publishers, 1973), p. 63. Reprinted by permission of the publisher.
5. Alfred J. Kahn and Sheila Kamerman, *Social Services in International Perspective* (Washington, D.C.: U.S. Government Printing Office, 1976), pp. 6–8.
6. See Harold Wilensky and Charles Lebeaux, *Industrial Society and Social Welfare* (New York: Free Press, 1958), p. 146.
7. Ralph Kramer, "Future of the Voluntary Service Organization," *Social Work* (November 1973), pp. 61–62. Paraphrased by permission of the National Association of Social Workers.
8. Ibid., p. 63.
9. Ibid., p. 62.
10. See, for example, Elizabeth Wickenden, "Purchase of Care and Services: Effect on Voluntary Agencies" in Neil Gilbert and Harry Specht, *The Emergence of Social Welfare and Social Work* (Itasca, Ill.: F. E. Peacock Publishers, 1976), pp. 149–162.
11. Kahn and Kamerman, *Social Services*, p. 4.
12. National Conference on Social Welfare, *The Future for Social Services in the United States* (Columbus, Ohio: National Conference on Social Welfare, 1977).
13. See, for example, Ray Valle and Lydia Mendoza, *The Elderly Latino* (San Diego: Campanile Press, 1978).
14. Charlotte Towle, *Common Human Needs* (New York: Family Service Association of America, 1952).
15. This entire section on research is broadly based on Sidney Zimbalist, *Historic Themes and Landmarks in Social Welfare Research* (New York: Harper and Row, 1977), pp. 73–231.

16. "Poverty Level is Raised Because of Price Levels," *New York Times,* April 10, 1979, p. B-6.
17. Ibid., pp. 123–127 and 139–174.
18. Harold McPheeters and Robert Ryan, *A Core of Competence for Baccalaureate Social Welfare and Curricular Implications* (Atlanta: Southern Regional Education Board, 1971), p. 15.

SELECTED READINGS

Boyer, Ruth. *An Approach to Human Services.* San Francisco: Canfield Press, 1977.

Dolbeare, Kenneth, and Dolbeare, Patricia. *American Ideologies.* Chicago: Markham, 1971.

Eriksen, Karin. *Human Services Today.* Reston, Va.: Reston Publishing Co., 1977.

Galinkin, George. *Public Welfare in Montana: A Personal View.* Washington, D.C.: College and University Press, 1975.

Howard, Donald. *Social Welfare: Values, Means, and Ends.* New York: Random House, 1969.

Keith-Lucas, Alan. *Giving and Taking Help.* Chapel Hill: University of North Carolina Press, 1972.

Macarov, David. *The Design of Social Welfare.* New York: Holt, Rinehart and Winston, 1978.

Robson, William A. *Welfare State and Welfare Society.* London: George Allen and Unwin, 1976.

Romanyshyn, John. *Social Welfare: Charity to Justice.* New York: Random House, 1971.

Towle, Charlotte. *Common Human Needs.* New York: Family Service Association of America, 1952.

Wilensky, Harold, and Lebeaux, Charles. *Industrial Society and Social Welfare.* New York: Free Press, 1958.

Zimbalist, Sidney. *Historic Themes and Landmarks in Social Welfare Research.* New York: Harper and Row, 1977.

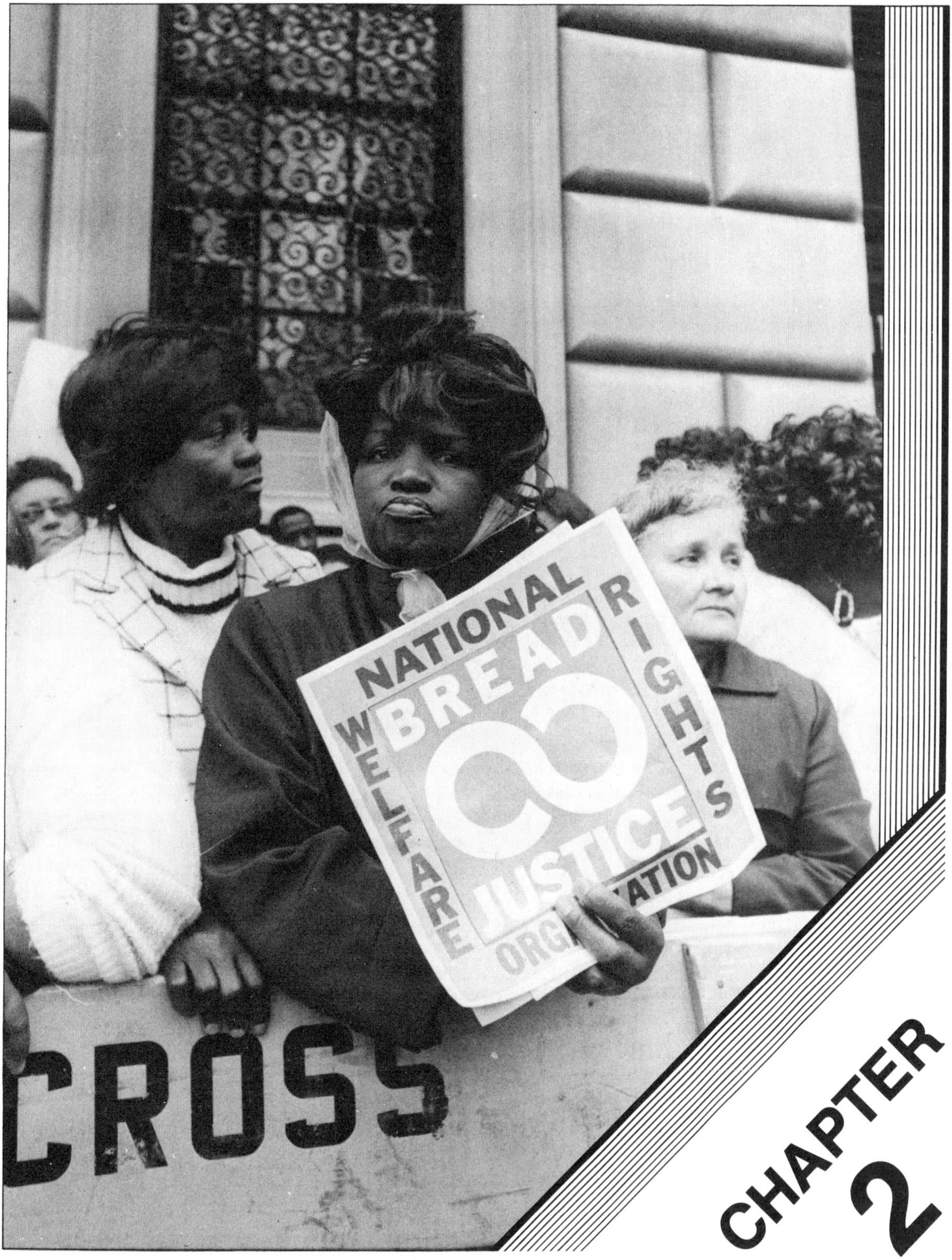

CHAPTER 2

A Brief History of Social Welfare

The present social welfare institution cannot be understood adequately without being aware of its history. This history is characterized by attempts to develop social welfare structures in response to social needs, much as our own structure continues to develop to meet the needs of our time. The nature of human culture is to accumulate and build on the experiences of the past, and many of the values and services that are part of our contemporary social welfare system have their roots in earlier times. Whether or not these traditional approaches to social problems continue to be appropriate is difficult to answer, but a knowledge of the sources of these approaches is essential to an intelligent decision about their current applicability.

The purpose of this chapter is to help readers acquire basic knowledge of the historical development of social welfare services and strategies. In tracing this development, the values underlying various events and decisions are made explicit. Information about the specific social welfare programs created by the Social Security Act and its subsequent amendments is provided in some detail. The information in this chapter is presented in a way that is intended to help the reader develop analytical skills appropriate for evaluating social welfare programs and to develop skills in relating values to policy development and service-delivery strategies.

The Bases of Social Welfare

There are two characteristics of the human condition that make social welfare an integral part of our humanity. The first is that compared to most other animals, human beings are poorly equipped instinctually. They are helpless at birth and for a relatively long period thereafter, depending on others for the nurturance necessary for their physical survival. The most characteristic feature of the human organism is its ability to learn and adapt. We learn our behavior, making it possible for us to learn the ways of whatever culture we happen to be born into and allowing us to move from one culture to another if necessary. Thus the second important characteristic of human beings is created, namely, that our humanity resides in our interaction. We become human, that is, participants in an ongoing social unit, by interacting with others and learning appropriate behavior. This interaction not only teaches us what to do, but also ultimately gives us a sense of ourselves—we acquire a group identity and a position within that group on the basis of our interaction with others.

Our need both for nurturance and social interaction makes us dependent on others. In social welfare terms, if we are going to talk about improving social functioning and minimizing pain, it can only be accomplished socially. Ultimately our dependence on others can itself be a source of personal breakdown and suffering, but even in those cases the cure lies within the social network. Human groups are functional for their members and no doubt always have been. By banding together, human beings ensure their basic survival in terms of protection and reproduction. Beyond that, the group makes possible the highly complex social patterns we take for granted today.

The first human group to emerge was probably the family, a group reflecting people's sexuality and need for protection. The family can be considered the earliest social welfare unit, and it continues to be a basic welfare resource. Most societies have had extended family units, that is, families made up of three or more generations and a variety of kin members. The family form dominant in the United States today, the nuclear family, is made up of two generations, adults and their children. Compared to the extended family, which has many family members who can work together to provide for each other's needs, the nuclear family's human resources are limited. In a later chapter we will see why the nuclear family is an important family form in America today, but the early extended family provided a more useful social unit that identified rights and responsibilities within a fairly large unit. In later societies, tribes were sometimes equated with the family concept, providing a way of extending the network of responsibility for the needs of others to a larger unit. Originally the family was the only social welfare unit; however, it was gradually supplemented with other social structural resources until today our society is a complex network of social welfare services of which the family is only one. Even today the family holds a special place in the social welfare system, and families have the right to make decisions that other social welfare units are legally prevented from counteracting (see Exhibit 3-3, "Battered Freddy," in the next chapter).

Early Social Welfare Services Outside the Family: The English Heritage

The church was perhaps the earliest formalization beyond the family of a concern for the poor, the sick, and the aged.[1] The Judeo-Christian beliefs expressed in the Old and New Testaments, which commanded that the needy be served, were instrumental in early church-provided social welfare services through its network of parishes and monasteries. Only as the development of national governments gradually broke the power of feudal and church landholdings were these services substantially reduced in importance. Today, the church continues to be instrumental in providing social welfare services, informally through its church helping programs, and more formally through social agencies with religious affiliations.

In the 1500s early attempts were made to formalize and unify social welfare services beyond churches, monasteries, guilds, and other benevolent groups.[2] In the Tudor period, the parish (the local governmental unit most analogous to contemporary counties) organized the provision of charity by parceling out responsibility for the poor to both religious and secular organizations. Gradually, a series of societal changes related to the beginnings of the Industrial Revolution created a strain on the existing systems of private charity and eventually led to their modification. Three of the most significant changes associated with the early roots of the Industrial Revolution were the breakdown of the medieval feudal system, the centralization of political power in national governments, and the displacement of church power by secular government. As church funds available to meet the needs of persons displaced from feudal estates declined, the power of local and ultimately national governmental units to care for the poor increased.[3]

As England became the world's greatest wool-producing nation, the wool trade became more productive than farming, with much land being removed from cultivation and given over to grazing. This displaced many workers from the land and was a force lessening the economic feasibility of the feudal manorial system. This in turn decreased the need for people previously in the service of nobles. These dislocations occurred at the same time that monasteries were broken up and their resources confiscated, thereby greatly weakening one of the earliest welfare resources in a period of increasing need. By 1518 the swelling ranks of the unemployed was a serious-enough problem to generate efforts to block migrants and the unemployed from wandering around the countryside in search of work or aid. Although late in the sixteenth century the English commission responsible for studying unemployment noted that the societal conditions of grazing enclosures and erratic commerce were the main causes of unemployment, thereby removing the blame from personal shiftlessness, the large numbers of persons displaced were considered a problem in their own day.[4]

In an attempt to protect themselves against these vagrant and starving people, the more affluent passed legislation to control the moral and social order.[5] The Elizabethan Poor Law of 1601 was an important early piece of such legislation.[6] This legislation established three categories of the poor—the helpless, the involuntarily unemployed, and the vagrant. The helpless, or needy by impotency of defect, were the aged, decrepit, orphaned, lunatic, blind, lame, or diseased. The involuntarily unemployed, including those made poor by misfortunes such as fire, robbery, or being "overcharged with children," were set to work or sent to a house of correction.[7] The vagrant, including drifters, strangers, squatters, and beggars, were ostracized. Each parish felt responsible only for its own members. Since the social dislocations of the time created forced vagrancy for many people, the fact that the Poor Law encouraged parishes to ostracize nonmembers tended to create a group of the poor who belonged nowhere. This has led some later observers to blame the Poor Law for having caused many of the poor to remain vagrants.[8] The Settlement Act of 1662 further legitimated the concept of a residence requirement, a carryover of which was one of the qualifications for public assistance in the United States until the Supreme Court decision in 1969 (*Shapiro* v. *Thompson*) that declared it unconstitutional.[9]

The parish welfare structure legitimated by the Poor Law consisted of four main parts: *Almshouses,* sometimes called indoor relief because assistance was provided in a facility established for that purpose, were provided for the helpless, a group considered legitimately needy. *Outdoor relief*—assistance provided in the recipient's own home—was provided for the aged and handicapped helpless, also a group considered legitimately needy. *Workhouses,* or houses of correction, were provided for the ablebodied needy, a group bearing the stigma of being shiftless.[10] Children of destitute families were *indentured*—that is, removed from their own homes and placed with a family in the community that agreed to provide room and board in return for the child's work. Although indenture seems cruel by contemporary standards, and it is true that many children were exploited by the families that agreed to support them, at the time it was believed that removing children from destitute families would both provide for their physical needs as well as give them appropriate role models. The legacy of these practices remains in our current social welfare structure in outdoor relief, which forms the major part of our public assistance system, and prisons and other total institutions, which carry on the traditions of ostracism, stigma, and forced work of the houses of correction. Whatever the social conditions of the time that created widespread need, the service structure established by the Poor Law implied that poor peoples' needs were at least partly their own fault.

The Elizabethan Poor Law of 1601 had several other significant components: It recognized the desirability of national coverage and administration of public welfare, a feature of many contemporary public programs. It never accomplished total national coverage, however, and the parish continued to be the local unit through which the legislation was administered. Each parish had an overseer of the poor appointed every Easter by the justice of the peace. Social welfare funds were obtained through voluntary contributions and a public land tax. The Poor Law tried to strengthen the family unit, which was felt to be the foundation of the community. It made parents and grandparents responsible for their children (unless married) up to the age of twenty-four for boys and twenty-one for girls. If relatives could not care for orphaned or abandoned children, they were apprenticed or indentured. Finally, ablebodied individuals were set to work in special public factories, establishing the principle still used today that the more people working, the less the tax burden on the affluent. If the ablebodied refused to work, they were sent to a house of correction. Ultimately, the competition between private and public factories led to the demise of the latter, but the work ethic for the poor has remained in many other guises.

As the number of needy increased, attitudes changed, and by the 1700s harsher laws and the narrowing of poor relief occurred. The attitude in workhouses became more punitive. Virtue was tied to thrift, industry, sobriety, and wealth, and poverty and dependency were further stigmatized. Amendments to the 1601 law went so far as to evict anyone from the parish who might "become" dependent. In 1776, Adam Smith published *The Wealth of Nations,* in which he advocated the amassing of wealth. People should operate to the best of their ability with minimal societal restraints—laissez-faire capitalism. Though he did not call for the end of the poor laws, he felt that giving freely to people would only result in dependency and misery.[11] Others followed in pointing out the evils of supporting those in need, with Thomas Malthus in 1798 arguing that population growth would soon outrun food production. Further impetus for making relief more punitive was the rise of Protestantism in Europe and England. It stressed the importance of individual effort, rather than the charity and the help-your-neighbor attitude of the Judeo-Christian tradition. Gradually the punitive aspects of the poor laws came to be stressed over their rehabilitative components.[12]

Social conditions worsened between 1740 and 1850 as the Industrial Revolution gained momentum. The shift from agriculture to technology continued; the population greatly expanded and the numbers needing to be clothed and fed shot up rapidly. The uncontrolled growth of towns and factories created many new social problems. In response to increasing need, the Speenhamland Act was passed in 1796. It broadened relief by making aid available when one's wages fell below a subsistence level. This subsistence level was based on family size and food costs, and it was called the "bread scale." The Speenhamland Act was probably ahead of its time in trying to establish an approximation of a guaranteed income, but the direct cause of its failure turned out to be the greed of the law-abiding citizens. Since employers knew that workers would get at least the bread scale no matter what wages they were paid, the Speenhamland Act had the effect of driving wages down, thereby increasing welfare costs. This unfortunate situation is an early example of how well-meaning and humane social legislation is sometimes abused and exploited by the affluent so that it benefits them rather than those in need. College students' abuse of food stamps and industrial contractors' exploitation of Office of Economic Opportunity contracts are two recent examples of this same process.

After the postwar depression of 1815, poverty was widespread and it became apparent that broader political changes were essential.[13] Taxes to support the Poor Law had tripled by 1832, and the law was called "a bounty of indolence and vice" and "a universal system of pauperism."[14] In the New Poor Law of 1834, the ablebodied poor were to receive no relief except for employment in workhouses. Outdoor relief was sometimes granted in an attempt to maintain the family at home, but relief payments were usually meager because they were supposed to supplement income rather than replace it. Widows and the aged constituted the two groups receiving the majority of aid. Despite the lower payments provided, the New Poor Law was praised for its more orderly, firm guidelines, which were less open to misuse, and for speeding up special reforms in the medical, housing, and sanitation areas.[15] Nevertheless, its restrictive and punitive features were evident.

To summarize the development of social welfare in England from 1601 to 1834, we have seen that the poor laws sought to stem disorder during rapid economic and social changes that made many members of society dysfunctional. The legitimately needy were distinguished from the shiftless and criminal, and involuntary unemployment was grudgingly accepted as a necessary consequence of industrialization. Only in the 1700s, when wealth became a virtue, was poverty considered a sin and a vice. The Industrial Revolution brought insecurity to many while others achieved wealth; but those who had prospered because of the economic changes were reluctant to take a charitable attitude toward those who had not. The poor were a burden with whom few wanted to contend.

The Colonial Social Welfare System in America

Considering the conditions of life in the colonies, it was not at all surprising to find many people in the 1600s and 1700s in need of public assistance and charity. Some of the original settlers were paupers, criminals, and indentured servants whom England was trying to dispose of, while others were seeking religious freedom, adventure, fortunes, or a new life. The colonists often landed in America in poor financial condition. They turned to subsistence farming as a livelihood or sought work in the early cities, such as Boston, Philadelphia, and Charleston.

Since the value system and conditions of life in the new country were compatible with the negative attitudes toward dependency that had been developing in England, the English Poor Law of 1601 and the Law of Settlement and Removal of 1662 were adopted. The public did acknowledge its responsibility to protect and care for the needy, but this did not mean that the needy were accepted or understood.[16] Throughout its history the United States has reaffirmed this responsibility to care for the needy, but along with it the fear has persisted that public care of the needy fosters dependence.[17] Carried over with the Poor Law were the practices of residence requirements, parental responsibility, classification of the needy, and indoor and outdoor relief. Residence requirements in the colonies included the practices of "warning out" (the turning away of persons who might become dependent) and "passing on" (transporting people to their legal residence if they became dependent).[18] Assistance was provided in four ways: private citizens could be paid to house the destitute (similar to foster care today); the destitute could be auctioned off to the lowest bidder; the needy could be placed in almshouses; or they could obtain outdoor relief. The ablebodied were required to work, a practice finding increasing popularity in our contemporary assistance systems in spite of its illogicality given a lack of jobs (see Exhibit 2-1).

EXHIBIT 2-1 *The Work Fallacy*

It continues to be a popular belief that large numbers of people who receive social welfare benefits can and should be working. The facts, now as in the past, say otherwise. Exhibit 2-4 demonstrates that most recipients of financial aid cannot work. This exhibit demonstrates two other reasons why work is not always the answer. First, jobs are not always available, especially for minority groups like blacks. Second, as Karen's father illustrates, many jobs pay wages inadequate for a normal family life, and thus a person may work full time and still be poor (these people are called the employed poor). Karen's story, with frustrated job searches and family life supported by several incomes because one job pays too little, is not that uncommon, especially for minorities. It certainly demonstrates that forcing people to seek jobs is not the answer if there are no jobs to be had or if people are physically or socially unable to work. Finally, the CETA program itself is analyzed, showing how the functioning of the economic institution may impede the ability of disadvantaged groups to find employment even though society attempts to structure social welfare programs for this purpose. What, in your view, is the possibility for someone in Karen's situation being helped by the CETA program? Do you know of other programs that might be helpful to her?

WORK OPPORTUNITIES FOR BLACKS

The Labor Department reported today that the unemployment rate rose two-tenths of a percentage point in August [1978] to 7.1 percent of the work force, and said that the increase reflected almost exclusively higher unemployment among black workers. . . .

The unemployment rate among black workers moved from 13.2 percent in July to 14.5 percent in August, which matched the highest post-World War II level for jobless blacks.

6.1 PERCENT FOR WHITE WORKERS. Among white workers, the unemployment rate was 6.1 percent in August. Altogether, the number of jobless people rose by 180,000 last month to 6.9 million. Many of those joining the unemployment rolls were laid off from their jobs, according to the Labor Department.

Unemployment was high among all categories of black workers, but the jobless rate among black teen-agers, 40.4 percent, was called "extremely high" by the Labor Department's Bureau of Labor Statistics.

The bureau also reported that the ratio of black to white jobless rates "continued its recent updrift to the unusually high level of 2.4 to 1 in August," meaning that 2.4 black workers were without jobs for every unemployed white worker.

Meanwhile, total employment rose by 210,000 bringing the number of working Americans to 90.8 million in August. All of the increase occurred among white workers, both adults and teen-agers, according to the report.

Source: Excerpted from Philip Shabecoff, "Blacks Bear Brunt of Jobless Rate Rise to 7.1% for August," *The New York Times,* September 3, 1978, p. 1.

KAREN'S STORY

Karen Gibbs, a 14-year-old brought up in the barrenness of the South Bronx, doesn't really know what a job is all about.

But she knows she wants one, and has to have one. She wants one badly enough, in fact, to have set out three times in three days to stand in line in the pale, pre-dawn light along with thousands of other teenagers to vie for a summer job.

She has seen other youngsters faint, she has seen fights break out, she has watched her 12-year-old sister, sent to accompany her by their worried mother, become so frightened by an atmosphere of confusion and competitiveness that she refused to go back.

Karen is one of nearly 500,000 teenagers in New York City who, according to Federal estimates, qualify for 60,000 seven-week summer jobs paying a top of $55.20 a week.

Last week as the taking of applications began, tens of thousands of teenagers thronged registration centers, many standing overnight in near-freezing weather. At times the crowds were so large that the centers did not open, or did so in confusion and disarray.

A spokesman for the city said that, by last Tuesday, 50,000 14- to 21-year-olds had sought summer jobs in the program, which began as the Neighborhood Youth Corps in 1964 and became part of the Federal Comprehensive Employment and Training Act (CETA) a decade later. Selected centers are to continue taking applications at least through May.

Ask her why she wants the job so badly and the reply from the shy slender eighth grader is immediate: "School clothes," for herself and three younger sisters and a younger brother . . . .

But before she sets foot in any store, she said, she is anxious to be able to give some money to her parents, Mr. and Mrs. Willie T. Gibbs of 1778 Vyse Avenue, who try to make a life for a family of seven on Mr. Gibb's earnings of $8,500 a year as a machine operator in Long Island City . . . .

Source: Excerpted from Judith Cummings, "South Bronx Girl Caught in Maze of Summer Job Plan," *The New York Times*, April 15, 1977, p. B-1.

She has an ambition. When she grows up, she said, she wants to be a nurse, largely because she once saw one working in a hospital. "But my mother," she said sadly, "tried to talk me out of it."

Her mother, Earline, her face displaying a little embarrassment and a lot of protectiveness, explained:

"You have to go to school too long to be a nurse or doctor or anything like that. She said she wanted to go to college, but I told her we didn't have the money for anything like that."

Reflecting on her daughter's future options, Mrs. Gibbs paused for a long moment and said, finally:

"A day-care center, that's the only job I know. Because we knew somebody who worked there before. The rest of the jobs, I don't know."

The family had fled to the Bronx from a larger apartment in Harlem when, as Mrs. Gibbs described it, the "junkies" started asking Karen and Yvan, then 8 and 6 years old, "to hold a jump rope on their arm while they shoot up, or a belt or something."

Now they live in a small, three-room apartment, with the four older children doubling up in the single bedroom while their parents sleep on a foldout sofa in the living room.

School (Intermediate School 84), despite the girl gangs that menace the halls and walkways, is something Karen generally likes. She particularly enjoys a science teacher who regales classmates with questions like, "Aren't I gorgeous?" and bestows a reward on the pupil who gives the appropriate answer. Science, she said, is her favorite subject.

A little money would make lots of things possible, young Miss Gibbs said, like the books she could buy to substitute for "the movies I don't get to see," and the school voice club, which she says she can't join because it calls for a $2 fee.

Mrs. Gibbs tries to augment her husband's take-home pay of $146 a week by purchasing $131 worth of food stamps for $95 every two weeks. The family appears to be classically working-poor and securing one of the Federal jobs for Karen has become a family project.

Frightened by the sisters' stories of the disorder of the first days at the job center, Tremont Methodist Church at 1951 Washington Avenue, Mrs. Gibbs walked her daughter the mile and a half to the center and back herself last Tuesday, keeping her 12-year-old sister home from school to mind the younger children.

The family was cut off from public assistance a couple of years ago when Mr. Gibbs, recovering from a bout with tuberculosis, began to earn some money again.

"Welfare said we didn't need no more help, so they cut us off," Mrs. Gibbs said. After weeks of taking days off from work to try to press an appeal for supplementary funds at the welfare offices in Manhattan and after being repeatedly told to come back later, Mr. Gibbs decided he could afford no more unpaid days in waiting rooms, and gave up.

CETA IN OPERATION

The Nation's largest single program to combat unemployment is now before Congress for review and reenactment. Authorized by the Comprehensive Employment and Training Act (CETA), this $11 billion program currently addresses two kinds of unemployment, long term and short term. By 1979, an estimated 1.5 million employment and training opportunities will be available through CETA programs.

Because of its size and funding, CETA has great potential to reduce unemployment and financial hardship among those groups usually hardest hit by long periods of joblessness—namely, women, minorities, and the poor. But it is for these very groups that the program has not met expectations.

For example, statistics show that while the number of minority people living in poverty increased from 1976 to 1977, minority representation in CETA programs actually declined significantly. And although women last year accounted for almost two-thirds of those living in

---

Source: Excerpted from Judy Heisher, "CETA's $11 Billion," in *The Civil Rights Digest*, Spring 1978, pp. 3–9.

poverty in this country, less than half of those enrolled in CETA programs were female.

At the same time, the women and minorities who were enrolled in CETA programs tended to be concentrated in training efforts and jobs at the lower end of the skill and pay scale, thus helping to perpetuate the discriminatory employment practices of the past.

The question now before Congress, therefore, is whether and how to improve the situation. The answer from social welfare experts, civil rights activists, and a growing number of economists is to reserve all future CETA jobs and services to the most disadvantaged in terms of length of unemployment and income. Such a move (called "targeting") would greatly increase the enrollment of women, minorities, and the poor.

These efforts must, however, be coupled with Labor Department action to ensure that the targeted groups receive fair treatment in the types of training, salary, and jobs they receive through the CETA program. Unfortunately, there currently exists a great deal of opposition to using the targeting concept in the largest of CETA programs now underway.

In 1973, when CETA was first enacted, the bulk of the available programs did emphasize service to the long term unemployed and those who have a hard time becoming employed even when jobs are in good supply. These programs created in CETA's earliest days attack the roots of persistent joblessness, namely, lack of education, training, or job experience, and help participants compete more effectively for jobs. They are referred to as the CETA "structural" jobs programs and those in need of services are called the "structurally unemployed."

Among the groups targeted for enrollment in these structural programs are the poor, women, minorities, the elderly, the handicapped, the disabled, youth, exoffenders, and those lacking in education. To enhance their employability, the structural programs provide skill training in the classroom along with on-the-job experience and subsidized employment in the public sector. The training experiences are supplemented by supportive services like counseling, aptitude testing, day care, and transportation to strengthen participants' chances of finding and retaining jobs. Most of the services and training are carried out by State and local governments called prime sponsors.

How CETA grew

Another newer and larger component of the CETA program, however, has become more important over the past several years with the increase in the national unemployment rate and is now funded at three times the level of the structural programs. This newer component is designed to pick up the slack in the job market caused by "down-cycles" in the economy (recessions) by providing temporary federally-subsidized jobs or public service employment in nonprofit agencies and State and local governments. Unlike the structural programs, these "countercyclical" programs do not provide training or supportive services, and are not aimed exclusively at the disadvantaged. Instead they seek to employ those out of work due to changes in the economy, the so-called "countercyclically unemployed."

Because of a variety of circumstances, the CETA countercyclical program enrolls predominantly white, male, educated, and skilled workers, and the rapid growth of the program in size and funding has all but eclipsed the training and targeting efforts of the original structural program. Many in Congress and the Administration are concerned over this turn of events and its impact on the Nation's poor, minorities, and women. Through job training and placement, CETA's structural program efforts were to provide a ticket out of poverty and a way off the welfare rolls. Now, however, the bulk of CETA funding is going to help support the better-educated white male.

There are other disturbing facts before Congress as it considers the fate of this multibillion-dollar program. While the Labor Department consistently reports female, minority, and youth unemployment at two and three times the level of white, adult males, the true extent of joblessness and poverty among these groups remains obscured because many continue to be undercounted and thus underrepresented in the Nation's labor force, census, and unemployment data. Thus, CETA currently lacks the necessary measurement tools with which to accurately develop and target its programs. Foremost among these tools is a measure of "discouragement."

Discouraged workers, as the name implies, are those who have given up looking for work because they believe none is available to them. Since they are not seeking employment, they are considered to be out of the labor force and therefore are not counted as unemployed. The meager statistics available on the participation of black males in the labor force show that discouragement is particularly severe among this group.

Measuring "underemployment" is yet another means of identifying need. As it is now defined, an underemployed person is either working part-time and seeking full-time employment, or is a member of a family whose combined earned income is some fixed percentage below the "lower living standard" income determined by the Bureau of Labor Statistics. At present no reliable method exists of accurately counting the number of underemployed persons, but it is generally believed that minorities and women suffer most from underemployment.

Nor do existing measures of unemployment include data on income as a test of actual need. Many workers now classified as unemployed are eligible for unemployment insurance (UI) and/or have an annual family income, despite periods of temporary unemployment, well above the lower-living standard level. Such a means-tested measure of unemployment would help identify those suffering the greatest hardship and thus help target CETA resources. If current statistics are any indication, the CETA program would have to significantly increase services to minorities and women in order to adequately address the situation.

Though originally the concept of self-help was strong, two major events helped to modify these early beliefs. Between 1760 and 1820, the French and Indian Wars left many families fatherless and drove frontier people to seek safety along the coast. Unemployment increased and wages fell as a result, while bad crop years, low yields, and other natural catastrophes made costs skyrocket. These conditions created need under circumstances that called into question the New England Puritan values of self-sufficiency, the goodness of work, piety, and the strength of the family.

A series of bloody revolutions at the end of the eighteenth century, of which the American and French are the most famous, created societies more equalitarian than ever before. The greater power of the common people over the social institutions that governed their lives generated the rise of Romanticism. Romantic ideals countered ascetic Puritan beliefs with a faith in the goodness, uniqueness, and value of each individual, thereby supporting attempts to increase individual autonomy and provide basic social welfare services to all. The depression after the Napoleonic Wars (1815–1821), the growing population, and the arrival of over six million immigrants between 1820 and 1860 were all factors that supported the adoption of some of the practical implications of Romanticism.

These effects were first felt in prison reforms, starting with the opening of the Walnut Street Prison in Philadelphia in 1790, followed by greatly improved conditions in almshouses. Almshouses became important as poor men's hospitals, a development fostered by the large number of immigrants who arrived destitute, ill, with language barriers, and encountering difficulty finding work. These immigrants were highly motivated and usually needed temporary care until they could regain their health and become somewhat acclimated to their new society. In response to such needs, medical care in almshouses was usually excellent, with some of the greatest physicians in the country working in them. Manhattan's Bellevue Hospital, Philadelphia's General Hospital, and Baltimore City Hospital were all originally almshouses.

Though many thought the residents of almshouses were capable of work, studies showed this to be false. In Philadelphia's Blockley Almshouse in 1848, only 12 percent of the men and women were ablebodied. Nevertheless, there was growing criticism that almshouses were too costly, too crowded, had unhealthy conditions, and were ineffective in reaching the needy whose pride would not let them be confined in an almshouse. These criticisms stimulated a period of vigorous social reform from 1830 to 1860. Thoreau, Emerson, and other intellectuals recognized the need for social reform and stimulated attempts to establish experimental social communities to find better ways of life. Brook Farm and the Oneida Community were two examples of their day, while the communes of our day continue the search for more satisfying community contexts.

In the Jacksonian era, 1830–1846, movements to correct the social ills of industry, eliminate religious intolerance, and provide better treatment of the insane increased.[19] Education, women's suffrage, temperance, trade unionism, and slavery were other important issues of the time that reflected society's struggles with early industrialization and the values of freedom and democracy. There continued to be conflicting views on welfare. Some felt that hard-working individuals should not have to pay taxes to support the idle, while others felt that those people who had once contributed to society should be aided in troubled times. Some felt volunteer charities should be the only source of aid, while others believed that volunteer charities were too limited and unstable to bear the sole responsibility for aiding those in need. While these issues were being debated, the evidence of need included antirent wars staged in New York; constant looting and burning in opposition to depressed economic conditions in Baltimore; and Boston's need to cope with a massive influx of Irish immigrants.

New Patterns of Helping: The Legacy of the 1800s ◀

From 1860 to 1900, the population of the United States rose from 31.5 million to 76 million, with 13.7 million being immigrants. The Industrial Revolution was having a profound effect on the United States during this period, and the nation was rapidly becoming a large, urban society increasingly cognizant of its many problems. During the 1800s, social welfare progress occurred in three major spheres: public social welfare services; private social welfare services; and services for special groups.

Progress in Public Social Welfare

Starting in 1857, outdoor relief became more generally accepted and replaced many almshouses. This resulted from studies that showed it to be less costly than help provided in almshouses, as well as an increasingly prevalent belief that those temporarily in need should not be subjected to the degrading conditions of almshouse life. Outdoor relief payments were small, however, since many continued to believe that low payment levels would encourage recipients to seek work in spite of evidence indicating that the majority of the needy could not work.[20] Relief payments in cities were usually in cash, but in rural areas relief was usually given "in kind" (giving the actual products, such as food and clothing, instead of money to buy these items).[21]

The Civil War and its aftermath led to other changes in the public welfare system. In this period of intellectual and social upheaval, the equality of all men and the struggle between competing political and economic systems became issues of high priority, with profound moral consequences. Congressional response to these issues included the passage of the Morrill Act and the establishment of the Freedman's Bureau in 1865. The former gave states land grants to build colleges and other public facilities. The latter was created to help the needy, especially ex-slaves, by providing financial assistance and free education in the South.[22] It was supported by the first federal tax legislation to care for the poor, a clear governmental declaration of its responsibility for citizens who were the pawns of the political and economic dislocations of the Civil War.

Progress in Private Social Welfare: The Charity Organization Society

In spite of progress in the public sphere, the limited help provided in the 1880s was strained to the limit by such events as the depressions of 1815–1821 and 1837–1843, as well as the panics of 1847 and 1857. Soup kitchens, collections through newspapers, and old clothing and bread funds were used to supplement public relief channels, but it became clear that more organized procedures would be more effective. An early attempt at such organization appeared in 1817. The New York Society for the Prevention of Pauperism stressed prevention and rehabilitation within a rather moralistic framework for dealing with problems. The New York Association for Improving the Condition of the Poor (AICP), founded in 1843 and subsequently copied in several other cities, was modeled after the New York Society for the Prevention of Pauperism, and superseded it. This association developed a classification for the needy: those who were needy by "unavoidable causes," by "own improvidence and vices," or by laziness. Like the society on which it was modeled, the AICP felt intemperance was a main cause of poverty. However, it realized that social reform was as important as moral reform, so in addition to moral preaching, attempts were made to improve sanitation and housing, and to lessen alcoholism, promiscuity, and child neglect.

The associations were in turn superseded by the development of the Charity Organization Society (COS). Begun in England in 1869, COS opened its first United States affiliate in Buffalo in 1877. By 1892, America had ninety-two COS's. Care in investigating claims, meeting individual needs, and providing minimal relief payments was stressed. COS also sought to coordinate private social welfare services to avoid costly duplication. Help was to be provided only to the "truly needy."[23] Case records were taken, and agents increasingly found education helpful in preparing such records. The workers kept accounts of all persons receiving aid and made regular visits to recipients. Paid agents were used to check up on welfare recipients. The COS's followed the teaching of Josephine Shaw Lowell as espoused in her book *Public Relief and Private Charity.* She believed that all relief should be voluntary, and made unpleasant enough so that few would stoop to ask for aid. Lowell believed that almshouses and workhouses should be rehabilitative, with those working there finding moral regeneration.

Lowell's relief system was based on some insidious values. Her underlying belief was that most needy people were capable of work, a belief no truer then than it had been earlier or is today. She also continued to distinguish between deserving and undeserving poor, and used a means test to determine eligibility for aid. Such values and practices continue to undermine contemporary efforts to formulate an adequate social welfare system, and as such were unfortunate parts of Lowell's work. However, she did make some beneficial changes to the practices then existing. The individual was considered for relief according to that person's personal set of circumstances, although if a person was found worthy of aid, the charity of relatives, the church, and others was sought first. A scarcity of other resources eventually led the COS organizations to have their own relief funds, and since few people volunteered to visit relief recipients, both the investigation of claims and the visiting of relief recipients became the job of a paid agent. These agents formed what might be called the first social workers in our current use of that name, being paid helping persons using a specified set of procedures to investigate need and provide resources to meet that need. This development was greatly aided by the work of Mary Richmond, a major figure in the COS in the United States. In 1897 she called for the establishment of a training school for professional social workers, and she subsequently formulated the first statement of the principles of social casework.

The COS also played an important role in the development of welfare in the United States in other ways. It countered the harshness of Social Darwinism* by focusing on individual circumstances that might create

---

* Social Darwinism was an extension of Darwin's biological concept of the survival of the fittest to the social world. The theory asserted that the poor and helpless were inferior to those not in need, and therefore to help them would be to perpetuate weakness. This idea completely ignored the social system as the cause of need.

need. It influenced and enlisted the support of scholars from university campuses, and set standards of case evaluation by which all charity and relief organizations could be measured. COS also offered auxiliary services: an employment bureau; a savings and thrift class; a loan office; a workroom; legal aid; a day nursery for working mothers; and visiting nurses. The establishment of the first State Board of Charities in Massachusetts in 1863 established a trend that resulted in sixteen states having such boards by 1897. These were public agencies modeled after the private Charity Organization Societies. They improved conditions in facilities for the needy, and created special services for children, the handicapped, and the mentally disturbed.[24] They also tried to counteract the excessively moralistic and restrictive aspects of COS practices, supporting outdoor relief as the most effective and humane way to provide help. However, the battle over the effects of outdoor relief continued into the new century, as Lowell continued to contend that it would lead to shiftlessness and dependence, and many states vacillated between outdoor relief and almshouse care.

Other Private Social Welfare Developments

In response to continued assertions by some groups that outdoor relief did not properly discourage the temptation to take help instead of trying to improve one's condition, other solutions to the relief problem were sought. The settlement house movement caught on as a possible alternative, and in 1887, Neighborhood House in New York, Hull House and the Northwestern University Settlement in Chicago, and the South End Settlement in Boston, were opened. They were community centers that met special community needs for practical education, recreation, and social cohesion. They were especially supportive in helping immigrants get a foothold in America. They formed ties with universities and the community in which they existed, and proved more understanding of the causes of poverty than the COS. In addition, Hull House, under Jane Addams's leadership, was able to offer auxiliary services, such as a free kindergarten, a day nursery, a playground, clubs, lectures, a library, a boarding house, and meeting rooms. Settlement houses, then, exemplified a community approach to problem solving.

We are just emerging from a long period in which a psychological approach was thought to be the most effective one to adopt in the solution of human problems. The limitations of such an approach in terms of problem abstraction, loss of client power, reduced quantity of services, and inequitable distribution of services have led many contemporary social welfare practitioners back to a more community-focused approach. Contemporary indigenous movements to reduce inequality and improve the quality of life in society are logical successors to the principles established in the settlement house movement. Today we speak of consumer advocacy, participation of the poor, community organization, and the like.

While the terminology may be contemporary, the ideas were sown in the earlier community settlement house movement.

Progress in the provision of services for special groups moved ahead in several areas during the 1800s. As American society industrialized, distinctions between the laborer and the industrial manager were becoming more apparent. It became increasingly evident that the old moral code of an individualistic, agrarian society was being applied to the practices of a corporate and industrial society.[25] Social Darwinism was the philosophy of the time, and it discouraged governmental intervention in the realm of business. The formation of groups such as the National Labor Union in 1866, the Knights of Labor in 1878, and the American Federation of Labor in 1886, was the result of workers' attempts to organize to protect themselves against such beliefs and their results. These organizational attempts were vigorously and often violently opposed by managerial and entrepreneurial groups. Recent efforts of Cesar Chavez, to organize migrant farm workers in spite of economic and social reprisals by the food industry as well as other union groups gives some flavor of what early organizational efforts were like.

The needs of the physically and mentally ill were also issues at midcentury. The American Medical Association (AMA) was founded in 1847, giving powerful support to early attempts to improve standards of medical care and practice. Movement of mentally ill prisoners from houses of correction to mental hospitals in 1844 improved their chances for receiving humane treatment. However, President Pierce vetoed legislation in 1854 that would have provided federal money to build homes for the mentally ill, in spite of Dorothea Dix's eloquent appeals. From our contemporary perspective, the AMA may be seen as maintaining professional privilege as much as supporting standards of medical practice, and the wisdom of Dorothea Dix's attempts to remove the mentally ill from the community into isolated mental hospitals may be questioned. However, at the time, the formation of the AMA was seen as a positive act, and the refutation of Dorothea Dix's goals slowed reform considerably.

Children and prisoners were two final groups for which services were improved during this period. Legislation passed in 1878 prohibited the removal of children from their homes solely because of poverty, while legislation in 1887 and 1890 improved the procedures used when children had to be placed in foster homes or large residential facilities. Reform schools to rehabilitate youthful delinquents were developed, and juvenile courts were established in 1899. Related to these changes were more general prison reforms resulting in the separation of male and female prisoners, and attempts to eliminate political influences in jails and prisons. In 1891, the National Conference of Charities and Correction (now the National Conference on Social Welfare)[26] recommended maximum and minimum sentences, a reformatory system, encouraging prisoners to learn a trade, letting the disabled practice their trade within the institutions, rewarding good behavior, keeping total records of each prisoner, giving classroom instruction, and allowing prisoners to attend regular religious services. As can be seen, more humane care was slowly being attempted for additional groups in society. Events like the atrocities documented in the Arkansas prison system and the spectacular Attica prison disaster in New York State serve as periodic reminders of the as yet inadequate nature of attempts to deal more humanely with all human beings regardless of their problems or offenses.

▶ Social Welfare in the Twentieth Century in the United States

Before 1900 the stigma of poverty was keenly felt, a result of Social Darwinism and the COS blaming dependency on personal failure. In spite of the progress toward an adequate social welfare system, substantial challenges remained as America moved into the twentieth century.[27] After 1900 the developing social and biological sciences helped people realize that social, economic, and other environmental factors played large roles in people's lives.

Between 1900 and 1925 the population of the United States reached 100 million, with 50 percent of the people living in cities. The United States had become an important industrial nation and world power, attaining unique prosperity and wealth; the gross national product (GNP) reached $104.4 billion just before the stock market crash of 1929. The publication of Robert Hunter's *Poverty* in 1904 showed that the growing society was developing a new regard for the poor. Hunter's statistics on the prevalence of unemployed men, low wages, and poor working conditions showed the poor to be victims of unfortunate circumstances rather than moral inadequacy. After John A. Ryan published *A Living Wage* in 1906, the value of more than a minimum standard of living became more accepted. He and other economists calculated what a family needed to live comfortably, and the discrepancy between the then-current wage scale and the estimated living wage was enormous.

Immigrants, though they did not comprise the entire group of unemployed, continued to form the majority of them. The communication problem, slum conditions caused by overcrowding, and the fear of a great number of men flooding the labor force caused much adverse feeling toward the new arrivals. The pressure became so great that in 1921 legislation was passed that set strict quotas on further immigration.[28] The 1924 Immigration Act further restricted and controlled immigration.[29] Unfortunately, such legislation did not raise wages, and did not stem the increasing migration of impoverished farm families to the cities in search of work.

In the period from 1900 to World War I, a group of concerned citizens called Progressives sought to expose the evils of low wages, long hours, bossism, health hazards, and other problems facing the poor in the cities.

Social workers also tried to help, and at the 1912 Conference on Charities and Correction, the Committee on Standards of Living and Labor recommended a liberal list of much needed reforms. Among them were the eight-hour workday for women, children, and some men; a six-day workweek; and an end to work hours at night.[30] In 1912, Woodrow Wilson took office on the platform of New Freedom, and before the outbreak of World War I he pushed strongly for reform. He encouraged the passage of the Federal Reserve Act and the Sixteenth Amendment (which established the federal income tax), the setting up of the Federal Trade Commission, legislation creating an eight-hour workday for railroad workers, laws against interstate transportation of goods made by child labor, and the Clayton Antitrust Act of 1914.

Children were of prime concern in the early 1900s. Theodore Roosevelt held the first White House Conference on Children in 1909. It dealt with the care of dependent children, and one of its outcomes was the formation of the Children's Bureau in the Department of Labor in 1912.[31] The bureau, in the capable hands of Julia Lathrop and Grace Abbott, carefully regulated the laws and reforms concerning children's rights in this country.[32] President Wilson held the second White House Conference on Children in 1919, which resulted in the Maternity and Infancy Act of 1921 (Sheppard-Turner Act).[33] In 1930, President Hoover held the third conference, which produced the Children's Charter. The charter emphasized the child's need for love, security, and understanding, as well as for protection, recreation, proper schooling, and preparation for adulthood. The fourth conference was held in 1940 by President Roosevelt. The topic was children in a democracy, and concern was for economic and social security for each child.[34] In 1918, the Children's Bureau identified another gap in services to children in its study of the existing juvenile courts. It found only a few acceptable. Reforms that resulted included hearings held in the judge's private chambers under informal conditions (i.e., no warrants or indictments); the provision of probation services; and special detention centers and psychiatric services.[35] Unfortunately, the unintended effect of these well-meaning reforms was to deprive juveniles of their basic legal rights, and many of these practices have since been abolished by the courts. Special health services for children were also sought, and by 1934 thirty-seven states had developed programs for diagnostic services, medical treatment, and convalescent care for crippled children.[36]

By the 1920s reformers had generated a greater awareness of the need that often resulted from such factors as poor sanitation facilities, low wages, poor safety precautions in industry, and various other occupational hazards. Unemployment, illness or incapacity, death of the breadwinner, and old age were also accepted as legitimate causes of need. Work-related problems were especially obvious in early factory systems, and by 1920 forty-three states had passed workmen's compensation laws.[37] However, many of these laws were ineffective and there was no uniformity in coverage or administrative structure from state to state.[38] This legislation was especially important for being an early form of social insurance, a type of social welfare program that was to be used widely in the Social Security Act of 1935.

Workmen's Compensation is a program to cover work-connected injury. Each state is required to develop its own program, as does the federal government to cover federal employees. The program is considered a cost to an employer of doing business, and employers are required to have a plan with a private insurance company, a state-run plan, or be self-insured. Although the scope of coverage, benefit provisions, and administrative procedures vary by state, in all states covered workers injured on the job receive benefits from the employer's insurance plan. Workmen's compensation is a plan that does not entail a direct cash grant out of public monies. Instead, employers have paid into a fund from which workers are paid in the event of injury on the job. As with any insurance, some employers pay in more than their workers ever collect, while others have workers collecting more than the employer paid. This sharing of risk is characteristic of any insurance plan. It is easy to see how a particularly salient problem of the time, industrial safety, combined with a social welfare program that did not disrupt societal values of self-reliance, resulted in a workable solution to the problem. When the need for the Social Security Act was recognized in the 1930s, it is little wonder that the Congress turned first to the social insurance concept.

Worker's compensation is a good program to use to examine some characteristics of the relationship between the states and the federal government with respect to social welfare policy. In recognition of states' rights, a basic principle of the society's political structure, each state has developed its own workmen's compensation plan within broad federal guidelines. This has led to variations in coverage among states that result in unequal benefits: residents of different states get different benefits. This trade-off of nonuniform and therefore inequitable programs in return for maintaining state autonomy is one that characterizes several other important programs, Aid to Families with Dependent Children being another major example.

State autonomy in welfare policy also makes it possible for some states to have programs that others do not, creating another type of inequality among states. In the Aid to Families with Dependent Children program, for example, some states allow families with an unemployed father to be living in the family, while others will not provide benefits if there is an employable adult male present, unemployed or not. The effect of this difference in programs is that in some states families can remain together while receiving AFDC benefits, while in others men must abandon their families in order for the family to receive help.

On the other hand, state autonomy often has a beneficial impact on national programs by allowing for state experimentation that may ultimately result in national legislation. Workmen's compensation is a case in point, since it was the recognition by individual states of the need for compensation for work-related accidents that finally led to the legislation requiring all states to have such programs. Once again the close interaction between the social welfare institution and the other major social institutions is illustrated.

Social welfare programs were gradually developed to aid various special groups in addition to those already mentioned. By 1920 forty states had passed acts to aid needy mothers, and soon after, similar aid was made available to the aged. Lobbies were formed to improve facilities for the destitute aged, and by the Depression this was one of the most powerful groups pushing for social security.[39] Unfortunately, other needy groups were not as successful in organizing to protect against the low level of aid and geographically variable coverage.

The early 1900s saw the continued growth of voluntary organizations financed by dues, donations, and subscriptions. Some of the best-known groups were the Boy Scouts, Girl Scouts, National Tuberculosis Association, American Cancer Society, Camp Fire Girls, Goodwill Industries, the National Association for the Advancement of Colored People (NAACP), and the National Child Labor Committee.[40] Another voluntary organization, the Red Cross, performed important functions under the directorship of Harry Hopkins during World War I. It provided a communications link between service personnel and their families and assistance to needy dependents of servicemen. It also advanced money to families that had not received their allowance from the Soldier's and Sailor's Insurance Law of 1919, which was supposed to protect the enlisted person's family from hardship resulting from the person's military service.[41] Charitable trust funds were also growing during the early 1900s. Some of the best known were the Rockefeller and Carnegie Foundations, the Rockefeller Institute for Medical Research (1901), the General Education Board (1902), the Carnegie Foundation for the Advancement of Teaching (1905), and the Russell Sage Foundation (1907).[42]

The Impact of the Great Depression ◀

The Great Depression of the thirties forced a change in the nation's thinking about social welfare and related values. The developing society had carefully nurtured values of self-reliance, initiative, hard work, and thrift, and was proud of its reputation as the land of opportunity where an individual could make a personal fortune—the classical rags-to-riches philosophy. It followed that anyone who had not been successful had not worked well or wisely enough, or had been improvident. Although there had been increasing recognition of some of the social causes of personal misfortune, there was still a very basic belief that for most people work and thrift would lead to success. The Great Depression shattered this dream. For the first time, people who had worked and saved, who had been proud of their accomplishments and were recognized in their communities as being fine citizens, had their savings wiped out. People who had always worked and who desperately wanted to work could no longer find jobs. It became painfully clear that there was something wrong with a value system that said that anyone who tried hard enough could work and prosper. It was no longer a situation in which individuals were in control. Social events were preventing people from working and were generating massive need. The American value system would never be the same again, and it was this change that made possible the sweeping changes enacted during Franklin D. Roosevelt's New Deal.

The Depression also answered once and for all the question of whether relief should be primarily public or private. The crisis was so widespread that private agencies could not hope to alleviate the unemployment and resulting need.[43] It was this impetus that finally made the federal government assume the major responsibility for economic stability and personal security. As it became clear that the private sector could not control business cycles, the government had to step in. No longer was the government that goverened least necessarily the best; strict laissez-faire capitalism had failed. The lack of economic opportunity and resources were clearly responsible for poverty and unemployment, particularly in the cases of youth, the aged, women, minority groups, and farmers,[44] and only the federal government had the power to step in to stem the rising tide of business and banking failures. The Great Depression was the major reason for poverty coming to be seen as a societal rather than an individual problem.[45]

Early Social Welfare Responses to the Great Depression

The Great Depression encouraged many changes in the administration and financing of outdoor relief. It stimulated increased public works and work-relief programs, an expanded categorical approach to relief, and eventually a new program of social insurance and social assistance.[46] To help with unemployment relief, some state governments established emergency relief administrations,[47] while the Wagner-Rainey bill of 1932 authorized the Reconstruction Finance Corporation to make loans to states for public works and unemployment relief.[48] In 1933 President Roosevelt established the Federal Emergency Relief Act (FERA), appropriating $500 million for grants-in-aid to states for work relief and unemployment relief. When FERA was abolished in 1936, it had allocated over $3 billion to assisting states.[49] In November of 1935 President Roosevelt created the Civil Works Agency, administered by FERA, "to give work to able-bodied poor."[50] The Public Works Administration was also formed, with goals to increase the demand for heavy or durable goods and to stimulate purchasing power. In spite of their good intent, the flurry of such experimental and often hotly contested legislation ultimately proved incapable of dealing with the need for a new approach to social welfare in the United States.

Legislation following the Great Depression constituted what was termed the New Deal, and it accelerated the increase in the amount of public control imposed on the nation's economy. "The New Deal, however, was more concerned with the social repercussions of industrialization, rather than with more narrowly economic problems."[51] While much of the early legislation passed in immediate response to the Great Depression was at least partially successful in alleviating need, it soon became clear that a more fundamental and enduring change in the nation's economic and social welfare structures was necessary. Such a plan, the Social Security Act, was proposed by President Roosevelt and was passed by the Congress in 1935. Two social insurance programs were established on the national level to meet need created by old age and unemployment: Old Age and Survivor's Insurance (OASI, or Social Security), a federal system of old-age benefits for retired workers; and a federal-state system of unemployment insurance. The program also provided for federal grants to states to help them provide financial assistance to the aged, the blind, and dependent children. Some health services, social services, and vocational rehabilitation were also included. "The creation of a foundation of social insurance was laid, and areas previously considered the exclusive province of the private sector were brought under the scrutiny of a democratic government."[52]

The Social Security Act of 1935: The Enduring Legacy of the Great Depression

The Social Security Act laid the foundation of the present public welfare system in the United States. Its major significance lay in two major categories of programs that it established: (1) social insurances; and (2) grant programs. The social insurance programs were seen as much more desirable than the grant programs, since as in all insurances the recipients of the benefits had contributed to them, while in the grant programs recipients received money taken from general revenues (obtained from tax revenues). In a society still trying to encourage self-sufficiency, hard work, and thrift, much less stigma was attached to a social welfare program in which individuals could be seen as simply receiving their own money back. Receiving a direct grant from noncontributed money carried the stigma of receiving something for nothing, something which one had not earned. Since the current structure of social welfare services is still built on these programs, and apparently will be until some form of guaranteed income is legislated, it is worthwhile to take a closer look at the Social Security program and the grant programs that accompanied it.

Social Security was intended to provide for need during old age when earning capacity was minimal. Payment levels were never intended to be sufficient to meet living costs in and of themselves, but were to be supplemented by personal savings—a direct attempt to maintain values of self-reliance and thrift. Although social security payments have steadily risen, they remain low enough to require some supplementation. (See Exhibit 2-2, on pages 72 through 78, for a detailed examination of how the current Social Security System operates.)

Social Security was intended to provide for need during old age and for the survivors (widows and children) of workers. Since it would take some years for the Social Security trust fund to be developed from the contributions of workers, the grant programs (which used current tax revenues) were included in the Social Security Act to meet the needs of those who were already aged, disabled, or dependent at the time of the passage of the legislation. It was assumed that these grant programs would decrease in importance as more and more persons were covered by the new Social Security program. Social phenomena, such as rural to urban migration, family disintegration, and regional pockets of poverty (Appalachia and native American areas especially) created an enduring need for these programs that was not originally anticipated.

Social Security has since been expanded to include disabled workers and their dependents, and certain health benefits for recipients. This is why the program is now called the Old Age, Survivors, Disability and Health Insurance Program (OASDHI).

EXHIBIT 2-2 *Social Security in Operation*

The following data give a picture of current levels of Social Security operation. Table 1 shows the contributions paid by employers and employees on the specified taxable earnings. Note that both employee and employer contributions are only made on earnings as shown—any earnings above this level have no Social Security contributions taken out. It is for this reason that Social Security is called a regressive tax, since lower income groups pay a larger percentage of their income in the tax than do higher income groups. For example, in 1978 a person earning $15,000 in taxable income would have Social Security contributions withheld on all of it, whereas a person earning $50,000 would have Social Security contributions withheld only from the first $17,700. Table 2 shows the number and percentage of people covered by Social Security (coverage is determined by length of work in a job in which Social Security contributions have been made). Table 3 shows the number of beneficiaries receiving Social Security payments, and the average amount of payments. Two concluding sections discuss some of the current issues raised by the Social Security program in general, and with respect to women in particular.

TABLE 1 Employer and Employee Contributions to Social Security

Year	*1960*	*1965*	*1970*	*1973*	*1978*	*1980*
Taxable earnings base	$4,800	$4,800	$7,800	$10,800	$17,700	$25,900
Tax rate that employers and employees each pay	3.0%	3.625%	4.8%	5.9%	6.05%	6.13%

Source: U.S. Bureau of the Census, *Pocket Data Book: USA 1973* (Washington, D.C.: U.S. Government Printing Office, 1973), pp. 183–84.

TABLE 2 Social Security Coverage (in millions of persons)

Year	*1960*	*1965*	*1970*	*1971*	*1975*
Covered persons	59.4	65.6	72.1	72.9	78.0
Percent of paid employed	88.0%	89.1%	89.5%	89.4%	90.1%
Not covered	8.1	8.0	8.5	8.6	8.6

TABLE 3 Social Security Beneficiaries and Benefit Levels

Year	*1960*	*1965*	*1970*	*1975*
Number of beneficiaries (in millions)	14.8	20.9	26.2	31.8
Average monthly benefits to family groups (in 1975 dollars) for:				
▶ Retired male workers	$148.80	157.80	179.70	225.00
▶ Disabled workers	$344.00	350.40	368.80	444.00
▶ Widowed mothers	$350.10	383.20	406.50	478.00
▶ Widows/widowers without children	$107.50	128.80	143.00	194.00

Sources: The data for Tables 2 and 3 are from Social Security Administration, *Your 1978 Social Security Deduction,* pp. 2–3; Social Security Administration, *Program Introduction* (revised January 1976); and *Social Indicators 1976,* p. 133.

GENERAL ISSUES IN THE SOCIAL SECURITY PROGRAM

Social Security provides the bulwark of income for 30 million people: the retired, the disabled, and survivors. It provides assurance of protection to 95 percent of children in the event the family provider should die. Nearly all of the aged are receiving or are eligible for benefits, and 80 percent of the population between 21 and 64 are covered in the event they should become seriously disabled. It is a matter of deep concern if the system supporting this structure of protection should be deficient. While even the most ardent supporters recognize gaps and deficiencies and have proposals for improvement, the Social Security "problem" is not as serious as many of its critics profess. The program is sufficiently complex that few people are able to evaluate the criticisms and to distinguish between legitimate concerns and the destructive criticisms which, in some instances, are aimed at liquidating the program.

Source: Washington Bulletin 23 (October 14, 1974): 173–76.

Fiscal Solvency of the System

Critics of the system and many of its friends have noted that the "trust fund" is not the basic source of paying benefits. Social Security is different from some private insurance plans. The trust fund has funds to pay benefits for a period of less than a year. This time period has been diminishing. In 1957 it had the capability of paying benefits for a period in excess of three years. It is evident that the trust fund is a contingency fund and that current income is used to pay current obligations. There is nothing wrong with this for the income is tax revenue and its collection on a regular basis is assured by the authority of the U.S. government. Misleading Social Security literature has used the term "trust fund" in a manner that suggests something more than this.

Although critics have made much of this point, conventional economic thought is that it is not only impractical but dangerous for the Social Security trust fund to be fully funded. If it were, the government would have immense sums to invest, more than the entire national debt and enough to dominate the private security market. The trust fund or contingent fund is composed of U.S. government securities. This has led some critics to say that the trust fund is composed of worthless "I.O.U.s." The trust fund holds such securities just as any bank or private fund would and receives interest on the securities at a fair rate. The trust fund is not the basic source of payments to beneficiaries, and such payments are not endangered.

The long-term trend is in the direction of a fiscal problem. Social Security's tax system and benefit structure are premised upon a birth rate higher than is evident and upon a growth in real wages that has not materialized. The low birth rates for the past ten years suggest that in the next century the ratio of workers to retired persons will be reduced problematically. Since the currently employed support the retired there must be a sufficient number of workers for every retired person to make the system secure. In 1947 there were twenty-two workers for every beneficiary. By 1972 there were only three. Also the many benefit increases provided to compensate for price increases have been financed in a manner that creates increasing obligations to pay higher benefits to many of those currently employed. Benefit increases have been financed by increasing the wage base and requiring higher wage earners to pay taxes on more income. Currently the law provides that when benefits are increased in the future (and the law assures that benefits will keep up with price) there will be automatic increases in the level of wages subject to tax . . . This will require a continued increase in the tax base, and this is dependent upon a growth in real wages. . . .

Equity of the Retirement Test

This test, which has been subject to severe criticism, is one of the ways Social Security determines who is to receive benefits. Social Security is not a program of assured annuities. It is a program of protection for those among the aged who are not employed. Since this is a "social" security system it is appropriate to skew the system to achieve certain social objectives. The test of whether an individual is working is a substitute for a means test. It identifies those who are most likely to be in need. A true means test would also have to include a test of resources, and this is avoided because studies of the income and resources of the aged show that those who are not working are the least likely to have sufficient resources to support themselves. While there are older people who have significant resources but are not employed, to ferret them out would require a full means test for everyone.

The law has established that the amount of money an individual has earned shall be the test of retirement. Currently (1974), the test figure is $2,400 a year, and this represents liberalization. In the past criticism of the retirement test has been blunted by raising the amount of earnings the individual may have and still be considered out of the work force. The amount of additional earnings that reduce benefits has also been liberalized. Now each $2 of earnings above the $2,400 reduces benefits by only $1. This has not stilled the attack on this particular provision. Some people want the test removed entirely. That is possible but could be accomplished only by a general reduction in benefits or an increase in taxes or some combination of the two. The people who would benefit by the abolishing of the test are those who are least in need.

In the criticism of the retirement test some unfair comparisons are made. It has been stated that the test figure is below the poverty level. It is true that $2,400 is below the poverty level, but an individual who is earning $2,400 can receive a full Social Security benefit, and currently it cannot be less than about $100 a month. The retirement test, when applied to an individual who has $250 a month in earnings, means that this person can receive the full benefit minus only $300 a year. Many critics of this provision are people who want to retire from their regular employment and supplement their Social Security by part-time employment. If earnings from such employment run over the retirement test level, they are not eligible for benefits. Thus the group most affected are highly skilled workers, with a relatively high standard of living, whose needs and expectations are legitimate but whose claim on a "social" security system cannot be equal to the claims of the lower income group.

Inequities in the Social Security Tax

It is generally recognized that the Social Security tax is inequitable. It is a tax on "the first dollar" of earnings. It taxes earnings no matter how small. It does not take into account family size or how many wage earners there are in the household. It differs from the income tax, which does take into account these items plus excessive medical expenses and other factors. Since the Social Security payroll tax is less equitable, why is it used? Taxes have to be imposed in an acceptable way. The payroll tax was acceptable in 1935 because Social Security was conceived as a worker-employer investment in the worker's retirement. At that time the trust fund concept was conceived as the mechanism for payment of benefits. The trust fund was shifted to a contingency fund some years after the program started. This method of taxing is also easier to administer.

A more basic consideration is the feeling that the program is more secure if taxes collected are used for benefits. Although it is true that Social Security "contributions" are really taxes and go into the general treasury and are appropriated to pay benefits, nevertheless the relationship between the amount of taxes and the amount of the benefits is maintained. For a shift to a more equitable tax system one would have to assume the risk that Congress might not consider the Social Security obligation inviolate and might fail to appropriate enough to pay full benefits. This concern has permeated Social Security planning. This provision distinguishes Social Security from welfare in the public eye. Workers have been willing to accept the Social Security payroll tax because they feel it promises future security.

An unwillingness to risk loss of public support keeps the inequitable Social Security tax in place. There are many proposals to correct this. One . . . would provide for an adjustment in the 1040 tax form for low-income workers. They would receive a refund for Social Security taxes. Another . . . bill would reduce the payroll tax from 5.8 percent to 3.9 percent and have a general revenue contribution make up the loss. This would make the tax less inequitable but would not eliminate the problem. The . . . report of the Social Security Advisory Council may have some impact for it will focus on the entire problem of financing.

Other Inequities

Critics have identified other inequities. Some of these are not reasonable and tend to overlook the fact that Social Security is an insurance program. Instances are cited of individuals who made contributions and received no benefits. Illustrations include the situation of someone who works for a year and pays taxes and then dies with no resultant beneficiary rights for his wife and dependents. This occurs because the worker has a marginal relationship to the work force and the law requires six quarters of coverage before survivor benefits will be paid. Another illustration is the individual who works a whole lifetime and dies before retirement without dependents. This contribution is "lost" inasmuch as the worker cannot include any of the Social Security rights in a will. The amounts contributed are used in the system to help finance benefits for others. Illustrations are given of individuals who contribute little but receive a great deal. The best examples are the older persons who made small contributions because much of their work experience was during the period when the tax rate was low. A retiree who started work in 1937 and worked at full taxable wages would have paid in a maximum of $5,200. This is contrasted with someone who is now working at a wage equal to the (1975) taxable wage base ($13,200) and continues in that status for thirty years who will have paid in about $21,660 and will receive benefits less generous as related to what was contributed than the already retired worker.

There is no doubt that these are valid examples of inequities in contribution versus benefits. The justification for the "grandparenting in" of the older worker is that the alternative was to have a large welfare program. The available mechanism was the state-operated Old Age Assistance program, which was not able to carry the responsibility. It can be argued that those already old should not be penalized for the failure of the nation to have anticipated their needs by broadening the Social Security program while they were working and could have contributed to its cost.

Criticism has also focused on some of the provisions that tend to exclude or delay potential benefits. Among these obstacles is the requirement that a disabled applicant must wait five months before receiving benefits. Congress determined that the program was for the permanently and totally disabled. The waiting period is one of the ways of establishing that fact. This is a serious problem for disabled persons. It can be eased but at a cost.

Married vs. Unmarried Beneficiaries

A long-standing source of complaint is the different status of married and unmarried beneficiaries. This seems to discriminate against working wives. The problem arises because of a provision that offers especially generous treatment for the wives of retired workers. The wife of a retired worker is recognized in the benefit payment for that worker by a 50 percent addendum. If a woman is unmarried and has worked or if she is married and has worked, she may receive no more in benefits than a nonworking wife, although she has contributed to the system. Under the law the wife with a separate Social Security account has her benefits compared under both provisions of the law (addendum to husband's benefits and independent beneficiary), and she receives the amount of the larger benefit. The married woman who did not work is in a favorable position for the receipt of retirement benefits. However, the employed woman received protection against disability in her working years while her counterpart who stayed home did not. The employed woman who was also assured of benefits for her children in the event of her death, which the unemployed woman was not. Critics have made proposals to combine in some fashion the benefits accruing to the woman who worked with the benefits she is entitled to as a spouse. This proposal has some validity but would involve additional cost.

While the law makes an assumption of wifely dependence upon the husband, it does not make a similar assumption about the dependence of the husband on the wife. For a wife's benefits to be increased 50 percent for a dependent husband proof must be submitted. No proof is necessary for the husband's benefits to be increased for his wife. A similar situation prevails in the event of the death of a spouse. The Equal Rights Amendment (now, in 1979, only three states short of approval) would undoubtedly have an effect on this situation. The many intricate provisions of the Social Security Act would be subject to examination against the criteria of equal treatment of men and women, and some changes would be required.

Level of Benefits

A persistent criticism is that for many people, especially those in the lower wage level, the Social Security system cannot promise enough retirement income for a decent level of living. Benefits are related to level of earnings. The minimum primary insurance amount is now $94 a month. A recently enacted provision assures a somewhat larger amount for low-paid workers who have a record of many years of covered employment. That special minimum can be as high as $170 a month. The average benefits paid are reflective of the many people who retired years ago and whose benefit calculation was based on low earnings characteristic of the times. The many increases that Congress has voted have been motivated by a desire to help these people. Although the benefit level is constantly rising, prices also continue to rise, and the situation of many beneficiaries remains critical.

A factor that aggravates this situation is the increasing proportion of applicants who retire at an earlier age with reduced benefits. Currently more than half of the applications for benefits are made by persons who are below the specified retirement age of 65 (62 for widows). Men and women workers may apply at age 62 and widows at 60 with benefits reduced 20 percent. Studies show that it is the workers with the poorest work records, lowest earnings, and poorest health who apply for early retirement. Even if they had postponed retirement to avoid the 20 percent reduction they would still have had a low benefit because their wage records were below average. "Retirement" is perhaps the wrong term to use in describing such individuals. They are generally out of work and without resources. For them Social Security is a form of unemployment relief. The employment market has increasingly discriminated against older workers, especially those with marginal skills.

No provision is made for this situation. Early retirement at reduced benefits costs the system nothing, for the reduction of 20 percent is actuarily calculated to assess the cost to the beneficiary. Should retirement without benefit reduction be offered to all at an earlier age? Strong arguments can be made to support that point of view. but if this is done there remains the question of the effect on the composition of the work force and the further erosion of the ratio of retired workers to employed workers. One possibility is to consider early retirees a part of the unemployed group and offer some coverage under unemployment insurance, relieving the Social Security system of a responsibility it is not equipped to handle.

General Considerations

Some of the possibilities for changing and improving the Social Security system have been identified, and there are many others. Few improvements can be made without costing money. Since there is no general tax revenue in the Social Security program, any additional cost would have to be assessed to employed persons. It is difficult to determine which of the proposed changes is the most urgent and which should be enacted with a tax increase. Many of those impatient with the slowness of change have urged the introduction of general revenue money in Social Security. The arguments against this have been presented. The pressures are so great that some breach in the position held for the past thirty-nine years is likely.

WOMEN AND SOCIAL SECURITY

With approximately 50 percent of all women in the United States in the labor force,[a] with divorce rates climbing,[b] and with increasing numbers of unmarried women the heads of households,[c] OASDHI (Social Security) is an increasingly important program for women. Yet there are a number of reasons why it is presently less effective for women than for men. As noted earlier, workers must be employed a certain number of quarter-years in jobs covered by Social Security in order to qualify for benefits. However, women's work careers tend to be much more sporadic than those of men because of their responsibilities as wives and mothers.[d] In addition, they are more

[a] *Washington Social Legislation Bulletin,* 34, May 22, 1978, p. 1.

[b] Ronald Federico, *Sociology*, 2d ed. (Reading, Massachusetts: Addison-Wesley, 1979), p. 371.

[c] National Association of Social Workers, *The Encyclopedia of Social Work* (Washington, D.C.: NASW, 1977), p. 358.

[d] Linda S. Rosenman, "Unemployment of Women: A Social Policy Issue," *Social Work* 24 (January 1979): 20–24.

likely to work in jobs still not covered by Social Security, such as domestic work or babysitting jobs. Therefore, they may not work enough quarters in covered employment to qualify for OASDHI benefits.

Even where they are covered, they are likely to receive lower benefits, because women generally hold lower-paying jobs than men (see Exhibit 5-10). This problem is worsened by the problem working wives face in having their benefits calculated in conjunction with those of their husbands (discussed earlier in this Exhibit). These inequities make OASDHI relatively ineffective in combating the institutional factors that create higher poverty rates for women than for men.[e] Whatever solutions are to be found for the issues currently facing OASDHI, they must reflect the fact that the role of women in society has changed substantially from that which existed when the Social Security Act was conceived and enacted.

[e] NASW, op. cit., p. 1033.

It should be emphasized once again, however, that the intent of the Social Security Act was to supplement people's incomes and savings when they reached retirement age, rather than to provide enough for them to survive solely on the benefits.

Social Security, being an insurance program, requires that working persons who are covered in the program contribute part of their salary to the Social Security trust fund. Employers also contribute to this fund for each employee. The fund is then used to pay benefits when an individual qualifies. Note that Social Security is work-related (only persons working can contribute, and they have to have worked for a specified period of time in an approved work context before they or their dependents qualify to receive benefits). Exhibit 2-2 provides data on Social Security contribution rates, benefit levels, and beneficiaries.

The second social insurance established by the Social Security Act of 1935, unemployment insurance, was intended to be a temporary income maintenance program during periods of temporary, involuntary unemployment. Each state has its own unemployment insurance program, established with federal guidelines, and has established its own methods of computation of benefits, maximum benefit amounts, and maximum benefit duration. The program is supported by a payroll tax paid by employers on a specified amount of earnings per employee. It is administered by the federal government, which collects part of the tax (through the Internal Revenue Service) for administrative expenses and to support the U.S. Employment Service. The remainder of the funds are held in trust for each state to use in paying benefits. Benefits are based on earnings or employment experience during a recent, specified base period, which varies by state. Recipients must register at the state employment office, seek work, and be available for work. Since each state has its own program, there is variability between states, and not all persons are covered, especially many low-income, unskilled, marginal participants in the work force whose work history is often too unstable to qualify them for coverage. Nevertheless, the program has been subject to minimal criticism, and has proved somewhat flexible in adapting to fluctuating economic conditions, with states being especially hard hit by depressed economic circumstances able to extend the duration of benefits and the level of benefit payments.

By far the most controversial programs in the Social Security Act were those providing the nucleus of the present public assistance programs. These were direct grant programs for the blind, dependent children, and aged persons not covered by Social Security. These programs were controversial because recipients received direct cash grants from tax revenues rather than the money they had previously paid into a fund, as was the case with the social insurances. Because the public assistance programs were so controversial, they were restricted to helpless groups with obvious need: the destitute aged or blind, and needy dependent children. A program of grants to the partially and totally disabled was added later. These grant programs involved complex federal-state cooperative arrangements in an attempt to support a governmental system that sought to leave as much power as possible at the local level, where it is assumed that the needs of the people can be more easily expressed and assessed. The federal government established certain broad guidelines governing these grant programs, which all states had to meet. For example, any program had to be offered uniformly to all citizens throughout a state. In general these federal guidelines sought to assure that there would be some level of uniformity and equity within and between programs, but specific characteristics of the programs, including major eligibility requirements and benefit levels, were left to the discretion of each state. We have already seen that this results in inequitable benefits among states.

Funds supporting these grant programs came from a combination of federal, state, and local general revenues. In 1968 an average of 66.1 percent of the total cost (payments and administrative costs) was federal money, 28.8 percent was from the state, and 5.1 percent was local money. The amount of federal funds is determined according to the characteristics of the state's program, the state's ability to meet the costs, and the general economic condition of the state. Withholding federal funds is one of the major ways in which the federal government can attempt to convince a state to comply with federal guidelines, but this power is limited by the ability of states to threaten to eliminate altogether one or more of the programs.

It has already been noted that the Social Security Act emphasized social insurances as a more acceptable way of providing for peoples' needs, since they are compatible with values of self-reliance and thrift. The grant programs were always minimal in scope and benefit levels, and concentrated on groups that were obviously helpless. The minimal nature of these programs also reflected the original belief that they would be temporary, and that persons receiving benefits from them would gradually be covered by OASDHI instead. To emphasize clearly the difference between the desirability of insurances and grants, the latter always had a "means test," requiring recipients to prove that they had no other resources or source of support. Recipients of social insurances did not have to do this. The only requirement was that they fell into the appropriate category; for example, that they be over 65 and retired, in order to collect Social Security. The difference was obviously one of entitlement and stigma, since the means test made it clear that recipients were receiving a handout because of their inability to provide for themselves, whereas recipients of an insurance benefit had simply claimed their rightful benefit.

In January 1974, the programs for the blind, disabled, and aged were transferred to a completely federally funded and administered program called Supplemental Security Income (SSI), leaving the Aid to Families with Dependent Children (AFDC) as the only major federal-state grant program for public assistance recipients. This action illustrates once again societal values at work, reflecting society's continued struggle with the work ethic and a belief in personal responsibility. Although AFDC dealt with a helpless group—dependent children—it also had to contend with the adults caring for the children. This created a host of potentially difficult value issues—mothers having children out of wedlock, fathers who abandoned their legitimate or illegitimate children, mothers staying home to care for the children rather than working, and so on. Society has tried to deal with these issues by imposing a variety of restrictions on AFDC recipients at one time or another. The program still remains a federal-state one with variable eligibility requirements and benefit levels, indicating that the value issues are still troublesome. Transferring the grant programs for the aged, blind, and disabled to a federal program with less restrictive eligibility requirements and higher benefit levels suggests that some criterion of worthiness continues to operate in our social welfare system. The aged, blind, and disabled can be clearly defined as helpless and are therefore helped with a minimum degree of stigma. Dependent children and their guardians, however, mix helplessness with an assortment of other less acceptable values and behaviors, and society's assistance to them comes grudgingly and minimally. Only when a guaranteed income is provided for all will the issue have been resolved once and for all. Exhibits 2-3 (pp. 81–82) and 2-4 (pp. 83–86) may help to illustrate the differences between SSI and AFDC.

AFDC and Supplemental Security Income Compared EXHIBIT 2-3

Some of the differences between AFDC and the Supplemental Security Income program are illustrated in the following data, which look at eligibility requirements and benefit levels, as well as administrative procedures. The stigma against AFDC recipients turns out to be a costly one for them, and illustrates the importance of values in the determination of social welfare programs, a fact as true today as it has been throughout the development of social welfare concepts and programs.

	AFDC	*SSI*
Eligibility Requirements		
Age	Under 21 years. If 16 or 17, must be regularly enrolled in and attending school; if 18 or over and under 21, must be regularly and successfully attending high school, college or university, or a course of vocational or technical training.	None, except for the aged category (age 65+)
Residence	Child is making his home in the state.	U.S.A.
Need	Deprived of parental support or care by reason of death, continued absence from home, or physical or mental incapacity of one or both parents, and living with relatives listed in federal act as interpreted, or in foster care as permitted under the federal act.	65 or older Blind Disabled
Financial/ Property Eligibility	Ownership of real property used as a home does not of itself disqualify. However, in determining need and amount of payment, resources (shelter, rent, etc.) from such property are taken into account. Real property not used as a home and all personal property (savings, cash value of insurance, bonds, and any other cash reserves) are limited to $1,100 for adult and one child, plus $50 for needy spouse and for each eligible child up to $2,000 maximum. When application or budget does not include needy adult, limitation on reserve for one child is $1,000; for two children, $1,100; with $50 for each additional child in family unit up to $2,000 maximum. (Administrative) May have equity in essential motor vehicle not to exceed $1,000; excess equity plus equity in the loan value of non-essential motor vehicles and non-essential personal property such as cameras, television sets, etc. are treated as reserve. Transfers of property must be made at fair market value; the proceeds are treated as a reserve.	Assets of $1,500 for single person. $2,250 for couple excluding house with market value under $25,000. Household goods, personal effects, insurances, car. Nonwage income over $20 a month reduces benefits. Wage income over $65 a month reduces benefit $1 for each $2 earned. Living in someone else's home usually reduces benefits.

	AFDC	*SSI*
Administration		
State	State Board of Social Services[a] (policy-making), for aged and disabled.—Seven members appointed by Governor for 6 years, overlapping terms, one to be a woman. Commissioner appointed by Board, with Governor's approval and serves at pleasure of Board. State-supervised program.	None. Administered by the Social Security Administration (federal), and checks sent directly to recipient. Apply at Social Security offices.
Local	County Department of Social Services (100). County Board of Social Services—usually 3 members, 1 appointed by Board of Commissioners, 1 by State Board, and 1 by the other two for 3-year overlapping terms; in 51 counties, 5-member boards. County Director appointed by County Board of Social Services.	None (see above)
Financing	Assistance costs: State and local funds. Source of state funds: general fund. Of nonfederal share, state not less than 50 percent, local not more than 50 percent. Administrative costs: Nonfederal share, state and local funds. State's participation varies according to county's financial ability (on an equalizing basis) from a small percent to 50 percent of the balance after having deducted federal participation.	General funds of the U.S. Treasury (Social Security funds are not used to pay SSI).

Average Benefit Payments
(per month)

	Family	*Recipient*	*One Person*	*Married Couple*
North Carolina	$130.24	$41.55	Uniform throughout U.S.A.:[b]	
Mississippi	51.08	14.37		
New York	294.38	85.37		
California	215.27	67.01	$177.80	$266.70
Montana	145.63	48.59		
Indiana	136.27	42.09		
Arizona	125.43	35.31		

Sources: The data on Supplemental Security Income is taken from U.S. Department of Health, Education, and Welfare pamphlet No. SSA 74-11000 (January 1974), and the data on AFDC in North Carolina is taken from pages 76 and 77 of *Characteristics of State Public Assistance Plans—January 31, 1973* (Washington: U.S. Government Printing Office, 1973). North Carolina data are illustrative, since each state's plan is somewhat different. Data on comparative payments by state are taken from *Public Assistance Statistics—April 1974* (Department of Health, Education, and Welfare Publication No. SRS 75-03100), Table 4 (unpaginated).

[a] Operated within Department of Human Resources.

[b] May be higher if state supplements federal SSI payments, or lower if recipient has other income as noted above. These figures are for 1978.

Welfare Myths EXHIBIT 2-4

A good indication of the value conflicts involved in AFDC can be seen by the fact that the federal government feels it necessary to distribute brochures about welfare "myths" in an attempt to minimize resistance to the AFDC program. One such leaflet is reproduced below, and each of its myths embodies a societal value which is threatened by the AFDC grant program. Can you translate the myths into their underlying values? How many of these myths did you hold? Do the facts convince you? Why or why not?

Myth. Welfare people are cheats.

Fact. Statistics reported by states indicate that four-tenths of one percent of welfare cases are referred for prosecution for fraud. The number of cases where fraud is established is even smaller. However, the states do not have a comprehensive means of detecting fraud, and some fraud undoubtedly is undetected. Nevertheless, the direct evidence available indicates that the amount of deliberate misrepresentation by welfare recipients is small. Errors due to other factors are a larger problem in the present welfare system.

Early results of a new reporting system on eligibility and payments show that about 5 percent of the nation's welfare recipients were ineligible for benefits received. Most of the errors were identified as honest mistakes by state and local welfare agencies or by recipients, operating under complex rules that vary with each jurisdiction. More than half the errors were by agencies. State and local agencies seek to minimize errors but are handicapped by lack of staff in the face of rising welfare caseloads and costs.

The first report covers about half the national caseload and thus is preliminary. It shows about 5.6 percent of welfare families as ineligible. It also reveals that 14.6 percent of welfare families received overpayments and 9.7 percent received underpayments. . . .

Under welfare reform, new rules regarding both eligibility and payments would be applied uniformly across the country. Use of modern, high-speed computers would provide an advanced system for preventing most incorrect payments and would use Social Security numbers to cross-check for duplicate applications and unreported income.

Myth. Give them more money and they'll spend it on drink and big cars.

Fact. Most welfare families report that if they received any extra money it would go for essentials. A survey of welfare mothers showed that almost half would spend it primarily for food. Another 28 percent said they would spend any additional money on clothing and shoes. The survey found that 42 percent of mothers bought used clothing or relied on donated clothing to make ends meet. Seventeen percent of the mothers said their children occasionally stayed home from school because they lacked decent clothes and shoes.

Nearly 10 percent of the mothers in the survey said they would spend extra money on rent for better housing, and 13 percent said they would spend it on a combination of food, clothes, and rent.

Myth. Most welfare children are illegitimate.

Fact. A sizable majority—68.6 percent—of the more than 7 million children in welfare families are legitimate, according to data compiled by the Social and Rehabilitation Service.

To help welfare families avoid unwanted pregnancies, the government in recent years has made family planning services available to those who wish it.

Myth. Once on welfare, always on welfare.

Fact. Half the families on welfare have been receiving assistance for 20 months or less.

Source: "Welfare Myths vs. Facts" (Department of Health, Education and Welfare pamphlet SRS-72-02009, undated and unpaginated).

Length of Time on Welfare

Less than six months	17.4%
Six months to one year	17.8%
One to two years	20.8%
Two to three years	12.2%
Three to five years	13.7%
Five to ten years	11.6%
Ten years or more	6.1%

Two-thirds of families have been on the rolls less than three years. About one in five families (17.7 percent) have been on welfare for five years or more, and about one in sixteen families (6.1 percent) have been on the rolls ten years or more.

Current figures show that about 65 percent of cases are on welfare for the first time; about one-third of cases have been on the rolls before.

Proposed welfare reforms are designed to strengthen work incentives, eliminate barriers to employment, and thus help present recipients rejoin the work force as soon as possible.

Children per Welfare Family

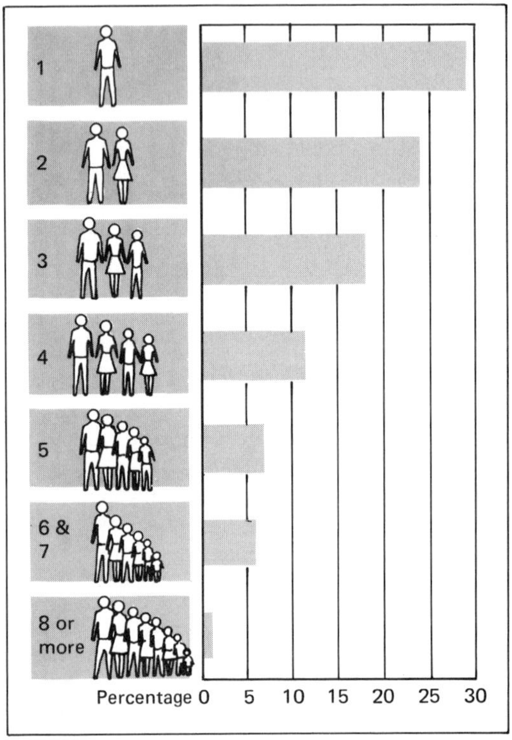

Myth. Welfare families are loaded with kids—and have more just to get more money.

Fact. The latest statistics for welfare families indicate that over half—54.2 percent—are comprised of one- and two-child families. This is a slight decline in two years: according to statistics gathered in 1969, only 49.6 percent of welfare families had one or two children and slightly more than half the welfare families had three or more children.

The typical payment for an additional child is $35 a month, hardly enough to cover the cost of rearing an additional child. A few states impose payment limits; families reaching that ceiling—usually a five- to six-person family—get no additional money for another child.

Myth. Welfare's just a dole, a money handout.

Fact. Money is necessary to a family lacking subsistence, but it usually takes more than just cash to help the typical welfare family get on its feet and back into the mainstream of society.

The Social and Rehabilitation Service asked welfare agencies what social services they had given to welfare families besides money. Here's what the agencies recently reported and the percentage of families receiving each kind of service (most families received at least one service):

- Health care advice and referrals (including Medicaid): 38.9 percent
- Counseling on financial and home management: 37.1 percent
- Employment counseling: 40.8 percent
- Services to secure child support: 28.4 percent
- Services to improve housing conditions: 27.2 percent
- Services to enable children to continue school: 17.5 percent

Other services which many agencies provide include those related to child welfare, vocational rehabilitation, and youth development. This range of social services has been found essential in helping disadvantaged people move toward independence and constructive living.

Welfare reform, among other things, would separate the administration of cash payments from the delivery of social services. The goal is improved social and rehabilitation services, more accessible services, and more coordinated services to those in need.

Myth. Most welfare families are black.

Fact. The largest racial group among welfare families—48.3 percent—is white.

Blacks represent 43.3 percent. Most of the remaining 8.4 percent are American Indians, Orientals, and other racial minorities.

Statistics show blacks comprise about 11 percent of the U.S. population, but 34 percent of the black population have incomes below the established poverty level, compared to 13 percent of the white population with incomes below the poverty level.

Myth. Why work when you can live it up on welfare?

Fact. The largest payment for basic needs that can be made to a welfare family of four (the typical family aided on AFDC) with no other income varies among states, from a low of $60 per month in Mississippi to a high of $372 per month in Alaska.

In July 1971, in all but four states, welfare payments, excluding payments for special needs, were below the established poverty level of $331 per month, or $3,972 per year, for a family of four. Unfortunately, some of the nation's working poor—ineligible for assistance under the present welfare system—earn less than the poverty level, too.

Each state establishes its own "need standard"—the amount required for the necessities of family living. A state standard may be below or above the poverty line. A state will use its "need standard" as a base for determining eligibility. However, 39 states pay less—some much less—than their own established standard of need. The federal government shares the cost of payments made by the states.

Welfare reform proposals—establishing a federal income floor nationally for welfare families—would provide an even base for payments. The working poor would get a cash assist as well, insuring that a family head would always be better off by working. Under welfare reform, family heads who are able to work would be required to make themselves available for jobs or job training. Penalties are provided if they fail to accept suitable jobs or training.

Federally Assisted Welfare Population
(as of October 1971)

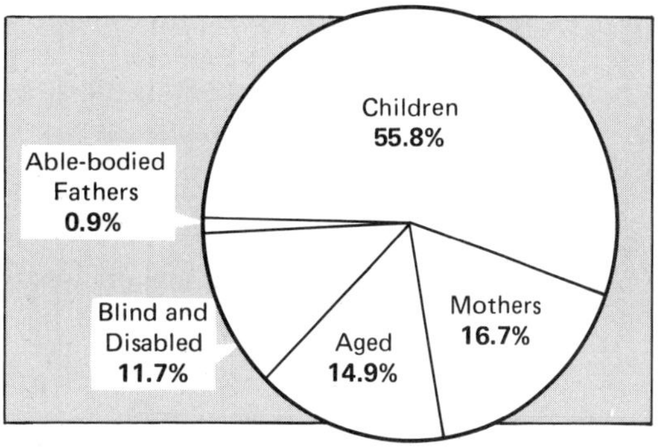

Myth. The welfare rolls are full of ablebodied loafers.

Fact. Less than 1 percent of welfare recipients are ablebodied unemployed males: some 126,000 of the more than 13.6 million Americans on federal/state-supported welfare (October 1971 statistics). All these individuals are required by law to sign up for work or work training in order to continue to be eligible for benefits. Prior to enactment of the new work-training law, government studies in three cities (Los Angeles, Milwaukee, and Camden) indicated that 80 percent of the ablebodied unemployed males on welfare did want to work. Nationally, among the fathers in this group, one in three was already enrolled in work training.

The largest group of working-age adults on welfare are 2.5 million mothers of welfare families, most of whom head families with no ablebodied male present. About 15 percent of these mothers work, and 7 percent are in work training. Many of the other mothers confront serious barriers to employment under the existing welfare system, such as lack of child care facilities, transportation, etc. With additional day care service and job training available, it is estimated that another 34 percent would be potential employees. About 4 percent of welfare mothers require extensive social and rehabilitative services to prepare them for employment.

The remaining 40 percent have little or no employment potential because they care for small children at home, have major physical or mental incapacities, or other insurmountable work barriers.

Factors in the Employability of Welfare Mothers
(From a 1969 study)

Needed at home to care for small children, have a long-term disability, etc.	40%
Employable if job training, jobs, and day care were made available	34%
Already employed full- or part-time	15%
In work-training programs or waiting to be accepted	7%
Need extensive medical or rehabilitative services before becoming employable	4%

Although the programs established by the Social Security Act in 1935 have been gradually expanded in scope and benefit levels, the basic structure of the Social Security Act has not been changed. As the number of recipients and program components have grown, so has the unwieldiness of the structure. This has been especially true of the one remaining public assistance program where federal-state sharing is involved—AFDC. The current administrative costs of public assistance are very high, as are the costs of the benefits themselves. Yet it is obvious that in spite of high costs, need is being inadequately met both financially and socially. The Social Security Act established the social acceptability of a national attack on need, but contemporary needs are probably too different from those in 1935 to be served adequately by legislation formulated and enacted forty years ago.

There are several areas in which the Social Security Act is presently inadequate:

1. It was limited in scope, reflecting the political and social realities of 1935. By its very passage, it paved the way for a more comprehensive view of needed social welfare legislation. New legislation will no doubt continue some parts of the 1935 act (such as Social Security and unemployment insurance), but it will probably change the whole basis for handling other social welfare needs (health care, financial assistance, social services, and so on). The Supplemental Security Income program is a step in this direction.
2. Contemporary society is vastly different from what it was in 1935. Rural-to-urban migration, civil rights progress, automation, and changes in educational opportunity have each had a significant impact on the nature of social life and the definition of social problems. New legislation must take account of these changes.
3. Funding and political realities have changed. The crisis in local and state fiscal affairs has shifted the burden of funding needs to the federal government. Patterns of cooperation and funding established

in 1935 will have to be reexamined and altered. Revenue sharing is an attempt to deal with this issue.

4. National priorities have changed. Minority groups are more vocal and more powerful. Domestic and foreign priorities are being reexamined. Affluence and its effects are being reevaluated. All of these priority adjustments must be reflected in national social welfare policy.

In summary, the Social Security Act of 1935 marked the recognition of governmental responsibility for needs in a new and creative manner. The act continues to support the basic framework of the social welfare system in the United States, but will probably continue to be supplemented or replaced by more contemporary legislation.

The period directly following the passage of the Social Security Act of 1935 focused mostly on World War II and its effects. As Russell Smith and Dorothy Zeitz put it in their book, *American Social Welfare Institutions* (1970), "The road to social change from F. D. Roosevelt's third inauguration in 1940 until the election of President John F. Kennedy in 1960 was circuitous at best and impassable at times."[53] The volunteer and public agencies were concerned with providing for the needs of men and women in the military, and their dependents, leaving postwar plans for the economy somewhat undirected. The Servicemen Readjustment Act of 1944 (better known as the G.I. Bill), which provided for medical benefits and a maintenance allowance for education, was the major social welfare legislation of the forties. During this period government support of social welfare was continued with few major changes. Foreign-policy concerns and ideological questions continued to be dominant in the fifties. As Smith and Zeitz point out, "Many social insurance measures and programs involving social spending were defeated in a rising tide of reaction against social legislation and a virulent anticommunist hysteria that convulsed the nation at midcentury."[54] Although revisions in the Social Security programs were made during both the Truman and Eisenhower administrations, radical innovations were rejected.

In 1953 Congress reorganized the welfare structure with the hope of gaining administrative efficiency and more coordinated planning. Modifications of the Social Security Act in 1954 and 1956 brought into the system many members of the labor force left out of the original act. Unemployment insurance coverage was broadened, and the amount of assistance and the duration of coverage were increased. The Social Security amendments of 1962 made significant funds available for the training of public assistance workers, and social services were added to financial aid in public assistance programs. The concept of public welfare as a rehabilitative program was stressed, maintaining the view of welfare as temporary until people could once again independently participate in a competitive society.

The Development of the Contemporary Social Welfare Scene

A new dimension of welfare began to come into focus in the fifties. In 1954, the Supreme Court found school segregation unconstitutional on grounds that "separate but equal" is inherently unequal, and ordered desegregation of the public school system "with all deliberate speed." President Eisenhower ordered federal troops to Arkansas to enforce integration of Little Rock Central High School in defiance of Governor Orval Faubus in 1957. The same year, Eisenhower signed the Civil Rights Act authorizing the Justice Department to bring to federal courts cases involving discrimination in voting. The Civil Rights Act of 1960 made legal action against state and local officials possible. These events ushered in a significant new period of social welfare growth. The Supreme Court's action established its role as a powerful force for social change and social justice. It has the power to mandate the enforcement of civil rights legislation and strike down legislation and interpretations of legislation that violate human rights. The use of this power has made it possible for progressive legislators and law-enforcement officials to act to preserve social justice when it has been threatened by persons motivated by bigotry, ignorance, or greed.

As the Supreme Court's actions changed the climate for social justice, courageous members of groups traditionally discriminated against were encouraged to accelerate their on-going quest for justice and equality. The blacks were the first to make major assaults against institutional inequality. Under the leadership of people like Martin Luther King and his associates, the 1950s and 1960s witnessed a series of nonviolent confrontations to demonstrate the existence of inequality and the need for social change. Blacks, often joined by white college students, carried out planned sit-ins at places of business that practiced discrimination. They organized peaceful protest marches to Washington, D.C., state capitols, and local power centers. They also carried out voter registration drives to help persons denied their legal voting rights through fraud and intimidation to exercise this right. These nonviolent attempts to enforce existing laws and to seek the passage of needed nondiscriminatory legislation were frequently met with harassment, intimidation, and physical violence (including murder) from law-enforcement officials and others. In spite of this, these courageous groups succeeded in gaining new legislation and widespread public support for their goals. By their successes, blacks stimulated similar attempts by other repressed groups, especially Chicanos, native Americans, and women.

Early in the 1960s, President Kennedy gave social problems the perspective of his New Frontier policies, and put problem-solving authority in the hands of concerned intellectuals. Social Security revisions were liberal; the Redevelopment Act was passed in 1961; and in 1962 the Manpower Development and Training Act was enacted. Food stamps were initiated as a new method of helping to meet the nutritional needs of welfare recipients. Kennedy's assassination burdened the American conscience, and enabled President Johnson to pass numerous pieces of social legislation. "The Great Society was envisioned as a perfectible society in which social justice [could] be created by the development of institutions to meet the needs of the citizens."[55] Under the Johnson administration the following legislation was passed: in 1963, the Mental Retardation and Community Mental Health Centers Construction Act; in 1964, the Economic Opportunity Act (the plan to mobilize the War on Poverty), and a civil rights act; in 1965, Medicare, Appalachia Regional Development Act, Department of Housing and Urban Development legislation, and another civil rights act; in 1966, a housing act; and in 1967, legislation further revising the Social Security Act.

The Economic Opportunity Act, which established the Office of Economic Opportunity (OEO) with its Vista, Job Corps, and Head Start programs, to name a few of the better-known ones, was one of the most significant acts of the times. For the first time, the "participation of the poor" in the power structure of the war on poverty was attempted in the form of community-action agencies. This new direction for welfare threatened local political structures and entrenched welfare organizations whose structures were poorly adapted to include client participation. The American dilemma of private versus common good arose again under the guise of federal and state funding conflicts, and in the shocking exploitation of OEO contracts by private contractors. Many communities had little experience in organizing to obtain grants, and they often deteriorated into many squabbling groups competing for resources to end their own deprivation. The lack of success of many programs reflected inadequate funding, inadequate planning, inadequate knowledge of needs, and inadequate client participation in planning.

The Office of Economic Opportunity was abolished in 1974 and replaced by the Community Services Program (CSA). Six basic programs are operated by CSA:[56]

1. *Community Action.* This program focuses on organizing and coordinating basic services at the local community level for the poor such as information and referral services, job training, child care, and nutrition training.
2. *Economic Development.* Efforts to help the rural and urban poor achieve community and business development are the focus of this program. It has funded small business enterprises, shopping centers, industrial parks, and housing projects, which are then used to house and employ poor people.
3. *Energy and Weatherization.* Precipitated by the energy crisis in 1973, this program helps the poor insulate and winterize their homes as well as to pay for high utility bills.

4. *Senior Opportunities and Services.* The aged poor are helped through this program working in conjunction with other services.
5. *Community Food and Nutrition.* This program seeks to reduce malnutrition by supplementing the food programs of other agencies and helping the poor to grow and preserve their own food.
6. *Division of State and Local Government.* This program works with state and local governments to improve the economic and other resources available to the poor by providing technical assistance to the community action agencies, to advocate for the poor, and to serve as a liaison with other agencies.

In addition to these changes, four programs were moved to other agencies: VISTA was moved to ACTION. Head Start was moved to The Administration for Children, Youth, and Families in the Department of Health, Education, and Welfare (HEW). The Follow-Through Program, which seeks to sustain the gains children make in Head Start, was moved to the Office of Education in HEW. Finally, the Native American Program, which seeks to facilitate efforts of tribes and Native American councils to coordinate and administer programs to assist the Native American groups (American Indians, Alaskan Natives, and Native Hawaiians) was also moved to HEW.

The Economic Opportunity Act underlined the need for more adequately conceptualized and implemented legislative solutions to the nation's welfare needs, the entrenched complexity of most social problems, and the obstacles created by the welfare bureaucracy itself. In spite of these problems, the Economic Opportunity Act succeeded in creating a new focus on community organization and planning, and a lasting involvement of users of social welfare services in decision-making about these services. It also proved the enduring value of some of the programs established on an experimental basis, such as Head Start. Exhibit 2-5 looks at some of the problems, failures, and accomplishments of the Economic Opportunity Act and the War on Poverty in more detail.

EXHIBIT 2-5 *The Legacy of the Economic Opportunity Act*

The War on Poverty, and the Economic Opportunity Act, which formed its foundation, was a massive and complex attempt to deal more adequately with poverty and a variety of other social needs. From its inception, the War on Poverty was mired in political and bureaucratic structures and problems that ultimately led to the dismantling of the Office of Economic Opportunity, created by the Economic Opportunity Act. Even so, the legacy of the War on Poverty is substantial. This excerpt provides a good summary of the importance of politics in the public decision-making arena, as well as the many and often conflicting influences on public social welfare programs.

Source: Excerpted from Mark R. Arnold, "The Good War that Might Have Been," *The New York Times Magazine*, September 29, 1974. Copyright © 1974 by The New York Times Company. Reprinted by permission.

It is clear now in 1974 that the original antipoverty strategy was based on a number of misapprehensions or beliefs that weakened its impact. One was that a class of Americans—the poor—could be singled out for special treatment without arousing deep resentment among others. . . .

This was, in fact, done with surprising success in many areas. But it was a mistake to have supposed that the system could be used to change the system—without arousing the system.

Yet, despite its difficulties, the antipoverty program introduced new techniques for coping with neglected problems, such as neighborhood-oriented health and legal services, preschool education, cooperative business enterprises, paraprofessional jobs and training programs that screen the hardest cases in, not out. It created, through establishment of local community-action agencies, new self-help institutions in the slums, enabling the poor to exert leverage on governments at all levels. It provided food, transportation, job training, health care, legal representation, homemaker skills, compensatory education and other basic human services to millions of needy Americans. It established career ladders for hundreds of talented minority-group members, among them representatives Ronald Dellums of California and Parren Mitchell of Maryland and Mayors Coleman Young of Detroit and Theodore Berry of Cincinnati. . . .

The Economic Opportunity Act was Johnson's first major legislative achievement as President. Its passage marked the beginning of one of the most prolific bursts of legislative activity in history. Within little more than a year after its passage, a historic civil-rights act, a voting rights act, the first omnibus program of aid to public schools and health insurance for the elderly all became law—testimony to Johnson's skill, to the nation's remorse over President Kennedy's death and to Congress's determination to bring to fruition the seeds of social policy planted in the New Deal. . . .

Behind the (proposed OEO legislation) message lay a titanic bureaucratic struggle involving almost a dozen agencies—Agriculture, Commerce, HEW and Labor among them—each eager to have its pet projects included in the poverty package sent to Congress. The basic choice was between a jobs-and-training approach, favored by Labor, and social services stressing community self-help, urged by HEW. The eventual compromise put primary reliance on community self-help, but with a strong youth-oriented employment component. A companion question—who was to run the new federal effort?—was harder to resolve. To settle conflicting claims, and take command of planning, Johnson turned to Shriver, director of the popular Peace Corps and a man whose links to the Kennedy family underlined Johnson's pledge of continuity. . . .

Johnson knew the agency would stir some trouble; it was to be an advocate for the poor within government, a prodder and goader of the great bureaucracies. At his insistence, it was set up in the executive branch and Shriver was made a Presidential Assistant as well as OEO director. "Sarge," the President said, putting a protective arm around him, "this thing can't survive less'n everybody knows when they're hitting it, they're hitting me. I'm your protection."

The Economic Opportunity Act gave the new OEO responsibility for operating some of the programs itself and for coordinating the often competing activities of the other agencies. Some of the major ones it ran were the community-action agencies, the Job Corps and VISTA (Volunteers in Service to America). The community-action groups, to be composed of all segments of a community, would attack local poverty with the help of $90 in federal funds put up for each $10 raised locally (the amount of Federal participation was changed by the 1974 amendments to 80 percent, decreasing gradually to 60 percent or, in some of the smaller agencies, to 70 percent). The Job Corps established residential training centers, for youth 14 to 22, where school dropouts with poor job prospects could complete their education and learn a trade. VISTA was to be a domestic counterpart to the highly successful Peace Corps; enrollees would work in migrant camps, Indian reservations, urban slums and rural outposts, helping the poor overcome their poverty. The Economic Opportunity Act also established a Neighborhood Youth Corps, within the Labor Department, to help keep youths in school, to provide help for migrant workers and small businessmen, to provide job-training for welfare mothers and to provide work-study grants to poor college students. New programs quickly joined the list: Head Start, a preschool program that emphasized attention to medical and nutritional as well as educational needs; legal services; and neighborhood health centers. . . .

Though prepared for some bureaucratic squabbling, Johnson was taken by surprise at adverse local reaction, and complained to Shriver: "Is OEO being run by a bunch of kooks, Communists and queers?"

Job Corps youths had been flown cross-country to camps without beds or programs. A half-million comic books were printed for recruitment purposes but were never distributed when it was discovered that earlier drives had generated 300,000 inquiries for only 1,000 job-training slots. Congressmen were fuming, by 1967, that the program was costing $8,000 per enrollee—more than it cost to send a young person to Harvard. . . . The trainees often clashed with local townspeople, indeed, rioted in some instances.

Community-action organizers, who had begun seeking to "strike down all the barriers," took aim at local merchants, slumlords, even Mayors. Local officials learned to their horror that they couldn't control community-action agencies. The act included the stipulation that such agencies should be public or private nonprofit enterprises, thus bypassing City Hall, and should be run with the "maximum feasible participation" of the people served.

There was another factor too. It was that many people took the rhetoric literally. Many of the tactics that drove Mayors and Governors to distraction—rent strikes, marches on City Hall, demands for more municipal jobs for minorities, even suits against welfare restrictions—were legitimate assaults on real sources of poverty. "I'll never forget the day in 1967 when the Supreme Court struck down state residency requirements for welfare eligibility," says Baker. The suit had been brought by OEO-supported legal services attorneys. "Many of our best friends on the Hill, in Governors' mansions, the Mayors' offices—they were all mad at us. This would cost them millions. They might have to raise taxes. Yet here was a decision that did more to alleviate poverty than almost anything else we had done. And that was always our quandary: how could we alleviate poverty without hurting the people whose support we needed to alleviate poverty?"

In 1966 and 1967, Congress enacted a series of restrictions, limiting salaries of antipoverty officials, putting a $6,900 ceiling on per-enrollee costs in the Job Corps, and permitting local governments to take control of community-action programs. These actions, coupled with a number of changes within the OEO itself, took much of the sting out of its activities. . . .

Back in June, 1966, Shriver's people worked up a 410-page four-year plan: By a combination of expanded services, stepped-up income maintenance and economic growth, two-thirds of the 36 million poor would be lifted from poverty by 1972, the remainder over the next four years. There was only one catch: Government antipoverty outlays would have to grow by $6.4 billion, or 28 percent, the first year, and $3 billion a year thereafter; OEO's own budget would quadruple from $1.7 billion in 1967 to $6.8 billion in 1972. Yet, the report said, the recommended increases were "less than the normal annual increase in federal tax revenues" in a prosperous economy and "would provide a real start" in the all-out war on poverty.

What happened, of course, was that the country got deeply involved in waging, and providing the funds, for another, hotter war. "Vietnam took it all away. . . ."

Charles Schultze, then L.B.J.'s budget chief, adds: "Rather than relying on economic growth to provide more antipoverty funds, he [Johnson] would have to raise taxes. He wouldn't do that. He could say he was raising taxes to finance Vietnam, but he feared the conservatives would use it as a club to kill all the Great Society legislation. By the time he decided to ask Congress for a tax hike [in 1968] he was afraid chances of getting it would be killed if people thought it was for the war on poverty." Thus, the four-year plan was never begun, and the nation never really adopted a goal for eliminating poverty, or a realistic strategy for meeting it. . . .

Shriver and his successor, Bert Harding, had already begun spinning OEO programs off to other agencies once such programs were deemed mature enough to survive in old-line bureaucratic settings without losing their poverty focus. OEO, after all, was to be experimental, not permanent. Nixon continued the process, sending Head Start to HEW, the Job Corps and other manpower programs to Labor. More transfers were to follow. . . .

In retrospect, it can be argued that if OEO had not pulled in its horns, it would not have survived as long as it has and many of its programs would not have survived at all. The showdown came in California, where Gov. Ronald Reagan compiled a report charging serious wrongdoing on the part of the statewide California Rural Legal Assistance and demanded that its funds be terminated.

CRLA was the prototype for dozens of the country's poverty law offices that served up occasional class-action suits along with a steady diet of routine divorce, housing and consumer cases. Acting on behalf of migratory and other poor farm workers in the state, it had brought one suit after another against state agencies and influential growers. Its legal victories had cost Reagan and his conservative supporters millions. The charges against CRLA were transparently politically motivated and were thoroughly discredited in 1971 by a panel of judges set up to investigate them, but the flap redoubled the Administration's determination to minimize controversy. It also provided a major push for detaching legal services from the OEO and placing them in a nonprofit government-chartered corporation where they could be better insulated from political attack. . . .

Richard Nixon's landslide reelection in November, 1972, affected OEO like no event since the escalation of the war in Vietnam. Federal outlays for the poor had doubled under Lyndon Johnson, rising from $7.9 billion in 1964 to $15.9 billion in 1969. They doubled again in the next six years, but virtually none of the increase went to programs authorized under the Economic Opportunity Act. Outlays for OEO programs in 1973 stood at the same level Nixon inherited in 1969: $1.9 billion. Most of the increase in funds for the poor under Nixon were not spent in training or service programs aimed at getting rid of poverty, but rather the funds took the form of direct financial assistance—in some cases available to nonpoor as well—such as Social Security benefit increases mandated by Congress, Medicare-Medicaid, the new federalized Supplementary Security Insurance, which replaced the "adult welfare" categories: aid to the aged, blind and disabled. The major exception was food stamps, a program which will have reached 15 million people in 1974 as compared with 1 million in 1969, and on which federal outlays soared, under Nixon, from $1.6 billion to $5.1 billion. . . .

In fiscal 1975, again the Administration had asked for no community-action funds. If the Mayors and Governors—and local administrators—wanted community action to stay in business, Arnett (the director of OEO appointed in 1973) told them, they'd better make their voices heard in Washington. They did.

What happened between last October and May 29 [1974], when the House acted, was unprecedented in OEO's history. The two national organizations that represent CAP [Community Action Program] directors and other friends of the program hired a high-priced lobbying team in Washington, headed by former Representative William Cramer, a one-time OEO critic. Letters proclaiming the virtues of community action poured in from 32 Governors, dozens of Mayors, Chambers of Commerce and more than a few of the 185,000 Americans who owe their jobs to the program. . . .

By a vote of 331 to 53 the House approved the Community Services Act, which kills OEO but preserves all programs in other agencies. . . .

Martin LaVor, a House Republican staffer who has followed OEO from its inception, explains the shift in sentiment: "Community action keeps the poor off the Mayors' backs. Some of them provide useful services, some are largely job-creating enterprises. . . . They create a buffer between the local power structure and the poor. Take them away and a lot of public officials will have problems on their hands they'd prefer not to have to deal with."

"It was a perfect way to resolve the issue," says Representative Albert Quie of Minnesota, the committee's ranking Republican. "The people who hate OEO could say, 'Look, we're getting rid of it.' The people who like the individual programs could say 'Look, we're keeping them.' Very often they were the same people."

The real questions raised by the short, unhappy life of the OEO transcend the fortunes of this or that program, this or that office. What indeed has it accomplished? What are its lessons? What does it take to eliminate poverty?

Certainly it has accomplished less than it initially promised. But it also seems clear that it achieved more than most Americans appreciate, changing city halls, welfare offices, housing officials and Congress in their treatment of the poor, bringing millions of poor into the political process and many of them into the decision-making process. It demonstrated that the public attention span is short and that, as Eli Ginzburg and Robert M. Solow put it in *The Public Interest:* "Social legislation needs a constituency larger than its direct beneficiaries" if it is to benefit the poor and the minorities, for they are, almost by definition, weak and powerless.

There were 23 million poor in 1973, according to the government's inflation-related price index ($4,540 for a nonfarm family of four); this is a third less than there were 10 years ago, when Johnson declared the poverty war. What's happened in the past decade has been a gradual maturing of often effective programs—accompanied by a diminished sense of national interest in the matter.

Box Score

COMMUNITY ACTION. 937 local "self-help" agencies . . . no longer organize rent strikes or city-hall marches as some did in the sixties, but provide a range of noncontroversial services to the poor: provide emergency assistance to the needy, channel welfare recipients into job training, find housing for the homeless, help for the homebound, run interference for the poor in dealing with local bureaucracies. . . . Employs a work force of 180,000, half of whom were formerly poor or on welfare. Cost: $330 million. Effectiveness: Mixed.

HEAD START. Comprehensive health, nutritional, and educational assistance to 380,000 preschoolers from low-income families. . . . Politically popular program whose frequently imaginative teaching techniques have rarely gained a foothold in public schools into which "graduates" are fed. . . . Children attending Head Start and its sequel, Follow Through, grades 1–3, score higher on achievement tests than those who don't. . . . Program is concentrating increasingly on home environment as the key factor in educational attainment. Cost: $430 million. Effectiveness: High.

JOB CORPS. Schooling and job training in a new environment for teenage school dropouts; program has undergone drastic changes from the sixties, maintains a low profile . . . boasts a 93 percent placement rate—in jobs, school or military service. But half of each year's 43,000 enrollees drop out within 90 days, and expenses required for residential setting keep costs per enrollee at more than $6,500 a year. Cost: $180 million. Effectiveness: Questionable.

LEGAL SERVICES. Employs 2,500 lawyers in 900 "poverty law" offices . . . provides free legal advice to persons meeting income guidelines up to a third above the poverty level . . . handles domestic, housing and welfare problems, consumer grievances concerning faulty merchandise, repossession threats and the like. . . . A few successful class-action suits against government agencies—lowering barriers to qualify for welfare, for example—have enraged many officeholders, but benefited the poor. Cost: $71 million. Effectiveness: High.

VOLUNTEERS IN SERVICE TO AMERICA (VISTA). 4,200 "domestic Peace Corps" volunteers spend two years working in health clinics, migrant camps, drug rehabilitation programs, senior citizens centers. . . . Well-established program now housed in ACTION, the conglomerate agency formed by the 1971 merger of all federal volunteer efforts, VISTA has shed its earlier controversial image, now gives its workers specific functions to perform. But program's inability to attract large numbers of volunteers with needed skills (plumbers, nurses) and $4,300-a-year cost of volunteer support has forced administrators to favor less expensive approaches to volunteerism. VISTA's cost: $22.8 million. Effectiveness: Mixed.

The first massive violence in the civil rights movement broke out in 1965 in Watts, a section of Los Angeles. Similar rioting later broke out in other cities. These riots reflected the accumulating frustrations with the steady but slow pace of progress achieved in civil rights. As greater social justice was attained, the remaining incidences of inequality and the poverty and humiliation associated with it were made even more visible—and perceived as even less tolerable. A period of conflict within the black civil rights movement developed. One side continued to argue for nonviolent protest, pointing to the real progress attained using this approach. Another view argued for a more activist—and, if necessary, violent—approach, pointing to the slow pace of progress and the high price blacks continued to pay in terms of poverty, illness, and discrimination. In April 1968, Martin Luther King was murdered in Memphis, Tennessee, weakening the forces pushing for nonviolence. Dissipation of the direct action through peaceful public protest phase of the civil rights movement was signaled by the ineffectiveness of the Poor People's Campaign in Washington, D.C., that same year. Thereafter, more militant and more politically sophisticated approaches were adopted, as exemplified by the National Welfare Rights Organization (NWRO). Formed primarily of public assistance recipients, it seeks changes in social welfare legislation to make benefits more adequate and equitable. It also seeks greater involvement of welfare recipients in social policy by organizing them as an effective political force. Unfortunately, by the early 1970s NWRO had lapsed into inactivity.

Students also had a period of militancy spurred by the escalation of the Vietnam War in 1966, the assassination of Robert Kennedy in the spring of 1968, and the invasion of Cambodia in 1970. "The SDS (Students for a Democratic Society), the leading group in campus unrest, in 1968 had only 250 chapters with 35,000 members, but could mobilize up to 300,000 supporters."[57] Not only the poor were organizing to demand a measure of influence in the nation's social policy.

The emerging new politics, social legislation, and living styles of the seventies seem to be seeking a way to make America a more just society. The New Left is a revolt against the bureaucracy of government, the depersonalization of universities, the inhumanities of war, the social and economic deprivation of minority groups and the poor, and the discrepancy in some areas between what America stands for and what it practices. The New Left has drawn its support mostly from college students, middle-class youth, and discontented blacks, and has emphasized community and social change.

Governmental responses to the problems posed by the Vietnam War, civil rights, and welfare reform have been slow and often ineffective. At present, "there is no clear definition of purpose, nor central direction in welfare effort as a whole. . . . Acceleration of programs toward the abolition of poverty seems unlikely."[58] President Nixon's resistance to school busing as an effective civil rights tool stimulated anti-busing legislation in

1972 that has seriously weakened school busing in concept and practice, a discouraging reversal of hard-won gains. Attempts to deal with the need for an overhaul of the nation's basic social welfare system have shown similar inconsistencies. Public assistance applicants must make themselves available for work as a condition for the receipt of aid, in spite of high unemployment rates, low wages, and the unsuitability of most assistance recipients for gainful employment.[59] The old question of welfare vs. workfare continues to live on in spite of centuries of experience that has repeatedly shown that most welfare recipients are unable to work because of age, illness, disability, or child-rearing responsibilities.

During the first half of the 1970s some significant legislation has been enacted that improves the social welfare service delivery system, while other legislation is more questionable, and some issues remain to be resolved through legislative action. As noted earlier, the Supplemental Security Income Program took effect in January 1974, and generally was a step forward in providing a uniform, federally administered guaranteed income program for the needy aged, blind, and disabled. The fact that the AFDC program was excluded from SSI is also to be regretted, however, since it continues to exhibit the many problems and inequities referred to earlier (see Exhibit 9-1 in Chapter 9 for more detail on welfare reform efforts).

Other legislation has begun the difficult task of changing society's inadequate medical system. Although American medical practice includes the most sophisticated technology available anywhere, society has been relatively ineffective in insuring that all of its members have access to adequate medical care. Whereas most highly industrialized societies provide comprehensive medical care to all of their members, Americans must purchase health care on an individual basis. This seriously discriminates against lower income groups. It also discourages people from utilizing preventive medicine, since medical checkups tend to be costly and are often not covered by medical insurance (insurances tend to cover services only in the event of an illness). The first problem, making medical care available to all, will not be a reality until a national health insurance plan is enacted by Congress (see Exhibit 9.2 in Chapter 9 for more detail on national health insurance proposals). The second problem, encouraging preventive medicine, has been addressed by legislation mandating the support of health maintenance organizations (HMO) as an alternative to health insurance, which is focused on the incidence of illness.

The HMO is an organization that contracts with individuals to provide comprehensive health services for a flat fee. This is thought to encourage persons to utilize services on a preventive basis since they are included in the fee paid the HMO, rather than utilizing services when an illness occurs as is the case with traditional health insurance plans. The HMO also has its own staff of medical practitioners (or contracts with such persons), enabling the HMO to exert more control over services and costs than is possible when an individual uses services provided by independent practitioners and organizations as is the case with traditional health insurance plans. It is important to note that the HMO is simply an alternative form of private health insurance; it is not a governmentally provided health insurance program.

Potentially significant legislation is Public Law 92-512, revenue sharing, passed in 1972. This legislation was part of Richard Nixon's so-called "New Federalism," an effort to transfer as much decision-making responsibility as possible back to the states from the federal government. "PL 92-512 provides for financial assistance to states and localities, one-third to the states, two-thirds to the localities. The localities are restricted in their use of funds to (1) 'ordinary and necessary capital expenditures' and (2) 'ordinary and necessary maintenance and operating expenses' in eight priority areas. These are public safety, environmental protection, public transportation, health, recreation, libraries, social services for the poor or aged, and financial administration."[60] Revenue sharing funds are not really new monies, since they are intended to replace, partially or totally, grants-in-aid, and funds for many grant-in-aid programs have been reduced with the advent of revenue sharing. Within the priority areas established by the federal government, the revenue sharing funds can be used at the discretion of the local and state decision-makers.

In theory, revenue sharing allows states and localities to allocate funds more wisely than is possible by the federal government, since these units of government are closer to the people and presumably more responsive to their wishes. However, Hardcastle notes the following:[61]

> *The trend represented by revenue sharing shows that nationally, a commitment to domestic programming, especially in social services, is simply not there. The political implications are clear. Federal protection for social services will be removed and they will have to compete with the entire array of fiscal demands for public funds. Mental health programs, for example, will have to compete for funds at the state and local level not only with child welfare services but also with street improvements.*

Revenue sharing marks a step backward in a process that had been developing for some time, namely increased federal planning and supervision of the social welfare system. An expanded role for the federal government in social welfare planning and supervision reflects the impact of large-scale social forces on individual and community functioning. The return to more local control opens up possibilities for less efficient and more inequitable use of funds, as well as an inability to see long-range human needs and plan appropriately for them. Social welfare has always been enmeshed in the societal need to set priorities in the use of relatively scarce resources. Revenue sharing reemphasizes the need for establishing priorities, but vests much of the decision-making power with those having perhaps the weakest grasp of the significance of their decisions.[62]

It is still too early to know how effective revenue sharing will be in meeting America's social welfare needs, but preliminary data are not encouraging. A National Revenue Sharing Monitoring Project sponsored by a coalition of the League of Women Voters Education Fund, the Center for Community Change, the National Urban Coalition, and the Center for National Policy Review, reports the following in a 1974 interim report:[63]

> *The general revenue sharing program intended to return "power to the people" to increase citizen influence and to make government more responsive to taxpayer pressure appears to be failing and failing miserably. Defenders of revenue sharing blame this failure on the narrowing flexibility in local budgets caused by increased costs of existing local government services. Many also cite concurrent federal categorical grant cutbacks or impoundments, and the pinch put on local budgets by spiraling inflation . . . but the widespread barriers to effective citizen participation which monitors reported are not explained by arguments about inflation or reduced federal spending. Citizen participation problems are built into the Revenue Sharing Act which does not specifically provide for such participation in local decision-making processes of allocation of these monies. The Act provides only that these monies be allocated in conformity with and through the same budgeting process established under local and state law. The assumption is that citizens participate in decisions as to how local revenues are spent and that this participation would be extended to revenue sharing expenditures as well. The assumption is erroneous. Citizens generally are not involved in complex local and state budgeting processes. Revenue sharing has not changed this fact of life.*

The result has been that "revenue sharing money was most often spent for the same purpose as local revenues have been spent in the past,"[64] yielding no particular benefit to social welfare services. Indeed, to the degree that grant-in-aid programs have been cut back, the net effect may be negative. While revenue sharing legislation is of great potential significance, perhaps the lesson from history it ignores is that we can't go backward. In the attempt to meet society's needs, it is rarely possible to resort to solutions that did or could have worked at an earlier point in society's history, because no society stands still. As of this writing, it appears that revenue-sharing legislation will be allowed to lapse in the next few years.

Legislation which has not yet been passed, but which is very badly needed, includes some type of guaranteed annual income, and national health insurance (see Exhibit 9.1). Part of the significance of the Supplemental Security Income Program is that for the first time it does establish a federal guaranteed annual income, at least for a segment of the population.

Proposals for such a guaranteed income for all Americans have covered a wide spectrum. Some of the major proposals have included the following:[65]

1. *Guaranteed Income.* A plan to supplement the income of individuals and families to insure that the annual income reaches a predetermined level. President Nixon proposed such a plan, the Family Assistance Plan, but it was not approved by Congress. There has been considerable debate about the level of income to be guaranteed, and whether all individuals and families would be included in the plan.
2. *Negative Income Tax.* A plan that again establishes a base income level, with those falling above it paying taxes and those falling below it being paid a supplement to reach that level. Somewhat similar to a guaranteed income, such a plan would also build in a work incentive provision, but unlike the above plan, it would be administered by the Internal Revenue Service.
3. *Children's Allowances.* A plan that automatically pays parents a cash allowance for each child. It is used in several other industrialized countries, and, contrary to some fears in this country, it has not led to an increase in the birth rate. But this plan discriminates against those without children, and, by automatically paying money to all parents, would in effect subsidize those not in need.[66]
4. *Social Dividend.* The least likely of all the plans, it would provide a universal payment to all regardless of income or status. It is the most costly of all the plans, but insures equal treatment to all and has no work provisions.

Whatever guaranteed income approach is ultimately selected, there is considerable feeling that America needs to move toward some such program. It is a contemporary expression of a belief that has been developing throughout the history of social welfare—namely, that society has a responsibility for the basic well-being of its members. Meeting peoples' economic needs is by no means equivalent to meeting their social needs, but it is a major step in that direction.

With the election of President Jimmy Carter in 1976, the climate for renewed progress in social welfare improved. The Housing and Community Development Act of 1977 included subsidies to low-income families as well as homeowners and the housing industry. It also extended the Community Development Block Grant program, and established a new Urban Development Action Grant program. This act sought to improve the quality of housing available, especially for the poor. The Juvenile Justice Amendments of 1977 extended the Juvenile Justice Act of 1974, and emphasized citizen participation, special-attention prevention-and-treatment programs, deinstitutionalization of status offenders,* and the monitoring

* A status offender is a youth who is apprehended for behavior that would not be an offense for an adult (such things as truancy and promiscuity, for example).

of separate facilities for juveniles. These amendments also extended the Runaway Youth Act. In 1978, the Child Abuse Prevention and Treatment Act Amendments and The Adoption Reform Act of 1978 were passed. The former strengthened the role of the National Center on Child Abuse and Neglect in contracting for research and for publishing results in the area of child abuse. It also established a new program on the sexual abuse of children. The latter established a National Adoption Information Exchange that will use computers to locate children who would benefit by adoption and to assist in placing them.

In spite of these advances, the mood of the country was mixed in the late 1970s. The Equal Rights Amendment was not passed within the time limit previously established, but Congress finally voted to extend that limit. The economic picture was darkened by inflation that proved difficult to control and that stimulated an atmosphere of economic conservatism with respect to social welfare expenditures. The passage of Proposition 13 in California, which limited the property tax and hence the funds available for public services, was one indication of this conservative mood. Affirmative Action efforts to protect educational employment and housing opportunities for minorities became less visible. Although states continued to make slow progress in legislation guaranteeing certain homosexual rights, some communities either repealed or defeated such legislation having to do with equal housing and employment for homosexuals. These antisocial welfare efforts had some well-known and visible proponents (Phyllis Schlaffley opposed the ERA, and Anita Bryant sought to deny homosexuals their rights), but they seemed to be part of an extensive, though rarely visible, right-wing reactionary network that was well organized and well funded. As always, efforts to improve social welfare services and structures met formidable opposition, yet achieved some successes even so.

▶ Chapter Conclusion

Expansion on the only meaningful frontier, that of individual people and their relationships with each other, is essential. Strengthening police and corrections structures in the nation cannot hope to solve the problem of social disintegration and individual malfunction. Although there is some reason to be proud of the nation's progress in conceptualizing and operationalizing social welfare, and although there is some optimism that current legislative trends are addressing basic needs, there is still much to be done. Millions continue to live in poverty. Inequality continues to be a way of life for many blacks, Chicanos, native Americans, homosexuals, and women. Social priorities continue to be questioned. Social welfare students and practitioners of today are living through a period of crucial importance to the future of social welfare in the United States. As is always the case, knowledge of the past will help all of us to make more intelligent decisions about the future. Exhibit 2-6 summarizes some of the major trends of the history of social welfare that will continue to affect the shape of the social welfare institution.

The Threads of History in Social Welfare EXHIBIT 2-6

To summarize this chapter's review of the historical development of the concept of social welfare, the major stages of welfare growth are presented on the following pages, along with a brief discussion of their enduring effects on social welfare concepts and programs.

Informal Welfare Structures

The highly formalized and specialized welfare structures we take for granted have their roots in informal attempts to meet people's basic needs. The family was the earliest structure in which this occurred, and, in spite of the highly formalized and professional programs that exist today, informal attempts to help others continue to exist and be important—the family, friendship groups, mutual aid groups. As long as the magnitude of need was small, and the definition of who was responsible for helping whom was narrow, informal welfare structures were adequate. When need and responsibility grew beyond immediate kin or friendship groups, more formal structures became necessary.

The Causes of Need

The incidence of need has generally been related to social conditions. The Industrial Revolution, including its earliest phases that broke up the manorial system, generated need of many kinds—housing, food, illness, and others. During periods of economic depressions, or during periods of war, it is common for people to experience need. Institutionalized inequality in whatever form—slavery; child labor, and indenture; lack of women's rights; and religious persecution, to name a few—serves to make people helpless and dependent. Although there is always some need caused by willful neglect and deviance, the lessons of history demonstrate that need is most often a social phenomenon. It is remarkable how resistant to these lessons some societies can be.

Categorizing the Needy

With the formalization of welfare services came the desire to categorize the needy in order to determine who qualified for what services (formalized in eligibility requirements). The Elizabethan Poor Law established three categories of the needy, which have proven remarkably long-lived. These categories, the services provided in each, and the present-day forms of both, are summarized below:

The helpless were persons who could not be blamed for being needy because of age, illness, or disablement. These persons received outdoor relief or were placed in almshouses. The helpless are still with us (the aged, dependent children, and the physically and emotionally disabled), and they continue to be considered worthy of assistance. Such aid today is normally provided in their own homes rather than in almshouses (although there are still some vestiges of almshouse-like residential facilities).

The involuntarily unemployed were persons who were the victims of misfortune, but who were generally ablebodied. They were usually sent to workhouses or houses of correction, where they were expected to work in return for help. The involuntarily unemployed are today generally helped through outdoor relief, although there is still a tendency to try to make receipt of aid dependent on going to work if at all possible.

The vagrant were persons without a stable place of residence. They were usually ostracized, or, if they had to be accepted by a community, placed in workhouses or houses of correction.

They were considered willfully indigent, and despised as a result. Vagrancy today has a somewhat different connotation. Persons who exist outside the normative structure are our contemporary vagrants, whether or not they are physically mobile—skidrow alcoholics, drug users, persons who have committed a crime, sexual deviants, etc. They are likely to inhabit the modern-day houses of correction—prisons and mental hospitals—and they continue to carry the scorn of their society.

PUBLIC AND PRIVATE RESPONSIBILITY FOR THE NEEDY. The enduring dislocations of industrialism created need on a scale beyond the resources of the informal welfare system. The result was the development of two types of structured social welfare: public and private. Publicly supported social welfare has always been the more important of the two because it is societal recognition of its responsibility to its members. Private social welfare depends on the personal sense of responsibility of individuals, and requires that they voluntarily forego some of their own resources to help others. In some this sense of responsibility does not exist, while in others available resources are too limited to allow any to be contributed to help others. Private contributions are also heavily dependent on societal economic health. On the other hand, until the 1930s private social welfare often met people's needs more adequately and comprehensively than did the then-minimal public system. Private services also served to stimulate the development of more adequate public services. However, public services have always been the barometer of societal attitudes toward the needy. Especially since 1935, public social services have come to dominate the society's social welfare system, reflecting changed attitudes toward helping.

Financial Aid, Social Services, and Special Groups

Two of the enduring issues in the provision of social welfare services have been deciding for whom society is responsible, and what needs should be met. Beginning with a focus on basic survival needs (food, money, shelter, health care) there has been a gradual expansion to include more socially oriented services—marital counseling, job skills, mental health, recreation, group participation, and the like. One way in which this has occurred is by focusing on special groups—children, the aged, the handicapped, the mentally ill, and prisoners—and developing a comprehensive network of services to meet their needs. This has generally led to a fragmented service delivery network (the aged are helped by programs different from those for children, or veterans, or the retarded), but still a gradually expanding network of increasingly comprehensive services has developed. Part of the reason for the initial focus on just one type of service (such as financial aid) or a special group whose needs seem so obvious (dependent children, for example) lies in society's struggle to define those who are deserving of need. Another part of the reason lies in changing and developing awareness of the causes of and solutions to need. And a third factor lies in historical accident—the existence of a Dorothea Dix, Jane Addams, or Michael Harrington to document need in a particular group, and often to fight for the development of services to meet identified need.

Professionalizing Social Welfare

There has been a progression in social welfare from informal services, to structured services, to structured professional services. Several factors have contributed to this progression: the increasing numbers of services provided and users served; the growth of the social sciences, making the measurement of social behavior possible and demonstrating the complexity of social behavior; and the expansion of the concept of social welfare beyond mere survival to include complex social behaviors. Although some other societies have well-developed social welfare systems that are informal in structure, in contemporary Western, industrialized societies the professionalization of social welfare is an indication of the society's commitment to social welfare goals.

The Quest for Social Justice

The very concept of social welfare suggests a concern with social justice in its attempt to share social resources with those in need. Early attempts to meet need were focused on physical needs for food, shelter, and nurturance. Gradually individual autonomy became another right recognized by society, and was reflected in a concern with adequate psychological functioning and personal care in such places as prisons and mental hospitals. The professionalizing of social welfare emphasized individualizing people and problems, so that services were adapted to individual needs. A much later development has been recognition of a need for social participation, the right of people to have input into social policy-making and service delivery. Paternalistic views of minority groups by majority groups are increasingly repudiated as unjust. Racial, ethnic, age, and sex groups are all being seen as having the right to determine their own destinies. Social justice means the right to equal participation in societal decision-making, and equal access to social resources. As the survival needs of people as physical beings have been more adequately met, society has been able to turn to the survival of people as social beings. Much of the future of social welfare will be in the development of a society characterized by higher levels of social justice.

STUDY QUESTIONS

1. What impact did the Industrial Revolution (including its earliest manifestations) have on the development of the social welfare institution? How did it affect the social welfare institution by affecting other institutions, such as the family? What type of new needs were created by such effects of the Industrial Revolution as new work patterns, new community structures, and new political forms?
2. Why was the Social Security Act such a significant piece of legislation when passed in 1935? Do you consider the Economic Opportunity Act as significant a piece of legislation in terms of its effects on the services provided and its impact on the way in which services are structured? Why or why not?
3. Taking a broad historical perspective, would you say that we have reason to be optimistic or pessimistic about the future of the social welfare institution? Do you think it will ever meet all the major needs people experience? Do you think it is now or will ever be an accepted part of the American social structure? Support your argument with specific historical references.
4. What is the current status of national health care legislation in America? Is there existing legislation or only proposals? Given the history of social welfare in this country, why do you think such legislation (or proposals) is either consistent or inconsistent with our whole approach to social welfare?

REFERENCES

1. Philip Klein, *From Philanthropy to Social Welfare* (San Francisco: Jossey-Bass, 1968), p. 10.
2. S. H. Steinberg, ed., *A New Dictionary of British History* (New York: St. Martin's Press, 1963), p. 280.
3. Blanche D. Coll, *Perspectives in Public Welfare* (Washington, D.C.: Government Printing Office, 1969), p. 2; Wallace Notestein, *The English People on the Eve of Colonization* (New York: Harper & Row, 1954), p. 245.
4. Samuel Mencher, *Poor Law to Poverty Program* (Pittsburgh: University of Pittsburgh Press, 1967), p. 11.
5. Klein, op. cit., p. 11.

6. Actually the Statute of Labourers of 1349 is sometimes regarded as the first poor law in England. For a good summary discussion of the breakup of feudal organization, and the replacing of church authority by secular power, see Paul A. Kurzman, "Poor Relief in Medieval England: The Forgotten Chapter in the History of Social Welfare," *Child Welfare* 49 (November 1970): 459–501.
7. E. M. Leonard, *The Early History of the English Poor Relief* (New York: Barnes & Noble, 1965), p. 16.
8. Mencher, op. cit., p. 12.
9. Russell Smith and Dorothy Zeitz, *American Social Welfare Institutions* (New York: John Wiley, 1970), p. 14.
10. Leonard, op. cit., p. 137.
11. Coll, op. cit., p. 9.
12. Mencher, op. cit., p. 27.
13. Steinberg, op. cit., pp. 174–75.
14. Coll, op. cit., p. 10.
15. Ibid., p. 14.
16. Ibid., p. 18.
17. Mencher, op. cit., p. 144.
18. Coll, op. cit., p. 20.
19. Nathan E. Cohen, *Social Work in the American Tradition* (New York: Dryden Press, 1958), p. 49.
20. Coll, op. cit., p. 30.
21. Ibid., pp. 36–37.
22. Smith and Zeitz, op. cit., p. 43.
23. Ibid.
24. Frank Bruno, *Trends in Social Work* (New York: Columbia University Press, 1957), p. 108.
25. Cohen, loc. cit.
26. Ibid., p. 7.
27. Coll, op. cit., p. 60.
28. Ibid., p. 63.
29. Walter Friedlander, *Introduction to Social Welfare* (Englewood Cliffs, N.J.: Prentice-Hall, 1961), p. 107.
30. Coll, op. cit., p. 63.
31. Friedlander, op. cit., p. 113.
32. Coll, op. cit., p. 72.
33. Friedlander, op. cit., p. 114.
34. Ibid., p. 116.
35. Arthur P. Miles, *An Introduction to Social Welfare* (Boston: D. C. Heath and Company, 1949), p. 200.
36. Ibid., p. 200.
37. Coll, op. cit., p. 74.
38. Miles, op. cit., p. 175.
39. Coll, op. cit., p. 81.
40. Richard H. Bremner, *American Philanthropy* (Chicago: University of Chicago Press, 1960), p. 117.
41. Bruno, op. cit., p. 232.
42. Bremner, loc. cit.
43. Coll, loc. cit.

44. Mencher, op. cit., p. 363.
45. Ibid.
46. Duncan M. MacIntyre, *Public Assistance—Too Much or Too Little?* (Ithaca: New York State School of Industrial and Labor Relations, Cornell University, 1964), p. 14.
47. Mencher, loc. cit.
48. Miles, op. cit., p. 219.
49. MacIntyre, op. cit., p. 15.
50. Miles, op. cit., p. 224.
51. Daniel Bell, ed., *The Radical Right* (New York: Anchor, 1964), p. 213.
52. Smith and Zeitz, op. cit., p. 101.
53. Ibid., p. 107.
54. Ibid., p. 108.
55. Ibid., p. 200.
56. Summarized from Jules Berman, "Equal Opportunities Act Amendments," *Washington Social Legislation Bulletin* 39 (August 14, 1978).
57. Smith and Zeitz, op. cit., p. 151.
58. Clair Wilcox, *Toward Social Welfare* (Homewood: Richard D. Irwin, 1969), pp. 360–77.
59. John Romanyshyn, *Social Welfare: Charity to Justice* (New York: Random House, 1971), pp. 173–75, 219–22, 231–32.
60. David Hardcastle, "General Revenue Sharing and Social Work," *Social Work* 18 (September 1973): 3–4. Reprinted by permission of the National Association of Social Workers.
61. Ibid., p. 7.
62. A good discussion of revenue sharing is in Max Frankel, "Revenue Sharing is a Counterrevolution" (New York: Sidney Hillman Reprint Series No. 36, Sidney Hillman Foundation).
63. "Monitoring Revenue Sharing," *Washington Bulletin,* Vol. 23, Issue 42, September 23, 1974, p. 170.
64. Ibid., p. 172.
65. A more complete summary may be found in Romanyshyn, op. cit., 258–90; and the President's Commission on Income Maintenance Programs, *Working Papers* (Washington, D.C.: Government Printing Office, 1969), Part III, pp. 407–55.
66. A clear comparison of children's allowances and the negative income tax is in Irwin Garfinkel, "Negative Income Tax and Children's Allowance Programs: A Comparison," *Social Work* (October 1968): 33–39.

SELECTED READINGS

The history of social welfare is an area that is exceedingly well covered in published materials. These works give a good overview, and the more recent books are thorough yet concise.

Axinn, June, and Levin, Herman. *Social Welfare: A History of the American Response to Need.* New York: Dodd, Mead Publishers, 1975.

Coll, Blanche. *Perspectives in Public Welfare: A History.* Washington, D.C.: U.S. Government Printing Office, 1969.

Feagin, Joe. *Subordinating the Poor: Welfare and American Beliefs.* Englewood Cliffs, N.J.: Prentice-Hall, 1975.

Gronbjerg, Kirsten. *Mass Society and the Extension of Welfare 1960–1970.* Chicago: University of Chicago Press, 1977.

Komisar, Lucy. *Down and Out in the USA: A History of Social Welfare.* 2nd ed. New York: New Viewpoints, 1977.

Leiby, James. *A History of Social Welfare and Social Work in the U.S.* New York: Columbia University Press, 1978.

Lubove, Roy. *The Professional Altruist.* New York: Atheneum, 1969.

Schottland, Charles. "The Changing Roles of Government and Family." In Paul Weinberger, ed., *Perspectives on Social Welfare.* 2nd ed. New York: Macmillan, 1974, pp. 120–35.

Smith, Russell, and Dorothy Zeitz. *American Social Welfare Institutions.* New York: Wiley, 1970.

Steiner, Gilbert. *The State of Welfare.* Washington, D.C.: Brookings Institution, 1971.

Trattner, Walter. *From Poor Law to Welfare State: A History of Social Welfare in America.* New York: Free Press, 1974.

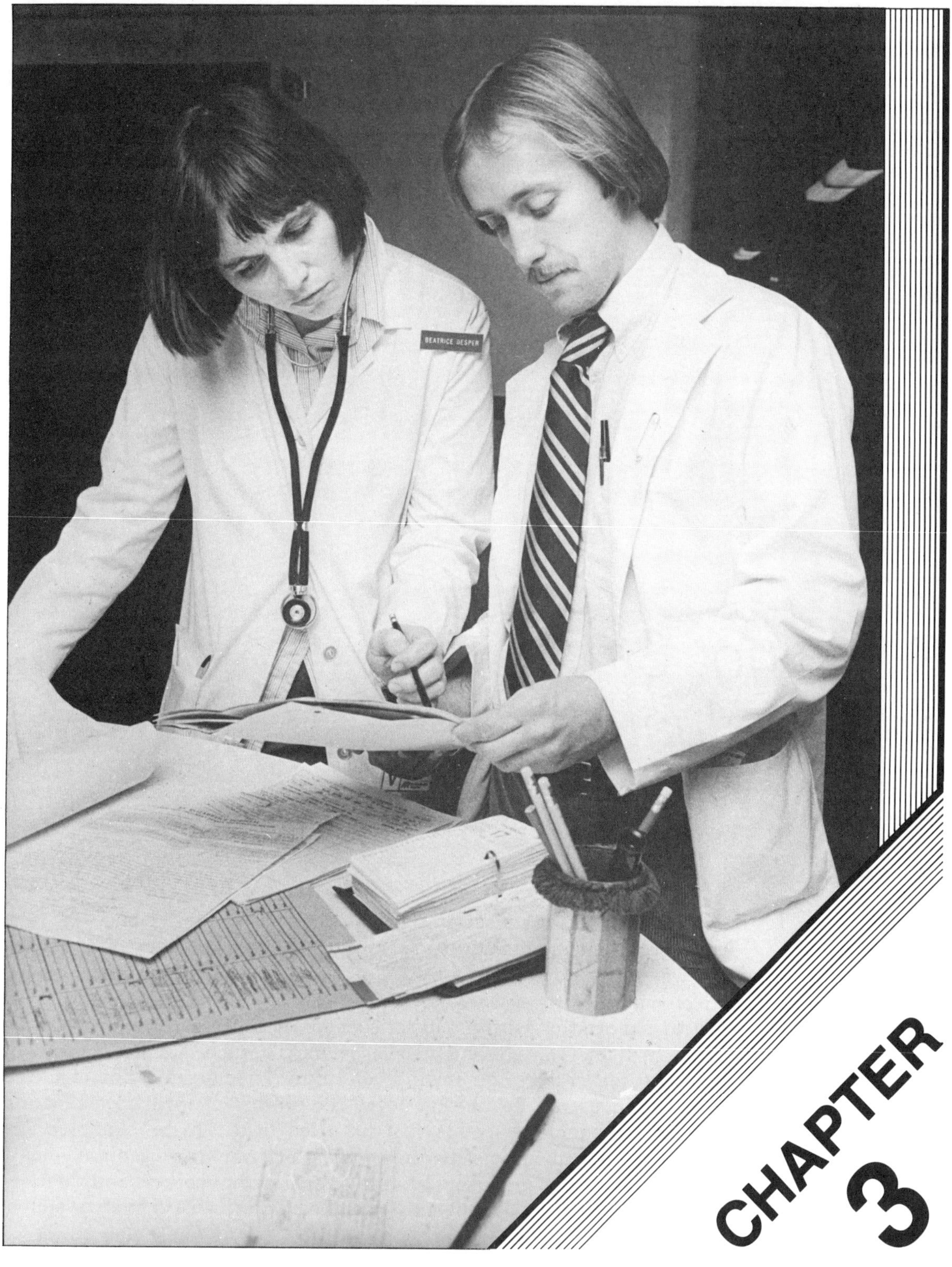

CHAPTER 3

Planning, Structuring, and Evaluating Social Welfare Services

Social welfare as a concept is only as good as its implementation. The concept is fundamental to the creation of a service delivery system, yet the way in which services are structured has an enormous impact on the effectiveness of those services. Remembering that social welfare is an institution existing within a larger societal institutional network, we can expect that the way in which social welfare services are structured will reflect societal values and practices concerning the organization of activities. The Industrial Revolution began the process of work specialization and mass production, events that have led to the highly complex and centralized bureaucratic structures with which we are all familiar today. These massive but impersonal forms of organizing workers and their activities have been adopted by most social welfare service delivery systems, in part because of their success in obtaining and expanding their societal mandate to provide a growing range of services. When over one million persons receive public assistance in New York City alone,[1] a highly sophisticated service delivery system is necessary. Consequently the social welfare practitioner has become a professional, a paid person working in an organizational setting with specialized training and a codified set of professional values and skills.

This chapter reviews basic social science knowledge about the structure and purposes of professions, formal organizations, and bureaucracies. It discusses the implicit values underlying each, as well as their implications for service delivery through professional and bureaucratic structures. It describes some potential value dilemmas faced by social welfare professionals and explores, in a preliminary way, some skills useful for clarifying and achieving professional objectives through bureaucratic structures. The chapter also presents a framework helpful in analyzing the effectiveness of social welfare programs—knowledge that facilitates the development of policy analysis skills and that is related to and helps explicate social welfare professional values.

The Bureaucratic Model of Organization ◄

The use of specialized large-scale forms of work organization is pervasive in contemporary American society. The society takes pride in the standard of living its citizens enjoy through mass production techniques. There have been problems in the use of these techniques in delivering services to people, however. When shopping it can be annoying to have to go to several sales persons and checkout counters to obtain all of the items one needs, although this system allows the store to maximize its sales and distribution efficiency. Dealing with a set of salespersons who are only trained in the sale of one particular item can also be frustrating, although it again permits the efficiency of in-depth specialized knowledge. While these situations are only annoyances to most of us, their prevalence in social welfare service delivery contexts can be serious obstacles to effective service delivery. People's problems tend to come in groups, making it difficult to provide specialized services, each of which deals with one problem or one aspect of a problem. (The case studies in Appendix C provide examples of this point.) The values of social welfare professionals also create problems within highly specialized service delivery systems, since they emphasize meaningful relationships with users and a commitment to solving people's problems—not part of them. It becomes evident that the interaction of the bureaucratic form of organization and social welfare professions is an area of considerable importance for the student of social welfare.

The bureaucracy is a way to formally organize a variety of people and activities into "a system of control based on rational rules."[2] When organizational goals and means can be specified, when tasks can be broken into their component parts and rationally organized, and when tasks can be organized into hierarchical spheres of control, a bureaucracy can be an extremely effective form of social organization. For example, the calculation and payment of Social Security benefits is relatively straightforward, and is generally conceded to be effectively accomplished by the Social Security Administration bureaucracy. Because the bureaucratic form of organization is the major one in contemporary American society, its pervasiveness encourages its use in all organizational contexts. Its appropriateness in social welfare contexts, however, depends on the nature of social welfare tasks to be performed and their suitability for the organizational characteristics of bureaucracies.

The formal characteristics of bureaucracies may be summarized as follows: (1) a high degree of specialization; (2) hierarchical authority structure with specified areas of command and responsibility; (3) impersonal relations between members; (4) recruitment of members on the basis of ability; and (5) differentiation of personal and official resources.[3] In the ideal bureaucracy, rational rules govern behavior, and individuals are expected to interact as organizational role occupants rather than as unique individuals. Given the above characteristics, a bureaucracy has several potential advantages: efficiency in the performance of set tasks in set ways by trained bureaucrats; predictable behavior; behavior that stresses competence more than personal feelings; and the possibility of rapid goal attainment given the trained personnel and routinized activity.

On the other hand, the bureaucracy has several potential disadvantages. It can become quite inefficient when its highly formalized structure must be changed. It can be inhuman in responding to the human needs of those within it, which can seriously affect the motivation of workers and in turn impair both the quantity and quality of productivity. Workers can become so highly specialized that they may be unable to adapt to new working conditions and tasks (trained incapacity), as well as losing sight of goals by focusing so intensively on the means (technicism). Finally, in an attempt to gain personal satisfaction and power from the basically impersonal, rational structure, various types of informal organization may arise.[4] Such organization may either supplement the formal organization and increase productivity,[5] or it may conflict with the formal organization and disrupt or restrict productivity.[6] Exhibit 3-1 uses an organization chart of the Department of Health, Education and Welfare to illustrate the complexity and formal structure of the typical bureaucracy.

The Structure of a Social Welfare Bureaucracy EXHIBIT 3-1

The Department of Health, Education and Welfare (HEW) has the primary responsibility for overseeing public social welfare services in the United States. It is supplemented by other federal departments that manage specialized services, such as the Department of Agriculture, which operates the school lunch, school milk, and food stamp programs, and the Department of Housing and Urban Development, which includes Model Cities, urban renewal, and mortgage loan insurance programs. In order to perform its many functions, HEW has a complex structure that is shown in Figure 1.

Each part of this overall structure has its own formal structure, illustrated by the three examples in Figure 2. Such elaborate and large structures always face potential problems in insuring coordination of individual parts (illustrated in Figure 3) and proper communication throughout the system. However, such structures seem to be the most efficient way to manage such a vast network of services in spite of their potential problems. These charts are excerpted from the *Washington Social Legislation Bulletin,* 6, March 28, 1977.

FIGURE 1 An Overview of the Structure of HEW

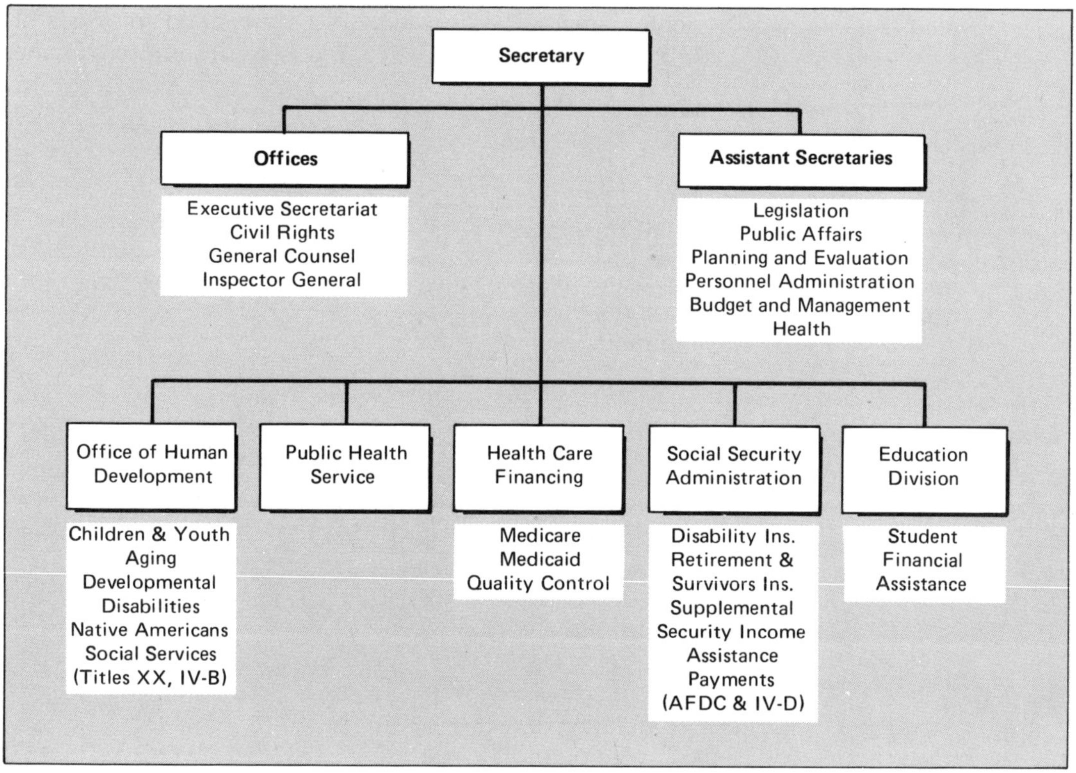

FIGURE 2 The Structure of Three HEW Subsystems

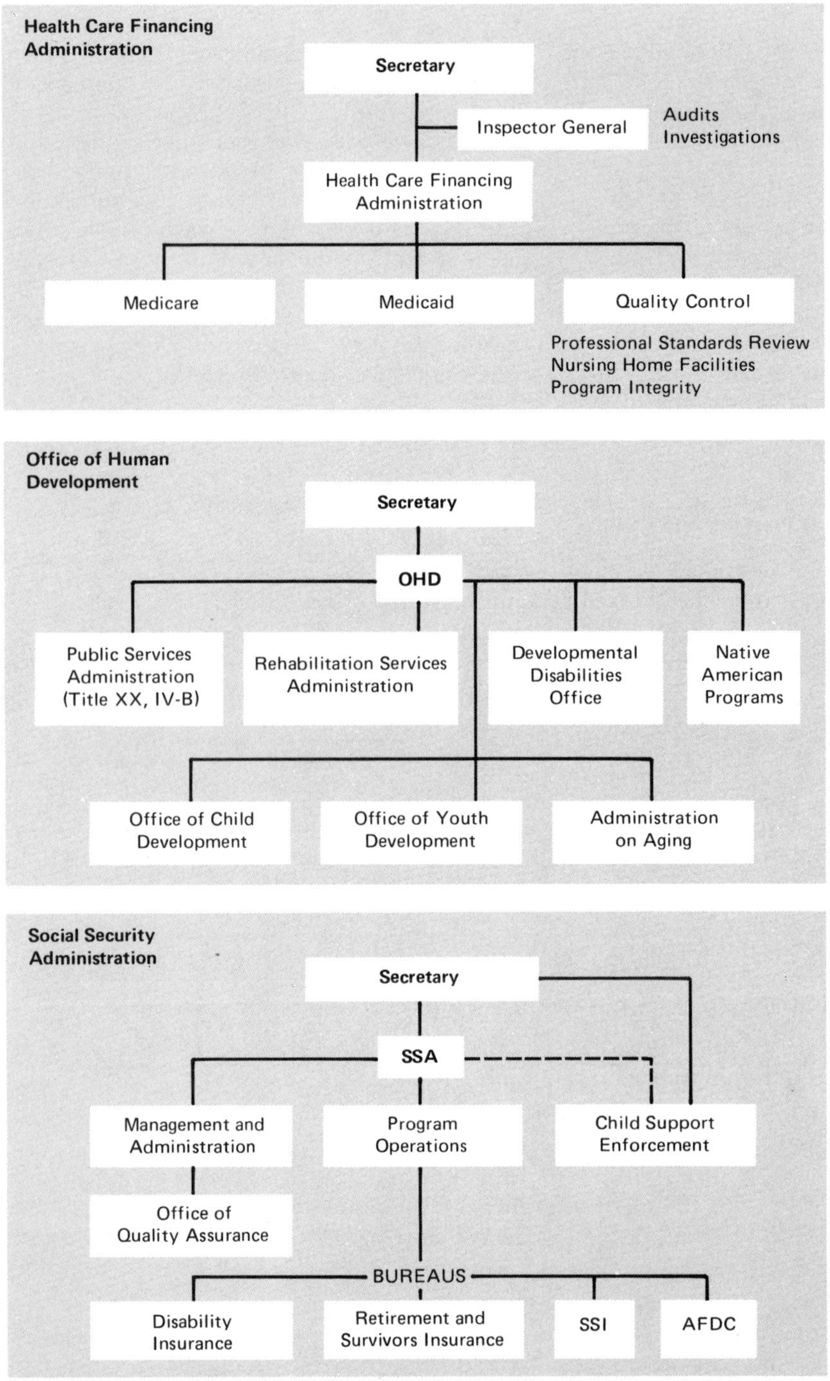

FIGURE 3 Intraorganizational Relationships Within HEW

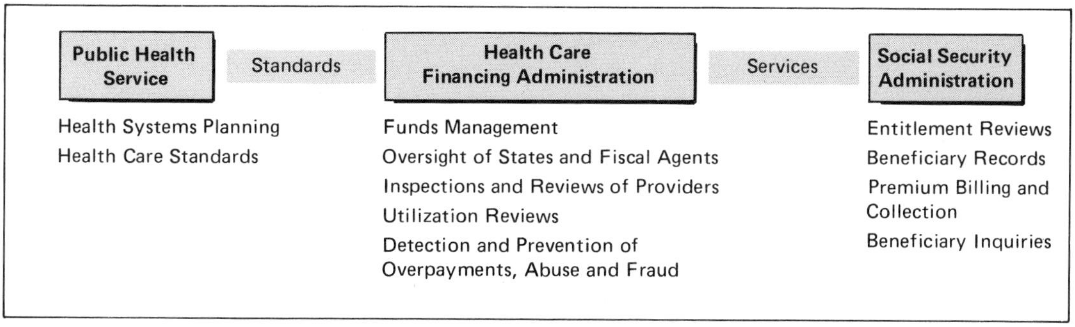

The Professional Model of Organization

In contrast to the formal, hierarchical structure and emphasis on predetermined goals and means, which characterize bureaucracies, professions have rather different characteristics. Hall identifies the following five characteristics of professions: (1) the use of the professional organization as a major reference; (2) a belief in service to the public; (3) belief in self-regulation; (4) a sense of calling to the field; and (5) professional autonomy.[7] Using the profession as a major reference can be seen in the various professional social welfare organizations, such as the National Association of Social Workers. They usually have local chapters that offer their members a full range of services and activities, including meetings to exchange information and plan professional activities, group life insurance, professional publications, certification, and group travel arrangements. It is through such mechanisms that the professional's identity is reinforced and maintained.

Using the profession as a reference combines with a belief in service to the public to make the specific organization in which professionals work less important than their professional missions. Dunbar and Jackson, talking about social workers working in free clinics, express the ideal of professional commitment: "Accomplishing a job and delivering a service are more important to them than hours, pay, professional status, recognition, or conventional agency procedures."[8] So, while a bureaucracy concentrates on procedures to help it most efficiently attain its objectives, professionals concentrate on meeting human needs within the framework of professional values, and the two are not always compatible.

A belief in self-regulation and professional autonomy results from the specialized knowledge bases and socialization procedures that characterize professions. For example, physical therapists have specialized knowledge of the human anatomy and technical skills derived from that knowledge.

Both are learned through a well-documented socialization process.[9] Professionals maintain that nonprofessionals are not equipped to evaluate their competence, since the nonprofessional has not mastered the specialized knowledge base. It follows that professionals must be trusted to evaluate each other, and impose necessary sanctions when appropriate. This in turn makes it difficult for the consumer to sanction the professional. However, professional organizations are sometimes too weak to be effective regulating bodies (social work, for example). In some rare instances, gross incompetence may be overlooked to protect the professional image from potentially intrusive legal action (medicine is a case in point). In these unusual situations, professional autonomy may interfere with service delivery.

A belief in service to the public and a calling to the field are important in creating a professional value system. Such values are often codified by the professional organization, and these set the standard for professional behavior. In the social service professions, such values usually emphasize the value of human life and personal integrity, the significance of knowledge, judgment, and self-awareness to help others in a professional way, and the equal accessibility of service to all who need it. For example, medicine has its Hippocratic Oath, and social work values emphasize client self-determination, confidentiality, and impartiality. Exhibit 3-2 looks at social work values in some detail.

EXHIBIT 3-2 *Social Work Professional Values*

The following is the Code of Ethics of the National Association of Social Workers (NASW), the social work professional association. Until 1969 only social workers holding the Master of Social Work degree were eligible for membership. In that year a membership category was created for graduates of B.A. social work programs approved (now accredited) by the Council on Social Work Education, reflecting the increasing differential use of manpower in the social welfare professions. This NASW Code of Ethics is a good example of the codification of professional values, although naturally in practice there may be some deviation from such values. At the time of this writing, the Code is being studied and debated and may be modified in the near future.

Social work is based on humanitarian ideals. Professional social workers are dedicated to service for the welfare of mankind; to the disciplined use of a recognized body of knowledge about human beings and their interactions; and to the marshaling of community resources to promote the well-being of all without discrimination.

Social work practice is a public trust that requires of its practitioners integrity, compassion, belief in the dignity and worth of human beings, respect for individual differences, a commitment to service, and a dedication to truth. It requires mastery of a body of knowledge and skill gained through professional education and experience.

Source: Reprinted by permission of the National Association of Social Workers, Washington, D.C.

It requires also recognition of the limitations of present knowledge and skill and of the services we are now equipped to give. The end sought is the performance of a service with integrity and competence.

Each member of the profession carries responsibility to maintain and improve social work service; constantly to examine, use, and increase the knowledge upon which practice and social policy are based; and to develop further the philosophy and skills of the profession.

This Code of Ethics embodies certain standards of behavior for the social worker in his professional relationships with those he serves, with his colleagues, with his employing agency, with other professions, and with the community. In abiding by the code, the social worker views his obligations in as wide a context as the situation requires, takes all of the principles into consideration, and chooses a course of action consistent with the code's spirit and intent.

As a member of the National Association of Social Workers I commit myself to conduct my professional relationships in accord with the code and subscribe to the following statements:

- I regard as my primary obligation the welfare of the individual or group which includes action for improving social conditions.
- I give precedence to my professional responsibility over my personal interests.
- I hold myself responsible for the quality and extent of the service I perform.
- I respect the privacy of the people I serve.
- I use in a responsible manner information gained in professional relationships.
- I treat with respect the findings, views, and actions of colleagues, and use appropriate channels to express judgment on these matters.
- I practice social work within the recognized knowledge and competence of the profession.
- I recognize my professional responsibility to add my ideas and findings to the body of social work knowledge and practice.
- I accept responsibility to help protect the community against unethical practice by an individual or organization engaged in social welfare activities.
- I stand ready to give appropriate professional service in public emergencies.
- I distinguish clearly, in public, between my statements and actions as an individual and as a representative of an organization.
- I support the principle that professional practice requires professional education.
- I accept responsibility for working toward the creation and maintenance of conditions within agencies which enable social workers to conduct themselves in keeping with this code.
- I contribute my knowledge, skills and support to programs of human welfare.
- I will not discriminate because of race, color, religion, age, sex or national ancestry, and in my job capacity will work to prevent and eliminate such discrimination in rendering service, in work assignments and in employment practices.

There are several problems that emerge from the bureaucratization of professional behavior. One is the need for bureaucratic structure versus the need for professional autonomy. A bureaucracy attempts to structure its positions in such a way that authority and responsibility are clearly specified. In this way, the organization has control over the behavior of its members, and intervention points are specified in the event that something goes wrong. This kind of structure automatically creates differences between participants in the organization. Since some have more power than others, there is an implicit or explicit assertion that some are more knowledgeable and skilled than others. This type of structure makes it very difficult to have the sharing between equals that a profession assumes. A profession recognizes that some of its members are more skilled than others, but the assumption is that all are at least minimally skilled, and that a continual process of member communication will serve to increase the skills of all. When professionals are forced to work in a superior-inferior relationship, as happens in many agencies using a supervisor-worker system, there is a real danger that there will be a loss of motivation in workers who have been trained to think autonomously. Barriers to innovation may also be created. This problem often surfaces in settings where one professional group is a minority in relationship to one or more others. John Wax's article exploring social work's power in a medical organization is an excellent example of this issue.[10]

A second problem is the need for bureaucratic structure versus the need for professional flexibility. The use of the profession as a major reference, belief in service to the public, and a sense of calling all demand a commitment to helping others on the basis of their need. Bureaucracies are concerned with specifying who is to receive service and under what circumstances—hours of work, forms to fill out, location of offices, qualifications of staff, allocation of resources, and so on. Stanton's study of the Pangloss Mental Health Association illustrates this problem when it describes a Christmas party for mental hospital inmates that meets bureaucratic needs and rules much more than client needs or desires.[11] The confrontation of bureaucratic rules and professional values is also seen in several major social welfare system problems:

1. *Gaps in service.* An agency sometimes offers only part of the services needed by a client, such as a Catholic Social Service agency that refuses to provide family planning information.
2. *Dividing the client.* In this situation, an agency divides up a client's problems into specialized parts, assigning different workers to deal with each part. Dividing the client and gaps in service can both be handled by referring clients to needed resources, but this requires follow-up to make sure that the referral has been successful. This often does not happen.
3. *Competition for resources.* Each organization seeks to preserve itself, and competes with other agencies for resources. Since each organization is accountable only for its own functioning, there is little encouragement for agencies to cooperate, although outside forces may require that they do so (United Fund drives or legislation mandating such cooperation, for example).

Exhibit 3-3 provides examples of some of these problems.

Battered Freddy **EXHIBIT 3-3**

The following case excerpt is an excellent example of the way in which formal organizations can, in the process of following all the proper procedures, fail in delivering needed services. However, in terms of fulfilling professional values, each was quite ineffective. This case is also a good example of many parts of the social welfare system being brought to bear on a problem, with several social service professions becoming involved. Note the ultimate reliance on the family to mobilize the social service network in a meaningful way, and the final ability of the system to act being based on the societal mandate given to certain professional systems (in this case the police) to forcibly intervene in the family. As the social service worker says, this is a serious decision requiring a great deal of evidence because of its police-state implications, and it illustrates the delicate societal decisions often encountered in social welfare work.

At 17, one year after his parents were arrested for child abuse and he had had the benefit of warm professional care, Freddy was 4 ft. 6 in. and weighed 75 pounds. One of Freddy's doctors said, "I think he can grow to about five feet now, maybe a little more. . . . But it's pretty certain he'll always be stunted."

Before his aunt swore out a warrant for the arrest of Freddy's parents on child abuse charges, Freddy's name slipped in and out of the files of three city agencies, a private organization for retarded children, and the police, all to no avail:

1. A policewoman visited the home and, noting Freddy was small for his age, referred him to a special school at Rosewood State Hospital. "However, there were no vacancies at the time," and contact was ended.
2. Since Freddy was first brought to public school at age 12, he was not allowed to register as a regular student, and was referred to the Department of Education's Psychological Service Division for testing and evaluation. Contact was ended when "the Psychological Services Division was completely unsuccessful in getting the parents to bring Freddy in for an evaluation. . . ."
3. The Psychological Service Division referred Freddy to a public health nurse who noted "that although he was 12 years old, he seemed no more than 5." She made several attempts to get the parents to bring Freddy to the Health Department's diagnostic and evaluation center, which they never did. After more than a year of frustrated attempts to have the boy taken to a doctor, and after an appointment at Johns Hopkins Hospital was broken by the parents, the nurse gave up.
4. The case was referred to the Baltimore Association for Retarded Children. After futile attempts at contact, "The Association notified the Health Department . . . that no progress could be made."
5. Referral was next made to the Department of Social Services. The worker there was allowed to take Freddy to the Department of Education for comprehensive psychological and intelligence testing. They recommended he be placed in a city school for trainable retarded children, but his parents refused to grant their permission. After another broken contact initiated by the parents, the Department of Education closed their file on Freddy. The Health Department did the same since it "had not been able to obtain evidence of physical maltreatment. . . ." This was followed by similar action by the Department of Social Services.
6. The warrant for the arrest of the parents was sworn out by Freddy's aunt.

Regarding this case, the agencies said:

HEALTH DEPARTMENT. "There was never any evidence of physical maltreatment that we could get a handle on. . . . If we sense a case of child neglect, we can only turn it over to Social Services;

Source: Adam Kline, "Battered Freddy's New Chance at Childhood," *Baltimore Sun Magazine,* October 11, 1970, pp. 20ff. Used by permission.

technically it would do no good to notify the school system of truancy, because he was never registered in a school to begin with. If there is any department that could have taken it to Juvenile Court then, it's Social Services, not us."

SOCIAL SERVICES. "A charge of contributing to the delinquency of a minor would be irrelevant. They kept him out of school, sure, but what school would have taken him anyway by the time it was brought to our attention? And not only that, he was almost 16, the age when school attendance becomes optional. If the parents weren't going to cooperate at that point, we felt there was nothing we could do. Look, it seems there was so much happening to the child, but we had no evidence of that; to tell the truth, we had no real evidence of anything other than that the boy was retarded and that they weren't doing anything to help him. The only way we could have found out more is by breaking down their front door, and this isn't a police state, we don't do things like that. The papers said the neighbors seemed to know what was going on, but, damn it, they never told us a thing."

A third consideration is the effects of bureaucratic functioning on the provision of adequate services. It was noted above that bureaucracies tend to develop certain characteristics, many of which can interfere with the provision of services. For example, technicism, trained incapacity and informal organization can all impede bureaucratic functioning under some circumstances. Besides these potential problems, the very structure of a bureaucracy can be a problem:[12]

> *Youths trying to get help from an agency encountered multiple barriers, intended or otherwise. Rigid eligibility requirements that involved filling out long application forms prevented many from starting the process, caused some to give up in the middle, and turned many others away who were determined to be ineligible for service. Being minors away from home prevented many from receiving medical treatment. Being drug-users prevented many from receiving help without risking arrest. Other obstacles blocking agencies' service to street people were the long waits for service, entailing waiting lists and appointments at a future date instead of the date of contact, the extensive records, including extremely personal and sometimes socially damaging information . . . and the . . . cold atmosphere and middle-class appearance of the agency setting.*

Structure is the very nature of bureaucratic functioning—it is what gives it its durability and organization. Yet it also gives it a certain inflexibility and creates something of a barrier between it and those who use it. Especially when dealing with certain client groups, such as the street people described above, or in certain types of emergency or sensitive situations, bureaucratic structure can effectively prevent or distort service.

Finding Ways to Make Professions and Bureaucracies Compatible

Having raised some of the rather serious issues of appropriateness of the bureaucratic form of organization for professional tasks and characteristics, the alternatives need to be explored. The fact that so much of the social system in which the welfare network exists is bureaucratically organized, and given the massive scale at which the social welfare system operates, strong pressures are exerted on both social welfare professions and organizations to embrace bureaucratization. But the problems social welfare bureaucracies have in specifying goals is being increasingly recognized. Without such specification, it is impossible to organize a rational bureaucratic structure. The problems inherent in bureaucracies are also being felt. The social welfare system is today faced with the challenge of finding ways to provide large-scale, complex, specialized services in a more flexible, responsive, and effective manner. Although this search is in its infancy, some exciting possibilities are emerging.

After some years of increasing centralization of planning and services, decentralization is being explored as one means of providing more accessible and less rigid and formal services. Departments of Social Services in some locations are establishing neighborhood branches to decentralize their service. In many communities, food stamps may now be sold in banks and other neighborhood locations rather than just at the Department of Social Services. Recreation programs are dispersing throughout many cities in the attempt to bring them closer to their users. This decentralization seems to hold a great deal of promise, but it is also limited. When highly specialized services are needed—psychological consultation or specialized medical care, for example—it will probably always be necessary to refer a client to a central facility, since the costs of having all services decentralized will probably remain prohibitive. Nevertheless, for the normal kinds of daily services people need, decentralization offers much hope as a way to enable professionals to function in a system that is structured and manageable, but also flexible and accessible.

A second promising experiment is with comprehensive neighborhood service centers that are not necessarily part of a large formal structure (as are the decentralized services discussed above). The free clinic is a model of this kind of organization. Dunbar and Jackson discuss the following characteristics of such facilities: [13]

1. *Trust.* Relations between professionals and users, and between professionals themselves, are characterized by compassion and acceptance regardless of the characteristics of the individual (unkempt hair, etc.) or his problem (drug use, etc.).

2. *Friendliness.* Professionals mingle with users on an informal basis, as well as having a more formal relationship with them. Users are not pressured and are free to make their own choices.
3. *Immediate service.* There are no waiting lists or eligibility requirements, although persons can make appointments if they wish to.
4. *Records.* Records are kept to a minimum in order to avoid labeling, protect users, and to minimize time taken away from working with the individual.
5. *Hours.* Hours are set which are responsive to the needs of the users. This usually means that there are evening hours instead of or in addition to daytime hours.

There are often ties between professional staff and more formally organized agencies, for referral purposes. The comprehensive neighborhood service center usually includes a range of professionals working together to provide as comprehensive a service as possible. They attempt to deal with people's needs as they exist rather than as organizations have planned for them. This tends to maximize professional commitment and self-regulation, and minimize formal structure. It can also lead to a scarcity of resources and lack of mandate by the larger professional and societal communities.

A third attempt to deal with the problems of the professional in the bureaucracy is the use of ombudsmen and indigenous persons. As was seen above, many problems of bureaucratic functioning entail a lack of accessibility, services that are too specialized, and obstacles to professionals operationalizing their commitment to provide service. One approach to these problems is to have a mechanism for users of a service to find out about services and have an advocate when they feel that their needs have not been met. The ombudsman accomplishes this, being a person or agency that reaches out into the community to identify need and help persons effectively use community services. This allows organizations to be as specialized and formal as they need to be and still provides a way for users not to get lost or crushed within them. It does not directly help professionals except that they are reassured that their services are reaching those needing them, and that bureaucratic obstacles are not seriously interfering with service. Indigenous personnel—that is, persons who live in the community being served—operate in a manner somewhat similar to ombudsmen in a social welfare agency. By being members of the community, they have greater knowledge about and access to it than would the typical professional person.

A fourth possibility is to work from within a bureaucratic structure to try to make it more compatible with professional objectives. A recent government report included the following order of priorities in modifying bureaucratic structures to increase agency effectiveness and worker satisfaction:[14]

1. agency goals—clear, common understanding of goals and commitment to them by agency personnel
2. agency policies—common understanding of policies by all personnel
3. communication adequacy—procedures and practices that insure timely transmission of required information to all personnel
4. supervisory practices—actions that enhance the autonomy, initiative, and professional commitment of agency personnel
5. agency-imposed constraints—reduction of excessive and unnecessary administrative controls
6. stability of work environment—avoidance of excessive turbulence within the agency through careful planning and communication of required changes in programs, policies, and personnel, and
7. structure—optimization of complexity and formalization through reduction of administrative levels and increase in supervisory span of control

There appears to be considerable management flexibility in making bureaucratic structures more responsive to the goals and needs of those who work within them. However, it is well known that large-scale organizations tend to generate their own inertia, and one of the problems facing attempts to change bureaucracies from within will be their power to resist such change.

Other strategies for making bureaucracies more responsive to professional and client needs have been proposed. Delbert Taebel has proposed the following, based on the strategy that the less dependent the client is on the bureaucrat, the more responsive the bureaucracy will be.[15]

1. *Political pressure.* Mobilizing professional and client resources to try to bring political pressure on bureaucracies to achieve change. This tactic has been used in a variety of ways, including sit-ins, nonviolent protests, lobbying, the creation of the National Welfare Rights Organization, and unionizing social welfare workers.
2. *Developing competitive structures.* To the extent that the social welfare service delivery system is a monopoly, this is a difficult strategy to pursue, although free clinics may be one possibility.
3. *Positive input.* Having professional and client groups support the useful aspects of the bureaucracy, building good will within the structure for use when there are grievances against it.
4. *Self-help programs.* A strategy for developing competitive structures as well as fostering autonomy and self-help. This is limited by lack of

resources and expertise, but might be made possible by obtaining grant monies and using volunteer professional assistance.

5. *Boycotting or overloading the system.* Boycotting the service delivery system is difficult because people usually are dependent on it for their basic needs. Overloading the system—that is, having everyone eligible request everything for which they are eligible—has been used as a successful strategy to force an organization to respond to the needs of professionals and clients. These strategies are perhaps more difficult to implement than earlier ones mentioned, but are nevertheless potential tools for change.

None of the attempts to overcome the limitations of bureaucracies discussed above completely solves the problems noted. Even in using these possible strategies, however, it is wise to exercise care in mounting too great an assault against bureaucracies. In spite of the problems that have been noted, the bureaucracy gives some semblance of order and objectivity to the massive, fragmented social welfare system, and gives it some strength relative to competing societal structures. Yet at the same time it can block the humane attainment of social welfare goals and in so doing erode professional motivation and performance. This leads to what can be called the professional's dilemma.

There are some fundamental decisions the professional must make in trying to reach a personal solution to structural conflict. The first is deciding how much of one's responsibility is to the agency for which one works and how much is to the clients one serves. If the balance of one's commitment is to the agency, then there will be a tendency to follow established agency rules rather than challenging those rules when they interfere with attempts to provide service to clients. For example, once when working with an unmarried mother, it seemed appropriate to have contact with the father of the child, who had been uncooperative in all previous attempts to meet with him. Since he worked at a job where he was paid by the hour, he was understandably reluctant to come to the office during the agency's hours, since they coincided with his work hours. The impasse was finally broken by arranging an appointment after agency hours, but this was against agency policy and required some considerable negotiation and special arrangements within the agency. Such agency rule-bending naturally carries risks, since bureaucracies tend to invest considerable normative value in their rules. The risks will be worth assuming only if service to the client is the primary consideration in a particular situation.

A related decision involves the extent of one's identification with an agency's goals compared to identifying with professional goals. When agency goals are dominant, there will usually be more willingness to follow agency procedures rather than adopting a more flexible approach to problems growing out of professional values and skills. For example, when working in a Catholic agency, in which it was against agency policy to discuss birth control with clients, a social worker had to deal with a woman having personal, marital, and child-rearing problems, and who was frightened of becoming pregnant again. Professional judgment suggested that birth control was an appropriate part of the helping relationship, at least until the other problems could be resolved, but agency policy forbade it. In this situation, the woman's own ambivalence about birth control was substantial, given that fact that she was Catholic, but it appeared that she was seeking some support to confront this issue in a way that would still enable her to maintain a healthy image of herself. Ultimately a discussion about planning and developing a plan for birth control did occur, but again, there were considerable agency repercussions.

A third decision involves the willingness to inconvenience oneself if necessary to help others. A desire to keep one's professional commitment within clearly delimited boundaries tends to make the order, predictability, and limited range of activities of the bureaucracy more appealing. A final decision relates to the commitment to follow social norms versus a belief in the appropriateness of norm violation when necessary. Adherence to the established social norms tends to make it more likely that the bureaucracy's inherently conservative qualities will be accepted.

Clearly these four decisions are related, and have related consequences. The professional who generally accepts the limits defined by the bureaucracy will tend to resist any information or pressures that suggest his or her work is ineffective. To the extent that such pressures exist, the worker may be tempted to minimize professional identification; or, if the pressures are great enough, the professional may resolve the problem by retreating into apathy or simply leaving the field. Decisions made favoring professional values and commitment are likely to generate substantial frustration with bureaucratic limitations. These frustrations can lead to frequent job changes in the search for a more acceptable structure, cynical exploitation of the bureaucratic structure to attain one's professional goals, or direct confrontation with the bureaucratic structure. Such confrontation can take many forms—personal actions, such as complaints or suggestions for more appropriate bureaucratic regulations; group actions, such as strikes, petitions, or informal organizations to counteract the bureaucratic structure; or group organization, as in the mobilization of consumer power to intervene in the agency structure, in political action, or in conjunction with other professional groups.

The ways in which the professional's dilemma can be solved are many and varied. Some are consistent with professional values, while others are closer to bureaucratic rules. Some are conservative, and others are more radical. Some involve quiet, personal thoughts; others include involvement in turbulent political and organizational activities. Which are selected comes down to a very personal decision based on one's financial and personal needs. Exhibit 3-4 illustrates how one doctor dealt with his dilemma.

There are no best solutions; there are only those that each person can personally devise and accept. Finding acceptable solutions is difficult and their impact will only be known when actually on the job. However, early recognition of the interaction between societal, bureaucratic, and professional values will foster a mature approach to the fundamental value and organizational issues that underlie the contemporary social welfare institution in American society.

EXHIBIT 3-4 *One Man's Solution*

The following story illustrates how each professional must accept responsibility for his own professional dilemmas, and how the creative professional can find solutions that are professionally sound, personally satisfying, and helpful to clients.

Dr. Richard E. Palmer, chairman of the American Medical Association's board of trustees, said recently that physicians were not trying hard enough to reduce medical costs.

One physician, perhaps the most unusual in the country, whom Palmer was not referring to is Dr. Richard Grayson, an internist who practices medicine in St. Charles, Ill., a town of some 10,000 people, 35 miles west of Chicago.

Dr. Grayson tells all his patients that if they judge the bills he sends them to be out-of-line, they can reduce them as they wish.

The Grayson method is to enclose with each monthly bill a [signed] note which reads: "My fee schedule is based upon standard medical practice in this area. However, for retired persons on limited pensions, or any others whose circumstances are difficult due to extensive illness, unemployment, or for any other reasons, I will reduce my fees."

"Under these circumstances," the note continues, "I suggest a 25 percent reduction, but more or less may be appropriate to your situation. No discussion is necessary—simply write the amount of reduction you choose on the statement with your remittance."

Dr. Grayson, 49, has been using this technique since 1969 when he read an article in *Medical Economics*. Recently he was publicized in *AMA Update*, the newsletter published by the American Medical Association, and reports, "I'm taking quite a bit of kidding from my colleagues. They're offering to send me all their poor-paying patients."

According to Grayson, "Money—or the lack of it—is the cause of emotional stress in some families these days. Emotional distress often leads to ulcers and other physical ailments. I see plenty of ulcer patients already; and I'd just as soon that my bills did not create more."

Grayson says that only 2 or 3 percent of his patients reduce the bills he sends out and that only one, a young father who had just lost his job, ever asked him to write off the bill.

Grayson modestly insists that he is neither altruist nor philanthropist. "I feel," he explains, "that arguments with patients about bills can interfere with my emotions for hours. It can stimulate all sorts of stress, and who needs that? Neither I nor the patient."

A rare physician, Dr. Richard Grayson. Are there many more like him?

Source: Parade Magazine, September 15, 1974, p. 21. Used by permission of Parade Magazine, Inc.

Accountability and Effectiveness in Social Welfare

The common theme unifying this discussion of the organization of social welfare services has been the effectiveness of those programs (see Exhibit 2-5, which assessed the impact of Economic Opportunity Act programs). As the system grows in size and complexity, the need for resources also increases. Because resources always involve policy decisions based on priorities, the social welfare system is increasingly being asked to prove its effectiveness and efficiency, thereby justifying the allocation of further resources to it. As Newman and Turem note, "Efficiency involves weighing alternatives against costs."[16] However, they further explain that "efficiency . . . does not mean that what is done is done for the lowest cost but that the ends achieved cannot be brought about in another way or an even lower cost."[17] These authors go on to assert that "the current crisis in social services is a crisis of credibility based on an inadequate system of accountability. Social programs are in trouble because they focus on processes and not results."[18] This assertion goes to the very heart of formal organizations—they can only be effective if they can specify their goals and the means to be used to achieve these goals. One of the persisting problems of social welfare organizations, and one that is being seriously attacked today, is their inability to specify exactly what actions will yield what results.

The whole question of accountability has created anxiety and resentment among many social welfare professionals. Indeed, Rosenberg and Brody entitled an article "The Threat or Challenge of Accountability."[19] In the attempt to meet criticisms raised against the social welfare service delivery system, management by objectives has become popular (often referred to as MBO). The fear that accountability and MBO raise in the minds of many social welfare professionals is that the search for proof of efficiency and effectiveness will yield a service delivery system that is arbitrary in its definitions of what services will be provided and limited in its perspective on human needs. This is a realistic fear. There have already been numerous examples of programs that, in their effort to prove themselves both efficient and effective, have focused only on users who showed the most potential for success and services that could be easily measured or counted—number who got jobs, number of housing units rehabilitated, number of children enrolled in school, and so forth. These programs may indeed have been very successful in performing such tasks, but one of the enduring problems of a social welfare system is to help those least able to understand and use services and to deal with those complexities of human functioning and need that are not so easily measured or so rapidly accomplished—curing mental illness, improving self-acceptance and feelings of self-worth, improving child-rearing values and behaviors, coping with permanent and total disability, and providing meaningful life patterns for the isolated aged, among others.

A hidden factor in issues of accountability is the impact of values. Decisions about criteria to use in determining successful service delivery reflect value judgments of what is important and how it can be measured. If success is defined as a closed case rather than as people improving their resources, a value judgment is being made about *what* is more important. When professional people themselves decide about the adequacy of a given service and end intervention on that basis rather than according to the user's perceptions, a value judgment is made about *how* to determine service adequacy and accountability. Exhibit 3-5 illustrates the impact of values on what and how accountability is determined. In evaluating effectiveness of services to American Indian families, removing the child is seen by the service delivery network as successful intervention (the how), and the number of children so removed as an indicator of success (the what). Therefore, from the service delivery network's point of view, these services are successful, even though the Indian children and families may evaluate them quite differently. Only if the users of services are the ultimate evaluators of services can this situation be changed, but this method is itself value-related. Service users will not be involved in evaluation and accountability procedures if they are seen as ignorant, demanding, or strange. When the diversity of human experiences is recognized and valued, accountability may take on new meaning in social welfare.

EXHIBIT 3-5 *American Indian Child Removal*

The following account of child removal practices with American Indian families raises a number of questions about values and their impact on service delivery. However, it is also a good illustration of how questions of accountability may be seen very differently by professional helpers and those they serve. After reading these excerpts, to whom do you think professionals are ultimately accountable: funding sources, the profession's values, or consumers? Why? How are value conflicts to be resolved?

Surveys of states with large Indian populations conducted by the Association on American Indian Affairs (AAIA) in 1969 and again in 1974 indicate that approximately 25–35 percent of all Indian children are separated from their families and placed in foster homes, adoptive homes, or worse . . . The disparity in placement rates for Indians and non-Indians is shocking. In Minnesota, Indian children are placed in foster care or in adoptive homes at a per capita rate five times greater than non-Indian children. In Montana, the ratio of Indian foster care placement is at least 13 times greater . . . In Wisconsin, the risk run by Indian children of being separated from their parents is nearly 1600 percent greater than it is for non-Indian children.

The Federal boarding school and dormitory programs also contribute to the destruction of Indian and community life. The Bureau of Indian Affairs (BIA), in its school census for 1971, indicates that 34,538 children live in its institutional facilities rather than at home. . . .

In addition to the trauma of separation from their families, most Indian children in placement

---

Source: Excerpted from William Byler, "Removing Children," *Civil Rights Digest,* Summer, 1977, pp. 19–24.

or in institutions have to cope with the problems of adjusting to a social and cultural environment much different from their own. In 16 states surveyed in 1969, approximately 85 percent of all Indian children in foster care were living in non-Indian homes. In Minnesota today, according to State figures, more than 90 percent of non-related adoptions of Indian children are made by non-Indian couples. Few states keep as careful or complete child welfare statistics as Minnesota does, but informed estimates by welfare officials elsewhere suggest that this rate is the norm. In most Federal and mission boarding schools, a majority of the personnel is non-Indian.

It is clear then that the Indian child welfare crisis is of massive proportions and that Indian families face vastly greater risks of involuntary separation than are typical of our society as a whole. . . .

In judging the fitness of a particular family, many social workers, ignorant of Indian cultural values and social norms, make decisions that are wholly inappropriate in the context of Indian family life and so they frequently discover neglect or abandonment where none exists.

For example, the dynamics of Indian extended families are largely misunderstood. An Indian child may have scores of, perhaps more than a hundred, relatives who are counted as close, responsible members of the family. Many social workers, untutored in the ways of Indian family life or assuming them to be socially irresponsible, consider leaving the child with persons outside the nuclear family as neglect and thus as grounds for terminating parental rights.

In the DeCoteau case, the South Dakota Department of Public Welfare petitioned a State court to terminate the rights of a Sisseton-Wahpeton Sioux mother to one of her two children on the grounds that he was sometimes left with his 69-year-old great-grandmother. In response to questioning by the attorney who represented the mother, the social worker admitted that Mrs. DeCoteau's 4-year-old son, John, was well cared for, but added that the great-grandmother "is worried at times."

Because in some communities the social workers have, in a sense, become a part of the extended family, parents will sometimes turn to the welfare department for temporary care of their children, failing to realize that their action is perceived quite differently by non-Indians.

Indian child-rearing practices are also misinterpreted in evaluating a child's behavior and parental concern. It may appear that the child is running wild and that the parents do not care. What is labelled "permissiveness" may often, in fact, simply be a different but effective way of disciplining children. BIA boarding schools are full of children with such spurious "behavioral problems."

Poverty, poor housing, lack of modern plumbing, and overcrowding are often cited by social workers as proof of parental neglect and are used as grounds for beginning custody proceedings. In a recent California case, the State tried to apply poverty as a standard against a Rosebud Sioux mother and child. At the mother's bidding, the child's aunt took 3-year-old Blossom Lavone from the Rosebud Reservation in South Dakota to California. The mother was to follow. By the time she arrived one week later, the child had been placed in a pre-adoptive home by California social workers. The social workers asserted that, although they had no evidence that the mother was unfit, it was their belief that an Indian reservation is an unsuitable environment for a child and that the pre-adoptive parents were financially able to provide a home and a way of life superior to the one furnished by the natural mother. Counsel was successful in returning the child to her mother.

Ironically, tribes that were forced into reservations at gun-point and prohibited from leaving without a permit are now being told that they live in a place unfit for raising their children.

One of the grounds most frequently advanced for taking Indian children from their parents is the abuse of alcohol. However, this standard is applied unequally. In areas where rates of problem drinking among Indians and non-Indians are the same, it is rarely applied against non-Indian parents. Once again cultural biases frequently affect decisionmaking. The late Dr. Edward P. Dozier of Santa Clara Pueblo and other observers have argued that there are important cultural differences in the use of alcohol. Yet, by and large, non-Indian social workers draw conclusions about the meaning of acts or conduct in ignorance of these distinctions. . . .

The decision to take Indian children from their natural homes is, in most cases, carried out without due process of law. For example, it is rare for either Indian children or their parents to be represented by counsel or to have the supporting testimony of expert witnesses.

Many cases do not go through an adjudicatory process at all, since the voluntary waiver of parental rights is a device widely employed by social workers to gain custody of children. Because of the availability of the waiver and because a great number of Indian parents depend on welfare payments for survival, they are exposed to the sometimes coercive arguments of welfare departments. In a current South Dakota entrapment case, an Indian parent in a time of trouble was persuaded to sign a waiver granting temporary custody to the State, only to find that this is now being advanced as evidence of neglect and grounds for the permanent termination of parental rights. It is an unfortunate fact of life for many Indian parents that the primary service agency to which they must turn for financial help also exercises police powers over their family life and is, most frequently, the agency that initiates custody proceedings.

The conflict between Indian and non-Indian social systems operates to defeat due process. The extended family provides an example. By sharing the responsibility of child-rearing, the extended family tends to strengthen the community's commitment to the child. At the same time, however, it diminishes the possibility that the nuclear family will be able to mobilize itself quickly enough when an outside agency acts to assume custody. Because it is not unusual for Indian children to spend considerable time away with other relatives, there is no immediate realization of what is happening—possibly not until the opportunity for due process has slipped away.

There are the simple abductions. Benita Rowland was taken by two Wisconsin women with the collusion of a local missionary after her Oglala Sioux mother was tricked into signing a form purportedly granting them permission to take the child on a short visit, but in fact, agreeing to her adoption. It was months before Mrs. Rowland could obtain counsel and regain her daughter.

It appears that custody proceedings against Indian people are also sometimes begun, not to rescue the children from dangerous circumstances, but to punish parents and children unjustly for conduct that is disapproved of. In a recent Nevada case, a Paiute mother had to go to court to recover her children following her arrest for a motor-vehicle violation. Parents of Nevada's Duckwater Band of Paiutes were threatened with the loss of their children when they sought to open their own school under an approved Federal grant and refused to send their children to a county-run school.

A few years ago, South Dakota tried to send an Oglala Sioux child to a State training school simply because she changed boarding schools twice in two months. In a report sent to us by a Minnesota social worker, she unashamedly recounts threatening her Indian client with the loss of her children if she is "indiscreet."

And it can be so casual—sometimes just a telephone call from an attorney or even the mere rumor that there is an attorney in the offing is enough to persuade a welfare department to drop the case. Sometimes it can be desperate. Ivan Brown was saved because the sheriff, the social worker, and the prospective foster parent fled when the tribal chairman ran to get a camera to photograph their efforts to wrest the child from his Indian guardian's arms.

In some instances, financial considerations contribute to the crisis. For example, agencies established to place children have an incentive to find children to place. In towns with large Federal boarding facilities, merchants may fight to prevent their closing. Not long ago, in response to political intervention, one boarding school in the Great Plains was being phased out as unnecessary because the children could do better at home. The merchants complained and, again as a result of political pressure, the full school enrollment was restored. Very recently merchants protested the proposed closing of Intermountain School with its large Navajo enrollment, despite the fact the closing was advocated by the Navajo tribe.

The contemporary thrust toward efficiency and effectiveness is good. If social welfare professionals seek to improve social functioning and minimize suffering, they must have some techniques to measure whether or not their actions are accomplishing these goals. If they are not, they must find new ways to try to deal with people's needs. With limited resources available to the social welfare system, it is a professional obligation to use these resources in the most effective manner. The accusation that there has been too much emphasis on process rather than results—that is, how many persons were counseled rather than how many persons that were counseled received some measurable benefit from such counseling—is a valid one, and will be explored in more detail later when looking at social work interventive methods. Yet the fact remains that it is very difficult to measure effectiveness in many cases, and more efficient alternatives are often unknown.

In the short run, social welfare systems must help society to understand the complexity of the human problems with which they must deal humanely and comprehensively, and resist pressures to reduce people and their problems to the most easily tabulated numbers. In the long run, the dictates of professional values as well as the very realistic pressures of funding and societal values make it imperative that social welfare professionals use all of their theoretical and research capabilities to find demonstrably more effective ways of utilizing societal resources to meet human need.

The examination of the organization of social welfare services already undertaken is one part of the search for more effective and efficient services, because the structure of services is a very important part of their success or failure. The knowledge upon which social welfare services are based, to be discussed in following chapters, is also an essential part of this effort—there simply is no place in our complex social welfare system for ignorant social welfare practitioners, no matter how sensitive and concerned they may be. But a third part of the search for greater effectiveness and efficiency is the development of meaningful criteria to use in evaluating social welfare services. How can we know if a service is meeting the needs of those it is trying to service? How can we know if all of those who need the service are receiving it? How can we know whether services are equitable? These are some of the issues involved in the evaluation of social welfare services, and to which we now turn.

Evaluating Social Welfare Programs ◀

Winnifred Bell has developed eight criteria helpful in evaluating the effectiveness of social welfare programs, whether public or private.[20] The greater visibility of the policy-making process in public programs makes it easier to apply Bell's criteria to such programs, but any program can be evaluated using these criteria.

Objectives. These are the purposes of the program as formally stated. A program may be successful in attaining these objectives, it may be partially successful, it may attain other objectives not planned for, or it may simply be unsuccessful. While the stated objectives guide one's evaluation of a program, the attainment of unanticipated objectives should be included in the evaluation of a program. In some cases they may be as important as the originally intended objectives.

Legislative authorization. This will normally be applicable only to public programs. Considering legislative authorization helps to relate programs to others created at the same time, as well as establishing a historical perspective for such programs. When programs fail, it is often because legislation did not build-in adequate implementation procedures. Exhibit 2-5, on the War on Poverty (in Chapter 2), is an example of this problem.

Source of funding. Funding is crucial to program implementation. In public funding, there is sometimes a distinction between legislation and the appropriation of funds to carry out the legislated program—both the authorizing legislation and the appropriations legislation are necessary for a functional program. Private funding may also have the duality of an agency recognizing a need for a program, but not having adequate resources to implement it.

Administrative structure. We explored, earlier in this chapter, the several ways in which administrative structure can influence program effectiveness. Such structural considerations include the internal functioning of an organization (specified goals and means, structural problems such as technicism, and the like), and the relationships between several organizations which may be involved in a program (cooperation between the Department of Agriculture and local departments of social services that operate Food Stamp programs, for example). The systems nature of social welfare is also significant in administrative structure. A program can be greatly helped or seriously hindered, depending on whether its structure provides for meaningful system ties. For example, when the Office of Economic Opportunity was created, it had strong presidential backing and the authority to initiate action in many parts of the social welfare system. In its last days, it had virtually no support and little power to gain the cooperation of other parts of the system.

Eligibility requirements. These determine who is eligible to participate in a program. If a program is institutional in scope, need is the only criterion for eligibility. The more residual a program is, the more stringent the eligibility requirements are likely to be, as was illustrated in the earlier comparison between the AFDC and SSI programs.

Coverage. Eligibility requirements establish the boundaries of the potential client population, while coverage refers to the number of those eligible who actually participate in the program. It is a good measure of the program's effectiveness in reaching the target population, and it is frequently the case that more people are eligible for a program than actually receive benefits.

Adequacy. Adequacy is a measure of the program's effectiveness in meeting the need of the target population. Sometimes programs are planned to meet only a percentage of the estimated total need, hoping to encourage self-help and to spread scarce resources as far as possible. However, the result is often a residue of unmet need, making the program inadequate in attaining its ultimate goal of need satisfaction. Many states, for example, pay AFDC recipients less than the budget calculated as necessary to meet minimum survival needs. Whereas some AFDC recipients are successful in finding some other source of help, many are not, with the unmet need being reflected in lead paint poisoning of desperately hungry children, and pregnant women suffering from malnutrition.

Equity. Whereas coverage is a measure of the actual population served by a program, equity measures the degree to which a program discriminates between categories of persons who qualify for coverage. One of the accusations against Social Security is that it is not equitable in its treatment of working married women, since they cannot receive separate Social Security payments upon retirement in spite of the fact that they made separate payments during their working years. Instead, they receive a payment tied to their husband's benefits, and this is less than they would receive if they collected their benefits independently (see Exhibit 2-2, the section on Women's Issues).

Exhibit 3-6 presents comparative data for Medicaid and Medicare. It is suggested that you take some time to use the above evaluative criteria to look at these two programs and try to evaluate their effectiveness. On the basis of your analysis, what changes do you think should be made? You might want to then compare your ideas with the material in Exhibit 1-9 (pp. 39–45), which presents data on cross-cultural social welfare programs. Looking at the ways in which other societies attempt to meet the needs of their citizens can be very instructive for our own society. Notice, however, that all societies face the same issue—what are the priorities in the allocation of social resources? When looking at Exhibit 3-6, you should also be alert to how it illustrates the differences between an insurance and a grant-in-aid program. Notice in particular how funding, administration, coverage, adequacy, and equity are affected.

EXHIBIT 3-6 *Medicare and Medicaid Compared*

The comparison of Medicare and Medicaid following is taken from an HEW pamphlet. It provides a concise listing of the differences between these two federal social welfare programs.

	MEDICARE	MEDICAID
Objectives	Providing protection from financial need caused by medical-care costs	Providing protection from financial need caused by medical-care costs
Legislative Authorization	Social Security Act—Title 18	Social Security Act—Title 19
Funding	As insurance program: MEDICARE HOSPITAL INSURANCE is financed by a separate payroll contribution (part of the regular Social Security withholding). MEDICARE MEDICAL INSURANCE is financed by monthly premiums. The federal government pays half and the insured person pays half. These monthly premiums now are: $5.80 from the federal government for each insured person; $5.80 from each insured person. MEDICAID can pay this $5.80 for those who qualify for MEDICAID coverage.	A grant program: MEDICAID is financed by federal and state governments. The federal government contributes from 50 percent (to the richest states) to 83 percent (to the state with the lowest per-capita income) of medical care costs for needy and low-income people who are aged, blind, disabled, under 21, or members of families with dependent children. Money is obtained from federal, state, and local taxes. States pay the remainder, usually with help from local governments
Administration	MEDICARE is run by the federal government. MEDICARE is the same all over the United States. The Bureau of Health Insurance of the Social Security Administration of the United States Department of Health, Education, and Welfare is responsible for MEDICARE.	MEDICAID is run by state governments within federal guidelines. MEDICAID varies from state to state. The Medical Services Administration of the Social and Rehabilitation Service of the United States Department of Health, Education, and Welfare is responsible for the *federal aspects* of MEDICAID.
Eligibility	MEDICARE is for people 65 or older. Almost everybody 65 or older—rich or poor—can have MEDICARE. Some people 65 or older can have both MEDICARE and MEDICAID.	MEDICAID is for *certain kinds* of needy and low-income people: ▶ the aged (65 or older) ▶ the blind ▶ the disabled ▶ the members of families with dependent children ▶ some other children Some states also include (at state expense) other needy and low-income people.

Source: "Medicaid, Medicare—Which Is Which?", Department of Health, Education, and Welfare (Washington, D.C.: U.S. Government Printing Office, July 1972).

	MEDICARE	MEDICAID
Coverage	MEDICARE paid medical bills last year for over 10 million people. HOSPITAL INSURANCE protected 20.3 million people. 19.8 million people were signed up for MEDICAL INSURANCE. This means that almost 10 percent of all the people in the United States have the protection of MEDICARE. MEDICARE is available everywhere in the United States.	MEDICAID paid medical bills last year for more than 18 million people who were aged, blind, disabled, under 21, or members of families with dependent children. In addition, some states paid medical bills for low-income people *not* aged, blind, disabled, under 21, or members of families with dependent children.
Adequacy	MEDICARE pays part—but not all—of hospital and medical costs for people who are insured. HOSPITAL INSURANCE pays inpatient hospital bills *except* for the first $68 in each benefit period. MEDICAL INSURANCE pays $4 out of each $5 of reasonable medical costs *except* for the first $50 in each calendar year—does not pay any of the first $50. MEDICARE HOSPITAL INSURANCE provides basic protection against costs of: ▶ inpatient hospital care ▶ post-hospital extended care ▶ post-hospital home care ▶ health care MEDICARE MEDICAL INSURANCE provides supplemental protection against costs of physicians' services, medical services and supplies, home health-care services, outpatient hospital services and therapy, and other services.	MEDICAID can pay what MEDICARE does not pay for people who are eligible for both programs. MEDICAID can pay the $68 MEDICARE does not pay in each benefit period for eligible people. MEDICAID can pay the first $50 per year of medical care costs and can pay what MEDICARE does not pay of the remaining reasonable charges for eligible people. MEDICAID pays for at least these services: ▶ inpatient hospital care ▶ outpatient hospital services ▶ other laboratory and x-ray services ▶ skilled nursing home services ▶ physicians' services ▶ screening, diagnosis, and treatment of children ▶ home health care services In many states MEDICAID pays for such additional services as dental care, prescribed drugs, eye glasses, clinic services, intermediate care facility services, and other diagnostic, screening, preventive, and rehabilitative services.
Equity	Tied to Social Security which has not achieved universal coverage and tends to be least likely to cover the unskilled, transient worker. Is available only to those 65 or older. While hospital insurance is automatic for those covered by Social Security, medical insurance is optional and requires an additional payment.	Does not apply in two states, and benefits are not the same in all states having programs. Tied to receipt of public assistance or Supplemental Security Income—public assistance is known to have incomplete coverage within the eligible population and to discourage participation through restrictive eligibility requirements and demeaning application procedures.

There is one additional criterion that can be used to evaluate social welfare programs, namely the degree to which user participation is involved. Participation can occur on at least two levels. The first is participation in planning, something which is rarely done. Since bureaucracies have specialized tasks organized into a rational, hierarchical structure, it is difficult for users of the services to have input into that structure. Decision-making processes that determine what those services will be and how they will be provided are usually not directly accessible to users. Bureaucracies that operate within a market system are presumed to permit user feedback through their decisions to use or not use the service offered. However, many social welfare service areas are not provided in a market system. If recipients of public assistance are unhappy with the amount of their benefits or the procedures governing the distribution of them, their alternative is usually no assistance rather than assistance from another source. It is for this reason that social welfare services have been called a monopoly. In Reid's words, "There is no market relationship between their producers and their primary consumers."[21]

In enumerating the problems that tend to result when social welfare services are provided in a monopolistic manner, Reid has pointed out the following concepts:[22]

1. Organizations not accountable to consumers often define service goals vaguely or not at all. When the goals are unclear the means to attain them cannot be precisely defined and often change.
2. Lacking accountability to consumers, organizations may allocate energy and resources in a way that is not consistent with the needs of service users. Since the organization is presumed to be worth preserving, it spends an inordinate amount of energy preserving itself rather than serving its users.
3. Clients (users) tend to be defined as irresponsible. With the emphasis of the organization so clearly internal, demands of users are seen as threats to the organization's goals, and therefore tend to be resisted. One way to do this is to rationalize user demands as irresponsible.
4. Workers get caught between their professional values, client demands, and organizational structure, becoming alienated from the agency and seen as adversaries by clients.

Reid goes on to suggest some strategies for the reform of the social welfare monopoly.[23] The first is to strengthen the influence of professionals within the organization and in service planning contexts. This runs into one of the problems with professions themselves. It was noted earlier that they are built on a specialized knowledge base, and are characterized by professional autonomy and self-regulation. This can result in professionals being detached from the people they serve, since by definition users lack the specialized knowledge with which to evaluate the service they are receiving from the professional. This potential for professional isolation from its users can serve to reinforce the monopolistic tendencies within social welfare delivery systems. A second strategy involves the development of countervailing power, that is, developing power structures that clients can use to have an impact on social welfare delivery systems. An example would be the National Welfare Rights Organization. There are obvious problems in the development of countervailing power. Users run the risk that they will be excluded from the services they may desperately need, and there are frequently inadequate educational and financial resources with which to develop viable countervailing power structures. An additional problem in the use of this strategy is the possibility that clients may use their power unwisely in terms of selecting services. However, as in all aspects of the helping situation, sometimes the right to assume responsibility for one's own life entails making mistakes as part of the growth process.[24]

The last strategy discussed by Reid is that of creating competing services, thereby allowing users to have an impact on the service delivery system by selecting the services they feel are most helpful. This would most directly strike at the monopolistic character of the social welfare delivery system. It could be operationalized through a system of vouchers that clients could use in whatever agency they wished. Since any agency, public or private, must at some point justify its existence in order to obtain resources, lack of selection by users would presumably seriously undermine an agency's ability to justify itself. This strategy would require that there be a meaningful choice of services for each need, so that someone needing income maintenance would be able to select from two or more agencies. This could result in a proliferation of agencies, and raises interesting possibilities for the use of advertising by social welfare agencies in order to attract users. Were this to be the case, the problems an uninformed consumer has in selecting wisely among alternative and highly advertised commercial products could invade the social welfare field. Obviously any strategy to reduce the disadvantages of a monopolistic social welfare delivery system will have its own set of problems and disadvantages, but they are worth thinking about in the quest for more efficient and effective services.

Different types of strategies for increasing the input of users into the services that so greatly affect their lives may be found in practices of other societies. Perlmutter, talking about Yugoslavia, notes that "the central organizing principle of its society is one of citizen participation or self-management within a highly decentralized structure."[25] An individual lives in a commune, which is "not merely a political unit, but a social-economic political community in which the citizen is represented both as an individual and as a worker."[26] Social welfare needs are met in such communities along with a range of other daily needs. There are managing bodies in these units which are "formed to include three constituencies: (1) users of the services; (2) the organizations providing the services; and (3) work-organization representatives. . . . Accessibility and participation are the guiding principles. Therefore the size, location, and even quality of service are designed to meet these objectives, even if this brings about a less professional program."[27] Professionals have their major impact in setting program standards, but citizens at the local level decide on the actual programs.

A similar approach is used in China, where there has also been decentralization and broad planning at the level of the central government. Local communities, however, choose the specific methods for implementing these planning decisions.[28] In addition, the principles of "self-reliance, mutual help, serving the people, and learning by doing" are basic to the culture, and they encourage a wide range of citizen participation.[29] For example, in talking about medical care in China, Sidel describes the system as follows:[30]

> *Since the Cultural Revolution many paraprofessionals have been trained to help give medical care and be a bridge between the general population and the medical professions. In the rural areas "barefoot doctors" have been trained in immunization, health education, and the treatment of minor illnesses. Barefoot doctors are peasants who receive approximately three to six months formal training and then work half time as agricultural workers and half time as medical workers; they are paid as full time agricultural workers. "Red Guard doctors," usually housewives, are the urban counterparts of the barefoot doctors, but are generally unpaid and work in neighborhood health centers under the supervision of fully trained physicians after only ten days' training. . . . The "worker-doctor" with one to three months' training works half time as a medical worker in his factory. Both in cities and rural areas "health workers" have been trained by and are directly responsible to barefoot doctors or Red Guard doctors. . . . All four categories of paraprofessional health personnel—barefoot doctors, Red Guard doctors, worker-doctors, and health workers—incorporate social service functions into their medical work.*

In such a system, there is no longer the wide gulf separating social welfare services from their users. Services are integrated into the fabric of life and are performed by many types of citizens, ranging from highly skilled professionals to minimally trained but professionally supervised paraprofessionals. The questions of social service monopolies, bureaucratic rigidities, and professional privileges fade in importance in such systems. The emphasis is on citizens helping citizens in a wide variety of ways and in a wide variety of contexts, but always so that they are meaningful to users and providers alike.

These cross-cultural examples lead into the second type of citizen participation, helping in the actual delivery of services. The Chinese approach obviously involves citizens in both the planning and delivery of services. In the United States, citizen participation in planning has been quite limited. The War on Poverty created by the Economic Opportunity Act attempted to generate "maximum feasible participation of the poor" in the planning and, to some extent, the carrying out of social welfare programs.[31] The demise of the Office of Economic Opportunity has reduced the thrust toward such participation, although there is still some level of citizen involvement in some social work programs and local educational planning. The picture is more optimistic in terms of citizen participation in the delivery of services, due to a new interest in the use of volunteers. In comparison with the kind of citizen participation existing in China, the use of volunteers in social welfare programs in this country offers rather limited opportunities, but is nevertheless an attempt to involve citizens in the social welfare system in a participatory manner.

The involvement of citizens in service delivery can have several benefits. In a large, specialized, industrialized society it is very difficult for different groups to have a realistic sense of the problems faced by members of other groups. Particularly in times of prosperity, it is difficult to understand that there may be pockets of poverty and social need. Members of majority groups may have trouble understanding that various kinds of discrimination occur, and they may only dimly perceive the effects of such practices. The sheer size and anonymity of the society make it very easy to lose touch with other people, and to lose a feeling of responsibility for what happens to other members of the society. Being a volunteer can provide the direct exposure to people and their needs which makes a citizen more understanding, empathetic, and willing to help. Volunteers can also help give programs a local flavor, so that users of services face friends and neighbors rather than what are considered to be faceless bureaucrats. This can be very useful in humanizing large, sterile bureaucratic environments, making the users of services more willing to cooperate in the helping process. Finally, volunteers can help to stretch resources. The realities of contemporary American society make it unlikely that adequate resources will ever be allocated to make it possible to eliminate need. Indeed, in most programs there are barely adequate resources to attain designated assistance levels, even though these normally fall far short of providing adequate assistance. Volunteers can be a way for programs to increase the personnel available to provide service, extending the type of service available and freeing more highly skilled professionals to do what they do best.

With all of its benefits, volunteerism as currently practiced in the United States is limited in effectiveness. It is not totally integrated into the service delivery system as is the case in China. It has not been conceptualized and organized in such a way that there is a comprehensive network of volunteers and paraprofessionals which feeds into professional helping contexts. Some agencies use volunteers more extensively and effectively than others, and there is evidence that sometimes volunteers are relatively ineffective and even manipulated by agencies for rather devious purposes.[32] In spite of these problems, volunteerism remains a viable and valuable way for citizens, users and nonusers alike, to participate in the important work of the social welfare institution. Returning to our original focus, the ability and willingness of an agency and a program to use volunteers and paraprofessionals to maximize the scope and effectiveness of its program may be considered another criterion usable in program evaluation. Exhibit 3-7 discusses the nature of the volunteer experience and tasks that volunteers can perform.

EXHIBIT 3-7 *The Volunteer Experience*

The following excerpt examines the characteristics that competent volunteers should possess, discusses the kinds of tasks involved, suggests skills necessary to be developed, and describes the relationship of the volunteer to the agency. It is interesting to note the use of the term "friendly visitor" instead of volunteer, a throwback to a term used before the development of social work as a profession when well-meaning citizens of a community undertook charitable activities. It illustrates one of the functions of volunteers, that is, helping to reduce the anonymity of welfare bureaucracies for clients so that they perceive themselves as dealing with friends and neighbors rather than impersonal specialists. How do the functions of volunteers differ from those of professionals?

We welcome you as a volunteer to aid in a Friendly Visiting Program among elderly or handicapped people. Without you this service would not be possible.

Your contribution is fourfold:

- It *enriches* the often cheerless and lonely life of an individual.
- It *supplements* the work of the professional staff.
- It is a *direct service* to your community.
- It enables *you* to grow in understanding and maturity.

Source: "A Guide for Friendly Visitors" (mimeographed pamphlet) (Guilford, North Carolina: Guilford County Department of Social Services). Used by permission.

What Is the Friendly Visiting Program?

The Friendly Visiting Program is an organized plan for visiting among people whose emotional and physical well-being is impaired by illness, injury, loneliness, or other misfortune.

Who Are the People Visited?

Elderly or handicapped people who live alone, in nursing or county home, or in any situation where warmth of friendliness is needed. All have one need in common—the need for someone to take a personal interest in them.

Who Are the Friendly Visitors?

Volunteers—intelligent, friendly, dependable men and women who recognize the value of this program to the persons whom they visit and as a service to the community.

How Does the Program Operate?

Your local Social Services Department staff find the need for this service among the people with whom they come in contact. If you want to volunteer you should contact the Social Services Department in your city or county.

Attendance at an orientation course is a prerequisite for each Friendly Visitor. This course, of no more than three sessions, is offered free of charge as the need arises.

The Friendly Visitor works with the agency caseworker or staff person requesting this service. The contact person provides the Friendly Visitor with further information and direction, has the story and pertinent facts about the person or persons to be visited and usually accompanies the volunteer on the first visit. Special emphasis is placed on matching interests on the basis of talents, hobbies, nationality. The Friendly Visitor reports directly to the agency contact person.

The above information pertains to Friendly Visitors volunteering as individuals or in connection with a group project.

What Do Friendly Visitors Do?

Create a warm and friendly relationship.

Chat of everyday affairs, except religion and politics.

Read aloud, write letters, play games, do puzzles.

Listen to and show respect for opinions and often-repeated stories.

Emphasize self-reliance but give assurance of help when needed.

Provide small, worthwhile jobs to do.

Assist with recreational activities.

Develop creative interests.

Admire and give importance to personal possessions.

Shop occasionally, with approval of the contact person.

Send seasonal greeting cards. Remember birthdays.

Take magazines, books, garden flowers, etc.

Cooperate with community affairs. Make posters, favors, place cards.

What Are the Duties of Friendly Visitors?

To observe the rules of the agency at all times.

To know and to keep within their privileges and limitations.

To visit regularly. If unavoidably detained, telephone. Should phoning not be possible, send an explanatory note.

To give full attention to the person visited.

To be a good listener. Consider the interests, likes and needs of each individual.

To refrain from discussion of controversial or depressing subjects.

To avoid criticism.

To guard against personal jokes and "talking down."

To respect names. It may be all there is left.

To help the older person assume responsibility for his own decisions.

To dress simply.

To keep confidential matters confidential.

To understand that all information about the residents, the staff, and the home are to be given out only by the person in charge. Publicity in any form is not the prerogative of Friendly Visitors.

What Qualifications Are Needed?

An *understanding* of and *liking* for elderly people.

A *sense of humor.*

Patience: Handicapped, confused, or senile persons are slow. Patience can go far to help a negative, irritable person to solve his own problems.

Tactfulness: To smooth over sensitive feelings.

Tolerance: To avoid unpleasant arguments.

Dependability: Disappointments are defeating.

Honesty: Admit mistakes. Don't be afraid to say you don't know.

Humility: Be willing to learn, and to accept constructive criticism with an open mind.

Generosity: Be willing for others to take the limelight.

Maturity: To communicate a sense of security and confidence. Understand that the elderly need to be useful and needed. They need to be loved and to have someone to love.

To recognize the spiritual values inherent in the warmth of friendliness.

Suggestions for Friendly Visitors

Establish a good rapport with the staff.

Check frequently with contact person to learn of developments.

Several visits may be required to gain the confidence of the persons visited.

Keep visits reasonably short. Do not stay through meal hours unless especially invited.

Be relaxed. When staying for only a few minutes do not appear hurried. Sit down in a chair where you can be easily seen. Do not sit or lean on the bed.

For the very ill, an affectionate pat may be better than a handshake.

Keep promises. Be careful what you promise.

Do not start anything that you are not prepared to carry through.

Refrain from talking in the corridors. Bits of conversation may be overheard, misinterpreted, and cause alarm.

Be a friend and companion. You are not expected to be a social worker, a pastor, a doctor, or a lawyer. Your visit means much to one who is shut away from normal family living. You may even be filling the place of the family.

Enjoy your visits. Cheeriness is contagious.

What Are the Responsibilities of the Friendly Visitors to the Agency?

To report regularly to the agency contact person. Any change in emotional, religious or physical problems should be reported immediately, and guidance and help requested.

To report to the contact person inability to accept or to continue an assignment once it has been accepted.

To recognize that Friendly Visitors supplement, not replace, the professional staff.

To avoid criticism of the policies of the agency.

To ask for a change if unhappy in the assignment.

Needs and Characteristics of the Elderly

The greatest contribution will be made by the volunteers who have a thorough understanding of the needs and characteristics of the elderly.

Some important factors are:

- Most older people are normal and have the same basic needs they have always had.
- They need to maintain their self-respect and as much independence as possible.
- Many have suffered loss of personal ties and are lonely. They feel rejected.
- They have to make adjustments continually to drastic and often tragic changes in their personal lives. These may include loss of husband, wife, or family; physical infirmities; changed economic circumstances; loss of employment and income; unfamiliar living arrangements; loss of community standing and influence. Many need reassurance. They are afraid of old age, of being alone, of illness, of not having enough money, or being pushed around. They fear death. They tend to be suspicious of anyone not connected with their own routine.

The Friendly Visitor can stimulate interest in the outside world and help renew a sense of personal dignity and worth.

Rehabilitation to self-care through personal attention, creative activity, physical exercise, and intellectual stimulation is worth all the time and effort that may be required.

Code of Volunteers

"As a Volunteer, I realize that I am subject to a code of ethics, similar to that which binds the professional. I, like them, in assuming certain responsibilities, expect to be accountable for those responsibilities. I will keep confidential matters confidential.

"As a Volunteer, I agree to serve without pay, but with the same high standard as the paid staff expect to do their work.

"I promise to take to my work an attitude of open-mindedness; to be willing to be trained for it; to bring to it interest and attention.

"I believe that my attitude toward volunteer work should be professional. I believe that I have an obligation to my work, to those for whom it is done, and to the community.

"Being eager to contribute all that I can to human betterment, I accept this code for the Volunteer as my code, to be followed carefully and cheerfully."

Chapter Summary ◀

This chapter has dealt with agency and program efficiency and effectiveness. The basic value systems and societal mandates discussed in the previous chapters enter into such considerations. But ultimately those values and mandates must be made operational, and that occurs through organizations that allocate resources and structure client and worker behaviors. Each professional has the responsibility to make sure that personal professional values are respected by the organization in which the person works, so that ultimately professionally sound evaluative criteria can be applied to the work. It is important to demonstrate to self, clients, and society that one's work is as efficient and effective as our present levels of knowledge and practice wisdom make possible. This evaluation cannot be complete without input from the users of the services, and the communities that support the services. Client participation in program planning and service delivery makes this possible. Again we cannot avoid the realization that the social welfare institution is part of a total societal system. In the attempt to help people to function more effectively many people and structures get involved. The wise use of social resources involves highly skilled professional judgment, but it also involves organizational structures and the participation of user groups and community citizens. In the long run, social welfare professionals are themselves citizens, and their work must reflect the needs of their fellow citizens.

STUDY QUESTIONS

1. After reading the material on the characteristics of professions, are you convinced that professions are different from any other occupation? Compare a profession to a nonprofession (being a secretary, for example), and see what differences you find. On the basis of your analysis, should professions have the degree of autonomy that they claim? If professions were less autonomous, what regulatory mechanisms would you suggest?
2. Read the "165 Howell Street" case in the appendix. Then consider the effect that the structure of services has on the services provided in this case. Would having less structure help, or would it create other problems? Can you think of more effective service delivery structures that would have been helpful in the Howell Street case?
3. Evaluating the effectiveness of social welfare programs is difficult. Make a list of the criteria noted in the book down one side of the page, leaving ample room between each. On the other side, briefly note why each criterion is or is not an accurate indicator of two things: (1) Is the recipient of the service actually functioning more effectively? (2) Did the professional worker do a good or bad job in helping the recipient of the service? If you find some of the criteria are not very helpful in answering these evaluative questions, what criteria seem more appropriate to you?

REFERENCES

1. In February 1971, there were 1,181,310 recipients of public assistance in New York City, according to Department of Health, Education and Welfare figures. *Public Assistance Statistics,* February 1971 (NCSS Report A-2, 2/71), p. 4.
2. Nicos Mouzelis, *Organization and Bureaucracy: An Analysis of Modern Theories* (Chicago: Aldine, 1968), p. 39.
3. Ibid.
4. Ibid., p. 99. He defines informal organization as "the structure and culture of the group, which is spontaneously formed by the interactions of individuals working together."
5. Ibid., pp. 102–103.
6. See Donald Roy, "Quota Restriction and Goldbricking in a Machine Shop," *American Journal of Sociology* 57 (1952): 427–42.
7. Richard N. Hall, "Professionalization and Bureaucratization," *American Sociological Review* 33 (February 1968): 92–104. See also Harold Wilensky and Charles Lebeaux, *Industrial Society and Social Welfare* (New York: Free Press, 1958), pp. 284–85.
8. Ellen Dunbar and Howard Jackson, "Free Clinics for Young People," *Social Work* 17 (September 1972): 34. Reprinted by permission of the National Association of Social Workers.
9. A classic example of occupational socialization is Howard S. Becker et al., *Boys in White* (Chicago: University of Chicago Press, 1961).
10. John Wax, "Developing Social Work Power in a Medical Organization," *Social Work* 13 (October 1968): 62–71.
11. See Esther Stanton, *Clients Come Last* (Beverly Hills: Sage Publishers, 1970), pp. 145–58.
12. Dunbar and Jackson, op. cit., p. 28.
13. Ibid., pp. 29–30.
14. Joseph Olmstead, "Satisfaction and Performance in Welfare and Rehabilitation Agencies," *Social and Rehabilitation Record* 1 (September 1974): 28.
15. Delbert Taebel, "Strategies for Making Bureaucrats Responsive," *Social Work* 17 (November 1972): 41–43. Paraphrased by permission of the National Association of Social Workers.
16. Edward Newman and Jerry Turem, "The Crisis of Accountability," *Social Work* 19 (January 1974): 15. Reprinted by permission of the National Association of Social Workers.
17. Ibid.
18. Ibid.
19. Marvin Rosenberg and Ralph Brody, "The Threat or Challenge of Accountability," *Social Work* 19 (May 1974): 345–50.
20. Based on material in Winnifred Bell, "Obstacles to Shifting from the Descriptive to the Analytical Approach in Teaching Social Services," *Journal of Education for Social Work* 5 (Spring 1969): 5–13.
21. P. Nelson Reid, "Reforming the Social Services Monopoly," *Social Work* 17 (November 1972): 47. Reprinted by permission of the National Association of Social Workers.
22. Paraphrased from ibid., pp. 47–50, by permission of the National Association of Social Workers and the author.

23. Ibid., pp. 50–54.
24. Alan Keith-Lucas, *Giving and Taking Help* (Chapel Hill: University of North Carolina Press, 1972), pp. 60–63.
25. Felice Davidson Perlmutter, "Citizen Participation in Yugoslavia," *Social Work* 19 (March 1974): 226. Reprinted by permission of the National Association of Social Workers.
26. Ibid., p. 228.
27. Ibid., p. 229.
28. Ruth Sidel, "Social Services in China," *Social Work* 17 (November 1972): 5. Reprinted by permission of the National Association of Social Workers.
29. Ibid., p. 6.
30. Ibid., p. 10.
31. Ralph Kramer, *Participation of the Poor* (Englewood Cliffs, N.J.: Prentice-Hall, 1969).
32. Stanton, loc. cit.

SELECTED READINGS

The problems of organizing and delivering social welfare services are major ones, and of crucial importance for the future of social welfare. The following sources examine various facets of these problems.

Brager, George, and Holloway, Stephen. *Changing Human Service Organizations.* New York: Free Press, 1978.

Bucher, Rue, and Strauss, Anselm. "Professions in Process," in Meyer Zald, ed. *Social Welfare Institutions.* New York: John Wiley, 1965, pp. 559–63.

Etzioni, Amitai. *Modern Organizations.* Englewood Cliffs, N.J.: Prentice-Hall, 1964.

Galper, Jeffrey. *The Politics of Social Services.* Englewood Cliffs, N.J.: Prentice-Hall, 1975.

Gilbert, Neil, and Specht, Harry. *Dimensions of Social Welfare Policy.* Englewood Cliffs, N.J.: Prentice-Hall, 1974.

Kahn, Alfred J. *Social Policy and Social Services* (Second Edition). New York: Random House, 1979.

Kahn, Alfred J., and Kamerman, Sheila B. *Social Services in International Perspective.* Washington, D.C.: U.S. Government Printing Office, 1977.

Prigmore, Charles, and Atherton, Charles. *Social Welfare Policy.* Lexington, Mass.: D.C. Heath, 1979.

Richan, Willard C., and Mendelsohn, Allan R. *Social Work: The Unloved Profession.* New York: New Viewpoints, 1973.

Shostak, Arthur. *Modern Social Reforms: Solving Today's Social Problems.* New York: Macmillan, 1974.

Stanton, Esther. *Clients Come Last.* Beverly Hills: Sage Publishers, 1970.

Steiner, Gilbert. *Social Insecurity: The Politics of Welfare.* Chicago: Rand McNally, 1966.

U.S. President's Commission on Income Maintenance Programs. *Background Papers.* Washington, D.C.: Government Printing Office, 1969.

Vinter, Robert D. "Analysis of Treatment Organizations," in Paul Weinberger, ed., *Perspectives on Social Welfare.* New York: Macmillan, 1969, pp. 428–43.

Wilcox, Clair. *Toward Social Welfare.* Homewood, Ill.: Richard D. Irwin, 1969.

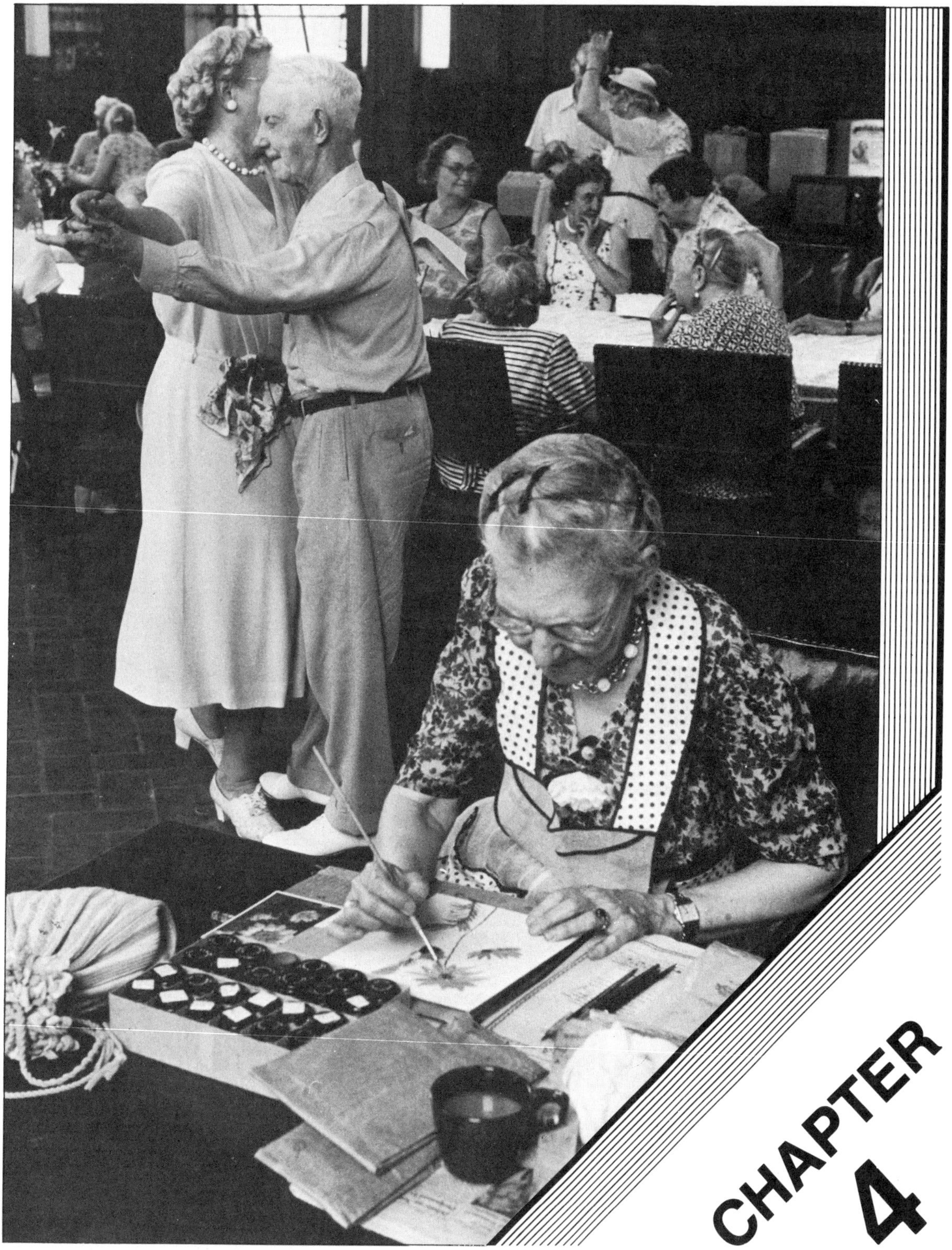

CHAPTER 4

The Knowledge Foundations of Social Welfare: A Framework for Analysis

Having already analyzed the structure of social welfare needs and services, it is clear that the knowledge needed to understand the social welfare institution is broad and extensive. The basic knowledge that is used by the social welfare professions generally comes from the social, behavioral, and biological sciences, especially sociology, psychology, biology, economics, political science, and anthropology. The social welfare professions use the knowledge generated by these theoretical disciplines, integrating and applying knowledge as needed to better understand and intervene in human behavior. From the experience social welfare professions have in using theoretical knowledge comes another kind of knowledge—practice knowledge. As theoretical knowledge is integrated and applied in practice situations, and as results from such efforts are analyzed, practice knowledge that describes the empirical effects of various kinds of intervention is accumulated. Social welfare professionals need to understand the basic theoretical knowledge so that it can be used in their own specific practice situations. They must also keep up to date on practice knowledge that, though still not highly developed, is growing and is already an important source of knowledge for social welfare practitioners.

The social, behavioral, and biological sciences use the scientific method to generate empirical data from which theories are generated and tested. The exacting rules of the scientific method minimize the frequency of inaccuracy and bias, as well as making possible the use of increasingly powerful methods of statistical and computer analysis. Each science specializes in certain parts of human and social behavior, a specialization necessitated by the complexity of people's actions in social situations. The problem for the social welfare professional is mastering the relevant areas of theoretical and practice knowledge, a lifelong task that can only begin in formal schooling.

This chapter does not attempt the impossible task of summarizing all of the knowledge needed by social welfare professionals. Instead, its primary cognitive objective is to provide a helpful framework for integrating knowledge from several different theoretical disciplines and applying it to social welfare concerns. In the next chapter a second related objective is to highlight the major knowledge areas that are most relevant to social welfare practice. The framework presented in this chapter will be helpful for integrating the knowledge areas summarized in the next chapter. It is assumed that the reader will have basic foundation knowledge in the social, behavioral, and biological sciences. The analytical framework and major content in these two chapters will then be a stimulus for readers to begin to use their existing knowledge in a more integrated and effective way, a cognitive and skill objective of these two chapters. As the integrating process occurs, readers will inevitably identify the need for additional theoretical and practice knowledge. This will, hopefully, begin to develop a commitment to lifelong learning through which this knowledge will be attained. The beginning development of this commitment is a major value objective of these chapters, along with the basic belief that professional helping rests solidly on knowledge as well as on motivation and skill mastery.

The understanding of three major areas—systems, human diversity, and the problem-solving process—will help to integrate our knowledge of the social welfare institution. We will now discuss each in some detail.

Systems ◄

The following material on systems adds to that discussed in Chapter 1. In talking about child-care research, Kenneth Kenniston states:[1]

> *First, no isolated type of behavior on the part of caregivers has any invariant effect on children: the consequences of any single kind of action depend on what* else *is happening between parents and children*

> *and on what they bring to their interaction . . . The earlier search for simple cause-and-effect relations (e.g., breast feeding produces optimistic children) has increasingly been abandoned for studies of the whole caregiver-child relationship in which each type of caregiver-child relationship is studied in the context of all other interaction patterns . . . The "ecology" of families is exceedingly complex. It includes everything from the quality of family housing to the job (or lack of job) of the parent; from the organization of the neighborhood to the parents' race; from the parents' sense of economic security (or insecurity) to their pride (or discomfort) in their heritage. These extrafamilial factors and forces affect children in two ways. In part, they directly determine the caregivers' behavior . . . And, in part, they indirectly determine the meaning a child assigns to any given pattern of caregivers' behavior.*

Kenniston's statement is an excellent illustration of the meaning and significance of systems for understanding human behavior. Biological and social behaviors occur in internally as well as externally linked systems, and thus attempts to understand a particular behavior must occur within the context of the systems of which that behavior is a part. We all know, for example, that our bodies are internal systems so that the actions of our heart affect the actions of our brains. We also know that what we eat, part of external systems related to food habits and availability of food, affects our heart through such things as hypertension, cholesterol levels, and so forth. Our social behavior is similar. The reinforcement we receive in our peer group affects what we do, and the peer group is itself affected by societal values relating to age groups, sex-role relationships, leisure activities, and a host of other things.

The study of social systems is a complex area that has produced theories from several disciplines,[2] as well as numerous attempts to apply them to social welfare contexts.[3] Much of the literature goes well beyond the level of detail needed by the average social welfare professional with only a baccalaureate degree. Yet it is essential that such a person have a firm grasp of the basic essentials underlying a systems approach to understanding the social welfare institution. Therefore, the following content about systems seeks to provide a level of understanding adequate for this social welfare professional.

Human life, as we discussed in Chapter 1, is organized into an interlocking network of structured relationships that begin with the individual and increase in size to the societal and even intersocietal levels. Each size level can be seen as a separate system; for example, systems of particular importance for social welfare professionals range from the individual (a biological/social system) to the family, the social welfare agency, and the community. Other even larger systems, such as social welfare professions and even the society as a whole, are important, but we will not elaborate on them here. Regardless of the size, a system is defined by the fact that it manifests four characteristics: boundaries, purpose, exchange, and networks. We will examine each of these characteristics separately, and then use them to illustrate the system characteristics and behavior of individual, family, social welfare agency, and community systems. As noted above, there are many other levels and types of systems. These particular systems have been selected for illustrative purposes because they are so central to the social welfare institution.

Boundaries. A system is an organized collection of activities and resources that exists within definable social and physical boundaries. For example, the human individual has internal processes that occur within the physically defined entity called the body. Similarly, a community has both physical (geographical) and social (who interacts with whom) boundaries. Boundaries are also important for defining membership, so that it is clear where one system begins and another ends.

Purposes. Systems have procedures that enable them to accomplish their objectives. One purpose is almost always survival, and the concept of *homeostasis* is used to refer to the balance between system components that give it stability. The human body has a state of "health," for example, at which point the body components are stabilized, so that the person is maximally functional. Systems usually have purposes in addition to survival—to become self-actualized for an individual or to deliver helping services for a social welfare agency. These purposes serve to focus the interactions and use of resources within a system, as well as guiding relations between systems.

Exchanges. Although systems have boundaries, they are usually permeable rather than closed. Systems need resources in order to function, and their functioning produces results of some sort (usually relevant to their purposes). Resources may come from within the system, but they often come from outside—these are called *inputs.* For example, people need to ingest food, families need shelter, and social agencies need a societal mandate. Systems *process* inputs in order to produce results of some sort—*output.* Communities, for instance, obtain input (money, food, people, and so forth) that is used to create a living environment for their members (output).

Networks. The exchanges that systems have occur with other systems, leading to networks of system relationships. This, of course, is why social welfare professionals have to understand human behavior systemically. The lack of availability of inputs from other systems can disrupt a system's homeostasis and lead to altered relationships with other systems. Children whose psychological and social needs are not met (part of the body system) by their family may develop disruptive behaviors (output) as a result. This

TABLE 4-1 An illustration of the Systems Approach

	Boundaries	*Purposes*	*Exchanges*	*Networks*
Individuals	The body	Survival Self-actualization Gratification	Input (food, air, nurturance) Output (energy, action) Process (breathing)	Impact (family members, peers, employers) These in turn affect inputs (money for food) and purposes (survival)
Families	Legally defined Kin (blood relatedness) Religiously defined	Preservation of family resources and traditions Socialization Economic	Input (money, societal mandate) Output (nurturance, socialization, work) Process (interactions of family members)	Impact (family members, school, workplace) These in turn affect inputs (decisions about a societal policy for families) and purposes (ability to socialize members)
Social Welfare Agencies	Legally defined	Provision of social welfare services Management of resources	Input (societal mandate, resources) Output (services) Process (employment practices)	Impact (social policy, public opinion) These in turn affect inputs (public support for social welfare) and purposes (resources to use in providing services)
Communities	Legally defined Geographically defined Defined in terms of social identity of its members	Organize economic, spatial and social sub-units	Input (money, media, policy) Output (goods, services) Process (services, social structure)	Impact (families, social agencies) These in turn affect inputs (policy) and purposes (social order)

will in turn alter the input and output of the family system. It is evident, then, that the output of one system has an *impact* on other systems. As each system experiences input-output-impact, it becomes enmeshed in networks of interdependence that relate to the input-output-impact of other systems. Professional helping efforts must reflect these networks so that appropriate and effective points of intervention can be selected.

The preceding material is a very simple systems analysis, but one which has direct applicability to the social welfare institution. Table 4-1 uses individuals, families, social welfare agencies, and communities to briefly illustrate the systems components discussed above.

An adequate understanding of the situations with which social welfare professionals work requires a systemic perspective. Child abuse is closely linked to group and social problems such as feelings of inadequacy as a parent, social isolation, and anxiety that can result from an event like the loss of employment. The functioning of social welfare agencies may be criticized by consumers who feel their needs are being met inadequately. At the same time, nonconsumer groups may feel that too many resources are being used by the agency. In order to survive and function effectively, agencies must be able to understand the social, political, and economic factors impinging on both groups and motivating their behavior. The interaction of systems is complex, yet most problems are created and resolved systemically. Therefore, an understanding of systems must be an integral part of the social welfare professional's practice activities. Exhibit 4-1 illustrates this point.

The Family Web EXHIBIT 4-1

The family, as one of the most important social institutions of our society, is a good barometer of societal changes. The systems nature of any society, including our own, is well illustrated in the following comments by Urie Bronfenbrenner, in which he talks about the impact on the American family of several changes in the society external to the family but very much related to its functioning.

The family, many experts lament, is dying. And no one cares, says Urie Bronfenbrenner of Cornell University, an expert in child development.

"Family is the primary institution we have," he said in a recent interview. "It certainly is the most effective and most economic system we have for making human beings more human."

"Family is important for nurturing not only the next generation, but everybody. They care for physical and emotional well-being, especially when an individual is young, old, sick, tired, or lonely."

"The number of families doing a good job is decreasing," he said. "What's caused it? An indifference. It's not deliberate, but we've had other things on our minds."

External situations, such as the economy, the increasing population, competition for jobs and a dwindling housing stock, have affected family life as much as changing attitudes and lifestyles.

"There are four principal areas of stress in today's society," Bronfenbrenner said. "They are money, conditions of work, television and the neighborhood."

Single-parent families and blue-collar workers are most affected by money, he said. In those households, employment can cause great tension. Employment also generates stress, particularly in households where both parents work.

"We have finally broken through our stupidities and are admitting that a larger proportion of society is entering the work world, but we've kept the old male work rules—9–5," he said. "We haven't come to terms with the fact that you can't be in two places at once."

Population reports show single parenthood has increased most rapidly among families with children under six, climbing from about 7 percent to 17 percent between 1948 and 1975. The

---

Source: "Other Things on Nation's Mind Put Home in Downward Spiral," *Greensboro* (North Carolina) *Daily News*, September 4, 1977, Section G, p. 1. © 1977 by The Associated Press. Reprinted by permission.

majority of these single parents are in the work force, and most are women.

Bronfenbrenner believes the overwhelming change in family life over the last 30 years is the emergence of the working mother. Government statistics show 37 percent of all married women with children under six were in the labor force in 1975, three times the number in 1948.

And with inadequate and sometimes costly day care facilities and babysitting services, many youngsters go unattended, Bronfenbrenner said. He calls these young people—with only the television and each other for companionship and guidance—"latch key children." They return from school to empty homes.

"Single parents also use television as a babysitter," he said. "But everyone's upset with what the children see on television and what TV does to them. The bottom line is that no one is home but the TV. Someone has to be home and active."

The fourth stressful area in family—the neighborhood—has fallen apart, he said. "The thing about having young kids is that you need help. And it's not the help you can get by telephone or across the town from a friend or relative," Bronfenbrenner said. "It's a neighborhood, because many of the support systems you need for parenthood have to be close by."

In any case, he says, priorities must be changed. "When families become as important to America as football or firearms, the divorce rate will take a deep plunge, nonreaders will cease to be a national problem, juvenile delinquency will experience dropouts, and neighborhoods will once again become a place for people of all ages to live together."

Finally, understanding systems is also crucial for social policy, which is the societal decision-making process that determines what *ought* to happen in society. Going back to Kenniston, "Policy and programs involve questions of *should*—normative and value issues—while research at best tells us only about what *is.* Thus, drawing policy conclusions from research findings necessarily involves the added step of invoking values about the kinds of people and the kind of society we cherish. No amount of research can choose or define these values for us."[4] Yet knowing what is happening is essential to our making decisions about what ought to happen. We cannot adequately know without a systems approach that places behavior in its full social context, and, within a systems approach, a functionalist view that helps to identify the hidden as well as the obvious relationships between parts of systems.

Systems are strongly influenced by the characteristics of the people within them. The person as a system is affected by genetically transmitted abilities and limitations, for example, as are families by the ethnic background of their members. Although systems share the structural characteristics discussed above, any particular system (such as a particular community) will have a unique set of people that affect its particular boundaries, purposes, exchanges, and networks. The fact that people are different leads to the concept of human diversity, which seeks to understand the reasons for those differences. The next section explores human diversity in some detail.

Human Diversity ◀

Human diversity refers to the continuum of differences between people and groups resulting from biological, cultural, and social factors. Diversity is a major characteristic of any society, but especially of industrialized societies. Therefore, any holistic understanding of human and social behavior must be grounded in an awareness and acceptance of how people's diversity affects their behavior. People do, of course, also share many similarities, classically formulated in Towle's "common human needs"[5] and Maslow's need hierarchy.[6] However, these needs get expressed many different ways because of biological, cultural, and social diversity. Other needs are differentially created by society as a result of societal values and structures. The result is a societal context in which people are differentially able to get resources to meet their needs as they see them.

Although each person is a unique combination of genetic and environmental characteristics and experiences, people are grouped according to particular characteristics that they possess in common with others. Since each person has many characteristics, each shared with some set of others, this person may be grouped in any number of ways. Characteristics and group memberships based on these common characteristics may be biologically determined and therefore ascribed, such as race and gender. Others are culturally and socially created and are more likely to be achieved, such as religious affiliation and marital standing. Still others, like ethnicity, are partly ascribed and partly achieved. As life goals and situations change, some characteristics and resulting group memberships may change, or their significance in a person's life may be altered. In general, ascribed characteristics are less likely to change than characteristics that are achieved, although the socially defined meaning and importance of an ascribed characteristic may change.

Since each individual comprises many characteristics, the composition of a group based on any one characteristic will include a wide range of people with respect to other characteristics. Women include those who are rich and poor, lesbian and heterosexual, physically handicapped and not handicapped, black, oriental, and caucasian. Therefore, a group that is different from others with respect to a particular characteristic (Puerto Ricans* as an ethnic group contrasted with Chicanos as an ethnic group)

* The terminology used to refer to the multiplicity of racial and ethnic groups in the United States is flexible and constantly changing and is subject to regional variations. Four major generic terms will be used in this book, with specific groups in each referred to as appropriate. *Blacks* refers to black Americans of African descent. *Native American* refers to American Indians, Eskimos, and Hawaiians. *Asian Americans* refers to Americans of Asian descent, including Japanese Americans, Chinese Americans, Philippine Americans, Thai Americans, and Vietnamese Americans. *Hispanic* (an Eastern term) and *Latino* (a Western term) refer to Americans with Spanish cultural roots, including Puerto Ricans, Mexican Americans

will itself have a wide range of internal diversity (among Puerto Ricans, racial mixtures, socioeconomic differences, gender differences, and so on).

In other words, there is as much difference within a group as between groups except with respect to the defining group characteristics (such as ethnicity) and factors directly related to them (such as cultural patterns). In addition, any group may change over time, as exemplified by the increasing willingness of the physically handicapped to fight for opportunities to engage in activities from which they were frequently excluded in the past (jobs, schooling, access to public facilities, and so forth).

Although people become members of groups because of a wide range of characteristics (tennis skill, left-handedness, avocational interests, and many others), group memberships based on certain characteristics become especially important in people's lives. Such group memberships affect the way people relate to the institutions of society, to other people, to other groups, to other members of their own groups, and to themselves. Groups that transmit cultural values to their members (such as ethnic groups) that significantly affect the assumptions that society makes regarding the typical behavior of their members (homosexual, for example) or groups whose members are limited in their ability to act in ways expected in social situations (such as the poor and the handicapped) are of particular importance for influencing the life experiences of their members. These groups are usually of most concern to social welfare professionals.

Groups have roles assigned to their members by society. These roles are frequently based on stereotypes about biological or cultural characteristics—for example, the elderly are forgetful and cannot be trusted with important tasks or Hispanics cannot speak English and are only suited to farm labor or factory work. These roles can become significant barriers to members of diverse groups since role definitions become part of the socialization performed by social institutions. This socialization may serve to perpetuate stereotypes and become a self-fulfilling prophecy by denying members of diverse groups opportunities to act differently. This point is well illustrated in Exhibit 4-2.

Being members of diverse groups means that the significance of social arrangements varies by group. The concept of normalcy may differ according to cultural values, life-style preference, or physical ability. Differences between a group's and society's definition of normalcy often leads to conflict and attempts to control or disadvantage members of diverse groups. Once "normal" is defined, alternative behaviors are "abnormal" or *deviant,* leading to a process of *stigmatization* that gradually tends to define the person so *labeled* as outside the acceptable bounds of social

---

(Chicanos), and Cuban Americans. Other racial and ethnic groups will be individually referred to as needed, such as Italian Americans. In referring to groups differentiated on the basis of sexual or affectional preference, the generic terms used will be heterosexual and homosexual, with homosexual men called gays and homosexual women called lesbians.

behavior. This easily becomes a self-fulfilling prophecy that makes it increasingly difficult for the stigmatized individual to be seen and treated as anything other than deviant and therefore unacceptable. For example, the concept of the intact nuclear family may be imposed on racial and ethnic groups as a condition of receiving financial assistance even though it violates cultural and social patterns in those groups.[7] The interaction between group members and society is constantly shifting as the group itself changes and as societal values change.

In order to understand the behavior of people from diverse groups, a dual perspective is needed.[8] One perspective is that held by those who belong to the group—their own perspective on what behavior is appropriate and "normal." The other is the perspective of outsiders who evaluate the behavior of members of a diverse group according to their own perceptions and standards. Understanding both views is necessary for understanding the behavior of oneself and others in social situations. Therefore, all behavior has to be seen within a general societal concern with whether a specific behavior is harmful to others. However, like all societal values, this value becomes politicized, so that the activities of certain groups are considered "normal" and acceptable even though there is evidence that they are harmful to certain other groups. We have already seen, for example, the negative effects of male dominance on women, yet such sex inequality is still considered acceptable by many people.

Agism and Imposed Disability **EXHIBIT 4-2**

Our society has often been characterized as youth oriented, in which the elderly are ignored and arbitrarily forced out of productive social roles. This behavior is imposed simply on the basis of age. It frequently has little relationship to the actual abilities of the people involved. The following excerpts illustrate this point, although points are made to show that our present misuse of the elderly need not continue.

The Gray Panthers are a national coalition of old, young and middle-aged activists and advocates working to expose agism's destructive web and to challenge all forms of age discrimination in our society. Agism does not just apply to the elderly. Agism is to see a person's problems as naturalistic and inherent to a chronological age, rather than the consequence of societal arrangements. All too often an individual buys such a belief and constructs a self-fulfilling prophecy of inadequacy.

The issue of agism provides Gray Panthers with the focus for commitment and action. There are four basic dimensions to agism: stereotyping, segregation, paternalism and victim-blaming.

Agism, like racism and sexism, is a method of stereotyping the behavior of the certain groups. Society stereotypes the old as "out of date," too slow, sickly, sexless or senile, unchanging, unemployable, etc. Society stereotypes the young as immature, irresponsible, unstable, inexperienced, over-sexed, impatient, etc. These stereotypes provide ready excuses for society not

---

Source: Excerpted from Margaret E. Kuhn, "Gray Panther Thoughts on Agism, Health Care and Worklife," *The Journal of the Institute for Socioeconomic Studies,* Autumn 1977, pp. 33–42.

to recognize the individual characteristics, contributions, and needs of the old and young.

Our laws and social structures reflect agism by segregating people from each other in efficient, chronological age categories from nursery school to nursing homes.

Paternalism emerges as a response to the segregation of stereotyped older and younger people. All too often the caretaker is an institution such as a school, retirement community, nursing home or boarding home.

Lastly, agism includes victim-blaming, where society's flaws become a social problem as society attempts to absolve itself from the responsibility. Services attempting to blunt pains of the aged seldom empower the victim, but instead reinforce powerlessness.

The Gray Panthers began in 1970 when six of us, friends forced to retire from national religious and social service organizations, decided to pool our efforts and help each other to use our new freedom responsibly. Our initial personal reactions to compulsory retirement were anger, shock, and loss . . . loss of friends, status, income, and purpose in living. We have seen the lives of once vigorous colleagues trivialized and wasted in retirement periods. The course of action we determined for ourselves was to use our knowledge and experience, our network of relationships, and our free time to work for broad-based social change.

Now, for the first time in United States history, the old will soon outnumber the young. Only a radical restructuring of society can solve in a civilized way the enormous problems created by this situation. The 24 million Americans 65 years old and older now comprise about 11 percent of the population. By the year 2010, or even sooner according to present trends, the percentage of older people may double. We see aging as a universalizing force in America—we are all aging. Society's response to these demographic shifts will profoundly affect people of all ages and human conditions. Although many older people need services, we work as advocates to understand and change the societal conditions that have made such services necessary—services which mostly serve to maintain and legitimize existing social structures. What some have described as "the plight of the elderly" will not appreciably improve without basic change in society. What follows are two examples of Gray Panther advocacy which we hope will be instructive to designers of social policy.

Health Care

The health care system gives priority to provider profits rather than user need. Gray Panthers, convinced of the dangers of the medicalization of health, have taken on the formidable task of confronting the medical industry. We have monitored and challenged it on these counts: the concentration of economic power and technology in the medical empires built by the billions of dollars from citizens' taxes and insurance premiums; and the interlocking of interests—the American Medical Association (AMA) with the manufacturers of drugs and hospital equipment, insurance carriers and medical centers with their hospitals, clinics, research laboratories and medical schools. There are artificial shortages of physicians created by the AMA limits on medical school certification and student admissions. We challenge their preoccupation with "sickness" care which treats diseases and grossly neglects prevention and maintenance measures for basic health and well-being. Americans of all ages are the victims of over-specialized services that fragment care and prevent holistic attention to the mental/physical/environmental factors. The neglect of the chronically ill and the disregard of the natural infirmities that come with the fragility of old age enrage us. Our crisis-oriented medical system excludes the old because many physicians do not wish to "waste their time on someone who's going to die anyway." Furthermore, they do not wish to deal with the bureaucratic procedures for Medicare and Medicaid reimbursement. Moreover, our unemployed and underemployed youth simply cannot afford the high cost of insurance premiums. This initial deprivation of health care may be the basis for poor health in old age.

Medical schools teach only the disease treatment model. That eliminates the most basic elements of health care, including nutrition, health education, personal responsibility for one's own health maintenance and awareness of pollutants. Furthermore, the disease treatment model does not provide effective care for the chronic, long-term illness of older people. Gray Panthers have reviewed the curriculum of medical schools and have petitioned at the annual convention of the AMA and the state medical societies to mandate courses in geriatric medicine and gerontology in medical schools. Only a limited portion of courses in family medicine and community health prepare medical students for work with older people. For example, with the omission of geriatric medicine in medical schools, young doctors are poorly equipped to diagnose many physiological conditions which can lead to irreversible mental impairment. Nearly 50 percent of the patients now in nursing homes due to mental impairment need not be there! Furthermore, we have asked the AMA to resume the tradition of house calls and family practice, to include consumer representatives on the various medical society governing boards, and to work with concerned citizens to reform nursing homes. Most of our petitions to the AMA are still disregarded. . . .

Worklife and Mandatory Retirement

The Gray Panthers have chosen the elimination of mandatory retirement as a primary objective because it is a positive step toward the amelioration of the elderly's diminished and degraded status. We have studied the effects of mandatory retirement on the mental and physical health of retired persons. As a result, we have testified at Congressional committee and state legislature hearings, appeared on television, addressed many public gatherings, and joined in class action court suits.

Mandatory retirement is a classic example of agism. It results in and perpetuates negative stereotyping that views old people as unproductive and only capable of rest and play. It creates artificial barriers between age groups and violates the workers' right to choose and to exercise control over their worklife. It forces many to live on reduced and fixed income. This exclusionary policy which arbitrarily views retired people as inadequate and incompetent makes them subject to paternalistic social programs. Economic deprivation and self-devaluation could be less of a problem if society permitted each person the choice either to retire or to continue to work. Hopefully, a change in retirement will impress a sense of empowerment upon the aging worker. If older people can choose to remain as workers in the mainstream of society, then they might more fully realize their ability to control their own lives and influence the direction of society.

The Gray Panthers have never been a "senior power" organization because the most important societal problems have implications that affect many sectors of the population, including the old. Furthermore, we realize that even after abolition of mandatory retirement, a new set of work-related problems may plague the elderly. It may well be that the end of mandatory retirement alone cannot stop stereotyping, segregation, rejection and the elderly's own self-degradation. Yes, elimination of mandatory retirement is important; however, it is just a first step toward a comprehensive reorientation, redirection and reformation of the Social Security system and income transfers . . . If we are to confront the problems of the aged and younger members of society, then we must think of solutions that are systematic and unified in nature.

All too often people confine and relate their thinking on mandatory retirement to the last stage of life. The earlier periods of life set the stage for the difficulties that confront the aged. The combined material of life experiences weaves a composite of personal development and difficulties. Hence, our problem-solving must first ask questions about how societal structure interacts with experiences of personal development. Gray Panthers advocate policies which encourage integrated life cycle experiences, rather than a set of separate, cage-like periods. People of all ages should experience education, work and leisure, rather than the age-segregated stages of school, labor, and retirement. . . .

Rather than seeing the end of mandatory retirement as the solution, we should consider a broad range of options that would make the structure of education, work, and leisure more flexible. A variety of options might include sabbatical leaves, part-time or shared work, and the facilitating of mid-career changes. Retirement could be optional and flexible. We could encourage those who desire to use some of their Social Security benefits before the age of 65 to take a sabbatical leave in search of education, training, and reevaluation of life directions possibly toward new careers. In the long run, we anticipate that workers of various ages will feel empowered by the choice to improve their work style. What will emerge is a new job fluidity and a new consideration of leisure time. They will see the possibility of exercising further control over the administration, organization and structure of the workplace.

▶ The Problem-Solving Process

Every helping effort undertaken by social welfare professionals must be built on an understanding of systems and human diversity. Such understanding is built on the mastery and integration of the basic biological, social, and behavioral science concepts discussed in the next chapter. However, systems and human diversity understanding must be used in an orderly manner if problem solving is to occur. This process ensures that all of the relevant persons and resources will be involved in the helping effort and that specific helping activities will be selected and carried out in a rational and purposeful way. It is important to understand the integrating significance of the problem-solving process. In order to understand all the elements of situations in which professional helping occurs, the systemic and human diversity characteristics of situations must be analyzed. This in turn results from the integration and application of biological, social, and behavioral science concepts that describe and analyze the various aspects of the situation-personal behavior, the cultural context, political and economic forces, and so on. These concepts are themselves derived from the use of systematic methods of social inquiry, especially the scientific method. Thus the use of the problem-solving process is the culmination of a vast body of research findings organized into concepts and then further integrated through the use of systems and human diversity as ways of holistically understanding situations.

The steps in the problem-solving process are as follows (throughout the significance of systems and human diversity is stressed):

1. Who are involved in the attempts to improve social functioning? What systems are relevant—individuals, social welfare agencies, communities, legal and/or political structures, and so forth?
2. What are the goals of these various participants? What aspects of human diversity influence these goals? How do the systems impact on each other and affect goals?
3. What resources are available for use in the helping effort? Each system has its own resources, and these are influenced by systems interacting with each other. In addition, the human diversity of the

persons within systems is a source of input to those systems—biological capacity, cultural values, informal support systems and self-help traditions, and so on.

4. What obstacles, real or potential, stand in the way of goal attainment? As with resources, systems and human diversity serve to organize conditions and resources so that they become resources or obstacles.
5. Who will agree to do what as part of the helping effort? Deciding this results in the plan for providing the help needed. Such agreement must reflect the way in which systems operate and interact, as well as the perspectives, preferences, and resources of diverse groups.
6. Time to carry out the plan is necessary.
7. Did the plan work? Were the objectives achieved? Why or why not?
8. What next steps are needed or desired? Having achieved one or more objectives, are other objectives now desired? If objectives were not obtained, are they to be abandoned or a new plan developed?

Analytical and Interactional Tasks by Phases of Problem Solving EXHIBIT 4-3

The following table has been modified to include the steps in the problem-solving process as discussed in this chapter. It presents a useful summary of problem solving as both an analytical and an interactional activity.

	Analytical Tasks	*Interactional Tasks*
1. Defining the problem (Who are involved?) (What are the goals?)	In preliminary terms studying and describing the problematic aspects of a situation. Conceptualizing the system of relevant actors. Assessing what opportunities and limits are set by the organization employing the practitioner and by other actors.	Eliciting and receiving information, grievances, and preferences from those experiencing the problem and other sources.
2. Building structure (What are the resources?) (What are the obstacles?)	Determining the nature of the practitioner's relationship to various actors. Deciding on types of structures to be developed. Choosing people for roles as experts, communicators, influencers, and the like.	Establishing formal and informal communication lines. Recruiting people into the selected structures and roles and obtaining their commitments to address the problem.

Source: Robert Perlman and Arnold Gurin, *Community Organization and Social Planning* (New York: John Wiley and Sons, 1972), p. 62.

	Analytical Tasks	*Interactional Tasks*
3. Formulating policy (Who will do what?)	Analyzing past efforts to deal with the problem. Developing alternative goals and strategies, assessing their possible consequences and feasibility. Selecting one or more for recommendation to decision-makers.	Communicating alternative goals and strategies to selected actors. Promoting their expression of preferences and testing acceptance of various alternatives. Assisting decision-makers to choose.
4. Implementing plans (Carrying out the plan)	Specifying what tasks need to be performed to achieve agreed-upon goals, by whom, when, and with what resources and procedures.	Presenting requirements to decision-makers, overcoming resistances, and obtaining commitments to the program. Marshalling resources and putting procedures into operation.
5. Monitoring (Did the plan work?) (Next steps)	Designing system for collecting information on operations. Analyzing feedback data and specifying adjustments needed and/or new problems that require planning and action.	Obtaining information from relevant actors based on their experience. Communicating findings and recommendations and preparing actors for new round of decisions to be made.

The problem-solving process is both *analytical* and *interactional.* Situations must be analyzed so that they can be understood in all their dimensions, especially in terms of the systems involved and the human diversity influencing the operation of these systems. Out of the analysis emerges the plan that then actually guides the interaction, the specific helping activities of those involved. Here, too, understanding systems and human diversity is essential if the proper kind of intervention is to occur that will make goal attainment possible. As noted earlier, ignoring the interplay of families and the workplace can render ineffective efforts to help battered spouses. Similarly, failing to modify communication to make it appropriate to different groups (such as the deaf, those who speak other languages, and so forth) is also inviting failure. Exhibit 4-3 summarizes the analytical and interactional nature of problem solving.

Chapter Summary

The social welfare professional has to be able to integrate knowledge so that helping situations can be understood conceptually, holistically, and practically. Systems, human diversity, and problem solving work together to help practitioners understand the meaning and the context of the people and situations they work with. Then components must be used together, so that they underlie every effort to understand practice-related events and situations. Every situation must be understood in its systems context; every situation is seen and experienced differently by members of diverse groups; every situation has to be approached in an orderly way that lays out its several dimensions analytically and behaviorally.

Although frameworks such as that described in this chapter help to bring coherence to complex situations, specific areas of knowledge are essential in order to understand the behaviors and structures to which a framework brings order and meaning. In the next chapter, three major areas of knowledge will be discussed: individual needs and functioning, the cultural environment, and the social environment. Together, these three areas provide the knowledge foundation for understanding systems and human diversity as discussed in this chapter. Therefore, these two chapters are best seen as two interlocking ways to approach one goal—understanding human behavior in order to improve social welfare structures and service delivery.

STUDY QUESTIONS

1. Using yourself as an example, analyze the systems that affect your behavior. Which systems influence you? In what ways do they do so? Do any of these systems interfere with your own personal objectives? If so, how do you attempt to overcome their interference? Do you ever use one system to help you deal with another?
2. Make a list of all the groups to which you belong, either by virtue of a physical or cultural characteristic or by choice. Which groups do you think have the most influence on your behavior? Which groups do you personally feel are most important to you—why are they so important, in your opinion? Selecting one of the groups to which you belong, how much do you share in common with the other members of that group? Do the differences between you and other members of the group ever create difficulties for you or them? Why?
3. Think about the problem that you as a student face related to choosing courses for next semester. How will you go about solving this problem? Will you collect information? If so, of what kind (think in terms of formal and informal information)? What process will you use to evaluate that information? What will your objectives be in selecting courses? What activities will you be committing yourself to in making your selection? Do you ever evaluate a semester's courses, either during the semester or at the end? How do you do this? If you do not do so, why not?
4. Consider racism as a social problem. What systems serve to create and maintain the problem? What characteristics of racial groups make it possible for problems to be created? What systems do you think should be involved in efforts to solve the problem? Why?

REFERENCES

1. Alison Clarke-Stewart, *Child Care in the Family* (New York: Academic Press 1978), pp. ix–x.
2. A good overview of systems theories may be found in Ralph Anderson and Irl Carter, *Human Behavior in the Social Environment* (Chicago: Aldine, 1978), as well as in Walter Buckley, ed., *Modern Systems Research for the Behavioral Scientist* (Chicago: Aldine, 1968).
3. For examples, see Edwin Thomas, ed., *The Socio-Behavioral Approach and Application to Social Work* (New York: Council on Social Work Education, 1967); Allen Mazur and Leon Robertson, *Biology and Social Action* (New York: Free Press, 1972); Richard Steiner, *Managing the Human Service Organization* (Calif.: Sage Publishers, 1977); and Allen Pincus and Anne Minahan, *Social Work Practice: Model and Method* (Itasca, Ill.: F. E. Peacock, 1973).
4. Clarke-Stewart, op. cit., p. xi.
5. Charlotte Towle, *Common Human Needs* (New York: Family Service Association of America, 1952).
6. J. D. Kidd, *How Adults Learn* (New York: Association Press, 1959), pp. 140–76.
7. See, for example, Carol K. Stack, *All Our Kin: Strategies for Survival in the Black Community* (New York: Harper & Row, 1974).
8. Dolores G. Norton, ed., *The Dual Perspective* (New York: Council on Social Work Education, 1978).

SELECTED READINGS

Anderson, Ralph, and Carter, Irl. *Human Behavior in the Social Environment.* Chicago: Aldine, 1978.

Monane, Joseph. *A Sociology of Human Systems.* New York: Appleton-Century-Crofts, 1967.

Monteil, Miguel, ed. *Hispanic Families.* Washington, D.C.: National Coalition of Hispanic Mental Health and Human Service Organizations, 1978.

Munroe, Robert, and Munroe, Ruth. *Cross-Cultural Human Development.* Monterey, Calif.: Brooks/Cole Publishing, 1975.

Norton, Dolores G., ed. *The Dual Perspective.* New York: Council on Social Work Education, 1978.

Reynolds, Vernon. *The Biology of Human Action.* San Francisco: W. H. Freeman, 1976.

Reul, Myrtle. *Territorial Boundaries of Rural Poverty.* East Lansing: Michigan State University Press, 1974.

Valle, Ray, and Mendoza, Lydia. *The Elderly Latino.* San Diego: Campanile Press, 1977.

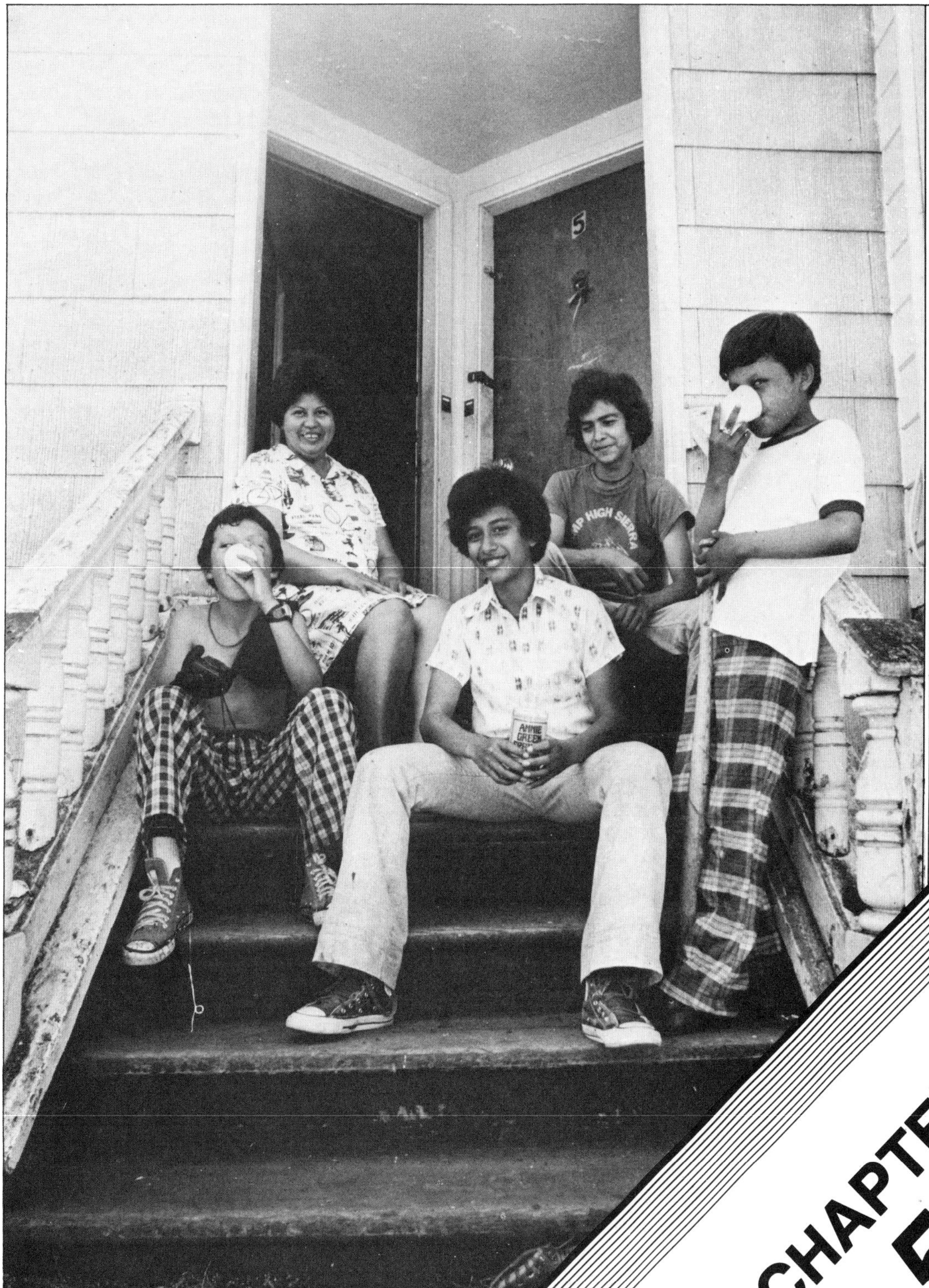

CHAPTER 5

The Knowledge Foundations of Social Welfare: Major Content Areas

Whereas the previous chapter developed a framework to use when looking at behavior and situations in order to understand them for the ultimate purpose of social welfare planning and intervention, this chapter will focus on specific content areas that the framework helps to integrate and apply. These content areas (such as sociology, psychology, political science, and so forth) are organized into three parts: knowledge that illuminates individual needs and functioning, knowledge relevant to the cultural environment, and knowledge about the social environment. Throughout this chapter, it will be useful to keep systems, human diversity, and the problem-solving process in mind: How do specific concepts (such as social stratification or the life cycle, for example) relate to understanding behavior systemically, the way human diversity affects behavior, and the way people work together to solve problems? Because most readers will probably have been exposed to each of these content areas in separate courses, a major cognitive and skill objective of this chapter is to help readers break down disciplinary boundaries in the application of knowledge to social welfare concerns. Throughout the chapter, the value objective of tying practice-related activity to a sound knowledge base will be evident.

It is impossible in one chapter to summarize and integrate the massive amount of scientific knowledge relevant to social welfare practice. This chapter will simply highlight especially useful knowledge content and stimulate the readers' abilities and readiness to make connections between theory and practice. Readers' liberal arts foundations, combined with their unique life experiences, provide a rich fund of knowledge out of which social welfare practice skills can develop. This chapter will try to start the lifelong process of making the necessary connections by looking at some criteria that may be helpful in selecting knowledge for practice and then discuss specific knowledge content areas.

Selecting Knowledge for Practice ◄

Values. Each of us has a value stance from which we approach the search for knowledge. For some, religious beliefs form an important part of their world view and their perception of cause and effect. For others, scientific methodology and empirically verified concepts and relationships are basic to their understanding of themselves and others. Still others may have an existential approach to the human condition. All of these attempts to understand the world are appropriate, but each will suggest bodies of theory that are compatible with it.

It is important to be aware of one's own values regarding acceptable sources of knowledge. This awareness not only aids us in our search for knowledge but also makes us aware of what knowledge we reject, and why. The following excerpts from an article discussing social work with American Indians illustrates what happens when a client group uses theory that has its foundations in tradition, while the professional uses theory based on practice wisdom or social science.[1]

> *The worker must not intervene unless the people request an intervention, and he is likely to wait a long time for such a request. The credentials of his profession, his position, status, knowledge, skills, achievements, and authority, though respected by the agency, are in most cases completely without merit among the Indians. Such things belong to Anglo culture and are not readily translatable into Indian culture. His standing in the Anglo community does not give him a license to practice intervention among Indian people . . . . In every case, the people utilize the established, functional, culturally acceptable remedy within their own native system.*

Evidence. A second criterion that can be used in choosing theory for practice is the evidence that supports it. Of course the whole question of what is acceptable evidence relates to values as discussed above, but however evidence is defined, that which is most strongly supported would appear to be the most promising as a basis for intervention. For example, within a scientific perspective, there is considerably more empirical evidence to demonstrate the effectiveness of behavior modification than psychotherapy. This might be one criterion to use in deciding between the two theories.

Practical Implications. Another way to choose between theories is the practical implications of each. For example, which theories suggest interventive approaches that achieve results more rapidly? At lower cost? With all user groups rather than with just selected ones? When faced with racial discrimination in a school, there are at least two competing sociological theories one could use. One says that values must first be changed, which obviously is a long, slow process. The other says that changing behavior will automatically change values, something that can be done much more rapidly (as President Eisenhower proved in Little Rock). Given that the first approach will take a generation or more to yield results, while the second approach may be used immediately and potentially be effective within a matter of a few years, one might wish to select the latter approach, all other things being equal (that is, if the second approach had much less evidence to support it than the first, one might not want to use it in spite of its rapidity).

Relevance. A final criterion usable in selecting theory is its applicability to the problem at hand. Out of the mass of existing social science data, certain segments will be most useful in dealing with a specific problem. Institutional discrimination and inequality has many causes, and many types of theory are relevant to its understanding. However, when dealing with a particular manifestation of it in a community, certain theory is more directly relevant than others. For example, when dealing with a large corporation's reluctance to hire the handicapped, focusing on corporate decision making makes more immediate sense than giving equal weight to less directly manipulable factors such as social processes that create prejudice and discrimination toward the handicapped.

▶ Individual Needs and Functioning

Social welfare is concerned with people, whether individually or in groups of various sizes. The structures of society are created by people as a way of fulfilling their needs, although of course these structures then generate their own organizational forces. People are complex unities or, in Perlman's apt description, biopsychosocial wholes.[2] People are born with genetically transmitted potential for biological growth, a potential that is socially shaped and, ultimately, socially evaluated.[3] In a culture that values bigness and strength in men, the small male will experience events that teach him to devalue his size. It does not matter whether the person is small because his parents passed on genes with limited body size potential (for example, his growth potential was fully achieved, but it was to be small) or because social conditions led to stunted body size (for example, the full potential for body size was never achieved).

One part, then, of the person's genetic inheritance is physical—size, neurological structure, organ health, and so on. As this "raw material" interacts with its social environment, the genetic potential is developed or stunted. Through this process, the psychological dimensions of growth occur. Although there are a variety of different theories of which needs can be called "common human needs," Maslow's hierarchy of human needs is well known and generally accepted: physiological needs (personal security and stability), belonging and love needs (affection, affiliation, warmth, and support), esteem needs (prestige, success, and self-respect), and self-actualization needs (seeking to develop all one's potential).[4] Furthermore, Maslow postulates that these needs are met in the above order, so that, for example, efforts to achieve self-actualization will not occur unless people's needs for belonging and love have been satisfied.

In the interaction between genetic inheritance and the social environment through which common human needs are met or ignored, the part of the psychological development generally called the personality develops. Here again, there are several theories to describe the process of personality, two of which have received the most attention: psychoanalytic and behavioral theories.

Psychoanalytic Perspectives

Sigmund Freud created a theoretical framework that attempted to unify the physiological and social events of the life cycle in a theory that explained personality formation and malfunction. "As a result of the specificity and generality of psychoanalytic theory, it seems fair to say that at the present time no theory of human behavior comes closer to accomplishing the full purpose of a behavioral theory; no other theory accounts for all the data of human behavior, its development, and its pathological deviations in terms of a basic set of postulates and derivations."[5] An added attraction of Freud's work was that it was relatively scientific for its time and capitalized on the emerging belief that human behavior could be scientifically studied.

Personality has been defined as "the sum of an individual's interrelated drives, temperament, and social roles; the unique . . . (combination) of characteristics which the individual manifests in his behavior."[6] Freud postulated that the human personality develops "through the stages of psychosexual development as the primary source of libidinal gratification shifts from the mouth to the anus to the genitals."[7] These stages are the oral, anal, phallic, latency, and adolescence. The major functioning personality units become differentiated as a result of stage development. These units, which Freud called "mental structures," are the id, ego, and superego. They may operate at one or more of three levels: the unconscious, the preconscious, and the conscious.[8] Since the Freudian personality is one with limited psychic resources (libidinal energy), the ego and superego grow by using energy originally utilized by the id.

Freud saw the personality developing as a result of two processes: the confrontation of the physical organism (id) with the social world, which results in the formation of the ego and superego; and passing through five stages in the course of the transformation of the physical organism into a fully socialized personality. The importance of the stages is that:[9]

> *Each stage can be thought of as confronting the child with a new problem, exposing him for the first time to a particular interpersonal relationship. . . . As a consequence of each stage, a certain amount of the individual's cathexes are fixated at that stage, and thus certain attitudes, fears, fantasies, defenses, and expectations are more or less permanently built into the personality. Major psychopathology results when excessive amounts of libido are fixated at an early development stage and the accompanying pattern of adjustment developed at that stage is maladapted to the demands of adult life.*

Consequently, we can see that the Freudian theory of personality development is a stage and conflict theory. The features of the personality develop through a series of stage transitions and grow out of the competition by each of the mental structures for its share of the existing libidinal energy. Exhibit 5-1 illustrates the major parts of the personality as described by Freud.

Freudian theory generated a number of "neo-Freudians" who modified and extended Freud's work in a variety of ways. For example, Otto Rank emphasized separation trauma as a motivating personality force,[10] and C. G. Jung developed his analytical psychology.[11] One of the neo-Freudians who has had considerable contemporary influence on the adaptation of Freud's ideas to social welfare contexts has been Erik Erikson.

Erikson's work is in part an attempt to elaborate the stages beyond adolescence, the last discussed by Freud. David Elkind says of Erikson:[12]

> *His descriptions of the stages of the life cycle, for example, have advanced psychoanalytic theory to the point where it can now describe the development of the healthy personality on its own terms and not merely as the opposite of a sick one. Likewise, Erikson's emphasis upon the problems unique to adolescents and adults living in today's society has helped to rectify the one-sided emphasis on childhood as the beginning and end of personality development.*

The Freudian Personality at a Glance **EXHIBIT 5-1**

Although an artificial construct for illustrative purposes, an effective way to see the scope of the Freudian theory of personality is in the following diagram. It schematically represents the three mental structures and the functions that each plays in the personality.* The total psychic (libidinal) energy within the system is fixed and it is a closed system; therefore, if the boundaries between any structures are to be changed, it will necessarily mean a redistribution of energy (which is why it is called a "hydraulic theory"). These structures develop in the process of moving through stages. Since the hydraulic nature of the system means one structure's gain is another's loss, defense mechanisms exist for each structure's use in trying to protect itself; hence the conflict nature of the system. Note that the id is completely unconscious, and the ego and superego have conscious, preconscious, and unconscious components.

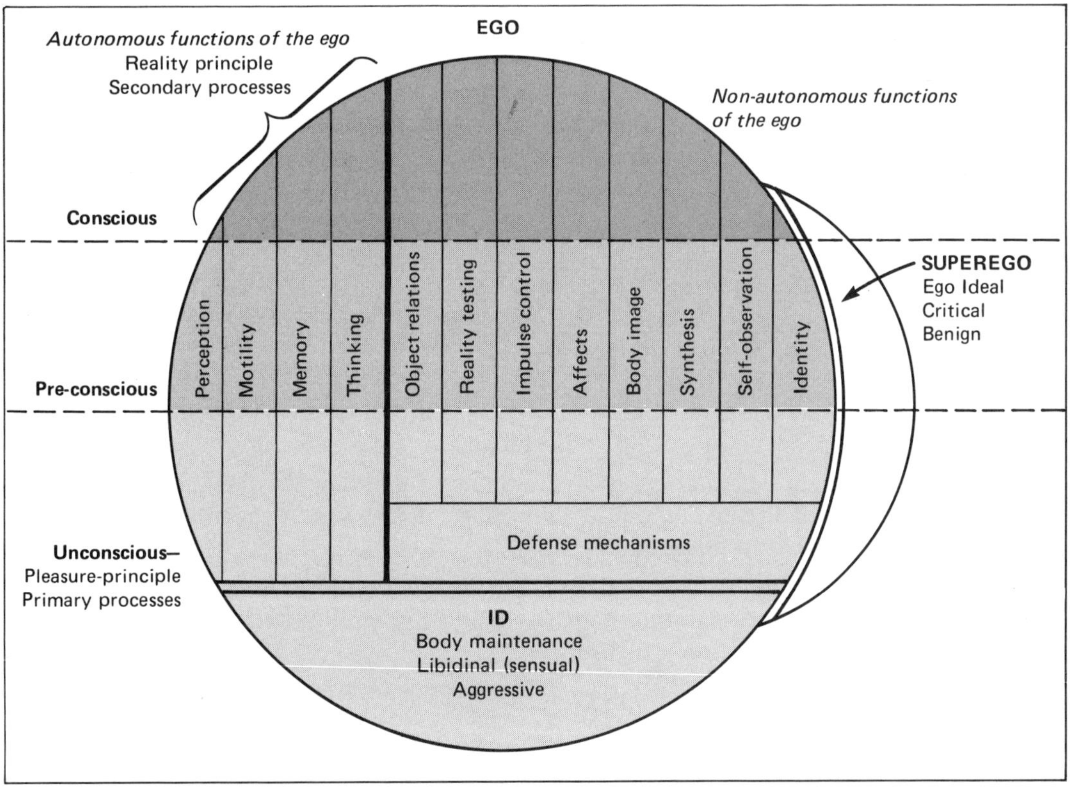

Source: From a lecture by Jack C. Westman, M.D., Professor of Psychiatry, University of Wisconsin, at the University of Michigan School of Social Work, October 23, 1962. Used with permission.

* For an elaboration of any of the concepts used, refer to Charles Brenner, *An Elementary Textbook of Psychoanalysis* (Garden City, N.Y.: Doubleday, 1957).

Erikson begins with "an epigenetic principle of maturation,"[13] which postulates that each individual has a physical timetable governing maturation. This timetable determines when libidinal energy will be shifted from one part of the body to another:[14]

> *This means that stages of development do not grow out of each other. For example, the stage when anal-type functioning is dominant does not result from the child-environment interaction necessary to successful passage through the oral stage . . . . The primary condition (for the oral to anal transition) is his maturational code, which determines when the focus of instinctual investment will be shifted from the oral to the anal zone. . . . But continuity between stages is so implied by the epigenetic principle insofar as each organ must already be a potential part of the ground plan in order for it to grow out of it and mature at the proper time.*

Erikson, then, is giving a different kind of emphasis to the biological component of personality from that assigned it by Freud. Whereas Freud saw the personality being shaped by a confrontation of internal biological and external social forces, Erikson says biological forces set a timetable to which social forces must adapt if the personality is to be a healthy one. Once a given biological stage is passed, the individual must move on, whether a successful social adaptation to the earlier stage has been achieved or not.

The combination of a genetic time clock and the fact that biological changes occur throughout the life cycle made it natural for Erikson to extend Freud's stages beyond adolescence. Erikson's eight stages are:[15]

1. *Oral stage.* Crisis of trust in the person on whom one is most dependent for one's sustenance.
2. *Anal stage.* Crisis of whether one will develop feelings of autonomy or shame and doubt about oneself, one's actions, and one's ability to be autonomous.
3. *Phallic stage.* Crisis of acquiring a sense of moral responsibility resulting from the initiative and consequent guilt in the resolution of the Oedipal problem.
4. *Latency stage.* Crisis of industriousness versus feelings of inferiority and overconformity.
5. *Adolescent stage.* Crisis of identity adoption versus identity diffusion.
6. *Genital stage.* Crisis of gratification from intimacy and solidarity versus isolation and withdrawal from relationships.

7. *Adulthood.* Crisis of caring for others and being a contributor versus self-absorption, stagnation, and interpersonal impoverishment.
8. *Senescence.* Crisis of ego integration versus despair.

Elkind summarizes the significance of Erikson's eight stages as follows:[16]

> *Their presentation . . . frees the clinician to treat adult emotional problems as failures (in part at least) to solve genuinely adult personality crises and not, as heretofore, as mere residuals of infantile frustrations and conflicts. This view of personality growth . . . takes some of the onus off parents and takes account of the role which society and the person himself play in the formation of the individual personality. Finally, Erikson has offered hope for us all by demonstrating that each phase of growth has its strengths as well as its weaknesses and that failures at one stage of development can be rectified by successes at later stages.*

Exhibit 5-2 (pp. 172–73) summarizes the major components of the stage theories discussed above.

Concurrent with the part of psychological development usually referred to as personality is the development of cognitive and perceptual abilities, also part of the person's psychological functioning. Cognition and perception are partially biologically determined—given adequate nutrition, stimulation, and physical care, they will develop within genetically set limits,[17] which of course may range from severe handicap (such as blindness or mongoloidism) to exceptional ability. However, cognition and perception are also partially socially determined, with personality development an important mediating factor. Here again, numerous theories prevail, ranging from Ellis' rational-emotive theory,[18] to Gestalt theory,[19] to a variety of learning based theories.[20] For example, Carl Rogers said, "A person learns significantly only those things which he perceives as being involved in the maintenance of, or enhancement of, the structure of self."[21] This is supported by a large body of research to show that people perceive very selectively,[22] and of course perception is closely tied to cognition. Rogers has developed his client-centered therapy based on the principles derived from these theories. It emphasizes clients' cognitive recognition of the sources of their behavioral difficulties, and it builds on ego and cognitive strengths to find solutions to them.

Behavioral Perspectives

Behavioristic theory asserts that behavior is learned in separate units (acts); that the units (acts) are related to each other; and that the units (acts) become established in the individual's behavior repertoire by means of external reinforcement.[23]

EXHIBIT 5-2 *Stages at a Glance*

This chart is an excellent summary of major stage theories, showing the relationship between physical and social development.

Psychobiological Development

Stage	*Age*	*Cognitive Functions*	*Affective Drives*	*Object Relations*	*Personality Structure*	*Critical Issues and Fantasies*
	Birth to 3 mo.	Congenital threshold of perception	Libidinal aggressive	Sucking Clinging Following	Primary Process	
		Smiles	Oral receptive—primary narcissism	Autistic	Pleasure principle	Omnipotence
	6 mo.			Symbiotic	Incorporation Projection	"To wish to have" "I am what I am given"
	9 mo.	Anxiety with strangers				Anxiety—loss of object (abandonment)
ORAL			Oral sadistic		Reality testing	
	12 mo.			Individuation		Oral triad—to eat, to be eaten, to die
	15 mo.	Thinking—phenomenistic (cause by contiguity)	Curiosity—see, touch, swallow		Reality principle	Trust vs. basic mistrust
	18 mo.				Denial (close eyes)	
			Anal sadistic—expelling, rejecting, destroying	Oppositional ambivalence		Passivity vs. activity
	2 yrs.	Magical thinking			Secondary Process	Control of self & environment
ANAL					Turning against the self	
	3 yrs.	Thinking—animistic causality (objects alive)	Anal retentive—possessing, withholding, exhibiting			Anxiety—loss of love, body contents
					Identification with aggressor	"I am what I wish"
	4 yrs.		Phallic	Oedipal complex	Denial	Autonomy vs. shame and doubt
		Dynamic causality (forces in object)				Castration anxiety
OEDIPAL					Repression displacement	Fantasies—birth, sex difference, primal scene
	5 yrs.				Sublimation Identification	Family romance Anxiety—Superego

Source: From a lecture by Dr. Mary Burns at the University of Michigan School of Social Work.

Stage	*Age*	*Cognitive Functions*	*Affective Drives*	*Object Relations*	*Personality Structure*	*Critical Issues and Fantasies*
	6 yrs.	Mechanical causality			Infantile amnesia	Initiative vs. guilt
	7 yrs.	Tell time Thinking—rational causality	Latency	Peers (same sex)	Reality principle	"I am what I can imagine I will be"
	8 yrs.		Auto-erotic	Teacher	Restriction of the ego Reaction formation	Develop individual skills
LATENCY				Parent surrogates	Undoing isolation	
	9 yrs.	Multiplication and division		Homosocial		Industry vs. inferiority "I am what I can do or learn"
	10 yrs.	Use dictionary		Devaluation of parental omnipotence and omniscience	Elaboration of superego	
	11 yrs.					Masturbation guilt, Oedipal fantasies
	12 yrs.		Puberty	Heterosocial		
				Peer group heroes Crushes	Asceticism Intellectualization	Anxiety—strength of drives
	13 yrs.	Thinking—formal operations	Genital		Regression Identification Altruism	
ADOLES-CENCE and GENITAL	14 yrs.	Heightened perceptual sensitivity				
	15 yrs.	Integration of associational traits		Distance vs. closeness	Individuality—ego-skill Superego—moral values Ego ideal	Oedipal complex revived Conflict of generations
	16 yrs.	Self-observation		Narcissistic object love	Acceptance of identifications Role experimentation	Parental vs. adolescent aspirations
	17 yrs.				Identity—self-esteem equals esteem of others	"I am what I am"
ADULT-HOOD TO SENESCENCE	18 yrs. Plus					Identity vs. identity diffusion

> *Central to the (behavioristic) conception of growth is the environmentalistic assumption that the source of all psychological phenomena is stimulation from the outside world . . .* [*and*] *psychological phenomena, like all other natural occurrences, are really physical in quality, or, at least, reducible to characterization in physicalistic terms.*

In a behavioristic perspective, acts are stimulated by the environment and are associated with each other into habits (learned behavioral patterns). Since acts are associational, behavior already learned does affect future behavior. "Stored associations influence the child's responses to environmental stimulation. The major (behavioristic) development hypothesis is therefore that early conditioned associations affect the child's behavior later in life."[24] Although the ideas of environmental influence on behavior and early behavior affecting later behavior are not incongruent with a psychoanalytic approach, the fact that no internal personality structure is specified is quite different from psychoanalytic theory. The focus on individual acts implies that they can be modified without a major realignment of the personality structure, a belief that is also quite divergent from psychoanalytic postulates.[25]

There are three ways in which behavioral theorists assert that behavior may be learned: classical (or respondent) conditioning, operant (or instrumental) conditioning, and imitation. Conditioning is most simply defined as the association of stimuli with responses. Classical (or respondent) conditioning is built on the principles of the unconditioned reflex and contiguity. An unconditioned reflex is an "innate response to stimuli,"[26] and the contiguity principle specifies that "the contiguity of two stimuli tends to give one of them the ability to elicit responses previously made to the other."[27] Classical conditioning, therefore, involves stimulus substitution. An unconditioned stimulus (one that evokes an unconditioned reflex) is paired with a conditioned stimulus (one that would not normally evoke an unconditioned reflex). Eventually the conditioned stimulus evokes the behavior previously evoked by the unconditioned stimulus. The famous Pavlov experiment illustrates classical conditioning, in which a dog was taught to salivate (a conditioned response) upon hearing a bell (the conditioned stimulus) after the bell has been associated with the presentation of food powder (the unconditioned stimulus).

Notice that there is a built-in limitation to the learning that may occur in classical conditioning. Since this type of conditioning depends on the existence of an unconditioned stimulus and response, only responses that already exist can be tied to different stimuli. Although classical conditioning is usable in social welfare contexts, a more flexible learning mechanism would clearly have greater utility.

Operant (or instrumental) conditioning is just such a tool. In operant conditioning, an individual's behavior is reacted to in some way by the environment (individuals can in some respects be their own environment).

Behavior that is responded to in a reinforcing way has the probability of its repetition increased. If the behavior continues to be reinforced it can be established as a habit. Operant conditioning may occur for randomly performed behaviors, or it may be shaped. Shaping starts with randomly performed behavior, successively reinforcing it and eliminating it as new behaviors closer to the ultimately desired behavior occur and are in turn reinforced and eliminated. Shaping is discussed in more detail later in this chapter.[28]

> *There is one major difference between classical and instrumental (operant) conditioning. In classical conditioning, an action that is already a response to a stimulus can be put under the control of a [different] stimulus by contiguity of the two stimuli. In instrumental conditioning, an action that is not tied to any specific stimulus can be put under the control of a stimulus by rewarding the action consistently when it is performed in the presence of the stimulus. Thus, randomly occurring actions can be made into reliable, controllable responses or regularly recurring actions.*

Two of the major issues in operant conditioning are the nature of the reinforcements and the schedule (frequency) of reinforcements. It is believed that individuals are ready to respond to stimuli in different ways at different times (called the drive state) and that different drive states have different drive stimuli. Therefore, there is no general uniformity of conditioning states; what will be reinforcing will vary between individuals and by drive state of any given individual. Although candy may be a generally effective reinforcer for the average child, it will not be for certain children, and will be less effective for any given child at some times than at others. Clearly, the individual's past reinforcement history will be important in understanding the crucial question of what is reinforcing for that individual, and this in turn is tied to cultural values and behavior patterns. Without such knowledge, the practitioner's ability to control behavior in an operant context is limited. A further complication is that the frequency of reinforcement also affects the learning that occurs. It has been experimentally shown that the frequency and patterning of reinforcements produces different learning patterns, again suggesting that the operant conditioning context is more complicated than might at first be assumed.[29]

A third behavioristic learning device is observational learning, or imitation. Observational learning "describes the fact that people can learn behavior patterns merely by watching other people perform them, that their own acts can be reinforced or inhibited by observing reinforcements and punishments to other people, and that they can acquire conditioned emotional responses to stimuli which accompany a painful stimulus to another person."[30] Whether or not observational learning occurs through imitation is affected by the individual's history of reward for imitation, history of reward deprivation, level of self-esteem and general dependency, and drive state. Observational learning may occur in primary or secondary contexts (that is, direct viewing or via a mechanical medium such as television).

Bandura and Walters suggest four major behavior modification techniques based on behavioral principles:[31] Most directly related to conditioning as a learning process is *positive reinforcement*—the teaching of behavior through the manipulation of positive reinforcements (rewards). The environment commonly dispenses rewards that enable social learning to occur in many societal contexts. Social welfare practitioners may manipulate rewards in purposeful ways to strengthen existing behaviors that are rarely or randomly performed. For example, a common problem of many marginally employable persons is their lack of skill in job interviews. In such a case, the helping person could use positive reinforcements to strengthen those behaviors appropriate to the job-interview context, such as punctuality, style of dress, and so on.

Whereas positive reinforcement is a powerful tool in strengthening and maintaining behavior, *extinction* is a tool usable in weakening and eliminating behavior.[32] Thomas defines the use of extinction as "withholding the reinforcer when a response, previously reinforced by that reinforcer, is emitted."[33] In many respects, extinction is the opposite of positive reinforcement and is based on the same principle—that behavior will be performed when it results in gratification for the actor. Extinction is a planned process of making sure that the reinforcement that previously occurred (thereby maintaining the behavior) no longer occurs. Under such conditions, the basis for the future performance of the behavior will be eliminated and the probability of its future occurrence reduced until it is eliminated altogether. Exhibit 5-3 illustrates the use of extinction.

A third behavioral technique is *counterconditioning,* sometimes called reciprocal inhibition. "The fundamental principle in using counterconditioning therapeutically, is to establish a response which is incompatible with a maladaptive response so the latter is eliminated."[34] Counterconditioning is a tool usable in eliminating undesirable behavior. It is based on the obvious fact that one cannot do two incompatible things at once. Rewards are provided to strengthen the desired behavior, which are more attractive than the rewards maintaining the undesired behavior. Counterconditioning frequently includes desensitization, which involves the purposeful manipulation of the stimulus evoking the undesired behavior. It is first presented in mild forms so that the resulting undesired responses are relatively weak and thus readily extinguishable.[35] As the desired behavior is progressively more strongly established, the stimulus evoking the undesired behavior may be presented in its normal form. The undesired response will now be more weakly reinforced than the desired response and will therefore be extinguished.[36]

An Example of Extinction EXHIBIT 5-3

A twenty-one-month-old boy . . . engaged in tyrannical tantrum behavior. The child would scream and fuss when put to bed and his parents couldn't leave the bedroom until he was asleep. The parents generally spent one-half to two hours simply waiting in the room until the boy went to sleep.

After it was determined that the tantrum behavior was sustained by the attention provided by the parents at bedtime, it was decided to institute a regimen of extinction. The treatment program was based upon research indicating that by steadfastly withholding reinforcers that sustain the behavior, there will eventually be a diminution of the behavior in question. It was decided to put the child to bed in a leisurely and relaxed fashion. Then, following the usual pleasantries, the parent was to leave and the door to be left closed. On the first night, the child screamed for forty-five minutes; on the second, he did not fuss at all; on the third, he screamed for ten minutes; on the fourth, for six; on the fifth, for three; on the sixth, for two; and, finally, after seven sessions, there was no screaming at all. In a follow-up, there were no side- or after-effects, and the child was found to be friendly, expressive, and outgoing.

Source: Excerpted from Edwin Thomas, ed., *The Socio-Behavioral Approach and Applications to Social Work* (New York: Council on Social Work Education, 1967), pp. 3–4. Reprinted by permission of the Council on Social Work Education.

The fourth major behavior modification technique based on behavioral principles is *modeling,* or observation learning. It results in new behavior when an observer faithfully reproduces a model's behavior that was not previously in the observer's behavioral repertoire. Observing a model can also serve to inhibit or disinhibit an observer's behavior, depending on the consequences to the model of his or her behavior. Inhibition, disinhibition, and response facilitation are not mechanisms for learning new behaviors. They involve already-existing behaviors being performed more or less frequently as a result of exposure to a model.[37] Modeling may occur when the model is physically present or when the model is presented vicariously, and characteristics of the model will affect the amount of modeling that takes place (the model's prestige and power, age, consequences to the model of his or her behavior, and so on).

Some have questioned the desirability of behavior modification techniques because of their obvious subversive potential. In a psychoanalytic approach, the talking through of the individual's problems and social history presumably insures at least a minimal recognition and acceptance of the behavior change process by the client. In the behavioristic approach, since behavior modification occurs through the manipulation of stimuli, reinforcements, and models, it is entirely possible for an individual's behavior to be modified without the person knowing it.

However, the resolution of the problem of misuse of a therapeutic tool does not lie in its abandonment. Doctors are known occasionally to misuse their techniques, but few would seriously propose that the techniques therefore be abandoned. The resolution of the issue in medicine lies in the strength of the profession to regulate member behavior, and this solution must be used in those professions using any form of behavior modification techniques. Ethical behavior is a professional responsibility, and it has its foundation in effective professional socialization and sanctioning.

A common goal of social welfare professionals is to achieve behavior change. Such change may result from therapeutic intervention with individuals or groups, or from social structural change that alters the environment in which individuals live, thereby facilitating individual and group behavior change. The social welfare practitioner cannot avoid the considerable responsibility entailed in behavior change. The practitioner must first be certain that efforts toward change, including methods and objectives, are acceptable to the people who will be affected by them. Having assured oneself of this, one is committed to the appropriate use of the most relevant and effective skill and knowledge at one's disposal in planning and executing change.

Comparing Psychoanalytic and Behavioral Theories of Personality

Although each proceeds differently, both psychoanalytic and behavioral theories of personality seek to link psychological development to social experiences. In that sense, they both emphasize systems, because they suggest that even at the level of individual growth and development one must understand the interaction of systems—in this case the biological system with the social systems impinging on it, such as the family, economic conditions, community resources, and so on. Both also relate to the problem-solving process in that they see human psychological development resulting from efforts to solve the problem (broadly speaking) of meeting needs. Out of the effort to find resources needed to grow and out of responses to such resources a solution is found—a personality that uses its cognitive and perceptual capacities to survive in its environment.

Unfortunately, neither theory of personality development explicitly addresses human diversity as a part of psychological development and functioning. This reflects the kind of ethnocentric thinking that has supported biased knowledge—we know a great deal about what has been defined as "normal" behavior in child rearing in middle-class families, but little about socioeconomic and ethnic variations.[38] We even know little about sex-related differences, including the interplay between the sex of the parent and the sex of the child.[39] Yet both psychoanalytic and behavioral theories would suggest that human diversity is important. Most basic is the biological uniqueness that is genetically transmitted—each person starts with a unique set of potentials, and therefore the developmental experience has to be differentially experienced.

In addition, both theories suggest that the social environment is very important. Obviously, these environments are strongly influenced by such variables as socioeconomic resources, ethnic values and behaviors, sex-related values, and many others. The fact that these differences exist and have an impact on behavior and development is not to say that they lead to "abnormal" development, an interpretation that has frequently resulted from ethnocentric interpretations of psychological theories (especially psychoanalytic theories). Variation from the norm is not equivalent to abnormality, although social definitions sometimes arbitrarily relate the two. Most psychiatrists would agree that a young female who seeks to engage in "tomboy" activities is not suffering from "penis envy"—she is simply responding to the interaction of genetic potential and socially created opportunities in her own way. To the degree that she is dealt with insensitively by her environment because of her uniqueness, however, she may indeed develop problematic behavior patterns (hostility, fear and anxiety, or destructiveness). These problems result from the social response to diversity, not from the diversity itself.

To summarize, individual needs are genetically derived and socially expressed. Through this interaction of individual's needs and social responses to them the individual develops a psychological structure with which to achieve one's ongoing needs. There are many theories that seek to explain this complex process. All of the major theories probably have some utility in doing so, although it is doubtful that any one is completely adequate. Theories vary in the degree to which they are empirically derived and supported, with psychoanalytic theories especially weak in empirical support. The utility of each theory is enhanced if seen within the systems, problem-solving, and human diversity described in the last chapter.

The Cultural Environment ◀

Culture is learned, shared, and transmitted behavior, the preserved experiences of a group that shape its thinking and future behavior. Culture consists of material objects such as housing, work tools, and dress, as well as nonmaterial components like values and ideas. The parameters of a group's orientation to its environment are defined by its culture, so that one group may focus on and especially value interpersonal relationships, whereas another may emphasize task accomplishment. This is why, as noted in the last chapter, culture is one source of human diversity. These cultural definitions of what is desirable strongly affect behavior because they tend to limit people's perceptions of what is even feasible. American Indian culture, for example, generally has such a strong respect for the physical environment that the Indians find it difficult to imagine that one possible adaptation to that environment is to use technology to dominate and control it. Yet non-Indian cultures routinely adapt in this way, wondering in the process why Indians have not become more "modern."

EXHIBIT 5-4 *Cultural Diversity in the United States*

The United States has always prided itself on its ability to accept and absorb persons from other cultures and societies. This has been an extraordinary part of this society's growth, and it has created an enormously rich culture resulting from the sharing between the many groups involved. The following data show the amount of immigration from major contributing countries during the period 1891–1975. These data demonstrate that most immigration has been from other Western cultures, although it should be pointed out that there has been significant immigration from certain non-Western cultures not shown in this table, especially Japan, China, and India, as well as the more recent immigration from Thailand and Vietnam.

Immigrants Admitted From Major Contributing Countries: 1891–1975

Years	*Total immigrants (thousands)*	*Major countries* Country	Number (thousands)	*Total immigrants during preceding decade as a percent of population at end of decade*	*Total U.S. population at end of decade (thousands)*
1891–1900	3,688	Italy	652	4.8	75,995
		Austria-Hungary	593		
		U.S.S.R.	505		
1901–1910	8,795	Austria-Hungary	2,145	9.6	91,972
		Italy	2,046		
		U.S.S.R.	1,597		
1911–1920	5,736	Italy	1,110	5.4	105,711
		U.S.S.R.	921		
		Canada and Newfoundland	742		
1921–1930	4,107	Canada and Newfoundland	925	3.3	122,775
		Italy	455		
		Germany	412		
1931–1940	528	Germany	114	.4	131,669
		Canada and Newfoundland	109		
		Italy	68		
1941–1950	1,035	Germany	227	.7	150,697
		Canada and Newfoundland	172		
		England	112		
1951–1960	2,515	Germany	478	1.4	179,323
		Canada and Newfoundland	378		
		Mexico	300		
1961–1970	3,322	W. Indies	470	1.6	203,235
		Mexico	454		
		Canada and Newfoundland	413		
1971–1975	1,936	Canada and Newfoundland	445	(X)	213,450
		Mexico	319		
		Philippines	150		

Source: Bureau of the Census, *Social Indicators 1976* (Washington, D.C.: U.S. Government Printing Office, 1977), p. LXIX. (Table originally taken from U.S. Department of Justice, Immigration and Naturalization Service, annual reports and unpublished data.)

X: Not applicable.

Cultures are operationalized through the social structures of societies, the actual organizations and rules established by a geographically located group with its own perceived identity. The cultural tradition generally holds more than is used at any given time, and it is constantly enriched through new experiences and exposure to other cultures. The various immigrant groups that settled in the United States had to adapt their cultural traditions, learned through their own languages and in societal institutions such as the family, education, and religion, to the new environment in which they found themselves.[40] These cultural traditions and resulting social structures had varying degrees of fit, and hence some adaptations were easier than others. In general, all Western cultures share more with each other than they do with non-Western cultures, and therefore exchange between Western societies is often easier. This is reflected in the traditional predominance of immigrant groups with Western cultures into the United States as demonstrated in Exhibit 5-4. However, immigration also reflects existing political and economic relationships between societies, as reflected in recent immigration to the United States from Vietnam (political) and Mexico (economic). Some sense of the differences between cultures, in terms of values, beliefs, and behaviors can be seen in Exhibit 5-5. Since this example is between two Western cultures (the United States and Cuba), it is easy to imagine the magnitude of the differences between even more dissimilar cultures.

The Cross-Cultural Migratory Experience EXHIBIT 5-5

Moving from one society or culture to another involves profound dislocations in thought and behavior patterns. The whole organization of one's perception of the environment, once taken for granted, is called into question. The natural, accepted behavior patterns may no longer be appropriate. Since our sense of self is closely tied to our security in being able to understand and function in the world around us, the person's whole personality structure may be threatened by cultural dislocations. The following excerpt describes the experiences of a Cuban family migrating from Cuba to the United States, and it is notable for the fact that the family members are well educated and come from a relatively affluent background.

Source: Excerpted from Myrtle Reul, *The Migration Episode and Its Consequences* (East Lansing: Michigan State University, 1972), pp. 72–94.

Maria Verona arrived at the Miami airport in August, 1960, with $75 in cash. The four children, who had always been cared for by servants, were eight, seven, six, and four years old. Only the two oldest could speak English, and only Luisa understood that they had left Cuba for a new home.

Luisa remembers some of the fears she had upon arriving in Miami. She helped her mother watch the other children and keep them together. It was the first time they had ever traveled without a maid, and she was terrified that something would happen to her mother. She knew that she, as the oldest, would traditionally have full responsibility for the care of the others, and she was afraid she would not know where to go or what to do. She remembers waking up at night and checking to see that her mother was still alive.

Maria's immediate concerns were how to cope with the problems of finding housing in a strange city, and how to manage the care of four children.

The youngest child was crying to go home to his own bed and the comfort of his nurse. She had never before been faced with the responsibilities of finding her own housing, making arrangements for utilities, or shopping for food. She had no idea what things cost or whether or not she was being overcharged.

She found an unfurnished house within walking distance of a school for $200 a month. She bought five cots and a stove and camped, awaiting the arrival of her husband. The children were homesick . . . .

Several weeks later when Carlos arrived in Miami, he was met by his family. He recalls the cultural shock of seeing his children "in public" barefoot and wearing shorts. He had never seen them look so disarrayed and so dirty before . . . .

The experiences in Miami were different from anything they had anticipated. The house was crowded with relatives who needed temporary housing. There was a limited number of beds and dishes. There was not enough privacy. These were all things they had never experienced before.

Carlos found that a doctor in exile, especially a psychiatrist, without proof of education and without having passed the examination of the Educational Council for Foreign Medical Graduates could not be considered for anything other than menial work. He was offered a job cleaning instruments, but he could not bring himself to take it. He decided to keep looking until he found a position in psychiatry.

Maria was more fortunate. She was offered a job as a social worker in the very same hospital where her husband was refused one in psychiatry.

Meanwhile, Maria's father, Dr. Estevoz, had arrived in Miami. Although he was well known in this country, he felt the need to prove himself just as he did when he was a young doctor at the University of Havana. It was almost as if the honors he had earned in a lifetime did not exist. He had to prove himself all over again because he was in the United States in a new role . . . he was an exile . . . .

In late December, a few months after his arrival, Carlos received information that a mental hospital in a southern state had an opening for a psychiatrist. He was told that a foreign physician would not need an examination if he made application by December 31. It was then December 30.

Carlos and Maria went to the mental hospital in Community X the next day. He was hired and scheduled to begin work in mid-January at $715 a month. He was pleased. They could manage well on such an income. Unfortunately he knew nothing about payroll deductions, and was unprepared at the end of January when he received a paycheck of slightly over $250 instead of the $355 he had expected for his first two weeks of work.

Although he was forty years old, this was the first time in his life that Carlos had ever actually been responsible for his own support or the support of others. He was conscious of his insecurity as he approached his new position. He felt confident of his medical training, but he was aware that he would need to prove himself in a strange community where the name Verona had no meaning . . .

There were many moments of insecurity in the early weeks at the hospital. On one occasion, an extremely ill patient threatened to report that he had made overtures toward her unless he did something she wanted. This is not an unusual situation for a psychiatrist to face and Carlos had handled it before with patients. But here he was a stranger, a foreigner, not yet established, and his wife and children were in Miami depending upon him. For the first time in his life he was not certain of his own position. He thought, "What will happen to me if this patient carries out her threat? What will the hospital officials believe?" He said his heart was pounding and his mouth was dry.

For the four Verona children, school adjustment in Community X was difficult. The greatest cultural shock was being treated as if they were different. They had never thought of themselves as being different, but now they were stared at. Sometimes they were treated as "poor refugees" and that was even worse. Luisa was told she looked like a "gypsy." She heard the word "Spick" for the first time and did not know its meaning. She was embarrassed to go to school wearing hand-me-down dresses that another student had outgrown.

The boys experienced more name calling than Luisa. They were constantly taunted with, "Castro, why don't you go back to Cuba where you belong? What did you want to come here for in the first place?" Later, those who did the most name calling became the best friends, but in the beginning everything was strange. The children felt as if they were between two worlds and not part of either.

Because each of us is raised in a particular culture, we grow up believing that what we do is "natural." When we are confronted by people who do things differently, it seems "wrong" or "strange" to us (although, of course, it seems "natural" to the other person). This tendency to see the world only from our own cultural perspective and to denigrate other cultures is called *ethnocentrism.* It is one of the major obstacles to sharing and cooperation between cultural groups, often leading instead to acts of *discrimination* (disadvantaging persons based on their group membership) that grow out of *prejudices* (irrational beliefs about categories of people). The inability to accept and appreciate cultural variation often leads to attempts to force the beliefs and behaviors of one cultural group on another.[41] For many years, it was considered desirable to seek a "melting pot" of cultures whereby the various cultures that make up United States society would meld together into one.

It has become apparent that efforts to combine cultures into one whole that eradicates many of the distinctive characteristics of each quickly gets into power-related issues. Who is to determine what aspects of which culture are to be preserved? Since new immigrant groups are by definition minority groups (as illustrated by the Verona family), they have little power to use in preserving those aspects of their culture that they consider valuable but which others may consider unimportant. The melting pot concept can easily become a justification for the reduction of cultural integrity to cultural stereotypes, and thus the Italian contribution to the pot is spaghetti and the black contribution is a delightful sense of rhythm.

An alternative view is *cultural pluralism,* in which each culture is seen as having its own integrity and right to preserve itself (if its members wish to). The society that results is a mosaic of many differently shaped and colored pieces that fit together into a complex, diverse, but integrated and interdependent whole. A pluralistic view avoids efforts to systematically destroy parts of cultures for the convenience of the dominant cultural group, thereby also avoiding the eroding of self-identity and feelings of self-worth that accompany such a process for members of the denigrated culture. These effects are poignantly described in Reul.[42] From a social welfare viewpoint, cultural pluralism is much more consistent with efforts to help people function more effectively by utilizing their own resources, rather than trying to replace their resources with those considered desirable by another cultural group. Sheehan[43] demonstrates the waste and illogicality of the latter approach, although her book also emphasizes that the development of social welfare services that respect and support a variety of cultures is a difficult and complicated process.

A final point about cultures is that they are best understood in terms of subcultures. Any but the least complex cultures have several internal subgroups that have modified the culture base in some ways and yet are still clearly identified as a part of the larger culture. United States society is an excellent example. There are cultural characteristics that are distinctly American[44] and which practically all subgroups in the society incorporate. At the same time, there are a multitude of diverse groups that have adapted the major aspects of the culture into distinctive subcultural patterns. An interesting recent example of this process is a study of homosexuals in the United States in which the data show that most homosexuals share many values and behaviors with heterosexuals and yet have created a distinctive life-style that is a functional adaptation to the social realities they face in a society that generally devalues homosexuality.[45]

A second important aspect of subcultures is that of their internal diversity. The very existence of subcultures demonstrates the enormous internal diversity within a culture, as explained above. However, even within subcultures there is usually considerable variation. Liebow's study of black street corner men[46] demonstrated this as has Sheehan's more recent portrait of the prison subculture.[47] The cultural roots of human diversity are deep, and they spread into a tangled web of complexity reflected within and between subcultures as well as larger cultures. The result is somewhat different cultural realities for the many groups within a culture. Since culture is such a pervasive force in the way people think, in what they believe and value, and in the way they act, the particular cultural context of the person or group with which the social welfare practitioner interacts has to be understood if helping is to occur.

The Social Environment

As noted earlier, cultural values, beliefs, and behaviors form the basis for the social structures created to organize social behavior. Consensus and conflict are ever-present forces in this process, because the diverse cultural elements in a society often have different behavioral imperatives. Although Anglo culture may not especially value the elderly, and therefore creates a relatively impersonal structure to care for them, Hispanic cultures value the elderly much more highly and press for social welfare services that personalize their needs and keep them within their local community.[48] These differences seek accommodation at the same time that basic consensus about societal goals and acceptable behaviors are sought. Conflict sometimes results, especially when each group approaches problems from a highly ethnocentric point of view and when one group has more power than the other.

As with personality development, there are a number of theories that seek to explain how social structures in societies are formed, operate, and change.[49] *Structural-functional* theories emphasize that social structures exist because they are effective for carrying out societal functions. These theories tend to focus on social stability rather than social change. The concepts of manifest and latent functions discussed in Chapter 1 are part of this theoretical approach. The *social conflict* theories then developed in order to give more emphasis to change. These theories see social structures emerging from struggles between various groups in society in the pursuit of their own self-interests. Although conflict theories do not dispute the fact that there are important social functions to be accomplished in a society, they believe that the structures that emerge to perform them are functional primarily for the most powerful groups in society. For example, doctors are more highly paid in American society than refuse collectors. Structural-functional theories would explain this in terms of doctors being more functional than refuse collectors—they preserve life, a basic necessity for society. As a result, they receive greater societal rewards in order to encourage people to undertake the long, rigorous training. Social conflict theories would explain the same fact in terms of doctors being more powerful—they have a powerful professional association (the American Medical Association) to fight on their behalf, and their threats to withhold basic life-sustaining medical services is more serious than threats not to pick up the garbage.

There are also other sociological theories to explain social structures and behavior. Evolutionary theories see inevitable developmental processes in social life that, analogous to biological principles, result in "birth" (the establishment of social structures), growth and development (increase in complexity), and decline. *Ethnomethodological* and *symbolic interactionist* theories see social life as highly situational, emerging from the interaction between people in the particular kinds of situations in which they find themselves. Nevertheless, all of these theories share a basic belief in the fact that social life is structured and that certain structural characteristics of society are basic (such as norms, roles, social control mechanisms, and others, which will be discussed later). This basic structure helps to explain much social behavior and therefore is very useful for social welfare professionals. However, the direct link between sociological/anthropological theories of social structure and their practice implications is less strong than was the case for the personality theories discussed earlier. Therefore, we will review concepts relevant to understanding the ways in which social structures influence behavior and raise implications for social welfare practice. However, the relationships between these concepts and practice will of necessity be more general than was the case with the personality theories reviewed previously.

Societies exist to facilitate the overall human enterprise—to help people accomplish more than would be possible without collective action. In order to do so, a structure of rules is created so that the many tasks that must be performed if the society is to function can be carried out with minimal overall disruption (although, as will be seen later, overall stability is often achieved at the cost of subgroup instability). The most basic rules of behavior, called *norms,* are associated with *positions,* groups of people who do the same thing (such as raise children, perform courtship rituals, work as a nurse, and so forth) in more or less the ways specified by society's norms. These are called *roles,* the behaviors associated with a position. Those who deviate from the generally accepted norms or positions are considered *deviant,* and they are thought to threaten the consensus and stability that societies seek. For example, the psychiatrist who uses the therapeutic relationship to obtain sexual favors violates the role associated with that position, and the skid row inhabitant who rejects the whole role/position structure associated with steady employment and related values of self-sufficiency is also defined as deviant.

Norms and roles are transmitted through *socialization,* the process of social learning. Socialization helps people learn how to fit into the structure of social relationships, although as the skid row inhabitants just discussed demonstrate, people may ultimately reject what they have learned. This can result from *role strains and inconsistencies,* the difficulties inherent in fulfilling many roles simultaneously. It may also result from mental illness that distorts social reality. Finally, it may result from the rejection of social relationships that people feel violate their cultural traditions, seeking instead opportunities to act out their own cultural imperatives (which have, of course, themselves been learned through socialization). For many reasons, therefore, becoming socialized can be a difficult process because inevitably the individual gives up some autonomy in order to fit into the group.[50] However difficult, socialization is an important social control mechanism because it seeks to make people automatically think in socially acceptable ways. When socialization is unsuccessful, other social control mechanisms are used to prevent or eliminate deviant activity. These include punishment, physical force, social ridicule, ostracism, and others.

Socialization occurs primarily through *social institutions,* a set of structures to which society has entrusted socialization in certain major areas of social functioning. Social welfare as a social institution has been discussed earlier in this book, and thus it will be discussed here only in relationship to other social institutions. The other major social institutions are the family, the economy, the political structure, education, religion, and the arts. The first four are especially relevant to social welfare and will be discussed at some length here, the first three in separate sections of the text and the fourth in conjunction with these three. Religion and the arts will be touched on in passing.

The Family as a Social Institution

The family is entrusted with the major social tasks of ensuring reproduction, the early care of the young, preparation of the young to enter the other institutions of society, the transmission of life resources, and meeting people's needs for intimacy and emotional support. Originally families were *extended* units of several generations, which allowed for intergenerational sharing but which became economically and geographically unwieldy in money (versus land) based urban economics. The *nuclear* family then became much more common; it is composed of smaller units that are more economically and geographically flexible and restricted in most cases to only two generations (parents and children). Other forms of the family have also developed in response to concerns about overpopulation, sex-role redefinitions, economic contingencies, and alternative life-styles. All of them seek to perform some or all of the societal functions assigned to the family.

The family is generally the first social institution the infant encounters for any significant period of time, and it is therefore of enormous significance to the child's development. Here the child is taught basic values and, depending on the kind of experiences encountered, develops the basis for self-identity. The child that is loved and respected learns to see the world as an exciting environment that can be productively managed. The ignored or overly protected child sees the world as threatening, whereas the abused child sees the world as cruel and violent. All of these perceptions tend to affect future growth directions, physically and emotionally, especially if they are confirmed repeatedly throughout childhood.

The family is also a unique carrier of cultural and social variables. The particular values and behaviors taught in the family reflect its cultural orientations toward other people and social behaviors and situations. A clear, although pathetic, example is provided in Exhibit 5-6. These values and behaviors are at least partially affected by social variables, such as socioeconomic resources and majority or minority group standing. Families with limited resources cannot make certain kinds of opportunities available to their members, and they can rarely socialize them to find other ways to obtain them. Because college may be out of the question economically, the child may be taught to value a job more than education. As a member of a minority group that is discriminated against, the child may learn that it is best to be docile and subservient. The cumulative effect of social disadvantage seems to be social isolation and frustration, with reduced participation in society's recreational and decision-making processes and greater acceptance of interpersonal aggression and abuse.[51]

EXHIBIT 5-6 *Sex, Physical Appearance, and Socialization*

The following letter written to Ann Landers is a pathetic reminder of how sex and physical appearance continue to be used as a basis for role allocations and the development of a sense of self through family socialization.

Dear Ann Landers:

I could never talk to anyone about this problem and I must tell it to somebody. It is getting me down.

My husband and I have been married 10 years. Our son, who is now 8, is a very handsome boy. He has my husband's eyes and smile, my nose, a great-shaped head, and strong jaw-line. Everyone remarks on his good looks.

Our daughter is 2 years old, and I am sorry to say she is the homeliest child I have ever seen. Nature really played a dirty trick on us. It would have been much better if the boy had been homely and the girl had been good looking. A girl needs beauty—a boy doesn't.

Our daughter inherited the worst features of both my husband and me. When people see her they don't know what to say. Occasionally someone will ask, "Is that your child, or is she adopted?" I know what they are driving at.

When our daughter is older we can have her protruding ears fixed, her chin built up and her nose remolded. Hopefully she will have a good figure. If she doesn't, there are several things a girl can do. But the growing up years are going to be very hard on this pathetic child. Please tell me how to face the future cheerfully. If you could name some movie stars who were homely youngsters, it would help a lot.

Star Crossed

Source: Ann Landers, *Washington Post,* April 15, 1971. Used by permission of Field Newspaper Syndicate.

The family is also a small group in which certain important role relationships occur and from which a great deal of learning occurs through role modeling. As a system, the family has to be understood in terms of its internal group dynamics as well as its ties to external systems. Adult relationships have to be understood in terms of each person's role conception, the reactions of others to the person's behavior, resources or lack of them, external pressures, and so forth. Similarly, parent-child relationships take place in a context that includes adult relationships, external input, and each person's role conception.[52] As with adults, parent-child relationships are interactional, with the parent reacting to the child's response to the parent's behavior, and vice versa. In addition, the total network of relationships between siblings and between each sibling and each parent affects all other family relationships.

The relationships between the family and other social institutions are many and significant. People learn basic language and interactional skills in the family that either facilitate or hinder their activities in other institutions, especially the educational institution. Personality and cognitive development, begun in the family, affect later motivation and skill as well as life aspirations, all of which relate to adult participation in the economic, political, and art institutions. Religious training in the family has an impact on value formation and use, which also relates to adult behavior.

The family, then, is a key social institution, entrusted with some of the most important activities necessary for individual growth and development as well as societal survival. Yet the family is undergoing perhaps unprecedented changes and stresses. For example, Sussman points out the following:[53]

> *The shift in composition of households from 1960 to 1975 is striking. Husband-wife households declined from 75 to 66 percent, households with no relatives of the head present increased 7 percent, and households composed of unmarried relatives increased from 10 to 12 percent. This shift coincided with a reduction in the mean household size of 3.33 persons in 1960 to 2.94 persons in 1975.*

The standard nuclear family is being increasingly modified and supplemented as more wives as well as husbands have careers, as more couples elect not to have children, as climbing divorce rates increase the number of remarried and single-parent families, as more people live together in same sex or opposite sex consensual unions, and as sex-role redefinitions make it easier for people to elect to live independently.

From the social welfare viewpoint, changes in family structures and functioning raise issues about the need for services. Can these variations in family structures still allow the family to perform the functions allocated to it by society? Clearly, some forms of the family are at greater risk in some areas—the single-parent family's ability to obtain needed resources to meet its members' physical and emotional needs, for example, or the ability of people living independently to meet their own needs in periods of medical or emotional crisis, or in old age. Yet change often brings with it innovative patterns of adaptation. There are many ways in which support networks can be developed among people living independently or in consensual unions, for instance, that provide the interpersonal caring and intimacy generally obtained in the family. In addition, more flexibility in family arrangements may actually reduce the need for some social welfare services if the alternatives allow people to find greater opportunities for growth and satisfaction and reduce feelings of entrapment and pressure. As women feel less pressured into and trapped within conventional marriages, for example, they may avoid potential problems of self-denigration, alcoholism, and acting out behavior toward their children.

Changes in the family provide an excellent example of the social welfare institution's focus on providing resources to help people function more effectively. Obviously, societal values support some family forms more readily than others at the present time. However, the social welfare professional needs to help society assist people achieve their own goals in whatever ways may be appropriate. No one family form is itself better or worse than others—each has its own strengths and weaknesses. The task is to build on the strengths and help overcome the weaknesses. People do have different goals for themselves growing out of their physiological, cultural, and personality differences. If society is to work on behalf of its members, and if social welfare is to participate in that work, knowledge about changes in family functioning will become part of the planning for better social welfare services. Changes in the family's relationships with the other major social institutions of society will also have to be taken into account in such planning.

The Economic Institution

As important as the family is for establishing many of the values and skills that will characterize adult life, the family's structure and functioning is heavily influenced by the economic institution. United States cultural values support a modified capitalistic free enterprise system[54] in which the marketplace is allowed to relate consumer demand to producer supply with relatively little governmental intervention. Laissez-faire refers to the lack of governmental intervention in market activities. In order to understand the way the market works, one must look at the mechanisms influencing production, distribution, and consumption.

One of the lasting effects of the Industrial Revolution was to make people dependent on wages. The tie to the land was broken, and self-sufficiency, at least for the bare necessities, was no longer feasible. In industrial societies a wage is received in return for work performed—the workers essentially sell their labor in the marketplace in return for wages that give them access to socially desirable resources. Basic resources are necessary for survival—food, shelter, and so on. Without adequate wages, life-sustaining resources may be inaccessible. This reliance on a wage sets up another potential problem situation.[55] Supply is based on demand, but demand is to some extent based on supply—that is, if there is no production, there is no need for workers, and hence there is no wage. If there is no wage, there can be no demand unless there is some outside influence to provide consumers with money, which then reestablishes the demand-supply-demand cycle. This outside influence is usually the exercise of government fiscal policy, primarily in terms of government spending, taxation, and manipulation of interest rates. The recession of the early and mid-seventies is an example. With declining demand, there was an excess of supply, which then resulted in widespread layoffs of workers throughout the economy, especially in the automobile, textile, and service industries. With large numbers of people out of work, demand declined further. The government then stepped in: an income tax rebate (which would immediately increase the individual's disposable income, that is, the amount of money available to be spent); a lowering of interest rates for loans, making more loan money available (also aimed at increasing spending by making it easier and less costly to purchase major items); and increasing government spending through the provision of public service jobs. These actions served to stimulate demand, which then helped reestablish the demand-supply cycle.

In addition to supply and demand, production is affected by other forces as well. These include the costs of production, including costs imposed by governmental regulation, competition, collusion, and the interdependence that exists between producers in a large, complex industrial society. Labor is an important cost of production, and technology is increasingly used to reduce labor costs. However, without work, people's wages disappear, and union-management collective bargaining efforts often revolve around management attempts to lower costs and union efforts to protect job security and adequate wage levels. Here the relationships between economic power, technology, and policy with social welfare are clear. Governmental regulation also seeks to balance the rights of producers, who have a right to a fair return on their financial investment, and the rights of citizens who should be able to expect safe and humane working conditions, safe and usable products, and a physical environment that is not fouled by industrial pollution. However, the costs of production created by safety regulation, for example, may increase the costs of a product that can then be beyond the reach of low-income people.

The competitive power of large producers makes it possible to drive out smaller producers, either through efficiencies possible in large-scale production processes or through collusion such as price fixing or having interlocking directorates.* When production power becomes concentrated in a few massive producers, their monopolistic power enables them to raise prices and at the same time reduce consumer choice in services and products. Finally, production is affected by the interdependence of producers to the degree that the services and products of one industry (steel, for example) are dependent on those of another industry (railroads to transport the steel to consumers).

Moving from production to distribution, we must first look at the effect of the existing production system on the market in which the products are to be distributed. A striking fact of this market in contemporary America is that it is characterized by wide disparities. Some persons are rich and have access to virtually unlimited products. Their demand is strong and constant. For others, the market is almost entirely out of their reach. They are poor and have access to very few products the market has to offer. Exhibit 5-7 (p. 193) illustrates the extent of maldistribution of resources in the United States.

Poverty is a painful subject for Americans, and one that is difficult to pin down. It is painful to realize that there are large numbers of poor people in the "richest country in the world." This creates some tendency to hide

---

* An interlocking directorate is when the same group of people serve as the directors of several companies.

the poor, to let them live their lives forgotten in the back corners of rural counties, Appalachian hills, Indian reservations, and urban ghettos. It also makes it difficult to decide what the society means by "poor." On one hand, an arbitrary figure can be used—below it people live in poverty and above it they do not. The figure often used is the money needed by an urban family of four to survive, set in 1979 at $6,700.[56] The limitations of this approach are obvious—is bare survival the goal of our society when we assess human need? Can poverty be so arbitrarily defined? Is it not more likely that, while families living on less than $6,700 exist in abject poverty, families living on $7,000 exist in poverty, although at a level less severe than their even poorer counterparts? Another approach is to look at *relative* poverty. It looks at how resources are distributed among all members of society, defining as the poor the group having access to the least resources.[57] This is a more realistic approach to the problem, because part of *being* poor is *feeling* poor, knowing that you are deprived of resources that others take for granted. Poverty is both objective and subjective. It is the objective reality that life lacks basic necessities—adequate food, shelter, social participation. It is also the subjective reality that one lives on the fringes of society, at the bottom of the social heap.

Regardless of how it is defined, poverty is considerably more than just an academic issue for several reasons:[58]

- *Poverty affects life chances.* The poor are disadvantaged in those areas of life that affect their basic physical survival, as well as those life conditions that affect the quality of their life. In other words the poor are likely to die at earlier ages than the nonpoor, to be victims of violent crime, and to incur more frequent and more serious illness.
- *Poverty affects life-styles.* The poor tend not to have access to the most desirable resources in society, such as education; pleasant, well-paying, and steady employment; and decent housing. They tend to feel socially isolated and to be conservative, feel helpless, and participate rarely in decision-making activities like voting.[59]
- *Poverty is related to minority group membership.* Poverty and minority group membership are interacting variables. People who possess socially defined criteria that are the basis for differentiation and *stratification** are much more likely to be discriminated against and therefore disadvantaged. One way such discrimination occurs is by restricting economic opportunity, leading to the relationship between minority group standing (often on the basis of human diversity discussed in the last chapter) and poverty. Of course, once poor, people fall into another group that is discriminated against.

* Stratification is the social process by which people are ranked on the basis of superiority, inferiority, and equality, usually through a system of social classes and/or castes.

Economic Reality in the United States EXHIBIT 5-7

The following provides a comprehensive view of poverty in the United States.

A recent report from the U.S. Census Bureau provides new information about the improved economic conditions of most, but not all, Americans. While the report indicates a decline in the total number of persons living in poverty, there are exceptions in the category of "unrelated individuals."

Most disturbing are the changes indicated from 1976 to 1977, where poverty increased for blacks of all ages, non-whites of all ages, white as well as all other children under 18, and non-white heads of households. And it must be noted that the poverty line represents an exceedingly meager level of income.

Persons Below the Poverty Level by Family Status, Sex of Head, and Race, 1957–77
(numbers in thousands of persons as of March of the following year)

	Number Below Poverty Level			*Poverty Rate*		
Year, Race of Head	*All Persons*	*65 Years & Over*	*Persons in Families*	*All Persons*	*65 Years & Over*	*Persons in Families*
All Races:						
1977	24,720	3,177	19,505	11.6	14.1	10.2
1976	24,975	3,313	19,632	11.8	15.0	10.3
1975	25,877	3,317	20,789	12.3	15.3	10.9
1973	22,973	3,354	18,299	11.1	16.3	9.7
1970	25,420	4,709	20,330	12.6	24.5	10.9
1965	33,185	NA[a]	28,358	17.3	NA	15.8
1960	39,851	NA	34,925	22.2	NA	20.7
1959	39,490	5,481	34,562	22.4	35.2	20.8
White:						
1977	16,416	2,426	12,364	8.9	11.9	7.5
1976	16,713	2,663	12,500	9.1	13.2	7.5
1975	17,770	2,634	13,799	9.7	13.4	8.3
1973	15,142	2,698	11,412	8.4	14.4	6.9
1970	17,484	3,984	13,323	9.9	22.5	8.1
1965	22,496	NA	18,508	13.3	NA	11.7
1960	28,309	NA	24,262	17.8	NA	16.2
1959	28,484	4,744	24,443	18.1	33.1	16.5
Black:						
1977	7,726	701	6,667	31.3	36.3	30.5
1976	7,595	644	6,576	31.1	34.8	30.1
1975	7,545	652	6,533	31.3	36.3	30.1
1973	7,388	620	6,560	31.4	37.1	30.8
1970	7,548	683	6,683	33.5	48.0	32.2
1965	NA	NA	NA	NA	NA	NA
1960	NA	NA	NA	NA	NA	NA
1959	9,927	711	9,112	55.1	62.5	54.9

Source: Washington Social Legislation Bulletin, 43, October 9, 1978, p. 171.

[a] NA = not available

There are a number of criteria that are used to assign people to minority, disadvantaged group standing, the major ones being age, race, ethnicity, sex, physical characteristics, and sexual preference plus, of course, economic resources. Some of these criteria are biological and others are socially created. Although all of them differentiate between groups of people, none of them need be used to stratify people—that is a socially created process. Assigning people to disadvantaged minority group standing almost always entails prejudicial attitudes as well as stereotyping, which ignores the wide range of diversity within these groups. Instead, the elderly are forgetful and too talkative, women are too irresponsible to hold positions of power, blacks are lazy and too fun loving, the Japanese are devious and too inscrutable, homosexuals are sexually promiscuous, and the poor don't really want a better life, anyway. Once categories of discrimination are established, the prejudices and stereotypes are difficult to destroy.

Discrimination is a complex value, economic, and political phenomenon. Through ethnocentric socialization, most people learn the prejudices of their elders and don't often stop to question them. These prejudices are often supported by economic fears that one's own position will be worsened if the situation of groups discriminated against is improved. This frequently leads to conservative political beliefs that create natural coalitions between economically fearful middle-class persons and persons of great wealth who depend on a supply of cheap, docile labor (which minority groups generally provide) to maintain their own wealth. Achieving greater equality in American society has been such a difficult goal to achieve because all of the social institutions work at some level to maintain inequality: the family socializes the disadvantaged to expect little, the economic system deprives them of resources, the political system has powerful coalitions against them, and education tracks them into "appropriate" job-related studies. To summarize this discussion of poverty, stratification, and other forms of institutionalized disadvantages, Exhibit 5-8 presents a series of illustrative tables.

EXHIBIT 5-8 *Life Chances and Life-styles of the Disadvantaged*

Although it is difficult to assemble data that has been reported in such a way as to be exactly comparable, Tables 1 through 7 demonstrate the effects of minority group membership on people's life chances and life-styles. Table 1 provides an overview of socioeconomic characteristics by race and ethnicity. Table 2 looks at life expectancy by race and sex, Table 3 at incidence of serious illness by race, sex, and income, and Table 4 at homicide victimization by race and sex. Table 5 analyzes years of school completed by race and sex, and Tables 6 and 7 do the same for occupation and unemployment. In aggregate, these data demonstrate that there are clear differences in American society that are related to various minority group characteristics. The data are from Bureau of the Census, *Social Indicators 1976* (Washington, D.C.: U.S. Government Printing Office, 1977), pages LXXI, 190, 198, 248, 302–3, 377, 381, and 548.

TABLE 1 Socioeconomic Characteristics of the White, Black, and Spanish-Origin Population: 1975

Characteristic	*White*	*Black*	*Spanish origin*[a]
Age			
Total population (in thousands)	182,500	23,785	11,202
Under 18 years	30.5%	40.0%	44.3%
18 to 64 years	58.9	52.7	52.1
65 years and over	10.5	7.2	3.6
Type of Residence			
Metropolitan areas	66.8	75.2	[b]81.4
Central cities	25.2	58.1	[b]49.2
Suburbs	41.6	17.1	[b]32.1
Nonmetropolitan areas	33.2	24.8	[b]18.6
Education			
Total persons 20 to 24 years old	104,065	11,096	4,762
Less than 4 years of high school	35.5	57.5	62.1
4 years of high school	37.3	27.0	22.9
Some college	27.2	15.5	15.0
Total persons 25 years and over	15,883	2,162	992
Less than 4 years of high school	14.0	28.3	40.6
4 years of high school	43.3	45.0	37.8
Some college	42.7	26.7	21.6
Size of Family			
Two persons	38.5	29.4	23.2
Three persons	21.6	22.7	22.5
Four persons	19.9	17.8	20.5
Five persons or more	20.0	30.1	33.8
Labor Force Status			
Total persons, 16 years and over	133,501	15,541	[c]6,724
In civilian labor force	82,084	9,123	4,024
	61.5%	58.7%	59.8%
Employed	53.7	44.0	47.1
Unemployed	7.8	14.7	12.7
Occupation of Employed Civilian Workers			
Total employed, 16 years and over	75,713	7,782	[c]3,510
White-collar workers	51.7	30.8	33.0
Blue-collar workers	32.4	39.3	46.7
Service workers	12.3	27.3	16.8
Farm workers	3.6	2.7	3.5

[a] Persons of Spanish origin may be of any race.
[b] Based on March 1974 Current Population Survey.
[c] Unadjusted data for March 1975.

TABLE 1 *(cont.)*

Characteristic	*White*	*Black*	*Spanish origin*[a]
Family Income in 1974			
Total families	49,451	5,498	2,477
Less than $5,000	11.1	31.5	21.6
$5,000 to $9,999	21.9	30.0	31.1
$10,000 to $14,999	25.1	19.1	24.3
$15,000 or more	42.1	19.4	23.1
Median family income (in dollars)	13,356	7,808	9,559
Persons Below Poverty Level in 1974			
Families with male head	5.5	16.6	16.6
Families with female head	27.6	55.9	53.2
Male unrelated individuals	18.3	29.9	29.0
Female unrelated individuals	26.5	51.9	40.7

Source: Adapted from U.S. Department of Commerce, Bureau of the Census, *Current Population Reports,* Series P-20, No. 292, March 1975.

[a] Persons of Spanish origin may be of any race.

TABLE 2 Life Expectancy at Birth, by Race and Sex: 1929–38 (Compared With 1969–74)

	Total			*White*			*Black and other races*		
Year	Both sexes	Male	Female	Both sexes	Male	Female	Both sexes	Male	Female
1929	57.1	55.8	58.7	58.6	57.2	60.3	46.7	45.7	47.8
1930	59.7	58.1	61.6	61.4	59.7	63.5	48.1	47.3	49.2
1931	61.1	59.4	63.1	62.6	60.8	64.7	50.4	49.5	51.5
1932	62.1	61.0	63.5	63.2	62.0	64.5	53.7	52.8	54.6
1933	63.3	61.7	65.1	64.3	62.7	66.3	54.7	53.5	56.0
1934	61.1	59.3	63.3	62.4	60.5	64.6	51.8	50.2	53.7
1935	61.7	59.9	63.9	62.9	61.0	65.0	53.1	51.3	55.2
1936	58.5	56.6	60.6	59.8	58.0	61.9	49.0	47.0	51.4
1937	60.0	58.0	62.4	61.4	59.3	63.8	50.3	48.3	52.5
1938	63.5	61.9	65.3	65.0	63.2	66.8	52.9	51.7	54.3
1969	70.4	66.8	74.3	71.3	67.8	75.1	64.3	60.5	68.4
1970	70.9	67.1	74.8	71.7	68.0	75.6	65.3	61.3	69.4
1971	71.1	67.4	75.0	72.0	68.3	75.8	65.6	61.6	69.7
1972	71.1	67.4	75.1	72.0	68.3	75.9	65.6	61.5	69.9
1973	71.3	67.6	75.3	72.2	68.4	76.1	65.9	61.9	70.1
1974	71.9	68.2	75.9	72.7	68.9	76.6	67.0	62.9	71.2

Source: U.S. Department of Health, Education, and Welfare, Public Health Service, National Center for Health Statistics, *Vital Statistics of the United States, 1973,* Vol. II, and *Monthly Vital Statistics Report,* Vol. 24, No. 11, sup. 1.

TABLE 3 Days of Disability per Person, by Selected Characteristics: 1973

Characteristic	*Restricted activity days per person*	*Bed disability days per person*	*Work loss days per person*
Total	16.5	6.4	5.4
Sex			
Male	14.7	5.3	5.2
Female	18.1	7.3	5.8
Race			
White	16.1	6.1	5.3
Black and other races	18.8	8.0	6.7
Region			
Northeast	13.9	5.5	5.2
North Central	15.5	5.8	5.2
South	18.4	7.4	5.9
West	18.1	6.6	5.2
Residence			
Metropolitan	16.3	6.4	5.6
Nonmetropolitan	16.9	6.2	5.0
Family Income			
Under $5,000	28.8	10.7	6.8
$5,000 to $9,999	16.5	6.5	6.3
$10,000 to $14,999	13.0	5.2	5.1
$15,000 or more	12.2	4.5	4.9

Source: U.S. Department of Health, Education, and Welfare, Public Health Service, National Center for Health Statistics, *Health, United States, 1975.*

TABLE 4 Victims of Homicide, by Race and Sex: 1940–73
(rate per 100,000 population)

	White		*Black and Other Races*	
Year	Male	Female	Male	Female
1940	5.0	1.3	57.1	12.6
1945	5.1	1.3	52.7	10.6
1950	3.9	1.4	49.1	11.5
1955	3.5	1.3	42.6	10.3
1960	3.9	1.5	41.9	11.2
1965	4.8	1.7	50.7	11.7
1970	7.3	2.2	72.8	13.7
1971	7.9	2.4	80.8	15.5
1972	8.2	2.4	83.1	14.8
1973	8.7	2.8	77.1	16.0

Source: Bureau of the Census, *Social Indicators 1976* (Washington, D.C.: U.S. Government Printing Office, 1977), pp. lxxi, 190, and 198.

TABLE 5 Years of School Completed by Persons 25 to 34 Years Old, by Sex and Race: 1964–74
(percent of the civilian noninstitutional population)

Years of school completed, sex, race, and age	*1964*	*1965*	*1970*	*1973*	*1974*
All Races—25 to 34 years					
Total					
Less than 8 years	7.2	7.3	4.5	4.0	3.7
8 to 11 years	25.8	24.7	21.7	17.9	16.2
12 years	42.6	43.2	44.0	43.9	42.7
College, 1 to 3 years	11.5	11.7	14.0	16.0	17.5
College, 4 years or more	12.9	13.1	15.8	18.2	20.0
Male					
Less than 8 years	8.1	8.4	5.4	4.5	4.1
8 to 11 years	25.5	23.1	20.4	17.0	14.8
12 years	37.4	39.2	39.5	39.3	38.6
College, 1 to 3 years	12.2	12.3	15.1	17.7	18.8
College, 4 years or more	16.9	17.0	19.7	21.5	23.7
Female					
Less than 8 years	6.4	6.2	3.8	3.5	3.4
8 to 11 years	26.1	26.3	22.9	18.8	17.5
12 years	47.6	47.1	48.3	48.3	46.6
College, 1 to 3 years	10.8	11.0	13.0	14.4	16.2
College, 4 years or more	9.0	9.4	12.0	15.0	16.4
White					
Total					
Less than 8 years	6.1	6.2	3.9	3.6	3.4
8 to 11 years	24.0	23.0	20.0	16.4	14.9
12 years	44.2	44.9	44.9	44.5	43.0
College, 1 to 3 years	12.0	12.1	14.6	16.5	17.6
College, 4 years or more	13.7	13.7	16.6	19.0	21.0
Male					
Less than 8 years	6.8	7.1	4.5	4.2	3.8
8 to 11 years	23.8	21.9	18.5	15.6	13.9
12 years	38.7	40.4	40.2	39.3	38.5
College, 1 to 3 years	12.8	12.7	15.8	18.3	18.9
College, 4 years or more	17.9	17.9	20.9	22.6	24.9
Female					
Less than 8 years	5.5	5.4	3.3	3.1	3.1
8 to 11 years	24.1	24.1	21.4	17.2	15.9
12 years	49.5	49.2	49.5	49.6	47.4
College, 1 to 3 years	11.2	11.6	13.5	14.7	16.3
College, 4 years or more	9.7	9.7	12.3	16.5	17.2

TABLE 5 *(cont.)*

Years of school completed, sex, race, and age	*1964*	*1965*	*1970*	*1973*	*1974*
Black					
Total					
Less than 8 years	15.5	15.2	9.8	6.9	6.2
8 to 11 years	42.1	39.2	36.8	31.7	28.5
12 years	30.0	30.6	38.4	40.9	42.3
College, 1 to 3 years	7.4	8.1	8.9	12.1	14.9
College, 4 years or more	4.9	6.8	6.1	8.3	8.1
Male					
Less than 8 years	18.4	20.0	13.3	7.8	7.0
8 to 11 years	42.1	34.7	37.4	29.9	26.1
12 years	26.7	29.4	35.0	41.7	41.5
College, 1 to 3 years	6.3	8.5	8.7	12.5	16.7
College, 4 years or more	6.5	7.4	5.8	8.0	8.8
Female					
Less than 8 years	13.2	11.4	6.8	6.2	5.7
8 to 11 years	42.1	42.9	36.3	33.2	30.5
12 years	32.7	31.5	41.4	40.3	42.9
College, 1 to 3 years	8.3	7.8	9.2	11.8	13.4
College, 4 years or more	3.6	6.5	6.4	8.5	7.4

Source: U.S. Department of Commerce, Bureau of the Census, *Current Population Reports*, Series P-20, Nos. 138, 158, 169, 182, 194, 207, 229, 243, and 274.

TABLE 6 Occupations of Employed Persons, by Sex and Race: 1960 and 1975

	Total		White		Black and other races		Male		Female	
Occupation	Number (thou-sands)	Percent of total	Number (thou-sands)	Percent of total	Number (thou-sands)	Percent of total	Number (thou-sands)	Percent of total	Number (thou-sands)	Percent of total
1960										
All workers	65,778	100.0	58,850	100.0	6,927	100.0	43,904	100.0	21,874	100.0
Professional, technical, and kindred workers	7,469	11.4	7,138	12.1	331	4.8	4,766	10.9	2,703	12.4
Managers, officials, and proprietors	7,067	10.7	6,889	11.7	178	2.6	5,968	13.6	1,099	5.0
Clerical and kindred workers	9,762	14.8	9,259	15.7	503	7.3	3,145	7.2	6,617	30.3
Salesworkers	4,224	6.4	4,123	7.0	101	1.5	2,544	5.8	1,680	7.7
Craftsmen and foremen	8,554	13.0	8,139	13.8	415	6.0	8,332	19.0	222	1.0
Operatives	11,950	18.2	10,536	17.9	1,414	20.4	8,617	19.6	3,333	15.2
Nonfarm laborers	3,553	5.4	2,602	4.4	951	13.7	3,471	7.9	82	.4
Private household workers	1,973	3.0	991	1.7	982	14.2	30	.1	1,943	8.9
Service workers, except private household	6,050	9.2	4,836	8.2	1,214	17.5	2,814	6.4	3,236	14.8
Farmers and farm managers	2,776	4.2	2,557	4.3	219	3.2	2,667	6.1	109	.5
Farm laborers and foremen	2,400	3.3	1,778	3.0	622	9.0	1,552	3.9	848	3.2
1975										
All workers	84,783	100.0	75,713	100.0	9,070	100.0	51,230	100.0	33,553	100.0
Professional, technical, and kindred workers	12,748	15.0	11,711	15.5	1,037	11.4	7,481	14.6	5,267	15.7
Managers, officials, and proprietors	8,891	10.5	8,493	11.2	398	4.4	7,162	14.0	1,729	5.2
Clerical and kindred workers	15,128	17.8	13,705	18.1	1,423	15.7	3,355	6.5	11,773	35.1
Salesworkers	5,460	6.4	5,218	6.9	242	2.7	3,137	6.1	2,323	6.9
Craftsmen and foremen	10,972	12.9	10,177	13.4	795	8.8	10,472	20.4	501	1.5
Operatives	12,856	15.2	11,042	14.6	1,814	20.0	8,971	17.5	3,885	11.6
Nonfarm laborers	4,134	4.9	3,349	4.4	785	8.7	3,777	7.4	357	1.1
Private household workers	1,171	1.4	728	1.0	443	4.9	30	.1	1,141	3.4
Service workers, except private household	10,486	12.4	8,590	11.3	1,896	20.9	4,370	8.5	6,116	18.2
Farmers and farm managers	1,593	1.9	1,538	2.0	56	.6	1,492	2.9	102	.3
Farm laborers and foremen	1,343	1.6	1,162	1.5	181	2.0	985	1.9	358	1.1

Average Annual Percent Change, 1960 to 1975

Occupation	*Total* Percent of total	*White* Percent of total	*Black and other races* Percent of total	*Male* Percent of total	*Female* Percent of total
Professional, technical, and kindred workers	3.6	3.4	6.6	3.7	3.3
Managers, officials, and proprietors	[a]–.2	–.5	1.8	.4	.2
Clerical and kindred workers	3.0	2.4	8.4	–.1	4.8
Salesworkers	–	–.1	1.2	.3	–.8
Craftsmen and foremen	–.1	–.4	2.8	1.4	.5
Operatives	–3.0	–3.3	–.4	–2.1	–3.6
Nonfarm laborers	–.5	–	–5.0	–.5	.7
Private household workers	–1.6	–.7	–9.3	–	–5.5
Service workers, except private household	3.2	3.1	3.4	2.1	3.4
Farmers and farm managers	–2.3	–2.3	–2.6	–3.2	–.2
Farm laborers and foremen	–1.7	–1.5	–7.0	–2.0	–2.1

Source: U.S. Department of Labor, *Employment and Training Report of the President, 1976.*

[a] Represents zero.

TABLE 7 Unemployment, by Major Occupational Group, Sex, and Race: 1964, 1969, and 1974 (in percentages)

Occupational group and race	1964 Male	1964 Female	1969 Male	1969 Female	1974 Male	1974 Female
White						
White-collar workers	1.6	3.3	1.2	2.8	2.0	4.2
Professional and technical	1.4	2.1	.9	1.9	1.7	2.8
Managers and administrators, except farm	1.2	2.1	.8	1.9	1.5	3.2
Sales workers	2.3	4.5	1.8	4.1	2.8	5.5
Clerical workers	3.0	3.8	2.0	3.1	3.1	4.6
Blue-collar workers	2.9	6.4	3.1	6.2	5.6	9.0
Craft and kindred workers	3.9	3.3	2.1	3.3	4.1	6.1
Operatives	5.1	8.8	3.2	6.4	(NA)	(NA)
Operatives, except transport	[a](NA)	(NA)	(NA)	(NA)	6.3	9.6
Transport equipment operatives	(NA)	(NA)	(NA)	(NA)	4.9	4.8
Nonfarm laborers	10.0	9.9	6.4	7.7	9.5	9.0
Service workers	4.8	5.7	3.5	3.7	5.2	6.0
Private household	([b])	3.1	([b])	2.9	([b])	3.7
Other service workers	5.7	4.3	3.5	3.9	5.2	6.4
Farm workers	6.1	2.6	1.4	1.4	2.0	3.1
Farmers and farm managers	.3	.9	.1	.1	.2	.7
Farm laborers and supervisors	6.1	2.6	4.2	1.6	5.0	3.8
Black and Other Races						
White-collar workers	3.3	6.0	2.5	5.2	4.6	7.0
Professional and technical	2.7	2.0	1.9	2.0	3.3	3.9
Managers and administrators, except farm	3.3	2.1	1.4	1.4	2.4	4.5
Sales workers	4.9	13.2	2.3	9.6	10.7	12.3
Clerical workers	4.2	8.3	3.6	6.5	6.1	8.0
Blue-collar workers	8.9	9.4	5.1	8.1	9.1	13.2
Craft and kindred workers	7.8	5.3	3.2	4.3	6.5	9.0
Operatives	7.1	13.3	4.8	8.1	(NA)	(NA)
Operatives, except transport	(NA)	(NA)	(NA)	(NA)	10.1	13.5
Transport equipment operatives	(NA)	(NA)	(NA)	(NA)	5.8	7.5
Nonfarm laborers	11.9	22.7	7.3	12.0	12.5	15.3
Service workers	8.8	9.7	5.9	6.2	9.2	8.0
Private household	([b])	7.3	([b])	4.5	([b])	5.2
Other service workers	8.3	8.8	6.0	7.4	9.2	9.1
Farm workers	7.7	9.1	3.3	13.3	5.9	7.3
Farmers and farm managers	1.6	[c]–	.1	.1	.8	–
Farm laborers and supervisors	7.7	9.1	4.4	14.6	7.9	7.6

Source: U.S. Department of Labor, Bureau of Labor Statistics, unpublished data.

[a] NA = Not available; introduction of new categories and definitions for operatives makes comparison of data impossible.

[b] Percent not shown where base is less than 35,000.

[c] – represents zero.

In addition to stratification and discrimination, the ability of producers to manipulate consumer demand is another reason for the maldistribution of income in the United States because the poor are usually more easily manipulated and are most severely affected by such practices. For example, through advertising, the poor are encouraged to purchase unnecessary or inferior products that they can ill afford. Price-fixing takes its greatest toll on the poor since they have the scarcest resources to work with. Unscrupulous credit practices inflate the prices of items purchased by the poor and may also make the poor more vulnerable to repossession if they default on a payment. Government practices can also inadvertently hurt the poor. For example, regressive taxes (that is, those taxes that take a higher proportion from the poor than the rich) further reduce the meager resources poorer people have available. Social Security is an example of a regressive tax. Social Security is withheld from salaries only up to a certain maximum ($25,900 in 1980). A person earning $6,000 a year has Social Security withheld from the whole amount of income, whereas someone earning $30,000 has the tax withheld from only the first $25,900 of that amount. There are many other factors that enter into the maldistribution of economic resources—lack of transportation, lack of consumer education, lack of choice in places to shop, and so forth. In many ways, the poor pay more.[60]

One of the functions of the social welfare institution is to help counteract the maldistribution existing in the economic institution. By supplementing the income of the poor, social welfare increases their access to desirable social resources. By educating the poor to more effective consumer practices, child-rearing methods, and homemaker techniques, social welfare helps the poor to use their money more wisely. By providing educational opportunities, by fighting discrimination in jobs and housing, and by stabilizing families in trouble, social welfare increases the opportunities for the poor to participate in the economic system. Social welfare strengthens the ability of the poor to function as both consumer and producer—knowing how to spend and having valuable skills to sell in return for a living wage. Even so, there are problems that develop from attempts by social welfare to find a more equitable solution to problems of maldistribution. One of the most important of these is a result of the attempt to provide social welfare services in a market system.

A public welfare system interferes with the operation of the market, and as such it is counter to society's modified free-enterprise economic values. This leads to attempts to minimize the disruption of the market by welfare, thereby preserving the market as far as possible and presumably minimizing resentment against welfare recipients. Such attempts include making welfare services either combinations of public and private services, publicly subsidizing private services, or specifically designing services so that they minimize interference with the market's operation. Health care for the aged is an excellent example of a welfare service provided partly publicly (Veterans Administration hospitals and other public hospitals) and partly privately (such as doctor's care, clinics in private hospitals, nursing homes). It also includes public subsidy for privately provided services, such as Medicare payments to doctors and hospitals, public-assistance vendor payments to nursing homes, and so on. The market is by definition not set up to protect those in need. It is a mockery of societal values to continue to believe that those who need extensive welfare assistance are able to be self-reliant, informed consumers in a free enterprise system.

The clash of free market and social welfare values inevitably creates resentment and discrimination against welfare recipients. Public monies spent on welfare must necessarily reduce the amount of such monies available for other purposes. The market model suggests that the same criteria used to evaluate private programs can and should be used to evaluate public programs. In one sense this is perfectly logical, since the public does have the right to get value for money spent. However, the difficulty of measuring human needs and appropriate services creates a tendency to concentrate on those services and persons most easily proved successful, a practice called "creaming."[61] Furthermore, the pursuit of efficiency tends to reduce complex problem clusters to simplified problems whose "solution" lies in a combination of money and chasing those needy persons alleged to be shiftless welfare exploiters from the rolls.[62] This is accentuated by societal values that stress individual achievement. They make it easy to believe that those who are in need have not tried hard enough and need a combination of opportunity and incentive. It becomes difficult to popularize the fact that data show the great majority of welfare recipients to be multiproblem persons with enormous disadvantages and obstacles to self-sufficiency.[63]

Inevitably, perhaps, this discussion has led into the third part of the economic system, consumption. Already referred to is what can now be made explicit, the distinction between personal consumption and social effects. For example, the maldistribution of income makes it possible for the wealthy to purchase products in the marketplace at will. However, the consequences are twofold: One, already discussed, is that the poor have very little power in the marketplace unless their resources are supplemented by the social welfare system. The other is the cost of such supplementation. Poverty leads to a range of problems. As long as society has a commitment to solve these problems, it must commit some of its resources to accomplish this goal. In other words, by allowing the wealthy to accumulate economic resources as they wish, society incurs the social costs of the waste of human ability, the loss of participation in the social system by part of the population, and the maintenance of that part of the social welfare system needed to deal with economic maldistribution. An underlying lesson of economics is that priorities must be established—society cannot have everything it wants. One of these priorities must be the balance between individual consumption and the social costs of that consumption.

The question of the costs of individual consumption takes on even greater significance in a world whose resources are increasingly being threatened with extinction. Overpopulation is a real threat, with starvation already a way of death in some societies. Energy stores are also limited, and their availability controlled by a handful of fortunate nations. More and more animal, bird, and fish species are nearing extinction. The effects of technology on the environment are increasingly understood—polluted rivers, fouled air, and poisoned soil. These effects are to a large extent the result of individual and corporate consumption decisions. The costs have so far been borne mostly by society. However, the costs are growing to the point that society itself cannot bear them—they are becoming world problems and world costs. These economic realities may ultimately extend the concept of social welfare beyond national boundaries and make the world community aware of its responsibility to all of its members.

The Political Institution

The American political system is structured to provide for the separation of powers. This occurs in four major ways. First is *separation of powers* within the federal government, which is divided into three branches.[64]

1. The *executive* branch. The presidency is the major component, although supporting offices include the vice-presidency and the cabinet. The executive branch provides overall national leadership in domestic and international relations, providing information about and initiating action to meet national needs. The executive branch also has the power to veto actions of Congress.
2. The *legislative* branch. The Congress is composed of two bodies, the House of Representatives and the Senate. The legislative branch has the responsibility for enacting legislation, which it can initiate, or which may be initiated by the executive branch. It also has the power to override presidential vetos.
3. The *judicial* branch. The courts exist as a forum within which to interpret law and individual behavior in relation to the law. It serves as a check for both the executive and legislative branches by its power to strike down legislation and actions it considers unconstitutional or illegal.

The Constitution of the United States was written in an attempt to create a federal government in which no branch would be able to gain excessive power over the others. Since members of the executive and legislative branches are the elected representatives of the people, a system was created that would minimize opportunities to seize personal power and create a totalitarian state.

The second major foundation to separation of power is a *federal-state sharing of powers.* Although a federal government was created to provide for general societal leadership and to meet the needs of all citizens, the several states were given the power to establish their own governing structures and to enact legislation and formulate policies governing the daily lives of their citizens. Federal power over states is limited, and states have representation at the federal level through their elected representatives and senators. The federal-state sharing of powers rests on the assumption that there are certain needs that states cannot meet themselves and which are best met for all of the states together at the federal level. However, it is also assumed that state government is more accessible to the people, who have the right to determine the majority of their own goals and appropriate means to attain them.

The third power base is the *political parties.* There are two main political parties, the Democratic and Republican. Other parties exist, but their significance in the political process has varied from election to election. Political parties serve as a means of involving people in the political process. They also express differing points of view, thereby giving citizens a choice of candidates representing alternative points of view in elections. Traditionally, the Democratic party has represented the views of those with more liberal social and fiscal beliefs, while the Republican party has tended to be more conservative. These traditional distinctions are increasingly difficult to make, however.

The fourth factor is the *electoral process* itself. The key people in federal and state government are elected, in theory representing the views of the major groups in society. The major groups are assumed to have the opportunity, through political parties, to work for the nomination of persons representing their views. The fact that there are many groups seeking representation can lead to two results: a proliferation of political parties, each representing an interest and putting forth its own candidates for election or coalitions between major groups. For a variety of financial and social reasons, the latter approach has generally been taken in America. The differing objectives of the Democratic and Republican parties have been thought to provide for the expression of different views by major groups in society.

The preceding discussion has obviously been a theoretical view of the American political system. In practice, there are many issues that arise from such a structure. One is that whatever the considerable virtues of a system built on the separation of powers, such a system tends to generate conflict. Since access to political power is important, there is considerable temptation to use whatever means available—legal or illegal—to gain access. For example, many persons who are elected to office at either the state or federal level have the power to appoint people to other positions, such as the president's power to appoint Supreme Court judges (if there is a vacancy). These appointments may be used to solidify one's own power and value system rather than to find the best person for the position. It is one of several ways that persons already occupying political office have an advantage in keeping it.

As with economic resources, political power is a valuable social resource that people seek to keep once they have it. The desire to keep power combines with the ability to use one's power to preserve it to disrupt the way a representative system responsive to organized coalitions would ideally work. In a society as diverse as ours, political representatives have to be responsive to a host of interests—right to life supporters as well as pro-abortion groups, manufacturers and union leaders, ethnic interests in addition to urban or rural advocates, the highway lobby versus mass transit supporters, social welfare reformers and persons who see social welfare as destructive of "free enterprise." How are representatives who wish to get reelected to represent each of these interests? Obviously it is impossible to do so; choices have to be made, but on what basis?

One obvious basis would be according to the representative's own values and beliefs. A second would be on the basis of empirical data showing the wisdom of a particular position, although value stances can rarely be so unequivocally justified. A third is in response to pressure groups. Those groups who can deliver votes at election time will have greater influence than groups who cannot reliably do so. Most political representatives no doubt respond to all of these decision-making strategies at some time or other, but if the desire to preserve one's political power is strong, responding to those groups that can help insure reelection will always be a serious consideration. This, of course, favors those groups with resources and expertise that are usable to organize people—disseminating the desired point of view, making personal contacts, providing transportation to the polls, organizing letter writing campaigns, and so forth. Poor, uneducated people do not have these resources, nor do those groups with little knowledge of the political system or little time from work for organizing activities.

The result is that certain groups can have a disproportionate influence on representatives. Groups advocating for decisions that favor business will generally be supported by those same businesses who can then write off the costs involved as a cost of doing business. The very wealthy, who have a substantial stake in many tax-related decisions, also have the resources to influence others—often in two ways, personally and by controlling a business. Although access to economic-related resources is an obvious advantage in the political process, there are other possible strategies. Sheer numbers is an effective weapon on election day, and any group that is large enough is a political force to be reckoned with. The lobby for the elderly is very effective for this reason (every voter is likely to support such issues since we all get old), as is the veterans lobby (not only is there a patriotic value support, most voters have family members or friends who are veterans). Other potentially large voting blocs are more or less ignored because they rarely translate their potential into votes: welfare mothers who do not know how to register or vote, ethnic groups that are intimidated by language problems and thus kept from voting, women who vote as their husbands suggest rather than on their own behalf, and homosexuals whose own self-image is so low that they see no point in supporting gay or lesbian rights.

Yet the fact that the political system is a representative one leaves open the opportunity for disenfranchised groups to develop the power and organization necessary to influence political representatives. This is a major function of the social welfare institution, which it performs in at least two ways: One is to serve as an advocate for the interests of disadvantaged groups by making data available about their needs, forming coalitions with powerful groups (such as the mass transit lobby support for urban transportation for the elderly), and personally talking to legislators to enlist their support. A second way is through organizing previously powerless groups so that they can make effective use of their voting power. The voting rights efforts of the blacks in the 1960s was a dramatic example of this strategy, one which is being repeated with other groups such as American Indians, Chicanos, women, and public assistance recipients.

Forming coalitions among minority groups can be an especially effective mechanism for influencing political representatives, but it is not easily accomplished.[65] It might seem logical for disadvantaged groups to band together to help each other, but further reflection identifies a number of problems. Cultural differences may make meaningful communication between groups difficult. Lack of experience in political activities often leads to reluctance to get involved and impatience with the detail and slow pace involved. Feelings of helplessness and internalized negative self-images often make it difficult to motivate disadvantaged people. Very practical problems like lack of a baby-sitter, the inability to read or write, and inability to get time off from work can also be obstacles. The political institution is part of a whole institutional fabric, and it cannot be understood outside of its larger systemic context. As long as the family and the educational institution socialize for failure, and the economic institution generates poverty and socioeconomic inequality, participation in the political institution will also be unequal.

In addition to the intervention of the social welfare system on behalf of minority groups and consumers in general, two other strategies have also become popular: the ombudsman and the development of countervailing power groups. American society today is so complex that many persons are unaware of services available, the structure of services, the political process, their rights as citizens, and so on. In the attempt to provide a link between individual people, with all of their lack of knowledge, fears, and prejudices, and the political and service structures that exist to serve them, the ombudsman concept was developed. The ombudsman is a person or group whose presence is made popularly known and whose purpose is to provide the information to help individuals find what they seek. Ideally, the ombudsman also seeks out problems in the provision of services or the involvement of citizens in the political process. Whether or not new problems are identified, the ombudsman helps citizens obtain what they wish in a system that is meant to serve them but which by its very scope may dwarf them instead.

Another method of overcoming some of these problems lies in the development of countervailing power: groups that can mobilize power to resist the power of others. Advocacy groups, such as Common Cause, can be effective lobbies on behalf of citizens who would have little power if they were not organized into groups. Consumer groups operate in a similar way, organizing consumers into structures that allow them to express and fight for their needs. Ralph Nader's work on behalf of consumers is a case in point. These kinds of groups have helped persons who have traditionally had little political and economic power to organize effectively on their own behalf.

Unfortunately, many social welfare professionals are poorly equipped to participate in the political process. Some fear that their jobs will be jeopardized if they participate, a fear that in some cases is very realistic. However, the alternative of having decisions made for the profession, which then may seriously weaken its ability to provide services, is not very attractive either. Even given the perceived desirability of participating, the problems the average citizen faces also confront the typical social welfare professional. Social welfare education has rarely included political action, and although this gap is being somewhat lessened today, the political action that is undertaken tends to be at the local level. Although very important, it must also be bolstered by national political action. A third factor is the current complexity of the welfare structure even for the professional welfare practitioner. The typical worker has limited tasks to perform and rarely has the opportunity to study the total welfare picture. Yet when welfare reform legislation is proposed, it is comprehensive and complex, leaving the practitioner uninformed about many details easily overlooked but of great significance. The fact that welfare professionals are often unable to see beyond their specialized interest to combine into a unified, more powerful social welfare lobby accentuates the problems the professions have in being active, effective political forces.

A final problem in the way of welfare professionals being politically active is again related to political sophistication. It is the lack of tenacity required to see legislation enacted and then implemented. Wilbur Cohen has well expressed the false optimism that can develop when working for legislation and the crushing disappointment when one's efforts fail. He also realistically discusses the need to accept such defeats and continue to work for change.[66] Even beyond the tenacity to get legislation passed, however, is the sophistication to know that legislation is only as good as the provisions for its enforcement. Wilcox repeatedly makes the point that so much good legislation has been relatively ineffective because of inadequate implementation provisions—lack of funds, lack of structures for enforcement and supervision, lack of legal support to untangle legal problems, and so on.[67] This helps to explain why, in spite of so much legislation in areas such as school desegregation, inequities still exist. Obviously, political tenacity has to go much further than simply the enactment of legislation, as difficult as that may be to achieve successfully.

▶ Putting It All Together: The Life Cycle

This chapter has attempted to review the major knowledge areas of particular relevance to an understanding of social welfare. It has sought a unified presentation organized around individual development, culture, and the social structure, drawing upon knowledge from the various biological, social, and behavioral sciences as appropriate. To conclude the chapter, the life cycle will be used to illustrate how the knowledge reviewed in the rest of the chapter is pertinent to a systemic, human diversity, and problem-solving view of human behavior.

The life cycle extends from conception to death and is a mechanism for defining levels of human development according to chronological age. In American society, commonly used life cycle periods include conception, birth, infancy (0–4 years), childhood (5–11), adolescence (12–15), young adulthood (16–20), adulthood (21–59), retirement and old age (60 to death), and death. Often there are socially structured quasipublic events (sometimes called rites of passage) that signify that an individual has moved from one point in the life cycle to another. For example, entry into school is clear recognition of childhood, and graduation from the primary grades and entry into junior high school is one marker of the transition into adolescence. Marriage is a significant social event acknowledging that the individual is assuming the responsibilities of adulthood, and retirement signifies the passage into old age. Having such social events to mark passage through the life cycle can help people recognize their developing social position. They also help others recognize these changes, enabling them to help in dealing with new situations and responsibilities. Each society has its own ways of defining important stages of the life cycle and its distinctive ways of recognizing their occurrence.

At each point in the life cycle, certain biological, cultural, and social forces come together. We have already seen that society seeks to have the functions performed that have been defined as necessary and desirable for its survival. On the other hand, people are learning how to make use of their genetically transmitted potential through interacting with the environment. The environment is itself culturally defined and operationalized through the social structure (roles, norms, positions, social institutions, and so on). Each of these—genetic inheritance, cultural context, and social structure—provide both resources and obstacles for the individual in the attainment of the societally defined tasks to be accomplished at each life cycle period. The individual faces a potential crisis when seeking to carry out the appropriate life cycle tasks—if successful (for example, if the resources are adequate) growth occurs and social dislocations are avoided, but if unsuccessful, growth may be slowed and problems may be experienced in a range of social situations. Since the periods in the life cycle are predictable, the potential crises or periods when the individual is at risk in particular ways are also predictable. Hence, social welfare services are often structured around the life cycle.

Some examples may help to make this clearer. We can begin with a diagram of the overall life cycle:

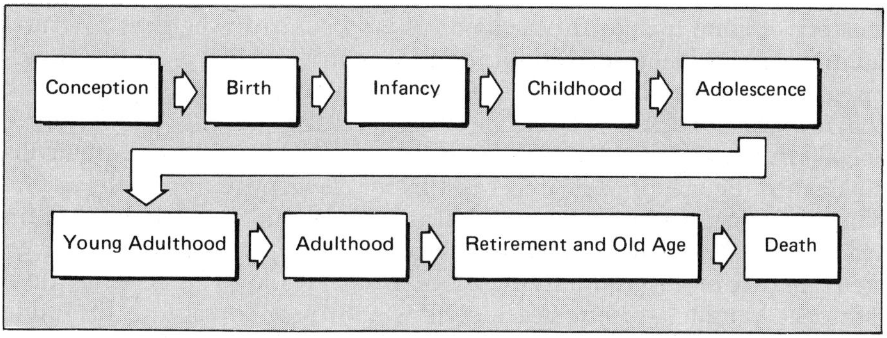

Each of these life cycle periods can in turn be pictured as follows, using adulthood as an example:

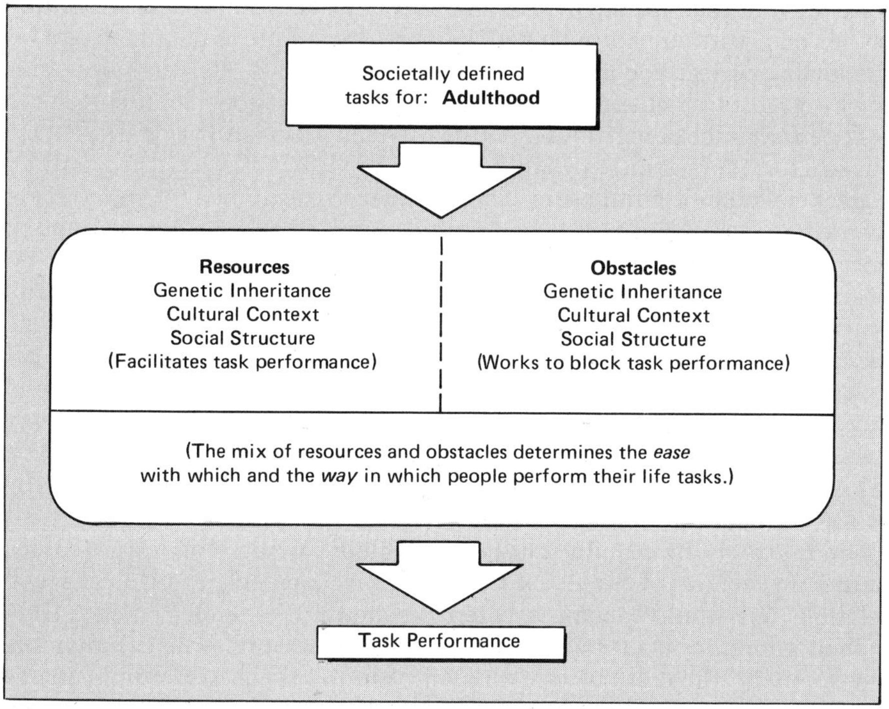

Working through this example, the societally defined tasks for adults generally relate to becoming economically self-sufficient, establishing intimate relations with others, living autonomously and in a way that is relatively stable and personally satisfying, having some conceptions of life goals, and utilizing oneself in ways that are productive and consistent with social norms. Common social rituals that provide recognition of having achieved adulthood are graduation from college, marriage, or getting one's own apartment. Thus the genetically inherited resources for the average adult include full musculature, fully developed speech and writing ability, mastery of complex cognitive processes, and control over physical functioning and appearance. Cultural resources might include values supporting personal self-reliance, beliefs about desirable jobs and life-styles, and concrete skills such as reading, writing, cooking, driving, and so forth. Social structural resources include the rituals marking passage into adulthood since they clarify role expectations for the new adult and those who interact with the adult. This could also include family help in finding an apartment, workshops to improve job performance, health insurance payments in case of illness, receiving a regular salary, and so forth. All of these resources would be useful for individuals striving to achieve life cycle tasks specified for adults in the United States.

Genetic obstacles to adult task performance would entail such things as physical handicaps, learning disabilities, and organically caused mental illness. Note that although obstacles may impede task performance, they do not necessarily make such performance impossible as demonstrated by the many perfectly competent handicapped adults. Cultural obstacles might be cultural values that give interpersonal relations dominance over task performance or beliefs about sexuality and procreation that emphasize supernatural forces rather than biological processes. Social structural obstacles can include family socialization when, for example, the male role is learned as incorporating spouse or child abuse, or when a homosexual is never taught how to constructively manage his or her sexuality. Other obstacles encompass widespread unemployment, a shortage of suitable housing, and lack of adequate day-care facilities for children. All of these factors impede the adult's attempts to function in socially expected ways.

Viewing the life cycle in terms of societal needs and cultural and social structural obstacles provides an integrated view of experiences, drawing upon a variety of social, behavioral, and biological science knowledge relating to psychological development, biological functioning, and the social context. It is also consistent with an analytical framework built around systems, human diversity, and problem solving. If all of the periods of the life cycle were to be analyzed using this approach, the web of social relationships would become apparent, as would their effect on each individual, information that would have direct practice relevance. Individual development, the cultural environment, and the social structural context are organizing concepts that should be equally useful for integrating specific knowledge in other areas of human life.

Chapter Conclusion ◄

Strategies to integrate knowledge derived from a wide range of social, behavioral, and biological science disciplines have been a long-standing need among social welfare professional practitioners. The problem has become even greater as these disciplines have developed ever greater and more sophisticated data and theories. The approach taken in these past two chapters is only a beginning effort, but one that will hopefully stimulate readers to explore their own solutions. One thing is clear, however—solutions must be found, because professional helping requires a range of analytical tasks that must be completed before client interaction occurs. Although both analysis and interaction require a wealth of knowledge, analytical tasks are especially closely tied to a broad range of knowledge from the social, behavioral, and biological sciences. Without knowledge, competent analysis is extremely unlikely, and without analysis, interaction is haphazard and uncertain.

In the next two chapters, professional helping will be explored at some length. First, professional helping as a process will be analyzed in terms of its objectives, activities, and participants. Then, specific helping skills will be presented in overview fashion—their detailed examination is the task of other courses that can adequately explore their conceptual complexities and problems of application. Since each social welfare helping profession has a somewhat distinctive set of specific helping techniques, a result of their rather distinctive helping objectives, social work will be used to provide a concrete example of a profession's helping skills. Other social welfare professions will share some of these skills with social work as well as having some of their own.

STUDY QUESTIONS

1. Select a life-cycle stage other than the illustration used in the text. Follow the model used in the text, identifying the major societal tasks for that stage, and next the genetic, cultural, and social resources and obstacles available in carrying out those tasks.
2. Select a current social problem that has particular relevance to the social welfare institution. Analyze how the five major institutions of society (the family, education, religion, and the political and economic institutions) relate to this problem in terms of helping to create, maintain, or solve it.
3. Assume that you are a social worker, and that one of your cases involves a 76-year-old woman whose husband has just died. She is concerned about being able to keep her six-room home, the adequacy of her income, and managing by herself. How might you analyze her situation, drawing upon biological, psychological, sociological, and economic knowledge?
4. After thinking about the approach to the knowledge base of social welfare taken in this chapter, in what areas do you feel your knowledge is most inadequate? How important do you think these knowledge gaps are for your future development as a professional helping person? Are there any possibilities open to you to fill in these gaps?

REFERENCES

1. Jim Good Tracks, "Native American Non-Interference," *Social Work* 18 (November, 1973): 33. Reprinted by permission of the National Association of Social Workers.
2. Helen Harris Perlman, *Social Casework: A Problem-Solving Process* (Chicago: University of Chicago Press, 1957), pp. 6–7.
3. See Allen Mazur and Leon Robertson, *Biology and Social Behavior* (New York: Free Press, 1972); and Vernon Reynolds, *The Biology of Human Action* (San Francisco: W. H. Freeman, 1976).
4. Ronald Holler and George DeLong, *Human Services Technology* (St. Louis: Mosby, 1973), pp. 123–124.
5. Alfred Baldwin, *Theories of Child Development* (New York: John Wiley, 1968), p. 375.
6. Arnold Rose, *Sociology: The Study of Human Relations,* 2nd rev. ed. (New York: Alfred A. Knopf, 1967), p. 729.
7. Baldwin, op. cit., p. 350.
8. For brief summaries of the Freudian approach, the following can be recommended: developmental stages, Baldwin, op. cit., pp. 351–73; and Charles Brenner, *An Elementary Textbook of Psychoanalysis* (Garden City: Anchor, 1957), pp. 16–32; levels of consciousness, ibid., pp. 35–37; mental structures, ibid., pp. 37–140.
9. Baldwin, op. cit., p. 351.
10. A representative work is Otto Rank, *Will Therapy,* translated by Jesse Taft (New York: Alfred A. Knopf, 1968).
11. A representative work is C. G. Jung, *Analytical Psychology: Its Theory and Practice* (New York: Pantheon, 1968).
12. David Elkind, "Erik Erikson's Eight Stages of Man," in Annual Editions, *Readings in Sociology, 74–75* (Guilford, Conn.: Dushkin, 1974), p. 14.
13. Jonas Langer, *Theories of Development* (New York: Holt, Rinehart and Winston, 1969), p. 33.
14. Ibid., p. 34.
15. Ibid., pp. 36–46.
16. Elkind, op. cit., p. 22.
17. Alison Clarke-Stewart, *Child Care in the Family* (New York: Academic Press, 1978).
18. Holler and De Long, op. cit., 125–126.
19. J. D. Kidd, *How Adults Learn* (New York: Association Press, 1976), pp. 150–176.
20. Malcolm Knowles, *The Adult Learner: A Neglected Species* (Houston: Gulf Publishing Co., 1973), pp. 30–63.
21. Ibid., p. 33.
22. Peter Day, *Methods of Learning Communication Skills* (New York: Pergamon Press, 1977), pp. 118–157.
23. Langer, op. cit., p. 52.
24. Ibid., p. 55.
25. An interesting attempt to relate psychoanalytic and behavioral approaches may be found in V. Meyer and Edward Chesser, *Behavior Therapy in Clinical Psychiatry* (New York: Science House, 1970).
26. Langer, op. cit., p. 56.
27. Baldwin, op. cit., p. 397.

28. Ibid., p. 398.
29. Albert Bandura and Richard Walters, *Social Learning and Personality Development* (New York: Holt, Rinehart and Winston, 1963), pp. 4–7.
30. Baldwin, op. cit., p. 428.
31. Bandura and Walters, op. cit., pp. 224–246; for applications of their theory, see Edwin Thomas, ed., *The Socio-Behavioral Approach and Applications to Social Work* (New York: Council on Social Work Education, 1967).
32. Edwin Thomas, "Selected Sociobehavioral Techniques and Principles: An Approach to Interpersonal Helping," *Social Work* 13 (January 1968): 12.
33. Ibid., p. 18.
34. Derek Jehu, *Learning Theory and Social Work* (New York: Humanities Press, 1967), p. 84.
35. Baldwin, op. cit., p. 430.
36. Ibid., pp. 424–554.
37. Ibid., p. 120.
38. Clarke-Stewart, op. cit.
39. Ibid.
40. See, for example, Oscar Handlin, ed., *Children of the Uprooted* (New York: George Braziller, 1966).
41. Dolores G. Norton, *The Dual Perspective* (New York: Council on Social Work Education, 1978).
42. Myrtle Reul, *Territorial Boundaries of Rural Poverty* (East Lansing: Michigan State University Press, 1974).
43. Susan Sheehan, *A Welfare Mother* (New York: Saturday Review Press, 1975).
44. Robin Williams, *American Society* (New York: Knopf, 1951).
45. Allan Bell and Martin S. Weinberg, *Homosexualities* (New York: Simon and Schuster, 1978).
46. Eliot Liebow, *Talley's Corner* (Boston: Little, Brown, 1967).
47. Susan Sheehan, *A Prison and a Prisoner* (Boston: Houghton Mifflin, 1978).
48. Ramon Valle and Lydia Mendoza, *The Elderly Latino* (San Diego: Campanile Press, 1977).
49. A basic overview of major sociological theories can be found in Ronald Federico, *Sociology,* 2d ed. (Reading, Mass.: Addison-Wesley Publishing Co., 1979).
50. Sigmund Freud, *Civilization and Its Discontents* (New York: W. W. Norton, 1961).
51. For illustrative data, see Bureau of the Census, *Social Indicators 1976* (Washington, D.C.: U.S. Government Printing Office), pp. 248, 302–303, 483–558.
52. Clarke-Stewart, op. cit.
53. Marvin B. Sussman, "Family," in *Encyclopedia of Social Work,* 17th ed. (Washington, D.C.: National Association of Social Workers, 1977), pp. 357–363.
54. Kenneth Dolbeare and Patricia Dolbeare, *American Ideologies* (Chicago: Markham, 1971).
55. A basic reference throughout this section is Richard Leftwich and Ansel Sharp, *Economics of Social Issues,* rev. ed. (Dallas: Business Publications, 1976).
56. "Poverty Level is Raised Because of Price Levels," *New York Times,* April 10, 1979, p. B-6.
57. Donald Brieland, Lela Costin, and Charles Atherton, eds., *Contemporary Social Work* (New York: McGraw-Hill, 1975), p. 90.

58. Leftwich and Sharp, op. cit., pp. 209–230.
59. Lucile Duberman, *Social Inequality: Caste and Class in America* (Philadelphia: J. B. Lippincott, 1976).
60. See David Caplovitz, *The Poor Pay More* (New York: Free Press, 1967).
61. Martin Rein, *Social Policy: Issues of Choice and Change* (New York: Random House, 1970), pp. 53–67.
62. Excellent discussions of moral perspectives used in evaluating the worth of recipients of public assistance may be found in John Romanyshyn, *Social Welfare: From Charity to Justice* (New York: Random House, 1971), pp. 41–46; and Gilbert Y. Steiner, *Social Insecurity: The Politics of Welfare* (Chicago: Rand McNally, 1966), pp. 108–140.
63. A good survey of some of the major contemporary problems in welfare is "The Welfare Industrial Complex," *The Nation*, June 28, 1971, pp. 808–811. See also President's Commission on Income Maintenance Programs, *Poverty Amid Plenty* (Washington, D.C.: U.S. Government Printing Office, 1969), pp. 13–41.
64. *Congressional Quarterly*, "Guide to Current American Government," Fall, 1970.
65. Ralph Kramer, *Participation of the Poor* (Englewood Cliffs, N.J.: Prentice-Hall, 1969).
66. Wilbur Cohen, "What Every Social Worker Should Know about Political Action," in Robert Klenk and Robert Ryan, eds., *The Practice of Social Work* (Belmont, Calif.: Wadsworth, 1970), pp. 334–346.
67. Clair Wilcox, *Toward Social Welfare* (Homewood, Ill.: Richard D. Irwin, 1969), esp. pp. 159–208. He notes the distinction between legislation and its implementation in looking at the difference between de jure and de facto segregation.

SELECTED READINGS

Alinsky, Saul. *Reveille for Radicals.* Chicago: University of Chicago Press, 1946.

Brown, Rita Mae. *Rubyfruit Jungle.* New York: Bantam Books, 1977.

Clarke-Stewart, Alison. *Child Care in the Family.* New York: Academic Press, 1978.

Heap, Ken. *Group Theory for Social Workers.* New York: Pergamon Press, 1977.

Galper, Jeffrey. *The Politics of Social Services.* Englewood Cliffs, N.J.: Prentice-Hall, 1975.

Kahn, Si. *How People Get Power.* New York: McGraw-Hill, 1970.

Leftwich, Richard, and Sharp, Ansel. *Economics of Social Issues*, rev. ed. Dallas: Business Publications, 1976.

Mazur, Allen, and Robertson, Leon. *Biology and Social Behavior.* New York: Free Press, 1972.

Reul, Myrtle. *Territorial Boundaries of Rural Poverty.* East Lansing: Michigan State University Extension Division, 1974.

Schumacher, E. F. *Small is Beautiful: Economics as if People Mattered.* New York: Harper & Row, 1973.

Segall, Marshall. *Human Behavior and Public Policy.* New York: Pergamon Press, 1976.

Sennett, Richard, and Cobb, Jonathan. *The Hidden Injuries of Class.* New York: Random House, 1972.

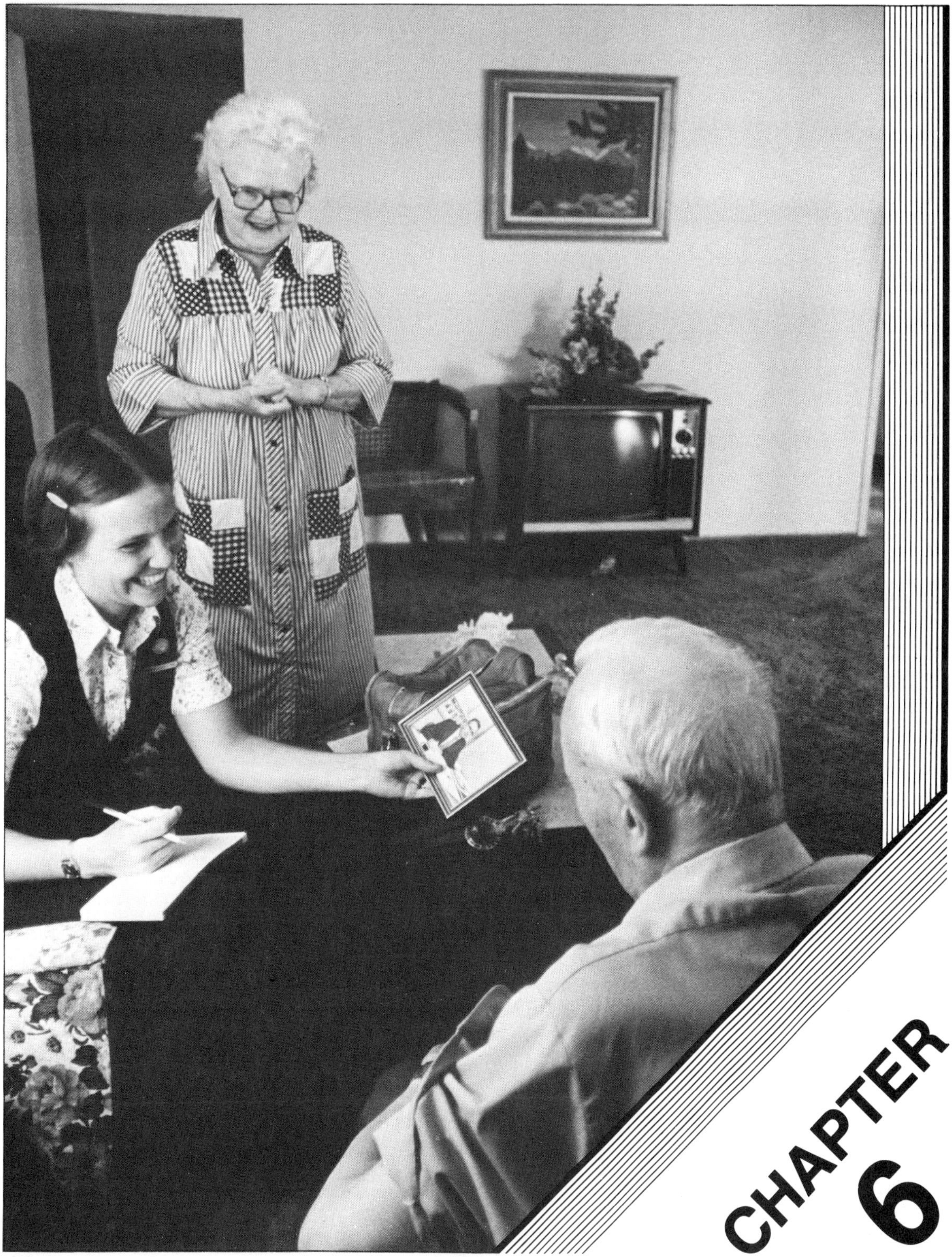

CHAPTER 6

An Overview of the Helping Process

As has been emphasized in previous chapters, the core of the social welfare institution is helping people function more effectively. Helping, however, occurs on many levels and in many contexts. The pervasiveness of the social welfare institution is partially a reflection of the fact that its helping function is found in so many places throughout the social structure, ranging from peer groups to the family to welfare bureaucracies. This chapter focuses on formal helping because most social welfare services and structures are built around this type of helping. However, it is important to remember that informal helping is now and has always been an extremely important part of the social welfare institution. The cognitive objective of this chapter is to provide an analytical framework to use in understanding formal helping as an interactional process. The value and skill objectives are to assist the reader to begin self-assessment in a conscious way. This includes developing a better understanding of the helping the reader has already done and examining carefully the demands of professional helping. Both are needed in order to better assess one's own motivation and suitability for the social welfare helping professions.

The Helping Process ◀

The components of the helping process can be listed as follows:[1]

1. People. Helping is a cooperative venture that involves at least two people, and often many more. Normally we think in terms of a person providing help (the *helper*) and a person seeking help (for convenience called here the *consumer*), although both helpers and consumers may be multiple people. The helper and consumer agree to work together to meet a need or solve a problem, and the work of both is essential to this process. The helper does not fundamentally solve the consumer's problem—people solve their own problems with the assistance of the helper. Helping, therefore, is a voluntary activity that both persons enter into. There are situations in which the consumer is ordered to seek help, as is the case when a delinquent youngster must see a probation officer. However, seeing a probation officer is far different from seeking help, because a probation officer cannot be helpful if the youngster refuses to accept the help offered (poor Veronica in Exhibit 1-6 is a case in point). In a sense, every helping situation is a *self-help* situation in which consumers use the resources provided by the helper to help themselves.

Helping may be informally or formally structured. In a book like this the focus is mostly on *formal helping,* in which specially trained helpers interact with consumers in situations specifically designed for that purpose. However, much helping occurs in *informal situations,* such as when friends try to be helpful to each other. Informal helping networks are extremely important because many people do not know about or are afraid of using formal helping structures. The results of informal helping efforts may be less predictable than formal efforts, but they are often very effective. In addition, many people tend to use formal helping structures only after exhausting informal helping networks.[2]

2. Place. Formal helping usually occurs through organizations specifically designed for that purpose. These are usually called social welfare agencies as a generic term, although they may have specific names as well, such as mental hospital, welfare agency, hotline, family service agency, Red Cross, and so forth. The organization designed for helping activities usually has basic resources needed in the helping process. These may include such things as clerical help, office space, recreational facilities, medicines, and books. Formal helping structures frequently provide help to people within the structure itself—a hospital room, an office, or a gymnasium, for example. The conditions under which help is provided can usually be more controlled in these settings, as when doctors have sophisticated medical equipment available in a hospital. However, their professional helpers may also go outside the structure to provide help. Meals may be taken to elderly people's homes, homemaker services may be provided for a struggling mother, a tenants' organization may meet in their own apartment building, and a social worker may sometimes go to a city council meeting to testify.

In informal helping situations, the place may be quite impromptu, unexpected, and even inappropriate. An automobile accident that occurs on a hilly dirt road requires that certain helping activities occur there or nearby. A distraught woman who has just been raped in a city park needs help either there or at the first point of contact with others from whom help is sought. Often help is required where resources have to be quickly improvised and where there may be many obstacles to overcome. Ultimately, however, the nature of the place is less important than the fact that help is found when sought.

3. Problem (need). The interactional nature of helping requires that there be basic agreement about what the problem or need is for which help is sought. Helping may be seen as a type of *contract* between the helper and the consumer, in which both agree to cooperate in order to reach a clearly specified goal utilizing defined resources. Unless such a contract is reached, the helper and consumer may only too late discover that they see the problem or need differently, and that their objectives are different. Even in the above-cited instance of rape, perspectives may be surprisingly different. The helper may assume that the woman is primarily concerned with getting medical care and physical protection and with contacting the police to try to apprehend the rapist. However, she may instead be most preoccupied by the wrenching emotional impact of her experience and her fears that loved ones may reject her.

The need for agreement between the helper and consumer raises the possibility that such agreement may in some cases not be achieved. What happens then? For one thing, helping cannot occur, because unless both parties agree and work together, helping is impossible. In formal helping situations, lack of agreement may result from the helper feeling inadequate to the task because of inadequate expertise, perceived inability to avoid emotional involvement, lack of needed resources, or some other factor. Lack of agreement may also stem from the consumer, who may distrust the helper's motivations, may question the helper's competence, or may simply feel uncomfortable with that particular helping person. If at all possible, the helper refers the consumer to a more appropriate person under these circumstances. In informal helping situations, lack of agreement usually results in a rather spontaneous and mutual disengagement between the potential helper and consumer.

4. Purpose. As we have already discussed, helping takes place for a purpose that has been agreed upon by the helper and consumer. There are, of course, many types and levels of helping, and everyone is both helped and helps others regularly. We may help someone who stops and asks us for directions, in the same way as we may seek help from others for this same purpose. We provide help by assisting a friend who is trying to decide on the appliance most suitable for his or her needs, and we seek help from friends by borrowing something we need. Professional helping people also provide help in more complex and difficult situations. Although we usually think about a particular concrete *task* that we are seeking to accomplish when we speak about a helping purpose, sometimes the helping purpose is to achieve a *process* goal. That is, rather than trying to accomplish a specific goal (getting money, meeting a suitable lover, filling out an application form, for example), we may instead be trying to develop the skills necessary to accomplish these things in the future (learn what resources exist, develop interactional skills, learn how to write, and so forth). Both task and process goals are equally important in helping efforts.

5. Helping activities. The helping process encompasses many specific decisions and activities, from the decision that help is needed through the actual interactions in which helping occurs. Although it is often overlooked, David Landy has emphasized the importance of the beginning of the helping process when help is sought.[3] Landy points out that the process of seeking help is often difficult and complex. It begins with a recognition that something is wrong, but such recognition is hampered by the common tendency to deny failing in some aspect of our lives. This is encouraged by a societal value system that preaches self-reliance and the belief that individuals can and should solve their own problems. Under these circumstances, it is not surprising that people often seek help only when they are desperate and when the problems are so complex that they are very difficult to solve. Seeking help is admitting that people have "failed" in coping with their problems, a situation others may also become aware of. The stigma attached to seeking help is one reason why people tend to turn first to the informal helping network: family, friends, or clergy. Here, problems can be discussed with minimal risk. Entry into the professional social service network implies that the problem is serious.

Landy also notes that the act of seeking help places consumers in a dependent position and requires that they relinquish some autonomy (answering endless questions, having to travel to an inconvenient agency location, keeping appointments, and the like). Being helped is often uncomfortable, involving confrontation with painful memories, unpleasant insights into oneself and others, and emotional stress. A person with problems may not be at all eager to temporarily endure more stress in order to achieve ultimate solutions. Talcott Parsons, a sociologist, has analyzed the role of people with physical illnesses. It seems very relevant in understanding the problem of the person seeking help in our culture, emphasizing the rights and obligations incurred in the process.[4] Landy's point, therefore, is to remind the social welfare practitioner that asking for help is a major step, and it is also likely to be stressful. Some of these stresses are vividly described in Exhibit 6-1.

Once the formal helping network has been entered, activities such as agreeing on purpose, working together on problem solution, and identifying task and process goals take place, as already discussed. Throughout the helping experience, resources are explored and used systematically. This is an exhausting and highly emotional undertaking because people react to their situation with feelings. Feelings are a natural and important part of the communication that occurs between a helper and a consumer. Our lives, and particularly the needs and problems in them, cannot always be looked at objectively and dispassionately. Our very identity as people is wrapped up in them, and specific events and objects take on meaning only through our perception of their significance for us. A man has gotten a divorce; that is an objective fact. But the meaning of that event lies in its perceived significance for him. Has it made him feel like a failure as a man? Does he fear that his relationship with his children will be destroyed? Is he anxious about his ability to care for himself, or about being lonely? As these feelings come out, the dimensions of the problems and needs around which helping must occur are visible.

EXHIBIT 6-1 *The Experience of Seeking Help*

In 1976, the Community Services Society of New York City sponsored a study of how the New York City Department of Social Services (DSS) was implementing existing procedures and regulations for applications for public assistance. The following case is one of the examples used in the report of this study. It is an excellent illustration of the difficulties people sometimes have in entering the formal helping network. Had the woman involved not been desperate, one could easily conceive her becoming so angry and upset that she would have ceased her efforts to find help. One could as easily imagine her dropping out of the helping effort if transportation to the agency had been especially difficult, as it is in many communities. As it turned out, this woman had the courage and stamina (plus help from ACCESS*) to persist in her efforts until she was successful. However, her account focuses attention on the procedures that are used in leading people to the social welfare services that have been created for their use. These procedures can become important determinants of the success or failure of helping efforts.

Mrs. B., an eighteen-year-old mother of one child, was nine months pregnant. She was separated from the father of both children and was staying with another man. The man told Mrs. B. that she had to leave because his wife was coming back to live with him.

Her father allowed her to stay in his home one night and a friend let her stay a second night. The next morning, June 8, she was "homeless" and

Source: Daniel Reich, *Applying for Public Assistance in New York City* (New York: Community Service Society of New York, 1977), pp. 22–23.

* ACCESS is a service to assist people apply for public assistance which is sponsored by the Community Services Society of New York.

went to the DSS Center to apply for public assistance. She was denied an application for public assistance because the worker said she had to have a place to stay before they could give her help. She should have been allowed to apply at the Center since her family was undomiciled. According to City Procedure 75-13, p. 10, the application for a homeless person "should be taken by the first IM Center at which the applicant appears." She was referred to Project ACCESS by an ACCESS worker, and ACCESS provided assistance so that she could have shelter.

On June 9, she returned to the Center but was told that she had to go to Family Court to report the missing father. On June 10, she returned to the Center but was told that because the room where she was temporarily staying was out of the district, she could not receive help from that Center. This again violated City Procedure 75-13, p. 10. DSS Central Office was called by ACCESS on June 10 to request intervention on this case by the administrative staff.

On June 15, Mrs. B. had her second child. She still had not received an application for public assistance. An appointment at the Center was made for June 18. On that date the applicant arrived at the Center at 9:00 a.m. but was told by the General Receptionist that she was too late to be helped. Mrs. B. finally received an application on her fifth visit to the Center on June 21. On June 22, Mrs. B. returned to the Center and was granted assistance.

Once the decision to seek help has been made and a working relationship between the helper and the consumer established, a variety of specific helping activities may be used. Concrete needs may be best met through activities to identify resources and link people with them: financial assistance programs, medical care, housing, physical security, and so forth. Task needs often involve activities to bring people together so that they can work collaboratively toward goal attainment. Process needs may require activities in the areas of teaching and learning as well as emotional support and development. The range of specific helping activities used by social welfare professional helpers is too enormous to be listed here (Chapter 7 looks at such activities in some detail for one profession, social work). What is relevant for this chapter's overview of the helping process is understanding that there are specific helping activities that are used in formal helping efforts.

6. Outcome. In evaluating the outcome of a helping effort, there are at least three general criteria that can be used: (1) Evaluation of involvement: were all of the relevant people involved, or did the helper try to do everything alone? As already noted, effective helping involves working with others, not dominating them. The consumer must have been involved to the fullest extent possible. Other persons who affect the consumer's situation should also be involved as appropriate (the systems perspective that everyone is tied into a network of activities). (2) Socioemotional evaluation: how did the people involved in the helping effort feel about it? Usually one is especially concerned with the perspective of the consumers—did they feel that the decision to seek help was a wise one? However, again using a systems perspective, the helper will also want to be concerned with the feelings of all those involved in the helping effort.

These people may at some time participate in other actions that affect social welfare activities (through the ballot box or by volunteering to work in a social agency, for example). (3) Task evaluation: was the need met or the problem solved? This, the most concrete way to evaluate a service, must always be a major part of the evaluation process.

Helping, therefore, is a complex interaction of two or more people around the use of resources to solve problems or meet needs. Although all of us are regularly involved in helping and being helped at many levels, the formal helping network requires a higher level of awareness, purpose, and skill in order to achieve more consistently effective results than can reasonably be expected from the informal helping network. Formal helping, however, should never be controlling. Controlling another's life and helping people to control their own lives are two different things, and only the latter strategy has any place among competent professional social welfare helping efforts.

The Helping Person

As much as it would be useful to be able to know exactly what the perfect helping person looks like, it is impossible to do. The reason is because there is no perfect helping person. The mix of person, problem, and purpose in the helping process is constantly shifting. The strengths that a particular helping person may have with one type of person (such as the elderly) or a particular type of problem (like child abuse) may be weaknesses with other people and problems. There are some general characteristics that experience has shown ought to be part of the professional social welfare helping person's overall personal profile, but the blend differs for each person. It is precisely the fact that each person is different which enables all persons seeking help, no matter what the problem or purpose, to find a helping person who can assist them. Each helping person has a "style," and as long as that style includes some strength along each of the dimensions that follow, one can predict that it will be effective most of the time:

1. Self-awareness. Helping people must know themselves reasonably well, and on the whole, they must like themselves. The motivations for helping others should revolve around a belief in one's own ability to be useful to others. The balance of personal strengths and weaknesses should allow the helping person to focus on working with others effectively. The values underlying the helping person's behaviors should support activities to help people take control over their own lives and to have access to needed societal resources. Interactional skills should be used consciously and skillfully. Because all of us have limits, the helping persons must know when their limits have been reached. To know that a given situation is beyond one's abilities is sensible; to persist regardless of one's abilities is dangerous and often harmful. None of us ever completely understands and knows ourselves, especially because we are constantly changing. Successful professional helping people know their own basic parameters, however.

2. Professional Commitment. The social welfare professional should have a strong commitment to the goals of social welfare and to the ethical standards of the particular social welfare profession (social work, nursing, criminal justice, and so forth). The professional helper has a fundamental drive to improve social and individual life conditions and reacts to situations of injustice and disadvantage. Commitment and self-awareness are closely related. The desire to participate in achieving the goals of social welfare means a constant evaluation of one's own professional behavior within professional standards of ethical behavior and practice competence. Professional commitment is not a blind, uncompromising assault on the institutions and structures of society that seem to be creating obstacles for people. It is instead a commitment and determination to work collaboratively with others to use professional knowledge, values, and skills to achieve the changes necessary to make it easier for people to achieve their life goals. Professional helping people work together; the world is too large and too complex for individuals to think that they can singlehandedly solve its problems, although each person can certainly make a (sometimes considerable) contribution to that overall effort.

3. Knowledge and practice skills. Professional helping activity is firmly grounded in relevant knowledge, and it proceeds through the use of carefully selected activities requiring specific skills. Some of the major knowledge bases of helping activities have already been discussed, and specific skills will be discussed in the next chapter. For now, it is sufficient to say that the social welfare professional knows how to identify or develop resources, use resources with and on behalf of people, interact skillfully with a wide range of people by understanding and respecting their cultural and life-style backgrounds, and constantly monitor helping activities to improve them. Helping is an activity that is carefully done. Strong feelings and a real commitment to improve people's lives are involved, but undisciplined emotion that ignores professional knowledge and skill is rarely successful.

4. Objectivity. Problems are frequently multifaceted and complex, and sometimes it is hard to separate the person from the problem. Nevertheless, if helping is to be effective, the helper has to be able to maintain perspective and be relatively objective about the problem and person with whom the helper is working. It is important that problems be *partialized,* that is, divided into their component parts so that a seemingly overwhelming whole can be solved piece by piece. Throughout this process, the goal of the intervention must be kept clearly in mind so that each piece fits into the whole. It is also important to separate the person from the problem, recognizing when one is dealing with a person and that particular person's reactions to a situation and when one is dealing with a situation whose dynamics may be tied to social and cultural structures and processes. Even when dealing with an individual, the helping person has to be sensitive and personal and yet still able to step back to carefully evaluate the person's strengths, needs, and weaknesses. It is possible to be objective without being impersonal. Being able to systematically evaluate a person and that person's situation can go on at the same time that the helping person is warm and caring toward the consumer. This duality of skills captures the meaning of professional objectivity.

5. Empathy. Empathy is the ability to comprehend another's subjective reality and feelings. Empathy is more objective than sympathy because it does not include sharing feelings with the other person; it is instead sharing an *understanding* of those feelings and their importance. This enables the helping person to understand without being overwhelmed by what may be very upsetting and immobilizing feelings. Empathy and support are necessary to enable the person who needs assistance to utilize resources—both personal and outside resources—to develop and implement a solution to the problematic reality.

6. Energy. Helping is an exhausting activity. Not only does it require the careful use of knowledge and skill, but it is also a constant drain on one's feelings and emotions. If there is a commitment to help, however, there has to be the energy to carry out the necessary helping activities. One of the common ways in which professional integrity is compromised is through the loss of energy, that is, being too psychologically or physically tired to care any more (sometimes called *burnout*). One way to avoid this is to emphasize the helping person's *enabling* role. As has been emphasized throughout this discussion of helping, the helper is not a rigidly controlling person. The helper's role is to facilitate the work of others, to enable the consumer and relevant others to understand resources and problems, to use resources more effectively, and to develop new skills. The helping person's own resources go much further for far longer if they are invested in cooperative and facilitative interactions with others.

7. Persistence and resilience. Helping can be a very discouraging endeavor. Sometimes problems are so complex that they seem overwhelming. Sometimes needs are so widespread that it seems they can never be adequately met. Sometimes people become so frightened by change that they become hostile and resistant. Sometimes painfully won gains are wiped out through an unusual or unanticipated event. And sometimes the progress is so slow that it is easy to forget it is even happening. Yet these are the realities of change. People are not always grateful for efforts to help them achieve their goals. There are many people who wish to block the goal attainment of others. The bureaucracies in which we live and work can sometimes proceed with excruciating slowness. In spite of it all, the helping professional has to keep working in a methodical way toward the goals of the helping situation and to keep finding better ways when the old ways are inadequate. Discouraged often, disappointed frequently, and tired daily, the professional commitment that supports the helping professional nevertheless provides the core motivation for trying again and again, seeking to be better and better.

What makes an effective professional helping person? There is, of course, no simple answer to such a question. There are many types of persons who make effective helpers. Keith-Lucas suggests the following:[5]

> *Courage, humility, and concern may then give us some characterization of the helping person. Other qualities such as dependability, patience, integrity, or a sense of humor are of course also desirable, or perhaps simply facets of these. Intelligence and imagination can be of help. But the helping person is an essentially human being, with many of the faults that all of us share. There is nothing ascetic or infallible about him or about his knowledge. He is disciplined but no automaton, sensitive but no seer, knowledgeable but not necessarily intellectual, unselfish but not self-denying, long suffering but no martyr. When we meet him we will probably like him but not, perhaps, be too impressed.*

Whatever the individual characteristics of the professional helping person, this person must possess self-awareness and be aware of any particular strengths and weaknesses, skills and deficiencies, preferences and pet peeves. As Keith-Lucas notes, all of us have limitations and weaknesses, and helping professionals are no exception. They must recognize their limitations so that these characteristics will not interfere with the helping process as they work.

Chapter Summary ◀

Given the complexity of industrialized societies, informal, unstructured helping networks are inadequate by themselves to cope with the magnitude and difficulty of many needs. The formal helping structures established through the social welfare institution have been created to meet the most pervasive and difficult needs. Helping is an orderly, planned activity that requires knowledge, skill, and certain personal qualities, many of which are shared by all of the individual social welfare professions. These shared elements of helping have been explored in this chapter. However, each social welfare helping professional also has a body of specialized helping skills that have been developed to deal with the particular kinds of needs handled by the practitioners in that profession. The next chapter looks at social welfare professional helping skills, using social work as an example of how each social welfare profession develops specialized helping skills based on its particular social welfare objectives.

STUDY QUESTIONS

1. Think about a situation in which you helped someone (remember that we help people in many small ways every day, and thus you need not try to think of a life-or-death situation). What feelings did you have about the person you helped? Why did you decide to try to be helpful? How did you think about yourself after helping this person? Were your efforts successful? Do you think the other person would agree with you in your evaluation of success or lack of it? Why or why not?
2. Now think of a situation in which you were helped by someone. How did it feel to need help? How did the person who helped you react to you? Do you feel that the person was successful in helping you? Do you think the other person would agree with you in your evaluation of success or lack of it? Why or why not? Do you find that your feelings about helping someone else are different from your feelings about being helped? If so, why do you think this is so?
3. Write out, in your own words and drawing upon your own ideas, what you think it will be like to be the kind of professional helping person you are considering becoming (or that you could conceivably think of becoming)—a social worker, special education teacher, nurse, physical therapist, and so forth. Then take another piece of paper and describe the qualities you have that you think would make you an effective helping person and those that you think might be problematic. Then compare your two essays—do you think you have the potential for becoming a professional helping person? If not, what kind of work do you think you could do well? As an extension of this exercise, interview someone who works in the profession you chose to write about. Find out from them what their work is like and what they do and don't like about it, and compare it to your view of the profession. How accurate was your view?

REFERENCES

1. The components of the helping process generally follow the framework in Karin Eriksen, *Human Services Today* (Reston, Va.: Reston Publishing Company, 1977), pp. 130–144.
2. David Landy, "Problems of the Person Seeking Help in Our Culture," in Mayer Zald, ed., *Social Welfare Institutions* (New York: John Wiley, 1965), pp. 559–574.
3. Ibid.
4. Talcott Parsons, *The Social System* (New York: Free Press, 1951), pp. 285–91, 476.
5. Alan Keith-Lucas, *Giving and Taking Help* (Chapel Hill: University of North Carolina Press, 1972), p. 108.

SELECTED READINGS

Keith-Lucas, Alan. *Giving and Taking Help.* Chapel Hill: University of North Carolina Press, 1972.

Rees, Stuart. *Social Work Face to Face.* New York: Columbia University Press, 1979.

Sheehan, Susan. *A Welfare Mother.* New York: Saturday Review Press, 1975.

Sheehan, Susan. *A Prison and a Prisoner.* Boston: Houghton Mifflin, 1978.

Stack, Carol K. *All Our Kin: Strategies for Survival in the Black Community.* New York: Harper & Row, 1974.

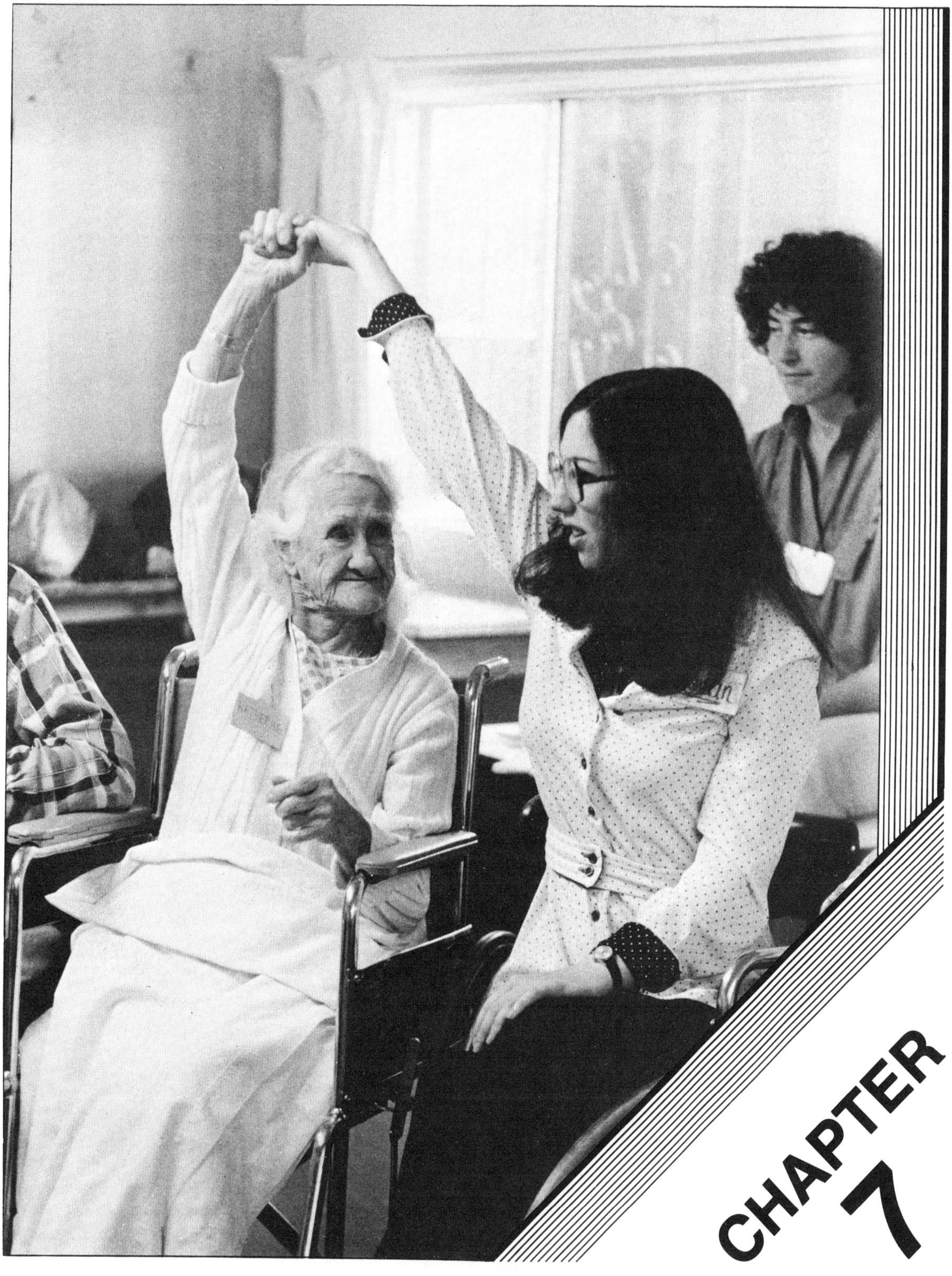

CHAPTER 7

Social Work Practice Methods

Social work is perhaps the most integrative of all of the social welfare professions. It looks at the total life space of the person needing help and attempts to identify and utilize the resources necessary to provide the help needed. Social workers utilize a whole range of more specialized social welfare services on behalf of their clients—medical, mental health, educational, rehabilitative, correctional, financial, and recreational services are some of the major ones. In order to link people with these services, social workers perform a variety of activities related to teaching and supporting people, as well as helping them to help themselves through concerted group activities. Underlying these activities are some basic skills having to do with communication, relating to others, planning and executing helping efforts, and professional self-awareness and self-assessment. Social workers are also involved in policy-related activities in order to expand the scope, quality, and availability of services to help people.

This chapter begins by examining the purposes of social work, for interventive activities flow from the profession's and society's view of its societal mandate. An overview of the development of various interventive methods and approaches follows, with an emphasis on the context in which they are developed. Finally, the chapter attempts to outline the most recent thinking about efforts to develop a set of integrated helping methods usable in the many practice situations in which social workers function. The knowledge objectives of this chapter include understanding the objectives of social work, the ability to describe the helping strategies that have been used in social work, and a grasp of current thinking about social work practice. Value and skill objectives include the ability to tie social work values to particular practice skills and approaches and the ability to evaluate critically the practice strategies that the profession has developed at various points in its history.

The Purposes of Social Work ◄

The purposes of social work were recently defined as follows:[1]

> *Social work is concerned and involved with the interactions between people and the institutions of society* that affect the ability of people to accomplish life tasks, realize aspirations and values, and alleviate distress. These interactions between people and social institutions occur within the context of the larger societal good. Therefore, three major purposes of social work may be identified:*
>
> 1. *To enhance the problem-solving, coping, and developmental capacities of people;*
> 2. *To promote the effective and humane operation of the systems that provide people with resources and services;*
> 3. *To link people with systems that provide them with resources, services, and opportunities . . . .*

This view of the purposes of social work makes clear its links to both individuals and the systems that affect their lives—focusing on only one or the other is not social work. This, of course, is consistent with what we know from the social, behavioral, and biological sciences—human behavior must be understood and manipulated as part of a complex whole. It is

---

* The institutions of society are defined as "including the family, education, religion, political and economic institutions, and the social welfare institution (including the health, legal, criminal justice, financial assistance, and social services systems and structures). The interactions between people and the institutions of society may include interactions between people within one institution (family members, for example), the functioning of one person in attempting to carry out institutional roles (an aged widow, for example), people attempting to interact with structures (a family seeking public assistance, for example), or institutional structures in interactions that influence people's lives (a social work agency's participation in the political process, for example)."

social work's unique purpose to understand this whole and to help people find ways to achieve satisfying lives within this realm, drawing upon specific services as needed.

Underlying this purpose of social work is a commitment to professional values (discussed in Exhibit 3-2). Social workers are defined as much by *how* they act as by *what* is done. For example, providing information is an appropriate social work activity, but it is social work only if it is done with respect for the other person's value and belief system and in a way that encourages mutual sharing and making maximum use of the knowledge that the other person already possesses. Professional social workers commit themselves to values as well as to the mastery of specific helping skills. Without the skills, social workers risk incompetence, but without the values they risk losing the whole purpose of trying to help another.

From these purposes, ten competencies that define the areas of expertise of the baccalaureate professional social worker have been derived. They are:[2]

1. *Identify and assess situations where the relationship between people and social institutions need to be initiated, enhanced, restored, protected, or terminated.*
2. *Develop and implement a plan for improving the well-being of people based on problem assessment and the exploration of obtainable goals and available options.*
3. *Enhance the problem-solving, coping, and developmental capacities of people.*
4. *Link people with systems that provide them with resources, services, and opportunities.*
5. *Intervene effectively on behalf of populations most vulnerable and discriminated against.*
6. *Promote the effective and humane operation of the systems that provide people with services, resources, and opportunities.*
7. *Actively participate with others in creating new, modified, or improved service, resource, opportunity systems that are more equitable, just, and responsive to consumers of services, and work with others to eliminate those systems that are unjust.*
8. *Evaluate the extent to which the objectives of the intervention plan were achieved.*
9. *Continually evaluate one's own professional growth and development through assessment of practice behavior and skill.*
10. *Contribute to the improvement of service delivery by adding to the knowledge base of the profession as appropriate and by supporting and upholding the standards and ethics of the profession.*

There is no consensus at the present time about the purposes and the competencies of professional social workers. The above formulation has been much discussed and widely accepted, but it is by no means the exclusive definition. However, it does yield an approach to helping skills that is integrated, coherent, and related to the knowledge discussed in Chapters 4 and 5. This approach is presented later in this chapter. First, some alternative approaches are surveyed, along with their origins, strengths, and weaknesses.

Traditional Approaches to Practice ◀

We live in a time when traditional ways of intervening to help people solve their problems are being reexamined. Although this may be upsetting to professionals trying to decide on their own interventive approaches, the history of social welfare interventive methods has been characterized by a continuing search for more effective helping techniques. We have already seen that helping has been a part of social life from the earliest records of human existence. However, when talking about interventive methods, we begin at the time when helping became a codified, professional activity rather than one left to the charitable impulses of friendly visitors.

Our earlier discussion of the charity organization societies noted that they served as a catalyst for the development of professional social work through their emphasis on individual case study and supervision.[3] The many changes the Industrial Revolution was creating stimulated the development of many kinds of helping—especially in the treatment of the physically and mentally ill. In these professions, the scientific base was obvious. This base was not so obvious in social work and other more relationship-oriented helping professions. As Lubove points out,[4]

> *A major source of irritation to social workers anxious to elevate their professional status consisted of those "many popular misunderstandings of social work, which identify it with nursing, with mental testing, with occupational therapy, with neighborliness." Psychiatry in the early twentieth century played a significant role in strengthening the social worker's conviction that she offered a distinct and valuable service which required specialized skill and training.*

This, combined with the charity organization society emphasis on case study, led to the dominance of casework (individual counseling) as an interventive method and a strong alliance between casework and psychiatry, especially Freudian psychoanalysis.

Other effects of the Industrial Revolution, including rapid urbanization, the rise of factories, and the shift from extended to nuclear family structures, created problems of illness, poverty, exploitation, mobility, and isolation that were obviously beyond the control of individuals or families. These problems were especially noticeable in the large numbers of immigrants that arrived on America's shores full of hope but often sick, homeless, and ignorant of the language and customs of their new country. In Jane Addams's words, "The Settlement (settlement houses, a type of community center), then, is an experimental effort to aid in the solution of the social and industrial problems which are engendered by the modern conditions of life in a great city. . . . It is an attempt to relieve, at the same time, the overaccumulation at one end of society and the destitution at the other. . . ."[5] Addams is asserting that another important focus of social welfare is to intervene in the social processes that create problems for individuals, rather than concentrating only on the individuals. Her statement also lays the foundation for social action as she talks about the need for a more equitable distribution of resources between the rich and the poor.

The social welfare professions, and social work in particular, began with two thrusts, the individual and the social. The attractiveness of the idea of scientifically based solutions to problems, plus the obvious complexity and political and economic risks of community development and social action, gradually led to a period in which casework dominated approaches to problem intervention. Nevertheless, the limitations of focusing primarily on a one-to-one interventive approach became obvious, and the community and social action heritage of social work were never completely lost. Gradually the need for a broader view of problem causation and solution led to the development of a group approach to problem solving, called group work, and the latent community and social action heritage found new expression in community organization. As social welfare professionalism increased, the need for administrative skills and research data also became evident, and they joined the ranks of important practice methods.

Because current social work practice includes a mix of traditional methods as well as new approaches to practice, the informed practitioner must at least understand the thinking behind each method. Therefore, the traditional methods of casework, group work, community organization, and management and administration will be briefly summarized. This overview will enable each reader to understand the major terminology and approach to practice used in each method. Next, a period during which a methods approach was seriously challenged by a role approach is briefly discussed. During this time, adapting a need to a method was rejected as less effective than adapting a variety of practice roles (rather than just one method) to a need. For example, rather than starting with casework (a method) and using it to try to solve whatever the need might be (marital counseling, more regular school attendance, economic assistance, or resources to change prejudicial and discriminating situations, for example), the social worker would start with the need and then use whatever practice roles are most appropriate and effective (such as advocacy, support, linkage, and so forth). The chapter ends with a reformulation of social work practice that, although building on the practice activities included in both the traditional methods and newer role approaches, focuses on the basic skills of the baccalaureate professional social worker as used in every practice situation.

Casework

There are many definitions of casework, reflecting the diversity of approaches possible. The Council on Social Work Education's definition is a concise summary of the basic approach: "a method of social work which intervenes in the psychosocial aspects of a person's life to improve, restore, maintain, or enhance his social functioning by improving his role performance."[6] Florence Hollis has said, "Central to casework is the notion of the person in his situation," [17] while Helen Harris Perlman talks of a "biopsychosocial whole"[8] providing the focus in casework. Perlman further explains that casework involves a person with a problem coming to a place where professionals use methods to help them.[9] Thus it can be seen that casework embodies the goal of improving social functioning, which characterizes social welfare as a whole. It does so by concentrating on one person in some depth, looking at the person's biological-psychological-social behavior in its social context. This is consistent with a systems approach as already discussed.

Casework, like most of the methods to be discussed, makes conscious use of helping, problem solving, and communication. It does so primarily on a one-to-one basis, concentrating on individualizing the situation of the person seeking help.[10] That is, the caseworker seeks to understand the specific biopsychosocial situation of the person with whom the caseworker is working. This includes the individual's personality structure and functioning, personal and social resources, typical behavior patterns in interaction with others, and real or potential problem areas. In doing this, the caseworker first seeks to obtain information through the skillful use of interviewing techniques. This information is called the *social history.* Although most characteristic of the beginning phase of the casework process, obtaining information continues to some extent throughout the relationship. This information is then interpreted, which is the process of *diagnosis.* In interpreting information, the caseworker begins with the information as presented by the client, including evidence of the meaning of the information for that person. Gradually the professional person places this information into a professional context, attempting to identify causes, effects, relationships, and possible solutions. Diagnosis is also something that continues throughout the casework relationship. As additional information is obtained it may affect interpretations tentatively made on the basis of earlier incomplete information.

Part of diagnosis is an assessment of the individual's situation. Whether there are any immediate crises that must be resolved, significant persons in the individual's life and environment, and available resources are explored. As situational assessment begins, the helping relationship begins to deepen, since the person seeking help must now take an active role in developing solutions to his or her problems. As planning for a solution is begun, the caseworker provides empathy, support, and information as appropriate. As a caseworker, one consciously uses a planned professional technique so that one can be of maximum help with as few of one's own problems as possible blocking communication and planning. As the person being helped selects solutions, the caseworker helps that person to implement the chosen plan.

Group Work

"When one gets down to the central core of what really happens that makes the group experience so meaningful and so useful, one discovers the simple truth that people with similar interests, similar concerns, or similar problems can help each other in ways that are significantly different from the ways in which a worker can help them in a one-to-one relationship. This is not to say that the group method is better—simply that it is different."[11] Put another way, "the group is the mediator between the individual and society. . . . Man can join with others in an effort to control what is happening to him."[12] The differences between casework and group work begin to emerge: (1) casework is usually a one-to-one relationship, while group work involves a worker and a small group of clients; (2) the worker-client relationship is the important process in casework, while in group work the group itself is the context and the process through which change occurs; and (3) casework and group work are methods with different requirements, and are most effective in the solution of different types of problems.

Group work builds on casework in that the group worker uses casework skills in relating to individual group members. It goes beyond casework when such relationships are supplemented by the interaction between group members, and as the structure of group activity generates social resources much greater than those available in a two-person group. Casework is more suited to problems involving extensive data-gathering, the discussion of strongly held feelings, and individual resource utilization. Group work is particularly effective in teaching interaction skills, achieving group goals, and providing recreation opportunities.

The American Association of Group Workers defines group work as follows:[13]

> *The group worker enables various groups to function in such a way that both group interaction and program activities contribute to the growth of the individual and the achievement of desirable social goals.*

The basic professional goal of group work is helping people function, and many aspects of the group process may be used to attain this goal. Wilson draws a distinction between groups with two distinct purposes:[14]

> *In [the task-oriented group], the group-enabler's primary responsibility is to support the group to accomplish its task; in [the growth-oriented group], the enabler's primary responsibility is to help members to use the group experience to resolve problems which are interfering with their personal growth and their social adjustment.*

Groups may exist, then, to accomplish group goal attainment or the social enjoyment and enrichment of its members. Wilson's emphasis on primary function suggests that one function may be dominant at any given time. However, she also implicitly recognizes that there are elements of both goals in all groups, as one would expect from the small-group literature reviewed earlier. Wilson also speaks of the professional person as an enabler in the group process. This concept is of great importance in interventive methods, and grows out of the professional value of client self-determination. Rather than imposing personal judgments on the clients, either individual or group, the worker helps the clients identify and develop knowledge and skills appropriate for the attainment of their goals.

Elaborating somewhat on Wilson, groups may be seen as focusing around member enjoyment (interest), the attainment of a specific goal through concerted group organization (concerns), or the use of the group as a therapeutic milieu (problems). As would be expected on the basis of small-group theory, different kinds of groups will have different structural characteristics. Vinter suggests that one needs to examine the following structural properties of a group to be aware of its purpose and potential: the social organization of the group patterns, roles, and statuses; activities, tasks, and operative processes; group culture, norms, and values; and the group's relationship to its external environment.[15] An example of the utility of this kind of analysis is Rapoport's identification of the following structural characteristics of therapeutic (problem-oriented) groups: democratization of decison-making; permissiveness in the discussion of behavioral problems; communalistic, tight-knit, intimate relationships; and confrontation, the use of the group as social reality.[16]

Such a structural analysis helps to understand how the group affects individual behavior, and helps identify goals consistent with the group's structure. In both Vinter and Rapoport the importance of external reality for the group is emphasized. No matter how significant the group may become for its members, they ultimately must transfer their new-found skills to the larger social world beyond the group. Even the group itself is affected by the environment in which it exists. For example, there may be organizational restraints in therapeutic groups, limited recreational facilities for pleasure groups, and a lack of appropriate community structures for groups seeking to achieve goals.[17]

Community Organization

Since communities are types of groups, community organization may be seen as an expanded form of group work. The latter typically deals with groups of fifteen and under, and the former with larger groups functioning in community contexts. This size distinction has inevitable implications: therapeutic goals are more difficult to attain, while task-oriented goals are more feasible. However, the attainment of goals assumes that a structure exists through which such goals may be sought, and this may not be the case in many communities. This gives rise to two major thrusts in community organization: (1) a task focus, in which the attainment of a community need is emphasized (a new playground, more social service agencies, political redistricting, and the like); and (2) a process focus, where the emphasis is on the building of viable, effective community structures in which people can work to accomplish their goals.[18] This latter focus is sometimes called "community development," in an effort to distinguish between the two major parts of community organization.[19] Actually the task and process distinctions that tend to surface in community organization underlie all social welfare practice. An interventive method attempts to solve specific problems while also trying to make it possible for the individual or individuals involved to be better able to solve the problems of the future.

Murray Ross's definition can be used to summarize community organization. He sees it as "a process by which a community identifies its needs or objectives, orders (or ranks) these needs or objectives, develops the confidence and will to work at these needs or objectives, finds the resources (internal and/or external) to deal with these needs or objectives, takes action in respect to them, and in so doing extends and develops cooperative and collaborative attitudes and practices in the community."[20] The community organization process entails identifying the problems that exist and for which there is a realistic chance of solution using community resources. Given that communities are commonly diverse in social composition, the various community components are likely to have their own definitions of existing problems, as well as their own order or priority for problem solution. In assessing stated problems, one wants to be sure to give all community groups a chance to express their views. The extent to which there is uniformity or competing views on significant problems (and the order of priority in their solution) can then be assessed.

Having studied the community, the worker begins the actual organization process. It is common to begin with a clearly specified task that has a high probability of successful accomplishment. This helps establish the belief that change is possible, and draws people into a "winning team."[21] In some respects this can be seen as a community-level expression of the value "start where the client is." Then one must begin with a workable group, those who are willing to participate and who have relevance to the tasks at hand. It is important not to alienate those not participating at the outset. The initial organization should be as nonantagonistic as possible, and leave the way open for the participation of others at a later time as that becomes feasible and desirable. With a task set and a working group organized, the strategy for attainment of the established goal becomes crucial. For some time community organizers automatically tended to think in terms of cooperative and conciliatory strategies that were clearly within the established community power structures. Rocking the boat was to be avoided for several reasons: fear that insurgent groups did not have the power to force the power structure to change; fear that the social welfare agencies involved in power tactics would be punished through withdrawal of community sanction and funds; and an ingrained respect for due process of law.

Several significant events changed these perceptions, and helped to make Ross's view of community organization as a tranquil, orderly process somewhat limited. First, as Michael Harrington and others pointed out, after decades of sporadic social reform, major social problems remained. Second, the black revolution made it abundantly clear that aggressive community organization and social action brought results that more passive, agreeable methods did not. Third, the black experience also stimulated more direct federal involvement in what were essentially community organization activities, so that the participants would be given some protection from retribution from the local community power structure. Fourth, the swelling magnitude of need threatened to topple many existing programs unless newer programs, more efficient and more acceptable to the recipients, were developed. Finally, the social welfare professions recognized that human need transcended job security, so that the risk of retribution against agencies and practitioners had to be run if programs consonant with professional values were to be obtained.[22] Community organization thus rapidly expanded its range of possible strategies to adapt to a variety of new community conditions and needs.

Administration, Management, and Research

In addition to casework, group work, and community organization, administration is often considered an important social work interventive method. As social welfare programs have become more and more complex, administration has become increasingly essential for the effective use of resources and for effective planning. However, administration has typically referred to a hierarchical kind of supervision which, although important, only deals with part of what is a larger need for the effective management of resources. Therefore, the term management will be used rather than administration in this discussion so that a broader range of management skills may be examined.

When discussing formal organizations and their effect on the structure of social welfare services in Chapter 3, it was noted that such organizations require careful planning so that means and goals relate to each other. We also saw that such organizations are characterized by hierarchical organization in which authority and responsibility generally flow from higher positions to those lower down in the organizational chart. This model is applicable to the majority of social welfare organizations.[23] The typical department of social services has a director, other administrative personnel, supervisors, workers, and support staff such as secretaries. The ultimate responsibility for organizing these people, and the resources they need for performing their tasks, is vested in the director. He or she must also work with specified planning groups at the community, county, state, and national levels when formulating agency policy and securing resources.

The kinds of administrative tasks just discussed are essential if the resources—human and financial—that society makes available for the performance of large-scale, complex social welfare services are to be properly managed. However, the management of resources takes place at practically all other levels of the organization, an idea which the professional model helps to make explicit. In a profession, there is considerable autonomy and internal control by the professional group itself. One of the implications of this is that professionals have considerable responsibility for effectively managing their own work load and resources. For example, social workers are assigned a caseload and a supervisor. The workers must then decide such questions as how to allocate their time between cases, how often to confer with the supervisor and for what purposes, how many appointments to make out of the office, and how much time to spend in a given interview. In a sense, then, each professional person is an administrator, making decisions about policy and resource utilization within the worker's own sphere.[24]

Any management attempt must be bolstered by data that measures the results of a given action or policy. Just as an agency must know how much it costs to provide services for how many persons, so an individual worker must know how much time is being spent filling out forms rather than interviewing clients. Data collection and analysis, the process of research, is generally thought of as highly formal. Much of it is, as when a sociologist like Jacqueline Wiseman does a study of skid-row alcoholics (see Exhibit 1-4). Individual workers, however, are constantly collecting data as they interview clients, talk with other professionals, and process forms.

Throughout all of these tasks, they are exposed to data which are relevant to the question of how effective their activity is and what tasks remain to be done (either by themselves, by their agency, by some other agency, or by society). The problem generally arises because the worker never takes the time to systematically organize the data and analyze it. Although the data concerning the use of time during the working day may be part of a worker's calendar, the data may never be analyzed to discover that more time is being spent filling out forms than providing services to clients.

Management and research are skills that pervade the helping effort. Agency administration and planning by specialized administrators will always be important to the development and carrying out of an effective social welfare structure. However, developing management and research skills by all professionals is also important if the day-to-day, increasingly complex activities they perform are to be effectively organized. In talking about accountability in Chapter 3, the importance of being able to demonstrate effectiveness was discussed. Research is a major way in which this is done, but it in turn is only as effective as the planning that makes data available. Professional helping persons need to be much more aware of the need for data. They must also accept responsibility for managing their resources—knowledge, time, skill, and all the rest—so the resulting data demonstrate that social welfare makes a significant difference in helping people to function more effectively.

Moving Beyond Traditional Methods ◄

Teare and McPheeters,[25] and Bisno,[26] have cogently discussed the problems of the traditional approach to interventive methods. They note that focusing on methods encourages a restricted view of problems and solutions, and tends to lead workers to be more concerned with their own methodological and bureaucratic problems than with the needs of the people they are trying to help. Bisno emphasizes these problems in the traditional approach by quoting Kaplan on the "law of the instrument":[27]

> *I call it* the law of the instrument, *and it may be formulated as follows: Give a small boy a hammer, and he will find that everything he encounters needs pounding. It comes as no particular surprise to discover that a scientist formulates problems in a way which requires for their solution just those techniques in which he himself is especially skilled.*

Bisno, in suggesting that the "law of the instrument" is applicable to social welfare practice, is saying that a worker's identification with one interventive method tends to limit his or her awareness of appropriate alternative techniques. He believes that it would be far more productive to begin with an analysis of the problem, and include all the possible ways to solve such a problem. Aside from the practical limitations of the "law of the instrument," Bisno also provides a thoughtful analysis of some of the theoretical problems growing out of the traditional approach.[28]

In developing a new perspective on interventive methods, Teare and McPheeters begin with the problem rather than the job. Once the problems have been defined and categorized, they focus on the tasks that could help to solve these problems. Then a rational way to group the designated tasks is developed.[29] This approach focuses on client needs, and allows the professional to distinguish clearly between the needs of the client, the professional, and the organization, all of which are important in the interventive process. The difference in approach, then, between the methods approach and the newer problem approach to interventive methods lies in the fact that the former often forces a problem into the method, while the latter tries to shape a method to solve a given problem.

Traditional marital counseling, for example, is commonly done by psychiatrically oriented professionals who talk to the couple and possibly their children in an office setting. The problem approach might try to identify the components of the marital problem and use a range of interventive approaches. These could include psychiatric counseling, reaching out into the community to find or develop recreational outlets for the children, helping the husband find job training or better employment to ease financial burdens, and mobilizing the couple and their neighbors to improve housing, since these issues can all be components of what is termed a marital problem. This comparison does not imply that the methods approach has been ineffective, but it does suggest that in many cases new perspectives can approach intervention in a more task-focused, flexible, creative manner than traditional approaches.

In attempting to identify the major problem areas requiring social welfare intervention, Teare and McPheeters list the following: health, education, employment, integrity of the family, money and financial resources, and integrity of the neighborhood and community.[30] The obstacles creating problems in these areas can be any of the following: deficiencies within individuals ("lack of education or training, inappropriate values, personal instability, poor physical health"); environmental deficiencies ("lack of resources or lack of access to them"); rigid or inequitable laws, regulations, policies, and practices (discriminatory practices, restrictive eligibility requirements, fraudulent contracts); and results of catastrophes.[31] Given these major problem areas and obstacles, four general functions of social welfare for meeting the identified needs are suggested by Teare and McPheeters: (1) promoting positive social functioning (promoting self-actualization); (2) preventing problems from occurring (providing accessible resources and developing skills in using these resources); (3) providing treatment (helping persons solve their problems); and (4) providing maintenance support for those unable to solve their problems.[32]

With the major problem areas, obstacles, and general goals of intervention specified, Teare and McPheeters develop nine "major objectives to social welfare activity," which can in turn be translated into specific tasks and ultimately clusters of tasks.[33]

1. *Detection*—"to identify the individuals or groups who are experiencing difficulty [at crisis] or who are in danger of becoming vulnerable [at risk] . . . [and] to detect and identify conditions in the environment that are contributing to the problems or are raising the level of risk."[34]
2. *Linkage or Connection*—"to steer people toward the existing services which can be of benefit to them. . . . A further objective is to link elements of the service system with one another."[35]
3. *Advocacy*—"to fight for the rights and dignity of people in need of help . . . [including] fighting for services on behalf of a single client, and . . . fighting for changes in laws, regulations, etc. on behalf of a whole class of persons or segment of the society. Therefore, advocacy aims at removing the obstacles or barriers that prevent people from exercising their rights or receiving the benefits and using the resources they need."[36]
4. *Mobilization*—"to assemble and energize existing groups, resources, organizations, and structures, or to create new groups, organizations or resources and bring them to bear to deal with problems that exist, or to prevent problems from developing."[37]
5. *Instruction-Education*—"to convey and impart information and knowledge and to develop various kinds of skills."[38]
6. *Behavior Change and Modification*—"to bring about change in the behavior patterns, habits and perceptions of individuals or groups."[39]
7. *Information Processing*—"the collection, classification, and analysis of data generated within the social welfare environment."[40]
8. *Administration*—"the management of a facility, an organization, a program, or a service unit."[41]
9. *Continuing Care*—"to provide for persons who need on-going support or care on an extended and continuing basis . . . in an institutional setting or on an out-patient basis."[42]

Teare and McPheeters then identify twelve "roles," tasks which professional helping persons may perform as they develop an interventive strategy to work with persons seeking help to solve a problem.[43]

Outreach worker. Reaching out into the community to identify need and to make sure referrals to other appropriate agencies are followed through. It is known that many people need and are eligible for services, but either do not know about them or are blocked from reaching them, such as old people who have no transportation, minority-group members who fear harassment, and people of many kinds who believe there is a stigma attached to accepting help. The outreach worker attempts to identify persons in need, and then help them to identify and reach social welfare services that can meet their need.

Broker. Knowing what services are available and making sure those in need reach the appropriate services. One of the results of the increased scope, complexity, and bureaucratization of social welfare services has been increased confusion and frustration experienced by users. The family doctor and house calls are things of the past. Large numbers of specialists now provide more expert but more impersonal treatment than did the general family practitioner. When emergencies arise, it is necessary to go to the emergency room of the nearest hospital, where treatment first depends on filling out certain required forms. Indeed, in many communities it is difficult to find a doctor who will accept new patients, so the person seeking medical attention may not know where to turn for help. The broker helps to deal with these problems, directing persons in need to available and appropriate services, explaining procedures, and providing assistance and support when procedures are lengthy and complicated.

Advocate. Helping clients obtain services when they might otherwise be rejected, and helping to expand services to cover more needy persons. The history of some social services, such as Aid to Families with Dependent Children, has been fraught with attempts to deprive potential recipients of their rights to the service for a host of usually moralistic excuses. The advocate works with such persons to insure that they receive the services to which they are entitled when they apply. Advocates also seek to expand services to meet the needs of groups whose needs are not being met with existing programs.

Evaluation. Evaluating needs and resources, generating alternative ways of meeting needs, and making choices among alternatives. There is an ongoing need for professionally trained persons to monitor the effects of existing programs, and to develop more effective ways to meet needs. The project undertaken by the League of Women Voters to monitor the effectiveness of revenue sharing in improving social welfare services, reported in Chapter 2 (footnote 63), is an example of the need to evaluate the effectiveness of a program.

Teacher. Teaching facts and skills. When discussing the helping relationship earlier in this chapter, it was seen that the helping person provides empathy and support to the person seeking help. Part of the support commonly offered is information needed to make a decision, and the development of skills to use in problem-solving—greater insight into one's own behavior, appropriate behavior and dress when having a job interview, childrearing and homemaker skills, and so forth.

Mobilizer. Helping to utilize existing services most effectively. Many persons and groups have potential resources that can be coordinated to develop more effective social welfare services. The mobilizer helps such persons and groups to accomplish this. For example, residents of a public housing project may feel that the project manager is providing inadequate janitorial and security services. If the manager refuses to provide more adequate services required by the residents, they may not know other techniques to get the manager to act. A mobilizer can help the project residents to understand the power they have in numbers, and the various strategies available to them to encourage positive action by the manager—such as rent strikes, sit-ins in his office, contacting other city officials, and picketing, to name a few possibilities.

Behavior-changer. Changing specific parts of a client's behavior. This is perhaps the closest role to traditional methods approaches, and would be exemplified by a psychologist who used a behavior modification program to end a child's bed-wetting.

Care-giver. Providing supportive services to those who cannot fully solve their problems and meet their own needs. Sometimes helping people to function more effectively must of necessity mean helping them simply to be more physically comfortable or to adjust to a permanently impaired level of functioning. For example, helping professionals who work with the aged in nursing homes generally have goals that focus on maintaining some level of physical comfort and social interaction in the face of physical and mental deterioration.

Consultant. Working with other professionals to help them be more effective in providing services. Here again the professional's responsibility to the profession is raised, with each professional utilizing his knowledge and skills for the benefit of other professionals as well as assisting persons and groups seeking help.

Community planner. Helping community groups to plan effectively for the community's social welfare needs. The professional's specialized knowledge base combines with daily experience to make such persons among the most informed and concerned about a wide range of community structures, community needs, and community resources. Professional social welfare persons have a responsibility to participate in community planning and decision-making structures so that their expertise will help the clients they represent have their needs met.

Data manager. Collection and analysis of data for decision-making purposes. The massive scope and complexity of the contemporary social welfare system makes sophisticated data collection a necessity if the system is to be properly evaluated. Rational decision-making is based on such data, as, for example, Social Security benefit levels are raised to keep pace with increases in the cost of living.

Administrator. The activities necessary to plan and implement a program of services. This may occur at the agency, community, state, and national levels and should be based on information provided by data managers and consultants. The scope and complexity of the contemporary social welfare system makes rational, carefully planned and structured administration a necessity. It is also well to reemphasize at this point the relationship of administration to management as discussed elsewhere in this chapter.

▶ Integrating Social Work Practice Methods

The reconceptualization of social work practice accomplished by Teare and McPheeters brought helping efforts much closer to the purposes of social work. Rather than having methods which tended to focus on only one part of the profession's mission, as tended to be the case with traditional casework, group work, and community organization, Teare and McPheeters showed how a variety of professional helping activities was needed in order to deal effectively with the systemic nature of human need. Their formulation is nevertheless built around problems and needs in the sense that care-giving was derived from a perceived problem, which then generated a need for emotional support, task assistance, strengthening coping mechanisms, or other activities as appropriate.

An alternative approach is to start with the competencies that every professional social worker must have in order to achieve the purposes of the profession (discussed earlier in this chapter) and then derive the practice skills needed to perform them. These competencies are used in every practice situation regardless of the problem or reason help is sought. The *way* in which they are used does vary by problem, however, as well as by the nature of the person or group seeking help. Since the competencies themselves come from actual practice as well as theoretical knowledge, this approach helps to link practice and knowledge. The remainder of this chapter will present a framework for integrating social work practice around competencies rather than problems. The reader is cautioned that this framework is still in the process of development; much of the social work practice community is still using the traditional methods or Teare and McPheeter's approach or some combination of both. This framework includes much of the substantive content of both these approaches, but organizes it differently and has different points of emphasis.

First, a word about organization. Six basic skills are presented as necessary for competent, professional social work practice: skill in communication, assessment, relating to others, planning, carrying out plans, and evaluating oneself and one's plans and activities. They will be discussed in this order for conceptual clarity, but the actual practice of social work involves considerable amounts of overlap and flexibility in the use of these skills. *Every practice situation entails the use of all of these skills,* whether individuals, groups, or communities are involved—each skill relates to all of these levels, and will be discussed to illustrate their use at each level. Each of the six basic skills includes a number of specific components. These will be described within the context of the appropriate basic skills, but here again, skill components are used very flexibly and interchangeably in practice. Finally, social work values and ethics underlie and give professional social work meaning to these practice activities. Each basic skill and any of its component parts must be used within the context of professional social work values and ethics in order to be social work. Otherwise, they are simply technical activities.*

Communication Skills

Communication is basic to any effort to understand people and situations, and to act in helpful ways. Communicating is a shared activity involving *senders* of information and persons who *receive* it.[44] The message exchanged is *encoded* by the sender and *decoded* by the receiver—that is, the sender puts the message in a form that seems sensible, hoping that the receiver will be able to understand it in such format. Often this is not the case. Interferences in the encoding/transmission/decoding processes, which are generally referred to as *static,* may block communication. Static includes the physical conditions in which the communication is attempted (a noisy room, for example), the transmission skill of the sender (such as knowing what the receiver wants to know and in what form the receiver can process the information), and the motivation and emotional state of the receiver.[45] Finally, communication involves *feedback,* the response of the receiver to the sender, which in turn evokes further responses by the sender, and through which ongoing communication occurs. To communicate effectively, therefore, our three basic concepts are again relevant: one has to understand the meaning of the system forces the sender and receiver are experiencing, one has to understand the diverse cultural and social realities that guide people's lives, and one must understand the problem that individuals are seeking to solve through their communication.

---

* Many of the skills described here are also used in other social welfare professions, and they become professional helping skills appropriate to a particular profession when used within the value and ethics framework of that profession.

Communication can be divided into two broad categories: direct interpersonal communication in which two or more people in physical proximity communicate with each other, and indirect communication in which an intermediary channel, such as written reports, are used. There are a number of mechanisms for direct interpersonal communication. Probably the most common is *body language,* the messages that people are constantly sending by the way they walk, dress, sit, smile, and so forth. Often we are not even aware of our body language—do you consciously walk a certain way, or decide when to breathe, or sit in a chair in a particular manner? Other activities we are generally more aware of, such as how we dress to make a certain impression. Yet, we have all had the experience of seeing someone walk by and forming an impression of that person, however fleeting, just on the basis of the body language that we rarely stop to plan in our own behavior. We are constantly communicating, then, often very unintentionally and with little effect (for example, no one is particularly interested in receiving our communication). At other times, though, body language can be an important part of the communication process—dating rituals, job interviews, and perhaps of great relevance to social workers, indications of anxiety and concern that users of social work services manifest.

Much communication is informal—we chat with family and friends in a relatively unplanned way, for instance. Other times, we communicate in a very structured, planned way. The most commonly used structured purposeful communication mechanism is the *interview.* Social workers frequently have to obtain information from people in order to understand problematic situations, people's life goals, available resources, and the functioning of relevant systems. Interviews are used for these purposes and may occur with people seeking help, with friends or family members, with colleagues who can be helpful in a particular practice situation, with political officials whose actions are relevant to people's needs, and in many other situations.

De Schweinitz distinguishes two types of interviews: objective, which are goal and task oriented (as when interviewing to determine eligibility for receipt of services); and therapeutic, which are more subjective and introspective (as when allowing clients to express their feelings).[46] Most interviews have elements of each, but to maintain an interview's focus it is often helpful to keep the distinction in mind. Exhibit 7-1 provides a useful summary of the major components of interviewing.

Social work direct interpersonal communication often has a teaching/learning function, because much of the purpose of social work involves making people more aware of resources, their own and those within social institutions. Carl Rogers has said, "We cannot teach another person directly; we can only facilitate his learning."[47] This reinforces the mutuality of teaching/learning, whereby each person involved shares resources with others (called *andragogy*) rather than one person being seen as the expert who commands the knowledge that others seek to get through a one-way

An Outline of the Interviewing Process **EXHIBIT 7-1**

Following is an outline of the interviewing process used in the Social Worker Technician program of the U.S. Army Medical Field Service School at Ft. Sam Houston, San Antonio, Texas. It is an excellent summary of the major components of interviewing, and it provides a useful overview of the activities that are part of skillful interviewing.

1. *Beginning of interview*
   a. Begin where the patient is
   b. Attempt to set patient at ease
   c. Attention to patient's comforts
   d. Efforts to establish rapport
2. *Interest in patient*
   a. Courtesy
   b. Treating the patient with dignity
   c. Individualize patient
   d. Warmth
   e. Tone of voice
   f. Demonstrated sincerity of involvement
   g. Attentiveness and eye contact
   h. Remaining patient-centered, not note-centered
3. *Drawing out affect*
   Encourage patient to express feelings, i.e., anger, sadness, warmth, joy, despair, hostility, and others
4. *Skill in responding to patient's behavior*
   a. Recognition and appropriate use of verbal communication
   b. Recognition and appropriate use of non-verbal behavior
5. *Clarification and consistency of role*
   a. Self-control of stress, prejudice, and judgmental feelings
   b. Appropriate appearance
   c. Conveying one's purpose in the interview
6. *Questioning technique*
   a. Proper balance between general and specific questions
   b. Questions which guide the patient in telling story in his own words
   c. Transitions
7. *Listening techniques*
   Proper use of silence which encourages the patient
8. *Ending*
   a. Brief summarization of interview content
   b. Opportunity for patient feedback on interview
   c. Proper explanation of future plan/view in regard to the patient

communication channel from teacher to learner (called *pedagogy*).[48] An andragogical approach requires a certain type of learning environment, which is characterized by respect for each person, participatory decision making, freedom of expression and availability of information, and mutuality of responsibility in defining goals, planning and conducting activities, and evaluating.[49] Teaching/learning, thus, is an important communication mechanism, but like any communication, it requires knowledge about the meaning of the content and context of the communication effort.

Direct interpersonal communication does not necessarily involve only two people. Often groups of people are involved, and in such situations additional skills are needed. The ways in which groups can be used to facilitate communication depend on the type of group involved. Groups whose purposes are recreational can provide teaching/learning opportunities within natural, nonthreatening contexts. The social worker's major tasks will be to stimulate ideas for activities, help obtain resources, and help isolates find acceptable positions in the group. Therapeutic groups can provide both teaching/learning as well as opportunities for the ventilation of feelings in a supportive, nonjudgmental context. Here the social worker may need to function to reduce the static that can result from strong feelings, especially anxiety and hostility, as well as to clarify and interpret communication content. Task groups help people to establish communication and be supportive of each other by identifying common objectives. In the process of working on tasks, these groups can help their members identify their own resources and find effective ways to use them in collaboration with others. The social worker can help members of task groups reduce static that results from suspicion, competitiveness, and prejudice, as well as assist them to establish communication channels with outside persons and groups (for example, those persons who can be helpful in achieving the group's tasks).

Groups can be used to facilitate communication (and other types of changes) only to the extent that their members perceive them to be worthwhile. This is most likely to occur under the following conditions:[50]

1. It satisfies needs and helps people achieve their goals.
2. It is perceived as supportive and accepting of its members.
3. Its members are congenial, and the group is perceived to be valued by outsiders.
4. Its members are involved in decision making affecting the group.
5. Those people who are participating in change efforts, either as facilitators of change or those to be changed, belong to the same group.
6. The group is perceived as attractive, in spite of whatever changes it may require of its members.
7. Group members see the need for greater communication or other changes.
8. The group supports efforts to develop changed behaviors in a nonpunitive way.
9. The group helps its members assess the success of their change efforts.

The group contexts that social workers function within are not restricted to client and client-related groups. Most social workers practice in organizations where they need to communicate with social work colleagues and colleagues from other social welfare professions. The individual and group communication skills used with clients are equally necessary with colleagues.

Finally, direct interpersonal communication also occurs through influence and persuasion. *Modeling* is a particularly common and effective communication device. Our behaviors are frequently observed by others who learn from them, sometimes because we intentionally attempt to model certain behavior, but often without our even knowing that modeling is occurring. For example, both child abuse and spouse abuse are apparently learned in many cases by having experienced or witnessed it in the family.[51] In general, modeling is effective communication if the model is perceived as attractive and if the model's behavior is rewarded.[52] Other forms of influence and persuasion result from the way in which communications are presented, such as whether both sides of an argument are discussed or just one side, the order of presentation of information, the use of graphic material, and relating communication to the receiver's frame of reference.[53]

In addition to direct interpersonal communication techniques, there are indirect techniques. Most indirect techniques involve the use of data and written information in one way or another. For example, social workers write case summaries, keep case records, and fill out a variety of agency forms. All of this material becomes a communication to someone (the receiver) when it is read. As in any form of communication, static can occur if the material is illegible, incomplete, poorly written, or otherwise ambiguous. Social workers also collect data daily as they go about their work. These data can be systematically collected and organized so that they "tell a story," or they can be ignored. Data that are systematized become potential communications to others for documenting service activities, identifying effective service delivery strategies, identifying unmet needs, and so forth. Here again, though, static can be significant. Data must be presented in a form and context appropriate to the receiver if it is to be usable. Sophisticated statistical reports will mean nothing to an agency director who cannot understand them, and accurate, important data will be rejected by judges or legislators before whom a social worker may be testifying if presented in a hostile, accusatory fashion.

Assessment Skills

Assessment is the process of organizing information in such a way that it is helpful in understanding a situation and ways of intervening in that situation. Assessment is *holistic* in that it seeks to analyze systematically who and what is involved in a particular situation while at the same time relating the situation to others which influence it. However, assessment also involves *partializing the situation* so that the parts that make up the whole are also systematically explored. For example, a social worker confronted with a battered wife's plea for help first has to obtain the information necessary to understand the woman's present situation—how is she handling the emotional stress? is she in further danger? does she have financial or other resources, such as a job, that can provide needed financial support or family and friends who could house her temporarily if needed? are there children involved? if so, where are they and what are their needs? The present situation is tied into a system of ongoing relationships, such as the family in this example, and these relationships are part of the present situation. On the other hand, the social worker cannot get so involved in the larger network of relationships that immediate needs get ignored.

Assessment is done with the people involved in the situation. Events have to be understood in terms of their meaning to the people that experience them. Without knowing these meanings, social workers risk imposing their own meaning, which may be quite foreign to the biological, cultural, or social characteristics of the people involved. Whether a sick and elderly person is seen as a burden or a readily accepted responsibility varies between groups, and the social worker's interpretation of the significance of such illness may be quite different from that of the clients. As information is obtained, it has to be processed for meaning with those who seek the social worker's assistance. The meaning not only reflects cultural differences as noted, but differences in life objectives as well. Assessing a situation in terms of possible intervention requires an understanding of how various alternatives relate to desired objectives. Objectives, like meanings, vary by individuals and groups. A better job that requires geographical mobility is not necessarily preferable to staying close to family and friends, and scientifically validated medical treatment is not always seen as more desirable than folk remedies or spiritual healing.

The same information has many interpretations, and the social worker must understand as many of them as possible. Obtaining an account of a child's fight with a friend from the child and the friend are both necessary. The similarities and differences between the account offer significant clues as to the various meanings of the event to the people involved. Sociologists refer to this as an ethnomethodological approach,[54] whereas psychologists have referred to it as a gestalt,[55] and others have spoken of an ecological approach.[56] The meaning for social work is the same: people place events in contexts that make sense to them. Adequate assessment requires an understanding of as many of these contexts as possible, and the people involved are the best interpreters of their own views. Of course social workers may also want to get the perspective of relatively unbiased observers precisely because their lack of involvement in a situation may provide yet another important sense of the event.

While information is being obtained, social workers use their own professional skill to put the various pieces together in such a way that intervention alternatives are suggested. Who else may need to be involved in further planning? How much insight do the various people involved seem to have into their own behavior and that of others? What resources and obstacles seem pertinent to the emerging goals for the intervention? However, being sensitive to and accepting of others does not mean having no ideas of one's own, or being afraid to exercise one's own professional judgment.

Skill in Relating to Others

Throughout the communication and assessment processes a relationship is being established (or, if things are not working well, not established). Here is a good point to reemphasize that helping is not a linear series of steps. Many things go on at the same time, and they are differentiated here only for conceptual clarity rather than to suggest that they happen in a particular order. The relationship is the bond that is developed between the professional person and those with whom the person interacts. This bond makes it possible to engage in mutual work on problems that are often difficult, psychologically painful, and emotionally and physically exhausting.

There are a number of factors that facilitate the development of relationships, although a relationship is something that partly develops from the unique chemistry between people. *Trust* is crucial, with both parties believing in the goodwill of the other. The client must believe that the professional person has the interest, commitment, and skill to be helpful. The client must also feel accepted as a person. The worker trusts that the client will try to achieve the identified intervention goals and will exercise good will within the realities of his life. *Nonjudgmentalism* is an important part of trust, especially for the worker. Clients must feel that regardless of how difficult, unpleasant, illegal, and even destructive the problem, they as people retain their basic self-worth and self-respect. As a representative of society, social workers have the obligation to inform people of behavior that is socially unacceptable and likely to lead to undesirable consequences. However, this must be in the context of the separation of behavior and self-worth. Behaviors may be unacceptable, but nothing can remove the basic worth and human rights of people.

Relationships also require *empathy,* the ability to understand the feelings of another. Experiencing need is fraught with many feelings—despair, embarrassment, fear, unacceptability as a person, and so forth. These are part of the situation, and they have to be dealt with during the helping effort. They can only be handled if they are recognized in a way that acknowledges not only their existence but also their meaning. *Mutuality* and *sharing* are also parts of relationships. Each party brings strengths, points of view, and goals to the helping effort. Through mutual exchange strengths can be maximized and help becomes more possible. This also allows for *self-determination,* the ability of people to decide what their life goals are. However skillful a social worker may be, no one has the right or the resources to control the lives of others. Through mutuality and sharing people are willing to work together without feelings of inferiority or incurring obligations that can never be repaid. Such feelings build resentment and hostility and block helping. Efforts to impose help on others will almost surely fail, whereas allowing people to work together to achieve goals maximizes helping efforts.

Interest and *confidentiality* provide encouragement for people to communicate in an open and frank way without fearing that information will be used inappropriately. The helping person's interest is strictly professional rather than voyeuristic, and thus whatever is shared is kept within the professional helping relationship rather than being used to add spice to one's personal conversations. Finally, a relationship is based on *listening, support,* and *realism.* One way interest is conveyed to another is through listening carefully to what is said, seeking clarification as necessary but avoiding repetition caused by inattention. Listening includes being sensitive to the many levels of, and mechanisms through which communication occurs, so that feelings and meaning are heard (and seen). Through interest, listening, mutuality, sharing, trust, and nonjudgmentalism the helping person supports efforts of others to communicate, to relate, and to engage in the helping process. However, supporting someone is different from false assurances. The successful outcome of an effort to organize a tenant's council cannot be guaranteed, but its members can be supported in their efforts. Persons with a terminal illness cannot be restored to perfect health, but they can be supported as they try to cope as constructively as possible. False assurances destroy trust and ultimately undermine a relationship, even though the helping person may want desperately to help others achieve their life goals.

Finally, there are special problems in relating to involuntary users of services. Sometimes groups of people are forced to accept social welfare services—criminals who are sent to prison, for example, or welfare mothers who must accept job training.[57] Frequently the provision of such services occurs in ways that violate one or more characteristics of a relationship—lack of confidentiality with prisoners, or lack of mutuality and self-determination among welfare mothers, for example. These situations create serious value and ethics dilemmas for social workers and seriously impede relating activities. The social worker is obligated to act as ethically as possible under the circumstances, explaining to the clients being helped what the limits of the helping situation are. Within these limits, the social worker may still be helpful, but the mutuality and sharing that is only possible when people are free to make their own decisions will inevitably be missing.

Planning Skills

Planning involves using knowledge to create a procedure through which goals will be sought. As has already been discussed, planning must involve the participation of those who will be affected so that people's rights to self-determination is respected and so that their cultural, biological, and social needs will be met in appropriate and acceptable ways. Knowledge is first analyzed to identify resources and obstacles and to predict as far as is possible what the effects of various helping strategies will be. Although helping a single parent get a job may solve financial needs, it may disrupt important cultural patterns with the parent's children, peers, and parents. Solving a community's need for safe, comfortable, low-cost housing with a high-rise housing project may lead to increased crime and broken neighborhood support networks.

After alternatives have been carefully considered in terms of available resources and obstacles, and foreseeable effects of various strategies considered, *contracting* occurs. A contract specifies what activities the various groups involved in the change effort will perform, what the time frame for the performance of these activities will be, and how and when assessment and evaluation will occur. The contract involves prioritizing, through which objectives are selected and then arranged for short- and long-term attainment. A large-scale goal, such as building a shelter for battered spouses, usually results from the attainment of smaller goals (such as partializing a situation, which was discussed earlier). It might be agreed, for example, that the local legal-aid office will clarify laws and policies about the establishment of a shelter for battered spouses, while the social worker will contact legislators and business people to interpret the need for such a shelter and seek funding for it. Meanwhile, the battered men and women might be organizing self-help support groups and seeking employment or job training to prepare for their own financial independence. Each goal is appropriate to each group and is reasonably small in scale. In the aggregate, they add up to the larger objective. Once again, the mutuality of the helping process is emphasized, as well as the right of individuals and groups to determine their own goals in ways that maintain their cultural integrity.

At the agreed-upon time, the progress of the helping activities has to be assessed and evaluated. Have objectives been attained? If not, *why* not—what should have been done differently? What planning is now necessary, building on experience from previous efforts? Planning, like all of the parts of social work practice, is not something that happens once. It is an ongoing activity that is responsive to the interplay of helping dynamics. As situations change, perhaps in part because some goals have been attained, strategies to attain remaining goals must also be modified.

Skill in Carrying Out Plans

This section discusses several activities that are important parts of the professional social worker's efforts to carry out the plans made with and on behalf of others. *Teaching and providing information* are activities frequently used by baccalaureate professional social workers. People often lack the information they need to find and use resources that could be helpful to them. For example, many young couples do not know that family planning counseling is available to them, and residents of a housing project may be unaware of their legal rights in situations where they encounter landlord difficulties. Social workers help people by providing relevant information that makes it possible for resources to be used. They frequently go further to make sure that these potential linkages are in fact accomplished by following up to make sure people who have been *referred* to services actually reach them. Indeed, in some cases the social worker may actually accompany a client or client group when contact with a resource or agency is attempted.

Making people aware of resources often entails teaching them skills related to information gathering and use. Although the social worker can tell people about services, they can also make them aware of sources of information (such as a community service directory or a community hotline) that they can then use in the future as needed. Similarly, people can be taught how to make best use of resources and services—how to dress for a job interview, how to check on eligibility, or how to utilize informal support systems in times of stress, for example. Teaching people how to better use themselves and their environment leads to personal growth and increased independence and control over one's own life. These are important social work practice goals that flow directly from professional values that respect people's freedom of choice and self-worth.

Sometimes people need to be *supported* during their efforts to learn about and use resources. Emotional support is helpful as people reach out to make contact with others, to develop personal support systems for themselves, and to participate in social and personal change efforts. Other people for whom support is necessary are those who face a short-term crisis (rape, a natural disaster, divorce, the loss of a loved one, and so forth) or who must learn to cope with a long-term debilitating illness, a handicap, or the prospect of death. All of these situations require the social worker to help the people involved clarify their respective situations, express their feelings about them, and explore the impact of their situations and their own behaviors on their future lives. They will also have to be helped to accept anxiety, resentment, inaction, and the need to depend on others as appropriate short-term responses to their situations. In the long run, of course, these feelings and behaviors will be modified so that more positive and productive self-concepts and behaviors are built. Even when a difficult situation cannot be challenged, people can develop their own best ways to cope with it. Hopefully these ways will enable them to continue to work toward their own life goals with positive and humane feelings about themselves and others.

Activities that *organize people and situations* are also basic for baccalaureate professional social workers as they seek to carry out plans. Organizing people entails helping people with similar objectives. For example, different racial or ethnic groups may have similar objectives—residents of an urban slum seeking better housing, or the residents of a rural community seeking more adequate medical care. Because the daily behavior of such groups may be dissimilar, everyone may lose sight of their common objectives. Therefore, once the social worker has helped the various groups involved identify their goals, the next step is the identification of areas of behavior compatibility. This enables the groups to identify common bases usable in getting to know each other, thereby recognizing their similarities as well as their differences. It is these similarities that will enable organized, concerted action.

Organizing people also necessitates the provision and clarification of information, as well as the facilitation of group functioning. People generally only attempt to do what they think is possible. Poor people who believe that their poverty is inescapable will become lethargic. The elderly who believe that no one cares about them will isolate themselves; and women who think they are incapable of competing with men in the workplace will only seek traditional women's jobs. As social workers help people identify their needs and realize that they can band together with others to meet them, they provide information about what is possible. This has to be supported by concrete information about services and strategies that can help turn shared motivation into organized action—ways to organize self-help efforts to meet some needs, for example, or ways to use collective action to press for changes as in a rent strike, an economic boycott, or a sit-in at the mayor's office.

Organizing people frequently involves some degree of conflict. Even helping people achieve some degree of consensus over objectives or strategies for collective action may lead to an airing of differences based on cultural values, previous experiences, or group priorities.[58] These differences can be healthy if they promote communication and greater understanding between groups. They become destructive when they are allowed to fragment groups and block the ability of groups to listen to each other. Conflicts between a group seeking something from another group can be even more serious in their consequences. Groups may become polarized so that any compromise is seen as weakness or defeat—union negotiations sometimes exemplify this process. Frustration generated by repeated unsuccessful attempts to organize to achieve objectives can lead to violence, as happened in the urban riots of the late 1960s. These are just a few of the potentially negative consequences of organizing people, and careful planning must occur if their unexpected occurrence is to be avoided. However, these extreme consequences reflect the power of organizing as a helping tool. Helping people to utilize their resources in a concerted way, forming coalitions with others as needed, is often the most effective way to achieve change, especially at the level of social policy, community functioning, and intergroup relations.

The great majority of social workers work in large-scale formal organizations like departments of social welfare, family service agencies, mental health centers, hospitals, and so forth. Therefore, professional social work practice requires *organization skills* if plans are to be carried out effectively. These organizations become the immediate system within which social workers work. Each has its own particular procedures including regulations specifying service delivery procedures (hours the agency is open, services available, eligibility criteria, and others), record-keeping procedures (what kind of records must be kept, who has access to them, what form of written, filmed, or dictated records are required, and so forth), and procedures to use in carrying out activities (forms to be filled out, use of the telephone, appropriate use of support staff persons such as secretaries, and how interviewing rooms can be reserved when needed, for example). These procedures are basic to organizational functioning, and no matter what a social worker may think about them, they must be used if the agency's resources are to be available to workers in their efforts to help others.

Although it often seems as if organizations have such highly structured procedures that the worker has little flexibility, that is not usually the case. It is virtually impossible to plan for every occurrence or to supervise every activity. Consequently, there are generally many areas in which workers have some degree of potential autonomy and in which they can creatively facilitate their helping efforts.[59] Although these opportunities can be important aids to professional functioning, it would be misleading to suggest that organizational structures need to be circumvented. Such structures serve to organize large-scale and complex behaviors so that helping activities are possible that might otherwise be unattainable. Working skillfully and creatively within organizations is an important ingredient of effective social work. When organizational structures impede service delivery, workers should seek to have them changed, but even then one needs to know how to use the organization to achieve internal change. Rarely are overt attacks against organizational structures effective, and more to the point, they are usually unnecessary because internal change mechanisms are available.

Skill in developing support systems. This ability has become an integral part of professional social work practice. Social workers routinely draw upon each other in many ways: informal advice, sharing of useful information, formalized supervisory structures, formally structured team networks that bring together persons with different but complementary specialized skills, and the use of professional associations to disseminate knowledge and support professional values. Organizations themselves are made up of many people, and thus in the course of the work day one interacts with colleagues both formally and informally. Even if this interaction were not so structured, however, professional helping is too complex to be a one-person activity. It is through the skillful use of one's own and other resources that people's needs are most effectively met. Even in private practice, the social worker has to be aware of the network of resources available.

Social work colleagues are obvious parts of a support system. They provide sympathetic listening, helpful practical suggestions, and active support when concerted action is needed. As already noted, social workers with different specialized skills may work together to attack a situation from a variety of perspectives, as when school social workers, medical social workers, and public assistance social workers work together to help a child and the family solve interrelated needs that may include truancy, illness, and poverty. Agency supervisors may also be part of a worker's support system, providing helpful expertise based on more extensive training or experience. Social work colleagues can also support each other through activities of professional organizations. Meetings provide continuing education in practice areas, as well as social interaction that is personally enriching and helpful in making contacts that may be useful in work situations. Professional associations also provide other vital functions, such as publishing journals to disseminate knowledge, developing professional standards of practice, engaging in lobbying efforts to enact legislation helpful to social work and the users of social work services, and monitoring practice to identify and censure practitioners and organizations that chronically violate professional standards.

The colleagial support system can also include non–social workers. For example, a medical social worker may be part of an interdisciplinary team of doctors, nurses, and rehabilitation specialists so that the range of needs of a patient and his or her family can be met. Even nonprofessionals, such as secretaries, volunteers, and family or community members are potential members of the professional's support system. These people contribute valuable parts of the total social work service, and their positive involvement helps achieve professional goals. It is obvious, therefore, that professional helping is a collaborative activity involving the creative sharing of multiple skills. The focus is on mutual sharing and help so that colleagues become a resource rather than either irrelevant or an obstacle. As romantic as notions of being *the* person to dramatically rescue a needy person may be, they are only fantasies. The reality of helping is making use of all of one's resources—one's own, the person's who seeks help, one's social work and social welfare colleagues, and others as appropriate.

Advocacy in policy making. A final major social work activity used in carrying out plans is advocating on behalf of others. Advocacy is interpreting unmet needs to persons and groups who have the resources to help meet them and then attempting to influence decision making on behalf of people in need. Advocacy is closely tied to policymaking, the process of deciding how societal or agency resources will be used.

In Kahn's words, policy is "the implicit core of principles, or the continuing line of decisions and constraints, behind specific programs, legislation, administrative practices, or priorities."[60] Since social policy lays the foundation for the services that will be provided and the manner in which they will be provided, it is a vital concern to all social welfare professionals. There can be no separation between direct practice with people seeking help and the formulation of policy because one affects the other. Social welfare professionals who avoid the thorny problems and the sometimes heated conflicts of the policymaking process leave the decisions about their work and the fate of those seeking help in the hands of others—many times in the hands of people ill prepared to make such decisions. Some of the possible professional roles involved in social policy are presented in Exhibit 7-2.

EXHIBIT 7-2 *The Advocate and Social Policy Formation*

Harry Specht talks of the formulation of social policy as one part of the social worker-advocate's task. He summarizes his discussion in the chart reproduced here, which shows how the advocate role can proceed from a perceived need to an institutional solution, and how this role relates to professional roles, tasks, and institutional resources.

Stages of Policy Formulation

Policy Stage	*Tasks*	*Institutional Resources*	*Professional Roles*
1. Identification of problem	1. Case-finding, recording, discovery of gaps in service	1. Agency	1. Practitioner
2. Analysis	2. Data-gathering, analysis	2. Research organization	2. Researcher
3. Informing the public	3. Dramatization, public relations, communications (writing, speaking)	3. Public relations unit, communications media, voluntary organization	3. Muckraker, community organizer, public relations man
4. Development of policy goals (involvement of other agencies)	4. Creating strategy, program analysis	4. Planning bodies, voluntary associations	4. Planner, community organizer, administrator
5. Building public support	5. Developing leadership, achieving consensus	5. Voluntary associations, political parties, legislative and agency committees	5. Lobbyist, community organizer, public relations man
6. Legislation	6. Drafting legislation, program design	6. Legislative bodies, agency boards	6. Legislative analyst, planner
7. Implementation	7. Programs-organizing, administration	7. Courts, agencies	7. Administrator, practitioner, lawyer
8. Evaluation, assessment	8. Case-finding, recording, discovery of gaps in service, gathering data	8. Agency, research organization	8. Practitioner

Source: Reprinted by permission of the National Association of Social Workers from Harry Specht, "Casework Practice and Social Policy Formulation," *Social Work* 13 (January 1968): 44.

Probably the greatest problem encountered in the policymaking process is grappling with the difficult issue of priorities. There are many worthwhile and important social tasks that need to be accomplished, of which social welfare is only one. When there are limited societal resources, how will the decisions be made as to the most necessary and the most efficient? Even within social welfare itself, establishing priorities is not easy. Should services for children have greater priority than services for the aged? Is the social return greater from income-maintenance services than from social services? Would a new hospital solve more problems than a new prison? There is no formula for answering these questions. The competitive nature of the American political system and the fact that resources are limited mean that there will be controversy and attempts to "prove" greater need by each group seeking those resources. But a great deal of "proof" is dependent on a value system that considers some things more worthwhile than others. One can demonstrate that millions of persons live in poverty, but if the societal value system places space exploration above the solution of poverty, or if it considers poverty a personal rather than a social responsibility, the "proof," however well supported by data, will make little difference in policy decisions.

Thus social policymaking begins with an existing value framework. It takes place within a competitive structure, each social need competing with the others for attention and the allocation of resources. Taking these factors into account, Kahn identifies several essential social policy dimensions:[61]

The basic objective of the policy. Programs may seek primarily to help the disadvantaged, or they may attempt to distribute resources more equally among all groups. "In general, a program that is sharply selective, focused on a deprived group . . . or available on a means-test basis, will have considerable redistributional impact . . . A universal program, whatever its other merits, may or may not be redistributional, depending on its attractiveness to poorer members of the community . . . and on the system of information and access that affects the actual pattern of utilization."[62] There is some tendency to think primarily in terms of social welfare as helping the needy, and it does do this to some extent. However, programs to meet the needs of all persons in society and to achieve a more equitable distribution of resources throughout the society are also important if the long-run results of social policy are to include an institutionalized social welfare system and a more just society. For example, the Supplemental Security Income program is very selective in addressing problems of the elderly, helping only the destitute aged. Social Security offers the elderly a much more comprehensive program that seeks to meet the retirement needs of all members of the society.

Sharply selective services tend to be less expensive in that a much smaller number of people will receive them. On the other hand, they can have substantial related costs. A selective program frequently has a cumbersome and expensive eligibility system included so that only members of the intended group participate in the program. This is true of a program like Aid to Families with Dependent Children, for example. Selective programs also tend to have more hidden social costs attached. Any program that differentiates between some groups as needy and others as not needy tends to stigmatize the former. This leads to the kind of humiliation food-stamp users experience in supermarkets when checkout personnel create a scene out of ignorance or in the attempt to make sure only food items are purchased (no soap, paper products, or other nonfood items). It may also lead to societal reaction against the groups receiving special services and consequent attempts to reduce or eliminate such programs. The fact that departments of social services find it necessary to publish pamphlets exploding "welfare myths" is an indication of their concern that AFDC recipients are being stigmatized and that their benefits may ultimately be threatened as a result (see Exhibit 2-4).

Deciding between consumption and investment. Policy is almost always caught up in the argument as to whether it is more efficient to meet immediate need or to invest in long-range programs that will ultimately reduce or eliminate need. It is very difficult to ignore immediate need—when people are starving, it seems heartless to give them seeds that will meet all their food needs in a year. On the other hand, immediate need is often so great that using resources to meet it would leave nothing for investment so that future need can be prevented. In many developing countries, for example, current levels of need are very high, and resources are very limited. Meeting current need would easily exhaust the country's resources, and future need would remain unmet. The nation's decision to concentrate its resources on economic and social development is probably wise for the long run. Yet the daily encounter with abject poverty and illness is hard to live with.

Frequently, the distinction between meeting immediate need and planning for the future is not so clear-cut, and both can be worked on simultaneously. Many of the Office of Economic Opportunity programs attempted to do both. Head Start, for example, met immediate needs for day care and educational enrichment, while also improving the child's chances of successfully completing later schooling. Similarly, many community development programs provide needed community resources while also helping the community organize itself and have a structure it can use to achieve future goals. On the other hand, a program may get bogged down in meeting one objective and never accomplish the other. AFDC meets immediate need, but it was hoped that it would also help recipients develop the resources and skills to become independent. In many cases, this never happened because of the inadequate level at which help was provided and the punitive restrictions built into the program.

Social utilities compared with individual services. Social utilities are basic services people need to function effectively in society. For example, physical protection, transportation, and education are all social utilities. These services cost money for society as well as for the individual users. Since they are usually subsidized out of general funds, everyone is supporting them whether they wish to or not. Social utilities take a collective approach to meeting human needs in recognition of the fact that group life depends on interdependence and cooperation. Individual services, on the other hand, are oriented toward the specific needs of individuals and are provided on an individual basis. Individualizing services tends to be expensive in comparison to collectively provided services. One way to meet this cost is to have individual services available on a fee basis. However, this discriminates against lower-income persons who then cannot afford the services. Individual services also tend to discriminate against the less-educated or socially involved who often do not know that services are available, or in some cases may not even be able to identify what their needs are. A social utilities approach is very compatible with an institutionalized social welfare system and an investment approach to the provision of services. Social utilities must be provided in order to maintain the kind of complex society in which we live, but the level of such services beyond those absolutely necessary is more debatable.

The manner in which services are delivered. Throughout earlier chapters of this book the point has been made that services can be provided in many different ways. Direct grants, in-kind payments, social insurances, personal counseling, and the structure of services have all been discussed. Deciding between the various ways in which services can be provided involves two kinds of questions. First there is the question of which kind of service will meet the need identified—are cash grants and social insurances equally able to solve the poverty problem? Yet there remains the question of efficiency—which of the alternatives solves the problem most efficiently, however efficiency is being measured (least financial cost, least user stigma, most user involvement, and so on). These two questions require somewhat different approaches.

Looking at services that will solve a problem can be a reasonably objective effort. If people are given money directly, will they in fact spend it on necessities, or will they spend it on luxuries or to support debilitating habits such as drug and alcohol use? It is possible to conduct research projects to answer such questions and to use the data obtained to select between various program types. Generally a given problem can be solved in more than one way, and thus after identifying those programs that do in fact solve the problem, it is then necessary to select the most efficient program. Here data may be of less use. A direct grant program may solve a problem along with an in-kind program, for example. The direct grant program is somewhat less efficient financially in that some of the money may be spent on luxuries. The in-kind program is efficient financially but less efficient socially because recipients of the service are deprived of a certain amount of autonomy and personal responsibility. Which program is most efficient? Obviously the answer to the question will depend on value judgments—whether money is more important than personal growth, for example—and upon the reality of the resources available. If the crucially scarce resource is money, it may be worthwhile paying the social costs and selecting the in-kind program. Determining the manner in which services are delivered becomes considerably more complicated than simple questions of fiscal efficiency.

Centralization of services and user participation. Related to many of the value issues raised above is the question of who makes social policy decisions. Obviously there are certain groups to whom society has given this responsibility—legislators and directors of agencies, for example. It has been suggested that all social welfare professionals, including direct service practitioners, should also be involved. In addition, many other kinds of persons might get involved in the legislative process, which is so often an integral part of policymaking. The segment not so often discussed is user or consumer groups, made up of those who will actually be affected by the policy decision. When looking at the complexities of the political process, some of the reasons for the lack of involvement of user groups can be identified—lack of resources, lack of education, lack of transportation, and the like.

Another reality of user participation, or lack of it, resides in the helping system itself. For one thing, concentrating on individual services and problems is not likely to encourage an approach that attempts to involve clients in larger social groups and processes through which they can have an impact on policy. For another, agencies sometimes find it easier not to involve users in policymaking. Organizations, in the attempt to preserve themselves with minimal problems and maximum efficiency, may try to keep everyone in neat categories. Direct service workers may feel too harassed to take the time to teach user groups policy skills, to work with them in the exercise of those skills, and to risk organizational displeasure if the consumer groups should come up with objectives opposed to those of the agency. Once again the point must be made that policy is grappling with priorities. How important is fiscal efficiency? How much influence should the values of societal and organizational decision makers have? How much risk can a worker or an agency afford to take? How important is the development of social awareness, personal growth, and the development of policy skills in user groups? Few professionals would deny that consumer groups ought to have some input into the policymaking that affects them, but there would no doubt be considerable differences in the priority assigned to that objective.

Accountability. Throughout this discussion, and at other points in the book, the issue of accountability has been raised. Obviously policymaking depends on it, because intelligent decisions must take into account the results of prior attempts to deal with problems. Accountability may take many forms—cost-benefit studies, operations research, performance contracts, and so forth. Such data are essential to knowing what is happening in the social welfare system and knowing where intervention is necessary to better achieve the system's goals. But there is no substitute for knowing what those goals are, and the data collected cannot help do this. Goals are related to data in that they are formulated partially on the basis of all existing information. However, they are also formulated on the basis of social values. Once the goals have developed from existing data and social values, accountability becomes meaningful in determining to what extent the goals have been attained. But accountability can never be a substitute for clearly formulated goals.

Advocacy may involve specific activities related to policymaking as well as other kinds of decision making that can affect people in need. As suggested above, understanding and knowing how to use social and agency policy is crucial. Clarifying needs and their causes and being able to communicate such information to others are also important. This frequently entails the ability to use data to document unmet need. Participating in activities that directly affect policymaking is also frequently possible. For example, communicating with elected representatives may impact on how they vote—Exhibit 7-3 summarizes the legislative process so as to illustrate ways in which social workers can influence the process.

The Legislative Process—Learning to Participate EXHIBIT 7-3

Although virtually all of us learned it in high school, can you recount the process involved in a bill becoming law? Do you know who your elected representatives are? Do you know how to write effectively to them to express your wishes? The answer to the second question can be found in a publication such as the *Congressional Quarterly Guide to Current American Government* (issued twice yearly at $4.00 an issue, available from the Congressional Quarterly, 1735 K St., N.W., Washington, D.C. 20006, and full of much more valuable information about our government). Summary answers to the first and third questions are given in the illustration and tips following. Another valuable reference for understanding the political system is Donald Herzberg and J. W. Peltason, *A Student Guide to Campaign Politics* (New York: McGraw-Hill, 1970).

Writing to Your Government: Tips

1. Write to your own Senators or Representatives. Letters sent to other Congressmen will end up on the desk of Congressmen from your state.
2. Write at the proper time, when a bill is being discussed in committee or on the floor.
3. Use your own words and your own stationery. Avoid signing and sending a form or mimeographed letter.
4. Don't be a pen pal. Don't try to instruct the Representative or Senator on every issue that comes up.

How a Bill Becomes Law

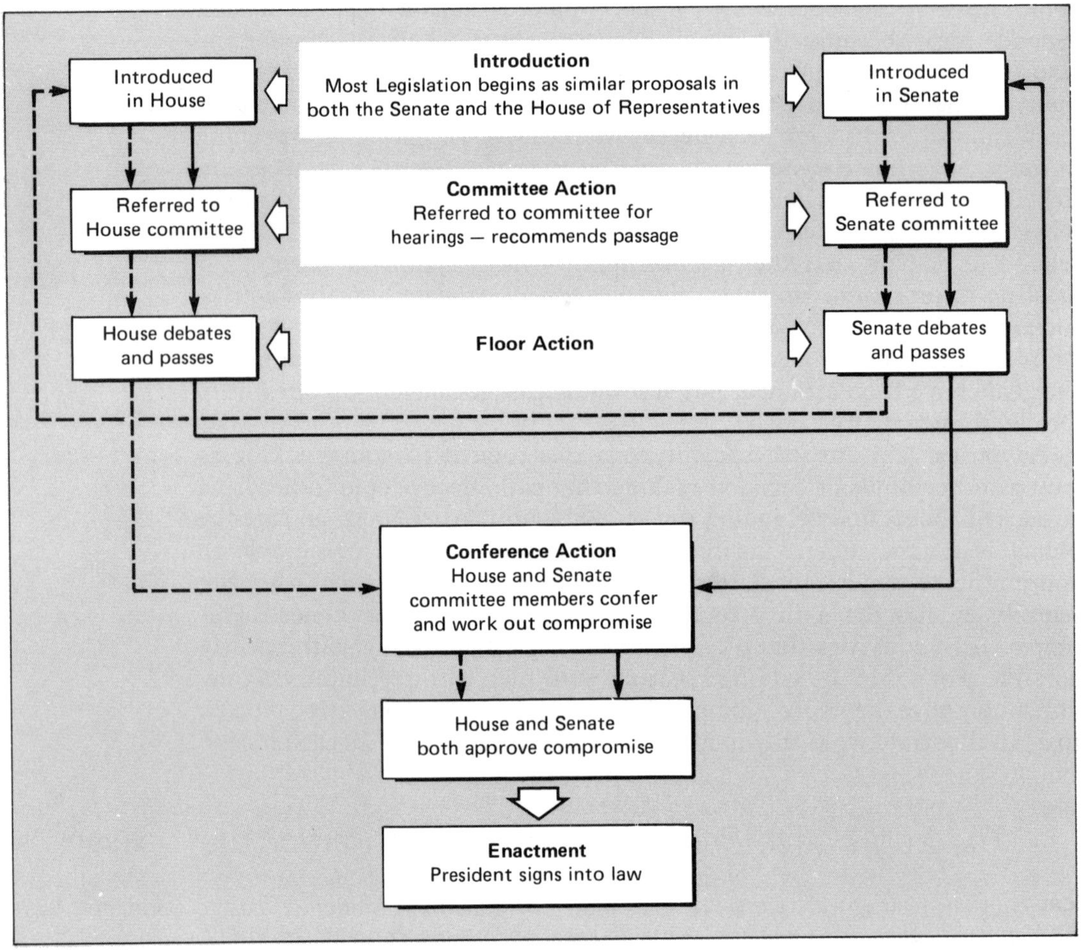

5. Don't demand a commitment before all the facts are in. Bills rarely become law in the same form as introduced.
6. Whenever possible, identify all bills by their number.
7. If possible, include pertinent editorials from local papers.
8. Be constructive. If a bill deals with a problem you admit exists but you believe the bill is the wrong approach, tell what you think the right approach is.
9. If you have expert knowledge or wide experience in particular areas, share it with the Congressman. But don't pretend to wield vast political influence.
10. Write to the Congressman when he does something you approve of. A note of appreciation will make him remember you more favorably next time.
11. Feel free to write when you have a question or problem dealing with procedures of government departments.
12. Be brief, write legibly, and be sure to use the proper form of address.

A 15-word telegram called a Public-Opinion Message (POM) can be sent to the President, Vice President or a member of Congress from anywhere in the United States for $1. Name and address are not counted as part of the message unless there are additional signers.

Social workers may also participate in public demonstrations in support of people in need, although care is needed to do so in ways that do not violate agency policies. Of course as a private citizen, and in one's nonwork hours, possible advocacy activities may be different from those engaged in while representing an agency as an employee.

Self-Assessment and Evaluation

The sixth and last basic baccalaureate professional social work skill to be discussed in this chapter is *self-assessment and evaluation.* Self-assessment is part of the professional's responsibility for his or her own behavior, and evaluation is part of any systematic problem-solving process. Because social workers are such important parts of the helping process, they have to be aware of how their behavior affects the actions of others. Do responses in communication efforts tend to be too quick, thereby discouraging others from fully expressing themselves? Do subtle ethnocentric attitudes and behaviors alienate certain groups and keep them from using services? Is practice seen in a competitive framework that blocks opportunities to work collaboratively with colleagues? Being able to analyze one's own behavior in order to accurately answer these questions requires a high level of *self-awareness,* the ability to look at oneself objectively but also gently. Coming to understand, accept, and change parts of one's own professional behavior is not a result of looking for "faults" and then "scolding" oneself into changing. It comes from a continuous attempt to be aware of one's own behavior, using professional expertise to understand it, and then developing a rational, realistic plan to change behaviors that are identified as needing to be changed. Indeed, it is exactly like using assessment and problem solving to help others!

Self-assessment is also greatly helped by the support system, the colleagues and others who can provide helpful information in a supportive way about one's professional functioning. It used to be common for social workers to undergo psychiatric analysis in order to develop self-awareness. Although this is still sometimes done, it is rare and generally unnecessary for the baccalaureate social worker. What is necessary is a willingness to grow as a professional and the ability to use one's support system to achieve such growth. Occasional mistakes are an inevitable part of professional functioning, but they lead to growth when they can be seen and understood in a patient, helpful, supportive environment. Interpersonal attacks and accusations lead to defensiveness rather than change and are not useful parts of the process of self-assessment. As with knowledge and skill mastery, self-assessment and growth as a professional person are lifetime commitments and processes.

Evaluation is an ongoing part of professional behavior. Comparing activities to objectives is always a relevant component of practice. Has needed information been obtained, or have efforts to influence decision making about a needed service been successful? Evaluation leads to ongoing planning to find better ways to achieve objectives, and thus the helping process involves continuous adjustments to more accurately respond to situations that may themselves be constantly changing. Unless evaluation is a part of the social worker's daily behavior, change efforts can drag on well past their period of utility and may easily slide into behaviors that promote dependency and apathy rather than growth and a focus on realistic needs and resources.

▶ Chapter Conclusion

This chapter has attempted to provide an overview of social work practice, the concrete skills that professional social workers use when seeking to help others. These are derived from the knowledge discussed in previous chapters, especially as that knowledge is filtered through professional social work values. The intent has been to provide only a broad overview of practice in terms of its historical development, its traditional methods, and a more contemporary perspective that emphasizes the basic skills needed in any intervention attempt. The ability to communicate, assess, relate to others, plan, carry out plans, and evaluate are parts of *every* practice effort whether with an elderly widower, a city council, an agency director, or a group of hostile teenagers. These skills are used somewhat differently in each situation, but the social worker's practice tools are common to all situations. Every practice situation requires analysis and intervention related to institutional systems that affect everyone. Our society is too complex to think that people can exist in isolation or that their problems do. It is the social worker's job to understand and intervene in that network of systems and relationships so that people may more fully identify and attain their life goals.

STUDY QUESTIONS

1. How would you define the ideal helping person? Include personal characteristics, knowledge possessed, and skills available to be used. If you aspire to be a social welfare professional, how do you rate yourself at present in terms of this ideal?
2. Go to a public place, such as a bus station, airport, or large post office, and observe the people you see. What kinds of different behaviors do you observe between those providing and those receiving help? Select someone and try to observe as many things about that person as you can. After doing so, try to construct a portrait of the person's life: Where does he live? Is she married? What kind of work does she do? Is he happy or sad? How could you go about getting additional information about this person if you had to? (Be sure to consider the range of human and nonhuman resources you could use.)

3. Review the basic skills that every baccalaureate social worker must possess as described in this chapter. Then evaluate yourself on each. Which do you already have to some extent and which have you just begun to acquire? Which do you use in your everyday life, and how could you use your daily experiences to further develop your social work skills? Which do you feel most comfortable with? Why?
4. Select a newspaper that you like and have daily access to. For six consecutive days, find at least one article in each issue that portrays a situation in which a social worker could be helpful. Write a short essay for each article describing what a social worker could have done in the situation described, trying to identify as many specific skills as possible. Then write a short summary essay describing the scope of social work as you see it.

REFERENCES

1. Betty L. Baer and Ronald Federico, *Educating the Baccalaureate Social Worker* (Cambridge, Mass.: Ballinger Publishing Co., 1978), p. 68.
2. Ibid., pp. 86–89.
3. Roy Lubove, *The Professional Altruist* (Cambridge, Mass.: Harvard University Press, 1965), pp. 1–54.
4. Ibid., p. 55.
5. Jane Addams, *Twenty Years at Hull House* (New York: New American Library, 1960), p. 98. See also pp. 90–100.
6. Russell Smith and Dorothy Zeitz, *American Social Welfare Institutions* (New York: John Wiley, 1970), p. 249.
7. Ibid.
8. Helen Harris Perlman, *Social Casework: A Problem-Solving Process* (Chicago: University of Chicago Press, 1957), pp. 6–7.
9. Ibid.
10. There are many good standard books that describe casework. The Perlman text already mentioned is one. Two well-known books are Florence Hollis, *Casework: A Psychosocial Therapy,* 2nd ed. (New York: Random House, 1972), and Carol Meyer, *Social Work Practice* (New York: Free Press, 1970). A concise discussion of the major casework concepts may be found in Jonathan Moffett, *Concepts in Casework Treatment* (New York: Humanities Press, 1968).
11. Emanuel Tropp, "The Group: In Life and in Social Work," in Klenk and Ryan, op. cit., pp. 176–77.
12. Janet Rosenberg, *Breakfast: Two Jars of Paste* (Cleveland: Case-Western Reserve University, 1969), p. 93.
13. Reproduced in Gisela Konopka, *Social Group Work: A Helping Process* (Englewood Cliffs, N.J.: Prentice-Hall, 1963), p. 14.
14. Gertrude Wilson, "Social Group Work: Trends and Developments," in Klenk and Ryan, op. cit., p. 170.
15. Smith and Zeitz, op. cit., pp. 253–254.
16. Ibid., p. 255.
17. The effect of the group's environment on its functioning is discussed in Lawrence Shulman, *A Casebook of Social Work with Groups: The Mediating Model* (New York: Council on Social Work Education, 1968), especially pp. 23–30

18. See Arthur Dunham, *The New Community Organization* (New York: Thomas Y. Crowell, 1970), pp. 4, 86. His relationship goals would be included under process goals in the framework being used here.
19. For a more detailed discussion of the distinction between community organization and community development, see ibid., pp. 175–179.
20. Murray Ross, *Community Organization: Theory and Principles* (New York: Harper & Row, 1955), p. 39.
21. Ibid., pp. 57–67, especially p. 62.
22. See Irwin Saunders, "Professional Roles in Planned Change," in Kramer and Specht, op. cit., pp. 269–284, especially p. 277.
23. See Harry Schatz, ed., *Social Work Administration: A Resource Book* (New York: Council on Social Work Education, 1970).
24. Focusing on the teaching of management skills at all levels in professional functioning is relatively new. One resource for further study includes Southern Regional Education Board, *Administration and Management Curriculum Development for Undergraduate Social Welfare Workers: Resource I* (Atlanta: Southern Regional Education Board, 1974).
25. Robert Teare and Harold McPheeters, *Manpower Utilization in Social Welfare* (Atlanta: Southern Regional Education Board, 1970), pp. 4–8.
26. Herbert Bisno, "A Theoretical Framework for Teaching Social Work Methods and Skills, with Particular Reference to Undergraduate Social Welfare Education," in Frank Loewenberg and Ralph Dolgoff, eds., *Teaching of Practice Skills in Undergraduate Programs in Social Welfare and Other Helping Services* (New York: Council on Social Work Education, 1971), pp. 72–78, 84–85.
27. Ibid., p. 84.
28. Ibid., pp. 75–77.
29. Teare and McPheeters, op. cit., pp. 7–8.
30. Ibid., pp. 11, 66–70.
31. Ibid., p. 12.
32. Ibid., pp. 17–18.
33. Ibid., pp. 19–21.
34. Ibid., p. 20.
35. Ibid.
36. Ibid.
37. Ibid.
38. Ibid.
39. Ibid., pp. 20–21.
40. Ibid., p. 21.
41. Ibid.
42. Ibid.
43. Ibid., pp. 34–35.
44. Peter R. Day, *Methods of Learning Communication Skills* (New York: Pergamon Press, 1977), pp. 1–20.
45. Ibid., pp. 41–48, 125–129.
46. Basic references for interviewing in social welfare are Annette Garrett, *Interviewing: Its Principles and Methods* (New York: Family Service Association of America, 1942); and Elizabeth and Karl de Schweinitz, *Interviewing in the Social Services* (London: National Institute for Social Work Training, 1962), pp. 9–11.

47. Malcolm Knowles, *The Adult Learner: A Neglected Species* (Houston: Gulf Publishing Co., 1973), p. 32.
48. Ibid.
49. Ibid., p. 83.
50. Ibid., pp. 87–88.
51. Alison Clarke-Stewart, *Child Care in the Family* (New York: Academic Press, 1978).
52. Day, op. cit., pp. 14–20.
53. See, for example, Herbert Abelson, *Persuasion: How Opinions and Attitudes Are Changed* (New York: Springer Press, 1959).
54. For a concise summary of ethnomethodology, see Peter K. Manning, "Language, Meaning, and Action" in Jack D. Douglas, *Introduction to Sociology* (New York: Free Press, 1973), pp. 296–300.
55. J. D. Kidd, *How Adults Learn* (New York: Association Press, 1959), pp. 133–176.
56. Ibid.
57. See, for example, Susan Sheehan, *A Prison and a Prisoner* (Boston: Houghton Mifflin, 1978), and Frances Piven and Richard Cloward, *Regulating the Poor* (New York: Pantheon, 1971).
58. Ralph Kramer, *Participation of the Poor* (Englewood Cliffs, N.J.: Prentice-Hall, 1969).
59. Robert Pruger, "Organizational Functioning as a Social Work Skill," in Baer and Federico, op. cit., pp. 149–168.
60. Alfred J. Kahn, *Social Policy and Social Service* (New York: Random House, 1973), p. 8.
61. Ibid., p. 93.
62. Ibid.

SELECTED READINGS

Baer, Betty L., and Federico, Ronald. *Educating the Baccalaureate Social Worker.* Cambridge, Mass.: Ballinger Publishing Co., 1978.

Combs, Arthur; Avila, Donald; and Purkey, William. *Helping Relationships: Basic Concepts for the Helping Professions.* Boston: Allyn and Bacon, 1971.

Goldstein, Howard. *Social Work Practice: A Unitary Approach.* Columbia: University of South Carolina Press, 1973.

Kadushin, Alfred. *The Social Work Interview.* New York: Columbia University Press, 1972.

Loewenberg, Frank M. *Fundamentals of Social Intervention.* New York: Columbia University Press, 1977.

Pincus, Allen, and Minahan, Anne. *Social Work Practice: Model and Method.* Itasca, Ill.: Peacock Publishers, 1973.

Siporin, Max. *Introduction to Social Work Practice.* New York: Macmillan, 1975.

Whitlock, Glenn. *Understanding and Coping with Real Life Crisis.* Monterey: Brooks-Cole, 1978.

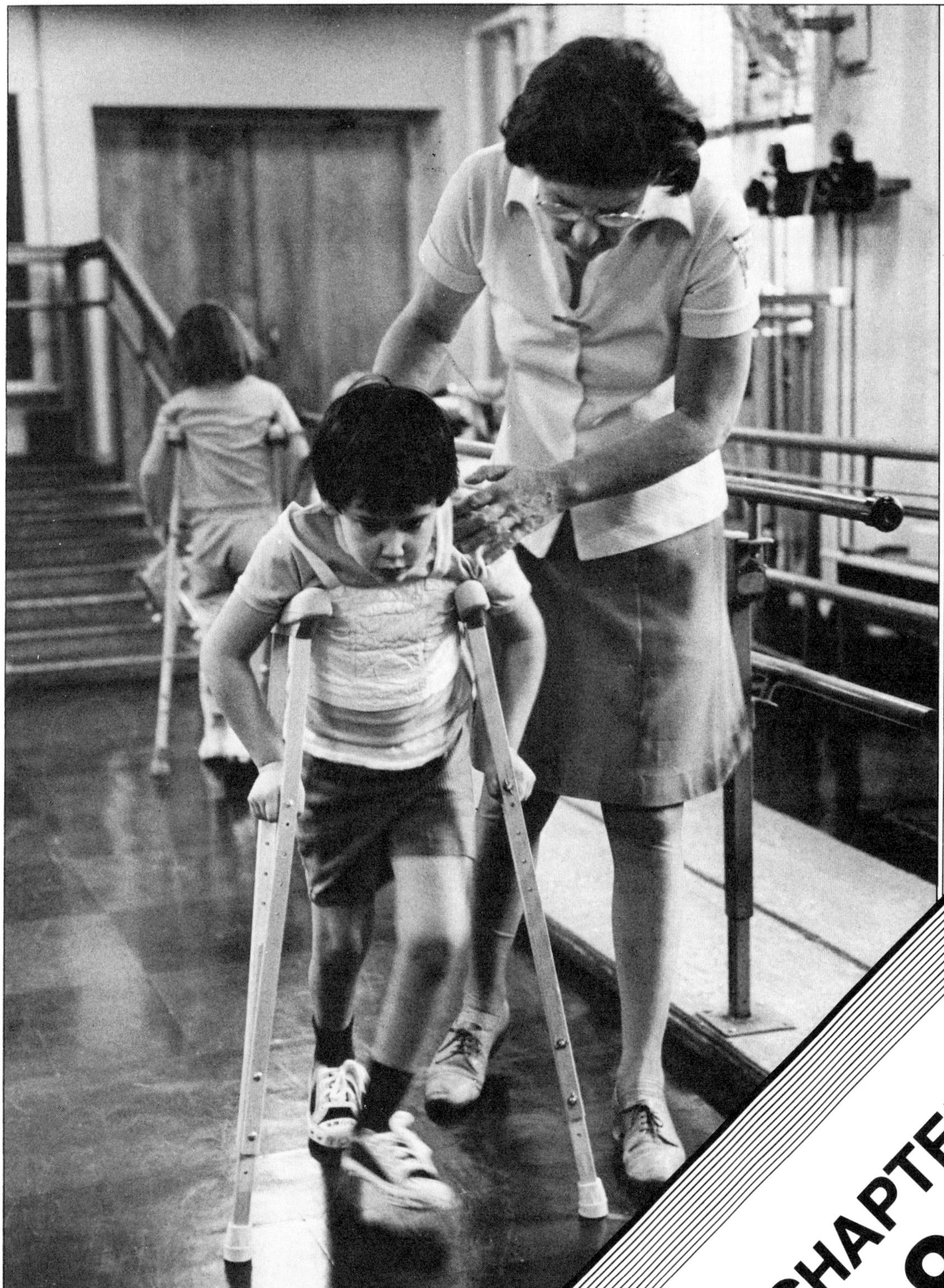

CHAPTER 8

Occupational Contexts

In studying the social welfare institution, we have been moving gradually from the general and theoretical to the specific and practical. We have looked at the values underlying social welfare, the knowledge that social welfare practitioners must have, and the skills that enable them to intervene effectively in problem situations. Now we look at where all of these come together—work settings.* Social welfare agencies are concrete structures through which society expresses its social welfare mandate by providing the authority and resources to perform social welfare services. Drawing upon theoretical knowledge and practice wisdom, agencies organize objectives and resources so that services are provided. Agencies differ considerably in their structure, their objectives, the resources available, their size, and in countless other dimensions. Consistent with our earlier discussion of organizational factors in the delivery of services, we would expect some discrepancies between agency objectives and agency functioning. For example, although the objective may be to provide services to those in need, most of the agency's resources may be spent de-

---

* For the purposes of this chapter, work settings will include social agencies and private practice.

veloping procedures that may actually discourage applications for help. Therefore, a basic task facing social welfare professionals is deciding which work context offers the kinds of experiences and opportunities they desire. This chapter is an attempt to look at some of the factors that should enter into that decision. As in the previous chapter, social work is used to provide concrete examples.

Education for Social Work

Before looking at these contexts of practice, brief consideration of educational preparation for various types of positions will be helpful. There are four basic educational levels to which jobs are related: high school, associate of arts (junior college), bachelor's degree (four years of college), and master's degree (graduate study). There are no countrywide, uniform standards governing the educational level required for particular jobs, but there are some generalizations that are more or less commonly accepted. Jobs requiring only a high school diploma are few and tend to utilize the worker's actual life experience in a certain social context. For example, a streetcorner worker who has contacts with juvenile gangs in a target neighborhood could be hired with only a high school degree (sometimes even less). Opportunities for advancement are quite limited, and pay scales generally low. At the associate of arts (AA) level, there is generally a technician focus. Such persons do relatively routine work under close supervision. There are increasing numbers of technician programs at the AA level in such areas as mental health, social work, and nursing, but actual available jobs are lagging behind the proliferation of such programs.

The bachelor's (baccalaureate) level has traditionally been the one from which most social welfare personnel are recruited. The baccalaureate-level practitioner often carries the major part of an agency's workload. In the past, the BA graduate with any major could move relatively easily into social welfare related jobs. Specialized bachelor's-level programs, in such areas as social work, criminology and law enforcement, and counseling, are now developing. As they develop, educators, practitioners, and students have begun to exert pressure on social welfare agencies to give preference in hiring and salary level to graduates of such programs. The master's-level graduates typically hold the positions of most responsibility, authority, and pay, and have the greatest choice of positions. The majority of the professional leaders in such social service professions as social work, teaching, and criminology will no doubt continue to have master's-level training. Naturally, this simple breakdown of educational levels does not easily accommodate some specialized training programs, such as medicine and law, but has general applicability to the social welfare field. Exhibit 8-1 provides data relating education levels to job types.

Factors Affecting Occupational Organization

Social welfare professionals practice in a wide range of agency settings, performing an equally wide variety of occupational tasks. There is no simple way of organizing the large, complex web of agencies, occupations, and activities. The factors to be discussed in this section are not mutually exclusive—any specific agency will be some combination of many of them. However, they do represent factors that can affect worker opportunities, activities, and restraints, and are worthy of consideration when attempting to chart a career or make a specific job selection. After looking at these general factors, the public social service agency will be looked at in some detail as an example of how these factors come together.

EXHIBIT 8-1 *The Maryland Social Welfare Picture—January 30, 1971*

To give some idea of a typical proportion of jobs at various educational levels in major social welfare professons, the results of a census of social welfare jobs are shown in the following table. While these data are several years old, the relationship between educational level and type and availability of jobs continues to be accurate.

Categories of Social Welfare Jobs by Level of Education Required, from Less Than High School Diploma through the Doctor's Degree

Occupational Category	*Less Than High School*		*High School Diploma*		*Special Training*		*Some College (No Degree)*	
	No. of jobs	Percent of category	No. of jobs	Percent of category	No. of jobs	Percent of category	No. of jobs	Percent of category
Supportive Aides	2638	83.6%	400	12.6%	72	2.3%	17	0.5%
Social Workers	—	—	—	—	1	—	2	.1
Correctional Workers	1	—	1876	74.6	—	—	—	—
Employment Workers	3	.3	158	14.8	—	—	22	2.1
Community Workers	46	5.7	243	30.2	122	15.1	64	7.9
Financial Asst. and Benefit Workers	—	—	98	16.6	—	—	278	47.8
Administrators	2	.4	7	1.3	—	—	135	28.0
Youth and Recreation Workers	6	1.2	12	2.5	—	—	5	.9
Health Related Workers	3	2.1	7	5.0	1	.7	1	.7
College Teachers of Social Welfare Subjects	—	—	—	—	—	—	—	—
Total	2,699	22.1%	2,800	22.9%	196	1.6%	523	4.3%

Source: Health and Welfare Council of the Baltimore Area, *12,000 Welfare Jobs: A One-Day Census of Social Welfare Jobs in Maryland, January 30, 1971—Part I* (Baltimore, Maryland: June 1971), pp. 24–25. Used by permission.

An occupational context with a long history in certain social welfare professional areas, such as medicine, but which is relatively new to others, such as social work,* is private practice. The private practitioner establishes an individual office but sometimes shares an office with other private practitioners. This person is free to establish areas of specialization, intervention practices (within general professional limits), and details such as fees, appointment scheduling, and so forth. As private practice increases in popularity, professional licensing assumes greater significance. It represents a way for users to have some confidence in the qualifications of a person who is represented as a medical doctor, psychiatrist, or social worker. Private practice has also stimulated some controversy over *third-party payments,* that is, payments from an insurance plan to a professional on behalf of a client. As more and more people have increasingly comprehensive medical and social insurances, having an arrangement whereby various social welfare professions are included in that insurance coverage is desirable. It enables users to seek a range of help without worrying about

* At the present time, the master's degree is generally considered minimal educational qualification for private practice (indeed, some state laws require the MSW in order to qualify for third-party payments described below). However, baccalaureate-level social workers may work in private practice under the supervision of those with advanced education.

Associate Degree		*Bachelor's Degree*		*Master of Social Work Degree*		*Any Other Master's Degree*		*Doctor's Degree*	
No. of jobs	Percent of category	No. of jobs	Percent of category	No. of jobs	Percent of category	No. of jobs	Percent of category	No. of jobs	Percent of category
10	0.3%	11	0.3%	4	0.1%	—	—	—	—
10	.3	1900	65.6	834	28.8	148	5.1%	—	—
—	—	639	25.4	—	—	—	—	—	—
—	—	864	81.2	—	—	17	1.6	—	—
9	1.1	249	31.0	46	5.7	27	3.3	—	—
—	—	208	35.6	—	—	—	—	—	—
2	.4	257	50.0	170	32.7	72	13.9	2	0.4
8	1.7	311	64.6	1	.2	8	1.7	—	—
15	10.7	113	80.7	—	—	—	—	—	—
—	—	—	—	31	50.0	2	3.2	29	46.8
54	0.1%	4,551	37.3%	1,087	8.9%	274	2.2%	31	0.3%

how they will pay for services received, and it assures the professional of payment without having to worry about the client's financial resources. In other words, both professional and user are free to concentrate on the problem. Developing an appropriate interventive plan and developing a sound helping relationship are foremost, rather than considerations of whether the help that is needed can be afforded.

In some respects private practice is a misnomer, since no professional works in isolation. Even though the professional may be free to establish a private office and conditions of work, the systems nature of human behavior makes it impossible to isolate social treatment from the social environment. Professionals normally depend on a network of professional relationships to use in their work. Medical specialists consult with each other about each other's patients and refer clients back and forth as appropriate. Social workers consult with psychologists, doctors, schoolteachers, and many others in trying to understand the problems brought by the person seeking help. They may also work closely with social workers in agency settings, such as those in departments of social services, in order to have access to needed resources. Again the professional model becomes important. All professionals must have access to other professionals, for stimulation, for consultation, for support. In an agency setting, this contact is usually a part of daily functioning. The private practitioner must find opportunities for this kind of contact through informal discussions, attendance at professional meetings, or structured working relationships with others. A commonly used solution to this need is for the private practitioner to work concurrently, part-time, in an agency. This is readily possible, since time in private practice is structured by the individual practitioner.

The private practitioner has some distinctive advantages and disadvantages in comparison to the professional working in a structured agency setting. There is considerable professional autonomy in deciding upon the kinds of clients and the types of problems to be worked with. There is also considerable flexibility in selecting interventive approaches to be used. For example, the private practitioner is free to experiment with a problems-focused approach at will, to try innovative helping strategies such as consciousness-raising groups with battered women, or to use techniques not commonly used in most agencies, such as behavior modification. This kind of professional freedom can be stimulating and enriching for the professional. Private practice can also be convenient and lucrative, since private practitioners may work out of their homes, and can establish their own fees.

On the other hand, the private practitioner can become isolated from the mainstream of professional activities, and lacks support in difficult and perplexing interventive situations. An additional potential problem is that the private practitioner's resources are limited, so one is dependent on agencies for certain resources, and it is sometimes difficult to establish workable ties to them. Doctors, for instance, must have relations with hospitals so that their patients can obtain beds. In many areas, there is considerable competition for the inadequate number of beds available, and the individual doctor may have difficulty obtaining the hospital resources needed. In a parallel situation, a social worker in private practice working with troubled families may need agency resources if it is determined that a child should be removed from an explosive family situation.

Moving now into factors related to working within an agency setting, the distinction between host agencies and agencies dominated by one profession bears a relationship to some of the issues in private practice. An agency dominated by one profession is one in which a profession, such as social work, dominates the work of an agency. A family-service agency would be an example. It is composed primarily of social workers, although it may also have other professionals on a full- or part-time basis, such as a psychologist who performs testing and consultation. A host agency is one in which there is a high level of sharing between the several professions that perform the ongoing work of the agency. A residential treatment center for the mentally disabled child would be an example. Such an agency would generally have social workers, psychologists, psychiatrists, and psychiatric nurses on its staff, as well as a range of paraprofessional staff persons.

Working in an agency dominated by one profession can be a reasonably comfortable and supportive experience, since the worker most commonly interacts with others who share similar professional training and beliefs. This can create real strength in a group of people whose work is mutually supportive. Each performs part of collectively formulated tasks in agreed-upon ways. On the other hand, this kind of strong professional support can result in isolation from different professions. This can be accentuated if the dominant professional group begins to see the other professionals that are occasionally used as less important than themselves. For example, hospital social workers sometimes complain that medical personnel, who dominate in most medical settings, use social workers to carry out predetermined plans rather than involving the social worker in planning as well as implementation. In general, though, increased experience with interdisciplinary planning and sharing is helping to minimize such dominant-subordinate problems.

The host setting offers a rich, multidisciplinary approach to problem-solving, which can be much more effective and comprehensive than the more limited perspectives likely in an autonomous agency dominated by a single profession. This can be enormously stimulating to all of the members of the interdisciplinary teams. In some cases, however, members of a given professional group can feel isolated from their profession. While it is exciting and stimulating to interact with professionals from other disciplines, sometimes interaction with and support from "one's own" can be comforting and helpful. Here again, the increasing use of interdisciplinary teams of professionals is helping to minimize feelings of isolation and loss of professional identity.

Another factor in describing agencies is whether an agency is public or private. To summarize briefly the points discussed in Chapter 1, public agencies—that is, those receiving public monies and administered by publicly elected or appointed officials—generally have a mandate bestowed by public participation through the political process. The services provided form the backbone of the society's social welfare structure, and, although funding is sometimes inadequate for the objectives identified, it is far greater than would be available without public funds.

Public agencies depend on public decision making for their mandate, and often work within rules that are complex and inflexible. Since public agencies may be attempting to meet several societal objectives at once—provide financial assistance, employment opportunities for disadvantaged minority groups, and career ladders for those with little formal education, for example—they may employ persons whose professional training and identification is limited. This is accentuated by the fact that some public pay scales are low, and working conditions are taxing—crowded facilities, old and deteriorated buildings, massive amounts of paperwork. Professionals with high levels of training and a very strong professional identification may look on public employment as a last resort.

Private agencies—that is, those supported primarily by privately contributed funds and administered by self-determined structures—generally have more flexibility than do public agencies.* Private agencies tend to be smaller, avoiding some of the problems of excess paperwork and overcrowding. Since they can determine their own objectives and procedures, they may hire only those with advanced professional training, and provide services to persons whose lifestyles are familiar to the persons providing services. Pay scales are often low, but are partially compensated for by generally pleasant working conditions and reasonably high levels of cohesion among the professional staff members. On the other hand, private agencies may have very limited resources, which can severely limit the scope and effectiveness of their treatment programs. The very pleasantness of their working conditions may reflect some disengagement from the more basic, complex, and unpleasant problems of a community and its residents. Interacting with other professionals may be pleasant and stimulating, but it does not necessarily make a contribution to attaining professional goals of opportunity and equity for all.

Although the distinctions between public and private agencies are very real, it is unfortunate that they have been so important in the past. Many professional people instinctively react against working in a public agency, feeling that it is doomed to result in poor quality service because of

* As noted in Chapter 1, private agencies are increasingly contracting with public agencies to provide services (a trend stimulated by Title XX legislation). This has tended to subject private agencies to some of the bureaucratic characteristics and pressures common in public agencies. Nevertheless, the general distinctions between public and private agencies discussed here are still relevant even though the two types of agencies are developing more and more commonalities.

frustration against a paper bureaucracy, inflexible rules, and loss of motivation. These are realistic concerns. However, there is little question that public social services will continue to grow in importance. If social welfare as an institution is going to have a major impact on this society, it will do so primarily through the public social services. This does not minimize the important contribution of private services. It is simply to say that there are major, probably unsolvable, restrictions on private services that are much less severe for public services. The social welfare professional of the future needs to think about how to use social welfare skills to help overcome some of the problems of public social welfare agencies. As will be seen when looking in detail at departments of social services later in this chapter, the services provided in the public sphere are far too important to be left to the least trained, least interested, or least competent professionals. Whatever the problems, there is no more important, diversified, or challenging area of social welfare practice than exists in public agencies.

Another distinction that can be made between practice contexts is between total institutions and community settings. *Total institutions* are those agencies which have total control over a group of persons who live within them. Examples include prisons, mental hospitals, juvenile correctional facilities, and certain types of medical facilities, such as sanitoriums for particularly disabling or communicable diseases. Access to total institutions is generally strictly controlled, with visitors having limited entry and residents having limited departure privileges. Community-based agencies generally have much less control and much freer access. For example, while a nursing home has total control over a group of persons who live within it, they elect to enter the home and may leave at will. They may also have persons visit them with minimal restrictions, and may leave the home for visits to others. Because total institutions are so highly restricted in terms of access, they are often located in isolated settings that further discourage visiting or other types of communication between insiders and outsiders. There has been a relatively recent increase in agencies that are, to some extent, between total institutions and community agencies—the halfway house. They are total institutions in terms of total control and reasonably rigid rules governing access, but are usually located in a community and have specified channels of communication between the community and their own residents. In many cases they are seen as a bridge between the total institution and autonomous community living.

Total institutions obviously have a high level of control over their (usually captive) client populations. This control may be necessary to protect the community, and to protect the individual clients. It offers opportunities to use treatment techniques that require such control—for example, many of the behavior modification techniques discussed earlier, where reinforcements must be closely controlled. However, they create real questions in terms of whether a helping relationship is truly possible. Helping is not control. It may be necessary to control people, but any helping professional will want to think through the implications of such control for the helping relationship. The isolation that exists between the total institution and the community also tends to deprive the professional helping person of commonly used resources. It is sometimes difficult to help someone to function more effectively in the social world when that person is isolated from that world. The halfway house tries to deal with this problem, providing an intermediate step during which the individual can attempt to use new skills in a carefully structured community context.

Total institutional settings also tend to be very expensive. In terms of professional priorities and planning, allocating massive amounts of scarce resources to total institutions, where problems tend to multiply and results tend to be minimal, is open to question. Community agencies avoid many of the above problems, yet in turn have the problem of coping with the interlocking web of social relationships all at once. Sometimes client control seems necessary, and sometimes it seems handy—but each social welfare professional has to decide whether he or she can function where it is practiced.

The final factor to be discussed in distinguishing between types of agencies is whether an agency is problem-focused or client-focused. Any agency has the organizational need to identify its objectives. Given the broad range of social welfare objectives, this is not easy. One reasonably concrete way to do this is to focus on meeting the needs of all persons or groups having a particular problem—such as poor health or housing. Another approach is to focus on a particular client population, dealing with the range of problems it might have—the aged, children, or migrant farm workers, for example. Not only does the adoption of one or the other focus help an agency to develop a set of goals, it also suggests an appropriate type of staff and interventive methods. An agency specializing in services to migrant farm workers may want to have a team of professionals on its staff—medical doctors to identify and treat illness, malnutrition, and related problems; homemakers to help with basic child care, the teaching of efficient home-care skills, and the provision of requested birth-control information; social workers to provide personal counseling, help obtain needed educational and financial resources, and provide assistance in planning for the future; and nurses to assist doctors and provide routine preventive health care and information. On the other hand, a family service agency that concentrates on personal counseling services for individuals and families would want to have a professional staff of social workers and psychologists.

The focus an agency adopts can have important implications for the range of activities the professional persons on the staff will perform. A client-focused agency is more likely to engage in a variety of activities related to the range of problems which any client group is likely to encounter. Although the agency may hire a variety of staff persons, each of whom specializes in the performance of certain professional functions, there are still likely to be some opportunities to engage in diversified interventive approaches. The social worker performing in the migrant farm-focused agency discussed above would most likely have opportunities for outreach, broker, planning, and advocacy activities, as well as performing more traditional roles such as care-giving and behavior-change. The social worker in the family service agency is likely to have a somewhat narrower range of interventive roles commonly used in the agency, focusing mostly on traditional casework and group work skills. Values and knowledge also enter into the equation, since some professional persons might prefer the diversity of working with a range of client groups—older people, teens, children, married couples—all in the same agency. Others might wish to focus on the multiproblem environment of one group, such as the physically handicapped.

Throughout this book there has been an attempt to encourage an active orientation to the study and practice of social welfare. Because values are involved, there are no simple answers. The answers to the difficult questions of what is social welfare and what it ought to be; how effective is the existing social welfare structure; what knowledge must be mastered if the social welfare institution is to be understood and effective interventive methods developed; and how intervention can best be conceptualized, are locked within each individual. Each helping person must grapple with the questions and seek the skills to answer them, working always within his or her value framework. It would be strange if the process of selecting one's own work context were somehow excluded from this framework of individual choice and values. Professional people must know what they want to do and where it can best be done. For some, the intensive control of the total institution offers opportunities to manipulate environment and behavior, which makes possible exciting behavior-change techniques. For others, the constantly changing panorama of a community provides excitement that can be maximized through private practice. For yet others, a tight job market may make it impossible to obtain the kind of job most desired. For all, however, maximum effectiveness depends on an understanding of the work context—its structure, its objectives, and the interventive opportunities within it.

An In-Depth Example: A Department of Social Services ◀

The preceding discussion has been somewhat abstract. To make it more meaningful, this section will look at a typical department of social services in some depth, hoping that such an examination will help to illustrate some of the issues involved in personally choosing an appropriate work context. We can only look at a typical department because they vary from state to state and county to county. A department of social services is typically organized on a county basis, with general supervision through a state agency. The state agency is, in turn, supervised by the federal Department of Health, Education, and Welfare, which has established some uniform guidelines that all departments must follow if they are to receive federal funds. The Guilford County Department of Social Services in Greensboro, North Carolina, can be used to exemplify the major characteristics of such an agency.

In terms of the categories used above, the typical department of social services is a public, community, problem-focused, autonomous social welfare agency. It employs social workers (including paraprofessionals, and sometimes consulting psychologists) to deal with a range of financial and social problems that may be experienced by persons of many kinds—infants, children, teens, adults, and older adults. It is community-based, often having branches at several points throughout a county, and typically has an extensive network of relationships with other social services in the community, such as hospitals, health departments, schools, the police and the courts, facilities for the aged, alcoholism treatment centers, state employment offices, and the like. The agency is part of the public social welfare system, being supported by federal, state, and county funds, and being accountable to a publicly elected or appointed body—in Guilford County, the County Social Services Board whose members are appointed partly by the County Commissioners (who are elected) and partly by the State Board of Social Services (whose members are appointed).

Services in a department of social services are divided into two parts: financial services, helping directly or indirectly to meet the financial needs of persons seeking help; and social services, meeting the nonfinancial needs of applicants. Previously, financial and social services were provided by the same workers in the agency, so that a family seeking Aid to Families with Dependent Children, a financial service, would automatically receive personal counseling, a social service. This is no longer the case. Today workers specialize in providing either financial assistance or social services. Some of the reasons for this separation are described in Exhibit 8-2.

EXHIBIT 8-2 *Understanding the Separation of Financial and Social Services*

In 1972, states were required to reorganize their departments of social services to provide for the separate provision of financial and social services. No longer did someone seeking financial help have to accept social services, such as personal counseling or homemaker services, and no longer was the image of the agency to be first and foremost the provision of financial aid. Now someone seeking just social services would be encouraged to apply. The actual separation has been slow and sometimes grudging—it is hard to change bureaucratic structures rapidly, and to reorient persons who have developed work habits and a professional identity based on an earlier model. However, the separation is now reality.

Source: HEW, *The Separation of Services from Assistance Payments*, Publication SRS 73-23015 (Washington, D.C.: Government Printing Office, 1972), pp. 5–8.

The objectives of separation are itemized below.

1. *To eliminate confusion about the relationship of the two functions to each other.* The public, welfare staff, and clientele are confused about the distinct purposes of the two functions. This stems mainly from the fact that policies are adopted which use financial assistance to achieve ends other than its principal purpose—meeting economic need. Persons who need, want, and are entitled to services sometimes refrain from applying for or accepting them because of the stigma they may attach to financial aid.

Referral sources see the welfare agency as relief-giving only. They do not consider it as a source of help in the solution of social problems of current, potential, or former recipients. This image must change if the agency's purpose is to be achieved. Statutory goals cannot be realized unless there is widespread awareness of the availability and utilization of services before, during, and after periods of assistance.

Separation will provide a framework which will promote clarification of the different goals of the functions, both in policy-making and in practice.

2. *To assure, to the greatest extent possible, freedom of choice in seeking, selecting, and accepting individualized services, except in situations where protective services are necessary.* Under policies adopted by welfare agencies, assistance recipients theoretically may accept or reject services as they see fit. Experience, however, demonstrates that in reality the client feels obligated to participate in any exploration the agency may wish to make of his social situation and to accept any service offered as a part of his recipient status. This option—his under policy in most instances—cannot be exercised under an integrated system. Although the objective of a completely voluntary service program cannot be achieved under the present law because of the many interrelationships which it establishes, separation will enhance the client's opportunity to choose freely without implied or assumed coercion.

3. *To achieve a higher quality of administration by attention to adequate planning, staffing, and financing for each component.* Where the same staff has carried the combined responsibility for income maintenance and service functions, the compelling necessity of providing individuals and families with the means to meet their needs has meant a certain continuing diversion of effort—away from providing services and toward the determination of eligibility. Both functions thus have been somewhat impaired. In each there is a blurring of the need for staff on the one hand, and financing, on the other. Essential continuity in both administrative and case-planning activity has been interrupted by this confusion: A fiscal crisis during the 1970–71 increase in caseloads resulted in suspension of services by some states and deployment of staff to determining eligibility for assistance payments.

When the two functions are administered through separate systems ("separate lines of authority" as required in the federal regulation), it will be possible to adopt program planning and financing methods which will preserve the integrity of each.

4. *To utilize staff more effectively by the creation of a structure which can make use of a wide range of personnel.* One of the most persistent problems plaguing public welfare has been the high rate of staff turnover. In the traditional public assistance operation, each worker, acting in both the investigative and service role, has had to perform a wide variety of tasks calling for many different skills.

Therefore, the educational and experience qualifications are set at the level required for the most difficult tasks. Separation will require the restructuring of positions and staffing patterns, so that many tasks now dubiously performed by social workers can be reassigned to persons with skills specifically related to those tasks.

5. *To make possible determinations of the costs and effectiveness of social services and income maintenance.* Under the present system, with the activities of staff inextricably entwined in carrying out the functions of assistance and services, it has been impossible to factor out the time and effort expended on either. In a separate system of service delivery, a variety of measurements can be established which can form the basis for sound program and fiscal planning, making accountability, in terms of "results," a reality.

The Social and Rehabilitation Service has underway two major projects directed toward this objective. One is conducting a cost analysis of social services under the public assistance and child welfare titles of the Social Security Act, and has, as one of its purposes, the provision of a basic foundation for future improvement in cost reporting and program budgeting. The other will produce a definitive blueprint for the periodic acquisition of data by which to judge the effectiveness of state and local social service programs.

6. *To facilitate the broadening of the scope of needed social services, including the development of service resources, by the development of a separate service operation.* Studies consistently show that the urgencies of financial assistance not only have overwhelmed the provision of social services; they have retarded the growth of new and different service. Moreover, where staff have adequately identified the need for a variety of services, the development of service resources has been slow, serving to discourage staff initiative. Although the law mandates the maximum use of other agencies in the delivery of social services through contractual arrangements, there has been comparatively little use of these resources. The creation of a visible entity of a social service unit or agency, with the allocation of identifiable staff resources to it, with the capability of working independently with other agencies, will preserve and promote the services program.

There is a range of specific services that are provided in the typical social service department. The following discussion is based on those provided by the Guilford County Department of Social Services, and is adapted from its brochure, "Services Available from the Guilford County Department of Social Services," issued in September 1972. Financial services may be broken down as follows:

Money Payments

Receipts of such payments is based on financial need as determined by state and federal policies and guidelines. Need must be demonstrated through an application process. The only direct money payment remaining in the department of social services is the Aid to Families with Dependent Children program, which provides financial aid to children under the age of 21 who are "deprived of parental support and/or care." In the past, social services departments also administered money payment programs for the destitute aged, the needy blind, and the needy disabled. However, these programs have now been taken over by the Supplemental Security Income program, which is federally administered.

Other Financial Assistance

These are programs that directly affect the financial resources of recipients, but are not direct money payments to them.

Food Stamps. This is a program that increases the food purchasing power of needy persons by enabling them to purchase stamps whose value is greater than the amount paid. The amount of stamps an individual may purchase, and how much they will cost, is determined according to state and federal guidelines. All persons who receive Aid to Families with Dependent Children receive or are eligible to purchase Food Stamps, but others who may not meet the criteria for AFDC may also qualify for Food Stamps—the elderly, college students, single persons, and so on.

General assistance. This program makes payments to landlords, utility companies, grocers, and others on behalf of individuals or families in need of temporary assistance—usually under emergency conditions. This program is funded and operated locally. Levels of assistance are generally low, and it is only intended to provide temporary help until a person can begin to receive assistance from some other more stable program.

Medicaid. This program makes payments to medical professionals for services rendered to the financially needy. Those receiving AFDC automatically qualify for Medicaid help, but non-AFDC recipients who cannot meet their medical needs may also be helped by this program.

Several programs exist that indirectly affect the financial resources of individuals and families. This would include programs such as foster care for adults and children, where adults or children that cannot remain in their own homes are placed in the homes of others who care for them. Foster parents or caretakers receive modest payments, to cover the costs involved, from the department of social services. Indirect assistance may also include programs such as day care, where payments are made to persons who care for the children of working parents that cannot afford to pay for such care, and family planning, where birth-control devices may be provided by the agency at no cost to the needy recipient.

Looking at the work implications of financial assistance programs for a moment, it is easy to see why they are often operated by paraprofessional personnel. The major tasks involved include the completion of forms, the fair and uniform application of regulations, the explanation of procedures, and the processing of applications. There are very few professional decisions that need to be made when carrying out these tasks, since regulations are usually very detailed and specific. The worker does interact with the applicant during the application process, and when eligibility verification is necessary, but the nature of the relationship is primarily informational. Interviewing skills are especially important, as is knowledge of forms and procedures and skill at extending personal support while completing the application process. However, empathy and the use of a variety of interventive skills are usually not important for the completion of these tasks. Consequently, highly trained professional social workers are generally not employed in the financial assistance section of a social services department, and typically find it a frustrating experience if they are.

Social Services

Social services are many and varied, some focused primarily on adults, and some concentrating on the needs of children or the aged. In all cases, the provision of social services requires higher levels of professional skill than do financial services. Because of the many services offered, each will be only briefly summarized (see also Exhibit 8-3):

1. Adoption services, which includes the investigation of applicants wishing to adopt a child, matching of prospective parents with children, providing informational and helping services related to child rearing, and follow-up services to verify that the adoption is successful.
2. Employment counseling, job placement, and referrals to job training.
3. Help in locating adequate housing, which may include outreach and advocacy functions focused on identifying areas of inadequate housing and the provision of more adequate housing.
4. Homemaker service programs, which involves helping homemakers to obtain or further develop necessary skills related to cooking, home care, proper nutrition, child rearing, and community participation.
5. Referrals to vocational rehabilitation programs.
6. Certifying eligibility for clinic services at the health department, and providing psychological assessment and testing services.
7. Disaster relief.
8. Cooperating with other agencies by providing information and referrals as appropriate. Agencies commonly worked with include other social agencies in the community (health department, private counseling and recreational agencies, public schools, and the like), local corrections personnel, the courts, other county departments of social services, and residential treatment centers in the state (such as mental hospitals).
9. Cooperating with out-of-town agencies needing information or verification of facts. Departments of social services are often contacted by an agency like Traveler's Aid, a branch of which may have been contacted by a client when experiencing difficulty far from home. This agency may need assistance in verifying facts and exploring available resources as part of developing the most appropriate interventive plan.
10. Adult services, such as protective services for vulnerable adults (the aged, the physically handicapped, and those with mental handicaps, for example), providing birth control and sterilization information when desired, and supervising adult group care settings (such as nursing homes).
11. Services for children. These are varied and include issuing work certificates for children between the ages of fourteen and eighteen (ages vary in different states), and processing applications for children needing specialized treatment such as that provided in schools

for the deaf or blind. As noted earlier, foster care services are provided, including the finding and licensing of homes, and supervising children placed in homes. An increasingly important function of child-care workers is the proper supervision of children lacking it in their own homes (juvenile delinquents, for example) and the protection of children reported as neglected or abused (called protective service).

A Typical Social Services Agency Organizational Chart **EXHIBIT 8-3**

This chart shows a typical social services agency's organizational structure, including the result of separating financial from social services. Naturally there will be some variation between states, but this model is reasonably representative.

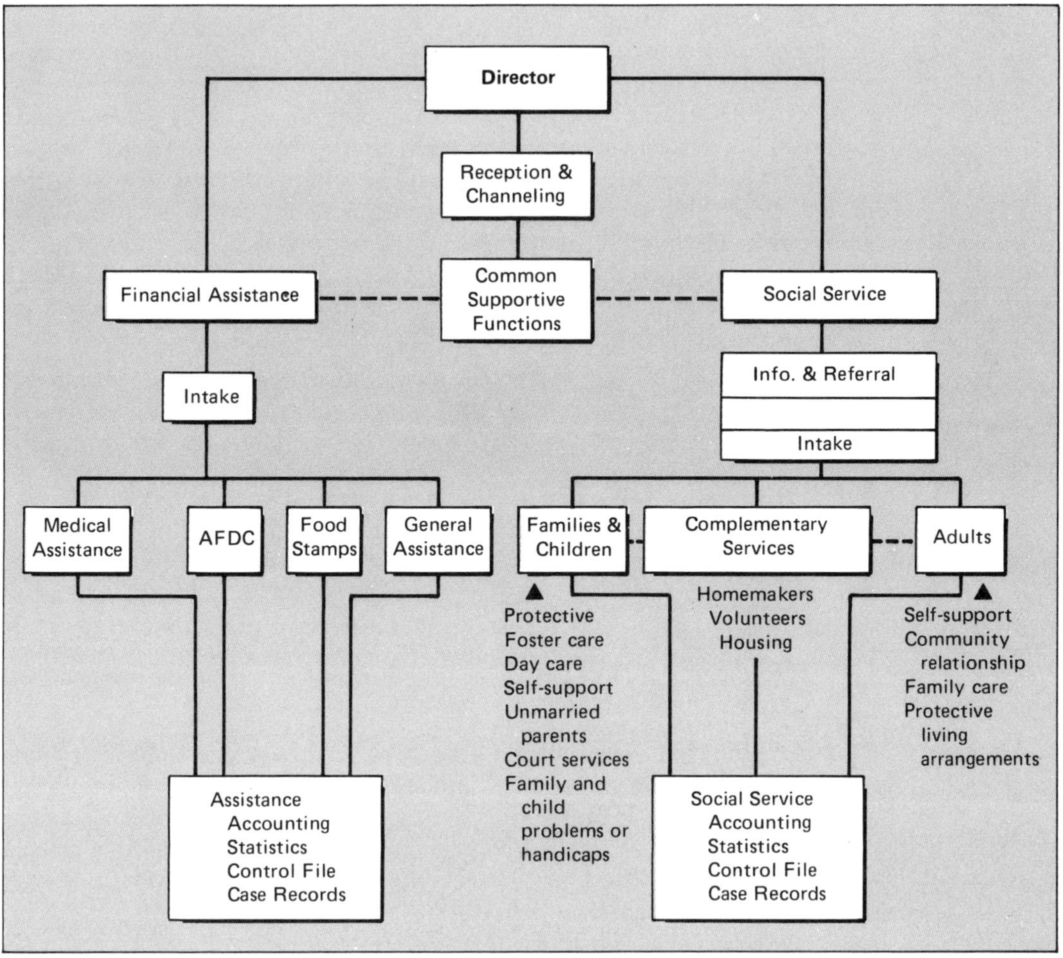

Source: Adapted from HEW, *The Separation of Services from Assistance Payments* (Publication SRS 73-23015) (Washington, D.C.: Government Printing Office, 1972), p. 98.

In the course of performing the many social service functions of the department of social services, the professional person has many opportunities to enter into a helping relationship with the persons seeking help. There is considerable room for the exercise of professional skills, and many opportunities to interact with a range of other community professional helping persons. Since it is impossible to predict how helping relationships will develop, the professional has considerable freedom to use individual judgment when working with a client. For these reasons, paraprofessionals are rarely used in providing social services except in certain cases where the tasks to be performed can be carefully structured in advance—homemakers, for example. From the professional person's point of view, the typical department of social services can be exciting and stimulating, offering a wide range of interventive and learning opportunities. Indeed, there are few agency settings that offer as many opportunities.

Against these advantages must be weighed the fact that social service departments are often large, impersonal, inadequately funded, and housed in crowded and depressing facilities. An additional drawback is that society's hostility toward social welfare values finds a generalized target in departments of social services—after all, are they not the ones that support the indolent poor at Cadillac standards? In addition, these agencies often deal with persons who have no other recourse, no other resources. This makes the task more difficult, since there are few supports to build on. It often creates a hostile client, desperate for help, yet fearful and defeated. Like any work context, the typical department of social services has advantages and disadvantages that must be weighed carefully.

▶ Social Welfare Jobs in the Future

Trying to predict personnel needs in social welfare is a risky endeavor. People's needs for services continue, but the society's willingness to fund such services is unpredictable in light of taxpayers' revolts around the country and efforts to restrict federal spending in order to achieve a balanced budget. Even under these uncertain conditions, however, some trends for the future can be identified that may influence the need for social welfare personnel:*

Demographic changes. The population continues to grow, creating a continuously expanding group for whom services are needed. In addition, the increasing proportion of the elderly in the population can be expected to increase the demand for services, given this group's need for physical,

---

* Basic references for this section are Sheldon Siegel, *Social Service Manpower Needs: An Overview to 1980* (New York: Council on Social Work Education, 1975), and *Occupational Outlook Handbook* (Washington, D.C.: U. S. Department of Labor, 1975).

medical, and recreational care, as well as help in relating to the family and economic institutions.

Changes in society's commitment. American society continues to expand the areas for which social welfare resources are deemed appropriate—for example, protective care for the young, the old, and battered women and more serious nondiscrimination efforts for women, homosexuals, and the handicapped. These commitments will require personnel in order to be operationalized.

Upgrading education and training. Many social welfare professions have, over the past decade, become much more organized. They have more clearly specified the education and training needed to perform tasks, and they have attempted to differentially use personnel so that levels of education and training are more logically related to tasks to be performed. One result is pressure to replace persons holding social welfare jobs who do not have professional training with those who do. This in effect increases job opportunities for trained personnel even though the total number of jobs available may not change.

Differential use of personnel. As noted above, many social welfare professions are more explicitly relating education and training to jobs. This may lead to shifts in job opportunities *within* a profession. For example, the tasks to be done may be seen as needing fewer persons with master's-level training and more persons with baccalaureate-level training. This can increase job opportunities for some and decrease them for others, all within the same profession. This process can be accentuated by financial cutbacks that encourage agencies to hire less costly personnel (who are generally those with less training). The effect may be to restrict the scope of services available, as well as to shift the job opportunities for different personnel levels.

What does it all add up to? Most projections see a continuing growth in social service personnel needs for the immediate future. For example, speaking of social work Siegel says:*

> *[Using a] . . . maximum projection of 402,000 social service workers means that about 153,000 would be baccalaureate level social workers [38 percent] and 121,000 would be those with some training in social work [30 percent]. This would be an increase from 1970 to 1980 of 54,000 with some graduate education and 68,000 baccalaureates, for a total increase of 122,000 new social work openings for the decade.*

* As quoted in *Encyclopedia of Social Work,* 17th ed. (Washington, D.C.: National Association of Social Workers, 1977), p. 1075.

Ironically the future of social welfare jobs is in part dependent on social welfare professionals themselves. Public policy decisions are crucial for creating—or eliminating—social welfare services and jobs. Social welfare professionals must work actively through their professional associations to influence these decisions in order that more adequate and better quality services be available for people. Secondarily, this will also serve to strengthen the need for and appropriate use of trained professional personnel. As has been emphasized throughout this book, the social policy arena is extremely important for professional functioning for every type and every level of social welfare professional.

Exhibit 8-4 presents "The Social Welfare Career Packet." It provides some basic information helpful to the person seeking to learn more about the work of social welfare. The social welfare institution is rich with work settings, each having its own distinctive blend of strengths and weaknesses. There is no substitute for assuming the responsibility for finding out about the work contexts possible, both through literature and through visits. Better yet, volunteering to work a few hours a week in an agency that seems interesting provides the inside view—the best view of all.

EXHIBIT 8-4 *The Social Welfare Career Packet*

The materials presented in this exhibit are taken from mimeographed handouts provided by the Health and Welfare Council of Central Maryland, Social Work Careers Service, Baltimore, Maryland. Although compiled a few years ago, they remain one of the best pictures of social welfare careers compiled to date.

Social Welfare Workers and Their Work

What Does the Social Welfare Worker Do? The social welfare worker is concerned with society and its social problems. He deals with the causes, the prevention, and the treatment of such problems. The social welfare worker may work with individuals, with groups, and/or the community. He may also work with adults, with teenagers, with children, or with all three.

At the present time our society is seeking new approaches to the increasingly serious questions of poverty, sickness, inferior education, urban ills, and racial injustices. Such new approaches are affecting, and will affect, the role of the social welfare worker. The student considering social welfare as a career, therefore, needs to know that if he enters the field he will become part of a dynamic but rapidly changing scene: new services are being offered and new methods are being developed to meet today's problems.

What Qualities Should the Social Welfare Worker Have? Social welfare needs those who are willing to accept the challenge of working in a field that is searching for ways to become more effective in solving the problems of an increasingly complex society. Social welfare requires individuals who have drive, imagination, intelligence, understanding, patience, and a genuine commitment to do the job. For those who are willing to invest in further educational preparation, this can be a most satisfying and rewarding career.

What Jobs are Included in Social Welfare? As stated above, social welfare encompasses a wide variety of jobs and job titles. Each category may or may not include workers on all educational levels from below high school through the Master's degree. The examples of job titles listed are representative samples only and by no means include all titles possible. Although there is considerable overlap with other fields and some lack of clarity in the structure of the jobs, most social welfare jobs fall into the categories listed below:

1. *Social Workers*—Includes social work and social work assistant positions. (Examples: Social Worker, Social Work Assistant, Psychiatric Social Worker, Medical Social Worker, and School Social Worker.) Community workers and group workers can be included in this category or in the appropriate category below.
2. *Financial Assistance and Benefit Workers*—Includes positions of those workers primarily responsible for determining eligibility for benefits including welfare, medical assistance, social insurance, veterans' benefits, etc. (Examples: Public Welfare Interviewer, Eligibility Technician, and Claims Representative.)
3. *Community Workers*—Includes positions of those working in social welfare planning and research (Examples: Community Organizer, Planning Assistant, and Researcher); those working at the neighborhood level to improve or stabilize conditions (Examples: Neighborhood Development Assistant, and Community Organizer); and race relations workers (Example: Assistant Intergroup Relations Representative).
4. *Employment Workers*—Includes positions related to job development, job counseling, vocational rehabilitation, and staff development. (Examples: Vocational Rehabilitation Counselor, Staff Development Assistant, Employment Counselor, and Job Developer.) Excludes personnel officers and school guidance counselors.
5. *Youth and Recreation Workers*—Includes positions of those whose duties primarily consist of working with groups for purposes of recreation or youth development. (Examples: Group Worker, Youth Worker, and Recreation Leader.)
6. *Correction Workers*—Includes positions both in the field of adult correction (Examples: Correction Officer and Correctional Classification Counselor), and juvenile correction (Examples: Youth Supervisor and Juvenile Probation Worker). Excludes those who are primarily law enforcement workers such as policemen.
7. *Specialized Health Counselors*—Includes positions of counselors working with specialized health problems (Examples: Alcoholism Counselor, Family Planning Counselor, and Drug Abuse Counselor).
8. *Supportive Aides*—Includes positions which are usually, though not exclusively, entry level positions open to those with a high school education or less and which support or augment the services of the Associate, Master's, or Bachelor's degree worker. (Examples: Homemaker, Day Care Aide, Social Service Aide, Relocation Aide, and Psychiatric Aide.)
9. *College Teachers* of graduate and undergraduate courses in social work and social welfare. (Examples: Professor, Assistant Professor, and Instructor.)
10. *Administrators*—Includes all social welfare administrative positions above the rank of supervisor. (Examples: Executive Director, Assistant or Associate Director, Division or Bureau Chief, Program Director, Project Director, and Coordinator.)

Exploring a Career in Social Welfare

Is social welfare the career for you? Do you think it might be, but want to know more about it? Will you like the work? Do you really have an aptitude for it? It's well to ask these questions now and there are a number of steps you can take to help find the answers for yourself.

First, review all of the information you can about a social welfare career. Your college or public *library* contains pamphlets and books about social work, recreation, corrections, job counseling, community organization, and other related helping occupations within the broad field of social welfare. *Your college vocational or placement office* also has such materials. The counselor in the placement office, or your college adviser, can help you plan which courses you should take to prepare for this career. He can also tell you whom to contact for additional information.

Sources of additional written career information include:

1. Social Work—Social Work Information Center, National Association of Social Workers, 1425 H St., N.W., Suite 600, Washington, D.C. 20005
2. Recreation—National Recreation and Park Association, 1700 Pennsylvania Avenue, N.W., Washington, D.C. 20006
3. Rehabilitation Counseling—American Rehabilitation Counseling Association, 1605 New Hampshire Avenue, N.W., Washington, D.C. 20009
4. Vocational Counseling—National Vocational Guidance Association, Inc., 1605 New Hampshire Avenue, N.W., Washington, D.C. 20009
5. Public Welfare—American Public Welfare Association, 1155 Sixteenth St., N.W., Washington, D.C. 20036
6. Child Welfare—Child Welfare League of America, 44 East 23rd Street, New York, New York 10016
7. Mental Health Careers—Mental Health Materials Center, 419 Park Avenue South, New York, New York 10016
8. Group and Neighborhood Work—National Federation of Settlements and Neighborhood Centers, 232 Madison Avenue, New York, New York 10016

Books, pamphlets, and information can help, but how do you really know if this is the career for you? How do you find out if you'll like the work; how will you know if you're suited for it? Career testing opportunities are needed to help you begin to answer these questions. *Volunteer work* is an excellent starting point—not just any volunteer job, however, but one where you can be involved with people; where you have a chance to see what a social service organization is doing; where you have an opportunity to talk with the workers in the agency; where you can have a small piece of the action yourself.

Volunteer work is available both for a few hours per week during the college year and for any time from a few hours to the entire week during the summer. Students can call any social agency in which they are interested to offer their services and inquire about the opportunities and requirements. Among those local organizations throughout the state that use volunteers are: community action agencies; groups working with retarded children; state mental hospitals; county or city departments of social services; youth serving organizations such as YWCA, Girl Scouts, Catholic Youth Organization, and Jewish community centers; bureaus of recreation; and the American Red Cross.

Another means of career testing while still in college is through *paid part-time jobs in the field of social welfare.* The number of such opportunities available during the school year is limited and students who volunteer in or live near an agency often have a better opportunity of securing those part-time jobs which are available. In addition your college placement office may have some listings of such jobs.

If you have a particular *skill which you can teach* you may be able to find a part-time job during the week or on Saturday working in a *recreation or youth serving agency.* In the process of teaching the skill, you will learn about the work of the agency, and very importantly, about your own ability to relate to and work with people, perhaps including those of backgrounds other than your own. Some of the skills for which there is a demand are: arts and crafts, ballet, sports, music, and swimming. To inquire about such opportunities call youth serving agencies near your home or college.

Paid summer work experience in a helping profession is one of the best ways of preparing for a social welfare career, although such work opportunities are limited in most areas. Some possibilities are the following:

1. *Summer Camps* provide an ideal opportunity for students to gain experience working with children. A number of camps, including both day and overnight camps, hire college students. The salary varies considerably from camp to camp. Students interested in camp jobs should seek further information from their placement office or the American Camping Association, Bradford Woods, Martinsville, Indiana 46151. Public libraries also have listings of camps approved by the American Camping Association.
2. *Recreation Departments* often hire high school and college students to work in their

summer programs. For example, Baltimore City Bureau of Recreation hires students seventeen years old and up as day-camp aides, playground aides, portable-pool guards, leaders for the handicapped, and traveling play leaders. Apply between January and mid-March at your local recreation department.

3. The *VISTA* program provides another means of testing an aptitude for a social welfare career. VISTA, Volunteers in Service to America, recruits, trains and assigns volunteers to work for one year fighting poverty in urban slums, on Indian reservations, in Appalachia, in mental retardation programs, etc. Applicants must be at least eighteen years of age and have no dependents under eighteen. The volunteers are sponsored by state and local agencies—public and private—and are paid only a minimum subsistence allowance and a $50 monthly stipend. For further information, write VISTA, Box 700, Washington, D.C. 20506.
4. Some large cities have *Summer Jobs in Social Work Programs,* in which young people are hired by agencies specifically so they can experience social welfare work first hand. To see if there is one in your city, contact the local chapter of the National Association of Social Workers, the local health and welfare council, or the local department of social services.

In summary, both information and career testing are essential in making a career choice. After such exploration you may or may not decide that social welfare is the career for you, but you will have a sound basis for your choice.

Social Welfare Jobs: Matching Training with Tasks

The field of social welfare can be entered at all educational levels from less than high school graduation through the Master's or Doctor's degree. Below is information about jobs and salary ranges at each educational level. Jobs may be in governmental service at the local, state or federal level, or they may be in private agencies such as those supported by the United Fund or other voluntary sources.

HIGH SCHOOL GRADUATION. A person with a high school diploma (and sometimes less) may obtain a beginning job in a social welfare organization such as a community action agency, a bureau of recreation, a department of housing and community development, a day care center, a department of social services, a child-caring institution, or a health service agency of a hospital. The student should be aware, however, that many of such jobs are available only to residents of certain neighborhoods or to members of the client group which the employing agency serves. Beginning social welfare positions are quite varied, but the worker usually does some of the following:

1. Goes out in the neighborhood to explain the services of the agency and to encourage the people to use the services.
2. Follows up clients who have been receiving the services of the agency.
3. When necessary, refers clients to other workers in the same agency or to other agencies for further service.
4. Helps the professional working with a recreation, community or therapy group, or with an individual or family.
5. Keeps simple records and reports.
6. Cares for and supervises children and/or adults in an institution, recreation center, or their own home.

Most workers with a high school diploma or less start at a salary of $4,500–$6,000 and receive increases with experience and training. Some of the positions provide for career advancement following additional experience, training, and/or formal education.

Some examples of the titles or jobs one may hold with a high school diploma are: Neighborhood Development Assistant I, Recreation Assistant, Health Aide I, Homemaker, Community Worker, and Youth Supervisor I.

ASSOCIATE OF ARTS DEGREE (TWO YEARS OF COLLEGE). A person who has an Associate of Arts degree (AA) may be employed in interviewing and beginning counseling positions with employment and manpower agencies, county and city departments of social services, hospitals and clinics, mental hospitals, and other organizations. He can work as a recreation leader, housing relocation aide, administrative secretary in a social agency, or serve as an assistant in urban planning.

The worker with an Associate of Arts degree often does some of the following:

1. Interviews clients and/or examines written information in order to determine eligibility for service including financial, medical, or other benefits.
2. Provides some of the services of the agency including elementary counseling.
3. The following duties are similar to those performed by workers with a high school diploma. The AA worker, however, usually would be assigned to situations of a more complex nature than those assigned to the high school graduate.
   a. Goes out into the neighborhood to explain the services of the agency, and to encourage people to use the services.
   b. Follows up clients who have been receiving the services of the agency.
   c. When necessary refers clients, whose problems indicate the need for such referral, to other workers in the same agency or to other agencies for further service.
   d. Helps the professional in working with a recreation, community, or therapy group, or with an individual or family.
   e. Keeps simple records and reports.

The salaries are varied, but most workers with an AA degree start at a salary of $8,000–$9,000. Most of the AA degree positions provide for salary increases and career advancement following additional experience, training, and/or formal education.

Examples of the titles of jobs one may hold with two years of college are: Public Welfare Interviewer, Health Aide III, Relocation Aide, Beginning Casework Assistant, Mental Health Associate, and Intake Interviewer. Some of the above jobs require additional experience beyond the AA degree.

BACHELOR'S DEGREE (FOUR YEARS OF COLLEGE). The largest number of employees in the social welfare field are those holding a Bachelor of Arts or Bachelor of Science degree. Although one may obtain a job in the social welfare field with a college major in any subject, many employers prefer someone who has majored or taken courses in the social sciences (sociology, psychology, social welfare, economics, etc.). Most of the provision of direct services to individuals, groups, and organizations is carried out by persons with a four-year college degree.

The worker with a Bachelor's degree and no experience usually does some of the following:

1. Provides specific services for clients, such as placement of a foster child; preparation for parole; preparation for hospital release; location of jobs, etc.
2. Assists clients and families, both individually and in groups, in discussing their problems and in developing and making the most of their abilities.
3. Assists clients in using agency, hospital, or community resources to help them solve their problems.
4. Works with a community, recreation, or therapy group.
5. Determines financial or service eligibility.
6. Gathers information, analyzes material, makes recommendations, keeps records, and submits reports.
7. Keeps in close contact with other agencies and organizations; makes referrals when necessary; works with other agencies concerning community problems.

The Bachelor's degree worker with no prior experience usually starts at a salary between $9,000 and $11,000. Some examples of the titles of jobs one may hold with a Bachelor's degree are: Casework Assistant I, Street Club Worker, Employment Counselor I, Assistant Intergroup Relations Representative, and Juvenile Probation Worker. Some of the above jobs require additional experience beyond the Bachelor's degree.

As the Bachelor's level worker gains experience, his duties become more complex. With considerable experience and increased responsibility, some Bachelor's degree workers earn as much as $12,000 to $18,000.

MASTER'S DEGREE. The Master's degree in social work (variously titled MSW, MSSA, MA, etc.) is often specified for positions in the social welfare field, although for certain jobs other Master's degrees are acceptable and sometimes preferred. The Master's degree in social work currently requires two years of college beyond the Bachelor's degree. Only a small percentage of employees in the field of social welfare possess a Master's degree. (In social work alone, only approximately 20 percent of all employees hold a Master's degree.)

The duties of the Master's degree worker may include the following:

1. Works with clients on more complex situations.
2. Develops and works with groups established for the purpose of therapy, personal development, and/or recreation.
3. Works with neighborhood or community groups to analyze their needs and develop plans to meet the needs.
4. Develops, coordinates, and evaluates programs and policies.
5. Supervises and trains staff.
6. Interprets the work of the agency through writing and speaking.

With experience, the Master's degree worker may advance rapidly either to the provision of direct service on a deeper level, to supervision, and/or to administration. In actual practice, outside of private agencies, very few persons with a Master's degree and experience are engaged primarily in the direct provision of services to clients. Advancement for Master's degree workers is almost always in the direction of supervision, staff development, planning, and/or administration.

Some examples of the titles of jobs one may hold with a Master's degree are: Social Worker I, Senior Community Organization Advisor, Counselor II, Juvenile Services Regional Supervisor I, Deputy Commissioner, and Assistant Administrator II. Some of the above jobs require additional experience beyond the Master's degree.

The Master's degree holder with no previous experience usually starts at a salary between $10,000 and $13,000. With increased experience and job responsibility a Master's degree worker may earn $15,000 to $25,000, and sometimes more.

Chapter Summary

Social welfare offers a wide range of career opportunities organized within the various social welfare professions. In spite of slowed growth in the national economy and continued ambivalence in societal values regarding professional helping, the outlook for social welfare jobs is promising. Most social welfare positions are in large formal organizations, a reality that speaks to the need to develop organizational skills as well as to have realistic expectations for the kinds of opportunities and limitations that exist in such settings. Finally, the availability of social welfare jobs tends to be unevenly distributed within and between states and regions, making geographical flexibility a significant factor in locating the kind of position that is desired. Although the opportunities for a rewarding social welfare career exist, each individual must first decide whether a career in social welfare is the kind of commitment he or she is willing to make.

STUDY QUESTIONS

1. In your community, visit a social welfare agency that interests you. What kinds of programs does it offer? What kinds of clients use its services? What kinds of professional and paraprofessional staff does it employ? What types of interventive methods are used in carrying out its programs? Would you enjoy working there? Why or why not?

2. Interview a social worker in your community. What frustrations and rewards has this worker experienced in the work? Would you find these frustrations tolerable? Would the rewards be adequate for you? Why or why not?
3. Make a list of the characteristics you would want in your ideal social welfare job. Then organize them in terms of the criteria used to analyze agencies in this chapter (for example, if you listed "working with children" you would put that under client-focused agency). Remember that the criteria are not mutually exclusive, so one of your characteristics might fit under more than one criterion. After doing this, what sort of agency seems ideal for you? Is there such an agency in your community? If so, visit it and see if, in practice, it seems as attractive as it does in theory. If there is not such an agency where you live, what compromises might you have to make to find a job in the "real world"?

SELECTED READINGS

The best sources of factual information about specific careers are those shown in Exhibit 8-4. The sources below are separated into (1) discussions of professional career issues; and (2) biographical-novelistic accounts of what being a helping person *feels* like. Many of these are available in paperback editions.

Collins, Alice. *The Lonely and Afraid.* New York: Odyssey, 1969.

Henry, William E. with John Sims and S. Lee Spray. *The Fifth Profession.* San Francisco: Jossey-Bass, 1971.

Hoejsi, J. E., T. Walz, and P. R. Connolly. *Working in Welfare.* Iowa City: University of Iowa School of Social Work, 1977.

Lubove, Roy. *The Professional Altruist.* New York: Atheneum, 1969.

Richan, Willard. with Alan Mendelsohn. *Social Work: The Unloved Profession.* New York: New Viewpoints, 1973.

Addams, Jane. *Twenty Years at Hull House.* New York: New American Library, 1960.

Beers, Clifford. *A Mind That Found Itself.* New York: Doubleday, 1948.

Crook, William H., and Ross Thomas. *Warriors for the Poor: The Story of VISTA Volunteers.* New York: Morrow, 1969.

Decker, Sunny. *An Empty Spoon.* New York: Harper & Row, 1970 (about urban education).

Densen-Gerber, Judianne. *We Mainline Dreams: The Odyssey House Story.* New York: Doubleday, 1973 (about drug addiction).

Fry, Alan. *How a People Die.* New York: Doubleday, 1970 (about native Americans).

Gell, Frank. *The Black Badge: Confessions of a Caseworker.* New York: Harper & Row, 1969.

Green, Hannah. *I Never Promised You a Rose Garden.* New York: Holt, Rinehart, and Winston, 1964 (about mental illness).

Greenberg, Joanne. *The Monday Voices.* New York: Holt, Rinehart and Winston, 1965 (about a vocational rehabilitation counselor).

Horwitz, Louis. *Diary of A. N.* New York: Dell, 1971 (about an AFDC child).

Hough, John. *A Peck of Salt: A Year in the Ghetto.* Boston: Little, Brown, 1972.

Milio, Nancy. *9226 Kercheval: The Storefront that Did Not Burn.* Ann Arbor: University of Micigan Press, 1970.

Thompson, Jean. *The House of Tomorrow.* New York: Harper & Row, 1967 (about unmarried mothers).

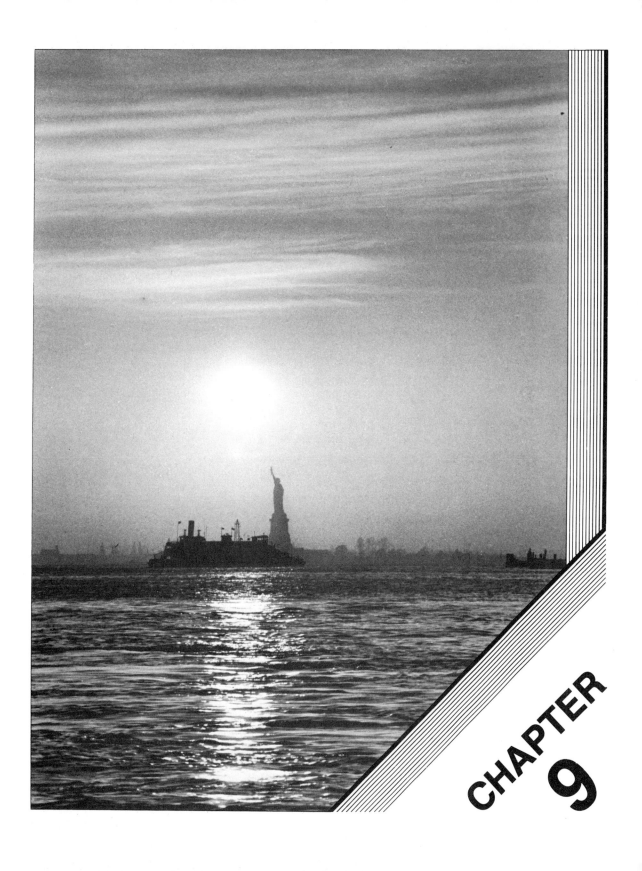

CHAPTER 9

Thinking Ahead

Looking ahead toward the future of social welfare in the United States, one must incorporate the perspective used throughout this book. Although there seems to be little doubt that social welfare is a firmly institutionalized part of the fabric of American society, fundamental social and professional issues remain. They are by now familiar: How are services to be provided most effectively? How are they to be funded? What kinds of services will be available to which people? What roles will social welfare professionals play in social policy and social planning? How will the various social welfare professionals resolve their own internal dilemmas and controversies? Looking ahead is always a risky endeavor, especially when dealing with a part of social life as volatile as social welfare. Nevertheless, there are some trends and issues that may suggest the future of social welfare in America. This chapter looks at several of them.

The knowledge objectives of this chapter are to make the reader aware of current social welfare issues as well as some of the major legislative proposals to resolve them. The skill objective is to further strengthen the reader's ability to obtain and evaluate information about issues and to assess policy proposals critically. Values are crucial elements of decision making, and the chapter emphasizes the value bases and implications of the issues and legislative proposals that are discussed. Here in this last chapter, the reader should try to apply the knowledge, skills, and values obtained in previous chapters as a beginning effort to look toward the future from the stance of a social welfare professional.

The Changing Societal Context of Social Welfare ◀

It is obvious that contemporary society is different from any that humanity has ever known, and that it continues to change with a rapidity that makes future predictions hazardous. These changes began in the Industrial Revolution, and have created a society whose complexity is staggering. People living in highly industrialized societies are presented with almost infinite choices and opportunities, but in return pay a price in the anxiety and bewilderment that often accompany such flexibility. Future demands placed on the social welfare institution can be expected to change as the needs of the people within society change.

There are several specific changes in the social structure which are likely to affect the provision of social welfare services in the future.[1]

A Shift from Relative Deprivation to Relative Abundance

The capacity of American society to produce goods and services has tended to raise people's expectations and aspirations. This has been accentuated by increasing success in eliminating some of the ascriptive barriers that previously kept certain groups from aspiring to much more than survival—racial and ethnic groups in particular. The mass media make it obvious that there is something available to gratify virtually every need and every whim. They further suggest that these items are available to all, or at least that everyone should aspire to have them. This society's emphasis on the biggest and best reinforces the belief that America has something for everyone; other countries may have scarcity as a way of life, but scarcity in this country indicates a problem of some sort rather than an inevitability. We expect to be comfortable, to have all of our needs met relatively easily, and to choose what we want when we want it. Sacrifice is no longer an accepted part of the vocabulary for the average American.

It has long been a goal of American society to provide "a chicken in every pot," and to some extent the society has attained this goal. Certainly the social welfare institution, with its emphasis on improving social functioning and minimizing suffering, seeks to help the society attain this objective. Still, abundance has its problems, and the social welfare system of the future can expect to deal with some of them. Abundance may be a way of life for some people, but many groups are still systematically deprived. As these groups are led to expect abundance and opportunity and reject deprivation and sacrifice, personal frustration, intergroup conflict, and individual and group-supported deviance can be expected. Aspiring to the rewards of abundance may also create a renewed interest in the legislative process as a way to redistribute societal resources more equitably. The social welfare practitioner of the future will no doubt be called upon to help individuals and groups participate in the political process as an interventive strategy.

There are other problems associated with abundance. A high level of personal affluence tends to use resources inefficiently—the American fixation on the automobile and convenience food takes a high toll in terms of poor energy utilization and the generation of waste. The costs of personal affluence must be borne by the society—a polluted river affects many people, and requires massive funding if it is to be cleaned. Social welfare will increasingly have as one of its responsibilities the monitoring of the use of social resources. Social planning that balances personal access and social costs is becoming essential. Furthermore, there is a tendency to equate abundance with the "good life." This may be true to the extent that people have enough to eat, adequate clothing and shelter, and access to a technology that spares them hard or dangerous work and personal discomfort. It is not the case, however, that affluence solves personal problems. Often the reverse is true. It is easy for a psychology of abundance to lead to greater and greater expectations for oneself and one's associates. The more one has and does, the more one wants and expects. Exploitative interpersonal relations can result, along with demands for personal freedom ("doing your own thing"), which make stable, mutually rewarding interpersonal relationships practically impossible.

Perhaps the greatest problem with abundance is that it facilitates goal displacement. When so much is possible it is easy to believe that affluence is not only desirable, but ultimately even necessary. The American automobile is truly an engineering marvel, offering swiveling front seats, couturier-designed upholstery, genuine Circassian walnut dashboards, and a rainbow of colors. But are these necessary? Do these features improve the value of the automobile for meeting the individual's needs in any fundamental way? Is the car any safer or more economical? Yet people aspire to absurdly luxurious automobiles because they are available, and may feel quite unhappy if economic circumstances force them to accept a less fancy but equally serviceable car. The point is that abundance is only as desirable as it is useful. If it brings us comfort and convenience without alienating us from ourselves and others, it improves the quality of life. If it distorts people's views of themselves, their friends and families, and their goals, it creates problems instead of progress. Technology is infinitely tempting, and many people succumb to its charms. When individuals lose their way and abandon appropriate goals and means, the social welfare system will need to be ready to help them reassess their lives and make appropriate choices.

An Increase in Structural Complexity

Industrial society is very complex. Each individual occupies many different positions, including those related to family, work, recreation, sex, and age. As was noted in Chapter 5, this multiplicity of positions can create conflicts and ambiguities which the social welfare system can help to avoid or mitigate. Since many positions are achieved (that is, chosen by the individual), the social welfare professions may also be needed to help people make choices among the various alternatives. This includes helping them to make their personal goals explicit, and analyzing the implications of various decisions. For example, the young person considering marriage while still in college can be helped to consider the possible effects on career choice and training, interpersonal rewards and strains, and obtaining needed resources. As always, the choice is the individual's, but the social welfare professional helps the person understand the sometimes confusing assortment of options and consequences.

Structural complexity also affects the provision of services in society, including social welfare services. The reliance on large-scale formal organizational structures and the use of computerized data collection, analysis, and retrieval methods can sometimes create service-delivery systems that are impersonal and inaccessible. If the marvels of technology are to be translated into usable services, the social welfare institution must help people to understand the services available to them, procedures for obtaining these services, and their rights as consumers. There are countless examples of the problems that can arise in a complex society—misunderstood and in some cases illegal credit practices; unintelligible food-dating codes; dealing with mistakes in computerized charge accounts, and many others. Even such basic rights as voting may be jeopardized by modern technology, as when an inexperienced person attempts to work a voting machine. Finally, of course, there are the procedures that make social welfare services themselves inaccessible—the complex eligibility requirements; exhaustive and highly detailed application forms; complicated insurance payment procedures; and centralized and isolated locations, to name some of the potential problems. Increasingly, the social welfare institution will have to be concerned with humanizing a highly specialized, efficient, but impersonal social world. Human values must not be lost in a display of sophisticated technological hardware or blind attempts to achieve organizational efficiency.

The Knowledge Explosion and Shifting Values

American society is increasingly a credentials-oriented society. Higher and higher levels of training are specified for many work positions, a natural consequence of increasingly sophisticated technological equipment and procedures. More and more knowledge is necessary to understand even the basic rudiments of everyday life—reading computerized printouts of books checked out of a library, or understanding food-dating codes, for example. Services previously provided by persons who would explain procedures if necessary are now provided by machines that permit no dialogue. Increasingly, knowledge is indeed power. We depend on specialists, and learn not to question their expertise. We read in the newspaper about issues we cannot really understand—should society invest in space exploration? The supersonic transport? Nuclear energy? At best, we can develop expertise in only a few areas. For the rest, we have to trust others, knowing full well that sometimes they cannot be trusted.

The knowledge explosion can have the effect of eroding our sense of involvement in the world around us. It may seem useless to worry whether billions of dollars should be spent to send people to the moon rather than improve public education, since we obviously cannot even understand the complicated issues involved. When a specialist deprives us of our right to self-determination, or dehumanizes us with his or her sophisticated knowledge and technology, it seems futile to complain. In the welter of confusing daily activities, it sometimes appears that we have all we can do just to take care of ourselves. There is little energy left to use in worrying about the problems of others. After a day of frustrations in impersonal and unstable work or shopping contexts, we may seek only to gratify ourselves. Values of commitment to people and life goals, careful planning to achieve these goals, self-sacrifice and sharing, and honesty can appear useless in a social environment that threatens our integrity and challenges us to preserve ourselves in the face of bewildering procedures and seemingly endless changes. The social welfare system must once again help individuals to better understand their environment, and to maintain their dignity and freedom within it. Social welfare must also strive to have an input into the social system so that human values are preserved and social processes are humane. Knowledge must be used for people, not against them. Social change must help people to function more effectively, not desensitize and dehumanize them.

In the remainder of this chapter, some directions the social welfare institution is apparently taking in trying to cope with its changing environment will be explored. First, new approaches to meeting people's basic financial needs will be considered. This will be followed by a consideration of social services as a way to help people meet their nonfinancial needs. Finally, issues facing social welfare professions themselves as they attempt to meet society's needs will be presented. The unprecedented rate of social change in contemporary American society has created problems and potentials that are difficult to comprehend. Trying to create a viable social welfare institutional structure under such circumstances is a challenge with serious implications for the future of social welfare in America.

Meeting Financial Need

Any attempt to revamp our procedures to meet people's financial needs runs head-on into some core questions: For whom is society responsible? To what standard of life is society committed, and do all groups in society have a right to the same standard? What groups have a responsibility to contribute to the needs of others? Who decides on the allocation of societal resources, and through what decision-making structures? Already some answers have been provided. Social Security has gradually been expanded in scope, and payment levels have been raised. Grants to the aged, blind, and disabled have been centralized and simplified so that recipients are helped with minimal harassment and uncertainty. Grant levels are more adequate than previously but are still unable to meet a living standard of basic dignity. Grants to families with dependent children are still low, contingent upon complex and often degrading eligibility and application procedures, and subject to societal scorn. There is still no comprehensive program to meet the financial needs of all members of this society, in spite of the fact that the fragmented, specialized programs that do exist have been slowly moving in that direction.

There are two areas of financial need that will almost certainly be more effectively dealt with through new legislation in the relatively near future: welfare reform and national health insurance. Welfare reform that would better meet people's financial needs while simplifying the structure of services, minimizing increases in costs, and supporting existing social values around self-sufficiency and work has long been debated in Congress. However, different groups have different objectives, and so far no compromise has been adequate to pass welfare reform legislation. Eveline Burns, an eminent social economist, has developed "The Ten Commandments of Welfare Reform," which combine the objectives of all the different groups involved in welfare reform:[2]

1. *The system must meet the income deficiencies of all needy people, including the working poor.*
2. *It must put money in people's hands when they need it.*
3. *The payment must be dependable and predictable so the recipient can budget his expenditures.*
4. *It must not offend the dignity and self-respect of applicants and recipients and should not involve highly detailed investigation of the applicant's personal circumstances.*
5. *It must not discriminate against the intact family or offer inducements to family break-up.*
6. *It must not discourage initiative or work incentive.*

7. *It must be sufficiently simple to permit effective and economical administration.*
8. *It must treat recipients, taxwise, the same as all other income receivers.*
9. *It must not involve heavy and markedly unequal financial burdens on state and local governments.*
10. *The costs must be kept to a minimum and preferably no higher than at present.*

Burns then goes on to ask whether these commandments can be kept, and her analysis shows many of them to be mutually exclusive:[3]

Many of the Commandments appear to be contradictory. It is obvious that satisfaction of the First Commandment will increase the size of the welfare bill, thus not fulfilling Commandment Ten.

For cost containment, Commandment Six is vitally important. If employable people can be encouraged to work through guidance, training, availability of jobs and the removal of deterrents in the welfare system itself, fewer people will need benefits. And better social services aiming to prevent or reunite broken families would reduce the costly AFDC caseload.

Welfare costs could also be reduced by abandoning the present effort to ensure that all persons in similar economic circumstances are treated precisely alike. The excessive degree of individualization fosters fraud and is costly and unworkable when dealing with millions of recipients. The remedy is to move to flat grants based on a concept of average need.

The Ninth Commandment, it is often assumed, can be satisfied by a federal takeover of all welfare costs through a system of uniform federally defined payments and nationally uniform eligibility conditions. Federal reinbursement of state supplementation due to higher living costs would relieve the burden on high-cost states. But states that choose to provide higher benefits because they are wealthier or more liberal should bear the residual burden themselves.

Satisfaction of many of the commandments would be difficult as long as the welfare system operates on a "gap-filling" basis. A system that undertakes to fill the gap between an applicant's income and some minimum income standard breaks the Sixth Commandment by discouraging earning. Attempts to avoid this by disregarding some fraction of earnings breaks the Eighth Commandment by taxing recipients at a higher rate than other people (a 25 percent disregard is tantamount to a tax rate of 75 percent). Larger disregards break the Tenth Commandment by making more people eligible and increasing the benefits of current recipients. In addition to its administrative complexity, such a system cannot yield predictable payments, thus breaking the Third Commandment.

As a result of her analysis, Burns feels that a major change is needed rather than relatively minor "reforms" if the various objectives for welfare are to be attained. The solution that she favors is a system of *taxable demogrants,* uniform payments that are lower for children than for adults, and which are made monthly to each individual regardless of the person's income. "At the end of the taxable year everyone would file an income tax return which would include the demogrant. Such a system would help the working poor as well as other needy persons. It would treat the needy, taxwise, in the same way as other receivers. There would be no inducement to fiscal desertion and family breakup. People would always be better off by working."[4] Although Burns's proposal is provocative and exciting, most welfare reform proposals being presented to Congress attempt to revise the existing structure. Exhibit 9-1 summarizes them.

Welfare Reform Proposals EXHIBIT 9-1

The increasing concern with creating a more efficient and humane system of financial assistance has led to a number of proposals for welfare reform. Summaries of some of the major proposals follow. It is easy to see how complex such proposals quickly become, in contrast to the relative simplicity of Burns's proposal. On the other hand, these proposals require a less drastic shift from existing programs.

Strategy	*Multiple Program Strategy*	*Carter Administration (to date)*
General Description	Seeks to work within the broad outlines of existing programs to improve coverage of intact families and working poor. Components of strategy include: (a) Refundable Tax Credit (RTC); (b) revisions to SSI and AFDC; (c) removal of Food Stamp purchase requirement; (d) introduction of Housing Allowance program to parallel food stamps.	A jobs and consolidated case program covering all families with children, single individuals, and childless couples.
Coverage	Universal coverage of all families and working poor such that all families receive adequate food and shelter without having to expend more than 25% of total income for housing or more than 30% for food.	Universal coverage without respect to family structure. Categorical treatment based on work test.

Source: Excerpted from the table in the National Association of Social Workers' *NASW News,* July 1977, pp. 24–25. This table reflects the major issues in welfare reform, and various possible strategies. When welfare reform legislation is finally passed it will no doubt respond to these issues, although it is impossible to know which strategies will be selected.

Strategy	*Multiple Program Strategy*	*Carter Administration (to date)*
Eligibility	AFDC—same as current system. Food Stamps—same as current system. SSI—same as current system. Housing Allowance—same as food stamps. Refundable Tax Credit—individual claiming deduction	Consolidated cash program—all those not required to work or for whom no private or public job is available and whose income falls below yet to be established levels. Jobs Program—all those required to work and whose income falls below yet to be established levels.
Work Requirement and/or Incentives	Varies depending on program RTC—work requirement not applicable. Housing—same as in current food stamp law. Food Stamps—same as in current food stamp law.	Two-parent families with children, possibly single-parent families with older children and other adults who are not aged, blind or disabled will be required to work. Special income disregards and tax rates will provide incentives to seek private sector employment.
Benefits	RTC—personal refundable tax credit of $200 disbursed quarterly. Housing Allowance—100% of fair market rent for standard housing—generally between $1320 and $3600 per year for a family of four with no other income —paid in cash. Food Stamps—same as current system with elimination of purchase requirement. AFDC—benefit levels determined by States. No national minimums.	Consolidated cash payment—replaces AFDC, SSI and Food Stamps. Amount of benefits varies according to family size and source of other income. Jobs—attempts will be made to provide public service employment or training, if no private sector job can be located. RTC—current RTC continued for all families with children.
Role of Federal, State, Local Governments	Federal: IRS & Treasury administrator RTC, 100% federally financed; HUD supervises state welfare agencies' administration of Housing Allowance financed from general revenue; same role as currently fulfilled in AFDC, SSI, Food Stamps. State: Continue basic state administration and current funding responsibility of AFDC; add administration of Housing Allowance.	Federal: Financing of minimum benefit and jobs program. Administration of consolidated cash program. State: Unclear. Local: Administration of jobs program.

Strategy	*Multiple Program Strategy*	*Carter Administration (to date)*
Role of Federal, State, Local Governments *(cont.)*	Local: Housing authorities assist in enforcement of fair market rent and standard housing stipulations.	
Linkage With Other Income Maintenance Programs	AFDC + SSI—count RTC as income and apply a 100% reduction rate. Housing Allowance and food stamps—neither program counts benefits of other as income, but both count RTC, AFDC and SSI as income; Housing Allowance replaces most current housing assistance programs. AFDC—treatment of Housing Allowance depends on state policy; rules for income and benefit computation would be standardized nationally.	AFDC, Food stamps and SSI consolidated into single cash payment. Medicaid—not specified.
Linkage with Social Service Programs	Not addressed	Not specified—Jobs program has implication for Day Care and other employment-related social services.
Comments	Cost—$12–16 billion Equity—some question about equity for childless couple. Adequacy—little change for present recipients; substantial increase in benefits for individuals and families not receiving AFDC. Administration—complexity is increased by addition of RTC & Housing Allowance. Fiscal Relief—RTC provides some fiscal relief to states.	Cost—no initial increase in cost, ($24.9 billion) Equity—reduces disparities between state benefits and between one and two parent families. Adequacy—unclear. Administration—administrative simplicity is a stated goal, complex benefit structure. Fiscal relief—minimal.

Triple Track	*National Governors Conference (Major Incremental)*	*Income Security for Americans (The Griffiths Proposal for Negative Income Tax)*
General		
Definition and treatment of low-income population according to three categories: (1) "working" poor (2) households with adult	Incremental approach using existing program and administrative structures to ultimately achieve universal coverage of all	A negative income tax approach to assistance providing for major changes in Federal tax structure and considerable tax relief and

Triple Track	*National Governors Conference (Major Incremental)*	*Income Security for Americans (The Griffiths Proposal for Negative Income Tax)*
General *(cont.)*		
expected to work but who does not have a job (3) households in which no adult is expected to work outside the home. Department of Labor and tax system provide support to unemployed and working poor.	low income persons. First steps are to mandate AFDC-UF (Unemployed Father) and eliminate purchase requirement for food stamps. (States given option to cash out).	consolidation of existing programs.
Coverage		
Categorical strategy with universal coverage of households without regard to family composition.	Uniform coverage of all eligible persons below an established income level; No distinction made between one and two parent families; Filing unit is the nuclear family. Phasing: 1st step—extended AFDC/AFDC-UF to all low income families. 2nd step—extend to all single persons and childless couples.	Universal coverage without regard to family structure.
Eligibility		
Working Poor—all extended families with at least one employed adult member and income below a fixed ceiling. Manpower—all extended families with an unemployed adult expected to work and an income below 150% of poverty line. Cash—single parent families with child under 12; caretakers of incapacitated or disabled adult; temporarily disabled.	Universal eligibility for income eligible families with children determined by application of nationally uniform eligibility standards. Accounting period not specified. Countable income: 70% earnings after $100/month disregard; 100% on other income after $20/month disregard.	Based solely on income determination relative to established national minimum standard.
Work Requirement		
Working Poor—no work requirement; Manpower—Refusal to accept a bona fide job offer after 30 days in program results in removal from track and loss of benefits; Cash—no work requirement.	All employable recipients are required to work or participate in a "work stimulation and training program." Refusal to accept a job paying the minimum wage would result in discontinuation of assistance.	No work requirement. Work incentive is offered through a 50% tax rate on earned income, as opposed to higher tax rates on other forms of assistance, and a proportional work expenses deduction.

Triple Track	*National Governors Conference (Major Incremental)*	*Income Security for Americans (The Griffiths Proposal for Negative Income Tax)*
Work Requirement *(cont.)*	Marginal tax rate: 70% in AFDC; 79% in AFDC plus food stamps. Flat dollar deduction for work expenses of $100 per month exclusive of child care costs. Each state would be required to develop such a program subject to federal review and compliance with minimum requirements—block grant.	
Benefits Working Poor—EITC varied according to family size and phased out at $12,000. Food stamps, increased minimum wage. Manpower—Placement assistance for a private sector job. Training or vocational education services. Placement in Public Service Employment job. Special Unemployment Assistance Benefit (two variations). Food stamps. Cash—National minimum benefit beginning at 75% of poverty level and phased into 100%. Unearned income taxed at 100% after small exemption. Food stamps cashed out.	Federal benefit floor set at $200/month for a family of four with state supplementation encouraged. Except for minimum, benefit levels determined by states.	Refundable tax credit of $225 per individual in all four-person tax paying units with income less than $23,500. Allowance for Basic Living Expenses (ABLE)—nationally uniform grant to qualified low income families and individuals; benefit level varies according to family type. Benefit reduction rate varies in relation to source of income ranging from 50% tax rate on earned income to a 100% tax rate on veterans' pensions and farm subsidies.
Government Role Federal: Financing and administration of programs to working poor; financing of manpower tract, expanded role for Department of Labor and tax system; federal and state financing of welfare tract; option of either federal or state administration. State: Partial funding of welfare tract; administration of manpower tract. Local: Varies according to state structure.	*Federal Participation Rate* Minimum grant—$200 100% $200–300 90% $300–400 50% $400 0% State: state administration, including determination of benefit levels beyond federal minimum.	Entirely federally financed and administered through IRS. (SSI would remain with the Social Security Administration).

Triple Track	*National Governors Conference (Major Incremental)*	*Income Security for Americans (The Griffiths Proposal for Negative Income Tax)*
Linkages (Financial)		
AFDC—Federally funded with minimum benefits set at 75% of poverty line initially. Coverage expanded to families not currently covered by AFDC-UF and general assistance. Food stamps—cashed out for welfare tract, and retained for manpower working poor with elimination of purchase requirement. SSI—Retained with mandate to maintain current benefit levels. Medicaid—Retained with revisions.	AFDC—Reformed to offer universal coverage of children and parents regardless of family composition. SSI—Retained as a separate program. Food Stamps—Continued but purchase requirement dropped —state option to cash out. Relocate to same administrating structure as income maintenance.	AFDC—Eliminated. SSI—Retained but somewhat altered. Food Stamps—Eliminated, replaced by ABLE. Medicaid—Not specified.
Linkages (Social Services)		
Proposal does stipulate the provision of child care and other services for all tracks but does not specify relationship or impact on current programs.	Options for handling child care costs: 1) Expansion of current Title XX funding earmarked for child care expenses associated with employment. 2) Creation of new title exclusively devoted to day care/child care costs and programs.	Not specified, but since program does not have a work requirement, it does not impose any undue burden on social services for the provision of day care and other work related services.
Comments		
Net federal cost—$11–16 billion; Equity—Reduces inequities among family types. Fiscal Relief—Substantial fiscal relief to states and localities. Adequacy—Only program with built-in escalation of benefit to poverty level; Administration—Complex, multiplies number of agencies a client must deal with.	Estimate Cost—federal net increases $10 billion. Equity—Reduces cross state disparities in benefits and inequities between one & two parent families. Adequacy—Benefit below poverty line. Administration—Maintains present structure Fiscal Relief—Substantial fiscal belief but varies with respect to level of state supplement.	Net Federal Cost Increase (in 1974 dollars) $12.9 billion. Equity—Program financially rewards the two-parent family. Adequacy—Benefit level substantially higher than present programs. Administration—Single agency. Fiscal Relief—Substantial fiscal relief.

The other area of coming change that relates to financial well-being is health insurance. Existing health insurance is private, with the exception of Medicare and Medicaid, which are available to those over 65 or those in financial need. Everyone else has private health insurance if they have any at all, and many people do not. The rapidly rising cost of health care makes serious illness a major financial threat for those without insurance. Even those who have insurance are endangered if the illness is major, because all existing health plans have limits to the amount and duration of payments. Most proposals for national health insurance seek to provide for basic and catastrophic coverage while simultaneously controlling costs. Because costs are controlled by the medical professions, the American Medical Association resists national health insurance proposals other than its own, fearing that professional autonomy will be lost if the other plans are implemented. The AMA claims that reduced autonomy will lower the supply and quality of medical personnel (and therefore health care) because financial and other incentives will be lessened, and it points to countries like England, in which national health insurance has had problems of adequacy of personnel, facilities, and patient satisfaction. On the other hand, costs continue to escalate beyond the reach of many people, thereby effectively reducing their access to health care. Some of the major proposals to deal with these issues are summarized in Exhibit 9-2.

Major National Health Insurance Proposals **EXHIBIT 9-2**

The following chart summarizes two of the major proposals for national health insurance. As with welfare reform, the strategies ultimately incorporated into national health insurance legislation cannot be predicted at the time of this writing, but the issues will no doubt remain the same.

	AMA (American Medical Association) H.R. 1818 Rep. Carter / S. 218 Sen. Hansen
GENERAL APPROACH	AMA would rely heavily on federal subsidies—tax credits and tax deductions—which, hidden to most taxpayers, would be added to tax bills. Subsidies would encourage purchases of private health insurance—under four separate plans having the same minimum benefit package. AMA would have

Source: Excerpted from a chart prepared by Professor Tom Fulton of the University of Missouri for the National Association of Social Workers and printed in *NASW News*, November 1977, pp. 12–13 (references are omitted in these excerpts and italics are added).

	AMA (American Medical Association) H.R. 1818 — Rep. Carter S. 218 — Sen. Hansen
GENERAL APPROACH *(cont.)*	federal responsibilities (for federal dollars and NHI results) filtered through state agencies. States would contract NHI administration out to private organizations affiliated with the health industry.
I. Coverage People covered Benefits covered Benefit package Catastrophic expense Preventive Mental health Long-term care Social work services Geographic coverage	People covered: Private health insurance "available" to everyone; actual AMA coverage 213 of 231 million (1980), leaving 3½ million with no insurance. Benefits covered: called "comprehensive," AMA would be more so than HIAA, less so than Health Security. Services "customarily furnished" but otherwise unlimited are: ▶ inpatient care in a general, psychiatric, or TB hospital; ▶ outpatient and emergency services; home health services; ▶ medical care provided by a physician, including preventive; ▶ dental care, children, age 2–6; emergency dental care for all. Limited (100 days): nursing facility care. Excluded: Rx drugs, eyeglasses, hearing aids. Catastrophic expense: income-related, maximum $2000 per year per family. *Social work services: not mentioned.*
II. Financing Progressivity Total cost; how we pay Taxes; hidden costs Premiums Deductibles, copayments Linkage of cost to quality	This bill would require the federal government to subsidize private health insurance and pay nearly all costs for low-income families. ▶ Subsidies would total $26 billion per year by 1980. Much would be hidden costs, including $5 billion in cash subsidies to employers. ▶ This financing by private insurance premiums is highly regressive. The 20% copayments are flat-rate, thus also regressive. ▶ Financing would not be used to improve the quality, distribution and cost effectiveness of health services.
III. Single Plan? Unified plan for all? No separate plan for poor? Means test?	AMA would have four separate plans for the purchase of health insurance from private carriers (1) for employees; (2) for the self-employed and nonemployed; (3) for some unemployed; and (4) for the aged and disabled, to supplement Medicare. All plans would provide the same benefits.

	AMA (American Medical Association) H.R. 1818 — S. 218 Rep. Carter — Sen. Hansen
III. Single Plan? *(cont.)*	▶ Separate plans would create negative impacts on health care. ▶ The AMA Means Test is notable. Based on federal income tax liability, it is universal and probably nonstigmatizing. However, the AMA use of it (a minute scale of 1% reduction for each $10 tax paid) is picayunish when compared with other federal subsidies, e.g., to employers.
IV. Federal Role Responsibility, accountability Intermediaries? Payment methods Cost-containment Administration of NHI Change in health system?	The federal role would be severely restricted. AMA has asked the government to tie its own hands, requiring itself to: ▶ subsidize the private health industry heavily ($26 billion); ▶ relinquish to private carriers nearly all controls of cost; ▶ continue methods of payment to providers similar to those for Medicare and Medicaid, which encourage, rather than restrain, cost inflation; ▶ omit any linkage between its funding and improvement in quality and distribution of health care resources and personnel; ▶ set nationwide minimum uniform private health insurance benefits as a basis for the AMA plan; and ▶ set up a physician-dominated Health Insurance Board to make "necessary" regulations and to set standards "for use by" state insurance departments.
V. Roles of Cooperating Organizations States Health care industry Consumer Social work policy role	States would have the important responsibility to determine whether carriers would be "qualified" to provide "qualified" standard minimum insurance, within any "necessary" regulations of the national board. Under AMA, the private health industry, with $26 billion in open-ended federal subsidies, would have prosperity, growth, and greatly expanded power to escalate inflation. Carriers would determine payments to providers, even procedures for auditing expenditures. Consumers (undefined) would be "consulted" along with carriers and providers in planning "any necessary" program to "maintain" quality. *Social work is not mentioned in the bill;* administration would be held within the health care industry.

	AMA (American Medical Association) H.R. 1818 — Rep. Carter S. 218 — Sen. Hansen
VI. Impact of the Proposal on Health Care Resources development Distribution of resources Alternate forms of delivery Quality assurance	*(Analyst's judgment)* This bill—by adding high inputs of federal money without commensurate government responsibility to assure quality care at reasonable cost—would build on the weaknesses of the health care system instead of its strengths. The bottom-line goal of the health industry is, understandably, profit and growth, and power to assure new profit and growth. The goal of government—to assure consumer and taxpayer concern for good health care actually available to everyone and costs distributed equitably—is needed as a countervailing force in NHI. The AMA bill does not provide this balance.
VII. Effects on Other Government Programs	Health programs for federal, state, and local government employees would be absorbed into the AMA employee plan for private insurance. Medicare would continue and be supplemented so as to equal benefits.
VIII. Phase-In	Dental care for children 7 through 17 years of age would be phased in over a 12-year period.

S.-3 Health Security H.R.-22 Rep. Corman	NHI for Mothers and Children S.370 Senators Javits, Cranston, Brooke and Humphrey
Coverage Truly comprehensive, single-plan health care system, financed/administered by Social Security to guarantee every American nearly entire range of health services as a right. "Working partnership," public and private elements. Goal is to eliminate financial/geographic barriers: no coinsurance, no deductions, no costly degrading means test. Built-in health resources development, quality assurance and cost containment. Castastrophic coverage explicit.	Like Medicare, this is partial NHI. It would provide comprehensive services to all children, and full maternal health services to women. Financing: wholly federal by social security payroll taxes and general revenues. Largely prepaid: no deductibles. No means test for eligibility. Federal responsibility for funds, and outcomes could be largely delegated to private organizations. Special provisions would reduce geographic and racial barriers to access, and would encourage "comprehensive maternal and child health practice."
People covered: Every resident of the United States—whether working, laid-off, not working, or retired—entitled to benefits as a matter of right. Benefits covered: Almost entire range of medically necessary personal health services,	People covered: All children under 18, and all pregnant women citizens. "Special population" benefits (transportation, care of dependents, and "social outreach assistance") for people in health manpower shortage areas, or who suffer high

S.-3 Health Security H.R.-22 Rep. Corman	NHI for Mothers and Children S.370 Senators Javits, Cranston, Brooke and Humphrey
including preventive and health maintenance services, castastrophic illnesses, full hospital and physician services, optometry, and podiatry. Most services as needed, without limit. Limited: dental care to age 15; private psychiatrist consultations, 20 per benefit period (BP); skilled nursing facility, 120 days per BP. *Social work services: covered only when on behalf of institutional provider and when paid by salary, stipend, or capitation.* Geographic coverage: Strong provisions for resources development and distribution would ultimately make all needed services available in practically all localities.	maternity/infancy risks due to poverty, discrimination, or cultural barriers. Health benefits covered. Except for some exclusions and limits, benefits are comprehensive, covering the range of preventive, remedial and rehabilitative care for children; and full maternity care for women (including full professional services and emergency hospital care for diagnosis and treatment of pregnancy and for injury or disease during pregnancy and 12 weeks thereafter). *Social work and mental health services for children are specifically included if provided in a public or nonprofit facility.* Limit: 60 days per year, each patient. Geographic Coverage: entire United States.
Financing Health Security would be financed by payroll taxes, federal general revenues, and a special health tax on unearned income. Sometimes Health Security is labeled the most expensive plan, but it is not: ▶ The total cost of health care under Health Security, AMA, would be nearly the same in 1981; but Health Security would then provide $12 billion more in health services than the others, and would restrain inflation much more effectively; ▶ Health Security would reduce hidden costs markedly more than the others. ▶ No one would pay hospital, doctor, or any other health bills.	Except for minor funding by copayments, financing would be wholly federal-half by payroll taxes, half from general revenues. Employers, employees, and self-employeds would each pay 1/10 of 1% of total earnings. This new feature—no limit on earnings taxed—would result in mildly progressive overall financing, when combined with mildly progressive general revenues. Hidden costs, in the form of income tax deductions for payroll taxes, would be increased. Copayments of 10% for some services (zero for other services and for families under the poverty line or receiving Medicaid) are comparatively modest, but would require a means test and would create hardship for many among the working poor. Financing is linked to improved facilities and quality.
Single Plan ▶ Health Security would set up a single, unified, universal NHI system. There would be no separate plan for the poor, no categories for any group, no degrading means test. ▶ Studies show that this single plan would save administrative costs, increase access to care, undergird improvements in the health care system, and provide the needed leverage for effective cost-controls. It would markedly reduce consumer confusion.	This NHI plan for mothers and children is, like Medicare, in the middle between the single universal plan for everyone and the loose group of separate plans. It would be a universal plan for part of the population. As such it has the advantages of unified national financing and no means test for eligibility. On the other hand, it would be in fact a separate plan, with complex, costly boundaries between itself and Medicare, Medicaid, existing maternal and child health services, etc. In its favor, the categories of this plan and Medicare are stable ones: there would be no frequent transfers due to age or diagnosis, as would be due to employment and income categories in AMA and HIAA.

S.-3 Health Security H.R.-22 Rep. Corman	NHI for Mothers and Children S.370 Senators Javits, Cranston, Brooke and Humphrey
Federal Role	
Under Health Security, the federal government would exert full responsibility for operations of NHI and full accountability for taxpayer money. It would do so through a Health Security Board, regional offices, local offices, advisory councils, consumer input, collaboration with states, and provision for appeals. Payments would be negotiated through annual budgets in advance, rather than retrospective as at present, for participating providers (both practitioners and institutional). Importantly, the payment would constitute payment in full: the participating provider could not charge more. The Congressional Budget Office states that a single NHI program covering the entire population (such as Health Security) could offer the greatest potential for controlling health costs.	The federal role would be to establish the plan, set guidelines and collect finances, then turn over to private provider organizations (intermediaries) some or all of the operations which are critical to cost-control and quality assurance (for example, determining amounts of payment, disbursing open-ended federal funds, making audits and determining whether services charged were necessary and actually delivered). Here, this bill is very similar to Medicare; and it would perpetuate and extend the vital weakness of Medicare—to delegate to private groups, federal functions critical to federal responsibilities. Provider charges would be set in advance (prospectively) and payments would constitute payment in full; but an important feature of cost-containment is missing, i.e., prospective budgeting.
Roles of Other Organizations	
States would have important functions: ▶ Collaboration with federal on health planning, health education; ▶ Responsibilities for licensing, professional training; ▶ By agreement to investigate whether providers meet requirements; The health care industry would enjoy prosperity and growth, but fewer windfall profits; private health insurance would supplement benefits. Consumers: "Persons who are representative of consumers" would be a majority on the National Advisory Council and on regional and local advisory councils. Their qualifications are stated: ▶ No financial interest in providing health services; ▶ Familiarity with the needs for personal health services; ▶ Experience with problems of furnishing such services; *Social work is not recognized for policy roles.*	State agencies are to be consulted, along with other groups, on the qualifications of hospital obstetric units, nursing homes, and home health agencies. Determining whether such institutions meet the qualifications could be delegated to states. Health Industry: The bill gives broad authority to USDHEW to provide assistance for malpractice reinsurance. Consumers: Persons "exceptionally well qualified as representatives of consumers of MCH (Maternal and Child Health) care services" and "having no financial interest in the furnishing of any health services" would be among a majority of nonprovider members on the National Maternal and Child Health Council. This group would study, recommend, and advise on the operation of the plan. *Social work policy input: not mentioned in the bill.*
Impact	
(*Analyst's judgment*) Health Security is decidedly more promising than AMA bill for a positive impact toward quality care for everyone at	(*Analyst's judgment*). If a patchwork rather than a complete NHI approach is deemed necessary, this Mothers and Children proposal, if without inter-

S.-3 Health Security H.R.-22 Rep. Corman	NHI for Mothers and Children S.370 Senators Javits, Cranston, Brooke and Humphrey
reasonable cost, equitably financed and distributed. Notably, two special provisions in the bill would reinforce the thrust toward that goal: ▶ A development fund to alleviate shortages of health resources; ▶ A Commission on Quality of Health Care, with authority to develop and promote standards for high quality care over the nation.	mediaries, would be a sound approach and would serve millions in high-priority groups. ▶ Payroll tax on all earnings is innovative, increases progressivity. ▶ Special outreach to high-risk and underserved people is innovative. ▶ The proposed Maternal and Child Health Practice, with funding, could become a major effective alternative form of service delivery.
Effects on Other Programs	
Medicare: supplanted. Medicaid would remain only to supplement Health Security and, at state option, provide long-term nursing home care, certain drugs, and adult dental care. Unaffected: Veterans Administration, military health services, WC.	This plan would take over from Medicaid, Medicare and the current Maternal and Child Health program all personal maternal and child health services now financed by those programs.
Phase-In	
No phase-in. Health Security would become effective as a whole at one time, but with expectations of growth in areas not covered, e.g., dental care for all ages, long-term care, and distribution of services to underserved areas.	Taxes would begin 1 January after enactment. Children's benefits would be phased in through ages 6, 12, and 17 at 2, 3, and 4 years, respectively after enactment. Special population benefits would begin at enactment, and maternal benefits two years later. All other provisions would be effective at enactment.

The Provision of Social Services ◀

Meeting people's financial needs is basic to their security, but it does not necessarily insure a satisfying level of social functioning. A society that truly meets the needs of its members must help them to function effectively in the wide range of personal and interpersonal behaviors that comprise a complex, industrial society. Whereas financial security has increasingly been delegated to the public social welfare network, social services continue to be provided both publicly and privately. Certain types of social services have been traditional—child welfare services, such as adoption, foster care, and protective care; vocational rehabilitation; physical therapy; personal and psychiatric counseling; recreational services; marriage and family counseling, and many others. In Exhibit 8-2 the separation of social services from financial services in public assistance was described, and it represents one current attempt to emphasize society's responsibility to meet its members' financial and social service needs. The Title XX amendments to the Social Security Act, signed into law in January 1975, operationalize this responsibility even further by providing for a variety of social services to a much wider range of persons than were previously eligible to receive such services in public agencies. Title XX is summarized in Exhibit 9-3.

EXHIBIT 9-3 *The Social Services Amendments of 1974*

The 93rd Congress passed a bill introduced by Senator Mondale, S. 4082, amending the Social Security Act to make social services available to more people. The legislation itself is many pages long, but a summary is presented below. Even this summary is long and complex, illustrating the knowledge needed and the patience required to study and understand important social welfare legislation.

Summary of Social Services Act

I. *Eligibility and Priority for Federally Reimburseable Social Services*

The bill provides special priority for recipients of AFDC and SSI and Medicaid by requiring that 50 percent of the federal social services funds used in a state be for services to such individuals and families.

The bill proposes that federal limitations on states in establishing those in a state eligible for federally assisted social services relate to the income of the individual or family, and would remove the requirement that recipients be classified as "former or potential welfare recipients." Federal matching for free services is available for people with incomes up to 80 percent of the median family income in a state (or the full national median, now $12,041, if less) adjusted for family size, and services at some fee up to 115 percent of the median income of a state. The $2.5 billion limit on federal payments will continue to apply.

II. *Defining Social Services*

The goals of the program are established as:

1. Achieving or maintaining economic self-support to prevent, reduce, or eliminate dependency.
2. Achieving or maintaining self-sufficiency, including reduction or prevention of dependency.
3. Preventing or remedying neglect, abuse, or exploitation of children and adults unable to protect their own interests, or preserving, rehabilitating, or reuniting families.
4. Preventing or reducing inappropriate institutional care by providing for community-based care, home-based care, or other forms of less intensive care, or
5. Securing referral or admission for institutional care when other forms of care are not appropriate, or providing services to individuals in institutions.

Social services would be defined by the state, required to be directed at the social services

Source: *The Congressional Record,* Vol. 120, No. 149, October 3, 1974.

goals with parameters for such definitions established by: prohibition against funding certain activities; prohibitions against reimbursing certain medical institutions for social services provided to those living in them (but other entities could provide social services to such individuals in such facilities); and, prohibitions against funding child day care not meeting standards. The draft bill also specifically names certain services as examples of social services but it is not intended to be an all inclusive list.

III. *Social Services Program Planning, Reporting, Evaluation, and Auditing*

Establishes new requirements for a state to conduct a program planning process to determine the services to be provided and who is to receive such services with primary emphasis on involvement by the citizens of a state. The Governor or such other officials as the laws of the state provide is responsible for publishing the services plan for comment and approving the final services plan for the program year. The state is also required to conduct evaluations and provide required reports to HEW and the public.

Ninety days after the end of the services program year an "annual social services program report" is approved by the Governor or other official designated under state law describing the services provided during the past year.

IV. *"State Plan" Subject to Prior Approval by HEW*

The state would submit for HEW approval prior to the beginning of the services program year a document which is still called a "State Plan." It would deal with state assurances regarding: fair hearings, confidentiality of information; designation of a single agency other than the Governor to supervise the administration of the state's social services program; no durational residency or citizenship requirement; and designation of state authorities for establishing and maintaining standards.

V. *Maintenance of Effort and Matching Provisions*

The bill establishes a maintenance of effort requirement for states which requires that the nonfederal share of its aggregate expenditures for the provisions of services during each services program year are not less than the aggregate expenditures for the provisions of those services during fiscal year 1973 to 1974 (whichever is less) with respect to which payment was made under the Social Security Act. The Governor is also to provide to the citizens of the state comparison of nonfederal expenditures between services program years.

Percentage of matching is not changed from present law, i.e.: 75 percent for all services except 90 percent for family planning services; 75 percent for training and retraining.

State matching may be in cash or in-kind by the state including provisions to the state by its political subdivisions. Private funds donated to the state are allowed to be utilized for nonfederal match but with certain restrictions.

VI. *Federal Evaluation, Research and Demonstrations, Program Assistance, and HEW Reports to Congress*

HEW is authorized to grant waivers under the proposed new Title XX for Social Services to any state now under the various titles of the Social Security Act and provide reports to Congress on the results of such research and demonstration programs.

[HEW] is also to provide to Congress prior to July 1, 1977 a report on the effectiveness of the social services program along with recommendations for improvements.

VII. *Effective Date of Regulations Published by the Secretary of HEW*

No final federal regulations for the program would be effective in a services program year for a state if the regulations are published within 60 days of the beginning of the state's services program year.

An issue of some importance in the provision of social services is the future of private social services. Title XX provides for cooperation between private and public agencies. As noted in Chapter 1, private agencies have increasingly contracted with public agencies to provide social services. Also previously mentioned is the leveling off of contributions to United Way campaigns, of necessity reducing the funds available to private agencies. It is reasonable to expect that private agencies will increasingly develop cooperative arrangements with public agencies so that the resources of each can be used to develop an effective network of comprehensive social welfare services. Social services are inherently more complicated than financial services, because they depend on an understanding of human behavior and effective mechanisms to change them when necessary. Meeting people's financial needs may encounter value obstacles and may become enmeshed in technical questions of how best to achieve a certain financial objective. However, it is a much less complex problem than changing human behavior. Therefore, part of the future of social services lies in the future ability of social welfare professions to find more effective ways of understanding and changing human behavior.

▶ The Future of the Social Welfare Professions

Obviously the social welfare institution is shaped by policy decisions made in political structures and in private agency board rooms. Yet the social welfare professions themselves also have a significant impact on the structure of social welfare. They train their members and develop standards to evaluate their work. They develop and support values that they seek to implement in the larger societal decision-making arena. They provide the daily, concrete social welfare services in ways that either help or do not help those in need. They interact with other social institutions and nonwelfare professionals to generate support for their goals. In a complex, competitive society, the social welfare professions are responsible for fighting for more adequate attainment of social welfare objectives. In order to carry out all of these functions, the social welfare professions themselves must be strong and must have clearly defined objectives and methods. The future of social welfare includes the future of the social welfare professions, and there are several issues that can be identified in trying to foresee the future of these professions.

The Changing Models of Professionalism

In the past, increasing professionalism was thought to lead to better professional service, but that assumption is now being questioned.[5] Professions have always claimed the right to be relatively autonomous. Working from the assumption that they were dedicated to public service, they claimed the right to formalize their own values, to identify their own objectives based on these values, to codify a specialized knowledge base, and to translate this knowledge into specialized practice principles and techniques. This emphasized the profession as self-monitoring, thereby protecting it from intervention by outsiders not oriented toward public service, or not knowledgeable about the complexities of providing helping services. By creating a group of cohesive, organized professionals, professions could become countervailing forces to work for changes in social policy that would improve the quality of life for America's citizens. The American Medical Association is often used as a model professional organization—strong, politically active, and effective in controlling standards of medical training and practice.

Against these advantages, some significant disadvantages of the professional model must be weighed. Highly organized professions can become elite groups with the power to protect their own interests. The same countervailing power than can be used to fight for needed social change can also be used to resist it if it threatens the profession's power. The American Medical Association has been heavily criticized for resisting national health insurance, for example. The Association argues that it will reduce the quality of medical service. Others argue that it may weaken the Association's power over what is currently a virtual medical monopoly, thereby improving service but weakening the organization. The point is that professional power can be used in many ways. If the assumption of public service turns out to be incorrect, professional power may be used to generate or perpetuate professional and personal privilege rather than improved social welfare services. Even the assumption of a public-service function has been questioned. Who should have the right to decide what is "public service"? Should a public assistance recipient decide what services he or she needs, or should a skilled professional make that decision? Should the medical profession decide that life should always be preserved as long as possible, or should each individual decide that for oneself? Should psychiatrists decide when a person is mentally healthy, or should the individual have some say in that determination? The power vested in professions to make very important decisions about what people ought or ought not do, what services ought or ought not be available, what groups should receive services or should be excluded, obviously affects the access that people have to social welfare services. If powerful professions are trying to protect themselves rather than concentrating at all times on service to the public, then their right to make these decisions should be questioned.

Even the professional's right to select knowledge and develop interventive methods based on that knowledge has been questioned. Some would question the validity of social science as a basis for understanding human behavior, for example. Movies portraying scientifically grounded behavior modification as an uncontrollable monster with inhuman effects raise this point. Being objective in dealing with people's problems has also been criticized as a dehumanizing approach to helping. Providing helping services in large, centralized bureaucratic settings has generated resistance and resentment. Most important of all, accusations have been made that social welfare professions simply attempt to control people so that they will accept the existing social system, rather than attempting to change the system itself so that it is more responsive to human needs.[6] Here again, professional autonomy is at issue. Should people participate in decisions about the kinds of service they are to receive? Should there be free clinics and neighborhood service centers rather than huge, isolated service structures? Should social welfare professionals be avowedly in the business of societal reform? Who does control the social welfare professions, and whose interests do they really represent? Exhibit 9-4 illustrates some of these issues.

EXHIBIT 9-4 *Kick, Kill, or Cure*

Moral issues related to trying to help others have been and will continue to be important in the social welfare professions. They are closely tied to the knowledge available for use in understanding behavior and developing change strategies—knowledge shapes moral values and vice versa. Social welfare professionals cannot be totally blamed for the effects that the imposition of moral values have on people, because they act within social standards as do most others in a society. Yet helping people do have a special responsibility to respect and understand diverse behaviors beyond that of nonprofessionals; it is part of their advocacy for others. This will become an increasingly important but difficult task in the future as our society struggles with attempts to guarantee social justice and human rights for all people as well as the backlash that such efforts seem to produce. The following account of a homosexual man's treatment illustrates the difficulties social welfare professionals face in meeting these challenges—it also illustrates why such efforts are so important.

Thanks to the gay liberation movement and the confidence and courage it has inspired, there is more of the "live and let live" attitude to homosexuals these days than there is of the old "kick, kill, or cure."

But it's important to remember that not long ago (and perhaps even today) the importance of being a "healthy heterosexual" was so great that some homosexuals sought a "cure" and some psychiatrists* reckoned they could do the job. . . .

The Programme of Treatment

The treatment consisted of two five-day sessions of drug therapy separated by nearly three months, and one out-patient session of electric shock therapy.

Source: Excerpted from Ralph Knowles, "Kick, Kill, or Cure," *Aequus*, May 1976 (Gay Liberation Front, Christchurch, New Zealand), pp. 10–12.

* The American Psychiatric Association no longer considers homosexuality an illness, although psychiatrists still treat homosexuals. Most do not use the aversion therapy described here.

The idea is to put the patient off his "antisocial" ways by "conditioning" him. This involves encouraging him to think about men and sex while making him violently sick, so that subconsciously his mind will connect homosexual activities with feeling ill and, therefore, avoid them.

First Drug Therapy Session

The stimulus used was erotic pictures provided by me and a tape recording based on incidents I had related. The tape began in a calm, neutral fashion, then concentrated on disgust and revulsion ending with the triumphant announcement that I was feeling sick—which was not surprising since at each session I was given an injection of a nausea-producing drug together with a measure of whiskey just to help things along. The combination certainly worked, as I was violently ill on every occasion—though I suspect they had to use increasingly large doses to produce the desired effect.

If you've ever been sick time and time again through the night until you can only dry retch and drool all over your clothes, you'll have some idea of what it's like.

I presume the conditions were usual—the room was bare of ornaments and colour, and the window was blacked out. No clean clothes or bed linen. No food. And no visitors other than the administering orderlies and the psychiatrist.

There was a pause of several hours after the first dose because, I gather, my blood pressure dropped dramatically; but, after that these little sessions continued every two hours day and night, with glucose and lime to prevent dehydration every other hour.

After about four days I begged the doctor to stop, but he asked me to continue, and when I eventually agreed, his manner changed and he announced that that was "it"! Apparently my agreement to go on meant that my will had been broken or, at least, that my determination to go through any kind of hell to be "normal" was now sufficiently strong.

The male orderlies suddenly disappeared. I was bathed and given clean pyjamas and linen. Flowers and curtains were provided by attractive female nurses, and my parents and friends were allowed to visit.

The Interim

The months that followed were University holidays during which all my friends, male and female, were away; and a gradually growing feeling of loneliness and desperation led to my spending a night on a coastal ship in port. Any port in a storm, they say, and it had certainly been a rough trip. That night remains in my memory bathed in a golden light (actually, the light came from a little radio in the steward's cabin; but let's go lyrical). I should have felt ill, I should have been disgusted and guilty, but, instead, I felt the relief of being back to normal, my normal.

Second Drug Therapy Session

The doctor didn't share my point of view, and a second session was suggested as a result.

One of the weaknesses of the first session was that it was aimed at deorientation rather than reorientation. The whole purpose was to put me off homosexual encounters, and nothing had been done to spur me on to heterosexual endeavours. It didn't work. The second session was modified accordingly. After it had finished I was given a hormone shot, an alluring heterosexual tape narrated by a husky-voiced woman, and some rather crude nudie picture books (this was before the more attractive *Playboy*-type literature was available).

Electric Shock Therapy

A few weeks later I visited outpatients for a short follow-up session using electric shock. Electrodes were applied to my hand, and when I had conjured up an interesting thought or two I signalled the doctor, who promptly closed the circuit. An electric current running through you does not help sexual daydreaming!

After a number of repeats, the doctor did not close the circuit, but the pictures in my mind vanished nevertheless in expectation of the shock. It is probably true to say that had this treatment continued, volts might have proved more effective than vomiting, and I might have been a sexless wonder today (or even "straight"!!).

However, we didn't persist with the attempt, and in spite of dire warnings about the disasters which lay ahead, I soon began a relationship which has now lasted eleven years . . .

Outcome (Positive)

It would be unfair to finish without making it clear that the experience wasn't all bad. First, I discussed my homosexuality with my parents for the first time on the eve of going into the hospital, and have kept it quietly in the open since, to everyone's obvious advantage. It was, then, the occasion of my "coming out."

And second, after the failure of the treatment I took stock of my situation and came to terms with myself and society calmly and finally, and have since been able to organize my life both in terms of career and relationships on a stable base of honest and welcome acceptance of being gay.

Conclusion

I would certainly never approach a psychiatrist again for similar or related treatment, nor would I advise anyone else to, regardless of how desperately they wanted to "change."

I consider this treatment psychiatrically crude and physically barbaric—not to mention medically ineffective, morally wrong, and socially outrageous.

The programme was outlined clearly to me, and I undertook it voluntarily; but I would be very angry if I learnt that someone more desperate to change, or more confused in his identity, was persuaded or encouraged to undergo it. I am pleased that there are signs that not all the psychiatric profession shares this doctor's views about homosexuality, heterosexuality, and the desirability of being "straight."

The issues are reasonably clear, but the solutions are much less so. The historical development of social welfare has shown that providing helping services to people requires much more than good intentions. It requires training, resources, and societal support. It also requires a commitment to helping, and a set of values that supports this commitment in practice. Professions are structures to provide such training, to obtain and effectively utilize resources, and to develop ways to operationalize commitment effectively. A profession must have some degree of self-protection simply because there are many competing structures in society fighting for the same social resources. The question becomes one of finding a level at which the profession can protect itself and still be open to input from the users of its services. It must not become so preoccupied with its own interests that it becomes disengaged from the needs of those it serves. Some strategies for doing this were discussed in Chapter 3, but the task has only begun.

It is naive to want professions and professional organizations to be totally responsive to users, and to have as their primary mission the reform of society. The professions and their users are much too dependent on society's mandate and resources to be able to challenge directly the existing social structure. However, professional commitment requires a more just society. This suggests that the professionals of the future must be astute political actors, who can work within the existing social structure to utilize available resources, and still find and use opportunities to affect social policy. They must also live their democratic values by involving the users of services in decision making about those services. Yet they must continue to use their specialized training to have their own input into decision making. As has been said many times earlier in this book, the social welfare professional of the future will have to be involved in far more than a peaceful 9-to-5 schedule of client interviews in an office.

Specialization and Integration

Two trends seem to emerge from current thinking about the future of social welfare practice. As noted earlier in this chapter, when looking at the changing shape of society itself, there is an increasing need for integrative kinds of services. Society has become so large and so complex that people can easily be lost within it. At the same time, there are many kinds of services available to help people function more effectively. The problem becomes one of helping people to find the services they need, and to help them understand the procedures necessary to obtain these services. This calls for a general integrative function within social welfare. This function includes many more specific functions, such as outreach, brokerage, mobilization, advocacy, and support. All help to individualize social welfare services. Services exist to be used by people. If they dwarf people, if they are inaccessible to those who need them, or if they are unknown to potential user groups, they are useless.

Kahn and Kamerman conclude, after an extensive study of the social services systems of eight countries, "There also may be evidence of convergence on the need for a 'generalist' practitioner or team at the core of the local service system. The picture remains mixed, but some countries do not see the possibility of a comprehensive and universal program unless there is at the front line, offering the core service, a person or unit with scope and range, not too tied to one intervention strategy or one type of response to need."[7] They go on to define the minimal baseline social services functions that such a generalist worker would perform in the course of serving all population groups:[8]

1. *Giving information and advice and making referrals about all of the social sector (human services, in the broadest sense).*
2. *Giving access to a range of social care services which enable handicapped, frail elderly, and disturbed people to remain in community living under some protection and with needed services and resources.*
3. *Providing front-line counseling, if only on a simple level.*
4. *Coping with emergency daytime, afterhour, weekend needs for housing, food, protection, institutionalization for the vulnerable*

aged, children, the mentally ill, and others—whether directly or by access to other community service personnel.

5. *Carrying out appropriate ongoing treatment, including efforts in individualized, group and residential contexts to bring about changes in adjustment, functioning, view of self or others.*
6. *Providing case integration, assuring that sequential service . . . or work with different family members within the personal-general social services or between programs in different systems . . . is mutually supportive and properly meshed.*

A recent baccalaureate social work curriculum development project in this country (discussed in the preface) reached similar conclusions about the functions of the entry level professional practitioner.[9]

The generalist is well suited to perform integrating functions as described in the previous paragraph, and therefore is a vital member of the professional team. However, as medicine discovered some time ago, there is also a need for specialists to deal with certain kinds of especially difficult and complex problems. Social work education appears to be moving in this direction by beginning to identify two levels of training: generalist training at the bachelor's level, and specialized training at the graduate level. A specialist might deal with something like services to the deaf, in which the ability to sign (that is, use manual symbols in place of speech) must be learned, as well as a great deal of highly technical knowledge about the causes of deafness, levels of deafness, and the relationship between levels of deafness and levels of social functioning. A generalist might assist a specialist in making use of the range of services available to a deaf family in a community (schooling, recreational services, vocational rehabilitation, and so on), and might make contact with significant nondeaf persons such as teachers and neighbors. The specialist would provide the major on-going service to the deaf person or family being helped.

The issue of specialized and integrated services can be related to the earlier discussion of models of professionalism. Service structures that combine generalists and specialists may maximize the professional's specialized training at the same time that it maximizes professional involvement in and awareness of user needs. As generalists seek to identify and develop services to meet needs, and deal with the problems of coordinating many kinds of services in a community, they are sensitized to issues in service delivery and have contact with a range of user groups. They can provide a valuable mechanism for organizing users so that they may have input into professional decision making. At the same time, the specialist draws upon knowledge and skills identified by the profession as appropriate for specific problem areas. Hopefully the specialist is working toward the profession's model of appropriate service, while the generalist is helping users to evaluate that model. While this potential exists, it will not be easy to attain if the relationship between general practitioners and specialists in medicine is indicative of the current ability of professions to utilize these two types of professionals creatively and for maximum benefit of the needy.

Professional Priority-Setting

However the issue of professional autonomy versus user input is resolved, the professions must not lose their ability to affect social policy. The social welfare professions are intimately acquainted with human need and problems in the structures developed to meet those needs. They must constantly provide data to support the need for more adequate services, and participate in the political processes out of which societal decisions emerge. America can become a welfare state in the best sense of that term—a society in which all members have opportunities to develop fully and function effectively, with services available to assist them when needed and desired. It is a basic responsibility of the helping professions to make sure that America's priorities are human priorities. Society's primary function is to provide services and resources for its members. Society must serve, and social welfare professionals must help it to understand and achieve the most effective ways of serving by participating in decision making at the national, state, county, city, and neighborhood levels. Without a societal decision to give priority to social welfare needs, the social welfare professions will not be able to function effectively to achieve their objectives. In this basic sense, the future of social welfare must lie in societal priorities that make comprehensive social welfare services possible. Exhibit 9-5 looks at the form that appropriate priorities might take.

Social Welfare Priorities for the Future **EXHIBIT 9-5**

In looking toward the years ahead, basic general priorities are needed to help us chart our course. This involves the delicate and difficult task of balancing the needs of all segments of a large and diverse society. Different groups in the society quite understandably emphasize different perceived needs and values. The following priorities were developed by social welfare professionals, representing a social welfare perspective on what our goals for the future ought to be. As with any policy issue, trying to decide what *ought* to be frequently generates controversy, and many non–social welfare groups would disagree with the priorities given here.

- Many government and welfare leaders are more aware of, concerned with, and will work harder to solve the problems of balancing economic with social interests. They recognize the astronomical increase in the power of government, as well as large private institutions—power to influence, intentionally

---

Source: John B. Turner, *Development and Participation: Operational Implications for Social Welfare* (1974). Reprinted by permission of the International Council on Social Welfare.

or not, every facet of an individual's life, almost on an hour-to-hour basis.

- More effective welfare programs are not likely to be forthcoming until citizens and politicians alike recognize that structural problems in a society are a major source of family and individual troubles, many of which require public solutions that offer useful incentives to individuals and families.
- Gains in women's rights will continue, particularly in employment and politics. Gains for migrant workers will quicken as the total number of workers is reduced, largely through mechanization of the industry. But many will face unemployment problems elsewhere. Progress for minority groups is harder to predict. It will probably depend on a more disciplined use of the political system. This in turn will depend on developing the internal strength of the minority communities to a far greater degree.
- There will be a much greater effort on the part of regional, state, and local governments to collaborate with each other and to sponsor human services. This development will usher in a greatly expanded era of collaboration among voluntary and governmental agencies.
- How to keep citizens informed on the one hand and provide the opportunities and structures for involvement on the other will continue to be a central issue in social development. Participation will increasingly come to be seen not as a solution, but as one condition for better solutions.
- For a while the unease about the increasing attention given by professions to advocacy vis-à-vis service functions will continue. It may even grow. However, when one remembers that the demand for advocacy is not limited to social work, it seems likely that new, more creative and more effective ways of helping people help themselves—to become their own advocates—will develop across the range of the social professions. Recognition and use of the ombudsmen is likely to grow.
- Professional training and experience are well on the way to routine inclusion of curricular materials on how to involve consumers and citizens, work with paraprofessionals, and work with related disciplines.
- Efforts to develop better research tools and capabilities will expand, and efforts will surely be made to coordinate basic areas of research exploration and development. Even though there is general agreement that government should have a more directive role in supporting research geared to social policy-making, important questions remain: What levels of government should spend the social policy research dollar, and what groups should carry out the research?

Chapter Conclusion

Achieving changes in social values sometimes seems a hopeless task. Although there is no question that the social welfare structure is solidly institutionalized in the United States, this book points out that adequate services are still needed in many areas. Certain basic social values must be changed if these needed services are ever to be feasible. The perspective of history is encouraging. When one thinks of the centuries it took to achieve the breakthrough of the Social Security Act, the lesson is clear—social change is slow and tedious. This country has made progress in social welfare. We do care for others in ways and at levels unthinkable not too many years ago. Yet we as a society still value individualism, discrimination, and laissez-faire capitalism, and these values often conflict with social welfare goals. Any projection that attempts to predict the resolution of this conflict would require a prediction about the future of the society. This is an impossible and perhaps sterile task. What the issue of value change in the future does suggest in a practical way is that all of us citizens will affect the values of the future. Values are made and can be changed. If we as human beings, citizens, and social welfare practitioners believe in certain values, we must fight for their adoption. It is a worthwhile project for the future of each of us.

It always comes down to us. We are society. We are the social welfare system. We are human beings. We make our own decisions. The study of social welfare is so wonderful because it calls to us to assume the responsibility of our human heritage by using ourselves to make the life of everyone better. It involves us totally: our feelings, our values, our ability to think, learn, and reason. It can be a life-encompassing task, or a part of other tasks. But it is there. The future? I hope that here, at the end of this book, the future presents itself to you in a different way from before. I hope that you see it as rich with many opportunities, theoretical and practical. Most of all, I hope you see it as an active challenge to assume the responsibility for making everyone's social welfare a part of your life.

STUDY QUESTIONS

1. Make a list of what you think the major problems facing members of American society will be in the next ten years. For each, list the social welfare services currently available to meet these needs. What areas of need remain unmet, if any? What predictions could you make about the future of the social welfare institution on the basis of this exercise?
2. Consider that the average college student has an active work career of approximately 40 years to look forward to. How do you assess the kinds of changes that seem likely in the social welfare professions over this time span? Does this affect your career planning? Why or why not?
3. Let us assume that circumstances made it impossible for you to enter a social welfare profession as a career. What would be your second choice for a career? How could you work to affect the future of social welfare in that career, and as a citizen of the United States?

REFERENCES

1. Many of the points made here are also dealt with in Edward R. Lowenstein, "Social Work in Postindustrial Society," *Social Work* 18 (November 1973): 40–47.
2. Eveline M. Burns, "Toward Welfare Reform in 1979," *The Socioeconomic Newsletter* (Vol. III, No. 8), September 1978, p. 4.
3. Ibid., pp. 4–5.
4. Ibid., p. 5.

5. Much of this discussion was stimulated by Jeffrey Galper, "Social Work as Conservative Politics," Module 55 (New York: MSS Modular Publications, Inc., 1974), pp. 1–33, especially pp. 3–9.
6. Frances Fox Piven and Richard Cloward, *Regulating the Poor: The Functions of Public Welfare* (New York: Pantheon, 1971).
7. Alfred J. Kahn and Sheila B. Kamerman, *Social Services in International Perspective* (Washington, D.C.: U.S. Government Printing Office, 1976), p. 368.
8. Ibid., p. 369.
9. Betty L. Baer and Ronald Federico, *Educating the Baccalaureate Social Worker* (Cambridge, Mass.: Ballinger Publishing, 1978).

SELECTED READINGS

Anderson, Odin W. *Health Care: Can There be Equity?* New York: John Wiley and Sons, 1972.

Clarke-Stewart, Alison. *Child Care in the Family: A Review of Research and Some Propositions for Policy.* New York: Academic Press, 1978.

Gilbert, Neil, and Specht, Harry. *Dimensions of Social Welfare Policy.* Englewood Cliffs, N.J.: Prentice-Hall, 1974.

Kahn, Alfred J., and Kamerman, Sheila. *Social Services in International Perspective.* Washington, D.C.: U.S. Government Printing Office, 1976.

National Conference on Social Welfare. *The Future for Social Services in the United States.* Columbus, Ohio: National Conference on Social Welfare, 1977.

APPENDIX A:

A Selective List of Federal Income-Maintenance Programs

The complexity and scope of the current United States social welfare service structure is difficult to grasp. Indeed, it is far too elaborate to include in an introductory text such as this one. However, to provide a sense of its massive, overlapping, and fragmented nature, fifty-five of the most important federal programs (of which there are almost 200) that seek to help people improve their economic position are listed alphabetically and briefly described in the pages following. Keep in mind that this is only a *partial* list of *federal* programs. It does not include social services (except as these relate to financial security), nor does it include any exclusively state or local programs, nor any private programs. You can see, therefore, why a complete listing of *all* social welfare programs would be so massive!

After studying this listing, what conclusions can you reach about the scope of social welfare? What groups can you identify as being major beneficiaries of social welfare? How does this listing help you evaluate the welfare myths in Exhibit 2-4?

AID TO FAMILIES WITH DEPENDENT CHILDREN

Social and Rehabilitation Service,
Department of Health, Education and Welfare

Public assistance to cover the minimum costs of food, shelter, clothing, and other items of daily living is provided on behalf of needy dependent children, generally in broken homes. Such children must be deprived of the support of at least one parent by reason of death, desertion, or incapacity. Benefits are paid directly to the children's parents or caretaker relatives in the form of cash, usually without restrictions on its use. Payments are monthly or semimonthly, in amounts varying according to each family's countable income and needs, as determined under state law. Benefits are funded by formula grants to state welfare agencies. Each state contributes from 17 to 50 percent of assistance costs, depending on its relative per capita income, as well as 50 percent of administrative costs. Each month, on the average, over 10 million recipients in over three million families are aided. Benefits are conditioned on need.

Authorization: Title IV of the Social Security Act, as amended, 42 USC 602 *et seq.*, 1301 *et seq.*
Budget Code: 75-0581-0-1-999
Catalog Code: 13.761
FY77 Expenditure (est.): **$5,718 million.** Includes over 10 percent for state and local administration and other support.

Source: Excerpted from William Lawrence and Stephen Leeds, *An Inventory of Federal Income Transfer Programs* (White Plains, N.Y.: The Institute for Socioeconomic Studies, 1978), pp. 20–205.

AID TO FAMILIES WITH DEPENDENT CHILDREN—UNEMPLOYED FATHER

Social and Rehabilitation Service,
Department of Health, Education and Welfare

Public assistance to cover the minimum costs of food, shelter, clothing, and other items of daily living is provided on behalf of needy dependent children in intact families. Such a child must be deprived of the support of his or her father by virtue of his unemployment. The father must meet certain requirements regarding past work history and must be at least partially unemployed. Benefits are directly paid to the children's parents in the form of cash, usually without restrictions on its use. Payments are monthly or semimonthly, in amounts varying according to each family's countable income and needs, as determined under state law. (Only half the states have elected to operate this program.) Benefits are funded by formula grants to state welfare agencies; and each state contributes from 17 to 50 percent of assistance costs, depending on its relative per capita income, as well as 50 percent of administrative costs. Each month, on the average, about 700,000 recipients in 150,000 families are aided. Benefits are conditioned on need.

Authorization: Title IV of the Social Security Act, as amended, 42 USC 602 *et seq.*, 1301 *et seq.*
Budget Code: 75-0581-0-1-999
Catalog Code: 13.761
FY77 Expenditure (est.): **$400 million.** Includes over 10 percent for state and local administration and other support.

ALCOHOL COMMUNITY SERVICE PROGRAMS

Alcohol, Drug Abuse, and
Mental Health Administration,
Department of Health, Education and Welfare

Alcoholics and problem drinkers are provided inpatient, outpatient, residential, emergency and after-care services in community-based facilities. Benefits are in kind, funded by grants to community mental health centers, their affiliates and other nonprofit agencies. Staffing grants meet a portion of the compensation costs of professional and technical staff in the initial operation of the facility. The federal matching percentage is somewhat higher in poverty areas, but the percentage in all areas decreases with each succeeding year. About 50 programs are to be supported this year. Although open to the general public in the catchment area, benefits are conditioned, in part, on need, because of a sliding-scale fee schedule based on family income.

Authorization: Part A, Section 203(e) of the Community Mental Health Centers Amendments of 1975, PL94-63, PL94-371.
Budget Code: 75-1361-0-1-550
Catalog Code: 13.251
FY77 Expenditure (est.): **$56 million.**

BASIC EDUCATIONAL OPPORTUNITY GRANTS

Office of Education,
Department of Health, Education and Welfare

Undergraduate students, enrolled at least on a half-time basis at public or private, nonprofit institutions of postsecondary education, are provided financial aid not exceeding one half of their needs, for as many as four years. Grant levels are determined according to the cost of education, as well as on the basis of student and family contribution schedules. Benefits are in the form of cash, funded through the institutions acting as disbursing agents. About two million students receive grants averaging close to $900 yearly. Benefits are conditioned on need and satisfactory continuance of education.

Authorization: Section 411 of the Higher Education Amendments of 1972, PL92-318, 20 USC 1070a.
Budget Code: 75-0293-0-1-502
Catalog Code: 13.539
FY77 Expenditure (est.): **$1,461 million.**

COMMUNITY ACTION

Community Services Administration

Low-income persons are provided a wide variety of services, planned and coordinated with local initiative by a community action (anti-poverty) agency, with the aim both of reducing poverty and its effects and of promoting self-determination. Services range from community organization and recreation to job development, training, placement and direct employment, to medical and dental care, emergency financial assistance, and housing. Benefits are largely in kind, funded by grants to 881 community action agencies, which must come up with 30 to 40 percent matching funds. Benefits frequently represent an enrichment of traditional public services adapted for a special subpopulation. Benefits are conditioned, in part, on need.

Authorization: Economic Opportunity Act of 1964, as amended by the Community Services Act of 1974, Title II of PL93-644, 42 USC 2790 *et seq.*
Budget Code: 81-0500-0-1-999
Catalog Code: 49.002
FY77 Expenditure (est.): **$346 million.**

COMMUNITY HEALTH CENTERS

Health Services Administration,
Department of Health, Education, and Welfare

Primary ambulatory health care is provided, and special and inpatient care arranged, for people in medically underserved areas, especially urban poverty areas. Benefits are in kind, funded by grants to state and local governments and nonprofit agencies, which use the funds for the development and operation of community health centers and for the acquisition and/or modernization of facilities. Local matching is determined on a case-by-case basis. Over 3,000,000 persons annually receive care in 164 community and 258 primary health centers receiving support under this program. Although open to the general public in the catchment area, benefits are conditioned, in part, on need, because of a sliding-scale fee schedule based on family income.

Authorization: Section 330 of the Public Health Service Act, as amended by Title V, PL94-63, 42 USC 254C.
Budget Code: 75-0350-0-1-551
Catalog Code: 13.224
FY77 Expenditure (est.): **$229 million.**

COMMUNITY MENTAL HEALTH CENTERS

Alcohol, Drug Abuse, and
Mental Health Administration,
Department of Health, Education and Welfare

All persons residing in a center's catchment area are eligible for mental health services, including inpatient, outpatient, emergency services, and partial hospitalization. Benefits are in kind, funded by staffing grants that meet a portion of the compensation costs of professional and technical staff in the initial operation of the center. The federal matching percentage is somewhat higher in poverty areas, but the percentage in all areas decreases with each succeeding year. About 280 centers are to be supported this year. Although open to the general public in the catchment area, benefits are conditioned, in part, on need, because of a sliding-scale fee schedule based on family income.

Authorization: Title II, Part A of the Mental Retardation Facilities and Community Mental Health Centers Construction Act of 1963, PL88-164, as amended by PL89-105, PL90-31, PL90-574, PL91-211, PL91-513, PL91-515, and PL94-63.
Budget Code: 75-1361-0-1-550
Catalog Code: 13.240
FY77 Expenditure (est.): **$79 million.**

COMPREHENSIVE MANPOWER AND TRAINING SERVICES

Employment and Training Administration,
Department of Labor

Unemployed, underemployed, and disadvantaged persons are provided training and manpower services through a variety of subprograms. Programs for special groups, such as migrant farm workers and Indians, are under national direction, while other programs are determined and administered by 400 state and local prime sponsors. Benefits are in kind, funded by formula grants to prime sponsors based on area income and unemployment data as well as previous grant levels. Typical programs include outreach, counseling, testing, work experience, vocational skills training (either in the classroom or on the job), remedial education, placement, and supportive services. A million enrollees are served annually. In most programs, benefits are conditioned, in part, on need.

Authorization: Titles I, II, and IIIA of the Comprehensive Employment and Training Act of 1973, PL93-203, as amended.
Budget Code: 16-0174-0-1-504
Catalog Code: 17.228, 17.230, 17.232, 17.234
FY77 Expenditure (est.): **$1,414 million.** Includes 15 percent for project administration and other support.

CREDIT FOR CHILD AND DEPENDENT CARE EXPENSES
Internal Revenue Service,
Department of Treasury

Indirect financial assistance is provided to taxpayers who must purchase child or dependent care services in order to work or to go to school. Benefits are in the form of tax relief, funded by allowing such taxpayers a credit of 20 percent of eligible expenditures up to certain limits, against tax liability. The credit cannot exceed $2,000 for one dependent and $4,000 for two or more. The credit may be claimed by a divorced or separated parent with custody of a child, and by married couples, if one spouse is disabled, or both are employed full-time or one is employed full-time and the other is a part-time worker or a student. Benefits are not conditioned on need.

Authorization: Section 214 of the Internal Revenue Code of 1954, as amended by the Tax Reform Act of 1976.
Budget Code: none
Catalog Code: none
FY77 Expenditure (est.): **$840 million.** Represents estimated FY77 revenue loss. Under former provisions, about 4 percent of such tax expenditures went to tax filers with adjusted gross incomes under $7,000; and 50 percent, to those between $7,000 and $15,000.

CRIPPLED CHILDREN'S SERVICES
Health Services Administration,
Department of Health, Education and Welfare

Physician services, including medical, surgical, corrective, diagnostic and after-care services, and hospitalization, are provided to children under 21 years of age who are crippled or suffering from conditions that lead to crippling. Benefits are in kind, funded by grants to appropriate state agencies which purchase appropriate services and care from hospitals and other providers. State matching of formula grants is required on a dollar-for-dollar basis. Over a half million crippled children are aided annually, including 100,000 with multiple handicaps. Benefits are not directly conditioned on need.

Authorization: Section 504 of the Social Security Act as amended, 42 USC 704.
Budget Code: 75-0350-0-1-551
Catalog Code: 13.211
FY77 Expenditure (est.): **$98 million.**

DAIRY AND BEEKEEPER INDEMNITY PAYMENTS
Agricultural Stabilization and
Conservation Service,
Department of Agriculture

Indemnity payments are provided to: (1) dairy farmers and dairy product manufacturers who have been directed to remove their milk or milk products from commercial markets because they contain harmful chemical residues; (2) beekeepers who have suffered losses of honeybees because of the nearby use of pesticides and other chemicals. Benefits are in the form of direct cash payments, without restriction on their use, based on the market value of the loss of the milk or dairy products and the replacement cost of the honeybees. Payments to beekeepers average slightly over $3,000. About 1,000 beekeepers and 20 dairy farmers make claims annually. Benefits are not directly conditioned on need.

Authorization: Titles II and VIII of the Agricultural Act of 1970, PL91-524, as amended by PL93-86, 7 USC 135b, 450j-1.

Budget Code: 12-3314-0-1-351
Catalog Code: 10.053, 10.060
FY77 Expenditure (est.): **$4 million.**

DEVELOPMENTAL DISABILITIES—BASIC SUPPORT

Office of Human Development,
Department of Health, Education and Welfare

Developmentally disabled persons (that is, those suffering substantial handicaps resulting from mental retardation, cerebral palsy, epilepsy, or other neurological conditions developed in childhood) are provided care, training, legal and other services. Benefits are in kind, funded mainly by formula grants to designated state agencies. The federal matching percentage is somewhat higher in poverty areas. About 50,000 individuals receive services annually. Benefits are not directly conditioned on need.

Authorization: Mental Retardation Facilities and Community Mental Health Centers Construction Act of 1963, PL88-164, as amended by PL91-517 and by PL94-103, the Developmentally Disabled Assistance and Bill of Rights Act.
Budget Code: 75-1636-0-1-500
Catalog Code: 13.630
FY77 Expenditure (est.): **$32 million.** About half these funds are to be used for planning, administration, facilities construction, and other support.

DISABLED COAL MINE WORKERS BENEFITS AND COMPENSATION

Social Security Administration,
Department of Health, Education and Welfare
and
Employment Standards Administration,
Department of Labor

Coal miners disabled by black lung disease and their dependents, as well as the widows of such miners and the dependent surviving children, parents or siblings, are provided monthly payments to replace income lost through disability or death. Benefits are directly paid to the beneficiary in the form of cash, without any restrictions on its use. Benefits on pre-1973 claims are funded by appropriations from general revenues to the Social Security Administration, and they represent 95 percent of program expenditures. New claims are the responsibility of the Department of Labor, and liability is shared with coal mine operators and their insurers. The basic benefit is $205 monthly for a single person, with increments for dependents, subject to other income in some specified circumstances. About 480,000 beneficiaries are aided annually. Benefits are not directly conditioned on need.

Authorization: Federal Coal Mine Health and Safety Act of 1969, PL91-173, as amended by PL92-303.
Budget Code: 75-0409-0-1-601, 16-1521-0-1-600
Catalog Code: 13.806, 17.307
FY77 Expenditure (est.): **$935 million.**

DISASTER ASSISTANCE

Federal Disaster Assistance Administration,
Department of Housing and Urban Development

Individual disaster victims in declared emergency and major disaster areas are provided shelter and temporary housing if displaced, assistance if put out of work, emergency transportation service, food coupons, grants to meet disaster-related expenses, and crisis counseling. Benefits are mainly in kind, funded by project grants to affected state and local governments and by the provision of federal facilities, equipment, and personnel. A substantial portion of the funds is used for repair and replacement of public facilities, for removal of wreckage and debris, and for essential work on public lands. No matching contribution is required, except for family and individual grant programs. Benefits are conditioned, in part, on need.

Authorization: Disaster Relief Act of 1970, PL91-606; Disaster Relief Act of 1974, PL93-288; Executive Orders 11749, 11795.
Budget Code: 11-0039-1-453, 86-3981-0-4-453
Catalog Code: 14.701
FY77 Expenditure (est.): **$387 million.**

DRUG ABUSE COMMUNITY SERVICE PROGRAMS

Alcohol, Drug Abuse and Mental Health Administration, Department of Health, Education and Welfare

Narcotics addicts, drug abusers, and drug-dependent persons are provided inpatient, outpatient, residential, emergency, and after-care services in community-based facilities. Benefits are in kind, funded by grants to community mental health centers, their affiliates and other nonprofit agencies. Staffing grants meet a portion of the compensation costs of professional and technical personnel. Project grants may meet a portion of operating costs. The federal matching percentage is somewhat higher in poverty areas, but the percentage in all areas decreases with each succeeding year. The goal is 100,000 treatment slots. Although open to the general public in the catchment area, benefits are conditioned, in part, on need, because of a sliding-scale fee schedule based on family income.

Authorization: Part A, Section 203(e) of the Community Mental Health Centers Amendments of 1975, PL94-63; Section 410 of the Drug Abuse Office Treatment Act of 1972, PL92-255 as amended by PL94-237.
Budget Code: 75-1361-0-1-550
Catalog Code: 13.235
FY77 Expenditure (est.): **$159 million.**

EARNED INCOME CREDIT

Internal Revenue Service, Department of Treasury

Indirect and direct financial assistance is provided to low-income workers who have dependent children. Benefits are in the form of tax relief and direct cash payments, funded by allowing the workers a credit against tax liability on certain amounts of earned income. The credit reaches a maximum at 10 percent of the first $4,000 of earnings; it is then reduced by 10 percent of all earnings above $4,000, thus phasing out at $8,000 of earnings (or adjusted gross income). Any credit in excess of tax liability is paid in cash to the worker. Over 80 percent of aggregate credits are returned as cash payments. Benefits are conditioned on need.

Authorization: Section 43 of the Internal Revenue Code of 1954, as amended by the Tax Reduction Act of 1975 and the Tax Reform Act of 1976.
Budget Code: 20-0903-0-1-604
Catalog Code: none
FY77 Expenditure (est.): **$1,070 million.** Represents estimated FY77 revenue loss of $215 million and direct outlays of $856 million.

EMERGENCY ENERGY CONSERVATION SERVICES

Community Services Administration

Low-income persons and the near poor are provided a variety of services to lessen the impact of the high cost of energy and to reduce energy consumption. Services include consumer education, legal assistance, transportation assistance to services and jobs, home weatherization to minimize heat loss, and crisis intervention (grants, loans, fuel vouchers or stamps) to prevent utility shutoff or lack of fuel. Benefits are mainly in kind, funded by grants to community action agencies and other public and private nonprofit agencies. The local share requirement, 25 to 30 percent, is waived for crisis intervention. Benefits are conditioned on need.

Authorization: Section 222a(12) of the Community Services Act of 1974, PL93-644, 42 USC 2790.
Budget Code: 81-0500-0-1-999
Catalog Code: 49.014
FY77 Expenditure (est.): **$242 million.**

EMPLOYMENT SERVICE

Employment and Training Administration, Department of Labor

Persons seeking employment are provided counseling, testing, and referral to jobs, appropriate training, or other services through 2,400 local offices. Specialized services are provided veterans, disadvantaged persons, youth, older workers, the handicapped, and rural residents.

Benefits are in kind, funded by formula grants to state employment security agencies. Over 14 million applications are processed annually, resulting in a million counseling sessions, a million tests administered and almost 5 million job placements. Benefits are not directly conditioned on need.

Authorization: The Wagner-Peyser Act of 1933, PL73-30, as amended, 29 USC 49-49n and 39 USC 338; Title IV, Section C of the Social Security Act of 1935, as amended, 42 USC 602 *et seq.* and 42 USC 1101 *et seq.*; PL93-508; PL93-618; PL93-203; PL93-112; PL94-567; PL94-45.
Budget Code: 16-0179-0-1-504
Catalog Code: 17.207
FY77 Expenditure (est.): **$614 million.**

EXCLUSION FROM CAPITAL GAIN ON HOME SALES BY THE ELDERLY

Internal Revenue Service,
Department of Treasury

Indirect financial assistance is provided, once in their lifetime, to elderly taxpayers who sell their homes but do not buy replacement homes. Benefits are in the form of tax relief, funded by allowing such taxpayers to exclude from consideration as income the capital gain realized on the sale of their residences. The exclusion applies to taxpayers of age 65 or older, on gains on the first $35,000 of adjusted sales price. This provision is intended to assist those elderly who wish to sell their houses and rent apartments or make other living arrangements, but the benefits are more concentrated among higher-income taxpayers. Benefits are not conditioned on need.

Authorization: Section 121 of the Internal Revenue Code of 1954, as amended by the Tax Reform Act of 1976.
Budget Code: none
Catalog Code: none
FY77 Expenditure (est.): **$40 million.** Represents estimated FY77 revenue loss. Under former provisions, about 10 percent of such tax expenditures went to tax filers with adjusted gross incomes under $7,000; and 20 percent, to those between $7,000 and $15,000.

FAMILY PLANNING PROJECTS

Health Services Administration,
Department of Health, Education and Welfare

Contraceptive advice and supplies and services, including physical examinations, diagnosis and treatment (but excluding abortions) are provided, with priority given to persons from low-income families. Benefits are in kind, funded by project grants to state and local agencies and nonprofit agencies to pay for services to persons who desire them, who would not otherwise have access to them and who are in need. Some local contribution is required toward project cost. Approximately 3,000,000 persons are to receive service this year. Benefits are conditioned, in part, on need.

Authorization: Section 1001 of the Public Health Service Act, PL78-410, as amended, 42 USC 300.
Budget Code: 75-0305-0-1-551
Catalog Code: 13.217
FY77 Expenditure (est.): **$121 million.**

FEDERAL CROP INSURANCE

Federal Crop Insurance Corporation,
Agricultural Stabilization and
Conservation Service,
Department of Agriculture

Agricultural producers are provided protection from crop losses caused by natural hazards, such as insect and wildlife damage, plant diseases, fire, drought, flood, wind and other weather conditions. Benefits are in the form of low-cost insurance, funded by U.S. Treasury capital stock and by the premiums paid by producers to the Federal Crop Insurance Corporation Fund. Many of the costs of loss adjustment, administration, and operation are not provided for in the premiums but through transfers from general revenues. Almost $2 billion in insurance is in force, covering 320,000 crops on 23 million acres in 1,500 counties. Benefits are not conditioned on need.

Authorization: Federal Crop Insurance Act, as amended, 7 USC 1501-1520.
Budget Code: 12-2707-0-1-351, 12-4085-0-3-351
Catalog Code: 10.450
FY77 Expenditure (est.): **$67 million.** Represents the FY77 expenses of indemnities, claims, operations and administration, less income from premiums.

FEDERAL-STATE UNEMPLOYMENT INSURANCE

Employment and Training Administration, Department of Labor

Workers in covered employment who are involuntarily unemployed, but able to and available for work, and who have accumulated enough work credits (based on time and wages) are provided weekly payments to replace their lost earnings. Benefits are paid directly to the individual in the form of cash, without restrictions on its use, funded through the states from the Unemployment Trust Fund, which is financed by federal and state taxes on employers' payrolls and by federal appropriations. Benefits are based on average past weekly earnings and may be reduced by any earnings during the overall period of unemployment, in accordance with state law. Benefits may be extended by two 13-week periods beyond the normal 26-week period, in times of higher unemployment. The federal government reimburses states for part of the costs of such extended and supplementary benefits. Benefits are not directly conditioned on need. About ten million beneficiaries will be aided this year, and over one third of them will require extended benefits.

Authorization: Social Security Act, as amended, 42 USC 501-503, 1101-1105; PL93-567, PL93-572 and PL94-45.
Budget Code: 16-0327-0-1-603, 20-8042-0-7-999, 16-0179-0-1-504
Catalog Code: 17.225
FY77 Expenditure (est.): **$13,490 million.** Includes 6 percent for state administration and other support. A quarter of the outlays are to be for extended and supplementary benefits.

FHA MORTGAGE INSURANCE

Federal Housing Administration Fund, Department of Housing and Urban Development

Through more than 30 subprograms, different categories of homebuyers and renters are provided assistance to live in standard quality houses, condominiums, apartments, and mobile homes. Benefits are in the form of favorable credit and down payment terms on housing, funded by FHA's insuring of private lenders against losses on loans used to finance the purchase, repair, rehabilitation, or improvement of approved properties and dwelling units. About $10 billion of insurance will be written on 430,000 units this year, resulting in a total outstanding balance in force of some $90 billion in mortgage insurance. Benefits are not conditioned on need.

Authorization: Titles I and II of the National Housing Act of 1937, PL73-479, as amended, 12 USC 1703, 1709, 1713, 1715, 1745.
Budget Code: 86-4070-0-3-401
Catalog Code: 14.108-14.140, 14.142, 14.151-14.155
FY77 Expenditure (est.): **$647 million.** FHA Fund capital outlays (acquisition of properties, defaults) and operating expenses in FY77 are to be partially offset by receipts from fees, premiums, property sales, and interest revenue. Estimated FY77 capital commitments are $1.03 billion.

FOOD STAMPS

Food and Nutrition Service, Department of Agriculture

Low-income households are provided increased food-buying power by purchasing food stamps with a face value that exceeds their cost. The stamps may then be used in participating retail food establishments at face value. The difference between the stamps' face value and their cost represents the benefit or "bonus" to a household, and the cost for a given value of stamps varies according to the household's size and adjusted income. Eligibility and benefit standards are national. Benefits may be considered to be in kind, funded by federal direct payments for a restricted use. States must pay 50 percent of administrative costs. On the average, over 17 million persons participate in the program each month; and the average "bonus" per person is about $24 monthly. Benefits are conditioned on need.

Authorization: Food Stamp Act of 1964, PL88-525, as amended by PL90-91, PL90-552, PL91-116, PL91-671, PL92-603, PL93-86, PL93-233, PL93-335, PL93-347, PL93-563, PL94-182, PL94-339, PL94-365, PL94-379, and PL94-585, 7 USC 2011-2025.
Budget Code: 12-3505-0-1-604
Catalog Code: 10.551
FY77 Expenditure (est.): **$5,474 million.** Includes 7 percent for state administration and other support.

FOSTER GRANDPARENT PROGRAM
ACTION

Low-income persons, age 60 and over, are provided part-time volunteer opportunities relating to the needs of children in residential and nonresidential facilities, including day care and preschool centers, and, more recently, in their own homes. The foster grandparents receive hot meals, stipends of $32 per week for up to 20 hours weekly, and other related services; the children receive supportive personal attention. Thus, benefits are in cash and in kind, funded by 90-percent grants to public and nonprofit private agencies. Approximately 15,000 foster grandparents serve about 45,000 children yearly. Benefits are conditioned, in part, on need.

Authorization: Title II, Part B of the Domestic Volunteer Service Act of 1973, PL93-113.
Budget Code: 44-0103-0-1-451
Catalog Code: 72.001
FY77 Expenditure (est.): **$40 million.** Includes over 20 percent for administration and other support.

HEAD START
Office of Human Development,
Department of Health, Education and Welfare

Preschool children from low-income families are provided comprehensive educational, health, nutritional, social, and related services in both full- and part-day programs, as well as in summer programs for children about to enter kindergarten, at community-based centers. Benefits are in kind, including social services for the family, and are funded by project grants to public or private nonprofit agencies. A 20-percent nonfederal share must be met in cash or in kind. About 350,000 preschool children are served annually in full-year, summer and experimental centers. Benefits are conditioned on need, and they include "hard" services (health care, meals, day care) as well as "softer" services.

Authorization: Title V, Part A of the Community Services Act of 1974, PL93-644, 42 USC 2921 *et seq.*
Budget Code: 75-1636-0-1-500
Catalog Code: 13.600
FY77 Expenditure (est.): **$486 million.**

HEALTH MAINTENANCE ORGANIZATION DEVELOPMENT
Health Services Administration,
Department of Health, Education and Welfare

Comprehensive, prepaid health care is provided to persons living in Health Maintenance Organization service areas. Benefits are in kind, funded by contract grants and direct and guaranteed loans to nonprofit agencies. Profit-making agencies in medically underserved areas may also receive such assistance. Local matching of 10 percent is required in all but medically underserved areas. Approximately 30 Health Maintenance Organizations serving 900,000 enrollees are to be brought into operational status this year. This program is meant to subsidize Health Maintenance Organization start-up costs, especially feasibility, planning and development efforts and initial operation. Benefits are not directly conditioned on need.

Authorization: Title XIII of the Public Health Service Act, PL78-410, as amended by the Health Maintenance Organization Act of 1973, PL93-222, and by PL94-460, 42 USC 300e.
Budget Code: 75-0305-0-1-551, 75-4435-0-3-551

Catalog Code: 13.256
FY77 Expenditure (est.): **$39 million.** Most of loan fund capital outlays in FY77 are to be offset by receipts (interest and loan sales). Estimated FY77 loan commitments are $60 million; grant outlays, $23 million.

HIGHER-EDUCATION WORK-STUDY
Office of Education,
Department of Health, Education and Welfare

Part-time employment (up to 40 hours weekly) is provided in educational institutions or in the public interest, for undergraduate, graduate or professional students whose resources, including parental contributions, are determined to be inadequate to permit them to study at their institutions of higher education. Benefits are cash compensation, funded by means of an 80-percent reimbursement of student's earnings by the federal government. Over 550,000 students are employed annually under this program. Benefits are conditioned on need; and, while the students are being compensated for work, this is a public employment program.

Authorization: Title IV, Part C of the Higher Education Act of 1965, PL89-329, 42 USC 2751-2752a; PL92-318.
Budget Code: 75-0293-0-1-502
Catalog Code: 13.463
FY77 Expenditure (est.): **$250 million**

INDIAN GENERAL ASSISTANCE
Bureau of Indian Affairs,
Department of Interior

Maintenance payments to cover the costs of food, shelter, clothing, and other items of daily living are made to needy Indians living on or near reservations, when such assistance is not available from state or local agencies. Benefits are in the form of cash, in amounts depending upon family size and needs, and without restrictions on use. Each month, on the average, some 65,000 Indians receive cash assistance. Benefits are conditioned on need.

Authorization: Snyder Act of 1921, PL67-85, 25 USC 13.
Budget Code: 14-2100-0-1-999
Catalog Code: 15.133
FY77 Expenditure (est.): **$64 million.**

INDOCHINESE REFUGEE ASSISTANCE
Social and Rehabilitation Service,
Department of Health, Education and Welfare

Recent refugees in alien status from Cambodia, Laos, and Vietnam are provided public assistance, medical assistance, and other welfare services for the needy, as well as a small amount of other social services. Benefits are both in cash (public assistance) and in kind, funded by 100-percent federal grants to state welfare agencies. The enabling legislation for this program expires during 1977, after which time needy refugees will be assisted through existing programs for the entire population. Benefits are conditioned on need.

Authorization: The Indochina Migration and Refugee Assistance Act of 1975, PL94-23, as amended by PL94-313.
Budget Code: 75-0570-0-1-604
Catalog Code: 13.769
FY77 Expenditure (est.): **$95 million.** Includes over 10 percent for state and local administration and other support.

JOB CORPS
Employment and Training Administration,
Department of Labor

Low-income youths, aged 14 to 21, are provided intensive educational and vocational training in a residential setting. Corps members also receive room and board, medical and dental care, work clothing, a monthly $30 living allowance initially, rising to over $50 subsequently, a readjustment allowance of $50 monthly for satisfactory service, as well as spouse and dependents allotments of up to $50 monthly. Benefits are in kind and in cash, funded by project grants to government agencies and private organizations. No local funding is required. Some 45,000 youths are trained, each for up to two years, at an average cost of $3,500 per year. Benefits are conditioned on need.

Authorization: Title IV of the Comprehensive Employment and Training Act of 1973, as amended, PL93-203, PL93-567, 29 USC 801 *et seq.*
Budget Code: 16-0174-0-1-504
Catalog Code: 17.211
FY77 Expenditure (est.): **$230 million.**

LEGAL SERVICES FOR THE POOR
Legal Services Corporation

Legal assistance is provided to low-income persons in most types of noncriminal proceedings. (Legal services funds may not be used in support of political activity, demonstrations, strikes, nor in cases involving abortion, military desertion, school desegregation, and homosexual rights.) Benefits are in kind, funded by payment to the corporation from general revenues for the salaries of staff lawyers and other expenses. The corporation raises substantial additional funds on its own. Approximately 3,000 attorneys in 700 offices handle a million legal matters annually. Benefits are conditioned on need.

Authorization: Legal Services Corporation Act of 1974, PL93-355, as amended.
Budget Code: 20-0501-0-1-751
Catalog Code: none
FY77 Expenditure (est.): **$125 million.**

MATERNAL AND CHILD HEALTH SERVICES
Health Services Administration,
Department of Health, Education and Welfare

Mothers, infants, and school-age children, especially in rural areas or areas with concentrations of low-income families, are provided comprehensive health care services aimed at (a) reducing the incidence of mental retardation and other handicaps caused by complications associated with childbearing; (b) reducing the incidence of infant and maternal mortality; and (c) promoting the medical and dental health of children and youth. Benefits are in kind, funded by grants to state health agencies for the purchase of inpatient care and health services in maternity clinics, well-child and pediatric clinics, special clinics for mentally retarded children, and other facilities. State matching of formula grants is required on a dollar-for-dollar basis. Almost two million children are served in well-child clinics yearly; almost one million receive dental care treatment; and over a half million women and 160,000 infants receive comprehensive prenatal and postpartum health care. Benefits are not directly conditioned on need.

Authorization: Section 503 of the Social Security Act, as amended, 42 USC 703.
Budget Code: 75-0350-0-1-551
Catalog Code: 13.232
FY77 Expenditure (est.): **$241 million.**

MEDICAL ASSISTANCE (MEDICAID)
Social and Rehabilitation Service,
Department of Health, Education and Welfare

Public assistance recipients and other low-income persons are provided inpatient and outpatient hospital services, laboratory and x-ray services, nursing home services, home health services for persons age 21 and over, early periodic screening and diagnosis and treatment for persons under age 21, family planning services and physicians services. AFDC recipients are automatically eligible in all states. SSI recipients in 35 states are automatically eligible, while in 15 states they must satisfy additional criteria. Medically needy persons (those with equivalent or somewhat higher incomes than, but characteristics similar to, AFDC and SSI recipients) are eligible in over half the states. Benefits are in kind, funded by formula grants to state welfare agencies for the direct purchase of approved services. Each state contributes from 17 to 50 percent of assistance costs, depending on its relative per capita income, as well as 50 percent of administrative costs. Over 24 million persons receive medical care annually. Benefits are conditioned on need.

Authorization: Title XIX of the Social Security Act, as amended; PL89-97; PL90-248; PL91-56; PL92-223; PL92-603; PL93-223; 42 USC 1396 *et seq.*
Budget Code: 75-0581-0-1-999
Catalog Code: 13.714

FY77 Expenditure (est.): **$9,859 million.** Includes 5 percent for state and local administration and other support.

MEDICARE—HOSPITAL INSURANCE

Social Security Administration
Department of Health, Education and Welfare

Except for specified deductibles and coinsurance, the reasonable costs of hospital and related care are paid directly to participating hospitals, skilled nursing facilities and certain other providers on behalf of persons who reached age 65 before 1968, disabled persons under age 65 who have been entitled to Social Security or Railroad Retirement benefits for at least two years or who have chronic kidney disease requiring dialysis or transplant, as well as persons who reached age 65 in 1968 or after with some but not sufficient work credit to qualify for Social Security or Railroad Retirement benefits. The latter group is assisted through general revenue transfers of almost one billion dollars into the Federal Hospital Insurance Trust Fund; the rest are financed by payroll contributions of employers and employees. Benefits are in kind, and approximately six million persons have benefits paid on their behalf annually. Benefits are not directly conditioned on need.

Authorization: Title XVIII, Part A of the Social Security Act, as amended in 1965 by PL89-97, and by PL90-248, PL92-603, PL93-233, PL94-182, and PL94-437, 42 USC 1395 *et seq.*
Budget Code: 75-0404-0-1-999, 20-8005-0-7-551
Catalog Code: 13.800
FY77 Expenditure (est.): **$15,314 million.**

MEDICARE—SUPPLEMENTARY MEDICAL INSURANCE

Social Security Administration,
Department of Health, Education and Welfare

Except for specified deductibles and coinsurance, the reasonable costs of physicians' services, outpatient and related care, are paid directly to participating providers on behalf of nearly all persons who are age 65 and over, as well as disabled persons under age 65 who have been entitled to Social Security or Railroad Retirement benefits for at least two years or who have chronic kidney disease requiring dialysis or transplant. Enrollees pay a monthly premium of $7.70, but some states have elected to pay the premium on behalf of certain qualifying individuals. The other half of the program's cost is met by general revenue appropriations. Benefits are in kind, and approximately 15 million persons receive them annually. Benefits are not directly conditioned on need.

Authorization: Title XVIII, Part B of the Social Security Act, as amended in 1965 by PL89-97, and by PL90-248, PL92-603, PL93-233, and PL94-182, 42 USC 1395 *et seq.*
Budget Code: 75-0404-0-1-999, 20-8004-0-7-551
Catalog Code: 13.801
FY77 Expenditure (est.): **$6,330 million.**

MILITARY NONDISABILITY RETIREMENT

Department of Defense;
Coast Guard, Department of Transportation

Regular and Reserve commissioned officers, enlisted members with 20 to 30 years active service, and certain reserve members are provided monthly cash payments to replace income lost through retirement. Payment amounts vary generally according to length of active service and pay grade at retirement. Benefits are in the form of cash, without restrictions on its use, directly paid to the beneficiary in amounts from 50 to 75 percent of basic pay at retirement. Benefits are paid through direct appropriation by Congress each year; there are no contributions from service member's military compensation financing this program. (As contributing participants, members are also eligible for Social Security benefits.) Close to one million persons receive payments monthly. Benefits are not conditioned on need.

Authorization: Officer Personnel Act of 1947; Army and Air Force Vitalization and Retirement Equalization Act of 1948; Career Compensation Act of 1949; PL85-422; PL88-132.
Budget Code: 97-0030-0-1-051, 69-0241-0-1-406
Catalog Code: none
FY77 Expenditure (est.): **$7,233 million.**

NATIONAL SCHOOL LUNCH PROGRAM

Food and Nutrition Service,
Department of Agriculture

Schoolchildren of twelfth grade and under, in participating public and nonprofit private schools, are provided low-cost, nutritional lunches at "full," reduced or no price, according to the family income of each child. Benefits are in kind, funded by formula grants and food donations to state educational departments, which in turn allocate the funds and food among participating schools. State and school district matching on a 3-to-1 basis is required, but schools receive additional assistance for free and reduced-price lunches served. Almost 4.5 billion lunches are served each school year, reaching 27 million children. Almost half the lunches are served at free or reduced prices to low-income children. Benefits are conditioned, in part, on need.

Authorization: National School Lunch Act of 1946, PL79-396, as amended by PL87-823, PL91-248, PL92-153, PL92-433, PL93-150, PL93-326, PL94-105, 42 USC 1751-1753.
Budget Code: 12-3539-0-1-604
Catalog Code: 10.555
FY77 Expenditure (est.): **$2,204 million.** Includes almost $500 million in distributed commodities.

NATIVE AMERICAN PROGRAMS

Office of Human Development,
Department of Health, Education and Welfare

American Indians and native Hawaiians and Alaskans are provided a variety of services to promote self-determination, self-sufficiency, community development, and to fill in the gaps left by other programs. Benefits are in kind, including manpower training and employment, housing, food, medical and social services, funded by project grants to tribal governing bodies and public and nonprofit private agencies. Generally a 20-percent local contribution is required. Over a half million native Americans benefit annually, including 150,000 in urban organizations in 36 states. Eighty percent of beneficiaries are low-income. Benefits are not directly conditioned on need.

Authorization: Title VIII of the Community Service Act of 1974, PL93-644, 42 USC 2991 *et seq.*
Budget Code: 75-1636-0-1-500
Catalog Code: 13.612
FY77 Expenditure (est.): **$42 million.**

PUBLIC LOW-INCOME HOUSING

Housing Production and Mortgage Credit,
Housing Management,
Department of Housing and Urban Development

Low-income families and elderly or disabled individuals are provided low-rent public housing that is decent, safe, and sanitary. Benefits are in kind, funded by project grants and direct loans to local public housing agencies for the purposes of acquisition (purchasing existing housing, procuring construction, letting contracts to private developers), subsidizing annual debt service payments, insuring adequate operation and maintenance, and modernization and expansion of facilities and services. There is no requirement for local matching; however, an indirect local contribution results from property tax abatements given local housing authorities. Benefits are conditioned on need.

Authorization: National Housing Act of 1937, as amended, PL75-412, 42 USC 1401-1435.
Budget Code: 86-0139-0-1-604, 86-0163-0-1-604, 86-0164-0-1-604, 86-4098-0-3-604
Catalog Code: 14.146, 14.147, 14.158
FY77 Expenditure (est.): **$1,112 million.** About 50 percent of outlays represent operating subsidies; and over 10 percent, acquisition and modernization expenditures.

PUBLIC SERVICE EMPLOYMENT

Employment and Training Administration,
Department of Labor

Unemployed and underemployed persons, generally in areas of substantial unemployment, are provided jobs in local public services. Preference is given to the disadvantaged, to the long-term unemployed, and to those who have exhausted, or were not eligible for, unemployment insurance. Benefits are in the form of cash compensation for work performed, funded by formula grants based on the number and percentage of unemployed in each state and locality of 100,000 population. The grants are used to finance the salaries, wages, and benefits of workers hired under the program. Generally, compensation is equivalent to that of the private-sector for similar work, subject to certain maximums. About 600,000 persons are employed in these positions. Benefits may be conditioned, in part, on need.

Authorization: Titles I, II, and VI of the Comprehensive Employment and Training Act of 1973, PL93-203, as amended by the Emergency Jobs and Unemployment Assistance Act of 1974, PL93-567.
Budget Code: 16-0173-0-1-504, 16-0174-0-1-504
Catalog Code: 17.232
FY77 Expenditure (est.): **$3,159 million.** Includes approximately 5 percent for local and state administration and other support.

REHABILITATION SERVICES AND FACILITIES—BASIC SUPPORT

Office of Human Development,
Department of Health, Education and Welfare

Persons with mental and physical handicaps, with an emphasis on the more severely disabled, are provided vocational rehabilitation services, including diagnosis and evaluation, counseling, training and employment services, assistance in paying for medical care and prosthetic/orthopedic devices, maintenance during rehabilitation, transportation, tools, equipment and supplies, reader services for the blind, interpreter services for the deaf, and small business opportunities. Benefits are mainly in kind, funded by formula grants to state vocational rehabilitation agencies which provide or purchase necessary services. Some state matching is required. More than one and a half million persons (including disabled recipients of public assistance) receive services annually; over 310,000 are rehabilitated. Benefits are not directly conditioned on need.

Authorization: Rehabilitation Act of 1973, PL93-112, as amended by PL93-516, PL94-230, 29 USC 701 *et seq.*
Budget Code: 75-1636-0-1-500
Catalog Code: 13.624
FY77 Expenditure (est.): **$733 million.**

RENT SUPPLEMENTS

Housing Production and Mortgage Credit,
Department of Housing and Urban Development

Low-income families that contain elderly or handicapped persons or that live in substandard or damaged units are provided good quality rental housing at rents equal to at least 25 percent of adjusted income. Benefits are in kind, funded by direct federal payments to owners of approved multifamily rental housing projects. These payments make up the difference between the tenants' partial rental and the market rent. This program was operated in conjunction with various mortgage insurance subprograms, with the rent supplement contract running for the life of the mortgage, or up to 40 years. About 300,000 units are eligible for rent supplements. New commitments will not be made under this program except when they cannot be accommodated under the Lower Income Housing Assistance (Section 8) program. Benefits are conditioned on need.

Authorization: Housing and Urban Development Act of 1965, PL89-117, 12 USC 1701(s).
Budget Code: 86-0129-0-1-604, 86-0139-0-1-604
Catalog Code: 14.149
FY77 Expenditure (est.): **$245 million.**

SOCIAL SECURITY—DISABILITY INSURANCE

Social Security Administration,
Department of Health, Education and Welfare

Physically and mentally disabled persons and their dependents are provided monthly cash payments, if the disabled person has worked for a sufficient period of time to be insured. Benefits may not be granted for the first five months of disability. Thereafter, payments are made throughout the period of disability to replace income lost through loss of work. Benefits are directly paid to the beneficiary in the form of cash, without any restrictions on its use, in a monthly amount that ranges from $108 minimum for a disabled individual to $992 maximum for a family. On the average, more than 2.5 million disabled persons and two million of their dependents receive such benefits monthly. As social insurance, benefits are not directly conditioned on need as much as on past contributions by which the program is financed.

Authorization: Social Security Act, as amended by PL92-603, PL93-66, and PL93-233, 42 USC 420-425
Budget Code: 20-8007-0-7-601
Catalog Code: 13.802
FY77 Expenditure (est.): **$11,625 million.**

SOCIAL SECURITY—RETIREMENT INSURANCE

Social Security Administration
Department of Health, Education and Welfare

Retired workers over age 62 and their dependents are provided monthly cash payments, if the retired person has worked for a sufficient period of time to be insured, and the payments are made to replace income lost through retirement. Benefits are directly paid to the beneficiary in the form of cash, without any restriction on its use, in a monthly amount that ranges from $86 to $399 for retired individuals and from $162 to $704 for families. On the average, more than 17 million retired workers and 3.5 million of their dependents receive such benefits monthly. As social insurance, benefits are not directly conditioned on need as much as on past contributions by which the program is financed.

Authorization: Social Security Act as amended by PL92-603, PL93-66, PL93-233, 42 USC 401-429.
Budget Code: 20-8006-0-7-601
Catalog Code: 13.803
FY77 Expenditure (est.): **$52,364 million.**

SOCIAL SECURITY—SURVIVORS INSURANCE

Social Security Administration,
Department of Health, Education and Welfare

Dependents of deceased workers are provided monthly cash payments, if the deceased worker had worked for a sufficient period of time to be insured; and the payments are made to replace income lost through his or her death. Benefits are directly paid to the beneficiary in the form of cash, without any restrictions on its use, in a monthly amount that ranges from $108 minimum for a sole survivor to $992 maximum for a family. On the average, 7.5 million survivors receive such benefits monthly. As social insurance, benefits are not directly conditioned on need as much as on past contributions by which the program is financed.

Authorization: Social Security Act, as amended by PL92-603, PL93-66, and PL93-233, 42 USC 401-429.
Budget Code: 20-8006-0-7-601
Catalog Code: 13.805
FY77 Expenditure (est.): **$18,888 million.**

SOCIAL SERVICES

Social and Rehabilitation Service,
Department of Health, Education and Welfare

Public assistance recipients and other low-income persons are provided social services to assist them to be economically self-supporting, to protect children and adults from abuse or neglect, to help families stay together, to prevent inappropriate institutionalization by providing alternate forms of care, and to arrange for appropriate institutionalization. Benefits are in kind, funded by 75-percent formula grants to state welfare agencies for allocation among local districts. Typical services are day care, foster or protective care, homemaking, family planning, and those related to health, mental retardation and drug or alcohol abuse. Day care accounts for approximately one third of expenditures; foster and protective care, for one sixth. Benefits are conditioned on need.

Authorization: Title XX, Part A of the Social Security Act Social Services Amendments of 1974, PL93-647, PL94-401, 42 USC 1397 *et seq.*
Budget Code: 75-0581-0-1-999
Catalog Code: 13.754, 13.771
FY77 Expenditure (est.): **$2,645 million.**

SUPPLEMENTAL SECURITY INCOME

Social Security Administration,
Department of Health, Education and Welfare

Blind and disabled persons, as well as those age 65 or over, are provided direct monthly cash payments, if their adjusted incomes and resources fall below specified national standards. Payments are made to bring the beneficiary's total income up to the nationally established minimum; benefits are in the form of cash, without any restriction on its use. The established minimum monthly income for an individual is $168 and for a couple $252, if living alone; but many states pay additional sums above the federally financed national minimum. On the average, about 4.4 million recipients are aided monthly, and about half are aged. Benefits are conditioned on need.

Authorization: Title XVI, Parts A and B of the Social Security Act, as amended by PL92-603, PL93-66, PL93-233, PL93-368, PL94-566, PL94-569, and PL94-585.
Budget Code: 75-0406-0-1-604
Catalog Code: 13.807
FY77 Expenditure (est.): **$5,299 million.** Excludes $1,515 million in state tax-levy supplementary payments.

SURVIVORS COMPENSATION FOR SERVICE-CONNECTED DEATHS

Department of Veterans Benefits,
Veterans Administration

Surviving widows, widowers, children, and certain parents of nondishonorably discharged veterans who died because of a service-connected disability are provided monthly payments which vary by family size, special needs, and the military pay grade and year of death of the veteran. Parents must meet certain income criteria for eligibility. Benefits are in the form of cash, funded by direct federal payments without restrictions on their use. Almost 90,000 dependent parents receive benefits, averaging $900 yearly, for veterans who died before January, 1957. Benefits are provided to about 65,000 other parents, 210,000 unmarried widows and widowers, and 110,000 children of those veterans who have died subsequent to January, 1957. Payments per case average almost $3,000 annually. Only for surviving parents are benefits directly conditioned on need. The pre-1957 program is distinct from the post-1957 one in rules and benefit levels. However, only 10 percent of expenditures are for pre-1957 coverage.

Authorization: 38 USC 321, 341, 410, 411, 413, 415 as amended by PL94-169, PL94-432 and PL94-433.
Budget Code: 36-0102-0-1-701
Catalog Code: 64.102, 64.110
FY77 Expenditure (est.): **$1,067 million.**

VETERANS COMPENSATION FOR SERVICE-CONNECTED DISABILITIES

Department of Veterans Benefits,
Veterans Administration

Non–dishonorably discharged veterans with service-connected disabilities, as well as the dependents of such veterans who are at least 50-percent disabled, are provided monthly payments which vary according to the severity of the disability. Benefits are in the form of cash, funded by direct monthly federal payments without restrictions on their use, ranging from $38 for a 10-percent disability to over $1,700 for loss of limbs or for blindness. Almost 2,250,000 disabled veterans receive compensation annually, for themselves and their 610,000 dependents, with an average yearly payment of just over $2,000. Benefits are not directly conditioned on need.

Authorization: 38 USC 310, 311, as amended by PL94-169, PL94-432 and PL94-433.
Budget Code: 36-0102-0-1-701
Catalog Code: 64.109
FY77 Expenditure (est.): **$4,796 million.**

VETERANS EDUCATIONAL ASSISTANCE
Department of Veterans Benefits,
Veterans Administration

Non–dishonorably discharged veterans with at least 181 continuous days of active service, any part of which occurred after January, 1955, or such veterans discharged after that date because of a service-connected disability, are provided financial assistance toward attaining an educational or vocational objective at an approved institution. Veterans are eligible for interest-bearing education loans of up to $1,500 per academic year, work-study allowances, tutorial assistance allowances and direct monthly payments, generally for no more than 45 months and varying from $292 for a single veteran to $396 for a veteran with two dependents, and $24 monthly for each additional dependent. Part-time educational efforts qualify for proportionate monthly subsistence payments. Some two million veterans receive direct payments that average almost $2,000 yearly. Less than 10,000 loans are made annually to veterans without sufficient funds to meet their expenses. Direct payments are not conditioned on need; loans are conditioned on need.

Authorization: 38 USC 1621, 1652, 1661, 1686 as amended by PL93-337, PL94-502.
Budget Code: 36-0137-0-1-702, 36-4118-0-3-702
Catalog Code: 64.111, 64.120
FY77 Expenditure (est.): **$3,683 million.** Estimated FY77 loan commitments are approximately $12 million.

VETERANS HOSPITALIZATION
Department of Medicine and Surgery,
Veterans Administration

Non–dishonorably discharged veterans with service-connected disabilities or diseases, those without service-connected disabilities unable to pay the cost of necessary hospital care, and those over age 65 or in receipt of a veterans pension are provided inpatient, medical, surgical and psychiatric care, related medical and dental services, and hospital-based home health care following discharge from inpatient status. Benefits are in kind, funded principally by means of the salaries and expenses of personnel assigned to VA hospital facilities. Approximately 1,210,000 veterans are treated as inpatients annually, with an average daily census of 76,000. Benefits are conditioned, in part, on need.

Authorization: 38 USC Chapter 17.
Budget Code: 36-0160-0-1-703
Catalog Code: 64.009
FY77 Expenditure (est.): **$2,862 million.**

VOLUNTEERS IN SERVICE TO AMERICA
ACTION

Community organizations in low-income areas are assisted in efforts to eliminate poverty and its effects through the provision of full-time trained volunteers who then live in the community. Depending on a community's needs and a volunteer's training and education, services provided relate to health, education, community development, housing, social services, and economic development. Benefits are thus in kind, funded by means of the subsistence allowances paid the volunteers. No local funding is required. Over 4,000 volunteers are working with some 500 sponsoring organizations; a majority of the volunteers are now recruited from the community in which they work. Benefits are not directly conditioned on need.

Authorization: Domestic Volunteer Service Act of 1973, PL93-113.
Budget Code: 44-0103-0-1-451
Catalog Code: 72.003
FY77 Expenditure (est.): **$23 million.** Includes over 20 percent for administration and other support.

WHEAT PRODUCTION STABILIZATION PAYMENTS
Agricultural Stabilization and
Conservation Service,
Department of Agriculture

Owners, tenants, and sharecroppers producing wheat are provided guaranteed incomes from that portion of their crops grown on acreage allotments. Benefits are in the form of federally financed direct cash payments, without restrictions on their use, based either on the difference between the average market price and a higher, government-established target price (deficiency payments), or on the loss incurred due to natural disasters which prevented any planting or the harvesting of at least two thirds of the normal allotment crop (disaster payments). The number of participating farms receiving payments varies from year to year depending on conditions. Last year, some 45,000 farms received an average of $1,300 each. (No person may receive more than $20,000 in one crop year from any combination of cotton, feed grain and wheat payments.) Benefits are not directly conditioned on need.

Authorization: Food and Agriculture Act of 1965, PL89-321, as amended by PL90-559, PL91-524, and PL93-86, 7 USC 1331-1340, 1379.
Budget Code: 12-4336-0-3-351, 12-3300-0-1-351
Catalog Code: 10.058
FY77 Expenditure (est.): **$111 million.**

WORK INCENTIVE PROGRAM
Social and Rehabilitation Service,
Department of Health, Education and Welfare, and
Employment and Training Administration, Department of Labor

Employable recipients of Aid to Families with Dependent Children (AFDC and AFDC-UF) are provided cash incentives, as well as manpower, employment and social services, to enable them to become self-supporting. Children under 16 or in school are exempt, as are disabled recipients and those required in the home for their care or for the care of preschool children. Nonexempt recipients may be provided assessment, testing, counseling, educational remediation, training, work experience and job placement (by the Department of Labor), as well as medical examinations and services, child care, transportation and relocation expenses (by the Department of Health, Education and Welfare). A $30 monthly stipend is provided, and approximately one-third of net monthly earnings is disregarded as income upon placement in a job. Benefits are in cash and in services funded by 90-percent formula grants to state employment services and welfare agencies. About a half million recipients receive services each year, and as many as 200,000 may be placed in jobs. Benefits are conditioned on need.

Authorization: Social Security Act, as amended by PL90-248, PL92-178, and PL92-223, 42 USC 602, 630.
Budget Code: 75-0576-0-1-504
Catalog Code: 13.748, 17.226
FY77 Expenditure (est.): **$365 million.**

APPENDIX B:
Social Work Personnel Standards

Although there are no national standards governing the training and employment of all social welfare professionals, various professional associations have attempted to develop such standards for their own profession. For example, the National Association of Social Workers (NASW) has developed recommended personnel standards to differentiate levels of education and professional responsibilities appropriate to each.[1] These are reproduced here in order to show how such standards are developed in a social welfare profession.* NASW has also developed a model licensing act that operationalizes personnel standards through legal recognition and enforcement. Because licensing is a function of each state, NASW has been working with states to enact such legislation based on its model. At the beginning of 1979, twenty-five states (including Puerto Rico) had legal regulation of some sort, including fifteen with licensing laws for social work. A number of others had bills before their legislatures.[2] These ongoing activities of NASW illustrate the increasing formalization occurring in the social welfare professions in an attempt to protect professional autonomy and improve service delivery.

In suggesting that social work titles be protected through legal regulation that prohibits their use by anyone other than persons meeting established professional criteria, and that practice be similarly protected through licensure, the profession is attempting to assure that persons calling themselves social workers and engaging in social work practice be competent to do so. Such legal regulation protects the consumer from incompetent practitioners and protects the profession's claim to set standards of professional practice. Professionals themselves are protected from competition with persons calling themselves professionals but who are untrained to provide professionally competent services. Professionals are also provided with a career continuum that provides them with incentive and flexibility.

Although there is little question that a clearly specified and closely integrated system of training, practice, and legal regulation of standards can be expected to have desirable effects on the level of service offered to clients, there are other less obvious issues involved in the strengthening of professional autonomy. As training procedures become more formalized, it is

* At the time of this writing, NASW is working on a revision of these standards.

increasingly difficult for persons who have skill—but who lack the formally specified training—to receive professional certification. This can be of particular importance to members of minority groups who may have had very valuable life experiences, but who may not have had the opportunity to pursue their formal education beyond grade school or high school. Women, too, may be affected, because they often have to drop out of school to raise families or may only be able to study or work part-time. Having preprofessional levels of professional recognition helps, but it still does not altogether overcome the rigidity imposed by formalized standards of training and practice.

Another potential problem with increased formalization is the potential isolation of the profession from the clients it serves. Users of services frequently lack the training that would qualify them for input into professional decision making as formally structured. Yet clients have a perspective on services that the professional cannot have, no matter how much training and experience the individual practitioner might have. After standards are established, especially if they are established by professional organizations that never have direct contact with users of the services, there is a tendency for them to become rigid. Behavior tends to be molded around the standard, rather than the standard remaining flexible to the needs of practitioners and users of services. The result is a potential for professional standards to become increasingly unrelated to practice realities, and thus professionals have the power to control practice in spite of beliefs by users and other nonprofessionals (or even some dissenting professionals) that the standards being used are irrelevant to people's needs.

Try to maintain a balanced analytical perspective when reading these standards. How do they help to strengthen social work practice? How might they serve to isolate the profession from its clients? How might they serve to isolate professionals from each other? Can you suggest any alternative standards or approaches to standards? On the whole, would you support the standards? Why or why not?

▶ Levels of Personnel*

This classification plan recognizes six levels of competence. There are two preprofessional levels, as follows:

- *Social service aide.* Entry is based on an assessment of the individual's maturity, appropriate life experiences, motivation, and skills required by the specific task or function.

* The material beginning here and continuing through page 364 is taken from "Standards for Social Service Manpower" (Policy Statement 4; Washington: NASW, 1973), pp. 5–19, and is used with permission.

- *Social service technician.* Entry is based on completion of (1) a two-year educational program in one of the social services, usually granting an associate of arts degree; or (2) a baccalaureate degree in another field.

There are four professional levels, as follows:

- *Social worker.* Entry requires a baccalaureate degree from an accredited social work program.
- *Graduate social worker.* Entry requires a master's degree from an accredited graduate school of social work.
- *Certified social worker.* Entry requires certification by (1) the Academy of Certified Social Workers (ACSW) as being capable of autonomous, self-directed practice; or (2) licensure by the state in which the person practices.
- *Social work fellow.* Entry requires completion of a doctoral program or substantial practice in the field of specialization following certification by ACSW.

Preprofessional Social Work

The two levels of preprofessional social work practice have distinct levels of competence:

Social service aide. Under professionally guided supervision or as part of a team, the social service aide performs various specified duties to help clients obtain and use social and related services, including obtaining information, providing specific basic information, aiding clients in agency procedures and services, and other supportive functions. The aide classification may cover a variety of specific service-related functions other than social service, but should be integrated with the performance of duties by other social service personnel.

Responsibilities require an ability to communicate freely, to understand and describe program procedures, to interpret the concerns and needs of clients, and to provide defined, concrete assistance with the needs of living. The aide must have knowledge derived from accumulated life experiences paralleling those of the consumer community, a capacity to learn specific skills taught through on-the-job training, and motivation to serve others. The minimum educational requirement for this classification is the ability to read and count, in addition to other individual skills necessary to carry out the tasks of the particular position.

Social service technician. As part of a team or under the direction of and close supervision by a professional social worker, the social service technician performs a wide variety of duties to facilitate the knowledge and use of social services. These involve disseminating information, obtaining information from clients, assisting clients in the use of community resources, obtaining information about assessing the impact and coverage of programs, carrying out specific program activities and tasks, and in other ways applying life experiences and knowledge derived from training in working with individuals or groups.

In carrying out these responsibilities, the social service technician must be able to make inquiries discreetly, provide clear information, understand and describe agency programs, recognize general levels of anxiety or reactions of fear, maintain emotional self-control, retain values, and provide services to assist clients with defined environmental problems.

The technician must have knowledge of the fundamentals of human behavior, specific agency operations, and specific communities and their social service programs and have skills in working with people, including the ability to communicate and empathize, attitudes of respect for individual and group differences, appreciation for the capacity to change, and the ability to use social institutions on behalf of consumers. The educational requirement is an associate of arts degree in a technical program of social services or its equivalent.

Professional Social Work

The four levels of professional social work practice also have distinct levels of practice and preparation:

Social worker. Under supervision, the social worker is responsible for professional service designed to sustain and encourage the social functioning of individuals or groups. The worker assists them to appraise their situation, to identify problems and alternative solutions, and to anticipate social and environmental consequences.

The social worker is guided by professional social work values, purposes of the service, prevailing organized knowledge, societal sanctions, and social work methodology. In carrying out responsibilities of the job, the social worker uses methods of disciplined inquiry based on interpersonal relationships involving cause and effect; interpretation of resources and their limits; intervention with related individuals or groups, colleagues, and other disciplines and organizations; direct counseling and services; and other related activities.

The social worker must have a beginning knowledge of human behavior and development, the social and economic environment, the social service system, and the factors that contribute to normal development and social and individual abnormalities, including symptomatology. The worker must be able to demonstrate a conscious use of social work methods, for example, skill in the use of specific techniques, such as interviewing, diagnosis, use of self-discipline, and use of social resources. The educational prerequisites for this classification are a baccalaureate degree from an undergraduate college or university with a social welfare program accredited by the Council on Social Work Education (CSWE).

Graduate social worker. The graduate social worker is responsible for providing professional, skilled social work services to individuals, groups, or larger social contexts and is capable of providing supervisory assistance to less advanced workers. Although the worker works under professional supervision, a significant portion of the work activity involves independent judgment and initiative.

The graduate social worker is guided by professional social work values, the purposes of the service involved, accepted theoretical and organized knowledge, societal sanctions, and social work methodology. In providing services, the graduate social worker uses methods appropriate to the situation, including a disciplined interaction based on a knowledge of interpersonal relationships of cause and effect, relevant professional literature and research to obtain necessary additional professional knowledge, the conduct of social research regarding the service or broad professional concerns, the interpretation of community resources and advocacy needed to assure the availability of resources, intervention with related individuals and organizations, the provision of therapeutic counseling directed toward clear goals, social action to increase awareness and to work toward the resolution of professional concerns, as well as other related activities.

The graduate social worker must have a theoretical and a beginning empirical knowledge of human behavior and development, a working understanding of social and economic realities and forces, a critical knowledge of social service systems, a familiarity with the nature and causation of individual and social abnormalities and an awareness of relevant community and professional organizations and related institutions. The worker must have demonstrated competence in at least one of the specialized social work methods and a knowledge of others. The educational prerequisite for this classification is the master's of social work degree from a graduate school of social work accredited by CSWE.

Certified social worker. The certified social worker is responsible for a wide range of independent social work activities requiring individual accountability for the outcome of service, including direct services to individuals, groups, or organizations; supervision of social workers and social service technicians; consultation at key points of decision making in the social services; interdisciplinary coordination; education and in-service training; improvement and development of services; and other activities requiring sensitivity and expert judgment.

Guided by the values of professional social work, purposes of the service, prevailing organized knowledge, societal sanctions, and social work methodology, the certified social worker uses methods of basic social research and planning, interpersonal therapeutic techniques, group and social organizational relationships, education and administration, and others as required by the clients or groups served.

The certified social worker must have both theoretical and empirical knowledge of human behavior and development and be familiar with the social and economic processes, the philosophy and operations of social services systems, the nature and causation of individual and social abnormalities, and the different relationships and responsibilities of professions, organizations, and societal institutions. The educational prerequisites for this classification are a master's degree from a graduate school of social work accedited by CSWE and certification by the ACSW as being capable of autonomous, self-directed practice.

Social work fellow. The social work fellow is capable of a wide range of independent social work activities requiring individual accountability for the outcome of service and special expertise in intensive services to individuals, groups, and organizations; administration and direction of programs and organizations; specialized consultation, planning, education, and decision making; and other activities requiring special combinations of education and experience. Having mastered the integration of social work values, the delineation of the purposes and policies of service, the integration of organized knowledge and practice, the testing of societal sanctions, and the incorporation of social work methodology, the social work fellow utilizes combinations of knowledge and skills in the following areas:

1. The direction and conduct of major research and planning efforts.
2. The application and extension of interpersonal therapeutic techniques.
3. The study and implementation of the objectives of groups or social organizations.
4. The expansion of educational and administrative theory and practice.
5. Other specialized endeavors based on social work expertise.

The social work fellow is required to have a broad knowledge of the field, with concentrations in specific areas. These areas include advanced knowledge of theories of and research in human behavior and development; the social and economic processes and their interrelationships; the nature and causation of individual and social abnormalities; and the planning of services involving the integration of professional, organizational, and institutional activities. In addition, the worker provides leadership in the planning, development and administration of social service agencies; analysis and formulation of social policy; research and the evaluation of social service delivery systems; advanced clinical practice, and education for social service.

The educational prerequisite for this classification is (1) a doctoral degree in social work or a related social science discipline, with at least two years of experience in an area of social work specialization; or (2) certification by ACSW and two years of experience in an area of social work specialization.

Guidelines

The standards have been prepared by NASW to provide a basis on which local and state NASW bodies, educators of social service manpower, administrators planning for or employing social workers, personnel specialists, and individual social workers may evaluate job classifications for social work and social service personnel.

Such evaluations should have two objectives: (1) to assure that classifications of existing job functions are related to the appropriate level of competence and educational preparation; and (2) to clarify and strengthen relationships among job classifications actually used to maximize the career potential in a setting or organization.

It is important to restate that the simple classification plan provided in these standards is not a substitute for the detailed and rational analysis of specific tasks required to establish accurately and professionally a staffing plan for social work manpower in an agency. It should, however, provide a means by which various staffing plans can be contrasted and interrelated for purposes of career planning and staff development.

A major purpose of these standards will be to assist in the development of curricula for social work programs appropriate to each of the defined levels. It is axiomatic that effective education requires definite educational goals. Both short-term training programs and more substantial educational programs should be directed toward specific vocational levels. Similarly, curriculum-building requires well-defined concepts of skills and competence. These standards are seen as a beginning step toward the more technically complete definitions required by educational planning. They should be adequate for general usage by personnel and staffing planners and for the administrative purposes of most agencies.

As a tool, it is hoped these standards will (1) achieve maximum effectiveness of and accountability in social service programs; (2) assure the appropriate use of qualified manpower; (3) provide opportunities for advancement in individual agencies; (4) facilitate the adaptation of workers transferring to other agencies; and (5) provide clear goals for the development of educational curricula.

Differential Use of Manpower

In applying these standards, the community social service system should be the initial focus of attention. For a comprehensive range of services to be provided in a community, a complete and appropriate use of manpower must be available. The combination of social worker classifications needed by an individual agency will be determined by the agency's size, functions, and technological development and by the available manpower. For example, in some agencies the nature of the functions would allow the use of social worker, technician, and aide levels, while in others the need for high discretionary or technical judgments might require a greater use of the certified social worker or graduate social worker levels.

In planning for the use of all social service manpower, emphasis should be placed on permitting individual employees to contribute as much as they can, according to their ability to practice. The opportunity to make meaningful contributions to the achievement of social service goals makes the difference between motivation for professional services and mere existence on a job.

To accomplish a differential use of manpower will require individual agencies, which comprise the community social service system, to cooperate formally in implementing a career ladder. Such a ladder must have two essential characteristics: (1) it should open doors to persons wishing to find a career in the social services and provide entry at each level of competence; and (2) it should provide the opportunity for career advancement, as well as for horizontal mobility. These characteristics will require programs of career recruitment, counseling, and meaningful staff development.

Job Levels

Because of the ordinal nature of this classification plan, several concepts concerning its application must be highlighted. As a general rule, a complexity-scale concept has been used. This means that an employee at any given level of competence should be capable of performing less complex functions but not be able to perform effectively those that are more complex.

Further, it should be recognized that there are qualitative differences among abilities at different levels. A social worker should be able to complete a survey schedule or interview clients for data to determine their need for agency services, while a certified social worker should be able to develop a survey design or to conduct counseling interviews involving complex marital adjustment problems. And there will be different performance levels within classifications that are dictated by such factors as length of service and demonstration of special abilities.

For a variety of reasons, agencies may find it necessary to define several grade levels within each classification level, primarily as a result of the differential activities within the agency. That is, certain clusters of work responsibilities might require unique abilities. However, additional levels should reflect two characteristics: (1) there should be a continuum of logical steps from one level to another, if possible, so that both responsibilities and opportunities for career advancement are clearly perceived; and (2) opportunity for advancement to a higher level should be possible for employees who can demonstrate an ability to perform such functions and who meet the prescribed qualifications.

Finally, all classification levels should provide salary levels commensurate with the functions performed and with the employee's performance. The salary structure should be commensurate with the standards for the field and reviewed annually for equity and for comparability both within the field and to the labor market generally.

Summary of Functions ◀

Social Service Aide

Functions. As part of a team or other professionally guided supervision,

- Interviews applicants for services to obtain basic data and to provide information on available services.
- Interprets programs or services to ethnic or cultural groups and helps such groups or individuals express their needs.
- Assists people in determining their eligibility for services and in assembling or obtaining required data or documentation.
- Participates in neighborhood surveys, obtaining data from families or individuals.
- Provides specific information and referral services to people seeking help.
- Conducts case-finding activities in the community, encouraging people to use available services.
- Provides specific instructions or directions concerning the location of services or procedures involved in obtaining help.
- Serves as a liaison between an agency and defined groups or organizations in the community.

Qualifications. Life experiences and knowledge of the community or special groups are the primary abilities required.

Although high school graduation is not always required and may be irrelevant, basic skills in reading, writing, and computation are important. A high school diploma may be required for certain positions.

A concern for people and a willingness to learn on the job are essential attitudes.

Social Service Technician

Functions. As part of a team or under close professional supervision,

- Conducts fact-finding and referral interviews based on an awareness of generally available community resources.
- Assists in helping individuals or groups with difficult day-to-day problems, such as finding jobs, locating sources of assistance, or organizing community groups to work on specific problems.
- Contributes to special planning studies from knowledge of a client's problems and viewpoints, as part of a project or planning unit.
- Helps assess the suitability or effectiveness of services by understanding and relating to the experiences and specific needs of a group.
- Provides coaching and special supportive role assistance to help groups or individuals use services.
- Provides specific instruction or direction to persons seeking services, as part of an outreach or orientation activity.
- Records data and helps collect information for research studies.
- Works with local agencies or workers regarding specific problems and needs for clients and agencies.
- Does emergency evaluations and provides emotional support in crises.

Qualifications. Completion of an organized social welfare program leading to an associate of arts degree or a bachelor of arts degree in another field.

Motivation to help people.

Social Worker

Functions. Using social work supervision,

- Provides social work services directed to specific, limited goals.
- Conducts workshops to promote and interpret programs or services.
- Organizes local community groups and coordinates their efforts to alleviate social problems.
- Consults with other agencies on problems of cases served in common and coordinates services among agencies helping multiproblem families.

- Conducts basic data-gathering or statistical analysis of data on social problems.
- Develops information to assist legislators and other decision makers to understand problems and community needs.
- Serves as an advocate of those clients or groups of clients whose needs are not being met by available programs or by a specific agency.
- Works with groups to assist them in defining their needs or interests and in deciding on a course of action.
- Administers units of a program within an overall structure.

Qualifications. Completion of an approved social work program awarding a baccalaureate degree.

Graduate Social Worker

Functions. Using consultative or routine supervision,

- Provides therapeutic intervention under supervision.
- Organizes a coalition of community groups to work on broad-scale problems.
- Is the social work component on a multidisciplinary team.
- Conducts group therapy sessions in a clinic setting.
- Provides consultative assistance with social services to a community.
- Develops and conducts research involving basic statistical techniques.
- Works on program planning for a major public agency providing social services.
- Is an instructor on a faculty of a school of social work.
- Administers a social service program.
- Serves as a team leader in a service unit.
- Works in a program planning section of a social service agency.

Qualifications. Completion of a master's of social work program in an institution accredited by CSWE.

Certified Social Worker

Functions. Using consultation, when appropriate,

- Serves as a team leader in a multidisciplinary therapy group.
- Provides psychotherapy to individuals and groups on an independent basis.

- Serves as a consultant to major social service and community action programs.
- Administers a social service program or agency.
- Teaches on the faculty of a school of social work.
- Plans and conducts research projects.
- Conducts program evaluation studies.
- Works as an independent consultant with industrial organizations to provide social work-oriented direction to employee service programs.
- Works as a community organizer or planner for a metropolitan coordinating body.
- Provides teaching supervision in a program providing intensive casework services.

Qualifications. Completion of a master's degree program in social work and certification by ACSW.

Social Work Fellow

Functions. In accordance with professional standards,

- Administers a major social service agency or program.
- Works as an independent consultant in private practice.
- Works as a psychotherapist in private practice.
- Is a professor on the faculty of a school of social work.
- Develops and directs a research program for a consultant firm specializing in social problems.
- Conducts independent research.

Qualifications. Completion of a doctoral program at an accredited school of social work or in a related discipline, with two years of specialization in an area of social work or certification by ACSW and two years of social work experience in the field of specialization.

REFERENCES

1. "Standards for Social Service Manpower" (Policy Statement 4; Washington, D.C.: National Association of Social Workers, 1973), pp. 5–19.
2. *Encyclopedia of Social Work* (Washington, D.C.: National Association of Social Workers, 1977), p. 1077, and personal communication with Myles Johnson on the NASW staff.

APPENDIX C

The Case File: Two Illustrative Cases

Two cases are presented here to illustrate for instructors and students how the values, knowledge, and skills discussed in the text manifest themselves in real social welfare situations. The cases are presented in their entirety and with no notes or supplemental material so that instructors may use them in whatever way they wish. As an aid to students, the following paragraphs highlight some of the major issues raised in each case:

The first case illustration, Mrs. R, focuses particularly on a systems approach in working with a family. In this case, the way in which problematic individual behavior may have its roots in and have an effect on the behavior of other individuals and groups is clearly illustrated. By using a systems approach, the worker utilizes many interventive points as she attempts to identify problems and resources and develop a helping strategy. Her efforts go far beyond Mrs. R as she looks at the individuals, groups, organizations (including professional social welfare organizations), and societal values and structures that impinge on the person for whom help is sought.

The second case illustration, 165 Howell Street, is an extended account of work with a group of tenement residents. It clearly illustrates how basic skills are used in one-to-one, small-group, and community contexts to develop an effective interventive plan. As with the case of Mrs. R, the importance of a systems approach in professional problem solving is demonstrated. Finally, 165 Howell Street shows how the community serves as a context for individual and group behavior, and how human diversity factors affect behavior in situations.

Case Illustration 1: The Case of Mrs. R ◀

Mrs. R, a black, forty-two-year-old, obese mother of ten children, was admitted to a state mental hospital. Prior to admission, Mrs. R, who has an eighth-grade education, resided with her husband and children in a six-room apartment in a deteriorated old building in the ghetto neighborhood. The family received a maximum AFDC grant, and Mrs. R earned a small

Source: Ben Orcutt, "Casework Intervention and the Problems of the Poor," *Social Casework* 54 (February 1973): 85–95. Used with permission of Family Service Association of America.

income from steady night work. The family managed poorly because their income provided only basic necessities. (They would be currently categorized as the "working poor.")

Mrs. R was diagnosed as a chronic schizophrenic, undifferentiated type. She was hospitalized at the request of the family court when at a court hearing both she and her husband were charged with child neglect. Her bizarre delusional responses led to recommendation of hospitalization. Mrs. R spoke of being unable to take care of her ten children, ranging from two-year-old twins to a fourteen-year-old daughter on whom she relied. Her child care was erratic, and at times she could not feed, change, or train the twins, nor could she touch or acknowledge any of the children. She refused to prepare her husband's meals and refused sexual relationships, fearing pregnancy. She used a contraceptive preparation which had been ineffective. Mr. R had withdrawn from her verbally and emotionally, and generally was away from the home. He had deserted her four years before, but returned when ordered by the court to face a jail sentence or return home.

Mrs. R is essentially nonverbal; her voice has a strained, unnatural sound. She distrusts people and is aloof and withdrawn. She complains of the heavy strain of family responsibility. Mr. R does not see himself as a helpmate and does nothing to maintain the family or marital relationship, nor does he give physical care to the children. Clinic appointments, school appointments, household chores and management, and discipline are left to Mrs. R. She says she resents this and her husband's criticism of her being a poor housekeeper, but she does not speak out about it. She tends to withdraw and appears apathetic.

The six school-age children all have learning difficulties and are in special classes at public school. One child, age ten, is severely retarded and cannot dress herself. All the children in the family are functioning below normal expectations. Little is known of Mrs. R's early life beyond the fact that she was the youngest of nine children and was born on a farm. She moved to the city with her mother during her teens after her father died. She worked in factories, was self-supporting, and lived with her mother until age twenty-six, when she married her present husband. Her mother has subsequently died, and there is no extended family in the city. In the hospital, in addition to appearing isolated, she evidences some delusional ideas.

This case illustration is similar to a magnitude of cases known to hospitals and to voluntary and public agencies that serve people from low-income groups in areas of a central city.

At the outset, one sees a family system in chaos and in transaction with a range of interlocking systems in the environment. The primary focus, as discussed here, would not be simply on Mrs. R as a new patient in the state hospital with an identified diagnosis of schizophrenia. The focus would be on Mrs. R as a component of her family system and the interlocking social systems, such as the hospital, the family court, Department of Social Services, the ghetto neighborhood, and public schools—and indirectly with the work system, where her husband is a structural part.

The unit of attention may shift with diagnosis and intervention, but primarily the focus is on the family in trouble. There is no attempt to minimize the fact that Mrs. R has a severe emotional illness. Her personality system is disorganized, with an overwhelmed ego that cannot successfully mediate the intrapsychic and environmental forces. Her individual dynamics should be assessed in concert with the dynamics of her family system and the transactions with other linking systems. With this focus, intervention is aimed at family equilibrium, differentiation, and growth in the family system. This practice does not imply that the R family system is seen and treated only as a family group, with help to Mrs. R accruing as residual to shifting the family dynamics in an improved equilibrium of the system.* It is important, however, to focus on change of functioning in the family as a dynamic, interactional unit, as well as change in the dynamics of Mrs. R's individual functioning. Intervention is aimed at both the family and individual systems. Treatment may be individual or family group treatment, or both.

The social caseworker who applies systems theory as a frame and focuses on the family unit, with Mrs. R as a component, will intervene in the following directions.

1. Build a trusting relationship with Mrs. R (person system) through regular contact, as a caring, dependable object whose quality of communication and tangible help can stimulate effective contact, a sense of trust, and self-worth. Dealing with her reality, its burdens, and a more realistic appraisal is aimed at improving her reality testing and expansion of ego-functioning.
2. Encourage Mrs. R, in dealing with ward and hospital systems, to participate and enlarge her object relationships and general functioning in her patient role.
3. Intervene in the hospital system to mediate problem situations, including access to knowledge of family planning, and serve as interpreter or advocate for the client in order to reduce stress and support hospital input for nurturance and change.
4. Involve Mr. R (family system) in a greater role of leadership as the sole parent in the home, as is consistent with his capacities and as the family transactions permit.
5. Intervene with the Department of Social Services agency system in the provision of a homemaker (paraprofessional) on a long-term

* The system purists are described by Christian Beels and Andrew Ferber, "Family Therapy: A View," *Family Process* 8 (September 1969): 296.

basis and bring routines into the home by which child care can be brought up to standard, without displacing Mr. or Mrs. R but by encouraging their support and accrediting parental strengths.

6. Intervene with housing authorities to provide adequate housing.
7. Intervene with the school system to mediate, interpret, advocate, or plan with school for children to maximize learning. The ten-year-old severely retarded child, who remains in the home, will need special planning depending on her functioning and the extent of care required.
8. Intervene with the family court to mediate and interpret family difficulties and enlist support for the family as a structural unit.
9. Intervene with the family as a group in assessment of family dynamics and with family group treatment as appropriately timed. The aim in treatment is to improve interpersonal relationships, facilitate appropriate communication and role-carrying, and shift the affective supports within the system to meet individual needs for growth and mastery of developmental tasks.
10. Enroll Mrs. R, as diagnostically indicated, in a formed group aimed at socialization and introduce the other family members who can benefit to community services offering group experience.

The social caseworker's diagnostic assessment of the individual/family and environmental transactions guides the intervention at varying depths in all of the linking systems to achieve reduction of frustration and to increase the supplies of energy and information that will stimulate exchange that is restorative and growth-producing. Systems concepts aid in depicting the fluid, interactional relationship within the person/family systems and those that interlock to form the environment for Mrs. R and the family. The functioning of Mrs. R as a component of her family system is conditioned by and conditions that of other members of the family. The homemaker who enters the family system must also be taken into account in the transactional processes. Serving as a dependable mother surrogate, the homemaker can be responsive to deep and feared dependency needs in Mrs. R's personality system which affect the entire family transaction.

The casework practitioner thus orchestrates a range of services combined with a therapeutic approach not only to strengthen Mrs. R's ego functioning, in individual work, but also to modify the functioning of the family unit. . . . The practitioner has responsibility to contribute from his knowledge of broad client needs to policies and development of a range of services, with delivery patterns that serve to prevent problems and to restore individuals and families, whose maladaptations are associated with substandard living. The aim must be to make available appropriately trained manpower, equipped to render direct helping services in a service network with sufficient resources. Professional knowledge, competence, and skill are basic requirements for the wide responsibilities of social casework practice at the hub of the wheel, especially aimed at poor, dysfunctional families alienated from the mainstream.

Case Illustration 2: 165 Howell Street

Part 1: Introduction

The project. The [Adelphi University] School of Social Work received a training grant from a federal agency and, in cooperation with the Southside Community House, assigned six graduate social work students to service tenement dwellers in the area. The tenements to be serviced were selected on the basis of past tenant participation in agency programs; this is not to say, though, that all tenants had a past relationship with the Community House. The number of tenants who had a past relationship varied from building to building. One of the selected buildings had been serviced in like manner for a few years previous to the initiation of this project by the agency itself, and its experience and interest were important to the decision as to which agency the school would cooperate with in the implementation of the proposal.

Though the original plan was to have one first-year student and one second-year student service a particular building, prior to the commencement of the work a decision was made to extend the service to six dwellings; and therefore, each of the six students was assigned to a separate dwelling. The basis for each tenement assignment was unknown to me; that is, I do not know why I was assigned the tenement I worked in rather than one of the other five.

Other factors were also important in the selection of these six from the many tenements that existed in the area. In each there were recognized multiple and complex social problems. These included poverty, overcrowding, discrimination, family disorganization, out-of-wedlock children, poor and deteriorating health, and emotional disturbance. In most of those selected there also were problems of mental illness and narcotics addiction, but I did not find such to be extensive in my tenement.

Social work servicing was to take the form of a generic approach with particular emphasis upon developing a tenant group in each building. Participation of all tenants was to be striven for, but this objective or goal would be subject to modification after more was learned about the building and the tenant system. Specific goals could not be formulated until more was learned about each tenement complex, but basic or broad goals were formulated prior to the initiation of service. The tenants in these buildings

---

Source: Louis Lowy, Leonard M. Bloksberg, and Herbert J. Walberg, *Teaching Records: Integrative Learning and Teaching Project* (New York: Council on Social Work Education, 1973), pp. 85–107. Reprinted by permission of the Council on Social Work Education.

were recognized as having experienced oppression, defeat, disillusionment, and despair. They were therefore in need of assistance in learning how to negotiate the complex bureaucratic structures which influenced them, in need of developing a stronger sense of community, in need of recognizing their true worth and abilities, in need of personal enhancement and development, and in need of developing a more positive image of the wider community and realizing their place in it.

The agency. As previously mentioned, the Southside Community House, an established agency with a long history of service to the community, embarked on such a program six years before this program began when it recognized that several disturbed youngsters using its program resided in the same building. The idea of working with all the families as a tenement social system was explored as an alternative to the more traditional plan of trying to work with each family as an isolated unit. Though the tenement program was funded from outside sources, the original program was undertaken at agency expense. Since the inception of this plan, graduate social work students have serviced the one particular building selected.

The tenement. The building was a five-story walkup with three apartments on each floor except the ground floor, which had two. All apartments facing front had three rooms, while those in the rear had five. Three years earlier, title of the building was transferred to the City Department of Real Estate, and at that time the building was partially renovated. Cockroaches were to be found in abundance throughout the building. Rats showed themselves infrequently. There was usually garbage in the halls, but not to any great degree.

The exterior and halls, though in need of paint and plaster, were in fairly good order. The complaints usually involved poor plumbing, holes in the floors and walls, defective utilities, and difficulty in getting anything fixed—from the front door lock to the rear room window sashes.

The group. One must understand that all the tenants were viewed as the client system to be serviced. The group which was formed not only was used to enhance the lives of those who actively participated, but was the vehicle used for reaching out to the others. Hopefully, the development of the group would have a positive effect on even those who were not participating members. Therefore, the group was not closed or limited; it was open to "other members." I personally preferred to view those adult tenants who had yet to participate, as members who would one day become active participants, rather than as possible members. This must be clearly understood, for it was important in my approach at all times. I have lost sight of the children, teenagers, or "visiting" adult males, but a focus was necessary and I decided to work with the strongest and most influential members of the entire client system: the mothers. For the purpose of this discussion, then, "the group" refers to only those who actively participated in group sessions.

Most of the members were there because of urban renewal and felt cheated that they had been displaced because of the building of housing projects and yet had been rejected in their many attempts to gain admittance to one. The large majority were dependent on the Department of Social Services for their economic needs, and all were dependent on the Department of Real Estate for their housing needs. In the tenement they had to cope with the lack of concern of the building agent; they had to watch what they said and did that might come to the attention of the DSS caseworker; they had to worry about what to do when someone became ill. The tenement is where they were, but all felt despair and defeat in being there.

The stresses which they had to endure came from almost anywhere. They could come from a large complex bureaucracy or from one's own child. They could come from inorganic as well as organic sources. Each tenant learned to deal with these stresses in his own way, but no one seemed to be able to get out from under. Seemingly, whenever one problem was solved, two others took its place. Assisting these people in understanding and developing skills in handling these stresses could not be done as swiftly as one hoped; it is a long process but a necessary one if these people are to be helped.

The history. Initially, I discovered that there were two major opposing family-based groups, friends of each group, and a few who had little or nothing to do with either group. These two groups comprised half of the tenement population. I decided the focus initially should be to bring these two factions together, and later to bring in the others.

During the early weeks neither group would meet with members of the other. I would hold two meetings on the same day. At one o'clock I would meet with the Waters group, then at two o'clock I would go up and meet with the Wards. Then both sides agreed to get together. On the day of the scheduled meeting everyone was either out shopping or sick. I then decided to concentrate on the mother-leaders, and they agreed to meet even though their daughters refused. Both mothers found something else to do at the time of the scheduled meeting, but it was finally held that day on fairly neutral territory: Olympia's third-floor apartment. Mrs. Ward went down two floors, and Mrs. Waters went up two. Then another meeting was set, but no one was at home on the planned day.

During the following week, Mrs. Ward contacted her best friend, Mrs. Moore, and Mrs. Moore told me she wanted to be included. One must note that Olympia is Mrs. Waters' best friend. The next meeting would be composed of the two mother-leaders and their respective best friends. Something happened before this meeting was held, though.

For almost three weeks the tenants had been without heat. Installing the new heating system was supposed to take five days, but unfortunately was dragged out to fifteen. On Monday, I received an "emergency call" from Edna and went to the building to learn that everyone was now angry enough to forget differences and do something. Mr. Ward agreed to go around with a petition and got almost everyone to sign. We then took it to a Community Council Legal Unit lawyer; I met him there after again calling Mr. Tubb, who "guaranteed" it would be taken care of that day. After speaking with the lawyer, Mr. Ward and I returned to the building to await the man who was supposed to finally okay the installation. For several hours Mr. Ward and I waited together in the doorway, to keep out of the rain and cold. Finally, the heat and hot water were restored.

When Wednesday came, all four came to the meeting at Olympia's, and Mr. Ward also joined us. When we attempted to relate the action he'd taken Monday, Mrs. Moore cut him off and said she didn't care to hear; she was there for other reasons. Gradually an argument developed and Mr. Ward left, cursing at Mrs. Moore. At the conclusion of this meeting I explained that I had asked the lawyer to talk with us at a next meeting. Mrs. Moore offered the use of her apartment.

Throughout all this beginning effort to get together, there was constant complaining about the building and its agent. There was a stated goal to meet with the man, and he had already agreed to it, but I felt the group needed further development before such a meeting could take place. The CCLU lawyer was part of this development. I met with him a couple of times before the meeting and agreed to what he would talk about, the questions I would ask, and his fostering of a group spirit.

At that meeting Mr. and Mrs. Ward, Sally, Mrs. Moore, Mrs. Waters, Faith and Olympia attended. They left this meeting stating they had to get together and stick together; "there can be no loose ends." The next meeting was also scheduled to take place in Mrs. Moore's, but a couple of days later I learned the Waters subgroup refused to return there because of Mrs. Moore's intoxication and insulting of Olympia. An agreement was reached to switch the meeting place to Edna's; even Mrs. Moore agreed, though I did not fully explain why the others wanted to switch. In this conflict the Wards stated they'd meet anywhere and saw justification for the others' not wanting to meet in Mrs. Moore's. This was quite a change of attitude for them.

The next meeting was held with the new DSS caseworker. I spent a few hours with him before the meeting, and he was very willing to help and understood what I hoped to accomplish. At the meeting he too fostered a group spirit and cohesion, but cautioned them about how to handle themselves with the building agent. He offered his support in their planned confrontation with the building agent, and he promoted good feeling between the tenants and himself.

Here I must restate one objective: to help the tenants negotiate the complex systems they are faced with. I tried to focus always on cooperation and communication. On one hand the meeting with the caseworker was intended to prepare them for the meeting with the building agent; but at the same time it was the big initial step in better communication and cooperation with the DSS.

The meeting with the building agent was one big "if"; no one even had a hint as to how it would turn out. In the two previous fairly formal meetings I felt secure about the outcome beforehand because of my contacts with the "guest speakers," but I had no lengthy discussion with the building agent beforehand. He was coming only because he felt "sorry" about the lack of heat in December. Neither the tenants nor I expected anyone other than Tubb, and they were even doubtful he would show his face.

Throughout this period of time I was developing relationships with the tenants. Since the day we waited in the cold and rain I had spent much more time with Mr. Ward; he had bluntly stated he wanted no responsibility, but would help me when he could. Primarily, I was trying to enhance his self-image and to "educate" him as to how we should deal with key persons. Previous to this he had usually cursed at me and treated me as part of the hated establishment.

Mrs. Moore was none too friendly from the beginning either, but we had a working relationship. Though she drank heavily, I responded to her as I would do to any other and would discuss the details of situations with her, though I was extremely doubtful that she could comprehend one word. I always had a sense that there was very strong racial feeling involved on the part of Mr. Ward and Mrs. Moore, but I believed I could not confront it until something was stated outright and a positive relationship of some kind had been developed.

Edna and Mrs. Waters were always friendly, but had long since learned not to get too involved" if someone came to help. Be nice to him or her, get what you can, but don't stick your neck out. The most fearful of any risk or conflict, though, was Olympia. Only after constant reassurance did she permit the first meeting to be held in her place, and as soon as the group was growing and things were happening, she flatly told me she was afraid and didn't want her apartment used. She was almost terror-stricken whenever someone mentioned "taking on" the building agent. She and Faith were the only two participating members who paid December rent even though all had agreed to stick together and not pay. That risk was too much for her. Our relationship was rather well established and she had found some support in me, enough to finally enable her to disagree with her subgroup prior to this meeting.

I had met individually with Helen only once prior to this session, but that talk was enough to change the image I had had of her when she was in the company of her mother and sisters. I was struck with her intellectual ability, her ability to understand her situation, and her methods of coping with it.

Mrs. Taylor was almost an unknown to me. Previously she had been so intoxicated that she didn't understand anything I said. I had asked Mr. Ward and Olympia to speak with her and try to motivate her. They succeeded, for she did finally come to the meeting with the DSS caseworker. She came to that session thinking I was the lawyer others had told her about. I finally convinced her otherwise.

The members. I will discuss only those who attended this session, but one must remember that there were other tenants and I did consider them as clients and, in a way, definitely part of the group.

Waters Subgroup.—*Mrs. Waters* lived in Apartment 1A, was the mother of Edna, Helen, and Faith, was a middle-aged Negro Methodist, was very religious. Her "adopted" children—Joe (12) and Vera (15)—lived with her. Her son, John, was the superintendent of the building, and the apartment actually belonged to him. She received DSS assistance for Joe and Vera. She declared a "Charleston divorce" from her husband years before, and he lived nearby with John. She could not read or write. Olympia was her best friend. Mrs. Waters had a bad heart and switched apartments with Helen (5C) because of this.

Our relationship was quite friendly, and she asked others to be as honest and truthful with me as she was. She found great comfort in her religion, did not promise and wanted to avoid conflict. She provided warm mothering to her daughters, and one by one they returned to her dwelling. Initially she was very much the sole leader of the group, but a sharing developed, especially with Edna.

Edna lived in Apartment 2A, was the twenty-nine-year-old mother of three small children, was a Methodist, was married but did not live with her husband, and received DSS assistance for the children. She recently had been hospitalized twice, yet she was the type who couldn't rest or relax. The diagnosis was yet to be made, but they thought she had heart trouble and she was taking medication. Her apartment, since her illness, was the hub of Waters activity.

Prior to her emergency call she was polite and cordial, but there was little strength to our relationship. After that call our relationship blossomed and she began to take more of a leadership role with the subgroup and the overall group as well. Of all of those in her subgroup, I felt she was the most interested in a group and wanted everyone to be friendly. She thought very much in terms of the group and influenced the others to think this way also.

Faith lived in Apartment 3B, was the mother of an eleven-year-old daughter, was in her mid-twenties, and was also a Methodist. Her husband lived with her, yet she received DSS assistance for the child. She just recently had moved into the building (four months before) to be closer to her mother, Mrs. Waters.

For the most part she was quite independent, spent most of her time in her own apartment cleaning, and appeared cool toward the others. She began to change, though. At the meeting with the lawyer, she came for herself; at this one she was more a part of the group. She had often said she wanted nothing to do with the group, but she was changing.

Helen lived in Apartment 5C, was the mother of one son, had just turned thirty, and also a Methodist. Though not as religious as her mother, she was the most religious of the daughters. Her male "cousin" was usually seen in the home and I became friendly with him after this session. She was very much attached to her mother and was rarely in her own apartment. She received DSS assistance for her child and had discussed a desire to return to work; she formerly had been a Youth Corps enrollee at the Alliance. Our relationship was good and I contacted the building through her [telephone]. She was willing to help and would participate, but was pessimistic about the outcome. As long as the group appeared together she would participate, but if conflict arose (which was the case) she retreated and said she would rejoin the group when the troubles were straightened out.

Olympia lived in Apartment 3C alone (her Egyptian husband had been deported four years before) and was a middle-aged, overweight black Catholic. Until her husband's deportation she worked as a domestic; she received DSS home relief assistance. We were trying to change her category, though, since she too had heart trouble.

She was highly dependent on others for everything, and avoided conflict for fear of losing friendship. She always kept her front door ajar for fear of dying and not being found for weeks. Any legal-looking paper threw her into a dither. Our relationship was good, but had been better in the past. I felt she was jealous because I had also developed a good relationship with others. She and Mrs. Moore had been the best of friends, but this turned into almost continual conflict, which was made-up two days after. She seemed to get involved in these arguments because the Waterses didn't like Mrs. Moore and she felt she must oppose Mrs. Moore in order to be "in" with the Waterses.

Ward Subgroup.—*Mr. and Mrs. Ward* lived in Apartment 5A and had eight children and two grandchildren living with them. Two daughters, Sally and Bonnie, lived in separate apartments with their own children; two other children were institutionalized. They had been receiving DSS assistance for almost twenty years. Both were middle-aged Negroes. Mr. Ward worked (and probably still does, part time) as an electrical draftsman until he was laid off. Then his heart went bad. He had just about attacked every caseworker up until that time. The previous caseworker said she hated the family and would go out of her way to give them as little as possible.

The Wards disliked the Waters group because they were not New Yorkers, yet got things the Wards couldn't get. To them the Waters family were newcomers making out better than they were. They saw the Waterses as snobbish and pretending to be better than they, yet John Waters was responsible for Bonnie's child and also her new pregnancy. Mr. Ward had always been called upon in case of extreme emergency, by everyone, including the Waters group. He apparently had been able to put aside his feelings when a real crisis hit, and everyone realized this.

Sally lived in Apartment 5B, right next to her parents. She had two very young children and was about twenty years old. She received DSS assistance for the children and also was a Youth Corps enrollee at the Community House.

She was extremely aloof and hard, and until recently hadn't spoken with her father in many months. She considered herself better than all the others in the tenement, had a "cousin" who provided her with fine clothes, etc., and saw herself getting out of the tenement as soon as possible. She demonstrated no liking for anyone, even her mother, and was very cool to me. Our talks were formal and fairly sophisticated—at her desire.

Mrs. Moore lived in Apartment 4B, next door to Bonnie. She had three sons, but only one was at home and she was then arranging to have him institutionalized. The eldest son, twenty-seven, had raped her daughter (then nine), ten years before and the girl had died in the hospital. The middle son was in "boarding school" in South Carolina. Her youngest son she accused of stealing her welfare checks. She was twice married and divorced and spent most of her time with her boy friend, Jack. She continued to receive DSS assistance for the children. Except for Mr. Ward, she was the only high school graduate of the group. Only once did I see her when she was not intoxicated.

Our relationship was conditional on my willingness and ability to help her with personal complaints. Through what happened in group sessions, though, we were very honest and frank. Every other tenant had verbalized that she had an inferiority complex and they pitied her, but she was not well liked, even by some Wards. From the beginning she was desirous of a working relationship, yet definitely not a friendly one. She never brought up the subject of race, but I felt she had deep, strong negative feelings toward whites.

Mrs. Thomas lived in Apartment 1B with her three teenage sons and received DSS assistance for them, was almost deaf in one ear, and had had four operations on her leg, was a middle-aged Negro, and was considered by all to be the one who drank the heaviest. One could almost always find her in the company of four or five drinking companions.

She was generally liked by all, and they believed she had suffered so much that she broke under the strain. Her son had been imprisoned with the Ward boy about the time her leg was injured. Before that she had been a hard worker, energetic and kind to everyone. Mr. Ward was one of her drinking companions, and he and Olympia stated that they felt the group was a success, for at the very least it had gotten Mrs. Thomas on her feet again and active as part of the group.

Outsiders.—*Mr. Tubb* was the building agent for the building. He was unwilling at first even to talk to me. Then we talked a few times on the phone, but still he refused to meet with me. Eventually he came to this meeting, though reluctantly. He refused to discuss the meeting beforehand and said nothing about the fact that his superior was also coming.

Mr. Ryder was Mr. Tubb's superior, and I knew nothing of him until the meeting.

Rocky was one member of a two-man team which did the small repair jobs around the building. I did not know he would attend either.

Part 2: Group Meeting—January 16, 1968

This meeting was to be the climax of the group's movement toward unity; it was to be a show of strength and solidarity. I also hoped to have the group members realize some of their potential and ability, see that they could assert some independence, and plan their next moves with as little intervention on my part as possible.

Though they had long asked to meet with the building agent, I doubted their stated actions once they would actually meet with him. All had said they would believe it only when it actually happened. On the one hand, they wanted to really let loose with him, and on the other, they feared the situation. It was an unknown and a risky one at that. Behind them lay the experience of a friendly outsider who met with them, then the DSS caseworker who represented that "machine" they hated and felt was always looking over their shoulders; and now they were to face the representative of the organization which aroused their most negative feelings.

Had they learned from these experiences? Had they fostered the feelings of security and competence that I intended they should? Were these enough to help them face today, realize their situation, and grow from it? I didn't know for sure, and my anxiety was showing. I went so far as to suggest an early lunch to my co-workers so I could get to the building early, urge a high attendance, check on their readiness, etc. At lunch I realized my own feelings and saw that such action would be contrary to what I hoped would result from the meeting. If the meeting was to stimulate greater independence, then that is what I would have to foster right from the start.

I arrived at Edna's apartment a few minutes before one o'clock, which was the time set for the meeting. She was well dressed and very anxious since no one else had come yet. If dress were any indication, I would say she felt the meeting was the most important to date. At earlier informal sessions she wore nightgowns, at the meeting with the lawyer a house dress, with the DSS caseworker a dress, and this time it looked more like evening wear or her Sunday best. As time went by her mother, Mrs.

Waters, came with Vera, who took the children downstairs. (This pattern was now well established and working well.) Soon after, Olympia came, followed shortly thereafter by Faith. "Where is everyone else?" was the common question. I suggested that, if they were worried about it, one of them should check on the others. (This would no longer be my function but theirs.) No one moved. Mr. Ward came in, asked for his wife, then went to get her. They continued to verbalize their anxiety about the others not being there. I remained silent, but I think I was just as anxious as they were. Finally, Edna took it upon herself to check on the others.

Meanwhile, Mrs. Thomas arrived and was helped in by a middle-aged man who quickly left after she was seated. She began jokingly yelling at me because of the postcard I'd sent. "I can get upstairs by myself, it's the getting down I can't do," she remarked. We all laughed and I realized she was "just what the doctor ordered." She was slightly intoxicated, and her remarks were very humorous. This light touch was what was needed at that point, and everyone took the opportunity, including myself, to release some of the anxiety through laughter. Edna returned with Helen and they joined in the fun. Now present were Edna, Helen, Faith, Mrs. Waters, Olympia, Mrs. Thomas and myself.

Mr. Tubb arrived, paid no attention to the tenants, came over to me, and, after a brief exchange of names, asked, "Are you going to hold the meeting?" His manner was more than abrupt, and I suggested his eyes speak for themselves. "Is this all?" he quipped. "We expect some more . . . that's what we're waiting for," I retorted. He then said his superior was waiting outside in a car and he went to get him. The tenants were extremely anxious at this point and began to move about. They said they couldn't believe it; "His boss too?" they asked. Edna rubbed her hands in delight about her chance to really tell them off. I reminded them of last week's session and what they said they would say today. Mrs. Waters and Olympia wondered where Mr. Ward was: "What's keeping him anyway? He should be here," said Mrs. Waters. I then asked about the other tenants. Yes, they had contacted the Puerto Rican families but no one could come. Also Mrs. Roland was out looking for a new apartment in the Bronx. "What about Mrs. Moore?" asked Edna.

I tried to reassure them, but they remained very anxious. I couldn't even reassure myself. Laughter worked before so I tried it again; I talked about the room, and they joked about the difference between "Charleston people" and other Negroes. Mrs. Thomas's remarks were beautifully funny, but then again anything probably would have seemed funny at that point. We all needed a good laugh.

Mr. Tubb returned and introduced me to his supervisor, Mr. Ryder, and the handyman who usually did the work in the building, Rocky. I then introduced them to the others. Olympia was still muttering, "Where's Tom?" I suggested we wait a few minutes for the others; Ryder said he was a busy man and either we begin or he'd leave; the others knew what time the meeting began, and the Department of Real Estate men were punctual. I began by explaining my interest, agency affiliation, and why we were holding this meeting. Mr. Ryder seemed not to be listening and asked, "Where's the lawyer?" I explained that he wasn't here, nor was he supposed to be, and strongly reiterated my point that he was here to talk with the tenants, not a lawyer or myself. "All right, all right, what's your problem?" he asked as he pointed at Mrs. Thomas. She was numb. I interrupted and told him this was no interrogation. "I know it isn't," he retorted, and pointed at Olympia and asked, "You got a complaint?" She almost fainted. I pulled his arm down and told him he was acting like a Gestapo officer and that he was here "to talk with" these people and not to yell at them. He said he didn't realize he was acting like that, but if that's how it looked, he'd stop. Then he asked me to "watch that I don't do it again." Then he put his hands under his legs to demonstrate his change of approach.

Again the harsh questions, but this time without the pointing. No one answered; they seemed perched on the limb of a tree. Then he loudly said, "See, this is a waste of time. They know they're treated right, they've no complaints, see for yourself!" He stood to leave. I sat way back and told him he was a "load of bullshit" and again told him the stupidity of his actions. I also mentioned that the tenants were doing the right thing in not talking. "Not until you really show a willingness to talk should they speak out." Then he asked if I were blaming him, and I said I was.

He sat down again and asked how he should act. I explained the difficulty of the situation because he'd already acted the way he had, but possibly he had now convinced the tenants that he wished to talk. I asked if anyone cared to say something. Dead silence. I suggested, in an asking way, that I relate Mrs. Moore's complaint since I had received her request to do so if she weren't present. I told the story. "Where is she?" Ryder quickly asked. I told him that this was not the point and asked if he'd really come to talk. "If so, explain it, not ask where is she," I told him. He looked at Tubb, and Tubb now had a quantity of official-looking cards in his lap. He sorted through them, then said three times his men tried to correct the situation but she was never at home.

This irritated Edna and she said that was a lie. Olympia supported her; they were finally talking. I decided to restrict my intervention from this point on. Then they all began to yell at once about these "supposed calls" with no one at home. Ryder turned to me "Now who do I believe?" he asked, holding his hands over his ears. Rocky yelled out that the tenants were wrong, and he was almost assaulted. Ryder intervened and told Rocky to keep quiet. "Where do we go from here?" Ryder asked. I refused to answer, quite loudly, and suggested he pose this question to the tenants. At this they resumed order.

As he began to ask them, Mrs. Moore came in. They all tried to fill her in at once. Mr. Ryder introduced himself. She took the floor and began to go over her complaint time and time again. Mr. and Mrs. Ward came in during this talk. Ryder promised to take care of it by Friday, but this didn't end her talking.

The others were getting annoyed at her. Mr. Ward was asked to talk by the others. Still Mrs. Moore would not stop; she was very drunk. We all sat painfully through this; at times I was asked to intervene, at others, Mr. Ward; side talks started. I continued to look at Mr. Ward, asking with my eyes that he intervene.

I was being torn apart inside, but I couldn't intervene. This was Mr. Ward's chance and I wanted him to seize it. He tried, he yelled at her, but still she continued. Then he made a motion to leave. Mr. Ryder pulled him back when he realized how much the others were pleading with him to stop her and not to leave. I felt sick to my stomach.

Then Mrs. Waters screamed at Mrs. Moore and told her everyone wanted Mr. Ward to speak. Mrs. Moore became silent. Mr. Ward began by thanking Mrs. Waters, then Mrs. Moore started in again. The others were almost out of their seats by then, but Mr. Ward gave her a dressing-down that quieted her. Then he began to relate his feelings. Mrs. Moore started in again; this time Olympia put her hand over Mrs. Moore's mouth and Mr. Ward continued. When he finished he looked questioningly at me. I said he had stated the problem very well but it might help if he gave some examples that would refute Mr. Tubb's records. In a low voice, "Give me some help . . . get me started," he asked. (Or was he telling me what to do? I'd like to feel it was the latter.) Then after I said, "the exterminator bit," he gave example after example.

Ryder then turned to Tubb and said he was taking control of the building "until I get to the bottom of all this." Mr. Ward was proud, very proud, and everyone could see it. I was jumping inside. He had taken that big step. Totally unlike him, he didn't use one curse, even at Mrs. Moore. At times he stood there like a meek lamb, worried, scared, unsure of himself. But he finally came through and provided the strength the others needed. I felt that no amount of "talking" about his position could have done for him what today's meeting was doing. I'd assist as I saw fit, but I would at least hesitate in interventions; I felt even more certain they could really declare some independence. In short, I was relieved.

Then Mr. Ward and Mr. Ryder began to go over the details of repairs and equipment. The list grew so long that Mr. Ryder promised to have a team of his men go through the entire building and fix everything and write down anything needed that they couldn't do. This brought responses from Mrs. Thomas, Edna, Mrs. Moore, and Olympia. Olympia really let loose. She refused to let his men in her apartment because they only "make things worse." Then she said Rocky did sloppy work. All the others disagreed and said his partner was a jerk, not him. Olympia stuck to her guns, stood yelling, and grabbed at Rocky. Edna and Helen tried to restrain her, but she quickly put them down verbally. Each had had a say, now she was having hers and she really brought this point home. They retreated and Olympia concluded her complaints. I had seen her angry before, but her taking on the whole group was almost inconceivable. Three times during her excited statements she remarked about her "bad heart" and "high blood pressure," but these remarks only affected Mr. Ryder; the others were now used to them.

Mr. Ryder said he would stay with his team and they wouldn't leave until the work was done to the tenants' satisfaction. Olympia then accepted his proposal and the others quickly followed. Then they began to praise Mr. Ward and talk among themselves.

While this was going on, Mr. Ward leaned over and whispered, "Should I bring up the rent?" and I winked in response. Then he stood in the middle of the room and told the story of no heat and no hot water in December. He concluded by asking where they [the tenants] stood on the rent. Mr. Ryder looked to Tubb and Tubb explained about the 33 percent. Ryder said, "Well, where's the problem? You're getting a 33 percent cut . . . I see no problem about the rent." Mr. Ward briefly spoke about the hardship it caused and concluded by emphatically stating that he wouldn't pay one cent of December's rent and that he'd only accept a 100 percent cut and nothing else. This really irked Mr. Ryder, and he suggested a 10 percent cut instead. I could not believe my ears, nor could Mr. Ward. Mr. Ryder went on to say they couldn't have everything they asked for and began to tell how expensive it was to keep up a building. With this, Mr. Ward pushed his way out. As the others attempted to bring him back, I talked with Mr. Ryder. I said 33 percent was already offered and saw no reason for lowering it. Then his attitude got the best of me and I lost my cool. I literally blew my stack and let him know how Tubb strung us along and how only the tenants suffered, while everyone else made money on the deal. Regaining control, I asked Helen to try to clear the air. I asked her because of her abilities and the way I thought she'd react.

She began by explaining what a good paying tenant she was and that she had no major complaints, but she couldn't permit the rent situation to be left as it was. In a low but firm voice she told of illnesses and hardships of the tenants, and then she too placed much of the blame on Tubb's faulty handling of the situation. When she finished, I added a few facts about specific attempts to correct the situation. It now became apparent that Mr. Ryder had not been told all the details, as Tubb had said he would do earlier.

Ryder was moved by Helen's talk and looked angrily at Tubb, then he asked if 50 percent would be acceptable. I said that the tenants would have to decide, and, as I told Tubb, the decision would be made at our get-together after this meeting. I then asked the tenants if they wished a change in plans. They did not and felt we should stick to our original plan.

Then he told us this 50 percent figure was not assumed; he'd first have to get permission, but in light of the situation, he felt he would get that permission. Mr. Ryder rose to leave, but I stopped him and we summarized the agreements reached today for all to hear. The primary ones were: He'd have an answer on the 50 percent cut in a few days; he and his team would go through the building next week; no punitive action would be taken against any tenant; the building agent would meet with us once a month and would have to report to Mr. Ryder on each session; Mr. Ryder would also visit some apartments today at the request of those tenants who wanted it.

I reminded everyone to come back for the get-together and thanked Mr. Ryder for coming, and then he assured me of his cooperation. As Rocky passed us he commented, "Now they like me . . . now they like me." Ryder laughed.

Informal session. I helped Mrs. Thomas downstairs and she said she could be told later about our get-together. She didn't want to go upstairs again after Mr. Ryder left. I rejoined the others in Edna's.

When I returned, I discovered that Sally had come down. This was the second time she had come after the meeting for the informal session. Edna, Helen, and Faith filled Sally in and seemed happy with the results. Then they began to discuss Mrs. Moore and verbalized their dislike of her coming intoxicated. Sally was laughing at their accounts; I was in the kitchen, but I could hear.

When I came back they asked me to talk about the meeting. I suggested we wait for the others before making any decisions, but we could begin to talk in the meantime. Helen asked if I felt things were really going to change. I said they already had and began to explain what it had been like in the building a few months before. Some interrupted with supportive statements and concluded with Edna's "Now we're really together . . . it's real . . . but we gotta stick together." Olympia started talking about the meeting.

I began to get back to Helen's question and explained our gains, but cautioned about what the actual results might be. We couldn't hope for too much, and a bumpy road lay ahead; but we had communicated, we had let them know we had a group that was concerned and willing to take action; we had gotten together. I reminded the Waters girls and Sally about their earlier feelings about each other, and how their mothers tried to get together because they possibly saw the merits of friendship. "You know, I don't hear any more remarks like that," I said, commenting on their previous refusals to see each other.

Then Mrs. Moore came back, listened a minute, then interrupted. She began by calling us all a bunch of nothings. "You're nobodies talking about nothing. You just talk; it doesn't mean nothing." I asked if she was angry with me and she said she wasn't. I said I was angry at her because I thought we'd reached a stage where we could talk frankly and I felt she was angry with me. She replied, "I'm not really angry with you. It's us. Why the hell do we need you? Who are you anyway, coming here? If we need you that only proves we're nothing, you're a white man. (The others cut her off and I asked her to continue.) I'm really mad at us. Why can't we hold a meeting without you?" she concluded.

I said that Mrs. Moore and I had talked about this before and that I wholeheartedly supported her views. "Why can't you hold meetings without me?" I asked. Olympia and Faith felt that they couldn't. Olympia said, "We're not strong enough yet, don't you see that?" Faith said I had the power to get things done and without me they were "lost." Mrs. Moore objected and began to repeat that I was white and she was a "Negro female." I began to respond when Olympia blew her top and said such remarks were out of order and called Mrs. Moore a drunkard. Mrs. Waters supported Olympia, but the others wanted to hear my reply. Olympia quickly left in a frustrated state. Only Mrs. Waters tried to stop her. I was tempted to also, but felt it best not to do so. Such action at the very least could be damaging to the group, particularly at this crucial point.

Then Mrs. Waters asked me to return to the earlier discussion about the meeting with Mr. Ryder. I said I felt it best to deal with Mrs. Moore's remarks instead and told them that just as we asked the white caseworker to spell out his philosophy, so too I should do the same today. "I'm white and you're all black. Now it's said out loud. Does it change anything? (Mrs. Waters pleaded for me to stop.) Maybe now that it's said we can talk more frankly. I don't know, sometimes I feel I don't belong here, and at others it's more like a second home. The thing is, you're a group now. I helped, but I, a white guy, shouldn't be in the front. You have to develop your own leadership. A black person should be your leader, not me. Let's face it, there's a hell of a lot happening these days, and if I stayed in the front, I'd be hurting you, all of you, and me too. I think you've got what it takes, you're ready. Just think about it a minute."

Edna broke the silence by yelling, "But Jack, you're our leader." Her mother, almost in tears now, said just about the same thing. Helen hit on another point I had hoped to get back to. She said this was a risky business and today they'd all stuck their necks way out. She wasn't prepared to do it again without me. She commented that I almost lost my cool a couple of times, but I'd gained control, something they couldn't do. She remarked, "I was watching you. I saw you struggling to keep calm. You warned him he was getting you hot under the collar. You realized what the risk was. I don't know if everyone here really knows even now."

I said a big part of this I'd failed to say; I wasn't going anywhere. I suggested I continue as I had been doing, but with a new twist. "From now on your leader will tell me what he wants from me. I'll help him or her all I can, and I'll remain available to all just as in the past."

Now Edna changed her view and began to praise Mr. Ward for both today's action and past ones. Helen played up the point that they also were crucial to today's success. Yes, I was needed, but they were gaining strength and should begin to realize this and do for themselves. She felt meetings should be held without me, so they could discuss things in their own way. I'd be told of the results, but not all that was said or how it was put.

Edna took the leadership and they began to formalize my future role as they saw it. Each had a say, even Sally, and gradually they defined specifically what I should do after they selected a leader. I would consult with "him." I'd continue to come to the more formal meetings, speak when I saw fit, but wouldn't lead it. After such meetings I'd tell them what was right and wrong and give them any information I thought they should have. I would also continue to see them individually and help in any way I could. I was pleased that they based many of these suggestions on their experiences with our group meetings. Edna, for instance, said it was a good idea to have me explain things after a meeting because it was working well. This was the third time we'd done this. I praised them on what they'd just done, explained what they'd done in moderately sophisticated language, and said I totally agreed with their decisions. Everyone was happy except Mrs. Moore.

She had more to say. She knew they were all talking in terms of Mr. Ward as the leader and she didn't like this. "Why him?" she asked. "I'm the one who got Jack—Mr. Benton—to come here. I'm the one who went around asking for help. You'd be no place without me. We wouldn't even be together here today if it weren't for me." Olympia came back as she was talking, and Olympia told Mrs. Moore to keep her mouth closed. The others giggled and Olympia looked at them sternly but proudly.

Helen asked how everything looked. I pointed out the great steps forward they'd taken, but again cautioned about bad days ahead. I'd be there to help, though, and they shouldn't feel too bad if I was asked to take a more active role. I hoped the situation would not arise, but if it did, they should remember it would only be temporary. They couldn't expect themselves to be a well-organized, sophisticated group overnight. They'd have to learn to deal with internal problems and conflicts, and if individuals had a fight, they'd have to stick with the group—even if with the persons in the room who had just fought with them. Faith and Olympia emphasized that either they would be a group or they would return to their "old ways" and live in their own separate "cat holes."

Then I asked Mrs. Moore if she had anything to say. She replied that she'd been told to be quiet. I said, "Well, if you think you should." She began to talk again about the leader. Edna interrupted and said they'd decide that later, not today, "since Tom ain't here now." Edna looked at me and explained that Mr. Ward was involved in "personal business" today, had come a long distance to be here for the meeting, and had had to get back. "That's why he left when he did, really." I acknowledged this.

Then Edna asked me about an earlier comment of mine concerning MacMahon Clinic; she wasn't sure what I'd said and felt we should discuss it before we ended the meeting. I said I would, but before I did, I just wanted them to be thinking about the rent decision. "This should be discussed too," I said.

Edna said she was concerned about her children's health. Helen felt the situation at the clinic was very poor, and Edna disagreed and related a recent incident. With that, Mrs. Moore jumped up and screamed that her daughter had been "murdered" there. This drew immediate silence. Edna broke it by first sympathizing with her and then explaining that things were changing now. Sally supported Edna, and Mrs. Waters asked that I speak.

I began by saying I felt the doctor who was used by most of them was unfit. I was amazed at their approval of this statement; I thought they liked him. I then went on to explain that someone from MacMahon Clinic was coming to talk with us and we should hear him out, even if we had strong feelings against MacMahon. Mrs. Waters pressed for my particular stand. I said, "If right now I was faced with only the two choices, I'd have to select MacMahon as the better one." This apparently satisfied them. Then they decided to hold off on the rent decision since Mr. Ward had a big voice in this and shouldn't be left out.

In concluding, Edna suggested that they adhere to the idea of moving the meeting place around. Mrs. Moore's offer was turned down since she'd already held one. Faith's offer was accepted and they remarked about gradually getting Mrs. Thomas to exercise more. Next time she'd have to make it up to the third floor.

Next, Edna suggested that from then on they have coffee and snacks at the meetings. "Coffee for Jack and snacks for me. How about it? Let's have some eats too. If they're really our meetings we should be able to do what we want at them—and have what we want at them too." Everyone agreed except Faith, who said she couldn't fix coffee. Edna said she'd take care of it. "Then it's fine with me," Faith concluded.

There would be no planned guest speaker at the next meeting; instead they would choose a leader, decide on what to do about rent, and plan following meetings. They began to leave one after the other, and I spoke to most individually before they departed. The general trend of each of the comments was how much of a success they felt the meeting had been.

Part 3: Early Contacts with Olympia—November 1, 1967

As I knocked on Mrs. Waters' door (receiving no answer) a short, very heavy black woman with very sharp and pleasant features walked down the hall and inquired, "Are you Joe?" I said I was and added, "But are you sure I'm the right Joe?" She smiled and asked if I was the one she was told to expect. "Aren't you going around meeting all the tenants?" She explained that Mrs. Waters had told her to expect me and expressed her desire to talk with me.

She explained that Mrs. Waters was around somewhere in the building and was about to help me find her when I suggested we talk. "Well, not out in the hall, I hope; that's not proper. Let's go up to my apartment," she said in response.

As we reached her apartment (3C) she stood rather motionless and seemed to be trying to catch her breath. I asked if she was feeling ill and she explained her poor health. "I just have to take my pill and then I'll be fine," she said as she opened the door. At her suggestion I went to the living room and waited for her to take her pill. The layout was the same as Mrs. Roland's apartment (the bathroom a few feet from the front door, then an open kitchen area, then the living room, and, at the far end, the corridor opening into the bedroom).

A few seconds later she joined me and had apparently undergone immediate transformation. Now she was alert and revitalized completely. (I thought this rather strange.) I complimented her on the appearance of the apartment and she thanked me, explaining that such cleanliness was proper. She added that possibly because others had children it was harder for them to keep things clean. I agreed but felt she meant me to think she was trying to be nice to the others but was really better than them. (At this point there was just an inkling, but I felt this definitely was the situation as our conversation continued.)

We then made the appropriate introductions and I explained my hopes of organizing a tenant group. Her name was Olympia. She said she should be glad to take part but doubted that many would participate. I explained who I had already seen and said they had reacted in a positive way for the most part. "Oh, Mrs. Thomas is interested?" she asked. I asked if there was a particular reason for her questioning tone, and she stated, "It's just that she's one of those I wouldn't think would want to, but I guess she can really use help. I'm glad to hear she's at least trying."

Then she changed the subject to her health and explained that she had an enlarged heart. She spoke of her Egyptian husband, who had been deported four years before (he had been deported four times), and said he had tuberculosis. When they discovered this about him they ("doctors") also made her take an X-ray and discovered no TB, but did discover an enlarged heart.

A number of times I attempted to get her to discuss any problems in the building but each time she changed the subject back to herself (her husband, her past life, her health, etc.). The talk was pleasant and rather frank, and I felt convinced she wanted me to like her and feel sorry for her and at the same time applaud her for what she had been able to do under difficult circumstances.

Under no circumstances would she tell me of other tenants, saying, "I can't speak for them. That wouldn't be right, would it?" Concerning her feelings she would only say, "I wouldn't want to give you a wrong notion. I think you should meet them and make up your own mind after you've talked to them." And when I asked who lived in a particular apartment (part of a stream of conversation), she said, "Oh, look at me, I never give out information and here I am talking to you this way. But I wouldn't want to give out any information like that, it wouldn't be right."

I felt that a rather positive relationship could be established without much difficulty and that she could very possibly be a great help to me and the others in a group. Though the conversation for the most part received its direction from Olympia, I was able to learn a great deal about her, her relationship with certain other tenants, facts about the building and its internal system. In a sense I felt as though we were playing a game. To any question, she would first have to maintain the privacy of others, then I'd rephrase it, then it would be permissible for her to answer (after I had first seen that she was a proper person and that it was customary for her not to talk about others).

November 3, 1967. For a while I didn't know which way to turn; Olympia wanted to control the conversation. At numerous points she revealed some of her needs; for instance, when we were talking about certain foods Mrs. Waters eats and makes, Olympia looked at me and said, "Now, you and I don't eat such stuff—do you?" They asked if I drank; I said I did. Olympia quickly added, "But not like they do around here; white people know how to hold their liquor. That's what you mean, ain't it?" I said that I had gotten plastered a few times, but she was right, it wasn't a habit with me (they howled with laughter). Olympia added, "The same with me. I don't drink no cheap wine, and I know how to hold it, and went into a long story about the many "fine restaurants" she drank in and didn't get drunk.

I had a constant feeling she was trying to play up to me. She wanted me to recognize her as being better than the others and a fitting person to socialize with "white folk."

November 8, 1967. We both came to the door (opposite sides) at the same time and I startled her. I explained about Mrs. Water's absence and Olympia said she couldn't attend the meeting anyway. She was ill with "an extremely bad cold." On invitation I went into her apartment and she fixed a cup of coffee for me. As happened at our first meeting, she set up a TV table in front of her living room chair (she suggested I sit there), then came the cup of coffee, two spoons and a creamer. A second later she came with sugar. "You know, I'll bet I'm the only one here with this kind of sugar (cubes)." I thanked her, but said I took my coffee without sugar. She replied, "Oh, I do too, sometimes. You know some people just can't take it that way." When she came back she sat at the dinette table. I got up, moved everything over to the table, returned the creamer to the kitchen, came back, and sat at the table with her.

She began to discuss her cold and how she and Mrs. Waters had gone to the clinic the day before. I felt the conversation was strained and commented on this. She replied, "It's just what I told you; you can't help these people. Look, even Mrs. Waters—she couldn't have forgotten." I explained that quite a few days had passed since we had planned this meeting. She said I should have come by and reminded people. I explained my earlier intent and said that something had come up at the office. I said, "Well, I guess it is a bit more than just partly my fault." "That's not it, it's the people here."

As we continued to talk I learned some of her true feelings. She explained how she had been dispossessed from her apartment on City Street in Brooklyn. The people in that tenement were warm and friendly. "But over here it's cold." I asked what she meant. Instead of answering she asked, "Is it like this all around the neighborhood?" I said she probably knew more than I about that, and asked in a leading but empathetic manner, "Is it everyone that's cold?" She spoke of Mrs. Waters in particular. "Even though we're best of friends, there's still something there, a coldness. Do you know what I mean? In Brooklyn we all cared for each other. If something happened to one of us, it happened to all. We helped each other and really loved each other. It was family, real family, not like here. Everyone here only cares about himself. They'll be friendly, but not real friends. Do you really understand what I'm saying?"

I said I had experienced a similar situation, but that it was even harder for her because she couldn't get away as much as she might like. I offered, "Probably sometimes you even feel trapped. But I think you have done a good job of making the best of things." That, she then explained, is what keeps her going. "Everyone needs a purpose. These people have children and the kids give them a purpose for living. But me, sometimes I wonder. But I do the best I can. That's my purpose, and to me its just as important. Everyone needs a purpose, right?" (She was deeply serious.) I said she was correct and added, "I think a big thing, though, is that we can all find much purpose if we just look around and maybe a little inside. It's there; I'm really glad you feel it, and I think you are being great. You know, I see you are one of the strong people here."

She then explained about some of the others and how even though they had children they didn't even try to help themselves or become better people. She asked very pointed questions, like "Whose fault do you really think it is?" and in a sense we argued. She felt most in the building were responsible for their own condition. "You can't blame the government or other people. Hell, it's them, it's their own damn fault." I explained that I couldn't find it in me to blame them. "It's just that some are stronger and able to take it, like you. And then some others are missing a little something, I don't know what. It's probably even different for each one. I can understand how you feel; after all, you live here and I don't. It's easy for me to say I'd rather understand than blame, but someone who lives here would really have to be a great person to be understanding and not get angry." Continuing after a pause, "You know, I think if I lived here I'd feel hurt—like the others are letting me down. I mean, they're human and so am I; they should care."

She then wanted to know if I felt hurt about the meeting's "falling to pieces." I said I'd be a damn liar if I said it hadn't bothered me; it had, but it "wasn't catastrophic." She asked, "What does that word mean?" I said, "In other words it's not the end of the world. It's a setback, but it's not a very bad setback. I didn't expect it, but I'm not going to give up. I'm like you. I'm going to keep on. You can't expect people to trust and like you right off the bat. They have to take their time, see what's happening first."

"But they should realize they have to do something too. The thing is that they don't even want help, some of them," she added.

The talk went on for some time and she revealed one great theme—her loneliness. She always spoke around the subject, and would probably not admit it if a direct question were put to her. I saw two major factors which I had to deal with: her health and her loneliness. It goes without saying that there were many tangentials to each area.

In discussing a meeting I suggested a change of strategy. I asked for her opinion about having only Mrs. Ward, Mrs. Waters, and herself meet with me the first time, instead of trying to get more tenants to the first meeting. She asked why I included her. She could understand about the other two, but not herself.

I explained that I felt she had much to bring to the group. As we continued she was hesitant about making any commitment. She realized Mrs. Ward's position without my saying anything and would permit her apartment to be used for the meeting. Other meetings including the other tenants would have to be held elsewhere. She didn't mind meeting with them, but she didn't want all of them in her apartment. She doubted that Mrs. Ward and Mrs. Waters would come to her place—"They never come in to see me, I always have to go to them"—but if I spoke to them and they agreed, it would be fine with her. We then went down to Edna's again.

I told them I'd come again next Wednesday, and went back upstairs with Olympia to get my coat. When we got upstairs we began to talk again. The discussion was serious and meaningful. The major point I wanted to make was to have her tell me she couldn't sleep at night. She said it wasn't that she was afraid of dying; it was that she is afraid of dying and not being found for weeks. She related a story from her past and explained that a friend had died and she had discovered it two weeks later. "I said goodnight to her and she must have just gone in and dropped dead." She screamed this last part and seemed to be in a trance. I tried to be sympathetic and reminded her of her friends. She said they really weren't friends and they wouldn't even bother coming up to her apartment. She then related a few instances when she was sick and no one had come to her aid. But she always kept her door ajar so she could "feel closer" to the others.

I said I wouldn't be by every day, but at least a couple of days a week, and I cared and would always stop in at least to say hello. She was apparently happy, but commented, "Why should I have to rely on you? They should care; they live here; people who live together should care about one another." She went on to say I must have a lot of things to do rather than be concerned about her—real important things. I said she was my concern and was one of those real important things she was speaking of. Her reply was a warm, friendly smile. I told her I'd be in again next Wednesday, collected all the data she had given me (her doctor, real estate agent, DW caseworker) as we talked, put on my coat, and let myself out.

November 10, 1967. After the meeting I went to Olympia's and she immediately asked about the meeting. I explained the "wait and see" situation. She quickly left that topic and began to talk about herself. Formerly she had been a maid and liked to work with rich people so she could have certain luxuries surrounding her. We discussed this at length, and our relationship became stronger with each talk.

At another point she explained that her doctor would not give her a note so that the Welfare Department would change her status from home relief to aid to the disabled. She told me of her "naughty" habit of using salt, though she was told not even to buy a shaker. As she put it, "Who can eat fried chicken without salt? That's just plain crazy." Also she confessed she should not be smoking—"doctor's orders."

We talked of her problem with the toilet and about her welfare check not coming—she had to go down on Mondays to pick it up in person. I explained my intention of contacting the caseworker and the building agent. She favored this, but impressed on me that they did their best and that both were liked by the tenants. "The last welfare person was just a horrible man. Don't do anything to get her [present worker] changed or mad at us," she commented. I reassured her and explained in detail of my intentions.

There were times during this talk when we laughed and joked. The feeling was friendly and I believe she saw me as an informal professional. I could relax and laugh, but the job of helping and organizing a group never left me and she realized this. I didn't come just to comfort and befriend her; I was there to get things moving on the path of organized self-help.

Part 4: Summary, February 1968—May 1968

1. Though no tenant left the building, there were two cases that were important in this respect:

Kathy Waters, daughter-in-law of Mrs. Waters, moved from the Bronx to stay with Mrs. Waters. With the help of Miss Tegran of the CCL Unit, Mr. James of the Martin Welfare Center, and Mr. Collins of the Southside Welfare Center, we were able to relocate her in a five-room apartment in Brooklyn. She then contacted her assigned welfare center in Brooklyn.

Delores Watson, a friend from Charleston, came to stay with Edna because of her family situation. She came with her four children. With the help of Mr. Collins and Mr. Curtis of the Southside Welfare Center, we were able to temporarily relocate her in a three-and-a-half room apartment in the area.

Both parents and their children frequent the buiding and in this respect, the Waters subgroup had expanded to include Edna (or Gertie), Helen, Faith, Olympia, Delores, Kathy, John Waters, and Mrs. Waters. As you can see, it was now a rather sizable grouping.

2. The group's contact with Mr. Tubb and Mr. Ryder of the Department of Real Estate proved fruitful during this period. The halls were painted and patched, toilet facilities were repaired for many, holes in apartments were patched, radiators were fixed, and those who requested them received new stoves and refrigerators. Much remained undone, though. Windows still had to be fixed and apartments were in need of painting.

A very positive working relationship was developed between the group and Mr. Collins of the DSS. Also, Mr. Curtis, unit supervisor, had a positive feeling toward the 165 Howell Street group and was helpful and ready to extend himself.

The group went through a very trying period, and Mr. Ward's leadership was challenged. As housing and welfare problems diminished in scope and intensity, the group turned inward and conflict was apparent in almost every meeting. Mrs. Moore was seen by the group as a destructive element in their quest for progress. Though all agreed she could be acceptable and helpful when sober, no one wanted any part of her when she had been drinking.

The Waters grouping grew in strength and number, but did not seek formal leadership. They felt it was a man's job. Joe Thomas was able to demonstrate some of his ability in leadership and was to be looked to in this respect. Mr. Ward, though the formal leader, lost the esteem and respect of the group and angered the others to the point where they no longer really wanted him as a leader.

Olympia began to speak out much more and confronted Mr. Ward a few times. She went outdoors more often and generally opened up quite a bit. The group provided her with a vehicle to grow and become more active and involved with others.

Faith, because of a number of specific actions, gained much respect, and possibly even Mr. Ward feared her ability and its recognition by the others.

Mrs. Cole of 193 Howell Street, a friend of Mr. Ward and Mrs. Thomas, became involved in the group and was a very active participant. Her relationship with the group did not rest solely with Mr. Ward.

3. *Goals*: (a) Though there had been some improvement in their living conditions, improvement as a concrete goal was not yet fully realized. (b) The goal to involve all tenants never crossed the racial barrier. There still remained two Puerto Rican families to be involved and the Ross brothers

in Apartment 2B. Their involvement was open to discussion. Perhaps it would be better to focus on individual family problems instead, including these three families, and view the present group as a secondary force; maintain the group, but focus on *all* families; possibly then, these others would join the group. Note: There was a problem of drug addiction in the Acevedo family. (c) Constant contact, even if not in person, was advisable. Other workers, too many others, came and went, with gaps between. I felt the worker should impart the sense that he was there all the time, even though he wasn't. Possibly, too, more attention could be given to the children and teenagers—or, if desired, they could be the new focus.

4. *Agencies and contacts*: Ed Collins of the Department of Social Services was helpful in regard to the group as a whole, as well as to its individual members. He was particularly helpful regarding Mrs. Moore and Kathy Waters. Because of work pressures, he often got bogged down. A call to him was all that was necessary for him to react positively and, if possible, quickly. At last contact there were two caseworkers assigned to the building, but Ed would probably be the real contact person for a while, even if he was no longer assigned there.

It goes without saying that Mr. Tubb and Mr. Ryder were involved with all tenants, but as leader, Mr. Ward had much more contact with them and was recognized by them as the leader of the building.

Though CCLU was involved for a period around the no-heat situation, Miss Tegran continued to help at a later date, specifically in the case of Kathy Waters.

Other contacts were not as intense or involving but of possible concern would be two parole officers: In the case of Nicholas Duke, the contact was Mr. Coshen; in the case of Mr. Ward, Jr., the contact was Mr. Femolo.

GLOSSARY

Glossary items are provided for the major theoretical and practice concepts discussed in the book. Specific programs (such as Medicaid, Supplemental Security Income, etc.) are not included in the glossary, but may be located in the subject index. Readers wishing to restudy any glossary items should check the subject index and then turn to the page(s) cited there.

Accountability Demonstrating that social welfare programs are effective in meeting needs. This usually requires that program objectives be clearly specified.

Achievement of positions The assigning of positions on the basis of individual ability (students who get the highest grades receive honors, for example).

Action system That part of a behavior change effort that works with the change agent system and the client system to influence the target system.

Adequacy The effectiveness of a program in meeting the needs of the target population (that is, the people the program is intended to serve).

Administration The effective management of professional resources and responsibilities in social welfare agencies and structures.

Advocate role Part of an interventive strategy, advocacy involves helping clients obtain needed services. This may require the implementation of new services.

Almshouse A facility to house those considered legitimately needy in which basic life-sustaining needs were met.

Ascription of positions The assigning of positions without consideration of an individual's abilities ("a woman's place is in the home," for example).

Autonomous social welfare agency An agency in which one profession dominates decision making and the provision of services.

Behavior-changer role Part of an interventive strategy, behavior change involves modifying specific parts of a client's behavior.

Behavioral psychology The branch of psychological theory that asserts that all behavior is learned in separate units (acts), that the units (acts) are related to each other, and that the units (acts) become established in the individual's behavior repertoire by means of external reinforcement.

Biopsychosocial whole Helen Harris Perlman's concept, which suggests that helping professions must understand the total person in that person's social environment. The helping relationship must include an awareness of the person's biological, psychological, and social characteristics and functioning.

Bread scale A subsistence level calculated according to food costs and family size, with welfare aid given if a family's income fell below that level. Public assistance budgets used today are a kind of bread scale.

Broker role Part of an interventive strategy, brokerage involves knowing services that are available and making sure those in need reach the appropriate services.

Bureaucracy A type of formal organization of people, tasks, and materials characterized by clearly specified goals and means and impersonal relations between those working in the bureaucracy.

Capitalist-Puritan value system The belief that people are responsible for themselves, and those who become dependent on others should be required to find ways to become self-sufficient.

Care-giver role Part of an interventive strategy, care-giving involves providing supportive services for those who cannot fully solve their own problems and meet their own needs.

Casework An interventive method that seeks to improve social functioning by concentrating on one person in depth, examining the individual's biological-psychological-social behavior within that person's social context.

Change agent A person who facilitates change.

Change agent system That part of a behavior-change effort that is composed of the change agent and the organization in or with which that agent works.

Charisma The personal qualities of an individual that enable that person to win the trust and loyalty of others.

Children's allowance The payment of a cash allowance to parents of children who are still minors.

Civil rights movement An ongoing attempt to achieve equal rights for all minority groups in American society. Most often this term refers to the attempts during the 1950s and 1960s to achieve racial equality for black people.

Classical (respondent) conditioning Acquiring a behavior by pairing an unconditioned stimulus with a conditioned stimulus.

Client A member of the client system; the person being helped.

Client-centered or nondirective therapy Developed by Carl Rogers, it adapts a psychoanalytic approach to focus on the client's perception of and feelings about the client's situation at any point in the life cycle. The helping person does not assume responsibility for and control over the person's situation in this therapeutic approach.

Client-focused agency An agency whose services are planned to meet whatever needs exist for a specified client population.

Client (user) participation The degree to which the persons who need and use a social welfare program have the opportunity to participate in program planning and evaluation.

Client system That part of a behavior-change effort that is composed of one or more persons who seek help or a change of some kind.

Collective bargaining The negotiation between a union and a business (or an entire industry) to establish mutually agreeable work contracts.

Collusion When several businesses agree to set prices or otherwise to jointly control the economic conditions within an industry. This interferes with normal market mechanisms, and increases the power of the businesses in the marketplace.

Community A spatially defined social unit within which there are identifiable patterns of social interdependence.

Community organization An interventive method that seeks to improve social functioning by using organizational and community groups to develop skills in identifying needs and organizing to meet these needs.

Community planner role Helping community groups to plan effectively for the community's social welfare needs.

Comprehensive neighborhood service centers Providing a range of social welfare services at centers scattered throughout a community. These centers are usually independently planned and operated, and are not usually under the control of a centralized administrative, bureaucratic structure.

Confidentiality Insuring that information obtained from and relating to clients is only used professionally and with the permission of the clients.

Consultant role Working with other professionals to help them be more effective in providing services.

Counter-conditioning (reciprocal inhibition) Eliminating a behavior by reinforcing a behavior that is incompatible with it.

Countervailing power structures Structures that arise to check or balance a lopsided distribution of power.

Coverage The number of people actually participating in a social welfare program.

Creaming When social welfare agencies concentrate on those services and users with whom they have been successful in the past, in order to legitimate the agency itself.

Curative social welfare services Services provided to solve an already existing problem.

Data-manager role Collecting and analyzing data for decision-making purposes.

Decentralization of services Dispersing social welfare services throughout a community so that they are more readily accessible to persons who may need them. Decentralized services are usually operated by a centralized administrative, bureaucratic structure.

Diagnosis Interpreting information from and about a client to understand his or her situation and the problems in it.

Diffusion The borrowing by one society of cultural elements from another culture.

Discovery An innovation providing completely new information.

Disposable income The amount of money available to be spent by an individual, household, group, or organization.

Dividing the client Dividing a person's problems into specialized subparts and assigning different professional persons or agencies to deal with each subpart.

Economic institution The major social structure to distribute the resources needed to produce, distribute, and consume goods and services.

Ego psychology An adaptation of psychoanalytic theory that focuses on the present, and utilizes the personality's rational processes to understand the problems of the present.

Eligibility requirements The criteria used to determine who is eligible to receive services in a social welfare program. Eligibility requirements may include such factors as age, income, employment status, parental status, and so on.

Empathy The ability to comprehend and sense another person's situation and feelings from that person's point of view.

Epigenetic principle of maturation Erik Erikson's theory, which asserts that each individual has a genetic timetable governing physical maturation.

Equity The degree to which a program is actually available to the people in the target population. Although in theory a program may specify a certain target population, in practice various characteristics may serve to exclude certain members of that population (lack of transportation to reach an agency to apply for service, for example).

Evaluative role Part of an interventive strategy, evaluation involves assessing needs and resources, generating alternatives for meeting needs, and making decisions among alternatives.

Extended family The form of the family comprised of three or more generations. It commonly also includes other blood-related persons.

Extinction Eliminating a behavior by not having it reinforced when it is performed.

Fiscal policy The government's intervention in the market to establish and implement economic policy.

Gaps in service When a social welfare agency or service network offers only part of the services needed by a person.

Grant programs Making a direct grant to a person to help meet the individual's needs (Supplemental Security Income, for example). Grant programs are usually funded by a combination of federal, state, and local tax revenues. Grants may also be in-kind, that is, providing a product (clothes, for example) rather than the money to buy the product.

Great Depression Starting with the Stock Market Crash of 1929, the Great Depression created massive unemployment, bank failures, and unprecedented need in the society. A series of programs were enacted to revive the economy and meet the human need created by the Depression. These programs comprised the "New Deal" of Franklin D. Roosevelt's administration, and included the Social Security Act in 1935.

Group dynamics Social behavior in small groups, including such factors as group composition, leadership, goal-setting, and cooperation or competition in group interaction.

Group work An interventive method that seeks to improve social functioning by using the small group as the context and process of change.

Guaranteed income Guaranteeing that the income of all persons or families reaches a predetermined level through a system of income supplements paid by the government to those whose income falls below this level.

Health Maintenance Organization A medical organization that contracts with persons to provide comprehensive health services for a flat fee. It is a type of health insurance.

Helping relationship The mutually desired interaction between a person seeking help and a professional helping person that is based on trust, respect, sharing, and mutual involvement in the problem-solving process.

Host social welfare agency An agency in which there is a high degree of sharing between several professions that participate in decision making and the provision of services.

Human diversity The ways in which people are different because of biological, social, and cultural characteristics.

Humanist-positivist-utopian value system The belief that it is society's responsibility to meet the needs of its members, and that most human breakdown is caused by societal malfunctioning.

Income-maintenance program A program that provides or increases the income available to a person or family.

Indenture Archaic practice of removing children from their own homes if their parents sought welfare help, and placing the children in more affluent families in return for the child's labor.

Indoor relief Providing welfare services to persons who reside in a facility for that purpose (originally almshouses, workhouses, and the like; today prisons, mental hospitals, rest homes, and so on).

Industrial Revolution Basic changes in the system of production in Western societies caused by the use of mechanical power in the production process in place of predominantly human or animal power. The roots of the Industrial Revolution go back to economic and social changes in the seventeenth century, with the main impact occurring in the eighteenth and nineteenth centuries. The revolutionary new use of mechanical power had far-reaching effects throughout the social structures affected.

In-kind payment Providing a person with a needed item (such as furniture) rather than the money to buy that item.

Institutional racism The comprehensive disadvantage created for members of a racial group by the systematic and cumulative discriminatory actions carried out within all of the major social institutions.

Institutionalized social welfare services Services that are an integral part of a social structure and are available to all societal members.

Interviewing Purposeful communication, including both verbal and nonverbal communication.

Invention An innovation created by useful new combinations of already existing information.

Judeo-Christian value system The belief that people have the right to make their own choices, but that society has the obligation to provide resources to help them do so and to aid them when the results of their choices create problems for themselves or others.

Laissez-faire capitalism First formalized by Adam Smith in 1776, the idea that minimal government regulation of the economic system promotes healthy competition and maximum efficiency. Most capitalistic societies of today have considerably more governmental economic control than that suggested by a pure laissez-faire system.

Life cycle The progression from birth to death through socially structured experiences related to chronological age. At each point in the life cycle the individual draws upon physical and social resources to solve the problems and achieve gratification.

Lobbyist A person paid to represent the interests of a person, group, or organization in the political and legislative processes.

Management by objectives (MBO) A technique to measure program effectiveness by specifying concrete program objectives, analyzing data to assess whether these objectives have been obtained, and making decisions about program structure and functioning on the basis of these data.

Market The economic mechanism that relates consumer demand to producer supply.

Means test A test of eligibility for aid in which the applicant must demonstrate that his or her financial resources are below the level specified by the program from which help is being sought.

Methods approach to intervention Fitting a problem to a preexisting method (such as casework).

Mobilizer role Part of an interventive strategy, mobilization involves helping clients to utilize existing services more effectively.

Modeling (observational learning) Acquiring a behavior by watching the behavior of others.

Monopolistic social welfare services The lack of choice in social welfare programs. Often only one program exists to meet a need (Aid to Families with Dependent Children, for example), leaving the person in need no choice in where he or she can turn for help.

Negative income tax A tax system in which those whose income falls above a predetermined level pay an income tax, while those with incomes below this level receive a supplement.

Nonjudgmental attitude Separating attitudes about a person from attitudes about that person's behavior. Although the behavior may be unacceptable, the person continues to be accepted as a worthwhile, autonomous individual.

Norms Rules for behavior.

Nuclear family The form of the family comprised of two generations, parents and their children. Under special circumstances, other blood-related or nonblood-related persons may be regular members of a nuclear family.

Ombudsman A person or agency that reaches out into the community to identify need and help people in need make use of appropriate social welfare resources (or develop such resources if they don't already exist).

Operant (instrumental) conditioning Acquiring a behavior by having it positively reinforced when it is performed.

Outdoor relief The provision of welfare services to persons who are living in their own homes. This is the major form of welfare services provided in this country today.

Outreach role Part of an interventive strategy, outreach involves reaching out into the community to identify need and to follow up referrals to service contexts.

Parish In Tudor England, the local governmental unit providing for public welfare services and payments. Roughly equivalent to our present counties.

Personality The individual's distinctive and regular manner of confronting and dealing with persons, problems, and situations.

Pluralism Competition among major groups in American society, which encourages each to participate in the political process to fight for its own interests. Through this competition, it is assumed that coalitions will be formed based on compromises that allow each group to have its major interests represented in the legislative process.

Policy The decision making that utilizes the political and administrative processes to identify and plan economic and social objectives.

Political institution The major social structure to allocate power through a system of government.

Position Named collections of persons performing similar functional behaviors.

Positive reinforcement Rewarding a behavior when it is performed.

Poverty Economic resources that are inadequate to provide the basic necessities of life as defined by a society. Poverty is both the objective reality that basic necessities are lacking, and the subjective reality that one lives on the fringe of society.

Power The ability of one person to influence others regardless of the wishes of the person being influenced. Bases of power include the ability to reward or punish, expertise, legitimacy, and identification (the ability to win the affection of the person being influenced).

Practice wisdom The understanding resulting from accumulated experience.

Preventive social welfare services Services provided before a problem exists, in an attempt to prevent the problem from arising.

Primary group A small group characterized by intensive, face-to-face interactions that permit the group members to express any aspect of their personalities.

Private income-transfer program Using monies voluntarily donated by one group for the benefit of other groups.

Private social service program A noneconomic social welfare service (such as birth-control counseling) supported with funds voluntarily donated.

Problem approach to intervention Developing a specific interventive strategy (method) in response to a specific problem.

Problem-focused agency An agency whose services are planned to meet the needs of any clients that have a specified problem or set of problems.

Problem solving That part of the helping process that involves the gathering of information, defining problem situations, assessing helping resources and obstacles, formulating a plan of action to solve the problems identified, and evaluating the success of the plan after it is carried out.

Profession An organization of specialists characterized by an emphasis on the use of specialized knowledge and skills to serve the public, and close colleague relationships to insure competence in professional training and performance.

Professional certification Recognition by a governmental agency or nongovernmental association of the fact that an individual has met specified predetermined qualifications.

Professional licensing Legal regulation of members of a profession. Licensing may be of two kinds: (1) title licensing—legal regulation specifying the qualifications necessary to use a professional title (who can call oneself a social worker, for example); (2) practice licensing—legal regulation specifying that certain professional activities may only be performed by members of a particular professional group. Practice licensing usually includes title licensing.

Psychoanalytic theory A theory of personality development that asserts that the three major personality structures postulated by the theory—id, ego, and superego—result from the competition between the demands of society and the attempts of the physical organism to find gratification. This competition progresses through biologically related stages, with the main outlines of the personality structure established by adolescence. Sigmund Freud is the founder of psychoanalytic theory, although more recent neo-Freudians have further developed his ideas.

Public income-transfer program Using public monies collected from one group for the benefit of other groups.

Public social service program A noneconomic social welfare service (such as marital counseling) supported with public funds.

Punishment Attempting to decrease the probability of a behavior's occurrence by removing a positive reinforcement or presenting an aversive stimulus.

Referral Sending a client to another social welfare resource when an agency is not able to provide the help needed. In some cases, clients may be referred to a more appropriate helping person within one agency. Referral involves the identification of a more appropriate resource and follow-through to insure that the client actually receives service as intended.

Rehabilitative social welfare services Services that are provided to solve an already existing problem, and to prevent its recurrence in the future.

Repossession When a store, bank, or credit company takes back an item purchased on credit because one or more payments have been missed.

Research The collection and analysis of data in order to assess the effectiveness of interventive efforts and the operation of any part of the social welfare institution.

Residence requirement Making the receipt of welfare benefits contingent upon residence in a specified geographic area for a specified period of time.

Residual social welfare services Social welfare services that are provided only to those who can prove need and who qualify by meeting restrictive eligibility requirements.

Revenue sharing Providing local communities with federal funds and allowing them to decide how they should be spent. Part of President Nixon's "New Federalism," revenue sharing is an attempt to increase community autonomy by imposing less federal influence on the programs that must be operated by communities.

Role Norms associated with a position.

Role ambiguity A lack of clarity in the definition or teaching of appropriate role behaviors.

Role conflict Conflicting role expectations existing in one or more positions simultaneously.

Role set Complementary roles that are defined in relationship to each other.

Role theory The study of how tasks are organized and distributed in society.

Rural community A community characterized by small population size, low population density, a relatively homogeneous population, and relative isolation from other communities.

Secondary group A group characterized by relatively impersonal interaction focused on the performance of specified tasks.

Separate but equal The provision of separate facilities, which are said to be of equal quality, for members of different (usually racial) groups. Most often used in maintaining racial segregation, and struck down as unconstitutional by the Supreme Court in 1954.

Settlement house A community facility to help residents meet their social, recreational, educational, and collective action needs.

Shaping Acquiring a behavior by the use of differential reinforcement and extinction to move from a spontaneously performed behavior via successive approximations to the new behavior.

Social change Change within a part of the social structure, without destroying the structure's identity.

Social Darwinism An extension of Charles Darwin's biological concept—survival of the fittest—to social life. Social Darwinism maintained that those who were needy were less fit than those who were not, and therefore should not be helped since the society would only be preserving defective individuals who could never be self-sufficient.

Social differentiation Socially defined distinctions between groups on the basis of ascriptive criteria (age, sex, race, and the like), or achieved criteria (income, occupation, education, and so on).

Social dividend A cash payment to all members of society regardless of income.

Social history Obtaining background information about a client that is then the basis of diagnosis and problem solving.

Social institution A cluster of positions, roles, and norms organized so as to meet a significant societal objective.

Social insurance Programs to meet people's needs, which are funded by contributions these people have made during periods when they are not in need (unemployment insurance, for example).

Social stratification A type of social differentiation in which groups are ranked on a scale of superior, inferior, and equal.

Social system An organized interrelated group of activities, each of which affects the others. In its broadest sense, *the* social system is the organization of the parts of the structure of a society in such a way that the functional independence that results enables the society to survive. Within *the* social system are a number of subsystems that are internally cohesive, but also affect each other.

Social utility A basic service needed for people to function effectively in society, and the provision of which is usually heavily subsidized by society.

Social welfare Improving social functioning and minimizing suffering through a system of socially approved financial and social services at all levels in the social structure.

Social work A socially legitimated profession that seeks to help people singly and in groups to meet their needs and achieve satisfaction in their daily lives.

Socialization Learning the culture in which one lives.

Socioemotional leader The main person in a small group who promotes group interaction and helps to maintain a cohesive interpersonal network within the group.

Starting where the client is Beginning the helping relationship at the point where the client feels the need for help. Intervention may ultimately shift to other areas, but this decision must be made in consultation with the client.

Separation of powers The organizing principle underlying the federal political structure, which provides a system of checks and balances to prevent one branch of the government from having controlling power over the whole structure of government.

Target system That part of a behavior-change effort composed of those people whose behavior must be changed if the goals of the change-agent system and the client system are to be attained.

Task leader The main person in a small group who helps the group achieve its goals.

Tax allowance Allowing an individual, group, or organization to exclude certain income from the total income on which tax is calculated.

Total institution An agency with total control over the clients who live within it, and somewhat isolated from the community in which it exists.

Urban community A community characterized by large population size, high population density, a heterogeneous population, and extensive ties with other communities.

Warning out The practice of refusing residence to persons seeking residence but who were judged by the community as likely to become dependent on welfare in the future.

Workfare The belief that those persons receiving financial aid should be required to work in return for this aid. Since the majority of financial aid recipients are incapable of working, for a variety of social and physical reasons, there is an inherent contradiction in this concept.

Workhouse or house of correction An archaic facility that housed those considered shiftless (illegitimately needy), in which the basic life sustaining needs were met in return for forced work.

INDEX

1 2 3 4 5 6 7 8 9 10